Chicano Students and the Courts

Critical America

GENERAL EDITORS: Richard Delgado and Jean Stefancic

Recent titles in the Critical America series include:

For a complete list of titles in the series, please visit the
New York University Press website at www.nyupress.org.

Chicano Students and the Courts

The Mexican American Legal Struggle
for Educational Equality

Richard R. Valencia

NEW YORK UNIVERSITY PRESS
New York and London

NEW YORK UNIVERSITY PRESS
New York and London
www.nyupress.org

Library of Congress Cataloging-in-Publication Data
Valencia, Richard R.
Chicano students and the courts : the Mexican American legal
struggle for educational equality / Richard R. Valencia.
p.   cm. — (Critical America)
Includes bibliographical references and index.
ISBN-13: 978-0-8147-8819-6 (cl : alk. paper)
ISBN-10: 0-8147-8819-X (cl : alk. paper)
1. Discrimination in education—Law and legislation—United States.
2. Mexican American students—Legal status, laws, etc.—United
States.   I. Title.
KF4155.V35 2008
344.73'0798—dc22   2008012218

New York University Press books are printed on acid-free paper,
and their binding materials are chosen for strength and durability.
We strive to use environmentally responsible suppliers and materials
to the greatest extent possible in publishing our books.

Manufactured in the United States of America

10 9 8 7 6 5 4 3 2 1

This book is dedicated to the Mexican American community and its struggle for educational equality, to all the Mexican American parents and their children who took their campaign for justice to the courts, and to the many civil rights attorneys—Mexican American, African American, Asian American, and White—who through their legal skills and hours of hard work made it possible.

Contents

Tables and Figures

Figures

Preface

Economist Thomas Sowell wrote in his chapter on "The Mexicans" (*Ethnic America: A History*, 1981), "*The goals and values of Mexican Americans have never centered on education* [italics added]" (p. 266).[1] Many other scholars and media figures have similarly asserted that Mexican American parents, particularly of low-socioeconomic status (SES) background, do not value education. The contention is that because the parents fail to inculcate this value in their children or demonstrate interest in helping the children with homework, Mexican American children tend to perform poorly in school (i.e., low academic achievement). These allegations cannot be taken lightly, as much evidence shows that when parents, of any ethnicity, become active participants in their children's education, they perform better in school.[2,3]

The myth persists that these parents are indifferent toward and devalue education. Valencia and Black (2002), for example, in the article "'Mexican Americans Don't Value Education!'—On the Basis of the Myth, Mythmaking, and Debunking," noted that the fallacy has appeared in sources as varied as (a) early master's theses (e.g., Gould, 1932; Lyon, 1933; Taylor, 1927); (b) published scholarly literature (e.g., Frost & Hawkes, 1966; Hellmuth, 1967; Marans & Lourie, 1967; Sowell, 1981); and (c) newspaper articles and columns. An example of the latter is The University of Texas at Austin law professor Lino Graglia's statement at a press conference on September 10, 1997. At that time, Graglia was chosen as honorary co-chairman of the newly established group, Students for Equal Opportunity —a group that was "tired of hearing only from supporters of affirmative action" (Roser, 1997, p. B1). At the campus press conference, where the new student group made its debut, Graglia stated,

> The central problem is that Blacks and Mexican Americans are not academically competitive [with Whites]. . . . Various studies seem to show that Blacks [and] Mexican Americans spend less time in school. *They*

have a culture that seems not to encourage achievement. . . . failure is not looked upon with disgrace [italics added].[4]

In an NBC *Today* interview, reporter Matt Lauer asked Graglia if he had any statistical backing for his cultural statements about minority students and educational achievement:

Graglia: I'm not an expert on educational matters.
Lauer: But you do agree with the statement that came out of yours that says they [Blacks and Mexican Americans] have a culture that seems not to encourage achievement?
Graglia: Well, I meant to say that there are some cultures, like some of the Asian cultures that insist more highly on the students going to school and achieving in school.

Asked by Lauer how he felt about the cultural issues that Graglia raised, Ramiro Canales (member of the Chicano/Hispanic Law Students Association at The University of Texas [UT]) replied,

Professor Graglia is not qualified to make cultural assessments. He is a law school professor and not a cultural anthropologist, and when he makes these generalizations they not only promote racial stereotypes but also distort reality as it is in Texas. I think both African American and Mexican American cultures promote success. I think that the parents of all the minority law students want their children to succeed.

The comments of Graglia, who has a long history of speaking out against affirmative action and busing for school desegregation (Roser & Tanamachi, 1997), drew national and international media coverage and swift denunciations.[5] Included among those who condemned his statement were UT School of Law Dean Michael Sharlot, UT Interim President Peter Flawn, UT System Chancellor William Cunningham, student organizations, professors, civil rights organizations, and lawmakers of color, some of whom called for Graglia's resignation (Martin, 1997; Roser & Tanamachi, 1997). Senator Gregory Luna, head of the State Hispanic Caucus, stated, "It seems we're in an era where the Ku Klux Klan does not come in white robes but in the robes of academe" (Martin, 1997, p. 1). UT students of color staged a sit-in at the School of Law and helped organize a political rally in which the Reverend Jesse Jackson, in front of five thousand people, lambasted Graglia (Roser & Tanamachi, 1997).

In addition to the available literature demonstrating that Mexican Americans indeed do value education and participate actively in their children's schooling, the Mexican American community's historical and contemporary struggle for educational equality has been long-standing and extensive.[6] This campaign has been so substantial that I am able to teach an entire undergraduate course, "Chicano Educational Struggles," on the topic at The University of Texas at Austin.[7]

Scholars who study Mexican American education follow one or two approaches (San Miguel, 1987; San Miguel & Valencia, 1998). The first approach, the "plight" dimension, explores what schools have done to Mexican American students (e.g., forced segregation), and how these children and youths have fared under oppressive conditions. The second approach, the "struggle" dimension, examines how the Mexican American community has developed and carried out campaigns for educational equality. As mentioned, Mexican Americans have demonstrated an indefatigable commitment in their struggle for a more equitable education. For those who continue to perpetuate the mythology of the Mexican American community's indifference toward and devaluation of education, they will henceforth have the present book with which to reckon.

This book consists of an introduction, a conclusion, and eight chapters that cover various categories of Mexican American–initiated school litigation. The chapters, in turn, proceed chronologically, beginning with the earliest lawsuits (e.g., "School Segregation"), and ending with the most recent (e.g., "High-Stakes Testing"). The introduction, "Understanding and Analyzing Mexican American School Litigation," provides a framework that serves as a theoretical tool to evaluate the positioning of race in lawsuits brought by the Mexican American community. In doing so, I draw from critical race theory, critical legal studies—especially the notion of indeterminacy, which I use to explain the discretionary nature of judicial decisions—and postcolonial scholarship.

"School Segregation," the subject of chapter 1, examines the long-standing legal struggle that the Mexican American community has mounted against segregated, inferior schools. Given that the early forced school segregation of Mexican American students became the crucible in which school failure of these children and youths originated and intensified over time, it is not surprising that Mexican Americans have committed a substantial amount of time and energy contesting school segregation. In undertaking research for this chapter, I identified thirty-five school desegregation lawsuits that Mexican Americans brought forth or in which they participated with African Americans, a tally that far overshadows the number of cases in the other categories (e.g., school finance; bilingual education; high-stakes testing) discussed in this book. In this chapter, I focus on the significant features of these lawsuits (e.g., *Mendez v. Westminster*, 1946; *Cisneros v. Corpus Christi Independent School District*, 1970), particularly showing how each case added new legal developments. This analysis helps us to understand how race played a central role in Mexican American–initiated desegregation litigation, particularly how Whites used their privilege to keep White and Mexican American students apart.

Chapter 2, "School Financing," examines another enduring educational problem facing Mexican American students—underfunded schools. The poor condition of schools in property-poor public districts sparked litigation beginning in the late 1960s, with Mexican Americans the main torchbearers. *Serrano v. Priest* (1969) and *Rodriguez v. San Antonio Independent School District* (1971), for example, were both initiated by Mexican Americans. *Rodriguez*, in particular, was part of a nearly four-decade-long interplay between the Texas courts and the Texas Legislature.

Chapter 3, "Special Education," covers the diagnosis and racialized placement of Mexican American children and other youngsters of color in classes for the educable mentally retarded (EMR). Often these children were, with some exceptions, false positives (i.e., incorrectly diagnosed and placed in EMR classes). A trinity of lawsuits brought forth by Mexican American, African American, and Yaqui Indian children who were erroneously deemed EMR—*Diana v. State Board of Education* (1970), *Covarrubias v. San Diego Unified School District* (1971), and *Guadalupe v. Tempe School District No. 3* (1972)—all ended in favorable consent decrees and helped to create a sea change in special education assessments.

Chapter 4, "Bilingual Education," begins with the 1848 Treaty of Guadalupe Hidalgo, which ostensibly guaranteed the language rights of Mexican-origin people. Such guarantees, however, were short-lived. Although the passage of the Bilingual Education Act (BEA) of 1968 laid a foundation for bilingual education, the BEA was underfunded and voluntary. As such, Mexican Americans had no recourse but to initiate lawsuits for their right to receive bilingual education. This chapter discusses eight key bilingual education lawsuits brought forth by Mexican Americans and shows how they helped to establish the right to bilingual education in the United States. In light of increasing anti-bilingual-education sentiment and withdrawal of federal support, this right is under siege.

Chapter 5 examines "School Closures." During the 1970s, over seven thousand public schools closed due to declining enrollment, inflation, and fiscal austerity. Given the racist nature of the United States and the overwhelming White composition of local school boards (and the political pressure to protect their constituencies), closures in many communities were racialized. This chapter examines three school closure lawsuits initiated by Mexican American plaintiffs: *Angeles v. Santa Barbara School District* (1979), *Castro v. Phoenix Union High School District* (1982), and *Diaz v. San Jose Unified School District* (1985). I have an insider perspective to this litigation, as I served as an expert witness in each case. In *Angeles*, *Castro*, and *Diaz*, high-enrollment Mexican American schools were chosen for closure while high-enrollment White schools were untouched —even though the White students were overwhelmingly responsible for the enrollment decline.

Chapter 6, "Undocumented Students," discusses the struggle of undocumented Mexican American children barred from public schools due to a change in a Texas state law in 1975, providing that only children who were citizens or legal immigrants could be enrolled. The judges in two foundational lawsuits—*Hernandez v. Houston Independent School District* (1977) and *Doe v. Plyler* (1978)—handed down opposite rulings, thus triggering a host of similar lawsuits of behalf of undocumented children in Texas. Eventually, these lawsuits were consolidated and reached the U.S. Supreme Court. In *Plyler v. Doe* (1982)—heralded by many as the high-water mark for Latino jurisprudence and deemed comparable in significance to *Brown v. Board of Education* (1954)—the Supreme Court ruled, 5–4, that the Texas law violated the Fourteenth Amendment rights of the undocumented children.

"Higher Education Financing" litigation comes in for examination in chapter 7. This area, as discussed, departs from the other topics covered in this book in that the target is higher education. Mexican American plaintiffs residing in the Border Region of Texas, an area of forty-one contiguous counties along the Texas-Mexico border and in South Texas, filed *LULAC v. Clements* (1992), asserting that although 20% of all Texans live in that region, it only receives 10% of the state's funds for higher education. The plaintiffs won, but the Texas Supreme Court reversed in

Richards v. LULAC (1993). The lawsuit nevertheless helped galvanize state-wide support for a more equitable system to fund higher education in the state of Texas.

"High-Stakes Testing" is covered in chapter 8. Beginning in the early 1980s, a national discussion centered on the "rising tide of educational mediocrity," which led to the standards-based school reform movement. The centerpiece of this campaign was high-stakes testing, a reform that called for a series of tests to decide grade promotion and graduation from high school. A major controversy erupted when high-stakes testing turned out to have a negative impact on students of color (e.g., higher rates of diploma denial to students of color, compared to Whites). In this chapter, I discuss several lawsuits initiated by Mexican Americans and others, complaining that high-stakes tests were racially discriminatory in impact. Two of these cases (*United States v. Texas*, 1985; *Association of Mexican-American Educators v. California*, 1996) arose when students of color were denied enrollment in teacher-education courses or denied certification after failing teacher-competency tests. In the third case discussed, *GI Forum v. Texas Education Agency* (2000), Mexican American and African American youngsters in Texas sued when authorities denied them a high school diploma because they failed to pass the graduation examination. I am able to contribute a sharp insider's perspective to this analysis here as I served as an expert for the plaintiffs, testifying on how deficit thinking racializes school failure among students of color. In particular, this case reveals that if students of color do not receive equal opportunity to learn, then their poor performance on high-stakes tests is reflective of inferior schooling —not inability to learn.

In the conclusion, "The Contemporary and Future Status of Mexican American School Litigation; What We Have Learned from This Legal History," I briefly discuss very recent litigation and lawsuits that Mexican Americans are likely to bring forth in the immediate future. Regarding recent litigation, I discuss lawsuits concerning within-school segregation in a racially diverse elementary school, and failure to provide bilingual education. Future litigation may center on (a) continuing inequities in interdistrict funding and (b) attempts by state legislatures to deny birthright citizenship to children born in the United States to undocumented immigrants. I close by reflecting on what we have learned from this legal history, particularly regarding how critical race theory can help us further understand race and education in the United States.

Acknowledgments

This book would not have been possible without the contributions of a number of individuals. I gratefully thank Deborah Gershenowitz, Senior Editor at the New York University Press, for her support throughout this project. Appreciation is also extended to Richard Delgado and Jean Stefancic, coeditors of the Critical America Series, for their support and encouragement. Special thanks go to Richard for his valuable editing suggestions. I offer my gratitude to two anonymous external reviewers who provided a number of excellent suggestions for improving the manuscript. I also extend my appreciation to Martin Tulic for his outstanding work in preparing the book's comprehensive and detailed index. This book was completed because of financial support from The University of Texas at Austin. I thank Dr. José E. Limón, Director of the Center for Mexican American Studies, and Dr. Manuel J. Justiz, Dean of the College of Education, for their research grants. My deep appreciation goes to the University of Texas Co-operative Society for awarding me a subvention grant to assist with the underwriting of this book. Very special appreciation goes to Dr. Bruno J. Villarreal, who served as my extremely able research assistant in facilitating the preparation of this project, particularly via his adroit skills in locating and helping abstract many of the legal cases. Thank you very much, Bruno, for your outstanding assistance.

To my wonderful wife, Marta, thank you for allowing me to bounce some ideas off you. Your excellent feedback is truly appreciated. Also, I extend my deep affection and gratitude to you for your unwavering support during the long process of undertaking this book project. And, as always, thank you Juan and Carlos, my twin boys, who were so patient while Dad did his writing. You're the best sons a father could have.

Introduction

Understanding and Analyzing
Mexican American School Litigation

Beginning with the *Romo v. Laird* (1925) school desegregation lawsuit in Arizona, for more than eight decades Mexican Americans have been engaged in a hard-fought legal struggle for educational equality.[1] Yet few scholars are aware of this long-standing struggle. Contributing, in part, to this unawareness is Mexican Americans' exclusion from much of the scholarship on civil rights history. Law professor Juan Perea (1997) has asserted that American racial thought incorporates an implicit "Black/White binary paradigm of race," which excludes Mexican Americans, "distorts history, and contributes to the marginalization of non-Black peoples of color" (p. 1213).[2] This binary has evolved to become a central point of discussion and critique in contemporary discourse. For example, Perea noted that even major books on constitutional case law have truncated history in such a way that the Mexican American struggle for school desegregation has been entirely excluded (see Stone, Seidman, Sunstein, & Tushnet, 1991). By contrast, in my own research on Mexican American desegregation lawsuits, I have identified thirty-five cases dating from 1925 to 1985 (see chapter 1, this volume).

The problem with the Black/White paradigm of race, which Angel Oquendo (1995) refers to as "racial dualism," is that it leads to the unfounded perception that Mexican Americans and other Latinos do not need access to the "machinery of civil rights law" (Ruiz Cameron, 1998, p. 1358). The reality is, however, that in the sphere of educational lawsuits Mexican Americans have indeed been quite active in civil rights discourse. To better understand and analyze this corpus of Mexican American–initiated school litigation, I employ a conceptual framework that draws from critical race theory, critical legal studies—especially the notion of legal indeterminacy—and postcolonialism.

Critical Race Theory

Critical race theory (CRT) began in the 1970s when a cadre of legal scholars, lawyers, and activists across the nation realized that the momentum of civil rights litigation had stalled (Delgado & Stefancic, 2001; Taylor, 1998).[3] A form of oppositional scholarship, CRT "challenges the experiences of whites as the normative standard and grounds its conceptual framework in the distinctive experiences of people of color" (Taylor, 1998, p. 122).[4] Some of the issues that CRT addresses are campus speech codes, disproportionate sentencing of people of color in the criminal justice system, and affirmative action (Taylor, 1998).

Now a growing field of scholarship with a large corpus of literature, CRT has gained widespread popularity in the field of education, especially among scholars of race and ethnicity.[5] Issues studied in CRT and education are diverse and include, for example, the experiences of scholars of color in the academy, affirmative action, educational history, families of color, tracking, the Western canon, hierarchy in the schools, and testing. In recent years, spin-off movements have separated themselves from CRT, including Asian critical race theory (AsianCrit; see, e.g., Chang, 1993) and Latina/Latino critical race theory (LatCrit). Similar to CRT, "LatCrit is concerned with a progressive sense of a coalitional Latina/Latino pan-ethnicity and addresses issues often ignored by critical race theorists such as language, immigration, ethnicity, culture, identity, phenotype, and sexuality" (Solórzano & Delgado Bernal, 2001, p. 311).[6]

Solórzano (1998), a prominent CRT scholar, has identified five themes, or tenets, that underlie the perspectives, research methods, and pedagogy of CRT in education. I also draw from Yosso's (2006) discussion of these points:

1. *The centrality and intersectionality of race and racism.* CRT begins with the proposition that race and racism are entrenched and enduring in U.S. society. Race "is a central rather than marginal factor in defining and explaining individual experiences of the law" (Russell, 1992, pp. 762–763). CRT calls for an examination of how race has come to be socially constructed and how the systemic nature of racism serves to oppress people of color while it protects White privilege. Although CRT in education focuses on race and racism, it also seeks to investigate how racism intersects with other manifestations of oppression (e.g., gender, phenotype, class, language, and surname).

(2.) *The challenge to dominant ideology.* Heterodoxy is another key element in CRT in education. Here, CRT challenges the orthodoxy, particularly regarding claims of the educational system and its views toward meritocracy, objectivity, color and gender blindness, and equal opportunity. Critical race theorists assert that these conventional and long-established concepts are actually camouflages for the power, self-interest, and privilege of the dominant group.

3. *The commitment to social justice.* CRT in education includes a firm duty to social justice and the elimination of racism. Critical race theorists posit that schools are political institutions, and therefore view education as a vehicle to end various forms of subordination, such as class and gender discrimination.

4. *The centrality of experiential knowledge.* CRT recognizes the great importance of experiential knowledge of people of color and that such knowledge is valid, appropriate, and essential to understanding, analyzing, and teaching about racism in education. CRT considers this experiential knowledge of students of color and their parents as a major strength and draws on various life experiences as communicated, for example, via biographies, family history, and films. Critical race theorists can also participate in this discourse by use of counterstorytelling (alternative or opposing narratives or explanations).

5. *The interdisciplinary perspective.* CRT in education challenges the ahistorical and unidisciplinary preoccupation of most analyses and argues that one can best understand race and racism in education by incorporating interdisciplinary perspectives. Critical race theorists in education frequently work across disciplinary borders, relying on multiple methods of inquiry so as to provide a sharper eye on the role of race and racism.

CRT provides a compelling theoretical framework for understanding and analyzing Mexican American–initiated school litigation. For example, as will be seen, the landmark *Mendez v. Westminster* (1946) desegregation lawsuit (see chapter 1) illustrates all five tenets for analysis. First, the *Mendez* case and the earlier Mexican American–initiated desegregation lawsuits insisted, in their legal arguments, on the centrality of race and racism in the lives of Mexican American schoolchildren. Second, *Mendez* challenged the dominant belief that segregation of Mexican American children was in their best interests, thereby exposing this traditional claim as a cloak of White self-interest and privilege. Third, *Mendez* represented a commitment to social justice beyond the boundaries of Orange

County, California. In this way, the ruling in *Mendez* helped to end the de jure segregation of Asian Americans and American Indians in California's public schools. As well, *Mendez* lent force to desegregation lawsuits concerning Mexican American children in other states, including Texas and Arizona. Fourth, *Mendez* wisely used the centrality of experiential knowledge of victimized Mexican American children and adults, as seen in the trial testimony. And, finally, *Mendez* used interdisciplinary perspectives and considerable collaboration. Mexican American plaintiffs, White expert witnesses, support from diverse organizations, including the National Association for the Advancement of Colored People, the American Jewish Congress, and the American Civil Liberties Union at the appellate level, all worked together to help plaintiffs prevail in *Mendez*.

Critical Legal Studies and Indeterminacy

A second approach to understanding and analyzing Mexican American–initiated school litigation is legal indeterminacy.[7] The position that the law is indeterminate, unpredictable, and discretionary is an essential feature of contemporary critical legal scholarship (Herget, 1995).[8] Legal scholar James E. Herget has noted that the term *legal indeterminacy*, which is a viewpoint or perspective about law, has the following characteristics:

1. The formal legal authorities (legislation, precedent, custom, scholarly doctrine) do not bind the courts in their decisions, and the judicial power may even be exercised to contradict those authorities.
2. The authoritative sources themselves contain ambiguous and contradictory principles.
3. Law is consequently not fixed and objective but indeterminate and subjective. An illusion to the contrary, i.e., that judges are strictly bound to follow the rules laid down elsewhere, is often perpetuated in orthodox legal thinking.
4. To explain the judicial process it is necessary to go outside the authoritative sources to other social phenomena. (p. 60)

If this view is correct, the norms and processes of the law are so diverse and antithetical in scope and goals that a lawyer or judge with honed skills can invariably turn to an "authoritative legal rule to justify any outcome they wish in a particular case" (Yablon, 1992, p. 1608). This idea that legal indeterminacy can lead to multiple outcomes in judicial decisions informs us, as legal scholar Linda Ross Meyer (1996) noted, that we need to be aware that the application of law is by no means an automatic deduction from firm, unwavering rules:

> What legal theorists now acknowledge with uneasiness, first-year law students with terror and confusion, and lawyers with prosaic calm is that there may not be a right answer to every legal question. Two reasonable minds, both analyzing the same set of legal materials, may differ as to their proper application. (p. 1468)

Legal scholar Gary Lawson (1996) has written an insightful article on legal indeterminacy in which he discusses its "cause" and "cure." Regarding the cause, Lawson begins by noting that a misunderstanding exists that *legal indeterminacy* is regularly thought to be synonymous with *uncertainty*. Lawson asserts that the two terms are not the same. Legal indeterminacy is a function of two elements: (a) the level of uncertainty about any specific legal claim and (b) the standard of proof that one needs to demonstrate a claim. With respect to the standard of proof, Lawson posits that one is unable to know whether uncertainty transforms into legal indeterminacy unless one knows the suitable standard. Legal indeterminacy is thus a function of both the degree of uncertainty and the applicable standard of proof: "The same amount of uncertainty will lead to more indeterminacy as the standard of proof is raised . . . and the same standard of proof will lead to more indeterminacy as the amount of uncertainty increases" (p. 417).[9] Indeterminacy concerning a particular legal matter arises only if the correct answer is so uncertain that the appropriate standard of proof cannot be met. We will later see how in a number of Mexican American–initiated school lawsuits some courts have considered the three standards of judicial review in deciding whether a legislative act has violated the Equal Protection Clause of the Fourteenth Amendment.[10]

Legal scholar Ken Kress (1989) asks, "Why do and should we care about legal indeterminacy?" (p. 285). If arguments about legal indeterminacy are indeed well-founded, then serious doubts arise about the likelihood of legal systems and adjudicative procedures being legitimate and nonarbitrary. Kress's point applies fully to Mexican American jurisprudence. Legal scholar George Martínez, in a 1994 article, "Legal Indeterminacy, Judicial Discretion, and the Mexican-American Litigation Experience, 1930–1980," shows that judicial decisions, either ruling in favor of or against

Mexican Americans, were frequently not ineluctable or compelled.[11] Martínez argues that unmasking the degree of judicial discretion in civil rights lawsuits is significant for two reasons. First, exposing the extent of that discretion helps bring to light how the courts have assisted or failed to establish the civil rights of Mexican Americans. Second, exposing "false necessity in judicial decision-making" (p. 559) by demonstrating how the ruling may have gone one way or another may help dismantle barriers to race relations reform.[12]

Postcolonial Theory

A third body of knowledge that is helpful in understanding Mexican American legal history is postcolonial theory. First developed in Asia, Africa, and now Latin America as a way of understanding the dynamics of colonialism and imperialism, postcolonial scholarship addresses such topics as language and the preservation of the native tongue. Writers in this tradition also analyze resistance, large and small, and collaboration with the overlords. They discuss the economics of colonial exploitation, the role of nationalism, and interracial sexuality and romance. Inasmuch as Mexican Americans are, in some respects, a colonized people whose lands were stolen and culture suppressed, this other great antisubordination tradition developing on the other side of the world may be useful as a tool of analysis.[13]

What follows next are comprehensive analyses of eight categories of Mexican American–initiated educational lawsuits. When appropriate, I integrate discussions of CRT, legal indeterminacy, and postcolonialism—the three bodies of thought that form the preceding conceptual framework.

1

School Segregation

The early forced segregation of Mexican American students became the crucible in which school failure of these children and youths originated and intensified.[1] The intentional separation of Mexican American students from their White peers in public schools began in the post-1848 decades following the Treaty of Guadalupe Hidalgo. The signing of the treaty and the U.S. annexation, by conquest, of the current Southwest signaled the beginning of decades of persistent, pervasive prejudice and discrimination against people of Mexican origin who reside in the United States (Acuña, 2007; Perea, 2003). Subsequently, racial isolation of schoolchildren became a normative practice in the Southwest—despite states having no legal statutes to segregate Mexican American students from White students (San Miguel & Valencia, 1998). In light of the long-standing status of school segregation and its detrimental effects on academic achievement, this topic has captured the interest of many scholars.[2] The early segregation of Mexican American students, however, needs to be contextualized in the larger realm of historical race relations in the Southwest. As a colonized people, Mexican Americans faced segregation in, or exclusion from, for example, movie theaters, restaurants, and public accommodations (e.g., swimming pools) (Acuña, 2007; Martínez, 1994). For many Mexican Americans, segregation spanned from the "cradle to the grave." There was forced segregation in maternity wards[3] and separate cemeteries for Whites and Mexican Americans (Carroll, 2003). The treatment of Mexican Americans as nonpeers allowed Whites to maintain their system of privilege and domination.

The number of Mexican American–initiated desegregation lawsuits far exceeds the number of cases in the other categories (e.g., school finance, bilingual education, and high-stakes testing) discussed in this book. I identified thirty-five germane desegregation lawsuits in undertaking research for this chapter. These cases are listed, chronologically, in Table 1.1.

TABLE 1.1
Mexican American School Desegregation Cases

Case	Year	State
1920s		
Romo v. Laird[b]	1925	AZ
1930s		
Independent School District v. Salvatierra[a]	1930	TX
Alvarez v. Lemon Grove School District[b]	1931	CA
1940s		
Mendez v. Westminster[a]	1946	CA
Delgado v. Bastrop Independent School District[b]	1948	TX
1950s		
Gonzales v. Sheely[a]	1951	AZ
Ortiz v. Jack[c]	1952	AZ
Barraza v. Pecos Independent School District[d]	1953	TX
Orta v. Hondo Independent School District[d]	1953	TX
Romero v. Weakley[a]	1955	CA
Cortez v. Carrizo Springs Independent School District[c]	1955	TX
Salinas v. Kingsville Independent School District[c]	1956	TX
Hernandez v. Driscoll Consolidated Independent School District[a]	1957	TX
Villarreal v. Mathis Independent School District[c]	1957	TX
1960s		
Chapa v. Odem Independent School District[b]	1967	TX
1970s		
Cisneros v. Corpus Christi Independent School District[a]	1970	TX
Perez v. Sonora Independent School District[b]	1970	TX
Ross v. Eckels[a]	1970	TX
U.S. v. Lubbock Independent School District[a]	1970	TX
Alvarado v. El Paso Independent School District[a]	1971	TX
People v. San Diego Unified School District[a]	1971	CA
Tasby v. Estes[a]	1971	TX
Thomas v. Bryan Independent School District[b]	1971	TX
U.S. v. Texas Education Agency (Austin)[a]	1971	TX
U.S. v. Texas (Del Rio)[a]	1971	TX
Arvizu v. Waco Independent School District[a]	1973	TX
Keyes v. School District No. 1 of Denver[a]	1973	CO
Morales v. Shannon[a]	1973	TX
Soria v. Oxnard School District Board of Trustees[a]	1974	CA
U.S. v. Midland Independent School District[a]	1975	TX
Zamora v. New Braunfels Independent School District[a]	1975	TX
Crawford v. Board of Education of Los Angeles[a]	1976	CA
1980s		
Mendoza v. Tucson Unified School District[a]	1980	AZ
U.S. v. CRUCIAL v. Ector County Independent School District[a]	1983	TX
Diaz v. San Jose Unified School District[a]	1985	CA

Note: Citations for cases listed in this table are located in the References.

[a] Published decision in official legal reporter (e.g., *Federal Supplement*) or in an alternative legal reporter (e.g., *Race Relations Law Reporter*). [b] Case filed in state or federal court but no published opinion. [c] Case filed in federal court but no findings. [d] Case not filed in state or federal court.

Texas's presence is clearly seen in this corpus of thirty-five cases; twenty-three (66%) were brought forth in the Lone Star State. In descending order, the remainder of the cases were initiated in California ($n = 7$, 20%), Arizona ($n = 4$, 11%), and Colorado ($n = 1$, 3%).

The lawsuits are all Mexican American initiated, except for a few cases (e.g., *Keyes v. School District No. 1 of Denver*, 1973), which African Americans brought forth and Mexican Americans later joined. Due to the sheer number of lawsuits and space limitations, I discuss fourteen representative cases, which are listed in boldface in Table 1.1. The discussions focus on the significant feature(s) of these lawsuits, particularly how each case added new developments in Mexican American desegregation litigation. The remainder of this chapter is organized as follows: (a) historical prevalence of school segregation; (b) school segregation: inferior schooling and adverse effects; (c) Mexican American desegregation litigation; (d) contemporary status of Mexican American school desegregation litigation and school segregation.

Historical Prevalence of School Segregation

During the post-1848 period, there were few school facilities for Mexican American children. [Local and state political leaders' lack of commitment to public schooling, racial prejudice, and political differences among Anglos and Mexicans accounted for this practice] (Atkins, 1978; Friedman, 1978; Hendrick, 1977; Weinberg, 1977). After the 1870s, the number of schools for Mexican-origin children increased dramatically due to popular demand, legal mandates, increasing financial ability, and a greater acceptance of the ideal of common schooling by local and state political leaders (Atkins, 1978; Eby, 1925; Ferris, 1962). This educational access occurred, however, in the context of increasing societal discrimination and a general subordination of Mexican Americans. Out of this relationship between society and education there emerged a pattern of institutional discrimination. The establishment of segregated, inferior schools for Mexican-origin children reflected this socially racialized arrangement of White dominance over Mexican Americans. For example, 90% of the schools in Texas were racially segregated by 1930 (Rangel & Alcala, 1972).

The increase in the Mexican-origin population and the escalating barrioization of Mexican American communities led to the entrenchment of Mexican American school segregation throughout the Southwest from the 1930s to the 1970s. In 1971, the Mexican American Education Study (MAES) report on the isolation of Mexican American students in the Southwest confirmed that the historical segregation of Mexican American students persisted (U.S. Commission on Civil Rights, 1971a). In 1968, one in two Mexican American students attended schools in which they constituted the predominant racial/ethnic group (i.e., 50% to 100% Mexican American enrollment); one in five Mexican American students attended schools that were 80% to 100% Mexican American. Later studies showed that Mexican American student segregation intensified from the MAES 1968 baseline date through the 1980s (Orfield, 1988a, 1988b).[4]

In sum, national, regional, and Southwestern reports provide ample data on the historical prevalence of Mexican American student segregation. Later in this chapter, I discuss the contemporary status of Mexican American school segregation.

School Segregation: Inferior Schooling and Adverse Effects

For the most part, segregated schooling for students of color frequently leads to inferior schooling and results. The Mexican American community recognized this bedrock principle long before the initiation of desegregation litigation. For example, in 1910, in San Angelo, Texas, the Mexican American community staged a "blowout" (school walkout), charging that the "Mexican" school was inferior in physical facilities and quality of instruction. The aggrieved parents demanded that their children attend the White schools. The school board, after hearing the charges and demands, decided against integration. Subsequently, the Mexican American parents boycotted their own school altogether. The boycott lasted through 1915, but to no avail. Some of the Mexican American children attended the local Catholic school and the Mexican Presbyterian Mission school (De León, 1974).

A number of studies and reports have documented the inferior conditions of segregated schools attended by Mexican American students in decades past (e.g., Calderón, 1950; González, 1990; Maddux, 1932; Menchaca & Valencia, 1990; Reynolds, 1933). For example, Menchaca and Valencia contrasted the Mexican and Anglo schools built in the mid-1920s in Santa Paula, California. The Mexican school enrolled nearly one thousand students in a schoolhouse with eight classrooms (grades K–8) and contained two bathrooms and one administrative office. On the other hand, the Anglo school enrolled less than seven hundred students and contained twenty-one classrooms, a cafeteria, a training shop, and several administrative offices. In short, the Mexican school had a much higher student per-classroom ratio and inferior facilities than the Anglo school.

Another example of such studies is Maddux (1932), who described schooling conditions for Mexican American children in separate classrooms in Weld County, Colorado. Mexican American children often attended "rooms . . . located in basements [of schools] with bad lighting and poor ventilation. The Mexican room in [the town of] Kersey is in the basement under the gymnasium," said Maddux. "When the gymnasium is in use the noise is deafening. . . . [In this school] the small children have to sit on cigar boxes" (pp. 34–35).

Although earlier scholars documented the inferior nature of segregated Mexican American schools, it has only been in the contemporary era that researchers have empirically examined the adverse academic effects associated with school segregation. Jaeger (1987), for example, investigated the relation between achievement test scores and percentage Latino (overwhelmingly Mexican American) and African American high school students in metropolitan Los Angeles (1984–1985 school year). He observed strong correlations: mathematics (−0.89), reading (−0.90), and writing (−0.85). That is, as minority enrollment increased, achievement decreased. The correlations between school enrollment percentage of White students and achievement test scores were likewise of very high magnitudes (0.80s), but in the opposite direction (i.e., as White enrollment in the high schools increased, test scores also increased). Finally, Jaeger disaggregated the data and found that the r's for percentage of Latino students and achievement were substantial (mathematics, −0.53; reading, −0.58; and writing, −0.53), but not as strong for the Latino/African American aggregate.

Espinosa and Ochoa (1986) examined the connection between Latino (overwhelmingly Mexican American) segregation and diminished achievement in California, using a large statewide sample (4,268 public elementary schools and 791 public high schools). Correlating California Assessment Program (CAP) scores (average of math and reading achievement) with percentage of Latino students in grades 3, 6, and 12, Espinosa and Ochoa found a strong relation between Latino concentration and CAP achievement (e.g., at grade 12 the observed r was −0.49).

A more recent analysis (conducted by the author) examined the relation between school segregation of Mexican American (and other Latino) and African American students and their academic achievement in the

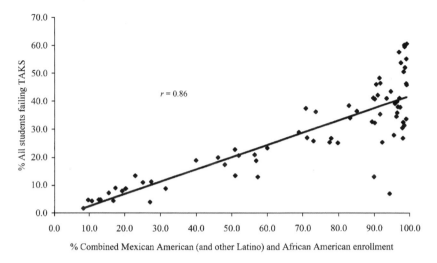

Figure 1.1. Scatterplot of Correlation between Percentage of All Students Failing All Tests on TAKS and Percentage of Combined Mexican American (and Other Latino) and African American Enrollment in Austin Independent School District Elementary Schools (*N* = 74). *Source*: Texas Education Agency (2003a).

Austin Independent School District (AISD). The AISD, the fourth-largest school district in Texas in the 2002–2003 academic year, enrolled 78,608 students (Texas Education Agency, 2003a). The racial/ethnic enrollments for Early Childhood Education to grade 12 were, in descending order: Mexican American and other Latino (51.6%); White (31.1%); African American (14.4%); Asian/Pacific Islander (2.7%); American Indian (0.3%). In this investigation, the correlational analysis was confined to the elementary schools (*N* = 74) in this highly segregated district.[5] The percentage of failure rates of all students on all Texas Assessment of Knowledge and Skills (TAKS) tests[6] was correlated with the percentage of combined Mexican American (and other Latino) and African American students in the seventy-four schools.[7] Figure 1.1 graphically illustrates that as the percentage of combined Mexican American/other Latino and African American enrollments increases in the seventy-four schools, the percentage of students who fail TAKS increases. The observed *r* of 0.86 suggests a very strong pattern of racialized academic achievement in the AISD.

Finally, school segregation and schooling problems are not confined to test score outcomes. For example, Orfield (1988a) found a −0.83 correlation between the percentage of Mexican American/other Latino and

African American students and graduation rate in metropolitan Chicago high schools. Furthermore, Orfield found a correlation of −0.47 between percentage minority high school students and percentage of students taking the college entrance examinations.

Another recent study (conducted by the author) demonstrated that school segregation of students of color is linked to higher dropout rates in the eleven AISD high schools (excluding one alternative high school); graduation rates for the class of 2003 were available for all eleven campuses (Texas Education Agency, 2004). The percentage of combined Mexican American (and other Latino) and African American students (grades 9–12) was correlated with campus graduation rates. The observed *r* was −0.94, suggesting a very strong negative correlation between percentage of students of color enrollment and rate of graduation in the AISD's high schools. An examination of two extreme schools (of the eleven) illustrates this relation. Johnston High School, a predominantly Mexican American/other Latino and African American school (combined 97.5%; 2.5% White), had a campus graduation rate of 68.2%. By sharp contrast, Bowie High School (predominantly White [70.2%]; 25.4% combined Mexican American/other Latino and African American) had a campus graduation rate of 93.0%. The above *r* of −0.94 means that Mexican American/other Latino and African American students who attend the more highly segregated high schools in the AISD have a lower probability of graduating from high school and subsequently of matriculating to college.

Mexican American Desegregation Litigation

As discussed, the number of Mexican American–initiated desegregation lawsuits far exceeds the number of cases in any of the other categories covered in this book. Therefore, the discussion here is limited to fourteen representative cases (listed in boldface in Table 1.1). All cases were litigated between twenty-three and eighty-three years ago. As such, the focus will largely be through a historical lens.

Romo v. Laird (1925)

This lawsuit is of particular interest because it is the first Mexican American–initiated desegregation case. Contrary to what many scholars have written, the *Independent School District v. Salvatierra* (1930) case in Texas is not the first desegregation lawsuit brought forth by Mexican Americans.

Adolfo "Babe" Romo, Jr., a Mexican American rancher in Tempe, Arizona (Maricopa County), filed this case (Muñoz, 2001). Romo sued the Tempe Elementary School District No. 3 on behalf of his four children, ages seven to fifteen years; defendants included Superintendent William E. Laird and others.[8] By design, the Board of Trustees required that the "Spanish-Mexican" children attend the Eighth Street School. This segregated school, designated as a Normal Training School, served as a training ground for student teachers enrolled in the teacher-preparation program at the nearby Tempe State Teachers' College. In the Eighth Street School, student teachers exclusively taught the children under the supervision of four "critic" teachers employed by the Board of Education of Tempe State Teachers' College.[9]

Plaintiffs complained in *Romo* that the teachers in the Eighth Street School "are inferior in attainments and qualifications and ability to teach as compared with the teachers . . . in the other schools of District No. 3, in that they have not completed their education and course of training in the work of teaching."[10] Plaintiffs sought a writ of mandamus requiring that the Board of Trustees allow them to enroll in the other (meaning White) schools of the district that employed certified and qualified teachers.[11] Plaintiffs particularly sought admission to the new Tenth Street School.

Defendants asserted that plaintiff children were entitled to admission to the other public schools of the district, but denied them enrollment in said schools due to pedagogical reasons. Defendants argued that because the Mexican American children were Spanish speaking, their English language development needs could be best met in a segregated school setting. Under state law, the district could segregate Mexican American children for instructional reasons, but not by race.[12]

Presiding Judge Joseph S. Jenckes ruled for plaintiffs, relying on *Dameron v. Bayless* (1912) (Supreme Court of Arizona), which was an African American desegregation lawsuit (initiated in Maricopa County, District No. 1). The court ruled:

> The law will . . . and does require that, after children arrive at the school building, it be as good a building and as well equipped and furnished and presided over by as *efficient corps of teachers as the schools provided for the children of other races* [italics added].[13]

In his judgment, Judge Jenckes ruled that plaintiffs were entitled to admission "on the same terms and conditions to the public schools of said Tempe School District No. 3, Maricopa County, Arizona, as children of other nationalities are now admitted."[14]

Although *Romo* is significant because it is the first Mexican American–initiated desegregation case, it exerted very little influence. Because it was not a class action lawsuit, only the Romo children benefited. Furthermore, days after the ruling in *Romo*, the Board of Trustees of the school district and the Board of Education of the Tempe State Teachers' College, at a joint meeting, decided that only certified teachers would be hired to instruct students at the Eighth Street School, and the student teachers would be allowed to observe (but not to instruct).[15] The immediate outcome in this policy change was the continued segregation of Mexican American children in the Eighth Street School, a practice that lasted until the 1950s (Muñoz, 2001). *Romo* is also important in this legal history because we see how school boards used the cloak of pedagogy—separation on language grounds—to isolate Mexican American from White children. This practice, used over and over, was, at its core, racialized segregation.

Independent School District v. Salvatierra (1930)

This case was the first Mexican American desegregation lawsuit in the state of Texas.[16] To best understand *Salvatierra*, some background information is in order.

Jesús Salvatierra and other Mexican American citizens and taxpayers, on behalf of their minor children, initiated *Salvatierra* in Del Rio, a community situated on the U.S.-Mexico border, 144 miles due west of San Antonio. In early January 1930, the Del Rio Independent School District's Board of Trustees (defendants, along with others) ordered an election to be held on February 1, 1930. The purpose of the bond election was to secure $185,000 to build a new senior high school and to remodel and enlarge the three elementary schools.[17] At that time, the district's four schools were located on an oblong, irregularly shaped unit of land, twelve hundred feet in length. At the east end, the senior high school and two elementary schools were located. An athletic field spanned the middle of the school property, and at the west end was situated the third elementary school, designated as the "Mexican" or "West End" school, which contained two rooms. The children in the West End school were in elementary grades up to the "low third." The school, constructed of brick and tile, was to be enlarged by the addition of five rooms and an auditorium.[18]

The trial took place in the District Court of Val Verde County; Judge Joseph Jones presided. Counsel for plaintiffs in this class action lawsuit were lawyers of the League of United Latin American Citizens (LULAC), the newly established Mexican American advocacy organization. LULAC's executive board selected the Del Rio Independent School District as a test case intended to bring an end to segregation in Texas (Balderrama, 1982). *Salvatierra* plaintiffs sought an injunction to prevent the district from enlarging the West End school. Plaintiffs' complaint asserted that the Board of Trustees exclusively and illegally maintained the West End school for Mexican American children and that the construction of new classrooms in the West End school would exacerbate such segregation in the district.[19]

In *Salvatierra*, plaintiffs acknowledged that the constitution of the State of Texas, adopted in 1875 and ratified in 1876, allowed for the segregation of White and "colored" children—colored meaning only "Negro." The statute read, "Separate schools shall be provided for the white and colored children, and impartial provision shall be made for both."[20] Thus, *Salvatierra* sought to determine the constitutionality of separating Mexican American children on racial grounds. The challenge to plaintiffs' attorneys, however, was to argue that the school district was illegally segregating Mexican American children under the "color of law," which is defined this way:

> The appearance or semblance, without the substance, of a legal right. The term usu. [*sic*] implies a misuse of power made possible because the wrongdoer is clothed with the authority of the state. *State action* is synonymous with *color of law* in the context of federal civil-rights statutes or criminal law. (Garner, 1999, p. 260)

Plaintiffs' claims asserted that although the law considered Mexican Americans legally to be "other White," the State was unlawfully segregating them under color of law.[21]

The District Court ruled in *Salvatierra* that the school district illegally segregated the Mexican American children, and thus the court granted an injunction of the new construction at the West End school. The school district appealed the decision to the Court of Civil Appeals of Texas, San Antonio; Judge J. Smith presided. The appellants argued, via testimony by

[handwritten annotation: argued segregation not for race but — migratory — language]

the school superintendent, that they did not segregate the Mexican American children based on race. Rather, the basis for the separation lay on two educational grounds. First, the superintendent noted that about half of the Mexican American children joined their parents in the migratory stream of picking cotton and working on ranches during part of the school year. As a result, the superintendent added, the children upon return to school were several months "retarded from the standpoint of enrollment,"[22] and thus for the children to receive efficient instruction they needed to be segregated in the Mexican school. Second, the superintendent testified that the Mexican American children required segregated instruction because of language needs. He commented,

The average Spanish speaking children [*sic*] know English as a foreign tongue, and consequently when you put him in a class with English speaking children and teach him according to the method of teaching English speaking children he is greatly handicapped.[23]

Therefore, the superintendent testified, Mexican Americans should be segregated on language grounds so as to be instructed by "teachers [who] are specialized in the matter of teaching them English and American citizenship."[24] Judge Smith cited state statutes and case law,[25] and noted that local school boards in Texas

have the power to manage and regulate the schools of their respective districts, to administer the affairs of those schools in such manner as in their judgment may most certainly accomplish the wholesome objects of our public educational policies. This discretion extends to the power to locate and construct the district schools upon such sites, and in accordance with such plans and specifications, as in their judgment seem best suited to the purposes of those policies.[26]

Following from this, the judge ruled that the school district was operating within its administrative power to manage educational matters as it saw fit. Although Mexican American students could not be arbitrarily segregated based on race, it was ruled that their segregation based on educational grounds was warranted and lawful. Judge Smith reversed the District Court's decision and dissolved the injunction. LULAC attorneys appealed to the U.S. Supreme Court, but the Court denied the writ of certiorari (request to be heard on appeal) on October 26, 1931, for lack of jurisdiction (*Salvatierra v. Independent School District*, 1931).[27] Valencia (2005) notes that the existing legal records do not reveal what eventuated after the Texas Court of Civil Appeals' decision. One could reason, however, that the Texas Supreme Court did not find error, leaving the Court of Civil Appeals' decision standing and subject to the U.S. Supreme Court's decision.

Texas's debut in desegregation litigation via *Salvatierra* was inauspicious. The presence of legal indeterminacy was particularly salient in this case. Martínez (1994) points out that the school district's two educational justifications for the segregation of the Mexican American children—late school entry due to migrant farm-working patterns and English language difficulties—were, at the core, race based and hence illegal. The existence of double standards, arbitrariness, and capriciousness were evident. With respect to the diminished school attendance resulting from the migrant farm-working life, the superintendent testified that "American English speaking children"[28] also came late to school. He stated, however, "No, I did not send any of those English speaking children who came in late over to the school where I sent the Mexican or Spanish speaking children."[29] With respect to the other justification for segregation—language needs—Martínez raises a valid point, which is that "There were no tests [used] demonstrating that the Mexican-American children were less proficient in English [than their White peers]" (1994, p. 576). In *Salvatierra*, the educational justification for segregation of the Mexican American was merely a smoke screen for the school board's race-based opposition to mixing young Mexican American and White children in the same classrooms. Within the context of CRT, we can see that the school board was more interested in maintaining White privilege than in providing educational equality for the Mexican American children. Although both the District Court and the Court of Civil Appeals ruled that Mexican American students could not be segregated on the basis of race, the educational justification (i.e., language needs) for segregation were a severe blow for years ahead in the Mexican American community's incipient campaign for school desegregation and integration. The language-deficiencies rationale for segregation of Mexican American children gained particularly notable strength on April 8, 1947, when the Texas Attorney General supported the *Salvatierra* court's holding:

> A school district may not legally maintain separate schools for pupils of Mexican descent where the segregation is based solely on race. But based

on language deficiencies and other individual needs and aptitudes demonstrated by examinations or properly conducted tests, a school district may maintain separate classes, in separate building if necessary, for any pupils with deficiencies, needs or aptitudes, through the first three grades. (opinion No. V-128; reported in Hinsley, 1968, p. 1109)

Alvarez v. Lemon Grove School District (1931)

Meanwhile, in California, a similar lawsuit was filed. *Alvarez* took place during the Great Depression in Lemon Grove, California, a small town located eight miles east of San Diego and fifteen miles north of the U.S.-Mexico border. At the time, Lemon Grove provided the Mexican-origin community with employment in a mining quarry and a railroad packing house. The town, however, was noted for its lucrative citrus business of growing lemons and oranges, producing annual sales of hundreds of thousands of dollars (Álvarez, 1986).

On August 13, 1930, the Lemon Grove School Board met to discuss problems at the Lemon Grove Grammar School, the only educational facility in town (Álvarez, 1986; Balderrama, 1982). The total enrollment of the school was 169 students, 75 (44%) of whom were Mexican-origin children. Most of the latter were first-generation American citizens by birth (Álvarez, 1986). Due to overcrowding, the school board voted to construct a two-room school, located in the Mexican American neighborhood, just for the Mexican American children. It appears that the overcrowding issue may have been a pretext for a far deeper motive—pressure from the White community to segregate Mexican American children from the White children.[30]

Subsequently, the district built the Mexican school. In a flagrant disregard of the Mexican American parents' and children's rights, the school board made no prior attempt to inform the families about the change in schools. The Mexican American children first found out on the morning of January 5, 1931, when they walked up to the front steps to enter Lemon Grove Grammar School, as they had routinely done so many times before.

Jerome J. Green, principal of Lemon Grove Grammar School, acting under instructions from the school trustees, stood at the door and admitted all pupils except the Mexican students. Principal Green announced that the Mexican children did not belong at the school, could not enter, and instructed them to attend a two room building constructed to house Mexican children. Dejected, embarrassed and angry, the Mexican children left the school and returned home [and informed their parents what transpired]. (Álvarez, 1986, p. 118)

The Mexican American parents were very upset about the treatment of their children and instructed them not to attend the so-called new school, which the children called *La Caballeriza* (the stable). On January 8, 1931, three days after Principal Green physically banned the Mexican American children from Lemon Grove Grammar School, the *San Diego Evening Tribune* published a news article headlined "75 Mexican Students Go on Strike" (Álvarez, 1988). The parents formed the *Comité de Vecinos de Lemon Grove* (the Lemon Grove Neighborhood Committee) and sought assistance from the larger Mexican American community. The committee also sought advice from Enrique Ferreira, Mexican consul in San Diego, who in turn arranged for two attorneys—Fred C. Noon and A.C. Brinkley from San Diego—to represent the parents in a lawsuit. Noon spoke Spanish fluently and was considered an expert in legal affairs regarding border relations (Álvarez, 1988).

Within a short time, on February 24, 1931, litigation of *Alvarez* began in the San Diego Superior Court, and lasted nearly four weeks; Judge Claude Chambers presided. Roberto Álvarez (on behalf of the other Mexican American children), ten principal witnesses in support of the plaintiff children, the school board, and school staff offered testimony.[31] The plaintiff's petition for writ of mandate "indicted each of the school board members for illegal segregation and commanded the admittance of all pupils of Mexican parentage and nationality to the main [Lemon Grove Grammar] school" (Álvarez, 1986, p. 129).[32] The petition stated that California had no statute allowing the segregation of Mexican American children based on race (as was the situation in Arizona and Texas, discussed earlier).

Defendants argued that in addition to the overcrowding issue at Lemon Grove Grammar School, the Mexican American children had certain needs and segregated instruction would be in their best interests. Specifically, defendants justified the segregation on educational grounds—that is, Mexican Americans' needs for Americanization, English language development, and a focus on basic instruction due to children's academic deficiencies. Plaintiff's strategy was twofold: First, they attempted to discredit the defendants' allegation about the Mexican American children's poor scholastic achievement and language deficiencies. For example, plaintiff Roberto Álvarez, who "was an exemplary student and spoke English well" (Álvarez, 1986, p. 125), provided key testimony. Second, plaintiffs' counsel sought to expose double standards in defendants' rationale that segregation of Mexican American children was warranted on educational grounds. For example, note the following exchange between Judge Chambers and a defendant:

> *Judge Chambers*: When there are American [White] children who are behind (in grade level), what do you do with them?
> *Answer*: They are kept in a lower grade.
> *Judge Chambers*: You don't segregate them? Why not do the same with the other children? Wouldn't the association of American and Mexican children be favorable to the learning of English for these (Mexican) children?
> Silence is the answer. (Álvarez, 1988, p. 46)

On March 30, 1931, Judge Chambers found that defendants had no statutory right under California law to segregate Mexican American children. Furthermore, he ruled that the education of these children in a separate facility retarded their Americanization and the English language development of the Spanish-speaking children. Judge Chambers ordered the Lemon Grove Grammar School to admit the children and to provide them with instruction on the same, equal basis with their White peers (Álvarez, 1986).

The *Alvarez* case is highly significant because it is the nation's first successful class action school desegregation court case. Notwithstanding this import, the case "was isolated as a local event, and had no precedent-setting ruling affecting either the State of California or other situations of school segregation in the Southwest" (Álvarez, 1986, p. 131).

Notwithstanding the incipient school desegregation litigative struggles in Arizona (*Romo*), Texas (*Salvatierra*), and California (*Alvarez*), the segregation of Mexican American students in the Southwest was entrenched by the early 1930s (San Miguel & Valencia, 1998; Valencia, Menchaca, and Donato, 2002).[33] Wollenberg (1974) notes, however, that

> By the mid-1930s, segregation of Mexican students was coming under attack. The Depression spawned attempts at social and economic reform, and these in turn created a belief that poverty and social disadvantages were caused by environmental factors subject to human remedy. (p. 322)

No further Mexican American–initiated desegregation lawsuits were filed from 1932 to 1945. By the early 1940s, however, the likelihood of Mexican Americans renewing their litigative struggle for school desegregation appeared to increase. Wollenberg (1974) comments,

> The doubts expressed about segregation in the thirties evolved into new convictions during the forties. By the end of World War II, spokesmen for California's educational establishment were vigorously condemning school segregation. The war had identified racism with Hitler and the Axis powers, while equality and justice were said to be the principles of the Allied cause. (p. 323)

The return of servicemen of color from World War II served as another factor that helped to reignite both the Mexican American and African American desegregation campaigns. The bravery and accomplishments of these men during the war were often unparalleled (Delgado & Stefancic, 2001). Indeed, scholars have documented that Mexican Americans, for example, were disproportionately represented among the casualties in World War II and that they were the most decorated ethnic group of the war (Morín, 1963; Ramos, 1998). Still, these servicemen—like their African American counterparts—returned home to experience the same discrimination and second-class citizenship that existed when they left to fight a war in the name of democracy (Klarman, 2004). Although these "valiant guardsmen of the American dream were forgotten, . . . these veterans stood prepared to struggle as never before for their rightful place as citizens of the United States of America" (Ramos, 1998, p. xvii). One such battleground became education, especially the desegregation of schools.

Mendez v. Westminster (1946)

Many scholars consider this case to be the most significant of the Mexican American desegregation lawsuits because its outcome had implications not only for California but for the Southwest and the nation. In 1943, at the height of World War II, Gonzalo and Felicitas Méndez and their children moved to his hometown of Westminster (Orange County), California, located thirty-five miles south of Los Angeles. At the time, a Japanese American family resided in Westminster and owned a sixty-acre farm. Unfortunately, the family members became part of over 120,000 Japanese American individuals to be rounded up and forcibly interned in concentration camps in the United States (Hayashi, 2004). A compassionate banker helped the Méndez family lease the farm from the Japanese American family. After considerable hard work, the Méndez family was able to make a relatively prosperous living by raising and selling lettuce, cabbage, peppers, and other types of vegetables (Ferg-Cadima, 2004; González, 1990).

Soledad Vidaurri, aunt of the three Méndez children, took Sylvia, Gerónimo, and Gonzalo, Jr., to the nearest school—Westminster Elementary School—to enroll them on the first day of the 1944–1945 school year (González, 1990). At that time, the school officially admitted only White students. The school also denied the Méndez children admission on the grounds that they were deficient in English, the common assertion that school boards had been advancing beginning with *Romo* (1925). This surprised Soledad, as her own children (Alice and Edward, Mexican American) attended Westminster Elementary. She later discovered that the school admitted her children because "of their light complexions and their last name, Vidaurri, which was French" (González, 1990, p. 150). This discrimination by phenotype and surname became a key issue in the *Mendez* case.

Immediately after Westminster Elementary School denied admission to her two nephews and niece, Soledad withdrew her own children from the school and informed Gonzalo and Felicitas what had transpired. Via communication between members of the Mexican American community and the school board, the Méndez family made several attempts to end school segregation. The board, however, was intractable (González, 1990). Subsequently, Mexican American plaintiffs filed a lawsuit that led to one of the most significant legal decisions in the annals of desegregation efforts in the United States. For the first time in history, plaintiffs succeeded in federal court to forbid segregation, using the argument that separate was *not* equal.

On March 2, 1945, five Mexican American fathers—Gonzalo Méndez, William Guzmán, Frank Palomino, Thomas Estrada, and Lorenzo Ramírez—filed suit on behalf of their fifteen collective children and five thousand other minor children of "Mexican and Latin descent."[34] Defendants in *Mendez* were four school districts: Westminster, Garden Grove, and El Modeno (located in relatively small rural towns in the citrus belt of southern California) and Santa Ana, a school district in Santa Ana (city of over forty thousand residents and the county seat of Orange County).[35] Joel Ogle, Orange County counsel, represented the defendant districts.

Unlike the Arizona, Texas, and California state court cases discussed earlier, *Mendez* was filed in federal court—the U.S. District Court for the Southern District of California (Central Division); Judge Paul J. McCormick presided. Thus, it was the first school desegregation case in which plaintiffs argued that separate was *not* equal in K–12 public schools because such segregation violated their rights under the Equal Protection Clause of the Fourteenth Amendment of the U.S. Constitution. This argument is what makes *Mendez* so distinct.

It is important to acknowledge that in the 1930s the National Association for the Advancement of Colored People (NAACP) had already adopted this federal court strategy for a series of higher education desegregation cases it was filing (*Pearson v. Murray*, 1936; *Missouri ex rel. Gaines v. Canada et al.*, 1938). Part of the NAACP's legal strategy was to win several of these higher education cases before testing the Fourteenth Amendment argument in K–12 cases (see Kluger, 1976). In sum, we need to be aware of the broader history into which *Mendez* fits. On the one hand, *Mendez* was *not* the first federal desegregation case, but it did push the agenda for using the Fourteenth Amendment argument in K–12 education. As such, the *Mendez* lawyer both may have been inspired by the NAACP legal strategy and may have contributed to it. *Mendez* is an example of one way in which the Mexican American and African American struggles were intertwined and reinforcing. This connection has not been fully acknowledged.

At the time of the *Mendez* case, the NAACP lawyers, including Charles Houston, Thurgood Marshall, and Robert Carter, were pursuing a different but somewhat parallel strategy to overturn eventually the 1896 *Plessy v. Ferguson* legal precedent. Based on a report issued by the NAACP in 1931, called the Margold Report (Kluger, 1976), and on the vision of Charles Houston, these lawyers were in the midst of a two-decade legal assault on segregation in schools that began with cases focused on the *inequality* of racially segregated schools, and not segregation itself until the 1950s. During the 1930s and into the early 1950s, the key NAACP integration cases involved Black students trying to gain access to graduate schools at prestigious state universities in Southern states that did not provide separate law schools or other graduate schools for students of color (see Klarman, 2004; Kluger, 1976).

In this way, the *Mendez* case fits into the center of the NAACP's meticulous road to *Brown* by directly questioning, in federal court, the validity of segregation itself within the K–12 public educational system just before the NAACP lawyers brought a series of cases that eventually did the same thing and culminated in the *Brown* decision. Yet, because appellants did not appeal *Mendez* to the U.S. Supreme Court, and because the final appellate court ruling tied the issue of segregation to California state law, this case could not set the same sort of legal precedent that *Brown* eventually did. Still, there remain many important similarities between the *Mendez* and *Brown* cases that suggest that the experience of the first case informed—directly or indirectly—the strategies of the second.

David C. Marcus, a civil rights lawyer from Los Angeles, served as the attorney for the *Mendez* plaintiffs; A.L. Wirin was co-counsel (Arriola, 1995). Marcus brought to this case his prior experience in desegregation litigation in federal court. He had represented Mexican American and Puerto Rican plaintiffs in a successful class action, known as *Lopez v. Seccombe* (1944), challenging segregation in a park and swimming facilities in San Bernardino, California. In this case, the plaintiffs argued that San Bernardino city officials had violated their Fifth and Fourteenth Amendment rights, especially the Equal Protection Clause, to full use of the public park and its facilities. *Lopez* was significant because it was the first time that the Equal Protection Clause had been used to uphold Mexican Americans' rights (Arriola, 1995).

Regarding the *Mendez* lawsuit, plaintiffs' allegations and desires for relief were, in a condensed form, as follows:

• Defendant school districts intentionally segregated children of Mexican and Latin descent via "rules, regulations, custom, and usage."[36] Thus, given that the segregative mandate of California (Section 8003 of the Education Code)[37] made no mention of children of Mexican descent, the districts were segregating Mexican-origin students "under color of law." Joe Ogle, defendants' counsel, strenuously argued against this allegation. As described in Wollenberg (1974),

> Joel Ogle replied that federal courts had no jurisdiction in the case, since education was a matter governed by state law. Moreover, Ogle claimed that the districts were not segregating children on the arbitrary basis of race or nationality, but for the reasonable purpose of providing special instruction to students not fluent in English and not familiar with American values and customs. Finally, he pointed out that in the case of *Plessy v. Ferguson* (1896) the Supreme Court had allowed states to segregate races, providing that the separate facilities for each race were equal. (p. 326)

• Both plaintiffs and defendants conceded "that there is no question of race discrimination in this action."[38] As such, plaintiffs argued that because Mexican schoolchildren are considered White, alleged discrimination was based not on race but on *national origin.*

• The Equal Protection Clause of the Fourteenth Amendment played a key role in the *Mendez* case. Plaintiffs' complaint was

> grounded upon the Fourteenth Amendment to the Constitution of the United States . . . [and] alleges a concerted policy and design of class discrimination against 'persons of Mexican or Latin descent or extraction' of elementary school age by defendant school agencies in the conduct and operation of public schools of said districts, resulting in the denial of the equal protection of the laws to such class of persons among which are the petitioning school children.[39]

• *Mendez* attorney Marcus employed a varied strategy by (a) questioning the state and federal legal bases of segregation; (b) having Mexican American community members who had attended the local schools speak to the extreme aspects of segregation; (c) underscoring, via testimony, examples of transfer denials; (d) having children testify to how attending segregated schools made them feel (Arriola, 1995); (e) using testimony of social scientists. Regarding this latter strategy, it appears that I am the first scholar to highlight the role of the social scientists as expert witnesses in *Mendez* by reporting on their testimony (Valencia, 2005).[40]

Marcus had two experts testify. They were Dr. Ralph L. Beals, Professor and Chairman of the Department of Anthropology and Sociology (University of California, Berkeley), and Mrs. Marie H. Hughes, former principal and Curricula Director in New Mexico. At the time of the trial, Hughes served as Curriculum Coordinator and Specialist in Education of Minority Groups, Public Schools, Los Angeles County. Hughes, who held a master's degree, had completed the residence work and academic work for a Ph.D. at Stanford University. The testimony of these two experts furthered the central argument that Marcus was trying to drive home with his other witnesses, namely that segregation retards the development of Mexican American children. A number of assertions ran through the experts' opinions. Beals's main points upon direct examination were the following:

• The segregation of the Mexican-descent students is at cross-purposes with Americanization. That is, segregation retards "the assimilation of the child to American customs and ways."[41]

- Segregation fosters antagonism in Mexican-descent children, feelings of being discriminated against, and hostility "to the whole culture of the surrounding majority group."[42]
- The separation of White students from Mexican-descent students reinforces "inferiority-superiority, which exists in the population as a whole."[43]
- Spanish-speaking Mexican-descent students lose ground in learning English in segregated settings. There is a "very widely known fact, that if you want to learn a foreign language you immerse yourself among people that speak that language, and do not stay among speakers of your own language."[44]
- English-speaking Mexican-descent children "lose some of their English facility"[45] in segregated settings with their Spanish-speaking peers.
- In sum, "segregation does retard the development of the child of Mexican descent."[46]

Hughes's testimony strongly bolstered Beals's expert opinions. She testified that the segregation of the Mexican-descent students (a) lessens their English language learning and Americanization development and (b) engenders feelings of inferiority. Of the two expert witnesses, Hughes's testimony appears to have been more valuable. Given that she had considerably more experience with Mexican-descent students (observing, developing curricula, and doing research), she was able to provide the court with deep psychological and linguistic insights. For example, with respect to the engendering of feelings of inferiority in Mexican-descent students, her testimony paralleled the arguments that were to be made later by Dr. Kenneth Clark in the *Brown* case. Hughes testified,

Segregation, by its very nature, is a reminder constantly of inferiority, of not being wanted, of not being a part of the community. Such an experience cannot possibly build the best personality or the sort of person who is at most home in the world, and able to contribute and live well.[47]

Regarding the educational value of having Spanish-speaking Mexican-descent children attend the same schools and classes as their White peers, she commented in her testimony,

The best ways to teach English is to give many opportunities to speak English, to hear it spoken correctly, and have reasons for speaking it, and to enlarge the experiences which demand English. That is, with any language you tend to learn the words of a given experience, and if your experiences are limited, your vocabulary will be limited. As the experiences are increased, as you meet more people from different kinds of homes and from different classes, different occupational classes, and so forth, then your language is naturally increased.[48]

On February 18, 1946—nearly a year after the *Mendez* case was filed—Judge McCormick handed down his decision. It was so far-reaching that it led to the end of *de jure* segregation of California's schools sixteen months later. The following are highlights of Judge McCormick's decision. First, regarding the core issue of jurisdiction, Judge McCormick noted,

> The defendants at the outset challenge the jurisdiction of this court under the record as it exists at this time. We have already denied the defendants' motion to dismiss the action upon the "face" of the complaint. No reason has been shown which warrants reconsideration of such decision.[49]

Nonetheless, Judge McCormick went on and explained why the federal court was justified to intervene:

> We think the pattern of public education promulgated in the Constitution of California and effectuated by provisions of the Education Code of the State prohibits segregation of the pupils of Mexican ancestry in the elementary schools from the rest of the school children . . . [and thus] the school boards and administrative authorities have by their segregation policies and practices transgressed applicable law and Constitutional safeguards and limitations and thus have invaded the personal right which every public school pupil has to the equal protection provision of the Fourteenth Amendment to obtain the means of education.[50]

Second, given that the defendants' attorney, Ogle, raised the *Plessy* case as justification for the separate but equal education of the Mexican American students, Judge McCormick had to respond to the *Plessy* doctrine, which was the prevailing law of the land since 1896. The judge, however, avoided direct reference to the constitutional issue of *Plessy* at this juncture. Rather, he based his decision on the California statute that disallowed the segregation of students of Mexican ancestry and on the Fourteenth Amendment's Equal Protection Clause. Yet Judge McCormick took an indirect swipe at *Plessy* in such a manner that this part of his decision is the singularly most important aspect emanating from *Mendez*. One observer, the Honorable Constance Baker Motley,[51] commented, "The district court's unequivocally strong language was radically new at the time the decision was issued."[52] Judge McCormick wrote in his opinion,

> "The equal protection of the laws" pertaining to the public school system in California is not provided by furnishing in separate schools the same technical facilities, text books and courses of instruction to children of Mexican ancestry that are available to the other public school children regardless of their ancestry. *A paramount requisite in the American system of public education is social equality. It must be open to all children by unified school association regardless of lineage* [italics added].[53]

Regarding this portion of the ruling, legal scholar Juan F. Perea argues that the federal judge rejected the entire underpinning of *Plessy v. Ferguson* and foreshadowed the reasoning of the Supreme Court in *Brown v. Board of Education*. Perea (1997) comments, "Where *Plessy* had reified segregation by disclaiming the Court's power to act to remedy social inequality, the *Mendez* opinion conveys a powerfully different understanding of equality that ultimately prevails in *Brown*" (p. 1244).

The third highlight of Judge McCormick's decision is his response to the so-called new integrationist educational theory proffered by social science and psychological experts who testified in *Mendez* regarding the harms of segregation (Arriola, 1995). The judge wrote, "It is also established by the record that the methods of segregation prevalent in the defendant school districts foster antagonisms in the children and suggest inferiority among them where none exists."[54] In reference to this part of Judge McCormick's opinion, Perea (1997) remarks, "The *Mendez* court also anticipated *Brown*, and rejected *Plessy*, in its understanding of the role of public education and the stigmatizing meaning and purpose of segregation" (p. 1244).

A fourth highlight of Judge McCormick's ruling: The defendant districts justified the segregation of Mexican-origin students by asserting that they based such separation on language needs and not race. As noted in the *Mendez* record, non-English-speaking students were "required to attend schools designated by the boards separate and apart from English-speaking pupils; that such group should attend such schools until they had acquired some proficiency in the English language."[55] The plaintiffs, on the other hand, alleged that the language segregation policy was a pretense for blanket discrimination against the students of Mexican ancestry, and thus the requirement was illegal: "The petitioners contend that such official action evinces a covert attempt by the school authorities in such school districts to produce an arbitrary discrimination against school children of Mexican extraction or descent."[56] Plaintiffs' argument clearly persuaded Judge McCormick. He noted,

> It has been held that public school authorities may differentiate in the exercise of their reasonable discretion as to the pedagogical methods of instruction to be pursued with different pupils [citing *Plessy v. Ferguson*]. And foreign language handicaps may be to such a degree in the pupils in elementary schools as to require special treatment in separate classrooms. Such separate allocations, however, can be lawfully made only after credible examination by the appropriate school authority.[57]

Continuing from this statement, Judge McCormick was highly critical of the districts' language assessment used in assigning Mexican American students to segregated schools. He added,

> No credible language test is given to the children of Mexican ancestry upon entering the first grade in Lincoln School. . . . The tests applied to the beginners are shown to have been generally hasty, superficial and not reliable. In some instances separate classification was determined largely by the Latinized or Mexican name of the child. Such methods of evaluating language knowledge are illusory and are not conducive to the inculcation and enjoyment of civil rights which are of primary importance in the public school system of education in the United States.[58]

Judge McCormick went one step further on the issue of language segregation, citing the integrationist educational theory. He wrote,

> The evidence clearly shows that Spanish-speaking children are retarded in learning English by lack of exposure to its use because of segregation, and that *commingling of the entire student body instills and develops a common cultural attitude among the school children* [italics added] which is imperative for the perpetuation of American institutions and ideals.[59]

In his ruling, Judge McCormick ruled that defendants discriminated against the Mexican-origin students and violated their rights under the Fourteenth Amendment. The judge ordered injunctive relief:

We conclude by holding that the allegations of the complaint (petition) have been established sufficiently to justify injunctive relief against all defendants, restraining further discriminatory practices against the pupils of Mexican descent in the public schools of defendant school districts. . . . The natural operation and effect of the Board's official action manifests a clear purpose to arbitrarily discriminate against the pupils of Mexican ancestry and to deny to them the equal protection of the laws.[60]

Reactions to this initial *Mendez* decision were swift and reverberated across the country. *La Opinión*, a Spanish-language newspaper in Los Angeles, interviewed plaintiffs' attorney David C. Marcus, who called the *Mendez* ruling *"una de las más grandes decisiones judiciales en favor de las prácticas democráticas otorgadas desde la emancipación de los esclavos"* [one of the greatest judicial decisions in favor of democratic practices since the emancipation of the slaves].[61]

A number of prominent law journals also noted Judge McCormick's decision, including the *Columbia Law Review, Harvard Law Review, Illinois Law Review, Minnesota Law Review,* and *Yale Law Journal*.[62] For example, a commentator in the *Columbia Law Review* (1947) acknowledged that *Mendez* was the first case to successfully assault segregation based on the Equal Protection Clause of the Fourteenth Amendment. The article noted that the courts had ruled in prior cases that if the physical facilities provided to each group were essentially equal, then students' humiliation as a result of being segregated to an inferior social status did not constitute discrimination. But the *Mendez* decision, the article argued, "breaks sharply with this approach and finds that the 14th Amendment requires 'social equality' rather than just equal facilities" (pp. 326–327). What was referred to as "social equality" in *Mendez* is strongly related to what were later called "intangible" factors in *Brown*. These same arguments were being made in the late 1940s in the higher education segregation cases brought by the NAACP as *Mendez* was winding its way through the courts (see Kluger, 1976). As such, *Mendez* portended the legal and integrationist theories put forth by the lawyers in *Brown*.

Attorney Ogle, upon advice from defendant school boards, brought forth the appeal of *Mendez* on December 10, 1946, to the Ninth Circuit Court of Appeals in San Francisco. By this time, the case had garnered national attention. Given that the separate but equal doctrine was at stake, reporter Lawrence Davies of the *New York Times* wrote that the appeal was "closely watched as a guinea pig case" (1946a, p. 6e).[63] In *Westminster v. Mendez* (1947), the appellant school districts filed a brief reasserting their arguments that the federal courts had no jurisdiction and that "separate but equal" is legal. Their brief stated,

> Education is purely a matter of state concern and that when the State has furnished all pupils within its jurisdiction equal facilities and equal instruction, it has not denied to any the equal protection of the law imposed by the Constitution of the United States.[64]

Meanwhile, five important and influential organizations submitted four amicus curiae briefs in support of the appellee Mexican American schoolchildren in *Westminster v. Mendez*. The groups were the NAACP, the American Jewish Congress, the Attorney General of the State of California, and the American Civil Liberties Union together with the National Lawyers Guild.[65] Each of these briefs was "planned as a piece of a puzzle, which would eventually give the court a clear picture of the wrongs of segregation, both in precedent and policy" (Arriola, 1995, p. 166). Using the lens of CRT, these joint efforts demonstrate the value of collaboration in the quest for social justice.

Thurgood Marshall, Robert L. Carter, and Loren Miller wrote the NAACP brief. Marshall and Carter later served as counsel for African American plaintiffs in *Brown v. Board of Education* (1954). The NAACP's amicus brief argued that the Ninth Circuit should invalidate segregation in public schools as a violation of the Constitution.[66] Given that Judge McCormick in the District Court had opened the door to argue against *Plessy* via his opinion that social equality, not separate but equal schools, is a paramount requisite in public education, the NAACP saw this as a grand opportunity to take on *Plessy*. The NAACP lawyers based their argument on three major points.

First, in *Plessy*, the Supreme Court accepted the "equal but separate" doctrine but limited its consideration to carrier accommodations (i.e., transportation of people). The brief noted that in "subsequent cases it has been *assumed* [italics added] that decisions have applied this theory to validate segregation in public schools."[67] The Supreme Court, the NAACP brief continued, has never stated such a validation because it had never addressed the constitutionality of public school segregation. Thus, the brief continued, the Ninth Circuit "is not bound by decisions of the Supreme Court to validate a segregated school system."[68]

Second, the NAACP showed, using empirical data, that in the seventeen states and the District of Columbia that had school segregation as universal policy, separate schools were not equal in terms of several critical measures, including per-pupil expenditures, and pupil-teacher ratios. For example, in nine of the seventeen states in which data were available, the per-pupil expense (in 1939–1940) for White and Negro pupils was $58.69 and $18.82, respectively.[69]

Finally, the NAACP argued that that equal protection of the laws cannot be realized in legally segregated schools because such segregation leads to inequality and fosters feelings of inferiority among minority groups. On this point, the NAACP brief echoed the views of the *Mendez* case's expert witnesses and foreshadowed the social science evidence that would be brought to bear in the *Brown* case. Kluger (1976), in his seminal book, *Simple Justice: The History of Brown v. Board of Education and Black America's Struggle for Equality*, states that the NAACP's amicus brief in the *Mendez* appeal "was a useful dry run" because it "tested the temper of the courts without putting the NAACP itself in the field" and drew added attention to the case, especially in several leading law reviews (pp. 399–400).

The American Jewish Congress (AJC), in its amicus brief, sought to avoid duplication of the NAACP brief. While the AJC strongly rebuked the *Plessy* decision, its brief focused overwhelmingly on ethnic relations and summoned up images of the recently defeated Nazi regime in Europe.[70] The AJC argued that the inferior status imposed on a minority group by the socially dominant group "is a humiliating and discriminatory denial of equality to the group considered 'inferior'" and thus violates the Constitution and U.S. treaties.[71]

The AJC also argued that any classifications according to color, race, national origin, ancestry, or creed that are based on "discriminatory social or legal notions of 'inferiority' or 'superiority'" are unreasonable and inadmissible.[72] The AJC brief continued, asserting that segregation by official state action of immigrant groups who lack facility in English violates immigration and naturalization laws and is "therefore an unconstitutional interference with a valid Federal regulation."[73] The AJC brief concluded with powerful language, especially in light of what Jews had all-too-recently suffered in Europe (also, see Arriola, 1995). The AJC brief concluded as follows:

> All discrimination is bad and humiliation of any human being because of his creed or language is unworthy of a free country. But none is so

vicious as the humiliation of innocent, trusting children, American children full of faith in life. Their humiliation strikes at the very roots of the
American Commonwealth. Their humiliation threatens the more perfect
union which the Constitution seeks to achieve. It is the awareness of that
danger and the desire to counteract it that has prompted the submission
of this brief.[74]

The tone in the brief's conclusion, plus the mention of the Nazi atrocities
in Europe, framed the AJC argument so as to capture the attention and
conscience of the Ninth Circuit (also, see Arriola, 1995, for his interpretation of the AJC brief).

The amicus brief jointly submitted by the American Civil Liberties
Union and the National Lawyers Guild (1947) overwhelmingly focused
its argument on the jurisdictional issue, supporting the original plaintiffs' claim that this case belonged in federal court.[75] This brief countered
appellants' reply brief that argued that the District Court did not have
jurisdiction to adjudicate disputes of state laws.[76] Meanwhile, the Attorney General's brief (Attorney General of the State of California, 1947),
short and narrowly focused, argued that the segregation of Mexican- and
Latin-ancestry children improperly contravenes state policy and thus violated the children's rights as guaranteed by the laws of the Fourteenth
Amendment.[77]

On April 14, 1947, in a unanimous 7–0 decision, the Ninth Circuit
Court of Appeals upheld the District Court judge's decision and thereby
paved the way for a remedy that called for an end to segregation in the
defendant school districts. Judge Albert Lee Stephens wrote the opinion
for the Ninth Circuit. Although the appellate ruling was a clear victory
for the Mexican American students in Orange County, California—and
it ended up having a broader impact across the state and the region—it
did not overturn the racist *Plessy* doctrine. Although the Ninth Circuit
had the opportunity to rule on the separate but equal doctrine, it refused
to address this significant issue (also, see Arriola, 1995; González, 1990;
Perea, 1997; Wollenberg, 1974). The Ninth Circuit took the route of judicial conservatism by ignoring many of the legal arguments presented by
the NAACP in its brief (Arriola, 1995).

Rather than taking on *Plessy*, the Ninth Circuit ruling addressed two
of the questions that were under consideration: "Are the alleged acts
done under color of state law, and do they deprive petitioners of any
constitutional right? The jurisdictional question is implicit in these two

questions."[78] In terms of the color of law issue, the Ninth Circuit ruled that in segregating pupils of Mexican ancestry, "the respondents 'did not hew to the line of their authority'; they overstepped it."[79] And thus, the Court ruled, "We hold that the respondents acting to segregate the school children as alleged in the petition were performing under color of California State Law."[80] As for the constitutional violation issue, the Ninth Circuit noted that via the defendant districts' action of forcing the segregation of schoolchildren of Mexican ancestry against their will, and contrary to the California law, the appellants violated the pupils' rights as provided under the Fourteenth Amendment to the U.S. Constitution. This violation occurred by "depriving them of liberty and property without due process of law and by denying the equal protection of the laws."[81]

Despite this good news for the Mexican American schoolchildren on whose behalf this case was originally filed, the Ninth Circuit chose to bypass the central legal and social issues of the day—namely, the separate but equal doctrine. In their decision, these federal judges were acutely aware of how close they were to taking on the constitutionality of *Plessy* and the laws of seventeen Jim Crow states.[82] They were also apparently aware of how rapidly the world and American society were changing in this post–World War II era. In the opinion rendered by the Ninth Circuit, Judge Stephens did acknowledge that the court's attention had been directed—in written and oral argument—"to the cases [e.g., *Roberts v. City of Boston* (1849); *Plessy v. Ferguson* (1896); *Gong Lum v. Rice* (1927)]—in which the highest court of the land has upheld state laws providing for limited segregation of the great races of mankind."[83] Notwithstanding the point that the Ninth Circuit was aware of the authority of these segregation cases, Judge Stephens wrote,

> There is argument in two of the amicus curiae briefs that we should strike out independently on the whole question of segregation, on the ground that recent world stirring events have set men to the reexamination of concepts considered fixed. Of course, judges as well as all others must keep abreast of the times but judges must ever be on their guard lest they rationalize outright legislation under the too free use of the power to interpret. *We are not tempted by the siren who calls to us that the sometimes slow and tedious ways of democratic legislation is no longer respected in a progressive society. For reasons presently to be stated, we are of the opinion that the segregation cases do not rule the instant case and that is reason enough for not responding to the argument that we should consider them in*

the light of the amicus curiae briefs [italics added]. In the first place we are aware of no authority justifying any segregation fiat by an administrative or executive decree as every case cited to us is based upon a legislative act. The segregation in this case is without legislative support and comes into fatal collision with the legislation of the state.[84]

The refusal of the Ninth Circuit to address *Plessy* was particularly disappointing to the NAACP (Arriola, 1995). Yet hope remained alive for an opportunity to challenge *Plessy* before the U.S. Supreme Court, as the civil rights groups that supported *Mendez* at the Ninth Circuit level anticipated an appeal by the appellant school districts. The appeal never materialized for at least two reasons: First, the affirmation by the Ninth Circuit was resounding and unanimous. Second, more than two months before the Ninth Circuit handed down its decision in *Westminster v. Mendez*, the California Legislature began considering a bill to end de jure segregation in the state (discussed in the next section). There would be, however, a more propitious time not too far down the line when the separate but equal doctrine was challenged. On December 9, 1952—five years and eight months after the Ninth Circuit handed down its opinion in *Mendez*—the U.S. Supreme Court heard the first oral arguments in *Brown v. Board of Education of Topeka*.

Next discussed is the broader impact of the *Mendez* case on California and on *Brown*, followed by coverage of two Mexican American–initiated desegregation cases (*Delgado* and *Gonzales*) that were influenced by *Mendez*. In this discussion, CRT in education becomes a valuable explanatory model to understand and analyze these impacts. Particularly salient are the CRT tenets that deal with (a) the exposure of racism at the state, regional, and national levels; (b) Mexican Americans' and African Americans' challenge to the dominant ideology of color blindness and equal educational opportunity; (c) the commitment to social justice by people of color as seen in the litigation struggles; and (d) the utility of people of color and Whites working together to improve education for all children.

Consequences for California. On January 27, 1947—about ten weeks before the Ninth Circuit affirmed the District Court's ruling on *Mendez* —California Assemblymen Anderson, Hawkins, Rosenthal, and Bennett introduced Assembly Bill (AB) 1375 (California Legislature, 1947; cited in Peters, 1948). AB 1375 intended to repeal the sections of the Education Code that allowed school boards to establish separate schools for certain Indian pupils and pupils of Chinese, Japanese, and "Mongolian" ancestry (see note 37, this chapter). The bill to repeal segregation easily passed the Assembly and Senate, and on June 14, 1947—two months after the Ninth Circuit affirmed Judge McCormick's ruling in *Mendez*—Governor Earl Warren signed the bill into law (Wollenberg, 1974). This is the same Earl Warren who, six years later, President Dwight D. Eisenhower appointed to become the fourteenth Chief Justice of the Supreme Court in 1953—the same man who authored the landmark Supreme Court opinion in *Brown*.

Did the amicus brief written by the Attorney General and Deputy Attorney General of California for the appellees of *Westminster v. Mendez* directly influence the repeal of the segregation statutes of the California Education Code? Arriola (1995) has contended that "The [*Mendez*] case brought public pressure on the State government of California to repeal all segregation laws on the books regarding Asians and Native Americans" (p. 199). Yet, ironically enough, although the *Mendez* case helped to end de jure segregation in California, Mexican American students remained highly segregated and became even more segregated over the decades following the ruling (see Hendrick, 1977; Valencia, Menchaca, & Donato, 2002).

Consequences for Brown. *Mendez* clearly influenced school desegregation jurisprudence in California and the Southwest (as discussed later), but how did *Mendez* help in shaping desegregation efforts at the national level, that is, in regards to *Brown*? This question can best be addressed by framing the discussion within two contexts: (a) the shifting nature of civil and human rights in the 1940s; (b) integrationist educational theory.

The Equal Protection Clause of the Fourteenth Amendment was in a state of flux in the 1940s (Arriola, 1995). Tussman and tenBrock (1949) summed up in their highly influential article that the Equal Protection Clause had been strangled during the clause's seminal period by "post-civil-war judicial reactionism [and was] long frustrated by judicial neglect" (p. 381). The authors noted that the Equal Protection Clause "appears to be entering the most fruitful and significant period of its career" and that the theory framing equal protection "may yet take its rightful place in the unfinished Constitutional struggle for democracy" (p. 381).

Some legal scholars contextualized the emerging optimism in the 1940s that civil rights would be advanced within the larger realm of human rights (see Klarman, 2004). Tussman and tenBrock (1949) commented that the Equal Protection Clause was amended to the Constitution "as a culmination of the greatest humanitarian movement in our history. It is rooted deep in our religious and ethical traditions. Is any other clause in the Constitution so eminently suited to be the ultimate haven of human rights?" (p. 384).

Thus, regarding *Mendez*, it is not surprising that human rights violations of the most heinous magnitude—the Nazi atrocities of World War II—became part of the record via the American Jewish Congress's amicus brief discussed earlier. Arriola (1995) has succinctly brought together the intersection of civil and human rights and *Mendez*:

> Contemporaries of the *Mendez* Court saw equal protection in a state of flux with the potential to head in a number of different directions. There existed a diverse body of case law that could allow the court to make a tremendous impact on American jurisprudence, that is if the courts were bold enough to look away from prejudiced precedent. . . . Equal Protection was in a state of metamorphosis during the 1940s and could have gone in any direction. The question was, which cases would lead the courts and which arguments would be persuasive. The NAACP and others hoped *Mendez* would be one of those cases, if not *the* case in the efforts to overturn segregation as embodied in the existing corpus of segregation precedent. (pp. 191–192)

Dudziak (1995), a critical race theorist, advances a less benevolent and more strategic view of the shifting optimism toward civil and human rights during this period. He argues that it was in the United States' self-interest, politically and economically, to end racial apartheid in this country. Dudziak notes that after World War II, racial discrimination in the United States received increasing attention from other countries and that newspapers throughout the world wrote about discrimination against visiting foreign dignitaries of color and American Blacks. It was a time when "the U.S. hoped to reshape the postwar world in its own image, the international attention given to racial segregation was troublesome and embarrassing. The focus of American foreign policy at this point was to promote democracy and to 'contain' communism" (p. 110).

More specifically, regarding school segregation, this critical perspective asserted that the United States could not tolerate a hypocritical image by fighting communism abroad and simultaneously supporting segregation stateside. Bell (1980) has coined this thesis "interest convergence" and applied it to *Brown*. This notion refers to when "the majority group tolerates advances for racial justice only when it suits its interests to do so" (Delgado & Stefancic, 2001, p. 149). It should be noted, however, that although the notion of interest convergence originated in the CRT literature, the idea has now entered the writings of mainstream scholars (e.g., Klarman, 2004).

Given this broader context of changing political times, coupled with favorable district and appellate court rulings, legal writings were ripe with discussions that *Mendez* could be the impetus for the Supreme Court to tackle, head-on, the reasonableness of the separate but equal doctrine. A commentator in the *Columbia Law Review* (1947) noted,

> The unwillingness of courts to challenge the reasonableness of a state classification [of segregation based on race] is now yielding where civil liberties are at stake. Since educational segregation on racial lines serves no desirable ends, a reappraisal of the validity of the practice is in order. A classification which might have been reasonable in the light of post–Civil War conditions may no longer be reasonable today. (p. 327)

A commentator in the *Yale Law Journal* (1947), writing about the Ninth Circuit's ruling in the *Mendez* case, stated that the case "has questioned the basic assumption of the *Plessy* case and may portend a complete reversal of the [separate but equal] doctrine" (p. 1060).[85] Furthermore, in the *Illinois Law Review* (1947), a commentator observed that given (a) the rising frequency of segregation cases challenging the validity of the separate but equal doctrine, (b) the economic fallacy of the notion of separate but equal facilities, and (c) the faulty position that segregation is not harmful, the Supreme Court "could be forced to grant certiorari and face this issue [of separate but equal] squarely" (p. 549). The commentator concluded, "In any event, the *Mendez* case and its companion cases raise this precise problem which the Supreme Court must consider and determine in any re-examination of the 'equal but separate doctrine'" (p. 549).

In sum, *Mendez* was litigated during a time when views toward civil rights were in a state of flux, and such civil rights were being inextricably linked to human rights. The *Mendez* victory—which extended "the scope of the Equal Protection Clause further than any previous decision from the federal courts involving educational discrimination" (*Minnesota Law Review* 1946, p. 646)—helped set a climate of optimism for a concerted Supreme Court challenge to *Plessy*. The late Honorable Constance Baker Motley, a member of the NAACP legal staff who helped prepare the briefs for the *Brown* case, wrote that on the cusp of *Brown* NAACP attorneys did not know if the prior cases involving Black students' access to predominantly White graduate schools (*McLaurin v. Oklahoma State Regents*, 1950; *Sweatt v. Painter*, 1950) would aid in the cases directly dealing with elementary and secondary schools. She further noted, "we all sensed from those [higher education] decisions and from a Ninth Circuit decision [*Mendez*] repudiating the segregation of Mexican children in California *that integrated education was an idea whose time had come* [italics added]" (Motley, 1991, p. 26).

In addition to this climate of optimism, the second way in which *Mendez* had consequences for *Brown* was the integrationist educational theory expressed by Judge McCormick's ruling. *Mendez* attorney David C. Marcus wisely used social scientists to testify that segregation led to negative effects on the educational and social development of the Mexican American children. Judge McCormick found that the segregative methods of the defendant districts "foster antagonisms in the [Mexican] children and suggest inferiority among them where none exists."[86] This reasoning led Judge McCormick to his historic opinion that equal protection of the laws is not provided by merely furnishing Mexican-descent children—in separate schools—equal textbooks, facilities, and instruction. "A paramount requisite in the American system of public education is *social equality* [italics added]" and "unified school association."[87] Thus, the judge ruled, public schools "must be open to all children by unified school association,"[88] meaning integration.

Commenting on Judge McCormick's argument about "social equality," a commentator in the *Yale Law Journal* (1947) wrote,

> Modern sociological and psychological studies lend much support to the District Court's views. A dual school system even if "equal facilities" were ever in fact provided, does imply social inferiority. There is no question under such circumstances as to which school has the greater social prestige. Every authority on psychology and sociology is agreed that the students subjected to discrimination and segregation are profoundly affected by this experience. (pp. 1060–1061)

The journal continued by citing a corpus of scholarly evidence as to how the dual system of education leads to negative consequences among children and youths (e.g., rage, inferiority complex, and discouragement of racial self-appreciation).[89] Furthermore, the *Yale Law Journal* noted, "These abnormal results, condoned by the implications of the *Plessy* case, deny the Negro and Mexican child 'equal protection of the laws' in every meaningful sense of the words" (p. 1062). Arriola (1995), a preeminent authority on *Mendez*, concluded, "In *Brown* and other cases, the courts would finally accept social science and policy as persuasive legal arguments, due in large part to the voluminous experimentation undertaken in the lower courts, similar to the appeal in *Mendez*" (p. 207).

Although it is not clear just how much of a direct effect the *Mendez* case and the social science research evidence employed by the plaintiffs had on the NAACP lawyers' decision to use similar evidence in the *Brown* case, it is clear that by the early 1950s, Thurgood Marshall and Robert L. Carter saw this evidence and the integrationist theory it promoted as crucial to their cause to end state-sanctioned segregation. According to Whitman (1993), "Thurgood Marshall and his chief assistants felt that psychological and sociological testimony would materially aid their cause" (p. 48). More specifically, Kluger (1976) states, "the NAACP's case would rest on the theory that school segregation itself contributed heavily to the psychic damage of black children" (p. 316).

This integrationist strategy, which proved so useful in *Mendez*, also served as the linchpin in *Brown*. On May 17, 1954, Chief Justice Earl Warren delivered the historic opinion of the Court. In the opinion, there were twenty-four words, in particular, he penned that became immortalized in our collective mind and led to the transformation of race relations as never seen before in the nation: "*We conclude that in the field of public education the doctrine of 'separate but equal' has no place. Separate educational facilities are inherently unequal* [italics added]."[90] And, as we know, the Warren Court ruled that because segregated schools cannot be made equal, plaintiffs were being "deprived of the equal protection of the laws as guaranteed by the Fourteenth Amendment."[91]

Although Chief Justice Earl Warren "omitted any reference to *Mendez* or, indeed, to Latino segregation at all" (Bowman, 2001, p. 1775) in his opinion, in the end *Mendez* and *Brown* are unmistakably connected. Namely, the *Mendez* rulings at the federal District Court and Ninth Circuit levels contributed to the "climate of optimism" that permeated this era. Second, the *Mendez* case showed the power of social science research in strengthening counsel Marcus's claim about the detrimental effect of segregation. This strategy helped to bolster plaintiffs' integrationist argument. Such testimony proved very useful in *Brown*.

Notwithstanding the thesis that *Mendez* served as an important precursor to *Brown*, why has *Mendez* seemingly slipped from the national consciousness? Several germane reasons help to explain this state of affairs.

First, the legal struggle against school segregation by African Americans has been considerably longer than the legal campaign undertaken by Mexican Americans. The genesis of African American desegregation litigation can be traced back to the mid-nineteenth century (*Roberts v. City of Boston*, 1849), followed by numerous cases (Bell, 1995). Mexican Americans, however, did not begin their long legal struggle against school segregation until more than eighty years later (*Romo v. Laird*, 1925).

Second, the law legally considered Mexican Americans as White in the United States, and Mexican Americans took advantage of the "other White" designation for about forty-five years in order to serve their interests in the early desegregation cases. Given these shifting social constructions of race experienced by Mexican Americans, coupled with the popular perception that Black-White racial tensions were more intense and oppressive compared to Mexican American–White relationships, *Mendez* likely has developed less import and visibility than *Brown*.

Finally, and most obviously, *Brown*, not *Mendez*, overturned *Plessy*. Had the appellants appealed *Mendez* to the U.S. Supreme Court following the Ninth Circuit upholding of the District Court—and had *Mendez* prevailed in the Supreme Court—then *Mendez* would be acknowledged as the landmark case that brought an end to the separate but equal doctrine in American schools.

Before we turn to the next case, *Delgado v. Bastrop Independent School District*, it would be informative to discuss further the inferior nature of "Mexican" schools—the core issue that gave rise to Mexican American school-desegregation litigation. This subject is expanded by discussing the documentation reported by Carlos I. Calderón (1950) in his master's thesis.

Calderón's work in Texas is important for two reasons. First, he undertook his observations during 1947–1949, a period that coincided with the significant *Delgado* case in Texas. Second, his report contains contrasting, detailed photographs of facility conditions at several segregated Mexican American and Anglo schools. Calderón's master's thesis consists of descriptive case studies of two Mexican American elementary schools and one Anglo elementary school in Edcouch-Elsa, Texas (located in the lower Rio Grande Valley, about fifteen miles from the Texas-Mexico border). The two Mexican American schools were Elsa and North Edcouch, and the Anglo school was South Edcouch (in the Edcouch-Elsa Independent School District).[92]

Calderón (1950) sought to compare the "quality and quantity of the facilities and services" (p. 14) of the schools attended by the Mexican American and Anglo children. To wit, he reported his observations on the following aspects:

- *Teacher-pupil ratio.* Calderón obtained data for the 1948–1949 school year, for grades 1 through 6. For South Edcouch (the Anglo school), the average enrollment per teacher per month (across all grades) during the school year ranged from twenty-five to thirty-eight pupils, with a grand mean of thirty-two pupils.[93] For North Edcouch (the Mexican American school), data analysis for the same comparison showed a range of twenty-two to seventy pupils, with a grand mean of forty-one students.[94] In sum, teachers in the Mexican American school (compared to teachers in the Anglo school) had, on the average, about ten more pupils to teach.

- *Classification and promotion practices.* As noted by Calderón, the general practice in Texas schools in the 1940s was that under normal conditions a student whose grades were satisfactory would advance one grade each school year. Although school officials employed this practice at North Edcouch and South Edcouch, the classification scheme differed between the schools. At South Edcouch, students attended "first grade" in the first school year, and upon satisfactory completion students advanced to "second grade," and so on. At North Edcouch, however, school officials institutionalized a different classification/promotion policy:

YEAR IN SCHOOL	GRADE LEVEL
first school year	beginners first grade
second school year	high first grade
third school year	second grade
fourth school year	third grade
etc.	etc.

Regarding this practice, Calderón aptly comments,

> Spanish-speaking children were compelled to spend two years in the first grade without regard to the ability of the student to do the work. A full year of the pupils' time was literally wasted and the student retarded, thereby making the pupil seem retarded in later years and even acquiring a feeling of inferiority due to the age factor. This was just another "traditional practice." (p. 20)[95]

- *School buildings.* The South Edcouch Elementary School, which housed all the Anglo students, consisted of a single, modern brick structure (see Figure 1.2). Also, a remodeled Army barracks served as a cafeteria and assembly hall. North Edcouch and Elsa Elementary Schools, which enrolled all the Mexican American students, had several buildings (cement-block rooms, wood frame structures, and old Army barracks),

Figure 1.2 (top). Modern Brick Structure: South Edcouch Elementary School (Anglo). *Source*: Calderón (1950, p. 23). Reprinted with permission of author. *Figure 1.3 (bottom).* Old Army Barracks: Elsa Elementary School (Mexican American). *Source*: Calderón (1950, p. 24). Reprinted with permission of author.

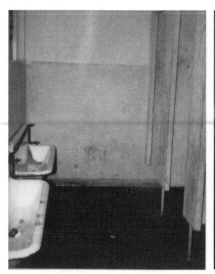 

Figure 1.4 (left). Indoor Rest Rooms with Stalls: South Edcouch Elementary School (Anglo). *Source*: Calderón (1950, p. 32). Reprinted with permission of author. *Figure 1.5 (right)*. Outdoor Rest Rooms without Stalls: North Edcouch Elementary School (Mexican American). *Source*: Calderón (1950, p. 32). Reprinted with permission of author.

housing various classes (e.g., beginners classes; fifth and sixth grades). Figure 1.3 shows an old Army barracks at Elsa. The two Mexican American schools had no lunchroom or cafeteria to serve the students. Thus, the children had "to walk at least six blocks to a restaurant to get their lunch or else go home, whichever was closer" (Calderón, 1950, pp. 34–35).

• *Rest rooms*. In South Edcouch, the White school, the rest rooms were located inside the building. The toilets were separated within stalls, and the floor was of mosaic tile (see Figure 1.4). By contrast, the rest rooms in North Edcouch and Elsa, the Mexican schools, were located outside the school buildings in an "out-house" fashion. The toilets were not separated by stalls, and the floor consisted of a rough cement texture. Furthermore, the rest rooms had no lights available, nor did they have windows to allow ventilation (see Figure 1.5).

• *Drinking fountains*. In the hall at South Edcouch there were two drinking fountains, one of which was electrically cooled (see Figure 1.6). At the two Mexican American schools, the only drinking fountains were located outside, on the playground (see Figure 1.7). Calderón (1950) notes

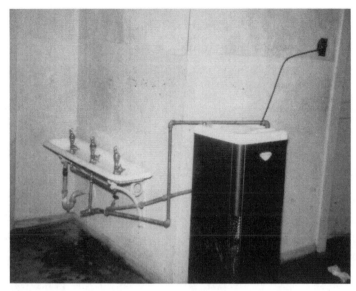

Figure 1.6 (top). Indoor Drinking Fountains with Electric Cooler: South Edcouch Elementary School (Anglo). *Source:* Calderón (1950, p. 30). Reprinted with permission of author. *Figure 1.7 (bottom).* Outdoor Drinking Fountains: North Edcouch Elementary School (Mexican American). *Source:* Calderón (1950, p. 30). Reprinted with permission of author.

Figure 1.8 (left). Shields on Bulbs for Diffused Lighting: South Edcouch Elementary School (Anglo). *Source:* Calderón (1950, p. 36). Reprinted with permission of author. *Figure 1.9 (right).* Bare Bulbs Used for Lighting: North Edcouch Elementary School (Mexican American). *Source:* Calderón (1950, p. 36). Reprinted with permission of author.

that having the water fountains outside the school buildings made "it impractical to make any attempt to drink water in inclement weather since there is no shed or any other means of protection for the children against the weather while drinking water" (p. 22).

- *Classroom lighting.* The Anglo and Mexican American schools lit their classrooms very differently. At South Edcouch, the classrooms were equipped with shielded light bulbs that, as Calderón (1950, p. 35) notes, "provided diffused, uniform lighting that minimized the glare of the bulb" (see Figure 1.8). By contrast, the classrooms at North Edcouch and Elsa were lit with bare bulbs (see Figure 1.9). Calderón (1950) voices this concern: "It is well known that bare bulb lighting is the worst in lighting in that it does not provide even lighting, but gives a glare that is harmful to the children's eyesight" (p. 35).

- *Medical and dental services.* The children at South Edcouch who required medical, dental, and optical attention received it on a regular basis. For the children at the two Mexican American schools, however, "it was almost impossible to get a physician to come to school for any purpose at any time" (Calderón, 1950, p. 35). Calderón notes that during his two-year observation the City Health Officer came to school once, and this was during a smallpox epidemic in which a doctor vaccinated the children. A dentist and optometrist promised to provide dental and eye care, respectively, but they did not come to the school during the time of Calderón's observations.

• *Intermural sports.* During his two-year study, Calderón reports that school officials did not allow the two Mexican American schools to play against the White school in a single game of athletics.

• *Band.* The children at South Edcouch received, on a regular basis, instrumental instruction under the direction of an able band director and music instructor. The children attending North Edcouch and Elsa never had the opportunity to receive such band or music instruction.

• *Busing.* Calderón (1950) also notes that White children from South Edcouch and the Mexican American children from North Edcouch and Elsa all took the same buses to school. Calderón observes, "The Anglo-American children usually sat in front while the Spanish-speaking children were traditionally seated in the rear of the bus" (p. 40). Calderón does not offer any discussion of what may best explain the segregated seating arrangement on the school buses. At least one possible explanation exists. Given the widespread social segregation in South Texas, perhaps the White and Mexican American children were merely following the Jim Crow policy of segregated bus seating—Whites in front, Mexican Americans in the back.

What can best be learned from Calderón's detailed case study, with its contrastive, revealing photographs and text? If one were to take only a single aspect of how the highly segregated Anglo and Mexican American elementary schools differed (e.g., diffused classroom lighting versus bare-bulb classroom lighting, respectively), perhaps a conclusion of inconsequentiality in the quality of schooling between the two ethnic groups could be drawn. Yet, if one were to piece together the entire parts of the mosaic (i.e., differences in teacher-pupil ratios; classification and promotion practices; quality of school buildings; rest rooms; drinking fountains; classroom lighting; medical and dental services; intermural sports; band instruction; seating assignments on the school buses), an inevitable conclusion of racialization results: in the facilities and services examined, the schools attended by the Mexican American children "were inferior in every respect when compared with those offered" in the school attended by the Anglo children (Calderón, 1950, p. 43). It was this frequent observation of inferior Mexican American schools in Texas and other communities in the Southwest that prompted desegregation litigation in decades past.

Delgado v. Bastrop Independent School District (1948)

This case co-occurred with the centennial of the Treaty of Guadalupe Hidalgo, and it was Texas's first Mexican American–initiated federal court desegregation case. Minerva Delgado (age six years old; first grade), and nineteen other Mexican American children attending grades 1 to 5 in public schools in Central Texas filed suit in the U.S. District Court for the Western District of Texas (Austin Division); Judge Ben H. Rice, Jr., presided.[96] Defendants included members of the Board of Trustees and the District Superintendents of Bastrop Independent School District, Elgin Independent School District, Martindale Independent School District, and the Colorado Common School District. The complaint also named L.A. Woods, the State Superintendent of Public Instruction, and the State Board of Education as defendants.[97]

The denial of Minerva Delgado's request to attend the White school, which was nearest to her home, prompted in part the filing of *Delgado*, a class action lawsuit. P.J. Dodson, Superintendent of Bastrop Independent School District, stated in his deposition,

> This past fall, the first day of school, one of our Latin-American students in the freshman class in high school called me that afternoon and said, "Mr. Dodson," [he] says, "Mama wants Minerva Delgado to go to the 'White' school." I said, "Why?" He says, "She is too far from the Latin-American school." "Does she speak English?" He says, "No, sir." "Does your Mother speak English?" He says, "No, sir." I says [sic], "She will have to go up there [Manor Ward School, designated for Mexican American children] until she can speak English well enough to do the work."[98]

The segregation of Mexican American children based on language status loomed large in *Delgado* (more on this later).

Delgado was to Texas as *Mendez* was to California: the goal in both cases was to bring an end to statewide school segregation. A cadre of powerful organizations and individuals backed the *Delgado* plaintiffs. Organizations included LULAC and the American GI Forum, a newly established (1948) Mexican American advocacy group for veterans. Notable individuals included attorney Gustavo ("Gus") C. García, whose star was rising,[99] and attorney A.L. Wirin, co-counsel in *Mendez*.[100] Dr. Héctor P. García, founder and leader of the American GI Forum,[101] and Professor George I. Sánchez—scholar, civil rights activist, and legal strategist—also assisted in the case.[102] Regarding how to approach the litigation of *Delgado*, Sánchez (1951, pp. 11–13) notes that although the *Mendez* decision was certainly far-reaching in its significance, he believed the case did not satisfactorily address at least several concerns germane to *Delgado*: (a) Given the complex makeup of communities, what actually is segregation? (b) To what extent can school communities go in segregating Spanish-speaking children in separate classes in the same building or campus? (c) If it can be shown that a school district is carrying on an unconstitutional practice of segregation, can the district be legally enjoined? Answers to these key questions were sought in *Delgado* filings, the trial, and during post-*Delgado*.

On November 17, 1947, plaintiffs filed the *Delgado* complaint[103] and the Memorandum of Points and Authorities[104] in federal district court. The legal bases of the complaint rested firmly on the district court ruling in *Mendez* as well as the upholding of that ruling by the Ninth Circuit. In its propositions of law, *Delgado* argued these two succinct points:

1. Such segregation [of Mexican-descent children] is illegal when there is no state constitutional or state legislative provision expressly authorizing it.
2. The cases upholding segregation of Negroes (upon the furnishing of equal accommodations) have no application because those cases uphold segregation of a different race; Mexican Americans are of the same race as Anglo-Americans.[105]

Given that the federal court decided these two points in favor of Mexican American plaintiff children in *Mendez*, *Delgado* counsel argued that these arguments should apply with equal force in Texas.[106] Under a second cause of action, *Delgado* plaintiffs sought $10,000 of damages per child ($5,000 for actual damages; $5,000 for punitive and/or exemplary damages).[107]

On June 15, 1948, Judge Rice rendered his opinion.[108] His favorable ruling for plaintiffs was not unexpected in light of the striking similarity of the facts and propositions of law between the landmark *Mendez* case and

Delgado, coupled with Attorney General Price Daniel's opinion of April 8, 1947 (see note 98, this chapter). In the final judgment, Judge Rice decreed the following:

- Based on "the regulations, customs, usages, and practices," the defendant districts in Central Texas segregated Mexican American children in separate classes and schools. As such, these actions are "arbitrary and discriminatory and in violation of plaintiffs' constitutional rights as guaranteed by the Fourteenth Amendment to the Constitution of the United States, and are illegal."[109]
- Defendants were "permanently restrained and enjoined from segregating" Mexican American pupils and "from denying said pupils use of the same facilities and services enjoyed by other children of the same age or grades."[110]
- It is within this order directly above that Judge Rice created, unfortunately, a loophole for the defendants. He wrote that the above injunction "shall not prevent" defendant school districts from maintaining "separate classes on the same campus in the first grade only," and such separation shall be for instructional purposes only. He also ordered that "scientific and standardized tests" shall be given to all students to ascertain whether they have "sufficient familiarity with the English language to understand classroom instruction in first-grade subject matters."[111]
- Finally, Judge Rice allowed "reasonable time" for defendants and other districts to comply with his order, "but in no event beyond September, 1949"—which was about fifteen months after he provided his final ruling in *Delgado*.[112]

What transpired after *Delgado* was as important as Judge Rice's ruling of restrainment/enjoinment of segregation itself. The ruling in *Delgado* helped to clarify the three questions Sánchez (1951) posed that *Mendez* left somewhat unclear (see earlier discussion). First, although segregation of Mexican American children was not allowable under state law (hence illegal), segregation brought about by custom and practice was also illegal. Second, the segregation of Mexican American children was allowable only under very narrow circumstances (children who had limited skills in English could be segregated only in the first grade, but in the same school attended by White students). Third, school officials throughout the state could be legally held responsible for approving and maintaining the segregation of Mexican American students. Hence, the court enjoined school officials from such segregation.

The *Delgado* ruling (with the exception of the proviso of language segregation, the second point above) constituted a historic victory for the Mexican American community of Texas. This climate of optimism elevated when subsequent to Judge Rice's ruling, Superintendent of Public Instruction, L.A. Woods—in concise wording—operationalized the *Delgado* decree in his "Instructions and Regulations."[113] Mailed to all Texas school districts, Superintendent Woods, in his dictum, mandated,

> You will take all necessary steps to eliminate any and all segregations that may exist in your school or district contrary to instruction and regulations. I shall take whatever steps are necessary to enforce these instructions and regulations and to prevent segregation of Mexican or other Latin American descent in the public schools as in the State of Texas as directed by the above-mentioned Court decree.[114]

Unfortunately, a comprehensive desegregation of Texas's schools never occurred. A period of noncompliance with the *Delgado* decree followed because of intransigence and subterfuge by state and local school officials.[115] Numerous tactics maintained this antidesegregation stand, including construction of new schools in Mexican American residential areas; gerrymandering of attendance zones; "free choice" options (for Anglos only); continued segregation of Mexican American first grades on separate campuses; token transfers of Mexican American students to Anglo schools.[116] On June 1, 1949, the Texas Legislature further exacerbated the execution of court-ordered school desegregation by shifting the powers of the State Superintendent of Public Instruction to a newly formed position, the Commissioner of Education, to be held by Dr. J.W. Edgar (Rangel & Alcala, 1972). L.A. Woods, who was elected as State Superintendent, was noted to be relatively sympathetic in working toward meeting the *Delgado* decree. By contrast, Commissioner Edgar, a professional educator who was appointed by Governor Beauford H. Jester, appeared "less willing to use the state power to dismantle segregated schools" (San Miguel, 1987, p. 129; also, see Rangel & Alcala, 1972, pp. 340–342). Although LULAC and the GI Forum identified numerous school districts that were out of compliance with the *Delgado* decree and raised these violations with officials,[117] the complaint process proved to be time-consuming and highly bureaucratic (San Miguel, 1987). Consequently, futility set in among Mexican American leaders, and desegregation litigation in Texas went into a hiatus until opportunities appeared more auspicious.

Gonzales v. Sheely (1951)

Three years after *Delgado*, this case arose, an Arizona desegregation lawsuit (U.S. District Court for the District of Arizona) in which "The principle established in Westminster School District of Orange County v. Mendez . . . appears to be controlling."[118] In *Gonzales*, Porfirio Gonzáles and Faustino Curiel, their four collective children, and three hundred children of Mexican or Latin ancestry were plaintiffs.[119] The Board of Trustees and principal of the Tolleson Elementary School District Number 17, County of Maricopa, were defendants. The complaint followed the same reasoning as *Mendez*: (a) segregation of the Mexican-descent students was executed "under color of state law";[120] that is, Arizona's Education Code did not mandate the segregation of Mexican-descent pupils;[121] (b) thus, plaintiffs argued, their equal protection rights—as guaranteed by the Fourteenth Amendment—were being violated.

Judge Dave W. Ling ruled in favor of the *Gonzales* plaintiffs. In a number of instances in his opinion, he drew—word for word—from the ruling of Judge McCormick in *Mendez*. For example: He broke from the doctrine of separate but equal, stating that the segregation of Mexican-descent children in separate schools constitutes a violation of the equal protection laws. Judge Ling wrote, "A paramount requisite in the American system of public education is social equality. It must be open to all children by unified school associations, regardless of lineage"[122] (cf. *Mendez v. Westminster* at 549). Second, he incorporated the value of the integrationist educational theory. He noted that the segregative methods of the defendant school district "foster antagonisms in the children and suggest inferiority among them where none exists"[123] (cf. *Mendez v. Westminster* at 549). Thus, Judge Ling commented, the "commingling of the entire student body instills and develops a common cultural attitude among the school children which is imperative for the perpetuation of American institutions and ideals"[124] (cf. *Mendez v. Westminster* at 549). Third, regarding the tests to assess language knowledge, Judge Ling criticized them by writing, "The tests that are applied . . . have been generally hasty, superficial and not reliable"[125] (cf. *Mendez v. Westminster* at 550).

Judge Ling ruled that defendants violated Arizona law and the laws of the United States (Fourteenth Amendment, Equal Protection Clause), and ordered a preliminary injunction enjoining defendants from segregating students of Mexican or Latin descent. Yet in his ruling the judge wrote (reminiscent of the *Delgado* ruling) that "English language deficiencies of some of the children of Mexican ancestry as such children enter elementary public school . . . may justify [curriculum] differentiation by public school authorities."[126] Judge Ling did note, nonetheless, this caveat: "Such separate allocations, however, can be lawfully made only after credible examination by the appropriate school authorities."[127]

The remainder of the 1950s saw a spate of desegregation lawsuits (predominantly in Texas) brought forth by Mexican Americans. These cases were largely inspired by federal court victories in the late 1940s (*Mendez* and *Delgado*) and in the very early 1950s (*Gonzales*). Excluding *Gonzales* (1951), Table 1.1 shows eight cases in the 1950s—nearly twice as many as are listed for the 1920s, 1930s, and 1940s combined.

Of these eight lawsuits, only two (*Romero v. Weakley* and *Hernandez v. Driscoll Consolidated Independent School District*) went the full legal gamut, from case filing in court to a published judicial opinion (federal district). These two cases are discussed later. In four of the other cases (*Ortiz v. Jack*; *Cortez v. Carrizo Springs Independent School District*; *Villarreal v. Mathis Independent School District*; *Salinas v. Kingsville Independent School District*), plaintiffs filed in federal court, but the court dismissed the suit without judgment.[128] In some of these cases, the outcomes proved favorable for Mexican American plaintiffs. For example, in *Cortez* (filed in Carrizo Springs, 104 miles southwest of San Antonio, Texas) plaintiffs accused the Texas Commissioner of Education, Dr. J.W. Edgar, of failing to comply with the *Delgado* decree. As such, *Cortez* plaintiffs sought a permanent injunction to end the segregation of the Mexican American students. The court dismissed the suit on June 13, 1955, when the Carrizo Springs Independent School District School Board agreed to stop engaging in segregation.[129]

The final two 1950s cases in Table 1.1 are *Barraza v. Pecos Independent School District* and *Orta v. Hondo Independent School District*, Texas cases filed in 1953. They differ from the other Table 1.1 cases, as plaintiffs in *Barraza* and *Orta* filed complaints with Commissioner of Education Edgar. In these earlier cases, plaintiffs "were required to exhaust administrative remedies before going to federal court" (Rangel & Alcala, 1972, p. 340). "Exhausting administrative remedies" involves first filing a complaint with the Commissioner of Education—in these instances, the school district was illegally segregating Mexican American students. If the Commissioner dismisses the complaint or rules for the school district, complainants can appeal the Commissioner's decision to the State Board of Education. If the State Board of Education upholds the Commissioner's decision, *then* complainants have exhausted all administrative remedies and can file suit in court.

For the most part, the administrative route proved futile for Mexican American complainants and their counsel. In *Barraza v. Pecos Independent School District* (located in far West Texas), Mexican American parents contended that the district approved the construction of East Pecos Junior High in the Mexican American section of town to segregate such students from their White peers. Although this plan clearly violated the *Delgado* decree, Commissioner Edgar "failed to find sufficient evidence of intent to segregate."[130] Segregation intensified over time. A decade and a half later (1968–1969) East Pecos Junior High was 100% Mexican American.[131] Similarly, in *Orta*, the Hondo Independent School District (located thirty-nine miles west of San Antonio), in 1952–1953, had "supposedly ended segregation in grades two through eight."[132] Yet Mexican American parents complained that the district reverted to segregation in these grades.[133] Commissioner Edgar admitted that sectioning of students had changed (from alphabetic use [apparently surname] to achievement test scores), but he held the change not to be arbitrary. He concluded that the evidence was insufficient to claim that the district was engaging in intentional segregation.[134] Next, there is brief discussion on two important Mexican American desegregation lawsuits in the 1950s—cases that saw the full course, from initial filing to judicial decision, in the federal courts.

Romero v. Weakley (1955)

Plaintiffs residing in the southern desert community of El Centro, California (located about ten miles from the Mexican border) filed this case in the U.S. District Court for the Southern District of California (Southern Division). Judge Peirson M. Hall presided. *Romero* is noteworthy on several accounts. First, Mexican American and African American plaintiffs, for the first time, joined as plaintiffs in a desegregation lawsuit.[135] Second, plaintiffs invoked the recent U.S. Supreme Court decision in *Brown v. Board of Education of Topeka* (1954) as controlling law in desegregation cases. Third, *Romero* raised an interesting jurisdictional question: Should desegregation cases in California rightfully be heard in state or federal district courts?

Plaintiffs in *Romero* argued that defendants, "under color of regulations, custom or usage,"[136] were maintaining separate schools in the El

Centro School District and Central Union High School District. Judge Hall, aware that the separate but equal doctrine of *Plessy v. Ferguson* (1896) no longer controlled, ruled that *Brown* did not apply in *Romero* because California had no state statute allowing school segregation.[137] Consequently, given that *Brown* did not control in the instant case and that no constitutional violation existed, Judge Hall ruled that plaintiffs' complaint "must be determined in the courts of the State of California prior to any consideration thereof by the Federal Courts of the United States."[138] He granted defendants' motion to dismiss, exemplifying another example of legal indeterminacy.

On appeal, the Ninth Circuit reversed and remanded *Romero*.[139] The appellate court ruled that a complaint of racial discrimination in public schools raises a constitutional violation; hence, *Brown* controls. Furthermore, the Ninth Circuit found that in its refusal to hear appellants' complaints, "the district court considers the case from a viewpoint exactly contrary to the obvious purpose of the civil rights legislation to give the litigant his choice of a federal forum rather than that of the state."[140] Unfortunately, we know little about the aftermath of the Ninth Circuit's reversal and remand of *Romero*. As noted by Salinas (1971), "Instead of going to trial, the case apparently was settled out of court" (p. 942).

Hernandez v. Driscoll Consolidated Independent School District (1957)

The Driscoll Consolidated Independent School District (DCISD) is located in Driscoll, Texas, a rural community in South Texas, twenty-three miles from Corpus Christi. At the time of *Hernandez*,[141] the DCISD averaged 288 students in all grades, of whom 70% were Mexican American.[142] First- and second-grade Mexican American children residing in DCISD filed *Hernandez* in the U.S. District Court for the Southern District of Texas (Corpus Christi Division); Judge James Allred presided. James DeAnda, a noted civil rights attorney who worked on behalf of Mexican Americans, was co-counsel.

Up to 1949, the DCISD maintained segregated schools for Mexican American and Anglo children. The school district abandoned this practice when it complied with the 1949 State Superintendent of Public Instruction edict of desegregation[143] and the *Delgado* decree. At the time of *Hernandez*, Mexican American and Anglo children attended the same classes in the same building and used the same buses, playgrounds, cafeteria, and restrooms.[144] Yet the ubiquitous segregation of young Mexican American children who were deemed "deficient" in English persisted. This was the basis of the *Hernandez* complaint. The DCISD defended such segregation in the first and second grades by proffering the all-too-familiar pedagogical argument that "those [children] who speak and understand the English language would be held back and retarded in their work [and] those who do not speak and understand the English language would be unable to learn the course of study prescribed."[145] Plaintiffs did not think it unreasonable to "have a good faith grouping for language deficiencies at least for the first year,"[146] but their counsel argued that the school district crossed the line. That is, the DCISD placed Mexican American children in separate classes in the first *and* second grades. Furthermore, the district forced the first-graders to stay in that grade a full three years before being promoted to the second grade.[147] In sum, Mexican Americans completed grades 1 and 2 in four years, while the Anglo children completed the same grades in only two years. Plaintiffs argued that the DCISD discriminated against the children on the basis of ethnicity, thus depriving them of their rights under the Fourteenth Amendment.

In addition to the expected defense that such separation by language was educationally efficient, defendants raised a counterclaim, arguing that the Mexican American parents' failure and refusal to speak English at home caused the entering children's lack of English proficiency. To remedy this, the counterclaim noted,

> Parent Plaintiffs and all members of the class they represent should be required by mandatory injunction, to the extent of their ability, to speak only the English language in the presence of their children who are of pre-school age or who are in the elementary grades, both while school is in session and during the summer vacation months, and such parents should also be required by mandatory injunction to prevent their said children from playing and associating with other children and persons who do not speak the English language.[148]

On January 11, 1957, Judge Allred ruled in favor of the plaintiffs, finding that the separate grouping of the Mexican American first- and second-graders was "purposeful, intentional, and unreasonably discriminatory"[149] and that such grouping was "directed at them as a class and is not based on individual capacities."[150] Regarding the centrality of individual differences among Mexican Americans, as well as among Anglo children, Judge Allred wrote,

> On brief defendants point out various bits of testimony by some of the minor plaintiffs which allegedly show their inability to speak or understand the English language. As observed by the Court at the conclusion of the evidence, these children appeared to be as bright as Anglo children of the same age; and, I add, their mistakes were no more than those that might have been made by any other child under the excitement or other emotions of a first appearance in court.[151]

Judge Allred cited *Salvatierra* (1930), *Mendez* (1946), *Delgado* (1948), and *Gonzales* (1951) as controlling, and commented that grouping by language must not be done arbitrarily but must be enacted "in good faith by scientific tests recognized in the field of education"[152] and must be administered to *all* children. Finally, given that Judge Allred found the defendants culpable, he denied their intrusive and appalling counterclaim.

The 1960s experienced a sharp drop in the number of Mexican American–initiated desegregation lawsuits. Table 1.1 shows only one such case —*Chapa v. Odem Independent School District* (1967). For a decade—from *Hernandez* (1957) to *Chapa* (1967)—not a single case was filed. What accounted for this decline in the filing of desegregation lawsuits during this period? Rangel and Alcala (1972) suggest that this dearth of cases may have been because court decisions (e.g., the *Delgado* decree) became so settled that school districts capitulated. Rangel and Alcala offer this example:

> Chicano parents in Crystal City, Texas, packed a school board meeting in 1960 and demanded an end to two segregated elementary schools. (Zavala County Sentinel (Crystal City, Texas) July 15, 1960, at 1, col. 6). As a result the grade schools were paired. (*Id.* July 22, 1960, at 1, col. 5). However, the school board refused to adopt rules dealing with discriminatory treatment of migrants. (p. 345)

Rangel and Alcala (1972) provide another explanation, which they believe more plausible: Mexican American attorneys viewed any further desegregation litigation as futile because of the widespread subterfuges used to bar effective relief.[153] Nonetheless, by 1967, school desegregation law had evolved, encouraging renewed enthusiasm within the Mexican American community in its struggle against educational inequalities—leading to the filing of *Chapa v. Odem* (Rangel & Alcala, 1972).

Chapa v. Odem Independent School District (1967)

Mexican American children living in Odem, Texas, a rural South Texas community located fifteen miles from Corpus Christi, filed *Chapa* in the U.S. District Court for the Southern District of Texas (Corpus Christi Division), with Judge Woodrow Seals presiding.[154] Attorney James DeAnda, who served as co-counsel in *Hernandez*, also served as counsel in *Chapa*.

The omnipresent "language handicap" separation of Mexican American children by school authorities was at the heart of the *Chapa* complaint. What appeared to be new, however, was plaintiffs' allegation that the language separation was a mere pedagogical deception. Plaintiffs argued that the Mexican American children had no principal or teacher with special training to teach the allegedly English-deficient pupils. Furthermore, two of the three teachers of first grade possessed neither degrees from college nor teaching certificates. Finally, the district superintendent admitted that the district separated most students without the use of achievement test data, and when tests were administered in 1955 and 1956, they tested only the Mexican American students (and only after separation). When the Anglo children were eventually tested, some of the students performed in the lower range of scores, yet the superintendent did not require them to attend the Mexican American school. Judge Seals requested further evidence on the issue of testing. In his final decision, the judge enjoined the Odem Independent School District from operating and maintaining a separate school exclusively for Mexican American students.

Table 1.1 shows that Mexican Americans filed numerous lawsuits (seventeen) in the 1970s, one less than in all other decades combined. The landmark case *Cisneros v. Corpus Christi Independent School District* (1970), in which Mexican American plaintiffs sought and gained protection under *Brown*, triggered this dramatic intensification of activity. Next discussed is *Cisneros v. Corpus Christi*, along with two related cases—*Ross v. Eckels* (1970) and *Keyes v. School District No. 1 of Denver* (1973). The penultimate case discussed is *Soria v. Oxnard School District Board of Trustees* (1974). Finally, this coverage closes with a discussion of *Diaz v. San Jose Unified School District* (1985).

Cisneros v. Corpus Christi Independent School District (1970)

This highly significant lawsuit stands next to *Mendez* in having wide-spread consequences. Years before the filing of *Cisneros*, José Cisneros and several fathers of children attending schools in the Corpus Christi Independent School District (CCISD) visited their neighborhood schools and were shocked by what they found. Mr. Cisneros recalled finding "Poor maintenance, dirty restrooms, windows that needed repair. . . . in further investigation we found that our school didn't have any teaching aids like projectors or tape equipment for language study."[155] The parents' inquiry expanded into other aspects such as teaching, curricula, and the overall quality of education that their children were receiving. The parents started attending school board meetings and were steadfast in pressuring the district to respond to their many complaints. Yet the parents' efforts were futile. Cisneros commented, "We honestly tried for approximately 2 years to fix those things . . . and we were just given the runaround."[156] Finally, out of frustration with the obstinate school board, Cisneros and twenty-five other Mexican American and African American fathers—all members of the United Steelworkers of America—filed suit against the CCISD on July 22, 1968, in the U.S. District Court for the Southern District of Texas (Houston Division), with Judge Woodrow Seals presiding. In *Cisneros*, plaintiffs claimed that the district was maintaining a dual school system.[157] The filing of this case resulted in the watershed *Cisneros* decision on June 4, 1970.[158] James DeAnda, who served as an attorney in *Hernandez* and *Chapa*, was co-counsel in *Cisneros*.

By the late 1960s, the use of the "other White" strategy in Mexican American desegregation lawsuits came back "to haunt Chicano civil rights attorneys" (Rangel & Alcala, 1972, p. 348). Beginning with *Romo* (1925), for more than four decades plaintiffs' attorneys in these cases relied heavily on the "other White/no statute" argument. Repeatedly, plaintiffs in these many cases asserted that (a) Mexican Americans were "other White" and (b) no state law existed to sanction their segregation. By the late 1960s, however, school boards turned the argument on its head: given that no state statutes provide for the segregation of Mexican Americans, then any such segregation is de facto in nature, not de jure. As such, school boards contended that Mexican Americans had no basis for an equal protection claim/lawsuit. *Brown*, the controlling authority in desegregation cases, could not be applied to Mexican Americans, the argument went, because in the absence of state laws allowing segregation, school boards could not be found culpable of intent, or de jure segregation. Furthermore, given that the law considered Mexican Americans as legally White, the CCISD (and other districts) desegregated their schools by pairing African American and Mexican American students and, thus, claiming that the district was unitary. Thus, attorneys for Mexican American plaintiffs needed to develop an equal protection argument so as to be protected under *Brown*. There lay the challenge in *Cisneros*.

In 1969–1970, the CCISD enrolled a total of 46,023 K–12 students in sixty-one schools. The district was nearly equal in the White and Mexican American enrollments, with respective percentages of 47.4 and 47.2; African Americans constituted 5.4% of the enrollment.[159] Given these proportions in this triethnic district, one would think that in the post-*Brown* era that the CCISD would desire and be capable of accomplishing desegregation. Yet massive segregation existed. For example, of the five high schools, three were predominantly White (ranging from 76.1% to 90.5%), and two were predominantly Mexican American and African American (ranging from 79.3% to 96.4%).[160] Extensive segregation also existed at the elementary school level ($n = 42$ schools). To examine a more detailed analysis of this segregation (conducted by the author), the data provided in the *Cisneros* opinion[161] were used to calculate an ethnic imbalance/balance analysis in the elementary schools.[162] The results showed that in 1969–1970, the CCISD had 85.7% of its elementary schools ($n = 36$) imbalanced (segregated) and 14.3% ($n = 6$) balanced (nonsegregated). Of the thirty-six imbalanced schools, sixteen (44.4%) were predominantly Mexican American/African American and twenty (55.6%) were predominantly White.

Plaintiffs based their claims in *Cisneros* on violations of the Fourteenth Amendment and Title VI of the 1964 Civil Rights Act.[163] Judge Seals determined that five issues were before the court.[164] To wit:

- Does *Brown* apply to Mexican Americans?
- If *Brown* applies to Mexican Americans, does it so apply in the instant case?
- Is CCISD a dual (segregated) or unitary school system?
- If CCISD is a dual system, is the segregation de jure or de facto in basis?
- If CCISD is a dual system, how can a unitary system be established and maintained (in light of recent Supreme Court and Fifth Circuit opinions)?

The defendants' responded:[165]

- *Brown* has no application to Mexican Americans.
- Even if *Brown* applies to Mexican Americans, the group has not been and is not presently segregated in the CCISD.
- Even if *Brown* has application to Mexican Americans, and if they have been and are now segregated in the CCISD, such segregation has been and continues to be de facto in nature, not de jure.

Due to space limitations, discussion is presented on two of the major issues described by Judge Seals. First, does *Brown* apply to Mexican Americans? In short, can Mexican Americans avail themselves of the Equal Protection Clause as African Americans can? Second, is the basis of segregation in the CCISD de facto or de jure in nature?

Regarding the question of *Brown*'s application to Mexican Americans, Judge Seals found that "These Mexican American students are an *identifiable, ethnic-minority class* [italics added] sufficient to bring them within the protection of *Brown*."[166] Testimony given by Dr. Thomas P. Carter, Dr. Héctor P. García, and Mr. Paul Montemayor heavily influenced Judge Seals's finding on this issue. Each offered convincing and lucid accounts of how Mexican Americans had been historically discriminated against as a class (in society generally and in schools) in the Southwest region, Texas, and the CCISD. Judge Seals also referred to a number of Mexican American–initiated lawsuits that spoke to the considerable amount of discrimination faced by Mexican Americans.[167] In addition to testimony regarding the widespread discrimination endured by Mexican Americans, Carter testified that they are a *readily identifiable minority group*:

> Looking at it culturally, they [Mexican Americans] are an identifiably different group with adherence to the Spanish language, certain physical characteristics that are more or less Indian or mistisaje [*sic*] or the blending of the Spanish and the Mexican. So, no matter how you cut it, you are going to come out as a minority, both from social science and from the legal point of view, and from the cultural point of view, and the racial point of view.[168]

In sum, the legal strategy of melding testimony on discrimination *and* ethnic identifiability proved to be powerful for plaintiffs. Judge Seals wrote, "Not only do I find that Mexican-Americans have been discriminated against as a class, I further find that because they are an identifiable, ethnic minority they are more susceptible to discrimination."[169]

With respect to the second central issue, whether the CCISD was de facto or de jure segregated, Judge Seals found the district to be dual in structure and was "a de jure segregated system maintained by state action."[170] While acknowledging that "some of the segregation was of a de facto nature because of socio-economic factors"[171] that caused Mexican Americans and African Americans to live in the "corridor,"[172] the dual school system of the CCISD "has its real roots in the minds of men."[173] The court came to this firm conclusion of the de jure segregation by noting that the CCISD school board engaged, for example, in gerrymandering attendance zones, building new and renovating old schools in the predominantly Mexican American and African American neighborhoods, and providing transfers plans that allowed the White students to avoid attending schools in the "corridor."[174]

In the end, Judge Seals ruled in favor of the plaintiffs and granted injunctive relief. To get on with the business of developing a desegregation plan, he ordered that a "human relations committee" be formed, consisting of twelve members (four Whites, four Mexican Americans, and four African Americans), to work with the CCISD school board.[175]

The CCISD was tenacious in its appeals, including a petition for a stay to the U.S. Supreme Court.[176] Yet, on August 2, 1972, the Fifth Circuit affirmed, en banc (by the full court), the district court's ruling that the segregation of Mexican Americans and African Americans was unconstitutional.[177] Notwithstanding the major legal importance of *Cisneros* in that Mexican Americans became protected under *Brown*, desegregating the CCISD schools proved problematic. After holding hearings in Corpus Christi in the post-*Cisneros* period, the Texas Advisory Committee to the U.S. Commission on Civil Rights noted, the CCISD "continues to maintain a segregated school district. . . . The school board and the superintendent have repeatedly denied the existence of segregation and steadfastly refused to develop workable plans for bringing about desegregation" (U.S. Commission on Civil Rights, 1977, pp. 76–77). On a final note, using the most recent data on Texas school enrollment (Texas Education Agency, 2005), I undertook an ethnic imbalance/balance analysis of the elementary schools in the CCISD. As of the 2004–2005 school year, the district's total enrollment was disaggregated by ethnicity as follows: Latinos, 75.5%; Whites, 16.7%; African Americans, 5.5%; other, 2.1%. Based on my analysis, the CCISD had 20.5% of its thirty-nine elementary schools ($n = 8$) imbalanced and 79.5% ($n = 31$) balanced. Of the eight imbalanced schools, two were predominantly Mexican American/African American and six were predominantly White. The number of current imbalanced schools is considerably lower than existed in 1969–1970 ($n = 36$) at the time of *Cisneros*. Rather than desegregation efforts by the CCISD, the reduction of imbalanced schools is more attributable to a sharp decline in the White student enrollment (from 47.4% in 1969–1970 to 16.7% in 2004–2005) and a substantial increase in the Mexican American enrollment (from 47.2% in 1969–1970 to 75.5% in 2004–2005).

Ross v. Eckels (1970)

Litigated at the same time as *Cisneros*, *Ross* is one of the longest desegregation cases on record—spanning twenty-seven years.[178] In 1956, the NAACP Legal Defense and Education Fund initially filed *Ross* against the Houston Independent School District (HISD).[179] The case ended in 1983 when the Fifth Circuit affirmed a 1981 district court decision ruling the HISD unitary, or desegregated.[180] Mexican American participation in *Ross* did not come about until 1970, and that is where we begin our discussion.

In the 1969–1970 school year, the HISD—then the sixth-largest school district in the nation, with 238,460 students and 230 schools—was reviewing seven possible desegregation plans (including the plaintiffs' plan).[181] The district population of students was 66.9% White and 33.1% African American.[182] The district estimated that approximately 36,000 students (about 15%) were "Spanish surnamed Americans," and they were statistically included in the White group.[183]

Of the seven possible desegregation plans under consideration for adoption, the district did not choose the plaintiffs' plan, as it relied heavily on massive busing (44,000 students daily) and was said to be very expensive.[184] Rather, the HISD selected the "equidistant zoning" plan, creating separate zones for elementary, junior high, and high schools. In turn, the HISD drew zone lines precisely equidistant between the adjacent schools and required each student to enroll in the school nearest his or her home.[185] The HISD contended that this plan was "completely fair and impartial"[186] and believed it the best strategy to achieve unitary status.

Plaintiffs appealed the district's equidistant zoning plan, claiming that their own plan had the better chance of unifying the district. The Fifth Circuit affirmed in part, reversed in part, and remanded the case with directions to the district court.[187] The appellate court found the equidistant zoning plan acceptable, but with modifications (i.e., the need to reduce the number of all–African American elementary schools).

In a critical dissent, Judge Charles Clark raised two points of injustice that are particularly germane here. First, he noted that the district's plan was "impotent" in that it excluded several "cut-glass," all-White areas.[188] Second, citing *Cisneros*, he commented on the "ominous" effect of pairing African American and Mexican American students, who were equally disadvantaged ethnic groups."[189] Judge Clark noted that it was "mock justice to force the numbers by pairing" the two groups.[190] He further commented that he would be extremely surprised to find a single teacher in the HISD "who would testify that the educational needs of these groups is advanced by such pairing."[191] In a final searing remark to his Fifth Circuit brothers, Judge Clark wrote, "We seem to have forgotten that the equal protection right enforced is a right to education, not statistical integration."[192]

The *Ross* pairing order included twenty-seven elementary schools, with only one being predominantly White.[193] In all, 14,942 African American, 6,233 Mexican American, and 2,368 White students were included in the pairing aspect of the HISD's equidistant zoning plan. Ergo, 21,175 of the total 23,543 students (89.9%) in the pairing order were students of color (Salinas, 1971). As such, the purpose of any desegregation plan—to attain a unitary school system—could not be realized by the HISD's equidistant zoning plan. Judge Clark, in his dissent, was not the only one concerned with this major issue of not providing an integrated and meaningful school experience for *all* students. In a case study of the HISD school integration issue—*Brown, Not White: School Integration and the Chicano Movement in Houston* (2001)—historian Guadalupe San Miguel, Jr., chronicled the Mexican American community's political response to the district's failed desegregation plan, including a 1970 boycott of the schools.

In 1972, Mexican American citizens who resided in the HISD sought, as a class, leave to intervene (enter) in *Ross* as a matter of right (Fed. R. Civ. P. 24[a][2]) and as a matter of discretion (Fed. R. Civ. P. 24[b][2]).[194] The district court, noting that the HISD historically and currently has considered Mexican Americans as White, denied both actions of the motion to intervene. The appellants, citing *Cisneros* and *U.S. v. Texas Education Agency* (Austin Independent School District),[195] prayed for the Fifth Circuit to reverse the denial of leave to intervene. Noting that because the "district court's ruling [in *Ross*] was based upon a legal premise which differed from the current rule of this circuit,"[196] the Fifth Circuit vacated the intervention denial and remanded the case "with directions to reconsider its action under the principles announced [by the Fifth Circuit] in the *Austin* and *Corpus Christi* decisions."[197] In this interesting development of legal indeterminacy, irony clearly surfaced. In the *Cisneros* and *Austin* cases, the Fifth Circuit favored Mexican Americans, yet in *Ross* their ruling on vacation and remand was equivocal. The Mexican Americans' legal status of being an identifiable ethnic minority group remained in limbo until the U.S. Supreme Court eventually decided the *Keyes* case.

Keyes v. School District No. 1 of Denver, Colorado (1973)

Like *Ross*, *Keyes* had a long and complicated history. In 1969, African American student plaintiffs attending schools in School District No. 1 of Denver, Colorado, filed *Keyes* in the U.S. District Court for the District of Colorado.[198] Culminating after twenty-six years, the district court finally declared the school district unitary in 1995.[199]

In 1969, School District No. 1 of Denver had 119 schools and a total enrollment of 96,577 students: 70.7% White, 15.8% Mexican American[200] (referred to as "Hispano" in Colorado), and 12.7% African American. The district court in *Keyes* found that for nearly a decade the school board of the district "had engaged in an unconstitutional policy of deliberate racial segregation."[201] Also, very importantly, Judge William E. Doyle in his district court decision drew some sharp differences between White and Mexican American students. The court noted that "Hispanos have a wholly different origin [than Anglos] and the problems applicable to them are different."[202] Furthermore, Judge Doyle commented on the similarities between African Americans and Mexican Americans. "One of the things which the Hispano has in common with the Negro is economic and cultural deprivation and discrimination [and therefore] the Hispano should receive the same benefit as the Negro."[203] Judge Doyle ordered the district to desegregate. Upon appeal, the Tenth Circuit affirmed in part, reversed in part, and remanded the case to the district court. The appellate court did not question the district court's ruling that Mexican Americans were not White.[204]

The U.S. Supreme Court granted a writ of certiorari on January 17, 1972.[205] Mexican American participation in *Keyes* began legally, per se, on May 22, 1972, when the Supreme Court granted MALDEF leave to file an amicus curiae brief.[206] The Supreme Court rendered its decision in June 21, 1973. The *Keyes* decision is quite important in at least three ways.

First, the Supreme Court had, for the first time in history, an opportunity to rule on a desegregation case that was not confined to the South. The justices were well aware of this geographic development. Justice Lewis F. Powell wrote in his individual opinion, "This is the first school desegregation case to reach the Court which involves a major city outside the South."[207] Second, the court ruled that in the absence of statutes allowing segregation, a district can still be found liable for intentional segregation if plaintiffs can show how school authorities carried out a systematic practice of segregation.[208] Third, Justice William J. Brennan, who wrote the opinion in *Keyes*, found "that the District Court erred in separating Negroes and Hispanos for purposes of defining a 'segregated' school. We have held that *Hispanos constitute an identifiable class* [italics added] for purposes of the Fourteenth Amendment."[209] The issue of whether Mexican American students are an identifiable ethnic minority class sufficient to bring them under the protection of *Brown* had been finally settled— and by the nation's highest court.

In the context of CRT, the decision in *Keyes* to view Mexican Americans as an identifiable ethnic group for purposes of desegregation demonstrates the centrality of race in explaining individual experiences of the law. From *Romo* (1925) to *Chapa* (1967), Mexican Americans utilized the "other White" strategy in desegregation cases, which worked to their advantage. Yet, in light of the systemic nature of racism in education and society, Mexican Americans were forced to seek protection as an identifiable ethnic minority group under *Brown*. As such, CRT assists us in examining how race became socially constructed in legal discourse in order for Mexican Americans to seek social justice.

Soria v. Oxnard School District Board of Trustees (1974)

This case, the last lawsuit of the 1970s to be discussed, illustrates how plaintiffs' attorneys were able to tie the knot between the historical source of segregation in the Oxnard public schools in the 1930s and present-day segregation in the early 1970s.

Mexican American and African American elementary schoolchildren living in Oxnard, California, and attending schools in the Oxnard School District (OSD) brought forth *Soria*, a class action lawsuit, in the U.S. District Court for the Central District of California; Judge Harry Pregerson presided.[210] Oxnard, a coastal community, is approximately fifty-four miles north of Los Angeles. At the time of *Soria*, the OSD was relatively small, consisting of twelve elementary and two junior high schools. The elementary schools enrolled 7,483 students (55% Mexican American/African American; 43% White; 2% other).[211]

Plaintiffs asserted that defendants maintained and perpetuated a racially imbalanced school system, thus depriving them of their Fourteenth Amendment rights. They demonstrated that in light of the ±15% rule-of-thumb formula, ten of the twelve elementary schools were imbalanced.[212] The pattern of imbalance was conspicuous. The eastern section of Oxnard, referred to as the *Colonia* (Spanish for "neighborhood" or "community"), was predominantly Mexican American and African American; all three elementary schools overwhelmingly enrolled students of color (81% to 96%). In the northwest sector, populated nearly exclusively by Whites, all three elementary schools were predominantly White (71% to 85%).[213] On May 12, 1971, Judge Pregerson, citing a number of cases as authority, found that the segregation in the OSD had "de jure overtones" and arose from such practices as location of new schools, student busing plans, and failure to adopt previous desegregation plans.[214] The court granted the plaintiffs' motion for summary judgment and noted that they are entitled to relief. Judge Pregerson gave the defendants twenty work days to submit a desegregation plan to the court. On July 21, 1971, the district court approved a plan and ordered the defendants to implement it.[215]

On appeal to the Ninth Circuit, appellants argued that "neighborhood population patterns" created the ethnic imbalance in the elementary schools, not the school board.[216] Appellants also declared that busing policies, selection of school construction sites, student assignments, and the like were "sound administrative determinations" and that no White students from the northwest schools were bused into the Colonia schools because of overcrowding in the latter.[217] The Ninth Circuit found the district court's conclusion that the school board's acts and omissions constituted "de jure overtones" was "inconclusive and vague on the question of the School Board's segregative intent."[218] The appellate court boldly noted that "the city of Oxnard [has not] ever maintained a 'dual school system' wherein students have been assigned to schools on account of race or ethnic background."[219] Finally, referring to the U.S. Supreme Court's decision in *Keyes* as authority, the Ninth Circuit vacated and remanded the case, ruling that the district court must apply the proper legal standard (i.e., de jure segregation) in determining whether the school board had committed a constitutional violation.[220] The district court–ordered desegregation plan, however, was left untouched, pending final resolution of *Soria*.[221]

On remand,[222] plaintiffs' attorneys certainly faced an arduous challenge: In light of the Ninth Circuit's ruling, how can counsel bring forth evidence that the OSD intentionally segregated its students? What transpired next was one of the most fortuitous and remarkable evidentiary findings one could imagine. Plaintiffs' attorneys, Joel Edelman and Herbert Nowlin, in their preparation for trial recalled that a reference in some materials to old school board minutes made mention of school segregation.[223] These minutes were of Oxnard school board proceedings taken during meetings from the mid- to late 1930s. Jack McCurdy (1975), *Los Angeles Times* education writer, commented,

> What unfolded during meetings in the . . . 1930s was a well-planned scheme of forced segregation which experts rank as one of the most blatant such episodes in school annals outside the South. The minutes of those meetings nearly 40 years ago . . . apparently constitute the first such evidence of a school board's systematic segregation of minority children in the Western United States. (p. 1)

In his opinion, Judge Pregerson liberally quoted from the school board minutes of the past. Minutes from August 7, 1934, November 4, 1936, and September 27, 1937, respectively, noted,

> Trustee Dockstader also brought up the matter of the segregation of Mexican children. After discussing the matter at some length it seemed to be the general opinion that complete segregation was impossible at the present time and that the matter was being handled in perhaps as satisfactory a manner as could be expected.[224]

> President Dockstader stated that the Board was in favor of the principle of segregation, although it might not be entirely practical at this time.[225]

> Taking the enrollment figures as presented at a previous meeting a typewritten plan was offered by Trustee Burfeind calling for all "Mexican" children living south of Fifth Street to attend the Haydock School, leaving all white and oriental children living south of Fifth Street in the Roosevelt and Wilson schools. The moving of Oriental children living south of Fifth Street to the Haydock School will be taken into consideration in case of future emergency, and no further shifting of pupils is intended. This plan is to be put into effect at an early date.[226]

The Oxnard school board minutes from November 1936 to June 1939 also indicated that the board established and maintained segregated class-rooms in racially mixed schools. School officials prevented White and Mexican American children from playing together by forcing them to have "staggered playground periods and release times" from school.[227] Plaintiff attorneys Edelman and Nowlin also had former superintendents of the OSD testify. One superintendent testified that Ramona Elementary School, located in the Colonia, had few conveniences. "Its floor consisted of blacktop rolled over bare earth, its illumination came from a single bare bulb, its roof leaked, its toilets were deplorable."[228] Another superin-tendent described one school as "literally no more than a chicken coop. It had a dirt floor, single thickness walls, very run down, some stench from the toilet facility."[229]

The old school board minutes strongly influenced Judge Pregerson's de-cision. He noted that at the first district court trial the "de jure overtones" he spoke of represented "visible branches" that indicated segregative in-tent. But, he continued, the discovery of the 1930s school board minutes by plaintiffs' attorneys exposed the "roots" of the board's discriminatory intent to segregate the schools.[230] Judge Pregerson ruled that from the "mid 1930's to the summer of 1971" the school board of the OSD "pursued a deliberate policy of racial segregation in its elementary schools."[231] He thus ordered that the segregation plan implemented on July 21, 1971, shall continue in full force and effect.[232]

Soria is another reminder that in CRT heterodoxy is a key element. In the 1930s, the OSD utilized a number of means to maintain the White privilege of the school board and the community. The OSD perpetuated the segregation of Mexican American and White students via, for example, location of new schools, gerrymandering, and racial separation in mixed schools. Although the old school board minutes did not surface until after three and a half decades, they were certainly helpful for plaintiffs' lawyers in *Soria* to mount an effective challenge to the orthodoxy and to expose the self-interest and privilege of the OSD school board.

Diaz v. San Jose Unified School District (1985)

This Mexican American segregation lawsuit was also lengthy, first filed in 1971, ruled on at the federal level in 1976,[233] and culminated with a Ninth Circuit ruling in 1988. I have considerable familiarity with the *Diaz* case, as I testified as an expert witness for the plaintiffs in the 1985 trial.[234]

The school district's desegregation plan included the closure of several high-enrollment Mexican American schools. I testified that the closures were not educationally sound decisions (see chapter 5, this volume, for a discussion of *Diaz* and other school closure lawsuits brought forth by Mexican Americans).

San Jose, California, is located about forty-two miles southeast of San Francisco. In 1985, the San Jose Unified School District (SJUSD) had a long and narrow shape, spanning sixteen miles north to south, and one and a half to four miles east to west. As were the schools, residential areas were racially isolated. The Mexican American population was concentrated in the downtown area (northern part of the district), and the White residents predominated in the suburbs of the southern part of the SJUSD.[235] In the 1984–1985 school year, the SJUSD enrolled 30,565 students in thirty-seven schools. The students were 57.0% White, 30.9% Mexican American, 8.4% Asian American, and 2.4% African American.[236]

In the initial complaint of 1971, Arnulfo and Socorro Díaz, parents and next friends of Fernando, Miguel, and Juan Díaz, and other plaintiffs (all junior high and high school students in the SJUSD) alleged that the school district operated and maintained a dual school system in violation of the Fourteenth Amendment.[237] Plaintiffs also sought a temporary retraining order to prevent defendants from completing construction of eleven elementary and two junior high schools as they would be imbalanced from inception.[238] Judge Robert F. Peckham, who presided over *Diaz* in the U.S. District Court for the Northern District of California (San Jose Division), ruled for the defendants on January 1, 1976, finding that "The evidence shows that defendant School District has adhered to a 'neighborhood school policy,' with the result that ethnic composition of the schools merely reflects residential patterns."[239]

On appeal, the Ninth Circuit vacated and remanded Judge Peckham's decision. The appellate court ruled that although "A neighborhood school policy is not constitutionally suspect,"[240] such a policy needs to be penetrated for examination in "the complete context in which the neighborhood policy was initially applied and enforced."[241] Thus, the Ninth Circuit found, "An inference of segregative intent arose from the appellants' proof."[242] On remand, Judge Peckham found again in favor of the defendants, ruling that the SJUSD acted without segregative intent.[243] On the plaintiffs' second appeal, the Ninth Circuit affirmed Judge Peckham's decision.[244] Judge Farris dissented, asserting that the SJUSD had plenty of opportunities to desegregate the schools but chose not to do so. He noted,

"More than twenty years have elapsed with no break in this continuing failure. This, in my opinion, is sufficient to support an inference of 'segregative intent.'"[245] Yet, in an interesting twist of legal indeterminacy, the Ninth Circuit, after a hearing en banc, found that the SJUSD had, in fact, acted with segregative intent in maintaining schools that were imbalanced.[246] The appellate court came to the conclusion by finding cumulative evidence that the district maintained and perpetuated segregated schools via a number of actions, for example, site selections of new school construction, faculty and staff assignments, and ignoring state guidelines in desegregation efforts.[247]

In 1985, Judge Peckham faced the task of addressing which desegregation plan to adopt—the district's or the plaintiffs'.[248] In July 1985, the SJUSD asked the district court to approve its desegregation plan. The plaintiffs argued that the plan did not go far enough in addressing the Ninth Circuit's mandate to desegregate the district. On August 27, 1985, Judge Peckham rejected the district's plan and ordered it to submit a comprehensive one. On September 30, 1985, the district did so, and on November 15, 1985, the plaintiffs responded with their own plan. The district filed a brief defending its plan and criticizing the plaintiffs' proposal.[249] Finally, on December 15, 1985, the district court commenced a ten-day hearing to decide an appropriate remedy.[250]

The school district's and plaintiffs' proposed desegregation plans differed significantly. In a capsule description,[251] the district's plan (a) employed a largely voluntary approach, (b) established four district-wide "dedicated" magnet schools and sixteen magnet "programs," (c) utilized majority-to-minority transfers, and (d) proposed some school closures. The plan's goal was to have 75% of the district's students attending desegregated schools in four to five years (by the 1990–1991 school year). By contrast, the plaintiffs' plan can be briefly described[252] as (a) emphasizing voluntary reassignments but also involving a mandatory element, (b) dividing the district into three vertical attendance zones, and (c) using "controlled choice" for regular school and magnet school/program assignments. The plaintiffs' plan would lead to 100% of the district's students being in desegregated schools in the first year of implementation of the plan.

Judge Peckham adopted, with modifications, the district's desegregation plan. Defendant's expert witness Dr. Christine Rossell's testimony that the plaintiffs' plan included a greater number of mandatory student assignments helped to influence the court's decision. Such assignments, she asserted, would create bitterness and divisiveness in the community and likely prompt White flight.[253] Judge Peckham ruled that the district's plan was a more moderate, thus appropriate, proposal, but he believed the district did not need four years to enroll only 75% of its students in desegregated schools. He ordered the district to enroll 90% of its students in such schools by December 31, 1989.[254] On appeal, the Ninth Circuit affirmed the district court's ruling.[255]

What is the contemporary status of imbalanced/balanced schools in the SJUSD? To address this, a racial balance/imbalance analysis (conducted by the author) was undertaken, using district data for the 2004–2005 school year (California Department of Education, 2005). Excluding alternative and continuation schools and very small programs (e.g., San Jose Community Middle School, $n = 15$ students) from the analysis, the district had forty-three elementary, middle, and high schools in 2004–2005; the total district enrollment consisted of 28.7% White students (compared to 57.0% in 1984–1985) and 71.3% minority students (70.9% being Mexican American/other Latino; combined minorities were 43.0% in 1984–1985). Using the ±15% formula, of the total forty-three schools, twenty-two (51.2%) were imbalanced (nine predominantly White and thirteen predominantly minority); twenty-one schools (48.8%) were balanced. In sum, although the White and minority enrollments significantly shifted since 1984–1985, the SJUSD continued to demonstrate substantial racial isolation, as similarly seen when the desegregation order was ruled on twenty years ago.

Contemporary Status of Mexican American Desegregation Litigation and School Segregation

Mexican American desegregation lawsuits have, as is the situation with African American desegregation litigation, for the most part, come to an end. The demise of school segregation litigation and subsequent remedies have come about through a long process of antidesegregation efforts by presidential administrations since 1968 (i.e., Nixon, Reagan, and George H.W. Bush), including the appointments of conservative federal court judges and policies of the Justice Department.[256] Also, some U.S. Supreme Court decisions in the 1990s resulted in severe blows for some court-ordered desegregation plans. For example, in *Board of Education of Oklahoma City v. Dowell* (1991),[257] the Supreme Court ruled that a school system could be declared unitary and supervision ended if, after years of compliance with a desegregation plan, the district had shown good-faith, reasonable efforts to eliminate any remaining effects of the prior discrimination. In sum, a district could be declared unitary, whether or not, in fact, it completely overcame its history of discrimination.[258]

These efforts to limit, and then eventually dismantle, school desegregation—coupled with the dramatic growth of the population of K–12 students of color, especially among Latinos (see Valencia, 2002a)—have resulted in widespread resegregation in our nation's public schools.[259] Regarding such patterns, Orfield and Yun (1999) found that one of the most important trends "is the continuation of a long and relentless march toward even more severe segregation for Latinos as they become our largest minority" (p. 11).[260] Orfield and Yun also found that *"Latino students are significantly more segregated than African Americans* [italics added] and segregation has been rapidly growing in the states where they have the largest enrollments" (p. 21).

In order to obtain a closer-grained analysis of contemporary school segregation, I examined the degree of racial isolation in Texas, the nation's second most populous state. The ±15% rule of thumb served as the formula. Because the public school enrollment of Texas's Early Childhood Education to grade 12 population is so large, with 4,335,815 students enrolled in 6,902 schools in 1,043 districts (Texas Education Agency, 2005), the analysis was restricted to the elementary school level. Due to the quantity of total elementary schools ($n = 3,707$), the examination only covered such schools in the fifty school districts with the largest elementary enrollments. This resulted in a subsample of 1,762 schools (47.5% of the total elementary schools). For the 2004–2005 school year, the number of elementary students captured in the top fifty districts amounted to 1,115,070 (a solid majority, 55.3%) of the state's total 2,016,310 elementary school students. This subsample of 1.1 million students in the 1,762 schools in the fifty school districts with the largest elementary enrollments contained 75.2% combined students of color (overwhelmingly Mexican American and other Latino) and 24.8% White. Several findings can be gleaned from this racial isolation analysis:

• Of the 1,762 elementary schools, 510 (28.9%) were imbalanced and 1,252 (71.1%) were balanced.

• Of the 510 imbalanced schools, 275 (53.9%) were predominantly White, and 235 (46.1%) were predominantly students of color.

• For the sake of interpretation, the meaning of the strong number and percentage of balanced schools ($n = 1,252$ and 71.1%) needs to be tempered with caution. That is, at first glance this looks quite favorable for desegregation purposes. The 71.1%, however, is misleading. Of the 50 districts, 27 (the majority, 54%) have very high enrollments of students of color (i.e., greater than 70%). For most of these districts, given the predominant enrollments of students of color, it is not surprising that one finds such a large percentage of balanced schools. For example, Houston, with a minority enrollment of 92.3%, has 165 of its 185 (89.2%) elementary schools balanced. Also, Brownsville, with a minority enrollment of 98.8%, has *all* of its 32 elementary schools deemed balanced.

• Imbalanced schools tend to be located in bi- or triracial districts that have discernible proportions of enrollments of Whites and students of color. For example, Austin, with students of color and White enrollments of 75.3% and 24.7%, respectively, has 60 of its 74 (81.1%) elementary schools imbalanced. Similarly, Humble, with White and students of color enrollments of 60.9% and 39.1%, respectively, has 13 of its 20 (65%) schools imbalanced. Finally, Amarillo, with students of color and White enrollments of 54.9% and 45.1%, respectively, has 26 of its 36 (72.2%) elementary schools imbalanced.

• In sum, racial isolation is clearly present in the elementary schools of Texas. Whether you consider nearly exclusive Mexican American districts (e.g., Laredo) in South Texas, predominantly White districts (e.g., Clear Creek) in Southeast Texas, triracial districts (e.g., Austin) in Central Texas, or mega, biracial minority districts (e.g., Dallas) in North Texas, Mexican American (and African American) and White students have little opportunity to attend the same elementary schools.

Conclusion

From the mid-1920s, beginning with *Romo v. Laird*, to the late 1980s, culminating with *Diaz v. San Jose Unified School District*, the Mexican American community has been indefatigable in its legal struggle against segregated schools. Likewise, the utter volume of desegregation lawsuits and complaints brought forth by Mexican American parents underscores the significance of these parents' striving unyieldingly for better schools for their children. Furthermore, using CRT as an analytical tool, the history of Mexican American school segregation is an attestation to the lengths that White-dominated school boards and White school officials—in their efforts to preserve privilege—went to prevent the integration of White and Mexican American children and youths. The historical forced segregation of schools created a host of conditions that led, and continues to lead, to school failure among many Mexican American students (Valencia, 2002b). It goes to say that if opportunity structures are racialized via school segregation, then racialized achievement patterns will result (e.g., higher dropout rates of Mexican Americans, compared to their White peers) (Valencia, Menchaca, & Donato, 2002).

Notwithstanding the protracted legal struggle that Mexican Americans have endured for desegregated schools, the current state of affairs looks bleak for any meaningful desegregation. There are, however, some research and policy suggestions that perhaps could serve as starting points to assist in reversing the intensification of Mexican American segregation and even to help promote integration (Valencia, Menchaca, & Donato, 2002). Some ideas include development of residential integration, a renewed interest in busing, expansion of federally funded magnet schools/programs, implementation of two-way bilingual education, and funding for teacher exchanges.[261] Certainly, these suggestions should at least be considered in segregated districts.

Epilogue

Shortly before this book went into production, the U.S. Supreme Court, in a 5–4 decision, dealt a severely debilitating blow to elementary and secondary school desegregation efforts in the high-profile case *Parents Involved in Community Schools v. Seattle School District No. 1* (2007).[262] On June 28, 2007, the Supreme Court—in a 185-page decision—struck down voluntary desegregation plans in Seattle, Washington, and Louisville, Kentucky, in which school districts used a student's race as a factor in school assignments. Appellants were White students who were denied their first choice of schools because the assignment would create racial imbalance. Appellants claimed that their equal protection rights under the Fourteenth Amendment were violated.

The cases before the Supreme Court were from the Ninth and Sixth Circuits, which affirmed the district courts' rulings that the desegregation plans were "narrowly tailored to serve a compelling government interest."[263] Chief Justice John C. Roberts, who wrote the majority opinion, commented, however, that "The districts have also failed to show that they considered methods other than explicit racial classifications to achieve their stated goals."[264] He elaborated,

> Our established strict scrutiny test for racial classifications, however, insists on "detailed examination, both as to ends and as to means. . . ." Simply because the school districts may seek a worthy goal does not mean they are free to discriminate on the basis of race to achieve it, or that their racial classifications should be subject to less exacting scrutiny.[265]

Justice Kennedy, who joined the majority, wrote a concurring opinion.[266] Differing from his fellow Justices in the majority, he noted that diversity is a compelling interest, a goal that school districts may pursue.[267] He also differed from his majority colleagues on the issue of race as a factor in desegregation efforts. He wrote that sections of the opinion by "THE CHIEF JUSTICE imply an all-too-unyielding insistence that race cannot be a factor in instances when, in my view, it may be taken into account."[268] Finally, Justice Kennedy's opinion offered some suggestions, other than systematic and individual race typing, for school desegregation.

> School boards may pursue the goal of bringing together students of diverse backgrounds and races through other means, including strategic site selection of new schools; drawing attendance zones with general recognition of the demographics of neighborhoods; allocating resources for special programs; recruiting students and faculty in a targeted fashion; and tracking enrollments, performance, and other statistics by race. These mechanisms are race conscious but do not lead to different treatment based on a classification that tells each student he or she is to be defined by race, so it is unlikely any of them would demand strict scrutiny to be found permissible.[269]

Justice Stephen G. Breyer wrote the dissenting opinion.[270] In his lengthy opinion (sixty-eight pages), he denounced the majority opinion, commenting that it undermined the promise of *Brown*—integrated education —and asserted that the decision "cannot be justified in the name of the Equal Protection Clause."[271] He also noted that the majority opinion was regressive: "the Court's decision today slows down and sets back the work of local school boards to bring about racially diverse schools."[272] In his conclusion, Justice Breyer noted that the majority opinion denied parents' wishes for their children to attend schools with fellow children of diverse races. He commented,

> The plurality is wrong to do so. The last half-century has witnessed great strides toward racial equality, but we have not yet realized the promise of *Brown*. To invalidate the plans under review is to threaten the promise of *Brown*. The plurality's position, I fear, would break that promise. This is a decision that the Court and the Nation will come to regret.[273]

It is difficult to ascertain the effect that the Supreme Court's ruling will have on the scores of other districts with voluntary desegregation plans. Only time will tell. What we do know, however, is that race, once again, comes to play a critical role in American education.

2

School Financing

The schooling process represents one of the most influential agencies of socialization in the lives of children and youths. Yet, as adults, few of us realize the enormous size of this "big business." Formal education employs more people than any other business in the United States (Brimley & Garfield, 2005) and is very costly. Expenditures for public elementary and secondary schools totaled $472.3 billion in fiscal year 2003–2004 (U.S. Department of Commerce, Bureau of the Census, 2006). The cost of education is also escalating due to, for example, increasing enrollment, inflation, and the high cost of energy (Brimley & Garfield, 2005). Thus, a major concern is the need to finance the nation's public elementary and secondary schools at an *adequate* level. The task of disbursing available funds in a fair manner to schools and to students, without regard to their location within the bounds of a state, is equally arduous and significant. "This is the principle of *equity,* or fairness" (Brimley & Garfield, 2005, p. 61).[1] The legal struggle for financing education equitably for high-enrollment Mexican American schools is the subject of this chapter.

Since the beginning of public education in the Southwest, Mexican American students have been shortchanged in the funding of their schools.[2] Reynolds (1933), in a regional study (*The Education of Spanish-Speaking Children in Five Southwestern States*) sponsored by the Office of Education of the Department of the Interior, reported, "Teaching materials adequate in amount and of the right kind for Mexican children are conspicuously absent" (p. 13). These historical financing inequities can be attributed, for the most part, to the rise of segregation between 1930 and 1960 (San Miguel & Valencia, 1998). A number of scholars have documented the financial neglect of Mexican American segregated schools during the pre– and post–World War II years (see, e.g., Calderón, 1950; García, 1979; Gilbert, 1947; also, see San Miguel & Valencia, 1998). For example, in 1934 the League of United Latin American Citizens (LULAC) issued a report on the condition of schools in the West Side barrio of San

Antonio, Texas (García, 1979). The teacher-student ratio in the West Side schools was 1:43, compared to a ratio of 1:36 in the Anglo schools.[3] Also, the report found the per-pupil expenditures to be $24.50 and $35.96, respectively, for the Mexican American and Anglo schools. Conditions deteriorated in San Antonio to such a degree that community activist Eluterio Escobar described (in 1947) the temporary wooden classroom buildings in the West Side schools as "fire traps" (García, 1979, p. 74). In sum, the racialized funding inequities of schools in the Southwest has a long history.

The struggle for equitable funding for segregated Mexican American schools finally manifested with two Mexican American–initiated lawsuits in the late 1960s—*Serrano v. Priest* in California and *Rodriguez v. San Antonio Independent School District* in Texas. These two cases triggered a flurry of school financing lawsuits in the 1970s through the 2000s (Brimley & Garfield, 2005).[4] As of February 2000, the supreme courts of thirty-five states have issued opinions on school finance lawsuits, with seventeen courts upholding the constitutionality of state funding systems, and eighteen courts declaring such systems unconstitutional (see Table 2.1).

In some cases (i.e., Arizona, Ohio, and Washington), the respective state supreme courts first ruled the state funding system as constitutional and later ruled it unconstitutional (see Table 2.1).

The following sections frame this chapter: (a) background factors of legal challenges in school finance reform; (b) *Serrano v. Priest*: on the path to the nation's first successful state school finance case; (c) *Rodriguez v. San Antonio Independent School District*: the elimination of the federal courts as a legal route for school finance reform; (d) *Edgewood Independent School District v. Kirby*: the reestablishment of *Rodriguez*; (e) Post–*Edgewood I*: interplay between the Texas Legislature and the Texas courts.

Background Factors of Legal Challenges in School Finance Reform

Dedham, Massachusetts, in 1648 levied the first property tax to fund local schools (Pulliam, 1987). Yet it was not until over three hundred years later, in the 1960s, that plaintiffs began filing lawsuits claiming that interdistrict differences in property value (wealth) created differences in the amount of funding available from property taxes for the education of children across districts.

TABLE 2.1
School Finance Litigation Decisions: State Supreme Courts
(as of February 2000)

State	Constitutional	Unconstitutional	Date
Alabama[a]		✓	1993
Alaska	✓		1997
Arizona	✓		1973
Arizona		✓	1994
Arkansas		✓	1983 and 1994
California		✓	1971
Colorado	✓		1982
Connecticut		✓	1977
Georgia	✓		1981
Idaho	✓		1975
Kentucky		✓	1989
Maryland	✓		1983
Massachusetts		✓	1993
Michigan	✓		1973
Minnesota	✓		1993
Missouri		✓	1993
Montana		✓	1989
New Hampshire		✓	1997
New Jersey		✓	1973 and 1990
New York	✓		1982
North Dakota	✓		1994
Ohio	✓		1979
Ohio		✓	1997
Oklahoma	✓		1987
Oregon	✓		1976 and 1991
Pennsylvania	✓		1979
Rhode Island	✓		1995
Tennessee		✓	1993
Texas		✓	1989
Vermont		✓	1997
Virginia	✓		1994
Washington	✓		1974
Washington		✓	1978
West Virginia		✓	1979
Wisconsin	✓		1989
Wyoming		✓	1980 and 1995

Source: Harris (2002, p. 33).

[a] The lower court ruling served as the final decision because the case was not successfully appealed by the state.

Two background factors served as catalysts for the emergent movement of school finance reform via litigation (Berke & Callahan, 1972). In February 1965, Arthur Wise, a doctoral student in the Department of Education at the University of Chicago, published a brief article titled "Is Denial of Equal Educational Opportunity Constitutional?" Wise's article appears to be the first published proposition asserting that inequities in funding of education might be unconstitutional. Wise's 1965 article formed the basis for his doctoral dissertation (Wise, 1967), which, in turn, led to his now classic book, *Rich Schools, Poor Schools: The Promise of Equal Educational Opportunity* (Wise, 1968). He analyzed U.S. Supreme Court decisions in three types of cases (i.e., race and education; indigent criminal; legislative reapportionment), and argued that discrimination in education based on race (e.g., *Brown v. Board of Education of Topeka*, 1954), discrimination in criminal proceedings based on poverty (e.g., *Griffin v. Illinois*, 1956), and discrimination in legislative apportionment based on geography (e.g., *Gray v. Sanders*, 1963) are all unconstitutional. Therefore, Wise asserted in his path-breaking book that discrimination in education based on poverty and geography is unconstitutional, leading him to proffer this argument: "Equality of educational opportunity exists when a child's educational opportunity does not depend upon either his parents' economic circumstances or his location within the state" (Wise, 1968, p. 146). In Wise's view, his suggestions could possibly serve as the foundation for the U.S. Supreme Court to form a legal doctrine that the quality of a child's education across school districts within a state cannot vary on account of wealth or geography. Subsequently, a number of attorneys, scholars, and organizations expanded, refined, and tested Wise's ideas (Berke & Callahan, 1972). The influential book by Northwestern University law professor John Coons and his associates (two law students at the time), William Clune and Stephen Sugarman, served as a second impetus for the incipient movement of school financing reform via litigation. In their 1970 book, *Private Wealth and Public Education*, Coons et al. sought to offer advice to future plaintiffs in school finance litigation. Plaintiffs' loss in *McInnis v. Shapiro* (1968) appears to have inspired Coons et al. Elementary and high school students attending schools in Cook County, Illinois, claimed that the state's financing scheme violated their Fourteenth Amendment rights. That is, the funding statutes allowed wide variations in the expenditures per students across districts (local districts could tax themselves above the minimum rate, thus leading to large variations). The plaintiffs asked for educational benefits according to the *individual needs* of students. In short, plaintiffs' proposed remedy called for individual districts to set their own tax rate, but any amount generated above the $400 baseline minimum would be captured by the State from property-rich districts and redistributed to property-poor districts. The court dismissed the case, commenting that the Fourteenth Amendment does not call for expenditures to be provided only on students' educational needs.

Furthermore, the court held that no judicially manageable criteria existed by which a constitutional directive could be enforced, and thus the case was nonjusticiable.[5] In light of the *McInnis* outcome, Coons et al. sought a more sophisticated and winnable strategy that plaintiffs could utilize in school finance litigation, namely:

1. Do not request from the court a determination of children's educational needs. Rather, confine your request for a finance system that is independent of district wealth. This has become known as the principle of "fiscal neutrality."[6] Coons et al. describe this precept as follows: "*The quality of public education may not be a function of wealth other than the wealth of the state as a whole*" (1970, p. 2).

2. Do not structure your lawsuit on a claim that the school financing system in question is racially discriminatory.[7]

3. Do not base your lawsuit on a claim that the school financing system of concern is discriminatory against the poor.[8]

4. In light of points 1–3, Coons et al. asserted, *Do* base your lawsuit on a claim of discrimination against *all* children in tax-poor districts, regardless of the children's race or familial wealth. As noted by Henke (1986), the Coons et al. advice in this context calls for the plaintiffs to vigorously persuade the court that "the combination of children in tax-poor districts, a protected class, and education, a fundamental interest, warrants shifting the burden to the state to show a compelling reason for the discriminatory treatment of children caused by differences in gross district wealth" (p. 9).

In sum, the legal doctrines developed by Coons et al. served, as we shall examine next, as the legal formulation adopted by the California Supreme Court in the landmark *Serrano v. Priest* (1971) decision.

Serrano v. Priest: *On the Path to the Nation's First Successful State School Finance Case*

Serrano v. Priest (Civil Action No. 938254, Superior Court, Los Angeles County, California, January 8, 1969; hereafter referred to as *Serrano v. Priest* [1969]) was the initial complaint in this significant Mexican American–initiated litigation, a lawsuit that eventually culminated in the nation's first successful state school finance case. As the case proceeded through the courts, the fundamental importance of education was deeply discussed and the financially discriminatory chasm between economically advantaged and disadvantaged school districts was exposed (Coon & Sommer, 1999).[9]

In the fiscal year 1968–1969, the revenues to fund elementary and secondary public schools in California originated from the following sources, listed in descending order by proportion: local property taxes (55.7%), state aid (35.5%), federal funds (6.1%), and miscellaneous sources (2.7%).[10] At that time, the chief source of revenue for funding public schools in California was, by far, the local property tax. Pursuant to the California Constitution (Article IX, §6), the Legislature authorized the governing unit of each county and city to levy taxes on the real property[11] within each school district "to meet the district's annual education budget" (Ed. Code, §20701 et seq.).[12] The amount of money that a district could raise depended mainly on its tax base—"i.e., the assessed valuation of real property within its borders."[13] And there lay the crux of the complaint in *Serrano v. Priest* (1969)—the assessed valuation of real property varied widely across districts. For example, in 1969–1970 in California, "the assessed valuation per unit of average daily attendance of elementary schoolchildren ranged from a low of $103 to a peak of $952,156—a ratio of nearly 1 to 10,000."[14] The assessed valuation per unit of average daily attendance of high school students ranged from a low of $11,595 to a high of $349,093—a ratio of 1 to 30.[15]

John Serrano, Jr., growing up in a working-class family, had at one time lived in East Los Angeles, an unincorporated section of Los Angeles County.[16] In 1967, his oldest son, John Anthony, entered first grade in a school located in the immense and, then, "property rich" Los Angeles Unified School District (LAUSD). Although assessors classified the district as property rich, the academic patterns of Mexican American students attending LAUSD schools were quite poor. For example, in a 1968 survey of Mexican Americans and White students in the sixth, ninth, and twelfth grades in twenty-three LAUSD schools, composite English and mathematics scores demonstrated racialized patterns. At all three grade levels, Mexican Americans showed lower and markedly lower achievement scores than their White peers. Likewise, at all three grade levels, White students had higher and markedly higher achievement scores than Mexican Americans (Grebler, Moore, & Guzmán, 1970, chapter 7, and Appendix C). In light of these lower academic achievement patterns for Mexican American students, it was not surprising that some parents opted out of the LAUSD and transferred to higher-performing districts.

At the time, Serrano, age thirty-nine, with a degree from California

State College at Los Angeles, was working as Director of Social Services at the Los Angeles Regional Center for the Developmentally Disabled. Serrano had concerns that his bright son, John Anthony, would not receive a challenging education at his present school. His son's principal advised him to enroll his son in a better school in another district. Consequently, the Serrano family moved to Whittier (California) and then settled in Hacienda Heights (California). Young John did well academically in the Hacienda–La Puente Unified School District (H-LPUSD), which in 1970–1971 was "property poor." Serrano, "by his own admission had chosen it [H-LPUSD] over a property-rich district [LAUSD] and was apparently satisfied with its services" (Fischel, 2004, p. 893). Interestingly, Serrano did not approach attorneys to initiate the *Serrano v. Priest* (1969) lawsuit. Conversely, a group of attorneys, working together to mount a major school finance lawsuit, recruited Serrano and other plaintiffs. Fischel (2004) notes that "Mr. Serrano freely admitted that his personal involvement was minimal, although he was ideologically committed to the case" (p. 893).

On August 23, 1968, Serrano filed *Serrano v. Priest* (1969) on behalf of his son, John Anthony (Domínguez, 1977). Soon after, other Mexican American plaintiffs from Los Angeles County joined the filing to form a class action lawsuit.[17] Defendants in the case included the State Treasurer (Ivy Baker Priest), the State Superintendent of Public Instruction (Max Rafferty), and the State Controller (Houston I. Flournoy). Defendants were also the Tax Collector, Treasurer, and Superintendent of Schools of Los Angeles County.[18] Judge Robert W. Kenny heard *Serrano v. Priest* (1969) in the Superior Court of Los Angeles County.

The plaintiffs' complaint set forth three causes of actions:

1. The California school financing system, by allowing between-school district disparities in the amount of revenue for education, violated the plaintiff children's equal protection rights under the Fourteenth Amendment and the California Constitution. As such, schoolchildren in the property-poor districts received markedly inferior educational opportunities.

2. Incorporating the first cause of action, plaintiffs claimed that the current financing system forced the parents to pay property taxes at a higher rate, compared to parents of other districts, in order to secure revenue that would be used to provide equivalent or lesser educational opportunities.

3. Incorporating the first two causes, the plaintiffs asked the court for a declaratory judgment that the present school financing system in

California was unconstitutional. In addition, the plaintiffs prayed for an order that would direct "defendants to make a remedial reallocation of school funds, and for an adjudication that the trial court retain jurisdiction to restructure the system if defendants and the state Legislature failed to act within a reasonable time."[19]

All defendants in *Serrano v. Priest* (1969) filed general demurrers[20] (challenges) to the complaint, maintaining that none of the three claims specified the facts sufficient to constitute a cause of action. In January 1969, Judge Kenny sustained the demurrers, with leave (permission) to amend. Plaintiffs did not amend their actions, and thus the trial court granted defendants' motion to dismiss.[21] Following their defeat in *Serrano v. Priest* (1969), plaintiffs took their case to the Court of Appeal of California, but, again, they were unsuccessful, as the appellate court affirmed the Superior Court decision (*Serrano v. Priest*, 1970).[22] In turn, plaintiffs appealed to the California Supreme Court. The appellants in *Serrano v. Priest* (1971; referred to in the literature as *Serrano I*) prevailed in this far-reaching decision, the first successful school finance case in the United States.

A major question before the *Serrano I* court, as well as other courts involving legislative actions, was: What standard of review should be applied in assessing whether a legislative act violates the Equal Protection Clause of the Fourteenth Amendment? The "rational basis" test applies to most legislation and mandates only that classification be "rationally related" to a "legitimate state interest" (Wilcoxen, 1985, p. 1107). Under this test, "laws are presumed valid and most laws survive review" (Wilcoxen, p. 1107). The "intermediate scrutiny" standard is a hybrid test that emerged in the 1970s. This quasi-strict standard requires a classification to be "substantially related" to an "important state interest" (Wilcoxen, p. 1108). By sharp contrast, the "strict scrutiny" test carries the most stringent requirements for review. Strict scrutiny is "very difficult to satisfy and few laws subjected to review under this standard will prevail" (Wilcoxen, p. 1108). In order for strict scrutiny to apply, plaintiffs must demonstrate that a particular state action (e.g., California's school financing scheme) either creates a "suspect class" or burdens a "fundamental interest." If plaintiffs can meet these requirements, then defendants can only rebut such challenges by proving that a "compelling state interest" justifies such treatment. Next discussed are suspect class, fundamental interest, and compelling state interest as they applied to *Serrano I*.

- *Wealth as a suspect classification.* The appellants in *Serrano I* asserted that the school financing system in California classified on the basis of wealth. The California Supreme Court found this proposition indisputable.[23] The Court noted that although the "foundation program" of the state's financing system provides $355 per elementary student and $488 per high school student, the school district's wealth, as measured by assessed valuation, determined educational expenditures.[24] To illustrate the differences in property wealth across districts, plaintiffs' lawyers presented select data in *Serrano I*, as shown in Table 2.2. For the four counties listed in Table 2.2, the assessed value per student in the property-wealthy district is considerably higher than the assessed value per student in the property-poor district, resulting in a higher expenditure per pupil in the former compared to the latter school district. Finally, the property-poor district is forced to levy a higher tax rate than the property-wealthy district. The Beverly Hills Unified School District (BHUSD) and the Baldwin Park Unified School District (BPUSD) in Los Angeles County (both listed in Table 2.2) illustrate these several comparative characteristics between property-poor and property-wealthy school districts. The BHUSD in the 1968–1969 school year had an assessed value per pupil of $50,885, about 14 times the assessed value per pupil of $3,706 in the BPUSD, resulting in an expenditure per pupil in the BHUSD ($1,232) of 2.1 times greater than the expenditure per pupil ($577) in the BPUSD. Furthermore, the tax rate in the BPUSD amounted to $5.48 per $100 of assessed valuation, 2.3 times higher than the tax rate of $2.38 per $100 in the BHUSD.

The respondents (defendants) argued that the expenditure per pupil does not accurately represent the wealth of a district because the tax rate

TABLE 2.2

Comparison of Selected Tax Rates and Expenditure Levels in Selected California Counties: 1968–1969 School Year

County and District	Number of Pupils	Assessed Value per Pupil	Tax Rate	Expenditure per Pupil
Alameda				
Emery Unified	586	$100,187	$2.57	$2,223
Newark Unified	8,638	6,048	5.65	616
Fresno				
Colinga Unified	2,640	33,244	2.17	963
Clovis Unified	8,144	6,480	4.28	565
Kern				
Rio Bravo Elementary	121	136,271	1.05	1,545
Lamont Elementary	1,847	5,971	3.06	533
Los Angeles				
Beverly Hills Unified	5,542	50,885	2.38	1,232
Baldwin Park Unified	13,108	3,706	5.48	577

Source: Adapted from *Serrano v. Priest*, 5 Cal.3d at 600 (Cal. 1971).

of the district partly establishes that expenditure.[25] Therefore, a district with a high total assessed valuation may levy a low tax rate, and eventually spend the identical amount per pupil as a property-poor district whose residents choose to pay a higher tax rate. The California Supreme Court in *Serrano I* found the respondents' argument meritless, noting that a property-rich district is favored because it can offer the same educational quality for its pupils with a lower tax rate.[26] Furthermore, property-poor districts are penalized because they are unable to raise their taxes high enough to equal the educational offerings of property-rich districts. Thus, the Court stated, "Affluent districts can have their cake and eat it too; they can provide a high quality education for their children while paying lower taxes. Poor districts, by contrast, have no cake at all."[27] Also, the Court in *Serrano I* embraced the fiscal-neutrality precept of the Coons et al. (1970) team, noting, "We have determined that this funding scheme invidiously discriminates against the poor because it makes the quality of a child's education a function of the wealth of his parents and neighbors" (rather than the wealth of the state as a whole).[28] Finally, the Court disagreed with the respondents' contention that de facto discrimination characterized the instant case. The Court found that governmental action, via the California Constitution and statutes, mandated in every detail the state's school finance system. In sum, de jure discrimination drove the instant case, and the State discriminated "on the basis of the wealth of a district and its residents."[29]

- *Education as a fundamental interest.* The appellants also asserted not only that the finance system in California differentiates on the basis of wealth but that it directly and substantially affects a "fundamental interest," specifically education.[30] Respondents contended that previous cases (e.g., *Hargrave v. McKinney*, 1969) in which the court held that education is a fundamental interest had no precedential value because these cases failed to consider education in the context of discrimination based on wealth. Rather, racial segregation or total exclusion from schooling formed the context of such cases.[31] The Court in *Serrano I* noted, however, that both itself (e.g., *San Francisco Unified School District v. Johnson*, 1971) and the U.S. Supreme Court had recognized education as a fundamental interest (*Brown v. Board of Education of Topeka*, 1954).[32] The *Serrano I* Court commented on the indispensable roles that education plays in modern society, noting that the twin themes of the importance of education—for the individual and for society—are vital to consider. "First, education is a major determinant of an individual's chances for economic and social success in our competitive society; second, education is a unique influence on a child's development as a citizen and his participation in political and community life."[33] The Court did note, however, that although previous decisions on the fundamental importance of education were not legally controlling on the issue before it, such decisions remain persuasive in their accurate factual account of the importance of education.[34]

• *The financing system is not necessary to accomplish a compelling state interest.* In the Court's last step for applying strict scrutiny,[35] it had to determine whether California's school finance system, as structured, was essential to effectuate a "compelling state interest."[36] The respondents argued that the compelling state interest lay in strengthening local control over public education by (a) granting local districts administrative power to control their schools and (b) promoting local control over the amount of money to be spent on education.[37] The Court rejected the respondents' argument of local control by noting, "We need not decide whether such decentralized financial decision-making is a compelling state interest, since under the present financing system, such fiscal freewill is a cruel illusion for the poor school districts."[38]

Finally, the California Supreme Court in this case did not find that the state's school financing system was unconstitutional, but merely that the trial court erred in granting defendants' demurrers. Given that no trial was held to decide the merits of the case, plaintiffs' allegations, if true, would meet all the requirements of strict scrutiny and render California's school financing system unconstitutional. As such, the California Supreme Court reversed the trial court's judgment and remanded it with directions to countermand the demurrers and to allow defendants an appropriate time to answer.[39] The decision in *Serrano I* immediately attracted the attention of the California Legislature. Lawmakers passed Senate Bill 90 (SB 90) and Assembly Bill 1267 (AB 1267), modifying the state's school financing system so as to meet constitutional muster.[40]

Judge Bernard S. Jefferson reheard the *Serrano* case on remand (Civil Action No. 938254, Superior Court, Los Angeles County, California, September 3, 1974). Ivy Baker Priest, lead defendant in the original case, was now deceased, but the court continued to use the title *Serrano v. Priest* for reasons of consistency and convenience. The trial began on December 26, 1972, and proceedings lasted more than sixty days, producing nearly four thousand pages of testimonial transcripts.[41] Litigants agreed that all germane provisions of the California Constitution, state and administrative codes, pertinent federal statutes and regulations, and any modifications from the enactment of SB 90 and AB 1267 would apply to the instant case (see note 40, this chapter).[42]

On September 3, 1974, Judge Jefferson entered his opinion,[43] ruling that the state's public school financing system for elementary and secondary schools, as it stood after the adoption of SB 90 and AB 1267, violated the equal protection provisions of the California Constitution.[44] The trial court held that substantial disparities in per-pupil expenditures across school districts resulting from differences in local taxable wealth will continue to occur under SB 90 and AB 1267.[45] The court's reasoning included, for example, these assertions:

- Above the foundation program,[46] local wealth is the primary determinant of the amount of revenue generated for a given tax rate.
- The amount of revenue from permissive override taxes[47] is solely determined by the amount of wealth available to a school district.
- Basic aid is anti-equalizing, actually widening the gap between low-wealth and high-wealth districts.
- Convergence of revenue limits with the foundation program occurs slowly, and may never occur, as a result of the voted override provision.[48]

The trial court applied the strict scrutiny test and concluded that the state's school financing system was not necessary to the attainment of any compelling state interest and therefore invalid.[49] The court also stated that it would retain jurisdiction over the case to allow the Legislature a six-year period to devise a financing plan that would equalize per-pupil expenditures within a band of $100 per student.[50] On October 28, 1974, the court denied defendants' motion for a new trial. The second appeal to the California Supreme Court followed.

The California Supreme Court handed down its decision in *Serrano v. Priest* (1976), referred to as *Serrano II*, on December 30, 1976—after what appeared an indeterminate duration. In a 4–3 vote, the Court affirmed the trial court's judgment, concluding that the lower court's holding was grounded solidly and accurately on the *Serrano I* decision in which the Court determined that the state's school financing system failed to withstand strict scrutiny. Therefore, "*Serrano I* constitutes the law of the case."[51]

Following the *Serrano II* decision, the California Legislature took the California Supreme Court's ruling seriously and passed a new law, AB 65, intended to correct the state's unconstitutional school financing scheme. Passed in June 1977, AB 65 has been described by one scholar as "extraordinarily complicated" (Guthrie, 1983, p. 214). It contained abstruse aspects such as "'breakpoints,' 'squeeze' and 'double squeeze' factors, 'base revenue limits,' and 'adjusted base revenue limits.' When enacted it was probable that more persons in California understood Einstein's theory of relativity than could comprehend AB 65" (Guthrie, 1983, p. 214). Scarcely a year after the enactment of AB 65, on June 6, 1978, the California electorate passed Proposition 13. This radical transformation limited the property tax rate throughout California at a uniform 1% of market value. California immediately felt the financial consequence of Proposition 13, which led to the withdrawal of $7 billion in local property tax money (Guthrie, 1983). One unanticipated consequence of Proposition 13 was that California's local school district control over revenue was virtually eliminated and substituted by nearly full state funding. "By 1979, the legislature was paying more than 80 cents out of every school support dollar" (Guthrie, 1983, p. 214). Furthermore, although the lengthy *Serrano* saga enhanced school funding equity in California, overall funding for public education began to decline. During the 1975–1976 school year, and prior to *Serrano II*, California ranked eighteenth in the country in per-pupil expenditures. Nearly twenty years later, during the 1994–1995 school year, however, the state ranked forty-first (Hirji, 1999).[52]

In 1986, seventeen years after the initial filing, the *Serrano* chronicle came to an end. In *Serrano v. Priest* (1986), referred to as *Serrano III*, the Court of Appeal of California (Second Appellate District, Division 2) found that the Legislature had done all that was reasonably attainable to lessen disparities in per-pupil expenditures to negligible differences. The court ruled that the state had met the standard as set forth by Judge Jefferson, trial court judge, in 1974. That is, "Disparities have, by any measure, including the $100 band, been reduced to insignificant differences in 1983."[53]

Rodriguez v. San Antonio Independent School District: *The Elimination of the Federal Courts as a Legal Route for School Finance Reform*

The *Rodriguez v. San Antonio Independent School District* (1971) case eventually led to a 1973 landmark U.S. Supreme Court decision in the history of school finance litigation. *Rodriguez*, a lawsuit filed by Mexican

Americans, stands alongside *Serrano* as perhaps one of the most important school finance cases in history (see Yudof & Morgan, 1974, p. 391).
Based on the extant literature, it appears that *Rodriguez* is the most well
known of the school finance lawsuits.[54] John Dayton and Anne Dupre,
legal scholars, noted that *Rodriguez* may be "the most significant [U.S. Supreme Court] decision regarding public schools since *Brown*" (2004, p.
2352). In this section, a capsule account is provided of what transpired in
Rodriguez and the appeal to the U.S. Supreme Court. Within the context
of CRT, *Rodriguez* and its progeny represent a vigorous commitment by
plaintiffs to social justice, as the case endured a nearly four-decade-long
interplay between the Texas courts and the Texas Legislature.

In the late 1960s, Texas public schools experienced serious inequities
in school funding across school districts, and such funding was greatly
racialized. For example, in 1967–1968 students in predominantly Mexican
American districts received about three-fifths of the funding provided to
their counterparts in predominantly White districts (U.S. Commission
on Civil Rights, 1972a, p. 25). Furthermore, in the 1969–1970 school year,
Texas ranked forty-ninth of fifty states in disparities in per-pupil expenditures. Texas had a high and low per-pupil expenditure of $5,334 and $264,
respectively, resulting in a "high/low index" of 20.2 (calculated by dividing $5,334 by $264; see Berke & Callahan, 1972, p. 33, Table 3). The time
was propitious for improvements, as the Texas Legislature had not dealt
with school finance reform since 1949.[55]

The Mexican American discontent with school funding inequities
erupted, as a case in point, on May 16, 1968, when four hundred students
at Edgewood High School in San Antonio participated in a school walkout (or "blowout") and demonstration (Orozco, 2001; Sracic, 2006). The
students marched to the school district administrative offices, carrying a
list of grievances that included complaints of a lack of qualified teachers
and insufficient supplies. Demetrio Rodríguez, lead plaintiff in *Rodriguez*,
noted that the litany of problems ranged "from Bunsen burners to broken
windows" (Sracic, 2006, p. 20). Furthermore, even health concerns arose,
as bats infested one floor of the school (Sracic, 2006). The political protest
carried out by the students helped galvanize the parents who subsequently
formed the Edgewood District Concerned Parents Association (EDCPA),
whose goal was to address specific problems in the district's schools
(Orozco, 2001). These concerned Mexican American parents complained
angrily of the neglectful and inadequate education their children were
receiving, taking aim at the massively overcrowded classrooms, teacher

shortage, inferior physical facilities, and the dearth of basic instructional materials. The root of these many problems, the parents asserted, was the lack of adequate funding (Yudof & Morgan, 1974). In due course, William Velásquez—a well-known activist in political and labor movements—put the EDCPA in touch with lawyer Arthur Gochman (Orozco, 2001; Sracic, 2006).

A cadre of Mexican American parents, mostly mothers, initiated *Rodriguez*. Demetrio Rodríguez, a World War II and Korean War veteran and a sheet-metal worker employed at nearby Kelly Air Force Base, served as lead plaintiff (Pratt, 2002; Sracic, 2006). Rodríguez participated in a number of Mexican American advocacy organizations, including the American GI Forum, LULAC, and the Mexican American Betterment Organization in San Antonio (Orozco, 2001; Sracic, 2006). The plaintiffs' children attended elementary and secondary schools in the Edgewood Independent School District (EISD), one of the seven public school districts in the San Antonio metropolitan area.[56] The EISD, located in the core-city sector in a residential neighborhood that had little industrial or commercial property, enrolled approximately twenty-two thousand students in its twenty-five elementary and twelve secondary schools. About 90%, 6%, and 4% of the student population were Mexican American, Black, and White, respectively.[57]

The following discussion covers the chronology of interplay between the Texas Legislature and the Texas courts with respect to the *Rodriguez* and subsequent *Edgewood* litigation. Table 2.3 lists the pertinent dates and developments from the filing of *Rodriguez* in mid-1968 to the Texas Supreme Court's historic ruling in *Edgewood Independent School District v. Kirby* (1989). Seven parents and eight children filed *Rodriguez* (hereafter referred to as *Rodriguez I*)[58] in the U.S. District Court for the Western District of Texas (San Antonio Division) on July 10, 1968, alleging an unconstitutional denial of equal educational opportunity under the Equal Protection Clause of the Fourteenth Amendment. A three-judge court was impaneled to hear the case. Initially, the complaint named the seven school districts in the San Antonio metropolitan area and the Attorney General of Texas as defendants. San Antonio Independent School District was the lead defendant (Yudof & Morgan, 1974). It soon became evident to both litigants and the three-judge panel that *Rodriguez I* held ramifications far beyond San Antonio, "for, in reality, the whole statewide system of financing education was under attack" (Yudof & Morgan, 1974, p. 392). Consequently, the State Board of Education, the State Commissioner of

TABLE 2.3

From Rodriguez I *to* Edgewood I: *Interplay between the Texas Legislature and the Texas Courts*

Date	Development
7/10/68	*Rodriguez v. San Antonio Independent School District* (*Rodriguez I*) is filed in the U.S. District Court for the Western District of Texas (San Antonio Division).
12/23/71	Three-judge panel court in *Rodriguez I* rules for plaintiffs. Defendants appeal directly to U.S. Supreme Court (*Rodriguez II*).
3/21/73	In a 5–4 vote, U.S. Supreme Court reverses district court's ruling.
1973–1983	Texas Legislature makes feeble attempts to address growing disparities between high- and low-property wealth districts.[a]
5/23/84	MALDEF files *Edgewood v. Kirby* (*Edgewood I*) in 250th District Court of Travis County. Judge Harley Clark presides.[b]
6/30/84	Texas Legislature passes House Bill 72, increasing state aid for poor districts. MALDEF decries bill as "intolerably illegal," amending its suit, and seeking additional funding for poor districts.[b,c]
1/20–4/8/87	Judge Clark hears *Edgewood I*.[b]
4/29/87	Trial court rules for plaintiffs, ordering the Texas Legislature to correct funding inequities by 9/89. Defendants appeal.[b]
12/14/88	Third Court of Appeals reverses trial court decision, 761 S.W.2d 859 (Tex. App.– Austin 1988); appellants appeal.
5/31/89	Texas Legislature passes Senate Bill 1019, increasing school funding; signed 6/16/89.[c]
7/5/89	Texas Supreme Court begins hearing of *Edgewood I*.[a]
10/2/89	Texas Supreme Court, in 9–0 decision, rules for appellants, 777 S.W.2d 391 (Tex. 1989); orders Texas Legislature to formulate new financing system by 5/1/90.

[a] Cárdenas (1997). [b] Acosta (2001). [c] Texas Legislature Online (2006).

Education, and the Bexar County (San Antonio) Board of Trustees were added as defendants.[59] Given the statewide implications of the *Rodriguez I* lawsuit, the case changed to a class action "on behalf of school children throughout the State who are members of minority groups or who are poor and reside in school districts having a low property tax base."[60] In September 1969, the court denied defendants' motion to dismiss the *Rodriguez I* complaint. Yet the court stayed additional proceedings to allow the Legislature a chance to address the state's school finance concerns. In January 1971, the Legislature convened, but made no headway on the school funding problem. Following the adjournment of the 62nd Legislature, Gochman, now with the assistance of other attorneys, began the final preparations for the *Rodriguez I* trial (Yudof & Morgan, 1974).[61]

Plaintiffs complained in *Rodriguez I* that Texas's system of school financing violated the Equal Protection Clause of the Fourteenth Amendment by abridging their fundamental interest to education and creating a suspect class based on wealth.[62] As discussed later, these two elements triggered the strict scrutiny standard.

Dr. Joel S. Berke, plaintiffs' expert, presented data from a statewide sampling of 110 school districts to demonstrate the relation between the amount of taxable property per pupil and actual level of per-pupil expenditures. These data, on which the trial court relied, are presented in Table 2.4. The data show a positive correlation between value of taxable property per pupil and per-pupil expenditures. As well, the data in Table 2.4 demonstrate a negative correlation between percentage of minority students in the district and per-pupil expenditures. Although not shown in Table 2.4, Berke also testified that the ten wealthiest school districts in the state (above $100,000 in taxable property per pupil) had an equalized tax rate of only 31¢ per $100 of assessed valuation. By sharp contrast, the four poorest districts (less than $10,000 in taxable property per pupil) were burdened with an equalized tax rate of 70¢ per $100 of assessed valuation.[63] Nonetheless, the richest districts with their low tax rate were able to yield a per-pupil expenditure of $585, while the poorest districts with their high tax rate were only capable of raising a per-pupil expenditure of $60.[64]

Another tactic that the *Rodriguez I* plaintiffs utilized to establish the existence of interdistrict disparities in school funding was to compare EISD, one of the seven defendant school districts, with nearby Alamo Heights Independent School District (AHISD), a city within the city of San Antonio.[65] Throughout the *Rodriguez* litigation, the EISD and AHISD were compared "to illustrate the manner in which the dual system of finance operates and to indicate the extent to which substantial disparities exist despite the State's impressive progress in recent years."[66] From a CRT perspective, it was essential for plaintiffs' lawyers to highlight these stark comparisons to demonstrate the centrality and intersectionality of race

TABLE 2.4
Relations between Value of Taxable Property, Minority Enrollment, and Per-Pupil Expenditures

Market Value of Taxable Property Per Pupil (number of districts)	Percentage Minority Students	State and Local Revenues Per Pupil (in dollars)
Above $100,000 (10)	8	815
$50,000 to $100,000 (26)	32	544
$30,000 to $50,000 (30)	23	483
$10,000 to $30,000 (40)	31	462
Below $10,000 (4)	79	305

Source: Adapted from *San Antonio Independent School District v. Rodriguez,* 411 U.S. at 16 (1973).

and class in San Antonio. Table 2.5 presents the sharp funding disparities between the EISD and AHISD. In the 1967–1968 school year, EISD had an enrollment of 90% Mexican American students, while AHISD had an enrollment of about 81% White students. The average assessed property value per pupil in AHISD was more than $49,000—about eight times the amount of the average assessed property value per pupil of $5,960 in the EISD. This disparity led to a difference in the per-pupil expenditures across the two districts, with the AHISD spending nearly twice the amount per pupil compared to the EISD. These disparities in school funding translated into superior schooling conditions in the AHISD. Table 2.6 speaks to this. Based on a number of selected indicators of educational quality, the AHISD—compared to the EISD—enjoyed a much more favorable situation. The AHISD had higher professional salaries per pupil and a higher percentage of teachers with master's degrees. The AHISD also had a lower percentage of total teaching staff with emergency credentials and a lower pupil-to-counselor ratio. In all, these gross differences in school funding and resultant educational quality led the trial court in *Rodriguez I* to note in its opinion the following generalizations:

> There was expert testimony to the effect that the current system tends to subsidize the rich at the expense of the poor, rather than the other way around. Any mild equalizing effects that state aid may have do not benefit the poorest districts. For poor school districts educational financing in Texas is, thus, *a tax more spend less system* [italics added].[67]

TABLE 2.5
Financial Disparities between Edgewood Independent School District (EISD) and Alamo Heights Independent School District (AHISD): 1967–1968 School Year

District	No. of Schools (and Enrollment)	Racial/Ethnic Proportion (%)	Average Assessed Property Value Per Pupil (in dollars)	Equalized Tax Rate (in dollars)	Per-Pupil Expenditures (in dollars)
EISD	37 (22,000)	Mexican American (90) Negro (6) White (4)	5,960	1.05	356[a]
AHISD	6 (5,000)	Mexican American (18) Negro (< 1) White (81)	> 49,000	0.85	594[b]

Source: Data are from *San Antonio Independent School District v. Rodriguez*, 411 U.S. at 12–13 (1973).

[a] The local tax rate of the EISD yielded $26 per pupil above the $222 contributed by the Minimum Foundation Program; federal funds provided another $108 for a total per-pupil expenditures of $356. [b] The local tax rate of the AHISD yielded $333 per pupil above the $225 contributed by the Minimum Foundation Program; federal funds provided another $36 for a total per-pupil expenditures of $594.

TABLE 2.6

Selected Indicators of Educational Quality: Comparisons between
Edgewood Independent School District (EISD) and Alamo Heights
Independent School District (AHISD), 1968

District	Professional Salaries Per Pupil (in dollars)	% Teachers with M.A. Degrees	% Total Staff with Emergency Credentials	Pupils Per Counselor
EISD	209	15	47	3,098
AHISD	372	40	11	645

Source: Adapted from Berke and Callahan (1972, p. 36, Table 5). Copyright © by Emory University School of Law. Adapted with permission of Office of Student Publications, Emory University School of Law.

Regarding *Rodriguez I* plaintiffs' assertion that education is a fundamental interest, the trial court—quoting from the historic *Brown v. Board of Education of Topeka* (1954) decision—noted that the vital nature of education for the citizenry rests at the nucleus of nearly twenty years of school desegregation litigation.[68] The court also commented that in light of the crucial importance of education, both to the individual person and the greater society, the defendants are required to demonstrate a compelling state interest that is induced by the present classifications generated under Texas's school finance scheme.[69] In sum, the defendants' case failed to pass the strict judicial scrutiny test.

On December 23, 1971, three months after the *Serrano I* decision in California, the three-judge trial court in *Rodriguez I* rendered its ruling—a benchmark decision in favor of the Mexican American community and other Texans residing in property-poor school districts. The court found merit in plaintiffs' claim that the current system of school financing in Texas deprived their class of equal protection under the law as per the Fourteenth Amendment. Relying in part on the *Serrano I* decision and the principle of fiscal neutrality, the court found that the defendants failed to demonstrate a compelling state interest for the current classifications based on wealth. Furthermore, the defendants failed even to substantiate a reasonable basis for the classifications.[70] The court also noted that the defendants' assertion concerning the advantage of granting decision-making power to local districts is simply unsubstantiated.

They [defendants] lose sight of the fact that the state has, in truth and in fact, limited the choice of financing by guaranteeing that some districts will spend low (with high taxes) while others will spend high (with low taxes). Hence, the present system does not serve to promote one of the very interests which defendants assert.[71]

The *Rodriguez I* court ordered the Texas Legislature to restructure the state school finance system in such a way that it does not violate the equal protection provisions of the U.S. and Texas Constitutions.[72] The court, however, stayed its mandate for two years in order to allow the defendants and the Legislature time to make the school finance system comply with the applicable law. The court retained jurisdiction over the case and informed the defendants that it would fashion its own remedy if the State failed to provide an acceptable plan.[73] Given what was at stake, loss of local district control, and the onerous challenge of restructuring the state's school finance system in an equitable manner, it was not surprising that the defendants appealed the district court's ruling.

Via a special procedure, the appellants appealed their case directly to the U.S. Supreme Court, and on October 12, 1972, it heard the oral arguments in *San Antonio Independent School District v. Rodriguez*—hereafter referred to as *Rodriguez II*.[74] In light of the monumental ruling in *Serrano I* in California and given that *Rodriguez II* was the first, and only, school finance equity case heard in front of the U.S. Supreme Court, the proceedings captured the eyes of the nation. On the side of the appellants, the Attorneys General of thirty states filed amicus briefs urging reversal of the *Rodriguez I* decision.[75] Some of the wealthiest suburban districts in the nation also filed amicus briefs on behalf of the appellants (Yudof & Morgan, 1974). For the appellees, dozens of organizations (e.g., the NAACP Legal Defense and Education Fund, the National Education Association, and the American Civil Liberties Union) filed amicus briefs urging affirmance of the *Rodriguez I* decision.[76] "On the sidelines, more than fifty attorneys representing the cream of American law firms, filed amicus briefs seeking to protect the interests of bondholders, while seeking neither affirmance nor reversal" (Yudof & Morgan, 1974, p. 400). To sum up, the U.S. Supreme Court's pending ruling in *Rodriguez II*, one way or the other, would result in monumental implications for state school finance schemes across the country. An affirmance by the Supreme Court would provide a landmark victory for advocates of equity in school financing. On the other hand, a reversal would deliver a crushing defeat for these supporters.

The appellants, finally recognizing the seriousness of the case, hired Charles Alan Wright, an eminent constitutional scholar and law professor at The University of Texas at Austin (Yudof & Morgan, 1974). Wright, who argued the case for the appellants, and his legal team had a basic strategy: demonstrate that the appellees' proposition—wealth is a suspect classification and education is a fundamental interest—lacked constitutional support. Therefore, the strict judicial scrutiny test is inappropriate and the rational basis test should be applied. Wright, in his oral arguments as well as his brief, tried to convince the Justices that if they affirmed *Rodriguez I*, cases challenging the distribution of state and city noneducational services would inundate the Court. Finally, appellants did concede that the state had a mandate to provide a minimum education to each student, but contended that the Texas education code was already doing so under the Minimum Foundation Program (Yudof & Morgan, 1974).

Arthur Gochman, the attorney who filed *Rodriguez I*, argued the case for the appellees. His strategy was to underscore that Texas's school finance system chiefly injured poor children who attended schools that were inferior to schools in property-wealthy districts.[77] Gochman also asserted that education is extremely important because it provides a means of socioeconomic mobility and inculcates democratic values. Education, he contended, is also positively associated with exercising one's First Amendment rights and informed voting. In short, education is a fundamental interest. Furthermore, Gochman refuted the claim that Texas provided an adequate minimum education for students, pointing out the reality that not a single school district in the state could support its schooling program exclusively from the Minimum Foundation Program (Yudof & Morgan, 1974). In regards to the appellants' claim of no demonstrable correlation between the amount of educational expenditures and educational quality,[78] Gochman argued that "the burden of proof should be on the state to show that resource discrimination was harmless, since the premise of the Texas school financing system was that the quality of education was related to the level of expenditures" (Yudof & Morgan, 1974, pp. 400–401).

On March 21, 1973, in a closely divided 5–4 vote, the U.S. Supreme Court reversed the district court's ruling in *Rodriguez I*. Justice Lewis F. Powell, who wrote the opinion for the majority,[79] principally adopted the two basic arguments put forward by Professor Wright. The majority reasoned this way:

1. *Wealth as a suspect classification.* One of the threshold questions regarding the applicability of the strict scrutiny test is whether an identifiable class can be defined. In the instant case, the suspect class was one

based on wealth. The majority opinion wrote that neither the appellees nor the district court proved that the Texas school finance system discriminates against the poor. The majority noted, "Appellees have made no effort to demonstrate that it [the school finance system] operates to the peculiar disadvantage of any class fairly definable as indigent, or as composed of persons whose incomes are beneath any designated poverty level."[80] Furthermore, the majority stated that there is reason to believe that the poorest families in Texas are not necessarily grouped together in the poorest property-wealth districts.[81] In sum, "Discrimination against poor districts did not mean discrimination against poor people" (Yudof & Morgan, 1974, p. 400). As such, the majority opinion could not accept the proposition that poverty is a suspect classification.

2. *Education as a fundamental right.* Regarding this second threshold question, the majority commented that the importance of education for the individual and society is undisputed. Yet the opinion noted that education is not among the rights afforded explicitly under the U.S. Constitution. Furthermore, the majority did not find any basis that education was implicitly protected.[82] The Justices who formed the majority also stated that even if they were to concede that education is a constitutionally protected right, the deprivation of education of appellee schoolchildren was *relative*, not *absolute*—thus no fundamental right was being denied. The opinion found that Texas schoolchildren were receiving, under the Minimum Foundation Program, "an opportunity to acquire the basic minimum skills necessary for the enjoyment of the rights of speech and of full participation in the political process."[83]

In sum, the majority found that the instant case was a particularly inappropriate one in which to apply the strict scrutiny standard. The opinion noted that the Texas school finance scheme was neither "irrational" nor "invidiously discriminatory." The plan was not a result of "hurried, ill-conceived legislation."[84] Therefore, the majority disagreed with the district court's ruling that the appellants lacked a rational basis for the state's school finance program. As such, the Texas funding system satisfies the rational basis test, and is thus constitutional.[85]

Justice Thurgood Marshall, well known for his dissents during his tenure as a U.S. Supreme Court Justice, filed a powerful sixty-five-page opinion in *Rodriguez II*—eleven pages longer than the majority opinion. Over his career as an Associate Justice on the Supreme Court (1967–1991), Justice Marshall was faced with the Court's majority increasingly retreating from remedies that he believed were essential to combat the country's legacy of racism. Justice Marshall, referred to as the "Great Dissenter," used dissenting opinions to voice his anger and disappointment (Arlington National Cemetery Website, 2006). Here are several of Justice Marshall's key points of dissent in *Rodriguez II*:

- *Educational adequacy.* As discussed earlier, the appellants asserted, and the majority opinion was persuaded, that Texas's Minimum Foundation Program provided funds for a basic and adequate minimum education for all students. Justice Marshall commented that the Supreme Court has never suggested that just because some "adequate" amount of benefits is dispensed to all, any discrimination resultant of those provided services is therefore constitutionally justifiable. Citing *F.S. Royster Guano Co. v. Virginia* (1920), Justice Marshall wrote, "The Equal Protection Clause is not addressed to the minimal sufficiency but rather to the unjustifiable inequalities of state action. It mandates nothing less than that 'all persons similarly circumstanced shall be treated alike.'"[86] He further noted that gross adequacy or inadequacy was not the issue, but rather inequality of educational opportunity that brings forth a question whether one's equal protection rights were being denied.[87]

- *Sufficient class.* The appellants faced another key question: Would the Supreme Court agree with the district court's finding that the suspect class was based on wealth? As covered earlier, the majority opinion ruled that appellees failed to prove that the school finance system in Texas discriminates against the poor. Furthermore, appellants contended that in constitutional terms the instant case entails nothing more than discrimination against the local school district, not individuals, given that state funds for education are provided to local districts. Justice Marshall disagreed with this premise by examining the ultimate consequence of such funding differences. He commented that a basic reality of Texas's school finance scheme meant that some Texas schoolchildren, compared to their more fortunate peers, were provided with substantially less educational resources. "Thus, while on its face the Texas scheme may merely discriminate between local districts, *the impact of that discrimination falls directly upon the children* [italics added] whose educational opportunity is dependent upon where they happen to live."[88]

- *Education as a fundamental interest.* The majority opinion in *Rodriguez II* held that education is not among the rights the U.S. Constitution explicitly provides to the citizenry. Nor is there any basis that education, as a right, is implicitly protected. On the other hand, Justice Marshall noted in his dissenting opinion that the fundamental importance of education has been extensively indicated by (a) the prior decisions by the Supreme Court, (b) the distinctive status that society affords public education, and (c) the pronounced relationship between education and some of our fundamental constitutional values.[89]

In the preface to his assertion that education is a fundamental interest, Justice Marshall presented a blistering critique of the majority opinion as to how his Brothers rigidly approached equal protection analysis. Stating that he "cannot accept . . . an emasculation of the Equal Protection Clause in the context of this case," Justice Marshall noted that the majority "apparently seeks to establish today that equal protection cases fall into one of two neat categories which dictate the appropriate standard of review— strict scrutiny or mere rationality."[90] Justice Marshall further commented that he could not accept the majority's strained efforts to show that fundamental interests, which demand strict scrutiny of the challenged classification, comprise only established rights that the Court is somehow required to recognize from the Constitution's text.[91] To make his point that the Court needs to allow a broader interpretation of what is a fundamental interest, Justice Marshall commented, "I would like to know where the Constitution guarantees the right to procreate."[92] He continued by asserting that some interests have been provided special judicial consideration when discrimination exists because they are, to some degree, interrelated with established constitutional guarantees.[93] Justice Marshall wrote, "Procreation is now understood to be important because of its interaction with the established constitutional right to privacy."[94] One of the most significant aspects of Justice Marshall's dissent in *Rodriguez II* is his assertion for the need for constitutional latitude in identifying fundamental interests (e.g., see Roos, 1974). Note the following equal protection analysis favored by Justice Marshall, which Roos terms a "sliding scale":

> The task in every case should be to determine the extent to which constitutionally guaranteed rights are dependent on interests not mentioned in the Constitution. As the nexus between the specific constitutional guarantee and the nonconstitutional interest draws closer, the nonconstitutional interest becomes more fundamental and the degree of judicial scrutiny applied when the interest is infringed on a discriminatory basis must be adjusted accordingly.[95]

In sum, the majority opinion in *Rodriguez II*, handed down between the time of *Serrano I* and *Serrano II*, had wide implications. The ruling unequivocally eliminated the federal courts as a legal path for school finance reform.[96] Rather than using the *Rodriguez* case to advance needed school funding equity, the Supreme Court delivered a devastating defeat to advocates of school finance reform in Texas and the nation as a whole. In Texas, the struggle for school funding equity languished for over a decade before *Rodriguez* was reestablished as a viable legal challenge. We turn to this account next.

Edgewood Independent School District v. Kirby (1984): *The Reestablishment of Rodriguez*

Following the U.S. Supreme Court's 1973 ruling in *Rodriguez II*, the Texas Legislature, operating under no legal orders, made feeble attempts to correct the ubiquitous funding disparities between high- and low-property-wealth school districts[97] (see Table 2.3 for the chronology of events that transpired). In 1975 and 1979, for example, the Legislature did make some changes in the state's school finance scheme. These included adjusting the formula used to compute the required state school funds. Also, under the State Equalization Aid program, the Legislature provided additional funding for property-poor school districts. Yet substantial differences in funding between property-poor and property-rich districts remained (Sracic, 2006). Justice Alberto González of the Texas Supreme Court (whom President George W. Bush later appointed as U.S. Attorney General) described the school funding status this way: "In some areas of the state, education resembled a motorcycle with a 1,000-gallon fuel tank, and in other areas it resembled a tractor trailer being fueled out of a gallon bucket" (Sracic, 2006, p. 126).

After more than a decade of legal inertia in Texas on public school finance, MALDEF reestablished *Rodriguez*, filing *Edgewood v. Kirby* (hereafter referred to as *Edgewood I*) on May 23, 1984, in the 250th District Court of Travis County (see Table 2.3).[98] Judge Harley Clark presided. Some of the original plaintiffs (including Demetrio Rodríguez) were joined by many parents and students. As well, sixty-seven other school districts joined the Edgewood Independent School District as plaintiffs. The defendants consisted of Dr. William N. Kirby (the Commissioner of Education), the State Board of Education, other State officials, and a number of school districts.

The bench trial in *Edgewood I* lasted from January 20 to April 8, 1987.

Plaintiffs claimed that the Texas school finance system violated several sections of the state's Constitution—Article I, §3 (equal rights), §19 (due course of law), and Article VII, §1 (efficient school system).[99] Drawing from the earlier *Rodriguez* deliberations, plaintiffs also presented data on the funding disparities between property-poor and property-wealthy school districts in Texas, as well as the effect of these differences on the quality of education. The plaintiffs relied on prior findings of fact in earlier litigation, in which the following was determined:

• The richest school district in the state has over $14,000,000 of property wealth per pupil, while the poorest district has about $20,000 of property wealth per pupil, a 700 to 1 ratio.[100]

• The one million students attending schools in districts at the upper boundary of property wealth, compared to the one million students attending schools in districts at the lower boundary of property wealth, have more than two and a half times as much taxable property wealth to fund their schools.[101]

• The three hundred thousand students enrolled in the highest-wealth schools have over 25% of the state's property wealth to fund their education, while the three hundred thousand students enrolled in the lowest-wealth schools have less than 3% of the state's property wealth to support their education.[102]

• Given the enormous disparities in district property wealth, in the 1985–1986 school year spending per pupil varied across districts, ranging from $2,112 to $19,333.[103]

• In light of the wide variations in interdistrict property wealth, the burdens imposed on taxpayers to support the education of their children differ greatly. In the poorest property-wealth districts, taxpayers must pay more than 20¢ per $100 valuation to acquire $100 per student. By sharp contrast, the taxpayers in the richest property-wealth districts needed to pay less than 2¢ per $100 valuation to raise $100 per pupil.[104]

• The poorer districts, compared to the wealthier ones, had a greater concentration of families living below the poverty level and families of ethnic minority background. For example, in 1980, Mexican Americans constituted 21% of the state's population. Yet Mexican Americans made up 84% of the population in the poorest districts.[105]

• The vast disparities in property wealth between property-poor and property-rich districts clearly affected the quality of education delivered. As noted in the *Edgewood I* legal record,

Greater financial support enables wealthy school districts to provide much broader and better educational experiences for their students, including such things as better facilities, more extensive curricula and more co-curricular activities, enhanced support through additional training materials and technology, better libraries and library professionals, additional curriculum- and staff-development specialists and teacher aides, more extensive counseling services, special programs to combat dropouts, parenting programs to involve the family in the student's educational experience, lower pupil-teacher ratios, and the ability to attract and retain better teachers and administrators.[106]

In *Edgewood I*, Judge Clark ruled on April 29, 1987, in favor of the plaintiffs. He concluded the following: (a) education is a fundamental right; (b) wealth is a suspect classification; (c) the existing school finance scheme in Texas is unconstitutionally inefficient; (d) the Constitution of Texas demands fiscal neutrality in the funding of public schools.[107] Finally, Judge Clark enjoined the germane state officials from enforcing the challenged statutes, but he stayed the injunction until September 1, 1989, to allow the Texas Legislature the opportunity to correct funding inequities.[108]

Not surprisingly, the defendants appealed the trial court ruling (see timeline in Table 2.3). The Court of Appeals of Texas (Third District, Austin) heard the case, with Justices Marilyn Aboussie, Bob Gammage, and Bob Shannon presiding. The appellants argued that education is not a fundamental right and that wealth is not a suspect classification. As such, they asserted, Judge Clark at the trial court had inappropriately applied the strict scrutiny standard in the equal protection analysis.[109] In a 2–1 vote, the Third Court of Appeals on December 14, 1988, reversed the trial court decision, relying heavily on federal case law concerning equal protection analysis, particularly *Rodriguez*.[110] The appellate court acknowledged appellees' argument regarding the importance of education but disagreed that education is a fundamental right under the Texas Constitution. Although education is specifically mentioned in the Texas Constitution, the Third Court of Appeals rejected the "nexus" analysis promulgated by appellees (i.e., education is necessary for the full exercise of fundamental rights like free speech and voting).[111] Judge Shannon, who wrote the opinion for the appellate court, cited *Hernandez v. Houston Independent School District* (1977) as precedential concerning the analysis of the validity of education as a fundamental right, arguing that the federal analysis via *Rodriguez* must be employed.[112] Consequently, appellees' claims failed.

Justice Gammage dissented, arguing that the Third Court of Appeals majority disregarded a number of findings of fact concerning the negative consequences that the Texas school finance system has on property-poor districts. He also pointed out that the majority, relying on *Rodriguez*, reasoned that education is not a fundamental right under the *federal* Constitution because it delineates no specific provision regarding education. The *Texas* Constitution, however, "explicitly recognizes that education is indispensable to the meaningful exercise of other fundamental liberties and rights, and *mandates* the legislature to make 'suitable' provision for an 'efficient' education system."[113] Appellees appealed to the Texas Supreme Court. In the meantime, the Texas Legislature passed SB 1019, which intended to increase school funding. Governor William P. Clements signed the bill into law on June 16, 1989 (see Table 2.3). Subsequently, the Texas Supreme Court began hearing *Edgewood I* on July 5, 1989.

After three months of oral arguments, the Texas Supreme Court in a unanimous 9–0 decision handed down, on October 2, 1989, a momentous ruling in favor of the appellants. Justice Oscar H. Mauzy wrote the opinion. For the first time in eighteen years—since the 1971 victory in *Rodriguez I*—property-poor districts in Texas reclaimed a solid legal triumph in the contentious sphere of school finance reform. The Texas Supreme Court's ruling in *Edgewood I* zeroed in on two major aspects: (a) the explicit funding disparities between property-poor and property-wealthy school districts and (b) the meaning of an "efficient" system of public education. A condensed discussion of these two points follows:

- *School funding disparities.* As with the district court, the findings of glaring disparities in interdistrict per-pupil expenditures as well as the differences of educational quality resulting from the unequal school financing in the state swayed the Texas Supreme Court. The Court underscored what the district and appellate courts noted: property-poor districts were "trapped in a cycle of poverty" from which there was no opportunity to escape.[114] Just to meet the minimum requirements to fund their schools, citizens in these impoverished districts (compared to property-wealthy districts) were forced to tax themselves at significantly higher rates, and the money raised had little positive consequence on improving the quality of education.[115] Commenting on the dramatic differences in the quality of educational offerings between property-poor and property-wealthy school districts, the Texas Supreme Court in its *Edgewood I* opinion used

San Elizario Independent School District (SEISD) as an example.[116] The SEISD offers "no pre-kindergarten program, no chemistry, no physics, no calculus, and no college preparatory or honors program. It also offers virtually no extra-curricular activities such as band, debate, or football."[117]

• *An "efficient" school system.* Article VII, §1 of the Texas Constitution states,

> A general diffusion of knowledge being essential to the preservation of the liberties and rights of the people, it shall be the duty of the Legislature of the State to establish and make suitable provision for the support and maintenance of an *efficient system of public free schools* [italics added].[118]

The Third Court of Appeals, in the *Edgewood I* decision, declined to address appellants' challenge under Article VII, §1, and concluded that "efficient" is fundamentally a "political question" not appropriate for judicial review.[119] The Texas Supreme Court in *Edgewood I* disagreed, however, commenting that the charge of providing an efficient system of public education in the state is not an area in which the state Constitution vests exclusive discretion in the Legislature. Rather, Article VII, §1, imposes on the Legislature an "affirmative duty to establish and provide for the public free schools," and this responsibility shall be accompanied by "standards."[120] The terms "suitable," "efficient," "essential," and "general diffusion of knowledge"—admittedly not precise in meaning—do impart a standard by which the Texas Supreme Court must gauge the constitutionality of the Legislature's actions.[121] The appellees contended that the term "efficient" meant a public school system that is simple and inexpensive.[122] The Texas Supreme Court once again disagreed, stating that the Texas Constitution required an "efficient," not a "simple" or "cheap" public school system. The framers of the state's Constitution did not intend a school system with huge funding disparities, but rather a system that provided a *"general* diffusion of knowledge." The current school system, as seen in the instant case, does not offer a general diffusion of knowledge. The system, as currently structured, is "limited and unbalanced," and "The resultant inequalities are thus directly contrary to the constitutional vision of efficiency."[123] Although the Texas Legislature has attempted, over the years, to reduce the funding disparities between property-poor and property-wealthy school districts, the Constitutional mandate of Article VII, §1 has not been met. Underscoring the gravity of the funding problems, Justice Mauzy noted that a comprehensive systemic reform is needed: "*A band-aid will not suffice; the system itself must be changed* [italics added]."[124]

To summarize, the Texas Supreme Court held that the state's school finance scheme is neither efficient from a financial standpoint nor efficient in providing for a general diffusion of knowledge throughout the state's numerous school districts. Hence, the present school funding system is in violation of the Texas Constitution. With lucidity, the Texas Supreme Court mandated, "Children who live in poor districts and children who live in rich districts *must be afforded a substantially equal opportunity to have access to educational funds* [italics added]."[125] The Texas Supreme Court reversed the judgment of the appellate court and affirmed the trial court's ruling, but with a modification. In light of the pending enormity of school finance reform facing the Legislature, the trial court's injunction was stayed until May 1, 1990, an extension of eight months.[126]

Post-Edgewood I: *Interplay between the Texas Legislature and the Texas Courts*

Over twenty years had lapsed since the filing of *Rodriguez I* in 1968. It is likely that residents of property-poor school districts and advocates for school funding reform in Texas felt that justice had finally prevailed with the Texas Supreme Court's historic 1989 ruling in *Edgewood I*. The Texas Supreme Court unequivocally mandated that all students, attending schools in property-poor and property-rich districts alike, must be provided an appreciably equal opportunity to gain access to school funds. At last, the time had finally arrived for funding equity in Texas public schools. Or had it? Unfortunately, this pursuit became entangled in a quagmire of interplays between the Texas courts and the Texas Legislature for the next sixteen years. Because of the length of this chronicle, a very brief sweep of these judicial/legislative interplays is provided. The chronology of events is listed (from "February/June 1990" to "May 26, 2006") in Table 2.7 (for varying degrees of coverage of these interplays, see Cárdenas, 1997; Sracic, 2006; Thompson, 2006; Torres, 2001; also see the newspaper accounts listed at the bottom of Table 2.7).

After the Texas Supreme Court's ruling in *Edgewood I*, the Texas Legislature in 1990 held four special sessions in attempts to address the Texas Supreme Court's mandate. The Legislature could not, however, devise a new and acceptable school financing plan. On May 15, 1990, Judge F. Scott

TABLE 2.7
*Post–*Edgewood I *Developments: Interplay between the Texas Legislature and the Texas Courts*

Date	Development
2/27–6/7/90	Texas Legislature holds four special sessions, but cannot devise a new school finance plan.[a,b,c]
5/15/90	Judge F. Scott McCown, replacing the retiring Judge Clark, appoints a master group to develop a financing scheme for the court to order implemented if the Legislature does not devise one by 6/1/90.[a]
6/1/90	Master group presents its plan that calls for the distribution on a county-wide basis of Available School Fund monies, and wealth-based distribution within each county.[a,b]
6/6/90	Texas Legislature finally passes Senate Bill 1, increasing state aid by $528 million; signed 6/7/90.[a,b,c]
7/90	MALDEF, in a repeat of *Edgewood I*, files *Edgewood II*, complaining that SB 1 is unconstitutional, as it does not substantially change the state's school financing system.[a,d]
9/20/90	Trial court rules for plaintiffs, ordering Texas Legislature to devise new plan within one year. State appeals.[a]
1/22/91	Texas Supreme Court, in a 9–0 decision, affirms trial court ruling, 804 S.W.2d 491 (Tex. 1991); gives Texas Legislature until 4/1/91 to devise new plan.
4/1/91	After Texas Legislature misses the deadline, Judge McCown schedules a hearing for 4/15/1991 to consider ordering the implementation of the masters' plan.[e]
4/12/91	Texas Legislature passes Senate Bill 351, creating 188 "County Education Districts" (CEDs); signed 4/15/91.[a,c,d]
5/3/91	Two groups of property-wealthy districts, led by Carrollton-Farmer's Branch ISD and Coppell ISD, file suit as plaintiff-intervenors, complaining that SB 351 violates several parts of the Texas Constitution. Original plaintiffs also challenge the constitutionality of SB 351, but with same previous *Edgewood* claims.
8/27/91	Trial court in *Edgewood v. Meno* (*Edgewood III*), upholds constitutionality of SB 351.[a] Intervenors appeal; original *Edgewood* plaintiffs align with State. Five cases consolidated under *Carrollton-Farmers Branch v. Edgewood*.
1/30/92	Texas Supreme Court, in a 7–2 decision, reverses trial court ruling in *Carrollton-Farmers Branch v. Edgewood*, 826 S.W.2d 489 (Tex. 1992), declaring SB 351 levies taxes and creates CEDs in violation of the Texas Constitution; gives Texas Legislature until 6/1/93 to devise new plan.
2/93	Texas Legislature enacts three constitutional amendments for voters to approve: (a) legalize CEDs, and give them authority to redistribute funds; (b) restrict the Legislature from enacting new school mandates without funding; (c) create state bond program for maintenance of schools.[a]
5/1/93	Voters reject all amendments.[a,b]
5/29/93	Texas Legislature passes Senate Bill 7, developing a wealth equalization plan based on "recapture" of funds from property-wealthy school districts; signed 5/31/1993.[a,b,c] Inappropriately nicknamed "Robin Hood" by the media, the appellation sticks.[f] Like *Edgewood III*, nine groups of plaintiffs from property-poor and property-wealthy districts challenge the law.
4/26/94	Trial court in *Edgewood IV* finds SB 7 constitutional.[a,b,c]
1/30/95	Texas Supreme Court, in a 5–4 decision, affirms trial court ruling, 917 S.W.2d 717 (Tex. 1995).
4/9/01	Four property-wealthy districts file *West Orange-Cove v. Alanis* in 250th District Court of Travis County, complaining SB 7 is an unconstitutional state ad valorem tax.[g]

(continued)

TABLE 2.7 *(continued)*

Date	Development
7/24/01	Judge McCown dismisses suit for failure to state a claim and ripeness. Plaintiffs appeal (*West Orange-Cove v. Alanis*, 78 S.W.3d at 541 [Tex. App.–Austin 2002, rev'd]).
4/11/02	Third Court of Appeals affirms trial court decision (*West Orange-Cove v. Alanis*, 78 S.W.3d 529 [Tex. App.–Austin 2002, n.r.e.]).
5/29/03	Texas Supreme Court reverses appellate decision, ruling that the trial court erred in dismissing appellants' claims, and remands for continued pleadings (*West Orange-Cove v. Alanis*, 107 S.W.3d 558 [Tex. 2003]).
12/1/03	*West Orange-Cove v. Neeley* filed in 250th District Court of Travis County. Judge John Dietz presides.[h]
9/15/04	Judge Dietz finds Senate Bill 7 unconstitutional on all but one claim. Defendants appeal.[i]
1/11–8/19/05	Texas Legislature fails to approve new finance plan after regular session and two special sessions.[j]
11/22/05	Texas Supreme Court, in 7–1 decision, modifies and affirms, in part, and reverses, 176 S.W.3d 746 (Tex. 2005); rehearing denied 12/6/05.
5/19/06	Texas Legislature, in 3rd special session, passes HB 3, shifting burden of school financing to tax overhaul.[g,k]
5/26/06	Judge Dietz declares HB 3 constitutional.[l]

[a] Cárdenas (1997). [b] Acosta (2001). [c] Texas Legislature Online (2006). [d] Saghaye-Biria (2001). [e] Blair (2006). [f] Robin Hood plan (2006). [g] Rendon (2001). [h] Copelin (2003). [i] Embry (2004). [j] Embry (2005). [k] Mortiz (2006a). [l] Mortiz (2006b).

McCown, who replaced retiring Judge Clark of the 250th District Court of Travis County, appointed a master group to develop a school financing scheme for the court to enact in the event the Legislature failed to devise a plan by June 1, 1990.[127] On this target date, the master group presented its school finance plan, which called for the distribution of funds on a county-wide basis of Available School Fund monies, and wealth-based distribution within each county.

On June 6, 1990, the Texas Legislature finally passed a school finance plan, SB 1, that it believed would pass constitutional muster. Under SB 1, signed into law by Governor William P. Clements on June 7, 1990, state funding for K–12 schooling increased by $528 million. Shortly after, in July 1990, MALDEF—in a repeat of *Edgewood I*, filed *Edgewood II*.[128] MALDEF's complaint asserted that SB 1 was unconstitutional, as it did not substantially change the state's school financing system. On September 20, 1990, trial court Judge McCown ruled for plaintiffs and ordered the Texas Legislature to devise a new plan within one year. The State appealed. On January 22, 1991, the Texas Supreme Court, in a 9–0 decision, affirmed the trial court's ruling and gave the Legislature until April 1, 1991, to devise a new finance plan.[129] After the Texas Legislature missed the deadline, Judge McCown scheduled a hearing for April 15, 1991, to consider ordering the execution of the masters' plan.

In the meantime, concerned by the possible enactment of the masters' plan, the Texas Legislature, on April 12, 1991, passed SB 351, creating 188 "County Education Districts" (CEDs).[130] Governor Ann Richards signed the bill into law on April 15, 1991—just thirty minutes before Judge McCown's hearing was to begin! Soon after, on May 3, 1991, two groups of wealthy districts—led by Carrollton-Farmers Branch Independent School District and Coppell Independent School District—filed suit as plaintiff-intervenors, complaining that SB 351 violated several parts of the Texas Constitution.[131] Likewise, the original *Edgewood* plaintiffs also challenged the constitutionality of SB 351, but with the same claims as in the original lawsuit.

In the next development in this seemingly interminable interplay between the Texas Legislature and the Texas courts, the trial court on August 27, 1991, in *Edgewood v. Meno* (*Edgewood III*) ruled that SB 351 was constitutional.[132] The property-wealthy-district intervenors appealed. Eventually, five cases that challenged the constitutionality of SB 351 on similar grounds were consolidated under *Carrollton-Farmers Branch v. Edgewood*.[133] In an interesting turn of events, the original *Edgewood* plaintiffs aligned with the State on appeal. On January 30, 1992, the Texas Supreme Court, in a 7–2 decision, reversed the trial court's ruling, declaring that Senate Bill 351 illegally levies taxes and creates CEDs, and thus violates the Texas Constitution.[134] The Texas Supreme Court gave the Texas Legislature until June 1, 1993—eighteen months—to devise a new plan.

The Texas Legislature, taking a tack not used yet, enacted three constitutional amendments for voters to approve. The amendments called for (a) the legalization of CEDs, granting them the authority to redistribute school finance funds; (b) the restriction of the Legislature from enacting new school mandates without funding; (c) the creation of a state bond program for the maintenance of schools. In light of the entire long-standing racial subtext of the *Rodriguez/Edgewood* case chronology, "It is interesting to note that at least one study indicated that voting on the amendment paralleled racial divisions, with the support for the amendment confined to African American and Mexican American communities" (Sracic, 2006, p. 130). On May 1, 1993, Texas voters soundly rejected all three amendments.

On the heels of this stinging defeat by the Texas plebiscite, the Legislature went back to the drawing board in an attempt "to craft a funding

scheme that might somehow navigate between the constitutional responsibilities announced in *Edgewood I* and *Edgewood II* and the corresponding limitations imposed by the court in *Edgewood III*" (Sracic, 2006, p.
130). On May 29, 1993—three days before the June 1 deadline established
by the Texas Supreme Court—the Legislature passed SB 7. Governor Ann
Richards signed the bill into law by on May 31, 1993. It developed a wealth
equalization plan based on "recapture" of funds from property-wealthy
school districts.[135] The media inappropriately nicknamed SB 7 "Robin
Hood," and the appellation stuck. In my view, the "Robin Hood" moniker
is classist, suggesting that money was being "stolen" from the rich and
dispersed to the undeserving poor. In reality, the new law was entirely
legal, being developed under the auspices of the court and passed by the
Legislature. As was the situation in *Edgewood III*, nine groups of plaintiffs
from property-poor and property-wealthy school districts challenged SB
7. About a month shy of a year from the signing of SB 7 into law, on April
26, 1994, the trial court in *Edgewood IV* found SB 7 constitutional, which
likely provided great relief for a frustrated Texas Legislature.[136] The Legislature also likely felt solace when, on January 30, 1995, the Texas Supreme
Court, in a 5–4 decision, affirmed the trial court's ruling.[137]

Notwithstanding this significant breakthrough in the protracted quest
for school funding equity in Texas, another major challenge arose. On
April 9, 2001, four property-wealthy school districts filed *West Orange-
Cove v. Alanis* in the 250th District Court of Travis County, complaining
that SB 7 is an unconstitutional state ad valorem tax.[138] Judge McCown,
on July 24, 2001, dismissed the suit for failure to state a claim and ripe-
ness. Subsequently, plaintiffs appealed.[139] Approximately nine months
later, on April 11, 2002, the Third Court of Appeals affirmed the trial court
decision.[140]

At a moment in time in which the thirty-three-year-old *Rodriguez* saga
appeared to have closure, another dramatic judicial/legislative interplay
unfolded. The Texas Supreme Court, in an 8–1 decision, reversed the appellate court's ruling, and remanded the case back to the trial court for
hearings.[141] The Texas Supreme Court ruled that the trial court erred in
dismissing appellants' claims, notably, (a) SB 7 is unconstitutional because
it mandates an illegal state ad valorem tax in order for school districts to
provide an adequate education for their students; and (b) school districts
lack any meaningful discretion in setting local property tax rates if even
one district must tax at the maximum rate allowable by the State in order

to meet state-mandated accreditation standards to comply with the constitutionally required "general diffusion of knowledge" clause.[142]

Finally, on December 1, 2003, plaintiffs had their day in court, filing *West Orange-Cove v. Neeley* in the 250th District Court of Travis County.[143] Judge John Dietz, replacing retiring Judge McCown, presided. Three groups of plaintiffs challenged the constitutionality of SB 7 on separate grounds. Group 1, consisting of West Orange-Cove and forty-six other property-wealthy districts, complained that SB 7 violated Article VIII, §1-e. Groups 2 and 3, consisting of Edgewood and 281 other property-poor districts, alleged that SB 7 violated Article VII, §1. On September 15, 2004, Judge Dietz ruled that SB 7 was unconstitutional. Not surprisingly, the defendants appealed.

Approximately four months later, on January 11, 2005, the 79th Texas Legislature convened. One of the hot-button issues for the legislators was, of course, school finance reform. Throughout the regular legislative session from January to May 30, 2005, and into two special sessions running from June 21 to August 19, 2005, called by Governor Rick Perry, the Texas Legislature unfortunately failed to approve a new school finance plan. The Legislature's inability to devise a constitutionally acceptable school finance plan met with frustration among Texas citizens. Jason Embry, journalist for the *Austin American-Statesman*, wrote, "With the final gavel falling Friday [August 19, 2005] to mercifully end the year's second special session, lawmakers must return to the people who sent them to Austin and explain why they haven't moved school finance changes and property tax cuts off of their to-do list" (2005, p. A1). Furthermore, Embry noted, "The mere mention of 'state Legislature' . . . elicited a roar of laughter from the half-dozen men playing billiards at the Round Rock Senior Center this week" (p. A1). Embry also wrote that Fred Bierschenk of Pflugerville commented, "It's frustrating to me that they could have a regular session and two special sessions and not figure out what to do with the schools. That's close to criminal. They're being paid to do a job, and they're not doing it" (p. A1).

On November 22, 2005, the Texas Supreme Court, ruling 7–1, modified and affirmed, in part, the trial court's ruling.[144] About six months later, at the end of a third special session, the 79th Texas Legislature finally passed HB 3, and Governor Rick Perry signed it on May 19, 2006. The bill fundamentally called for a reduction of property taxes, and a shifting of the school financing burden to a tax overhaul (Mortiz, 2006a). One week later, on May 26, 2006, Judge Dietz lifted his former ruling, noting that the HB 3 rectified the court's concerns (Mortiz, 2006b).

Presently, the lengthy judicial/legislative interplay over school finance reform in Texas may be over, as no one appears to be contemplating a legal challenge. As these final words are penned about this four-decade-old Texas school finance chronicle, the forty-seven property-wealthy plaintiff districts from the *West Orange-Cove* litigation conceded, in a legal filing, that HB 3 will allow schools some room for financial leeway in 2007. The lawyers for these plaintiffs, however, did raise serious concerns about whether the new school finance system would allow districts to fund their educational needs over the long haul (Embry, 2006). Estimates exist that funds acquired from the new taxes will result in a $25 billion shortfall of paying for the new school finance scheme over the next five years (Robin Hood plan, 2006). Yet the absence of a legal challenge does not mean that the controversy over school finance reform has ended in Texas. Perhaps all we can conclude at this point in time is, as Embry (2006) has commented, "School finance is out of the courts—for now."

Conclusion

The Mexican American community's legal struggle for equity in school funding has lasted for nearly four decades and is likely to continue, even with the apparent closure as seen in the most recent legislative/judicial interplay in Texas. Although the Mexican American people's campaign of nearly forty years for school finance equity has been shorter than the Mexican American community's sixty years of legal battles for school desegregation (see chapter 2), the school finance struggle has been more tumultuous. Legal indeterminacy, a major theme of the present book, has clearly characterized the school funding litigation war. Legal scholars John Dayton and Anne Dupre (2004) have captured this judicial discretion:

> As in all wars, the ultimate battle is for the hearts and minds of the people. But when this battle includes litigation, the initial war is for the hearts and minds of the judges. Litigants find themselves in a complex adversarial dance in which advocates for the state express the will of those with political and economic power and advocates for reform express the needs of those without financial means or political clout. Each side attempts to

get the court to join in their side of the dance and to share their vision in this protracted contest of competing ideals about education, taxation, and social justice. (pp. 2411–2412)

From *Rodriguez I* to the numerous variants of *Edgewood*, Mexican American litigants faced the courts' judicial indeterminacy. These decisions inform us in that they expose the extent to which judges assisted, or failed to assist, in protecting the rights of Mexican Americans. The U.S. Supreme Court's 1973 ruling in *Rodriguez II* exemplified such legal discretion. Although Justice Thurgood Marshall's dissent regarding a "sliding scale" analysis of equal protection can be interpreted as a powerful counterstory, the majority opinion's limited and rigid perspective in interpreting the Constitution was the death knell in promoting civil and social justice in the area of school finance reform.

From the vantage point of CRT, much can be learned (also see Alemán [2005], who applies CRT to the school finance political discourse). First, this corpus of litigation demonstrates the centrality of race, as well as class. The intersection of race and class is particularly salient because the litigants are not only Mexican American but economically disadvantaged as well. These are Mexican American children and their families residing in property-poor school districts who have little or no control where they live, and thus the quality of education provided to these children primarily becomes a function of local wealth. In CRT, a major tenet is heterodoxy—the challenge to the orthodoxy, or the status quo. In *Serrano*, we saw this challenge manifest in the legal principle of fiscal neutrality, the requirement that school funding shall be a function of the wealth of the state as a whole, not of the local district. This principle came to serve as the judicial sine qua non in promoting school funding equity in *Serrano* and numerous lawsuits across the country that followed.

In sum, disparities in school funding based on the racial and class profile of school districts still remain. A recent study revealed that of the forty-seven states investigated, thirty had lower per-pupil expenditures in districts at the highest quartile of poverty and above than at the lowest quartile and below. Also, thirty-one of forty-seven states with districts containing the highest percentage of students of color also had the lowest per-pupil expenditures (Dayton & Dupre, 2004). Notwithstanding data such as these, the picture is not entirely bleak. Dayton and Dupre have noted this positive monetary outcome of the school funding litigation wars: "The litigation since *Serrano* and *Rodriguez* has resulted in the reallocation of billions of tax dollars to poorer school districts and has transformed the public schools in some states to a degree second only to the transformation that followed *Brown*" (p. 2364).

3

Special Education

According to the most recent report from the U.S. Department of Education, Office of Special Education Programs (2002), in the 2000–2001 school year, approximately 12.7% (n=6.1 million) of the country's 47.8 million pre-K to grade 12 public school children (ages three to seventeen) were enrolled in special education programs in the fifty states, the District of Columbia, and Puerto Rico.[1] Students in special education (e.g., classified as having mild mental retardation or specific learning disability) perform below the norm on cognitive tests and other measures to such an extent that special intervention is necessary. Notwithstanding its importance in the nation's educational enterprise, the field of special education is not without its problems. One of the major, long-standing concerns has been that many Latino and African American students are inaccurately diagnosed as educable mentally retarded (also referred to as mildly mentally retarded). These racialized assignments to educable mentally retarded classes are the subject of this chapter.

With respect to special education students with alleged educable mental retardation, Mexican Americans have historically played a central role in allegations of faulty diagnoses and placements. The focus of this chapter is on three major lawsuits of several decades past in which Mexican American and other plaintiffs of color brought suit against school districts. In *Diana v. State Board of Education* (1970), *Covarrubias v. San Diego Unified School District* (1971), and *Guadalupe Organization, Inc. v. Tempe School District No. 3* (1972), Mexican American and other plaintiffs of color asserted that intelligence tests, among other assessment issues, were being used discriminatorily, resulting in an overrepresentation of students of color in classes for the educable mentally retarded (EMR).

This chapter is organized around the following sections: (a) the roots of Mexican American students in special education; (b) the entrenchment of group-administered intelligence tests; (c) the emergence of discriminatory allegations against intelligence tests; (d) Mexican American et al.

special education litigation: *Diana, Covarrubias,* and *Guadalupe*; (e) influence of Mexican American et al. special education litigation on federal
legislation and professional practices.

The Roots of Mexican American Students in Special Education

The testing, diagnosis, and placement of Mexican American students in
classes for "slow learners," and the accompanying concerns surrounding these assessments, originated in the intelligence testing movement of
the 1920s (Valencia, 1997a; Valencia, Villarreal, & Salinas, 2002). During
this era, schools routinely administered group intelligence tests to many
Mexican American children and youths. Based, in part, on these students'
typically lower test performances, school officials funneled them into programs that provided little opportunity for cognitive growth and academic
progress. As a case in point, let us examine what transpired in Los Angeles, California (see González, 1974a, 1974b, 1990, 1999).

During the 1920s, mass intelligence testing in Los Angeles was indeed
a big enterprise.[2] By decade's end (1928–1929), school personnel administered a total of 328,000 tests, for example, at the elementary level alone
(González, 1974a). Based on IQ test results, in large part, students were
placed in one of four types of elementary classes/rooms: *normal* classes,
opportunity rooms, *adjustment* rooms, or *development* rooms. Opportunity rooms were designed for both mentally superior children (opportunity A) and slow learners (opportunity B—children with measured IQs
above 70 but below the normal cut score). Adjustment rooms, on the
other hand, were structured for normal children (i.e., average interval IQ)
with specific skill problems (e.g., remediation in reading; "educationally
maladjusted" [most likely this was what we currently refer to as emotional
and behavior disorders]). Development rooms (sometimes referred to as
centers) were designed for children with IQs below 70; testing personnel typically referred to them as "mentally retarded" or "mentally deficient." González (1974a) noted that the median IQ for Mexican American elementary school-age children in Los Angeles in the late 1920s was
about 91.2.[3] Given the observed median IQ, he suggested that "there was a
very high probability that nearly one-half of the Mexican children would
find themselves placed in slow-learner rooms and development centers" (p. 150). In light of the estimation that Mexican American students

constituted only 13% of the student population in 1927 in Los Angeles City and County (Taylor, 1929; cited in González, 1974a), these children and youths were overrepresented in classes for the mentally subaverage (opportunity B classes) and for the mentally retarded (development centers) by 285% (calculated by Valencia & Suzuki, 2001, p. 17).

In addition to what occurred at the elementary school level, González (1974a, 1990) also researched the role of intelligence testing and its partial role in secondary school curriculum differentiation in Los Angeles schools. He comments, "By the mid-twenties a four-tiered tracking system, each with its specific teaching methods, curriculum, and educational objectives and consequences was in full swing" (1990, p. 83). The Division of Psychology and Educational Research, using mass IQ testing to identify the type of course work that allegedly would be commensurate with students' mental capacity, designed four curricular tracks: very superior, normal, dull-normal, and mentally retarded. Given the widespread belief that Mexican American children were not suited for "book study" and thus should be trained for "hand work" (see Stanley, 1920), Los Angeles schools undertook a racialized and systematic curricular plan of "training for occupational efficiency" for Mexican Americans, a term used by González (1990). The marriage between the educational system and local business partly led to the success of the Los Angeles vocational educational program. Vocational education partially modified its curriculum based on local labor needs (González, 1990). It was not uncommon for the Los Angeles Chamber of Commerce and the public school system to be bedfellows.

> The purpose of schooling became interwoven with, and in a number of ways, shaped by industry. The preparation of students to enter "the business and industrial world" was more than just a preparation for life. It was an education molded by business and industry. (González, 1974a, pp. 168–169)

What transpired in special education in Los Angeles public schools in the 1920s brought forth two significant issues: (a) the large overrepresentation of Mexican American students classified as mentally subaverage and mentally retarded, and (b) the placement of these students in special education programs of dead-end schooling that prepared the pupils for a life of menial labor. Decades later, in the early 1970s, these two issues resurfaced in California. Yoshida, MacMillan, and Meyers (1976) have commented on the overrepresentation and curricular issue this way: "The concern over possible violations of the civil rights of minority students was superimposed upon the smoldering doubts about the educational inadequacy of the EMR program" (p. 215).

The Entrenchment of Group Intelligence Testing

By the mid-1920s, group-administered intelligence (and achievement) tests were used with great frequency in U.S. public schools, and bureaucracies arose to handle the mass testing and use of test results.[4] The U.S. Department of the Interior, Bureau of Education (1926), published a survey reporting the frequency of homogeneous grouping and the use of group intelligence tests in classifying students to ability groups (cited in Chapman, 1988). Based on data from 292 cities with populations ranging from ten thousand to more than one hundred thousand, the percentages of cities reporting homogeneous ability grouping at the elementary, junior high, and high school levels were 85%, 70%, and 49%, respectively. The same report noted that 250 (86%) of the 292 cities surveyed used group intelligence tests in student classification. Thus, in the very short period between the publication of the group-based National Intelligence Tests in 1920 and the mid-1920s, American public schools had become highly differentiated in curriculum, and, by far, group intelligence and achievement tests served as the sorting mechanisms. By 1932, 75% of 150 large cities made curricular assignments of pupils using the results of intelligence tests (Tyack, 1974).

Continuing into the 1940s and 1950s, group intelligence testing in most of the nation's public schools became a routine practice. Writing during the fall of 1949, Benjamin Fine, columnist for the *New York Times Magazine*, commented,

> Between now and June, 20,000,000 children will be subjected to tests to measure their intelligence. This figure indicates the position of influence to which IQ—Intelligence Quotient—tests have risen in little more than a generation in American school systems. In nearly all, they are used in greater or lesser degree to determine when a child should begin to read, whether another should go to college, and if a third is likely to grow up

to be a dolt or an Einstein—that is, whether he is "worth worrying about" or "simply beyond help." (p. 7)

In short, beginning in the 1920s and escalating in usage in the '30s, '40s, and '50s, group-based intelligence tests were widely administered in the nation's public elementary and secondary schools. Group-administered intelligence testing had taken on a life of its own, and one relatively free of controversy—until the late 1950s.

The Emergence of Contemporary Discriminatory Allegations against Intelligence Tests

As discussed, the first phase of criticisms against intelligence testing vis-à-vis students of color unfolded during the 1920s.[5] The roots of the second, or contemporary, phase of the testing controversy traces back to the monumental U.S. Supreme Court decision *Brown v. Board of Education of Topeka* (1954), which struck down the *Plessy v. Ferguson* (1896) "separate but equal" doctrine. For a dozen years after *Brown*, southern school systems attempted to forestall, or even circumvent, the Supreme Court's desegregation mandate through innovative strategies (Bersoff, 1982):

> Many of these tactics relied heavily on the use of intelligence and achievement tests. For example, in one major southern city, black children were not permitted to transfer to a "white" school unless their grade level score on an ability test was at least equal to the average of the class in the school to which the transfer was requested. Each of these dilatory mechanisms was challenged in the courts by minority plaintiffs and eventually struck down as unconstitutional. (p. 1046)

Although plaintiffs prevailed in demonstrating how schools unconstitutionally used intelligence and achievement tests against African Americans in the goal of desegregation, "in no case was the validity of the tests themselves attacked" (Bersoff, 1982, p. 1046). The reason for this inattention to validity issues is that the judiciary had a preoccupation with whether standardized intelligence and achievement tests "were administered only to blacks or were used to make decisions solely on racial grounds" (Bersoff, 1982, p. 1046). Although such tests were routinely administered in the

South, and elsewhere, to Whites and students of color during the decade after *Brown*, grouping practices (i.e., curriculum differentiation) and subsequent concerns about varying access to equal educational opportunity did not capture judicial scrutiny.

In any event, the use of tests by southern schools to forestall the desegregation mandate sparked the second phase of the testing controversy in motion. With the advent of the Civil Rights Movement during the late 1950s and its peaking during the early 1960s, the rights of people of color became focal points of national concern. The role of group-administered IQ tests in the classification of students of color in the educational mainstream and the tributary of special education became part of this debate. Speaking of those years, Anastasi (1988) comments, "A common criticism of intelligence tests is that they encourage a rigid, inflexible, and permanent classification of pupils" (p. 67). So deep were these concerns that the New York City public schools, for example, discontinued the use of IQ tests in 1964 (Gilbert, 1966).

Hobson v. Hansen (1967) emerged as the first case that spoke to the legality of using group intelligence tests in the curricular assignments of students of color in the mainstream (i.e., *not* in special education). In *Hobson*, a federal district court in Washington, D.C., ruled in favor of the African American plaintiffs, finding that schools used standardized group "aptitude" (i.e., intelligence) tests, in large part, to place many such students in the lower tracks. Such practices, the court found, created significant racial disproportionality in curricular assignments and subsequently led to diminished educational opportunity for the plaintiffs, in comparison to their White peers (Bersoff, 1982). *Hobson* profoundly affected the use of intelligence tests and in educational decision making to this day. On this, Sandoval and Irvin (1990) comment,

> The court decided that the standardized *group* aptitude tests were inappropriate (i.e., not valid) because the tests are standardized on white middle-class children and could not be generalized to black children. This notion of standardization became the first legal definition of test bias or lack of validity. In the decision, the court particularly disapproved of the inflexibility of the tracking system, and its stigmatizing effect on black children. Because placement in a lower track was perceived to be harmful, the issue of equal educational opportunity was identified. In addition, the judge criticized the practice of using ability tests as the sole basis (or a major factor) for deciding on placement. (p. 89)

By the mid-1960s, the education of children with mental retardation grew to become a major undertaking, with more than 540,000 children across the country enrolled in special education programs (Goldberg, 1971). In local public schools, the enrollment of such children grew approximately 400% from around 1950 to 1970, and by 1970, public schools enrolled 90% of the nation's children with mental retardation. Furthermore, the overwhelming proportion of children with EMR were taught in full-time, self-contained special classes.[6]

Along with this dramatic growth in the population of students with mental retardation, a national concern arose about the overrepresentation of students of color and low-SES students labeled as EMR (Doll, 1962; Robinson & Robinson, 1965). In a frequently cited article, "Special Education for the Mildly Retarded—Is Much of It Justifiable?" L.M. Dunn (1968) turned the national limelight on the disproportionate numbers of minority and poor children placed in classes for the mildly, or educable, mentally retarded. He wrote,

> In my best judgment, about 60 to 80 percent of the pupils taught by these teachers are children from low status backgrounds—including Afro-Americans, American Indians, Mexicans, and Puerto Rican Americans; those from nonstandard English speaking, broken, disorganized, and inadequate homes; and children from other nonmiddle class environments. This expensive proliferation of self contained special schools and classes raises serious educational and civil rights issues which must be squarely faced. It is my thesis that we must stop labeling these deprived children as mentally retarded. Furthermore we must stop segregating them by placing them into our allegedly special programs. (p. 6)

The concern that school personnel may have incorrectly diagnosed students of color as EMR (i.e., false positives—students falsely identified as EMR who in fact are not) became the core of the overrepresentation issue. For example, based on her research in Riverside, California, Dr. Jane Mercer, sociologist, found that a substantial percentage of Mexican American and African American students classified as EMR were actually "quasi-retarded." She commented,

> Most of these normal-bodied persons who fail an intelligence test but have adequate adaptive behavior would be persons who lack the skills and knowledge needed to pass an intelligence test because they have not

been socialized in families that conform to the sociocultural mode for the community. (1973, p. 143)

In a similar vein, the President's Commission on Mental Retardation (1970) coined a social construction which defined mental retardation situationally, describing the "six-hour retarded child"—typically poor and of color—as follows:

> We now have what may be called a 6-hour retarded child—retarded from 9 to 3, five days a week, solely on the basis of an IQ score, without regard to his adaptive behavior, which may be exceptionally adaptive to the situation and community in which he lives. (Inside booklet cover, n.p.)

Concerns about labeling children in special education went beyond the mentally retarded. In the early 1970s, an organization conducted a national survey of the fifty state special education directors (State-Federal Information Clearinghouse for Exceptional Children, 1973; cited in Goldstein, Arkell, Ashcroft, Hurley, & Lilly, 1975). The survey reported that a slight majority (56%) of the directors indicated that "the major controversy in special education today involves labeling handicapped children and the related problem of where to place them" (p. 4).

Prior to the filing of *Diana v. State Board of Education* (1970), indisputable data surfaced in California illustrating the overrepresentation of students of color in programs for the EMR. Table 3.1 presents these disparity data. In the 1966–1967 school year, Mexican American and African

TABLE 3.1

Disparity Analysis by Race/Ethnicity for EMR Category:
California K–12 Enrollment, 1966–1967 School Year

Racial/Ethnic Group	Enrollment[a] (%)	EMR[b] (%)	Disparity[c] (%)
White	75.1	50.1	−33.3
Mexican American[d]	13.6	26.6	+95.6
African American	8.2	21.1	+157.3

Source: Adapted from Racial and Ethnic Distribution of Enrollment (Exhibit B), *Diana v. State Board of Education*, Civil Action No. C-70-37 (N.D. Cal. 1970).

Note: EMR = educable mentally retarded. K–12 = kindergarten through grade 12.

[a] % enrollment = percentage of racial/ethnic group in total K–12 enrollment.
[b] % EMR = percentage of racial/ethnic group in EMR program. [c] In the % disparity column, a minus sign (−) indicates underrepresentation, and a plus sign (+) indicates overrepresentation. Richard R. Valencia calculated the disparities. [d] The Mexican American group likely includes a small proportion of other Latinos.

American K–12 students were overrepresented in EMR classes by substantial proportions—that is, 95.6% and 157.3%, respectively. By contrast, White students were underrepresented by 33.3%.

Mexican American et al. Special Education Litigation: Diana, Covarrubias, *and* Guadalupe

Viewed through the lens of CRT, this corpus of litigation initiated by children of color underscores the centrality of race in the assignment of students to special education classes. This litigation also challenged the alleged "objectivity" of intelligence tests. Several years subsequent to the highly influential *Hobson* decision, plaintiffs of color brought forth a round of lawsuits alleging that intelligence tests were being used discriminatorily in the placement of such students in EMR classes.[7] These post-*Hobson* cases proved especially important because of the nature of the targeted intelligence tests. Bersoff (1982) comments,

> Despite *Hobson*'s implicit approval of individual testing, the [post-*Hobson*] cases now began to attack the stately, revered, and venerated devices against which all other tests were measured—the individually administered intelligence scales such as the Stanford-Binet and the WISC [Wechsler Intelligence Scale for Children]. (p. 1048)

This section covers a trio of post-*Hobson* cases initiated by Mexican American and other plaintiffs of color that took matters a big step further —assaults against *individually* administered intelligence tests. Although a number of scholars have covered one or more of the *Diana, Covarrubias,* and *Guadalupe* cases (e.g., Collings, 1973; Goldberg, 1971; Oakland & Laosa, 1977; Reschly, 1979; Ross, DeYoung, & Cohen, 1971; Vaughan, 1973), such coverages are limited in scope.[8] In all three lawsuits, filed in federal district courts, plaintiffs and defendants settled by consent decrees. Because these cases did not go to trial, and the judges wrote no opinion to publish in the *Federal Supplement,* scholars who have discussed *Diana, Covarrubias,* and *Guadalupe* have generally relied on secondary sources and not sought out the original legal documents. The discussion of these cases here is an exception. I secured, from the National Archives in California and Arizona, most of the legal material (e.g., initial complaint, filing of motions, affidavits, civil minutes, judges' orders, interrogatories,

TABLE 3.2
Disparity Analysis by Race/Ethnicity for EMR Category:
Monterey County (California) K–12 Enrollment,
1966–1967 School Year

Racial/Ethnic Group	Enrollment[a] (%)	EMR[b] (%)	Disparity[c] (%)
White	69.2	50.8	−26.6
Mexican American[d]	18.5	32.1	+73.5
African American	6.3	12.0	+90.5

Source: Adapted from Racial and Ethnic Distribution of Enrollment (Exhibit B), *Diana v. State Board of Education*, Civil Action No. C-70-37 (N.D. Cal. 1970).

Note: EMR = educable mentally retarded. K–12 = kindergarten through grade 12.

[a] % enrollment = percentage of racial/ethnic group in total K–12 enrollment.
[b] % EMR = percentage of racial/ethnic group in EMR program. [c] In the % disparity column, a minus sign (−) indicates underrepresentation, and a plus sign (+) indicates overrepresentation. Richard R. Valencia calculated the disparities. [d] The Mexican American group likely includes a small proportion of other Latinos.

correspondence between parties and the court, and settlements) germane to the three cases. The first comprehensive discussion of *Diana*, *Covarrubias*, and *Guadalupe* emerges from this research.

Diana v. State Board of Education (1970)

In Monterey County (California), where the plaintiffs in *Diana v. State Board of Education* resided, racial/ethnic disparities in the EMR category reflected the statewide pattern. Table 3.2 shows these data from Monterey County. Mexican American and African American students were overrepresented at rates of 73.5% and 90.5%, respectively; Whites were underrepresented by 26.6%.

Nine Mexican American students of varied ages served as plaintiffs in *Diana*. These children all attended the same self-contained EMR classroom in Soledad Elementary School in the town of Soledad, California (Monterey County).[9] Soledad is located in central California in the heart of the ninety-mile stretch of the Salinas Valley, referred to as the "world's salad bowl" (see www.BeachCalifornia.com/soled/html). Agribusiness is a multibillion-dollar industry in the Salinas Valley, and relies on farm workers to harvest the crops. Plaintiffs ranged in age from eight to thirteen years (mean=10.2 years, mode=11 years),[10] and all were from low-SES background (six of the nine children's representatives [parents] were farm workers).[11] Each child came "from a family in which Spanish was the predominant, if not the only, spoken language."[12]

In the 1960s, school psychologists in Monterey County school districts typically administered, for possible EMR placement, either the Wechsler Intelligence Scale for Children (WISC; Wechsler, 1949) or the Stanford-Binet Intelligence Scale (Terman & Merrill, 1960). The Stanford-Binet, first developed in 1916 with an all-White standardization group, underwent restandardization in 1937, and a second restandardization in 1960, using a norm group of exclusively 3,184 White children (Sattler, 1992). The WISC, first constructed in 1949 using an all-White group of 2,200 children, did not undergo a restandardization until 1974, several years after *Diana* (Sattler). An observed IQ score between 55 and 70 on the WISC and 52 and 68 on the Stanford-Binet resulted in placement in an EMR class.[13] In most California counties (including Monterey), these individually administered intelligence tests were "*given only in English* [italics added]."[14] Given the Spanish-language background of the nine plaintiffs and the administration of the intelligence tests only in English, it was not unexpected to read in the *Diana* complaint the following: "The I.Q. scores of the nine plaintiffs when tested solely in English by a non-Spanish-speaking tester ranged from 30–72 with a mean score of 63½."[15] This mean was 36.5 points, or about 2.5 standard deviations, below the standardization mean of 100 on the WISC and Stanford-Binet.

Plaintiffs' counsel contracted Victor Ramírez, an accredited California school psychologist, to conduct psychological evaluations of the nine student plaintiffs.[16] On November 1 and 2, 1969 (two months before the filing of *Diana*), Ramírez, a Latino English-Spanish bilingual, undertook his evaluations. He noted his assessment procedure as follows:

Each student was given the WISC test in Spanish or English. Each student was given the opportunity to respond in either language or in a combination of both languages. In addition, each child was given wide range achievement tests to measure academic progress, Peabody Picture tests (solely to determine in which language the child was most proficient), and, when indicated, a Bender Motor Gestalt. In addition, specific information about the child and his family was elicited insofar as that was possible.[17]

Ramírez's evaluations are particularly interesting in that he retested the plaintiffs in Spanish. These results are presented in Table 3.3 and can be summarized as follows:

1. Of the nine children, seven (Diana, Armando, Arthur, Manuel, Ramon, Ernesto, and Maria) had, on retest, a Full Scale IQ (FSIQ) higher

TABLE 3.3
WISC Retest Results (Spanish Administration)
for Nine Plaintiff Children

Child Name (and age)	WISC Scale IQ		
	Verbal	Performance	Full
Diana (8)	67	96	79[a]
Armando (8)	77	72	72[a]
Arthur (11)	94	86	89[a]
Manuel (10)	82	89	84[a]
Margarita (13)	62	83	70
Ramon (11)	81	75	76[a]
Ernesto (9)	71	92	79[a]
Maria (11)	74	87	78[a]
Rachael (11)	66	74	67
Mean	75	84	77

Source: Adapted from Psychological Evaluation of Nine Plaintiffs Conducted by School Psychologist Victor Ramírez (Exhibit A), *Diana v. State Board of Education,* Civil Action No. C-70-37 (N.D. Cal. 1970).

Note: WISC refers to the Wechsler Intelligence Scale for Children.

[a] Plaintiff scored above cut score (WISC IQ of 70) for EMR placement.

than the cut score (70 IQ) used by the district for placement of students in EMR classes.[18]

2. For these seven children, their FSIQs ranged from a low of 2 points (Armando) to a high of 19 points (Arthur) higher than the EMR placement cut score. The average number of points above the cut score for the seven children was 9.6 points.[19]

3. For the other two children who did not score above the EMR placement cut score, one child (Margarita) scored at the cut score, and the other (Rachael) scored 3 points below.

4. As a whole, the children's retest WISC FSIQs demonstrated significant gain scores. The complaint noted, "Diane [Diana] improved 49 points over an earlier Stanford-Binet test. Her brother Armando jumped 22 points. Three other children showed very substantial gains of 20, 14, and 10 points. The average gain was 15 points [one standard deviation]."[20]

5. In addition to the FSIQ, the WISC also contains a Verbal Scale IQ (VSIQ) and a Performance Scale IQ (PSIQ). The FSIQ is obtained from combining the score of the VSIQ and the PSIQ. The VSIQ, as its name indicates, is verbally loaded, measuring such knowledge as vocabulary, word similarities, and general information. The PSIQ, by sharp contrast, requires very little verbal knowledge (mostly confined to understanding test instructions) and measures, for example, skills related to using codes,

arranging pictures in the correct order, and using blocks to make specific designs. Given the difference in the behaviors sampled by the VSIQ and the PSIQ, an ample body of long-standing evidence shows that Mexican American children typically exhibit a profile of higher scores on performance scales compared to verbal scales (P > V) on various measures of intelligence.[21] This P > V pattern occurs when Mexican American children are tested on either an English or Spanish version of a particular instrument (see, e.g., Valencia, 1988, p. 86, Table 1), but the P > V gap is larger for the Spanish administration. Regarding the VSIQ and PSIQ scores of the *Diana* plaintiffs, the data shown in Table 3.3 demonstrate the ubiquitous P > V pattern for six (67%) of the nine children. The gap ranged from 7 IQ points (Manuel) to 29 points (Diana). The average P > V difference was 16.5 points, slightly more than one standard deviation.[22]

6. Ramírez's evaluations of the nine plaintiffs also contained achievement test results based on the Wide Range Achievement Test (WRAT; Jastak & Jastak, 1965).[23] Ramírez reported WRAT grade equivalents for Reading (Word Attack: Pronouncing Words), Spelling, and Arithmetic. The children's achievement scores are presented in Table 3.4, showing that for both the Reading and Spelling grade equivalents, eight of the nine children performed at grade 1 or lower.

The Arithmetic grade equivalents ranged from K.7 to 3.6, with a mode of grade 3. Although the children performed considerably lower on all

TABLE 3.4
WRAT Results for Nine Plaintiff Children

Child Name (and age)	WRAT Subtest Grade Equivalent		
	Reading[a]	Spelling	Arithmetic
Diana (8)	PK.1	1.2	K.7
Armando (8)	PK.2	1.2	K.9
Arthur (11)	1.9	1.8	3.2
Manuel (10)	1.9	1.8	2.6
Margarita (13)	1.7	2.2	3.4
Ramon (11)	2.3	1.8	3.6
Ernesto (9)	K.6	1.2	1.8
Maria (11)	1.5	1.6	na[b]
Rachael (11)	1.5	1.2	2.6

Source: Adapted from Psychological Evaluation of Nine Plaintiffs Conducted by School Psychologist Victor Ramírez (Exhibit A), *Diana v. State Board of Education,* Civil Action No. C-70-37 (N.D. Cal. 1970).

Note: WRAT = Wide Range Achievement Test. PK = prekindergarten. K = kindergarten. The numeral following the decimal in each of the grade equivalents is the month. For example, Margarita's grade equivalent (1.7) for Reading is first grade, seventh month.

[a] Reading score refers to Word Attack: Pronouncing Words. [b] na = not available.

WRAT subtests than the norms for the standardization group, the Reading and Spelling scores are of particular concern.

The cultural loading and highly verbal nature of these subtests partly explains the depressed scores on Reading and Spelling. The failure of the teacher in the special education class to challenge, academically, the children (who were all taught in the same class) appears to be another factor explaining the low scores of the WRAT. Each child had been in an EMR class for periods up to three years.[24] Regarding the very limited instruction provided to the children, the plaintiffs' complaint read,

> They [plaintiff children] are sometimes divided into two groups for teaching but that is the extent of differential treatment. Since there is only one teacher for the class, the two groups are taught simultaneously. The children spend substantial class time coloring in coloring books and cutting pictures out of magazines. Eleven-year-old Maria characterized the classroom activities as "babystuff." One of the younger children cries frequently making teaching in the class very difficult. While Arthur and the other plaintiffs in their EMR class receive this limited "3 R's" education, 98% of the school children the same age as Arthur have had 5 years of formal school training.[25]

Although lead plaintiff Diana's overall low performance on the WRAT was not unique compared to the other plaintiff children's scores, her WRAT profile (see Table 3.4) demonstrated the lowest grade equivalent on Reading (PK.1) and Arithmetic (K.7), and on Spelling her grade equivalent was tied with three other children for the lowest score (1.2). Sadly so, Diana's teacher never taught her the alphabet or numerals between one and ten. As Ramírez wrote in his report, "Present testing [of Diana] indicates severe academic deficiency in all basic skill areas with the inability to recognize the letters of the alphabet or produce numerals between 1–10 satisfactorially."[26]

In light of school psychologist Ramírez's psychological evaluations of the nine plaintiff children, he noted that because the strong majority of the children scored FSIQs (on retest) above the cut score of EMR placement, they were considerably more capable of doing stronger academic work than they exhibited on the WRAT. As such, he recommended reassignments for at least seven of the nine children.[27] The report on Manuel typified Ramírez's recommendations:

Manuel [who had a FSIQ of 84] showed no significant difference noted [on the WISC] between his verbal score [82] and performance score [89]. Present testing further indicates academic deficiencies especially in the areas of reading and spelling skills. Current findings do tend to indicate that Manuel is capable of functioning above his current program placement and, if given proper remedial help in some of the basic skills areas, could even make an adequate adjustment to a regular program.[28]

Meanwhile, the passage of House Resolution No. 444 had important bearing on *Diana*.

On August 6, 1969 the California Assembly passed House Resolution No. 444 recognizing that "a disproportionate number of children from such groups (minority groups) are assigned to classes for the mentally retarded." The Resolution calls upon school psychologists, school districts, and parents to undertake careful re-evaluation of all students then in EMR classes and "strongly urge(s) the State Board of Education to give attention and aid to proposals for changes in the structure of special education [MR] categories."[29]

Yet addressing the mandate of House Resolution No. 444 was slow in coming. As noted in the plaintiffs' complaint, "local districts have not undertaken to any procedure to remedy the current [EMR overrepresentation] situation."[30]

The impetus for the *Diana* lawsuit can be traced to September 1969, when one of the plaintiff children's parents brought attention to the district regarding the "unlawful EMR placement in Soledad."[31] On December 15, 1969, plaintiffs' attorney met with Soledad Elementary School Superintendent Wendell Broom. The parties reviewed the facts of the case to strive for an agreement as to how reclassification would occur. They also discussed the allegations of the complaint, including (a) the gain in IQ scores on the retest, (b) the statewide pattern of discriminatory EMR placement of Spanish-speaking Mexican American children, (c) the serious harm being caused to the children, and (d) the urgency of reclassification action. The complaint noted,

These findings confirmed his [Superintendent Broom's] own suspicion that unfair testing of Mexican-Americans occurs. He unequivocally indicated that he could reassign the children immediately after Christmas vacation to regular classes and that he could use existing facilities for high powered supplementary training in language and mathematics to correct past deficiencies caused by their improper placement so that the children would be fully integrated into the normal program as quickly as possible. Mr. Broom stated that the Christmas vacation provided the most opportune time for this transition as the school would devise a schedule during this period and the children in the school would accept the change as a natural one. He further assured plaintiffs that the tests already administered to the children would be sufficient so long as the psychologist [Victor Ramírez] who administered them was certified by the State of California.[32]

Within days, however, Superintendent Broom reneged on his promises, prompting the filing of the *Diana* lawsuit.

On December 30, 1969, 15 days after school officials had promised to reassign the children, an agent of the school district sent a letter to plaintiffs changing the school's position, indicating that a "complete study" would be necessary, and asking for further documentation. In spite of plaintiffs' warnings, in response, that any further delay in providing the children with a regular education would endanger their chances to make up for the three years of deprivation already suffered, the children upon return from Christmas vacation on January 5, 1970, were and are presently forced to stay in classes for mental retards.[33]

On January 7, 1970, plaintiffs' attorneys filed *Diana* in the U.S. District Court for the Northern District of California. Judge Robert F. Peckham presided. Filed as a class action suit, the plaintiffs in *Diana* constituted the nine students previously mentioned, a second group of four plaintiffs from the same families (see note 10, this chapter), and on behalf of all others similarly situated in California, representing two classes of children:

1. Bilingual Mexican-American children now placed in California classes for the mentally retarded.
2. Preschool and other young bilingual Mexican-American children who will be given an IQ test and thus be in substantial danger of placement in a class for the mentally retarded, regardless of their ability to learn.[34]

Defendants in *Diana* included the State Board of Education, Max Rafferty (the Superintendent of Public Instruction for the State of California), and Wendell Broom (Superintendent of the Soledad Elementary School District). Plaintiffs claimed their action under the Fourteenth Amendment, the Civil Rights Act of 1964 (42 U.S.C. 2000d, 200d-1), and the Elementary and Secondary Education Act (ESEA) of 1965 (20 U.S.C. 241).[35] The complaint listed nine points for declaratory and injunctive relief that they wanted Judge Peckham to consider in his order and judgment. In abbreviated form, the seven most germane of the nine points are the following:[36]

1. Defendants shall be restrained from placing any Spanish-speaking or bilingual child in EMR classes by administering an IQ test solely in English.

2. Defendants shall be restrained from either (a) refusing to accept the retesting results by Victor Ramírez, or (b) if defendants do so question the validity of said results, they shall be restrained from refusing to test the nine plaintiffs in both Spanish and English by a qualified bilingual examiner.

3. Defendants shall be restrained (a) from refusing to place plaintiffs in regular classrooms with intensive supplemental instruction in language skills and mathematics and (b) from refusing to expunge from plaintiffs' school records that they were in EMR classes.

4. Defendants shall be enjoined from placing in an EMR class any Spanish-speaking or bilingual child who scores, on the WISC Performance Scale, above the cut score for EMR placement.

5. Defendants shall be enjoined (a) from refusing to retest all Spanish-speaking and bilingual children in EMR classes in California, (b) from refusing to conduct such retesting in both Spanish and English by a qualified bilingual examiner, and (c) from failing to reassign children in accordance with points 3 and 4 above.

6. Defendants shall be enjoined from (a) placing any child younger than age ten years in an EMR class, and (b) placing any Spanish-speaking or bilingual child in an EMR class *unless* an IQ test—"standardized by culture in Spanish and English and constructed to reflect cultural values of the Mexican-American"[37]—has been administered, and the child scores below (as established by the test standardization) the cut score for EMR placement.

7. The plaintiffs declared, under several laws, that assignment of Mexican American students in EMR classes in California public schools "was

unlawful and unconstitutional and may not be justified by administration of the currently available IQ tests in English only to these bilingual and Spanish-speaking children schoolchildren."[38]

Plaintiffs and defendants settled *Diana* on February 5, 1970, when Judge Peckham signed a stipulation and order.[39] They agreed to ten major points, with far-reaching implications for the assessment and placement of Mexican American and other students of color in EMR classes in California and elsewhere. In brief, these points covered the following:

1. *Language assessment.* Students whose primary language is other than English shall be interviewed and assessed in both English and the primary language of the home.[40]

2. *School psychologist competence.* The school psychologist (or other qualified person) administering tests to a student whose primary language is other than English shall be competent in speaking and reading the primary language used by the student.[41]

3. *Approved list of tests.* Students shall be administered verbal and nonverbal individual intelligence tests chosen from a list approved by the State Board of Education.[42]

4. *Preeminence of nonverbal tests.* No student shall be placed in a class for the mentally retarded if he or she performs on a nonverbal intelligence test—or on the nonverbal section of a test including both verbal and nonverbal sections—higher than the cut score used by a school district to determine the classification of mental retardation.[43]

5. *Test normed on Mexican Americans.* Test developers in the State Department of Education are to undertake the norming of an individually administered intelligence test with the Mexican American school-age population in California as the target standardization group.[44]

6. *Parental consultation.* No student shall be assigned to a "special school or class, integrated program of instruction, or experimental program"[45] until the admission committee's recommendation is received and it is certified that the child's parent has been consulted as required by the State Education Code.[46]

7. *Multiple information collection.* In addition to the report prepared by the school psychologist, other germane information shall be collected and considered by the placement committee before a student is enrolled in a class for the mentally retarded. Such information shall include (but not be limited to) "a study of the cultural background, home environment and learning opportunities" of the student. Furthermore, "In no case shall placement in a class for the mentally retarded be based on a low score

achieved on an intelligence test without an evaluation of that score in light of the facts learned in the aforementioned studies."[47]

8. *Retesting and reevaluation.* Students currently enrolled in EMR classes, and who may be candidates for (a) continuance or (b) return to regular classes, shall be recommended only on the basis of evaluations standards, including any retesting that is deemed necessary. Such assessments shall be conducted pursuant to points 1–7, above. Children who are transitioned to regular classes shall be placed with children of comparable age, and the regular program supplementation should contain as much individual attention, small-group instruction, or other special attention as deemed possible.[48]

9. *Annual review.* The retesting and reevaluation stipulation described above in point 8 shall be a permanent feature of an annual review.[49]

10. *Significant variance.* The State Department of Education (SDOE) shall require all school districts to undertake surveys to ascertain the number and percentages of students, disaggregated by race/ethnicity, in EMR classes. In the event the SDOE finds a "significant variance" between the racial/ethnic proportions of EMR classes and the racial/ethnic proportions in the total district, the district is required to submit an explanation of the significant variance.[50]

Although none of the settlements reached in *Diana* were ever fully realized (e.g., the development of an intelligence test normed on Mexican American students), several far-reaching and positive outcomes resulted from the case.

1. *Decertification of students in EMR classes.* The first direct positive consequence of the *Diana* decision stems from the retesting and reevaluation requirement of the stipulation and order. In light of the class action nature of *Diana*, the retesting and reevaluation mandate affected thousands of students in California's public schools. In 1969, the reassessment of students in EMR classes began, and by 1973 the reevaluations of all such students were completed. From 1969 to 1973, about 11,000 to 14,000 students in EMR classes had undergone "decertification," the process of reevaluation and reassignment (Yoshida et al., 1976).[51] Furthermore, the absolute number of students in EMR classes, as shown in Table 3.5 (lines 2 and 4), sharply declined 37% from 55,519 (in 1969) to 35,110 (in 1973). This decrease of over 20,000 students (including 6,374 White, 7,581 Latino, and 6,268 African American students; see Table 3.5, line 5) can be partly linked to the *Diana* decision (i.e., the retesting and reevaluation mandate that led to decertification) and, in part, to other significant contemporary

TABLE 3.5

Changes in California EMR Enrollment by Race/Ethnicity: 1969 to 1973

	Race/Ethnicity					
	White		Mexican American (other Latino)		African American	
Enrollment Category	%	No.	%	No.	%	No.
1. Total Statewide Enrollment: 1969[a]	72.4	na	15.2	na	8.9	na
2. EMR Enrollment: 1969[a] (total = 55,519)	43.1	23,929	28.2	15,656	27.1	15,046
Disparity: 1969[b]	−40.5	na	+85.5	na	+204.5	na
3. Total Statewide Enrollment: 1973[c]	69.5	na	17.2	na	9.7	na
4. EMR Enrollment: 1973[d] (total = 35,110)	50.0	17,555	23.0	8,075	25.0	8,778
Disparity: 1973	−28.1	na	+33.7	na	+157.7	na
5. EMR Enrollment Change: 1969–1973[e]	+16.0	−6,374	−18.4	−7,581	−7.8	−6,268

Note: Percentage data in lines 1, 2, and 4 and totals in lines 2 and 4 are from Yoshida et al. (1976, p. 219, Table 1). Richard R. Valencia calculated all other numerals. na = not available or not applicable.

[a] Fall 1969. [b] In the Disparity row, a minus sign (−) indicates underrepresentation, and a plus sign (+) indicates overrepresentation. [c] Fall 1973. [d] June 1973. Available from California State Department of Education, Educational Demographics Office (Wayne Dughi, Researcher), September 16, 2003. [e] A minus sign (−) indicates a decrease, and a plus sign (+) indicates an increase.

lawsuits filed by students of color in EMR classes in California schools.[52] It appears that the decline (37%) from 1969 to 1973 of students in EMR classes can be attributed to the decertification process and the litigious climate of the time. School officials, fearing lawsuits, hesitated to enroll minority students in EMR classes. In short, the 20,000-plus student decline in EMR from 1969 to 1973 included the 11,000 to 14,000 count estimated by Yoshida et al., and the 6,000 to 9,000 students not placed in EMR classes due to school districts' fear of litigation.

Another germane point regarding the sharp decrease in students enrolled in EMR classes needs to be mentioned. Although the absolute number of students enrolled in EMR classes declined by more than 20,000 students from 1969 to 1973, the changes in the percentages of Latino and African American students—as shown in Table 3.5, line 5—were quite small. In 1969 and 1973, Mexican American (and other Latino) students constituted 28.2% and 23.0%, respectively, of the statewide EMR enrollment—a decrease of 18.4%. The percentages for African American students in 1969 and 1973 were 27.1% and 25.0%, respectively—indicating a decline of 7.8%. The point to underscore: Although the absolute numbers of Mexican Americans/Latinos in EMR classes decreased by 7,581 students from 1969 to 1973, and African Americans declined by 6,268 students in the same time period, both groups remained overrepresented in EMR classes in 1973. In sum, racialized patterns persisted. As shown in Table 3.5 (line 4, Disparity %), the overrepresentation of Mexican American/Latino and African American students were, respectively, 33.7% and 157.7%; White students were underrepresented by 28.1% in EMR classes. Furthermore, the 157.7% overrepresentation of African American students in 1973 was nearly identical to the 157.3% overrepresentation observed in the 1966–1967 school year (see Table 3.1), before the *Diana* lawsuit. This nagging overrepresentation of students of color in EMR classes was symptomatic of the SBOE's footdragging in meeting the significant variance mandate of the *Diana* stipulation and order (see note 50, this chapter).

2. *Some confirmation of inaccurate EMR diagnosis.* Plaintiff students in *Diana* asserted that school officials erroneously diagnosed them as being EMR. A study reported in Yoshida et al. (1976) provides confirmation that some of the decertified students may have indeed been false positives. In this investigation, 833 decertified students (80% Latino and African American) from twelve California school districts participated in the study.[53] The researchers first administered the Metropolitan Achievement Test (MAT), and then they calculated grade equivalents (GEs) for the decertified (D), regular class (RC), and EMR students. Yoshida et al. summarized the results as follows:

As measured by the MAT, the D students were performing lower as a group than their RC matches though higher than the retained EMR students. However, the distributions of GEs for the Ds and RCs showed considerable overlap indicating that many Ds may be achieving at comparable levels with some RCs. In teacher perceptions, the Ds were rated more unfavorably than the RCs in both achievement and social acceptance. Nevertheless, about one-third of the Ds were thought to be at least average or better than their regular classmates in achievement with almost 60 percent of the Ds similarly perceived in social acceptance.

Many of those teachers who did not receive transition aid reported that they: (a) did not know that the D was a former EMR who qualified for supplemental monies, (b) thought some D students did not require the special help, or (c) were unaware of the program. The first two reasons further confirm that some students were succeeding at a level which did not require some type of special help. (p. 232)

3. *1970 Memo from Office for Civil Rights.* On May 25, 1970, J. Stanley Pottinger, Director of the Office for Civil Rights (OCR) sent a landmark memorandum to all U.S. public school districts with more than 5% national-origin racial/ethnic minority group students. The memorandum, "Identification of Discrimination and Denial of Services on the Basis of National Origin," appeared to be triggered by the *Diana* outcome, mentioning compliance reviews by the OCR that found denial of equal educational opportunity to "Spanish-surnamed" students with limitations in English-language facility. One major part of the memorandum spoke to this compliance concern so central to *Diana*'s stipulation and order: "School districts must not assign national origin minority-group students to classes for the mentally retarded on the basis of criteria which essentially measure or evaluate English language skills" (35 F.R. 11595).[54]

Covarrubias v. San Diego Unified (1971)

Several years prior to the filing of *Covarrubias v. San Diego Unified et al.*, the racial/ethnic disparities in the EMR category in San Diego County, California, reflected the statewide profile in the 1966–1967 school year. Table 3.6 presents the data germane to San Diego County. The overrepresentation rates of Mexican American and African American students were 100.9% and 338.5%, respectively; White students were underrepresented in the EMR category by 34.4%.

TABLE 3.6
Disparity Analysis by Race/Ethnicity for EMR Category:
San Diego County (California) K–12 Enrollment,
1966–1967 School Year

Racial/Ethnic Group	Enrollment[a] (%)	EMR[b] (%)	Disparity[c] (%)
White	81.6	53.5	−34.4
Mexican American[d]	10.8	21.7	+100.9
African American	5.2	22.8	+338.5

Source: Comparisons of Two Methods of Calculating Rates of Enrollment in Special Education Classes in the State of California Public Schools for Selected Counties (Exhibit A), *Covarrubias v. San Diego Unified School District*, Civil Action No. 70-394-T (S.D. Cal. 1971).

Note: EMR = educable mentally retarded. K–12 = kindergarten through grade 12.

[a] % enrollment = percentage of racial/ethnic group in total K–12 enrollment.
[b] % EMR = percentage of racial/ethnic group in EMR program. [c] In the % disparity column, a minus sign (−) indicates underrepresentation, and a plus sign (+) indicates overrepresentation. Richard R. Valencia calculated the disparities. [d] The Mexican American group likely includes a small proportion of other Latinos.

In *Covarrubias*, seven Mexican American and thirteen African American students who were enrolled in EMR classes in various schools in the San Diego Unified School District composed the plaintiffs. The Mexican American children, all from low-SES background, came "from families in which Spanish is the predominant if not the only language spoken in the home."[55] The African American children, also from low-SES background, came from families in the San Diego "ghetto" in which "so-called 'Black English' is spoken."[56] At the time of filing the *Covarrubias* claim, the twenty plaintiff children—enrolled in EMR classes ranging from grades 1 to 9—attended six different elementary schools and one junior high school.[57]

In February 1970—ten months before plaintiffs filed the *Covarrubias* complaint—a state-licensed bilingual examiner independently retested the plaintiff children on a measure of intelligence. The examiner used "certain techniques tending to compensate for the bicultural and bilingual problems of plaintiffs."[58] Results of the retesting showed that all plaintiffs scored above the cut score for EMR placement, and in each instance plaintiffs scored higher on the performance section of the test, compared to the verbal section.[59] The complaint noted that in certain instances, the P > V difference was 29 IQ points. Furthermore, none of the plaintiffs had a PSIQ below the cut score of 70 for EMR placement, no child had scores in the 70s, eleven (55%) had performance scores above a 95 IQ, and four (20%) scored over 100.[60]

On December 1, 1970, plaintiffs filed *Covarrubias* in the U.S. District Court for the Southern District of California. Specifically, this class action lawsuit covered the initial twenty Mexican American and African American plaintiffs, plus all other such students of color "in the San Diego Unified School District who have been wrongfully placed and are wrongfully retained in the EMR program."[61] The San Diego Unified School District (SDUSD), the School Board of the SDUSD, and sixty "Does" (unnamed defendants acting in their capacity as officials of the SDUSD) were named as defendants in *Covarrubias*.

The plaintiffs claimed that the SDUSD had violated their right to an equal education, pursuant to the California Constitution (Article 9, § 5). In addition, plaintiffs' claim arose from violations of the Civil Rights Act of 1870, 1871, and 1964. The Civil Rights Act of 1870 provides, in part, for "legal action to accrue both in law and in equity for any person against whom any action has been taken under color of State law which is discriminatory in nature based on race or color."[62] This act also provided for the injured party to sue where it can be shown that "two or more persons conspired to deprive any person of equal privileges under the law."[63] The Civil Rights Act of 1964 contains specific regulations "that each school district has an affirmative duty to take prompt and effective action to eliminate . . . discrimination based upon . . . national origin, and to correct the effects of past discrimination (Section 6)."[64] Furthermore, this act requires *equal opportunity* in access to, for example, classes, instructional curricula, teachers, and textbooks.

Covarrubias plaintiffs prayed for injunctive and declaratory relief quite similar to the points raised in *Diana* (e.g., enjoining defendants from administering IQ tests or other assessments that do not properly account for plaintiff children's language and cultural backgrounds; enjoining defendants from placing any plaintiff in EMR classes via invalid IQ tests or methods; enjoining defendants from refusing to place plaintiff children in regular classes, with supplemental individual instruction in language, mathematics, and other subject areas).[65]

Taken together—and in the context of CRT and a commitment to social justice—*Diana*, *Covarrubias*, and *Guadalupe* formed a powerful set of cases in which plaintiffs of color sued for inappropriate EMR placement. We need to understand, however, the cases' individual contributions. *Diana* certainly laid the foundation for subsequent cases. *Covarrubias*, however, added new or expanded elements to the logic and legal strategy of plaintiffs' arguments regarding complaints. Likewise, *Guadalupe*, discussed later, added new elements.

Plaintiffs presented three new strategies in *Covarrubias*:

1. *Stigmatization.* In their complaint, plaintiffs argued forcefully that their inaccurate and thus wrongful EMR placement stigmatized them as being slow learners, inferior, and second-class individuals. Note the following:

> Plaintiffs are informed and believe these [EMR] records are available to future teachers and faculty advisors as plaintiffs progress through school, to governmental authorities, including recruiting offices for the various armed forces officer programs and even employers. The stigma attached to placement in EMR programs in the eyes of such persons reviewing plaintiffs' records is such as to virtually make objective evaluation of plaintiffs' accomplishments and potential impossible. . . . The stigma attached to the EMR notations on plaintiffs' records and the widening gap in actual learning combine to effectively deny plaintiffs any practical

chance to realize their potential in college, in armed forces' officer programs, in executive or management programs, or in various other areas of society through which members of minority racial groups have sought and been able to lift their standards socially and economically and to share part of the American dream of self realization and self help for a better life. . . . Plaintiffs have been confronted with taunts and derision by other children in and out of school by reason of their being wrongfully placed in EMR classes and have come to feel and will continue to feel a profound sense of guilt and shame over being considered second rate and inferior in their achievements and learning. This makes their adjustment to life and to school and to their role as so-called slow learners more difficult and introduces psychological problems into their already problem laden experience.[66]

2. *Monetary damages.* In light of the stigmatization charge, plaintiffs sued for monetary damages.[67] Their claim asserted,

The wrongful placement and retention of plaintiffs in EMR classes will inevitably result in their being cut off from economic gains available to children in regular school classes and will cut them off from any chance to be gainfully employed, and many will be forced into further humiliation of reliance upon public assistance. . . . As a direct and proximate result of the discriminatory action by defendants on the basis of plaintiffs' race and color in wrongfully placing each plaintiff in an EMR class and wrongfully and unlawfully retaining plaintiffs in said EMR classes when by right they should not be there, each plaintiff has been damaged far in excess of $10,000, the exact amount of which is not capable of exact determination at the present time, but plaintiffs will seek leave of Court to amend this complaint when the amount as to each plaintiff and each class member is ascertained.[68]

3. *Child and parental due process.* Plaintiffs argued that defendants concealed the EMR status of affected students from their parents. They also claimed that defendants withheld information regarding EMR assessment, placement consent, and nature of the program from the parents/guardians. The concealment charge noted,

Neither plaintiff children nor parents nor guardians were informed or knew of the meaning or significance of the EMR program of the defendants; of the manner of selection for such program, or the manner of determining continued placement of children in such program. No real, or meaningful, consultation with these parents or guardians was had by defendants, no real or meaningful consent was given. Neither the plaintiff children, guardians nor parents, have consented and they do not now consent; they withdraw any consent conceivably given to placement in such program or continued placement in such program.[69]

Following from this concealment allegation, plaintiffs asked the court to permanently enjoin the defendants from

Causing, instigating or participating in any misrepresentation or concealment to plaintiffs and others similarly situated, and to the parents of plaintiffs and others similarly situated, of the true and complete nature of placement and retention in EMR classes. Causing, instigating or participating in any act to obtain the consent of the parents of plaintiffs and others similarly situated for placement in EMR classes without providing a translator for those parents who are unable to fluently speak, read or understand English.[70]

In 1971, attorneys for the defendants and plaintiffs signed a settlement agreement, consisting of fifteen points.[71] Many of the stipulations were consonant with the agreements reached in *Diana*—for example, the district agreed to retest and reevaluate all students enrolled in EMR classes; administer both nonverbal and verbal intelligence measures; require parental consent for EMR placement; provide intensive and supplemental instruction to students transitioned to regular classrooms; require evaluations from bilingual certified examiners; and expunge the records of all students in EMR classes who were transitioned to regular classrooms.[72]

As discussed earlier, one major way in which *Covarrubias* broke from *Diana* dealt with due process. Of the fifteen points listed in the Settlement Agreement, several sections discussed the establishment and mandate of a watchdog group, the Citizens Committee (CC). This committee—which consisted, in part, of community members selected by MALDEF, NAACP LDF, and the Superintendent of the SDUSD—had, for example, the following charges: (a) upon request by the parents, review of all students assigned to EMR classes; (b) right of the CC to consult external testing experts; (c) right of the CC to review the operations of the EMR program; (d) right of the CC to require annual reports of the school district regarding the EMR program (e.g., racial/ethnic enrollment). A final point regarding the settlement agreement: with respect to plaintiffs' monetary damage claim of $10,000 (or greater), the settlement awarded the sum of $1 to the plaintiffs and members of the class similarly situated.

Guadalupe Organization, Inc. v. Tempe School District No. 3 (1972)

As seen in *Diana* and *Covarrubias*, students of color were also overrepresented in classes for the educable and trainable mentally handicapped in the Tempe Elementary School District No. 3, in the spring of 1971.[73] Mexican American students made up 17.8% of the total enrollment of the district but constituted 67.6% and 46.3% of the educable and trainable mentally handicapped enrollments, respectively.[74] These data showed Mexican American student overrepresentations of 279.8% and 160.1% in the educable and trainable mentally handicapped enrollments, respectively (calculations by the author).

The lead plaintiff in the instant case was Guadalupe Organization, Inc., a community-based, nonprofit organization that had as one of its goals the advancement of educational interests for the community of Guadalupe, Arizona (located about five miles from Tempe). Incorporated in 1946, Guadalupe Organization had 440 dues-paying community members in 1971.[75] The other plaintiffs included two groups of Mexican American and Yaqui Indian[76] children in Tempe Elementary School District No. 3. The first group contained twelve Mexican American and Yaqui children whom the district had assessed as having educable or trainable mental retardation and placed in classes for the mentally retarded[77] (the complaint was later amended to add two plaintiff children to the first group).[78] Each child came from a family in which "Spanish or the Yaqui Indian language was the predominant, if not the only, spoken language."[79] The second group consisted of seventeen Mexican American and Yaqui children with the same racial/ethnic and language background as the first group, but they were preschoolers about to enter school or already in school and were scheduled to be administered IQ tests.[80] The plaintiff class in *Guadalupe* also included all children similarly situated in Arizona:

1. Mexican-American and Yaqui Indian children now placed in classes for the mentally retarded.
2. Preschool and other young Mexican-American and Yaqui Indian children who will be given an I.Q. test and thus be in substantial danger

of placement in a class for the mentally retarded, regardless of their ability to learn.[81]

As in *Diana* and *Covarrubias*, in *Guadalupe* the district assigned the plaintiff children to classes for the mentally retarded based exclusively, or near exclusively, on the child's performance on a standardized IQ test (the WISC) administered solely in English.[82] Thus, given the plaintiffs' assertion that these inappropriate assessments led to inaccurate diagnoses and wrongful placement in classes for the educable and trainable mentally retarded, and in light of the positive outcomes of *Diana* and *Covarrubias*, a lawsuit was timely. From a CRT perspective, a challenge to the orthodoxy —the alleged objectivity and fairness of IQ tests—guided the *Guadalupe* legal strategy.

On August 10, 1971, plaintiffs' attorneys filed *Guadalupe* in the U.S. District Court for the District of Arizona. The numerous defendants included, for example, the Tempe Elementary School District No. 3, W.P. Shofstall (Superintendent of the Arizona Department of Education), Donald M. Johnson (State Director of the Division of Special Education), and Margaret Fauci (school psychologist employed by the Tempe Elementary School District No. 3).[83] Plaintiffs complained that defendants had violated their rights under the Fourteenth Amendment of the U.S. Constitution and Title 20 of the Elementary and Secondary Education Act of 1965 (20 U.S.C.A. §236, et al.). Plaintiffs also claimed that defendants had violated their rights under Arizona laws concerning students' right to an education and the education of exceptional children.[84]

As seen in *Diana* and *Covarrubias*, plaintiffs' prayers for injunctive and declaratory relief in *Guadalupe* were quite similar[85] (e.g., restraining defendants from placing any Spanish-speaking or bilingual child in a class for the mentally retarded based solely on an IQ test administered in English; enjoining defendants from refusing to place plaintiff children in regular classes, and such placement should include intensive supplemental instruction; enjoining defendants from placing any Spanish-speaking or bilingual child in a class for the mentally retarded if such child scores above the cut score on the Performance Scale of the WISC; enjoining defendants from refusing to expunge the record of plaintiffs' mentally retarded placement). Similarly to *Covarrubias*, *Guadalupe* plaintiffs also asked for monetary damages ($10,000) due to the stigma attached to the mentally retarded label. Regarding the raising of new or expanded elements in the *Guadalupe* complaint, plaintiffs went beyond *Diana* and

Covarrubias in the area of instruction in regular classes. Plaintiff children would be placed in regular classrooms, the complaint asserted, and "intensive supplemental *bilingual and bicultural training* [italics added] in language and mathematics to allow them to achieve parity with their peers as soon as possible.[86]

On January 25, 1972, both parties filed a stipulation and order, and on May 9, 1972, Judge Walter E. Craig approved and signed it.[87] The order required that the district assess the primary-language status of any student referred for placement in classes for the mentally retarded *prior* to intellectual assessment. Also, the assessments must include valid and reliable tests that do not stress spoken language.[88] In addition to these two requirements, the stipulation and order listed ten other permanent regulations,[89] many corresponding closely with the collective set of agreements resulting from the *Diana* and *Covarrubias* settlements. These stipulations included, for example, that school districts in the state with an excessive percentage of children (of any racial/ethnic group) in classes for the mentally retarded needed to offer a compelling educational justification for such disproportionality. Other requirements included parental due process, decertification of inaccurately placed children and subsequent assignment to regular classes, and expungement of mentally retarded placement record of decertified children.

As did *Covarrubias*, *Guadalupe* also broke from *Diana* by adding new or expanded elements in the settlement. First, the decree established a new cut score on an intelligence test, that critical score used to inform decisions about a student's possible placement in a class for the mentally retarded. The *Guadalupe* stipulation and order noted the following permanent regulation:

> It is recommended that no child be placed in a special education class for the educable mentally handicapped if (a) he/she scores *higher than two standard deviations below the norm* [italics added] on an approved verbal intelligence test in the primary language of the home; or (b) he/she scores *higher than two standard deviations below the norm* [italics added] on an approved nonverbal intelligence test or on the nonverbal portion of an approved intelligence test which includes both verbal and nonverbal portions given in the primary language of the home. Intelligence tests shall not be either the exclusive or the primary screening device in considering a child for placement in classes for the handicapped.[90]

The criterion of two standard deviations (30 IQ points) below the mean (100) on an intelligence test significantly reduced the probability of EMR diagnosis for post-*Guadalupe* intellectual assessments of students. The demarcation line for defining intellectual subnormality, or mental retardation, varied considerably during the early 1970s in the United States (Mercer, 1973). Depending on local usage, an IQ cut score of 85, 75, or 70 served as the criterion. Based on the normal distribution of IQ scores, scoring below a cut score of 85, 75, or 70 would likely lead to a diagnosis of mental retardation for 16%, 9%, or 2%, respectively, of the student population.

Guadalupe also went beyond *Diana* and *Covarrubias* by requiring the assessment of "adaptive behavior." Although *Diana* hinted at the measurement of adaptive behavior (see previous discussion of the *Diana* stipulation and order, point 7 covering "multiple information collection"), the stipulation and order in *Guadalupe* specifically referred to adaptive behavior. Note the following:

> No children shall be considered for placement in classes for handicapped children unless an examination of developmental history, cultural background, and school achievement substantiates other findings of educational handicap. *This examination shall include estimates of adaptive behavior* [italics added]. Such examination of adaptive behavior shall include, but not be limited to, a visit, with the consent of the parent or guardian, to the child's home by an appropriate professional adviser who may be a physician, psychologist, professional social worker or school nurse, and interviews of members of the child's family at their home. If the language spoken in the home is other than English, such interviews shall be conducted in the language of the home.[91]

The requirement of the assessment of adaptive behavior stemming from *Guadalupe* led to a major advancement in special education. Although special education scholars had conceived of the notion of adaptive behavior (e.g., self-help skills; personal independence) prior to the 1970s (see Doll, 1941; Heber, 1961), no one had truly honed its measurement (Oakland & Goldwater, 1979), nor routinely assessed it (Goldstein et al., 1975). The American Association on Mental Deficiency (AAMD) provided a slightly revised definition of mental retardation in 1973 in the sixth revision of the *Manual on Terminology and Classification in Mental*

Retardation: "Mental Retardation refers to *significantly subaverage general intellectual functioning existing concurrently with deficits in adaptive behavior* [italics added] manifested during the developmental period" (Grossman, 1973, p. 5). The operationalization of "significantly subaverage general intellectual functioning" meant performance of two or more standard deviations below the normative mean on a standardized test of intelligence (e.g., the WISC). Finally, although the AAMD retained the dual requirement of measuring intelligence and adaptive behavior from previous manuals, in the 1973 *Manual* there appeared to be a greater emphasis on the two-prong requirement. In closing, an interesting question to ask is, Did *Guadalupe*'s stipulation and order requiring (a) the use of a two standard deviation cut score (on an intelligence test) for identifying the mentally retarded and (b) the measurement of adaptive behavior have any direct influence on the 1973 AAMD *Manual*'s operationalization of subaverage intellectual functioning and the underscoring of the importance of measuring adaptive behavior? No direct evidence exists in the *Manual* to address this question. It does appear, however, that the writers of the *Manual* did make some statements suggesting that the litigious climate of the time influenced their writing. Note the following:

> All psychological tests measure samples of behavior, and behavior is influenced by the culture in which an individual resides. Deficits that emerge in test performance are often reflected in school work, job performance and other major life functions. To impugn tests because of their presumed cultural bias is to conceal the effects of cultural disadvantage, impede remedial action and solution of social problems. This alleged limitation of intelligence tests could in fact be its major value in assessing a child's performance in his *own* culture. This application of tests *across* cultures, however, unless properly standardized, is likely to lead to serious errors in individual diagnosis and the rates of mental retardation. (Grossman, 1973, p. x)

Influence of Mexican American et al. Special Education Litigation on Federal Legislation and Professional Practices

Diana, Covarrubias, and *Guadalupe*—all settled by consent decree—made their mark in shaping nondiscriminatory assessment guidelines. This influence particularly manifested in federal legislation requirements and in works describing professional standards.

Federal legislation. In 1975, Congress passed, and President Gerald Ford signed into law on November 29, 1975, Public Law (P.L.) 94-142, the Education for All Handicapped Children Act (*Federal Register*, August 23, 1977).[92] Many scholars consider P.L. 94-142 to be one of the most significant pieces of legislation regarding children and youths ever passed by Congress. Rueda (1991), for example, describes P.L. 94-142 as "the equivalent of a civil rights law for handicapped children" (p. 254). Morse (2000) comments that P.L. 94-142 is one of the most significant developments in the history of special education. Indeed, P.L. 94-142 is an extremely important contribution to the field of special education. Yet it should be emphasized that this act came about via a culmination of standards "laid down since 1971 by courts, legislatures, and other public bodies throughout the country" (Zettel & Ballard, 1982, p. 11).

The requirement of P.L. 94-142 that is most germane to our discussion is the section commonly referred to as the "nonbiased assessment" requirement (Reschly, 1979, p. 228). This mandate, specifically located in the congressional regulations regarding Protection and Education Procedures (PEP) of P.L. 94-142, reads as follows: "Testing and evaluation materials and procedures used for the purposes of evaluation and placement of handicapped children must be selected and administered *so as not to be racially or culturally discriminatory* [italics added]" (42 F.R. 42496, §121a.530,b). Of particular import to the discussion here is that a number of specific features of PEP (see §121a.530–121a.553) quote nearly verbatim the principles resultant from the *Diana, Covarrubias,* and *Guadalupe* cases, as well as from some of the right-to-education cases (see note 8, this chapter, for a comment on these latter cases). Reschly (1979) paraphrased these P.L. 94-142 PEP features, as follows:

1. Procedural safeguards which provide for informed consent and due process are required.
2. The assessment must be conducted in child's native language if at all possible.
3. Tests and other evaluation devices are validated for the specific purpose for which they are used, and administered by trained personnel.
4. Classification and placement decisions are *not* based on a single source of information (such as IQ) and areas of specific educational need are identified in the evaluation process.

5. Inferences about aptitude or achievement are not made from evaluation procedures which reflect the child's impaired sensory, manual, or speaking skills.
6. Assessment must be conducted in broad variety or areas and placement procedures shall draw upon information from aptitude and achievement tests, teacher recommendations, physical conditions, social or cultural background, and adaptive behavior. Further, information from the above sources must be documented and carefully considered.
7. Decisions are made by a multidisciplinary team with participation of parents.
8. Placement options are selected according to the principle of least restrictive alternative and an individualized educational program is developed.
9. The educational program is reviewed annually and a comprehensive reevaluation which meets the requirements stated above is conducted at least every 3 years. (p. 229)

Furthermore, in a recent volume commissioned by the eminent National Research Council (Donovan & Cross, 2002), scholars noted that the PEP regulations of P.L. 94-142 constitute the "greatest legal influences on the determination of special education need and eligibility for disability status" (p. 214).[93]

Professional standards. In addition to the judiciary and legislative bodies, professional associations have also been influential in improving assessment practices with children and youths of color (Oakland & Laosa, 1977). The Society for the Study of Social Issues, Division 9 of the American Psychological Association, offered one of the first attempts in this area in 1964 (Deutsch, Fishman, Kogan, North, & Whiteman, 1964). Although Deutsch et al. fail to suggest concrete and useful guidelines for assessing children of color, the authors do discuss several critical limitations of standardized tests germane to minorities. They are the following: Possible differences in test performance between minority-group children and the standardization group are due to problems associated with test reliability, predictive validity, and construct validity. Unfortunately, the discussion of factors that Deutsch et al. posit to explain the preceding psychometric differences in tests across "lower-class" and "middle-class" groups is based in deficit thinking, an endogenous model that blames the victim (see Pearl, 1997; Valencia, 1997b). Deutsch et al. describe low-SES minority children, compared to their middle-class counterparts (presumably children of color and White, respectively), for example, as "less verbal, . . . less motivated toward scholastic and academic achievement, less competitive in the intellectual realm, . . . less exposed to intellectually stimulating material in the home" (p. 132). Deutsch et al. do not present competing interpretations to explain intraracial differences in test performance, such as test bias, examiner bias, and opportunity to learn. Nor do the authors discuss the strengths of low-SES minority children (see, e.g., Swadener & Lubeck, 1995).

The best-known document that lays down standards for the promotion of sound and ethical use of tests and provision of evaluating the quality of testing procedures is the *Standards for Educational and Psychological Testing* (American Educational Research Association, American Psychological Association, & National Council on Measurement in Education, 1999).[94] Although the 1999 edition of the *Standards* makes no mention that P.L. 94-142 influenced it, it is more than apparent that this 1975 Public Law had some role in shaping the guidelines.[95] Chapter 7 ("Fairness in Testing and Test Use"), chapter 8 ("The Rights and Responsibilities of Test Takers"), and chapter 9 ("Testing Individuals of Diverse Linguistic Backgrounds") particularly demonstrate the influence of P.L. 94-142 on the *Standards*.

Examples of a specific standard from each of these three chapters from the *Standards* that are intended to promote sound and ethical use of tests vis-à-vis culturally and linguistically diverse groups of individuals are the following:

Chapter 7, Standard 3:
When credible research reports that differential item functioning exists across age, gender, racial/ethnic, cultural, disability, and/or linguistic groups in the population of test takers in the content domain measured by the test, test developers should conduct appropriate studies when feasible. Such research should seek to detect and eliminate aspects of test design, content, and format that might bias test scores for particular groups. (p. 81)

Chapter 8, Standard 4:
Informed consent should be obtained from test takers, or their legal representatives when appropriate, before testing is done except (a) when testing without consent is mandated by law or governmental regulation, (b) when testing is conducted as a regular part of school activities, or (c) when consent is clearly implied. (p. 87)

Chapter 9, Standard 3:

When testing an examinee proficient in two or more languages for which the test is available, the examinee's relative language proficiencies should be determined. The test generally should be administered in the test taker's most proficient language, unless proficiency in the less proficient language is part of the assessment. (p. 98)

In sum, the 1999 *Standards* provides, in part, some valuable guidelines designed to promote nondiscriminatory assessment. Given that *Diana, Covarrubias,* and *Guadalupe* influenced P.L. 94-142, which in turn influenced the *Standards*, these three cases, in an indirect manner, shaped the *Standards*.

Conclusion

The allegation that school officials falsely identified and classified students of color as EMR, resulting in overrepresentation in this special education category, ignited the legal struggles in *Diana, Covarrubias,* and *Guadalupe*—as well as the African American–initiated *Larry P.* case (see note 52, this chapter). Notwithstanding the legal victories, legislative requirements, and advocacy of professional organizations, overrepresentation in the EMR category remains racialized, and the disproportionality is particularly acute for African American students.

As discussed earlier, thousands of students in EMR classes (White and children of color alike) underwent decertification and were placed in regular classes following the outcome of *Diana* (see Table 3.5). Yet Mexican American/Latino and African American K–12 students in California continued to be overrepresented in the EMR category over the years. In the 2002–2003 school year, Mexican American/Latino students were overrepresented by 6.6%, and African American students were overrepresented by 42.7%. White students showed the typical pattern of underrepresentation (in this instance, 6.6%) (U.S. Department of Education, Office for Civil Rights, 2004).

For years, a number of scholars have discussed the data in regards to the nagging issue of the EMR overrepresentation of students of color (e.g., Artiles & Trent, 1994; Brady, Manni, & Winikur, 1983; Donovan & Cross, 2002; Finn, 1982; Meier, Stewart, & England, 1989; Patrick & Reschly, 1982; Valencia & Suzuki, 2001; Wright & Santa Cruz, 1983). Of these publications, Artiles and Trent provide an especially insightful analysis of the factors most likely contributing to the overrepresentation of students of color, particularly African Americans, in the EMR category. Artiles and Trent identify the core of the issue via a multivariate systemic analysis. The authors suggest that the following factors contribute to the overrepresentation problem: (a) contradictory legal outcomes before and after the passage of P.L. 94-142; (b) unresolved debate over the construct of intelligence and the measurement of mental retardation (particularly an overreliance on IQ and the deemphasis of adaptive behavior); (c) faulty referrals and assessment procedures (i.e., overreliance on the "medical model," a form of deficit thinking); (d) fallacy of the cultural diversity–disability analogy (i.e., the tendency of testing personnel to equate culturally diverse students with disabilities).

Indeed, the problem of overrepresentation in EMR classes of students of color remains a concern today. Awareness of this lingering issue deserves attention (see Artiles & Trent, 1994, for a comprehensive discussion of suggestions to solve the problem). Furthermore, we need to be aware that due to the collaborative legal struggles of Mexican American, African American, and Yaqui children and their parents, there are regulatory requirements (P.L. 94-142 PEP features) and professional standards (the *Standards for Educational and Psychological Testing*) that provide guidelines for nondiscriminatory assessment. CRT informs us that victimized groups of diverse backgrounds, who collectively work together toward a common goal (here, nondiscriminatory assessment), can form a strong and formidable union. Finally, the struggle for justice by the *Diana* children and parents (primarily farm workers), who initiated a sea change in special education, needs to be acknowledged. Morse (2000) identifies this oft-cited landmark case as one of "Ten Events That Shaped Special Education's Century of Dramatic Change."

4

Bilingual Education

The United States of America has been and continues to be a polyglot nation. Even before the arrival of European explorers, the indigenous people spoke more than five hundred languages in the geographic area presently known as North America (Lawerence, 1978). During the American Colonial period, linguistic diversity flourished, as seen in the many languages spoken (e.g., English, French, German, Finnish, Swedish, Polish, and Dutch; see Castellanos, 1985). Being bi- or multilingual during this period had clear advantages:

> Because of the many nationalities represented in Anglo America, as well as the many Indian nations that existed here, knowledge of two or more languages became a decided advantage for trading, scouting, teaching, and spreading the gospel, as well as for diplomacy. (Castellanos, 1985, p. 4)

Based on the 2000 U.S. Census, the population five years old and over spoke English and numerous different languages at home (U.S. Department of Commerce, Bureau of the Census, 2000a). These non-English languages, in quantitatively descending order, cluster in four categories: (a) Spanish or Spanish Creole; (b) other Indo-European languages (e.g., French [including Patois and Cajun], Italian, German, Yiddish, Russian, Hindi, Urdu); (c) Asian and Pacific Island languages (e.g., Chinese, Japanese, Korean, Laotian, Vietnamese, Tagalog); (d) other languages (e.g., Navajo [and other Native North American languages], Hungarian, Arabic, Hebrew, African languages).

Unbeknownst to many, bilingual education in the United States has a long history. Under an 1828 treaty, the U.S. government recognized the language rights of the Cherokee Nation (Leibowitz, 1980). In part, Article V of the treaty read,

> It is further agreed by the U.S. to pay $1,000 . . . towards the purchase of
> a Printing Press and Types to aid towards the Cherokees in the progress
> of education, and to benefit and enlighten them as people, *in their own*
> *language* [italics added]. (Quoted in Leibowitz, 1980, p. 57)

Following the treaty, however, President Andrew Jackson began a policy
in the 1830s of forced removal of the Cherokees from the eastern United
States (Crawford, 1995). The Cherokees, in turn, used the power of the
printing press to resist the removal, and the State of Georgia retaliated by
confiscating and destroying the press. During the forced relocation of the
Cherokees to Oklahoma, more than one-third of the tribe died during the
infamous "Trail of Tears" (Crawford, 1995). After settlement,

> The Cherokees established and operated an educational system of 21
> schools and two academies, which enrolled eleven hundred pupils, and
> produced a population ninety percent literate in its native language.[1]
> They used bilingual materials to such an extent that by 1852 Oklahoma
> Cherokees had a higher English literacy level than the White populations
> of either Texas or Arkansas. (Castellanos, 1985, p. 17)

Early school laws of the 1800s made no mention of the language of
instruction, yet in later years some states allowed bilingual instruction:
Territory of New Mexico (Arizona and New Mexico, 1850), Illinois (1857),
Iowa (1861), Kentucky and Minnesota (1867), Oregon (1872), and Colorado (1887) (Castellanos, 1985). During the early history of bilingual education, German Americans, in particular, vigorously founded schools in
which students were instructed in German, or bilingually in German and
English (Castellanos, 1985). Escamilla (1980) has provided an insightful
analysis of how the German American community in St. Louis, Missouri,
struggled, in the face of opposition, to develop successful German-English
public bilingual schools from 1870 to 1917.

As discussed later in this chapter, contemporary bilingual education
came about via a number of contextual forces in the 1960s, federal legislation over time, and *litigation*. The coverage here focuses on eight bilingual
education lawsuits filed by Mexican Americans. The chapter is organized
around the following sections: (a) the importance of the Spanish language
and bilingual education for Mexican Americans; (b) catalysts for the resurgence of bilingual education; (c) Mexican American–initiated bilingual education litigation.

The Importance of the Spanish Language and Bilingual Education for Mexican Americans

February 2, 1998, marked the sesquicentennial of the signing of the final draft of the Treaty of Guadalupe Hidalgo, the treaty that brought an end to the Mexican American War (1846–1848) and the annexation, by conquest, of over 525,000 square miles of territory by the United States (this annexation included present-day Arizona, California, western Colorado, Nevada, New Mexico, Texas, and Utah).[2] As noted by many scholars, the Treaty of Guadalupe Hidalgo signaled the beginning of persistent discrimination and oppression of Mexican-origin people (e.g., Acuña, 2007; Griswold del Castillo, 1990; Menchaca, 2001; Perea, 2003; Rendón, 1971). In the field of Mexican American Studies, 1848 has become a major point of demarcation in that 160 years ago, Mexicans living in the United States became a conquered people. Although Articles VIII and IX of the treaty respected and guaranteed the civil and property rights of Mexicans who elected to remain in the United States, such provisions proved illusory and were unfulfilled (Griswold del Castillo, 1990). To many Mexican Americans, the Treaty of Guadalupe Hidalgo is but another broken agreement, analogous to the U.S. government's violation of treaties it entered into with various American Indian tribes.

In the Treaty of Guadalupe Hidalgo, the language rights of Mexicans appear not to be explicitly mentioned, but rather the framers implied them. Although Articles VIII and IX of the treaty (see Appendix 2 in Griswold del Castillo, 1990, for the full text of the ratified treaty) do not clearly allude to language rights, it appears that the drafters assumed language rights under the "free enjoyment of their [Mexicans'] liberty" phrase of Article IX. This interpretation concurs with Crawford (1995) who comments, "While not mentioned explicitly, a guarantee of certain language rights was strongly implied" (p. 32). In any event, the tacit nature of mentioning Mexicans' language rights has led some scholars to express the treaty's foundational import in laying down the language rights and other rights of Mexicans. For example, Rendón (1971) notes, "The Treaty of Guadalupe Hidalgo is the most important document concerning Mexican Americans that exists. From it stem specific guarantees affecting our civil rights, *language* [italics added], culture, and religion" (p. 81).

Although the language rights of Mexicans stemmed from the Treaty of Guadalupe Hidalgo, such guarantees were short-lived. Within years of the treaty's ratification, the victors of the Mexican American War suppressed

Spanish, and the primacy of English emerged. Regarding language usage in the schools, San Miguel and Valencia (1998) note,

> The subtraction of Spanish from the schools occurred in two phases. In the first phase, mostly during the 1850s, Spanish was usually only limited to a medium of instruction in the schools. Both Texas and California, for instance, enacted legislation in this decade mandating the use of English in the schools and restricting the use of Spanish.[3] Anglo officials in New Mexico tried to enact an English-only law for the public schools during the 1850s, but were unsuccessful because of the large and politically strong Mexican American population.[4] During the second phase, from 1870 to the early 1890s, Spanish was prohibited in the public schools. In 1870, for instance, Texas and California passed English-language laws prohibiting its use.[5] A similar English-only law was passed in New Mexico in 1891.[6] Anglos' increased anxieties over the continued growth of minority groups and their increased impact on U.S. religion, culture, politics, and social life was the impetus for the passage of these laws (Calvert & De León, 1990; Hendrick, 1977, 1980; Macías, 1984). The passage of these English-language laws did not immediately remove Spanish from the schools, but it laid the legal framework for its successful removal over the next several decades. (p. 362)

Scholars of bilingual education frequently divide this field's history into two periods: pre–World War I and post-1960 (e.g., see August & García, 1988; Hakuta, 1986). During the interim of these two eras—from approximately the early 1920s to the late 1960s—Mexican American and other language minority students experienced widespread linguistic neglect and repressive language policies in the schools. Historically, school officials forced Mexican American Spanish-speaking students to face the ubiquitous situation of "sink or swim": learn English to survive; if you do not learn the language, school failure is imminent. Educators perceived Mexican American students who entered school as monolingual Spanish speakers as "problems" to be fixed. This deficit thinking orientation of educators affected a substantial proportion of the Mexican American student population. For example, in his 1930 book, *The Education of Mexican and Spanish-Speaking Children in Texas*, Herschel T. Manuel estimated that

> Probably 90 percent of the Mexican children who are enrolled for the first time in the schools cannot understand and speak the English language.

Language instruction is, therefore, one of the major aspects of the "Mexican problem." In teaching English to beginners the prevailing method employs English almost exclusively. (p. 150)

Exclusion of the Spanish language in Southwestern schools persisted well into the 1960s. Not only did the schools exclude Spanish from the curriculum as a means of instruction, some officials in the five Southwestern states (Arizona, California, Colorado, New Mexico, and Texas) institutionalized "No Spanish" rules regarding conversational use of Spanish between students in classes and schoolgrounds.[7] Based on a 1969 investigation conducted by the U.S. Commission on Civil Rights, titled the Mexican American Education Study (MAES), 41% and 66% of all Texas elementary schools surveyed discouraged the use of Spanish on schoolgrounds and in classrooms, respectively (U.S. Commission on Civil Rights, 1972b).[8]

Violations of the "No Spanish" rule often resulted in punishment of the transgressors. The MAES report of 1972 contains excerpts from essays written by seventh-grade Mexican American students in Texas in 1964. The students' middle school teachers asked them to recall their elementary school experiences regarding their teachers' attitudes toward speaking Spanish in school. Examples of these recollections were,

- *If we speak Spanish we had to pay 5¢ to the teacher or we had to stay after school. . . .*
- *In the first through fourth grade, if the teacher caught us talking Spanish we would have to stand on the "black square" for an hour or so. . . .*
- *When I was in elementary they had a rule not to speak Spanish but we all did. If you got caught speaking Spanish you were to write three pages saying, "I must not speak Spanish in school." . . .*
- *In the sixth grade, they kept a record of which if we spoke Spanish they would take it down and charge us a penny for every Spanish word. If we spoke more than one thousand words our parents would have to come to school and talk with the principal. . . .*
- *If you'd been caught speaking Spanish you would be sent to the principal's office or given extra assignments to do as homework or probably made to stand by the wall during recess and after school. . . .* (U.S. Commission on Civil Rights, 1972b, pp. 18–19)

Another form of punishment for violating the "No Spanish" rule resulted in "Spanish detention" classes. For example, as late as 1966, teachers in

```
┌─────────────────────────────────────────────────────────────┐
│            VIOLATION SLIP — SPANISH DETENTION                 │
│                                                               │
│  _____ was speaking                │
│                                                               │
│  (Student's name and classification)                          │
│                                                               │
│  Spanish during school hours. This pupil must report to Spanish │
│                                                               │
│  Detention in the Cafeteria on the assigned day. (The teacher │
│                                                               │
│  reporting should place the date on this slip.)               │
│                                                               │
│                                                               │
│                                                               │
│  _____   _____      │
│                                                               │
│  (Dates to report)                   (Teacher reporting)      │
│                                                               │
│                                                               │
│  Return this slip to Mr. _____        │
│                                                               │
│  or Mr. _____before 3:30 p.m.               │
│                                                               │
│                                                               │
│  9/66                                                         │
└─────────────────────────────────────────────────────────────┘
```

Figure 4.1. Reproduction of Violation Slip Used to Place
Child in Spanish Detention Class: Texas, 1968. *Source:*
U.S. Commission on Civil Rights (1972b, p. 19).

a highly segregated school in El Paso, Texas, ordered students who were
caught speaking Spanish during school hours to report to a Spanish detention class for an hour after school. Figure 4.1 is a reproduction of the
Spanish detention slip.

In conclusion, following the Treaty of Guadalupe Hidalgo and into
the 1960s, Mexican American students in public schools throughout the
Southwest commonly endured Americanization programs, severe restriction on the use of Spanish as a curricular vehicle, and the exclusion
of Mexican culture as an area of curricular study (González, 1990; San
Miguel & Valencia, 1998).[9] School officials intended these policies to ensure the hegemony of the English language and Anglo culture. Notwithstanding these oppressive policies, the implementation of bilingual education as an accepted and viable model of instruction for Mexican American and other language minority students resurfaced in the 1960s.

Catalysts for the Resurgence of Bilingual Education

Scholars have identified the 1960s as a highly significant period in the history of bilingual education. In his volume *Contested Policy: The Rise and Fall of Federal Bilingual Education in the United States, 1960–2001*, historian Guadalupe San Miguel (2004) discusses a number of contextual forces that helped break the ground for passage of the Bilingual Education Act of 1968.[10] Among the most important factors included (a) research findings on bilingualism, (b) the Civil Rights Movement, (c) federal social legislation, and (d) the emerging Chicano(a) Movement. To these, I would add the importance of the Coral Way bilingual education experience in Dade County, Florida. This section briefly discusses these five contextual forces, plus an important report by the National Education Association (1966) that helped to set off a chain of events that led to the enactment of the Bilingual Education Act.

Research findings on bilingualism. Prior to the 1960s, many researchers and educators held a common misconception that bilingualism had negative consequences on cognitive development. The literature on this topic can be traced back to the turn of the century, when social concerns arose in the United States about the intellectual abilities of the new immigrants who were bilingual or were developing bilingually (Hakuta, 1986, 1990).[11] "The legacy of this early research is the view that bilingualism causes cognitive retardation" (Hakuta, 1990, p. 49).[12]

In the early 1960s, research findings began to emerge that challenged the myth of bilingualism. Elizabeth Peal and Wallace Lambert (1962) of McGill University in Montreal conducted the most cited study of this period.[13] In their investigation, Peal and Lambert compared the intellectual abilities of "true," or balanced, ten-year-old bilingual children (French and English speaking) with their monolingual (French-speaking) peers (both groups were of comparable, middle-class SES backgrounds). The results showed higher intellectual performance among the bilingual children. Researchers have replicated such findings in over thirty investigations in different cultural settings (Hakuta, 1986, 1987), and such results showing the cognitive superiority of bilinguals over monolinguals continue to be found, for the most part (see Bialystok, 2001, for an excellent review of literature on the relation between bilingualism and cognitive development).

Civil Rights Movement. With the emergence of the Black-inspired Civil Rights Movement in the late 1950s and its peaking in the early 1960s, discrimination in all walks of life—e.g., housing, employment, health care, government, and education—became focal points of national concern.[14] Soon after, other activists of color and White sympathizers joined the African American struggle for equality. Among these supporters were language scholars, who along with other civil rights activists, asserted that discrimination goes deeper than race (San Miguel, 2004). National origin, gender, and religion also had importance.[15]

Given that the rubric of national origin subsumes language and culture, discrimination in this area took on particular significance for Mexican Americans and other language minority groups. During the Civil Rights Movement of the 1960s, scholars and activists began to agitate that the federal government had a responsibility to address all forms of discrimination, including inequitable treatment of language and culture in public K–12 education (San Miguel, 2004). Within the context of CRT, a focus emerged in the 1960s in which activists sought to investigate how racism intersects with other manifestations of oppression, particularly language and cultural oppression.

Social legislation. The Civil Rights Movement prompted a groundswell of enacted social legislation. These new laws "produced two avenues to bilingual education" (Malakoff & Hakuta, 1990, p. 31). First, Title VI (42 U.S.C. §2000d) of the 1964 Civil Rights Act (P.L. 88-352)[16] "ultimately provided the enforcement mechanism through which the courts could order that limited-English-proficient (LEP) students be served" (Malakoff & Hakuta, 1990, p. 31).[17]

The second pathway to bilingual education included President Lyndon B. Johnson's "War on Poverty," in which activists believed that fighting poverty served as a key vehicle in improving the low academic achievement of low-SES students of color (see, e.g., Castellanos, 1985; Malakoff & Hakuta, 1990; San Miguel, 2004). Supporters viewed the Economic Opportunity Act (EOA) of 1964 (P.L. 88-452) as the centerpiece of the War on Poverty. The EOA provided funding for a number of programs to combat poverty, including, for example, Volunteers in Service to America (VISTA), the Job Corps, Work Study, Legal Services, and Head Start. The Elementary and Secondary Education Act (ESEA) of 1965 (P.L. 89-10) surfaced as the other major federal legislation. Under Title I (20 U.S.C. §241a) of ESEA, funding became available for compensatory education for children of poor families. As discussed later, the 1965 ESEA was amended in 1968 as Title VII, or more widely known as the first Bilingual Education Act.

Chicano(a) Movement. The emerging Chicano(a) Movement of the mid-1960s also became a factor in advocating for bilingual education (San Miguel, 2004; also, see I.M. García, 1989, 1997; Navarro, 1995). This powerful social movement, initiated by many Mexican American individuals and organizations, emphasized ethnic solidarity, political and social change, and equality. Ignacio M. García (1997), author of *Chicanismo: The Forging of a Militant Ethos among Mexican Americans* (a book synthesizing the various phases of the Chicano[a] Movement), describes this social movement as follows:

> This social activism came to be known as the Chicano Movement, or Movimiento—the most traumatic and profound social movement ever to occur among Mexicans on the U.S. side of the Rio Grande. This movement caused a fundamental shift in the way Mexican Americans saw themselves, practiced their politics, and accommodated to American society.[18] (p. 3)

Student organizations within the Chicano(a) Movement provided particularly strong support for bilingual education. A case in point was the Mexican American Youth Organization (MAYO), the avant-garde of the Chicano(a) Movement in Texas, established in 1967 (Navarro, 1995). Given the long-standing and deplorable schooling conditions faced by Mexican Americans in Texas, MAYO struggled—from its inception—to improve the public educational system. With very limited success, MAYO used the political strategy of school boycotts (i.e., student walkouts of protest, sometimes referred to as "blowouts"). In Texas, MAYO helped to organize thirty-nine school boycotts between 1967 and 1970, with many student demands, including the end of the "No Spanish" rule and the implementation of bilingual/bicultural education (Navarro, 1995).

Coral Way bilingual/bicultural education experience. Many people are surprised to learn that Cubans, not Mexican Americans or Puerto Ricans, established the first bilingual education programs in the second historical period (post-1960 to the present). Following the 1959 Cuban Revolution, and the rise of Fidel Castro, thousands of fairly privileged refugees fled Cuba to Miami, Florida. Crawford (1995) describes the Cuban exiles this way:

> The early arrivals were Hispanics of European stock, light-skinned, and largely from the professional classes. Proud of their language and culture,

they brought with them education and job skills, if little ready cash. Many had taught school in Cuba, and the state of Florida helped them become recertified. Generous subsidies were available through the federal Cuban Refugee Program. (pp. 35–36)

The renaissance of bilingual education occurred in the Coral Way Elementary School in Miami (Dade County) in September 1963.[19] Architects of the initial program, funded by the Ford Foundation, structured the curriculum in grades 1–3 around a dual-language, biethnic model, in which teachers taught the Cuban children their morning lessons in Spanish and their afternoon lessons in English; for the American (English-speaking) children, teachers reversed the schedule (Crawford, 1995). Overall, the Coral Way experience proved successful, and its bilingual education approach spread to other schools in Dade County and soon attracted national attention (Castellanos, 1985). Mexican Americans in the Southwest and groups in other locations soon followed the influential Coral Way model:

Largely as a result of the Dade County experience, school districts in the Southwest began in 1964 to introduce bilingual teaching in schools with heavy concentrations of Mexican-origin pupils. Two bilingual programs were launched in Texas: (1) in the Nye School of the United Consolidated Independent School District in Webb County (outside Laredo), and (2) in the San Antonio Independent School District. In 1965 bilingual projects began in Pecos, NM, and in Edinburg, TX. In 1966, bilingual programs were established in the Harlandale Independent School District of San Antonio, in Del Rio, and in Zapata, TX; in Calexico and Marysville, CA; and in Rough Rock, AZ. The following year, bilingual programs were initiated in Las Cruces, NM and St. Croix, VI. (Castellanos, 1985, p. 73).

In addition to the five preceding contextual forces, the highly influential 1966 report by the National Education Association (NEA) also served as a key factor in the resurgence of bilingual education (Castellanos, 1985; Crawford, 1995; San Miguel, 2004). In 1965, the NEA approached a group of teachers in Tucson, Arizona—mostly Mexican American and Spanish speaking—who expressed interest in surveying and bringing attention to constructive approaches for teaching Spanish-speaking Mexican American students in the Southwest. The NEA also sought to place the spotlight on the educational plight of Mexican American students in the five

Southwestern states. In its report, *The Invisible Minority . . . Pero No Vencibles*, the NEA (1966) wrote in the foreword,

> The most acute educational problem in the Southwest is that which involves Mexican-American children. In the elementary and secondary schools of five states in that region—Arizona, California, Colorado, New Mexico and Texas—there are approximately 1.75 million children with Spanish surnames. Many of these young people experience academic failure in school. At best, they have limited success. A large percentage becomes school dropouts. (p. iv)

Although the NEA report clearly intended to publicize the educational neglect of Mexican American students in the Southwest, it appears that its major agenda provided survey results based on "visits to school districts where promising and innovative [teaching] programs for Spanish-speaking children were reported to be in operation" (p. v).[20] The NEA-Tucson Survey Committee visited and observed forty-five elementary, junior high, and high schools in the five Southwestern states.[21] In its report, the NEA showcased a small number of the better bilingual education programs from the five states, underscoring that bilingual education should be viewed as a key strategy to improve the educational lot for Mexican American students.

In late October 1966, the NEA brought together, in Tucson, bilingual teachers and other educators, researchers, legislators, special interest groups, and individual activists to discuss the findings of the NEA report and to plan political strategies (San Miguel, 2004). Senator Ralph Yarborough (D-TX) and Texas State Senator Joe Bernal also attended. Crawford (1995) observes, "Politically speaking, this [conference] marked the birth of the 'bilingual movement'" (p. 41). The NEA report unequivocally stated where bilingual education could find a statutory home—under the 1965 ESEA:

> It is hoped by all associated with the Survey that this report might stimulate action in the form of programs developed to more appropriately serve Mexican-American children. The suggestion is underlined by the fact that financial help is now available to help school systems move ahead. The provisions of recent federal and state compensatory education legislation make it possible for schools to develop programs for the Spanish-speaking which previously might well have been beyond their financial

reach. For example, opportunities for developing such programs are entirely within the scope of either Title I or Title III of the *Elementary and Secondary Education Act* [italics added] of 1965 (P.L. 89-10). (pp. v–vi)

On January 17, 1967, Senator Yarborough introduced S. 428, the federal Bilingual Education Act. He introduced his bill by commenting on how after the Treaty of Guadalupe Hidalgo, the Mexican American population in the Southwest became exploited and discriminated against and endured serious economic disadvantage. Yarborough also noted, in hard-hitting words, that school officials often victimized Mexican American students via language suppression:

> The most promising area for progress is in the field of education. Here Mexican-Americans have been the victims of the cruelest form of discrimination. Little children, many of whom enter school knowing no English and speaking only Spanish are denied the use of their language. Spanish is forbidden to them, and they are required to struggle along as best they can in English, a language understood dimly by most and not at all by many.[22]

Touting the importance of becoming bilingual via bilingual education, Yarborough commented,

> We have a magnificent opportunity to do a very sensible thing—to enable naturally bilingual children to grow up speaking both good Spanish and good English, and thereby to be in a position to go forth confidently to deal with the world, rather than retreat in embarrassment from a world which speaks a language which they can understand only imperfectly.[23]

Apparently prompted by the NEA report, Yarborough proposed to amend the 1965 ESEA (P.L. 89-10). Initially, the bill only targeted Spanish-speaking students (Mexican American and Puerto Rican), due to their numerical presence and their long-standing educational plight (Castellanos, 1985). Yarborough's S. 428 recommended,

1. bilingual education programs;
2. the teaching of Spanish as the native language;
3. the teaching of English as a second language;

4. programs designed to impart to Spanish-speaking students a knowledge of and pride in their ancestral culture and language;
5. efforts to attract and retain as teachers promising individuals of Mexican American and Puerto Rican descent; and
6. efforts to establish closer cooperation between the school and home; and other activities which meet the purposes of this title.[24]

Yet fellow legislators heavily criticized Yarborough's bill, noting that the target population was limited to Spanish-speaking students. Following S. 428, legislators introduced thirty-seven bills in the U.S. House of Representatives similar to Yarborough's. Finally, Congressman James Scheuer of New York rewrote S. 428 to include *all* non-English-speaking children (Castellanos, 1985). Congress passed this version in December 1967, and President Johnson signed it in January 1968. The enacted bill emerged as Title VII–Bilingual Education Programs (P.L. 90-247) of ESEA and became known as the "Bilingual Education Act." In its "Declaration of Policy" (§702), the Bilingual Education Act of 1968 stated,

> In recognition of the special educational needs of the large numbers of children of limited English-speaking ability in the United States, Congress hereby declares it to be the policy of the United States to provide financial assistance to local educational agencies to develop and carry out new and imaginative elementary and secondary school programs designed to meet these special education needs. For the purposes of this title, "children of limited English-speaking ability" means children who come from environments where the dominant language is other than English.[25]

Notwithstanding the monumental political victory by bilingual education advocates in getting the 1968 Bilingual Education Act (BEA) passed, the law suffered from a number of debilitating features (Castellanos, 1985; San Miguel, 2004). San Miguel identifies five problems, in particular:

1. *Underfunded.* Compared to the existing poverty legislation for compensatory education programs—which had a funding authorization of $1 billion—Congress funded the BEA with a mere $85 million (about 8.5% of the funding for poverty legislation).

2. *Categorical in nature and compensatory in intent.* The BEA placed priority on non-English-speaking children of low-income families (non-English-speaking children of moderate-income background were denied

services). Also, the BEA was remedial, or compensatory, in design, viewing non-English-speaking children as "educatively disadvantaged" and their language as a "linguistic handicap." The bill's objective was transition to monolingual English classes as quickly as possible. This deficit thinking orientation did not bode well for those advocates who wanted to develop additive bilingual education programs (i.e., developing *bilingual* students).

3. *Open-endedness.* The bill did not mandate or prescribe a specific curriculum or particular bilingual instructional strategies, thus leaving the instructional area very open to interpretation by funded local educational agencies.

4. *Ambiguity.* Closely related to the above weakness, the BEA lacked a clear purpose, leading to a nonexistent definition of fundable programs, which in turn led to some serious problems in fiscal responsibility (e.g., waste of scarce funds).[26]

5. *Voluntary basis.* Given that the BEA did not require the implementation of bilingual education for its targeted populations, local educational agencies participated on a voluntary basis. Due to the lack of a mandate, only a small number of eligible school districts took advantage of the bill's funding during the early years of the BEA's implementation.[27] The voluntary nature of programmatic participation through the BEA proved to be a key factor in triggering litigation during the early period of the 1968 BEA.

Mexican American–Initiated Bilingual Education Litigation

Of the various categories of educational litigation covered in this book, the area of bilingual education presents the greatest challenge in understanding and interpreting what transpired in this complex body of cases.

TABLE 4.1
Mexican American Bilingual Education Cases

Case	Year	State
Serna v. Portales Municipal Schools	1972	NM
Morales v. Shannon	1973	TX
Keyes v. School District No. 1 of Denver	1974	CO
Otero v. Mesa County Valley School District No. 51	1975	CO
Guadalupe Organization, Inc. v. Tempe Elementary School District No. 3	1978	AZ
Castaneda v. Pickard	1981	TX
Gomez v. Illinois State Board of Education	1985	IL
Teresa P. v. Berkeley Unified School District	1989	CA

TABLE 4.2
*Percentage of Schools Offering Bilingual Education and
Percentage of Mexican American Students Enrolled:
Southwestern States, 1969*

State	Schools Offering Bilingual Education (%)	Mexican American Students Enrolled (%)
Arizona	0[a]	0[a]
California	8.5	1.7
Colorado	2.9	0.7
New Mexico	4.7	0.9
Texas	5.9	5.0
Southwest	6.5	2.7

Source: Adapted from U.S. Commission on Civil Rights (1972b, p. 22, Figure 6).

[a] Less than one-half of 1%.

This holds true for at least two reasons. First, legal claims for the right to bilingual education can be made to the courts via several avenues: statutory bases stemming from legislation, rights under state constitutions, and the Due Process and Equal Protection Clauses under the Fourteenth Amendment (Grubb, 1974).[28] The filing of claims through various legal bases, coupled with the untested waters in this new arena of bilingual education litigation, led courts to use considerable judicial discretion in making rulings. When appropriate, this legal indeterminacy will be underscored as we go through the various lawsuits. Second, in some of the cases, complexly intertwined layers of remedy exist. For example, in *Keyes v. School District No. 1 of Denver* (1974), both bilingual education and desegregation plans were at stake. In this section, eight key bilingual education lawsuits initiated by Mexican American plaintiffs, listed in Table 4.1, are briefly discussed in chronological order.[29]

Serna v. Portales Municipal Schools (1972)

In its 1969 survey, a year after the enactment of the BEA, the U.S. Commission on Civil Rights (1972b) MAES reported that only an extremely small percentage of schools in the Southwest offered bilingual education programs and only a minuscule percentage of Mexican American students were enrolled in such classes. Table 4.2 shows these data for the five Southwestern states. For the five states, as a whole, only 6.5% of the schools provided bilingual education, and educators served merely 2.7% of the Mexican American student population in these classes. In three states

(Arizona, Colorado, and New Mexico), bilingual education reached less than 1% of the Mexican American student population. In sum, educators served about one in forty Mexican American students in bilingual education classes in the Southwest, meaning that the new BEA had little effect on the total Mexican American student enrollment in the Southwest (U.S. Commission on Civil Rights, 1972b).[30]

In light of the fact that participation in the 1968 BEA was voluntary and of the paucity of bilingual education programs, it was not unexpected that Mexican Americans would initiate lawsuits for the right to have bilingual education. The 1972 *Serna* lawsuit, the *first* bilingual education lawsuit filed by Mexican Americans, originated in Portales, a small town in eastern New Mexico situated about seventeen miles from the Texas border.

Portales experienced considerable racial tension between the Mexican American and Anglo communities throughout the 1950s, 1960s, and into the 1970s. Charges of racial prejudice and discrimination and resultant inequality faced by Mexican Americans, particularly in education, partly prompted the *Serna* case (Martínez, 1979). At the time of the filing of *Serna* in 1971, Portales, a residentially and educationally segregated community, consisted of four elementary schools (Lindsey, Brown, James, and Steiner) and one junior and senior high school. Lindsey, located in the predominantly Mexican American area north of the railroad tracks, enrolled 87% Mexican Americans during the 1971–1972 school year, and the other three elementary schools—located in the predominantly Anglo neighborhoods south of the railroad tracks—had Anglo enrollments of 78% to 88%. Mexican Americans constituted 35% of the total enrollment of the four elementary schools.[31]

The plaintiffs in *Serna*, a class action lawsuit, included four minor Mexican American students and the Chicano Youth Association, an unincorporated association whose goal was to work toward the elimination of racial discrimination, particularly in the Portales schools. MALDEF attorneys served as counsel for plaintiffs. Defendants included Portales Municipal Schools, specifically members of the Board of Education, the District Superintendent, and the principals of the respective elementary, junior high, and senior high schools. Judge Edwin L. Mechem adjudicated *Serna* in the U.S. District Court for the District of New Mexico.

The plaintiffs based their complaint on violations of (a) due process and equal protection rights guaranteed by the Fourteenth Amendment and (b) statutory rights under Title VI of the Civil Rights Act of 1964, specifically §601 (42 U.S.C. §2000d).[32] Although the district asserted that it had a bilingual education program in place at Lindsey, plaintiffs charged that defendants failed to provide adequate learning opportunities to meet plaintiffs' educational and social needs.[33] Plaintiffs also claimed that the curriculum at the highly predominant Mexican American Lindsey Elementary School substantially equaled the offerings at the three predominantly Anglo, middle-class, English-speaking elementary schools. Thus, "It is the similarity of these programs which is the crux of plaintiffs' claim of inequality of educational opportunity [experienced by the Spanish-speaking children]."[34]

Defendants argued that the bilingual education programs "established at Lindsey and the increase in the number of teachers with a Spanish surname indicate its awareness of the needs of the Spanish-surnamed children and constitutes sufficient affirmative action to remedy whatever deficiencies may have existed."[35] Plaintiffs' counterargument, shaped by expert testimony at trial, asserted that based on scores from intelligence and achievement tests, the students at Lindsey—compared to the students at the other three elementary schools—performed considerably lower, notwithstanding the district's remedial effort.[36] The expert testimony on test score differences and the plaintiffs' assertion that the district made feeble remedial attempts in addressing the educational needs of the Spanish-speaking children appeared to have influenced Judge Mechem's decision. He ruled for the plaintiffs, noting,

> Coupled with the testimony of educational experts regarding the negative impact upon Spanish-surnamed children when they are placed in a school atmosphere which does not adequately reflect the educational needs of this minority, as is found to be the situation in the Portales schools, the conclusion becomes inevitable that these Spanish-surnamed children do not in fact have equal educational opportunity and that a violation of their constitutional right to equal protection exists.[37]

Judge Mechem further remarked,

> The administrators of the Portales school district are aware of these conditions, have taken some steps to alleviate the problem, and have made positive improvements. These corrections, however, are not adequate. Under these circumstances, it is incumbent upon the school district to reassess and enlarge its program directed to the specialized needs of its Spanish-surnamed students at Lindsey and also to establish and operate

in adequate manner programs at the other elementary schools where no bilingual-bicultural program now exists. The fact that the other three elementary schools have a smaller Spanish-surnamed enrollment than Lindsey does not eliminate the requirement for such programs.[38]

Judge Mechem also ordered the school district to recruit and hire more Spanish-speaking teachers and to seek more funding for bilingual education programs. The judge gave the district ninety days to submit to the court its plan for remedial action pursuant to his requirements set forth in the opinion. *Serna* is of particular importance as it represents the *first* court-ordered mandate for bilingual education in the nation.

In compliance with Judge Mechem's order of November 14, 1972, defendants submitted a bilingual education plan. The basic features were the following:

• Bilingual education shall be provided for approximately 150 students (grades 1–4) at Lindsey for about thirty minutes daily.

• Title VII bilingual education programs shall be provided for about forty preschool children.

• Nearly all bilingual education program staff shall be Spanish surnamed.

• One Spanish-surnamed aide shall be provided at the junior high school.

• At the senior high school, an ethnic studies course shall be offered.

• Bilingual education funds from the State Department of Education shall be sought to provide (a) one bilingual-bicultural teacher for each of the other three elementary schools and (b) one such teacher or aide for the junior high.[39]

Subsequently, plaintiffs filed a motion for hearing to voice their objections to defendants' bilingual education plan. Judge Mechem granted the motion, and after presenting their objections, plaintiffs introduced their own plan. The essential features were the following:

• All Lindsey students in grades 1–3 shall receive bilingual education instruction for sixty minutes daily; all students in grades 4–6 shall receive forty-five minutes per day of such instruction. Via a testing system, the time allotted for instruction shall be adjusted.

• At James, Steiner, and Brown elementary schools, all Spanish-speaking students in grades 1–6 shall receive thirty minutes daily of bilingual education instruction. A testing program (as above) shall be implemented.

The program should become available to non-Spanish-speaking children if funding increases.

- At the junior high school, English-proficiency testing shall be done to determine if bilingual education is necessary.

- An ethnic studies course (elective) shall be offered at the senior high school in the 1973–1974 school year; the course should be continued and others added in the following years.

- Minimum curricula set forth (as noted by all the above) in the district's schools is not intended to limit the development of other bilingual education programs or course offerings.

- There will be concerted efforts by the district to increase bilingual education teacher hirings and program funding.[40]

Judge Mechem, after reviewing both parties' bilingual education program proposals, entered his final judgment by adopting the plaintiffs' proposal. Defendants promptly appealed the ruling to the Tenth Circuit Court of Appeals, presenting two grounds for reversal (*Serna v. Portales Municipal Schools*, 1974):

> First, appellants suggest that appellees neither have standing nor are suitable parties under Rule 23 to maintain this suit as a class action; second, that failure to afford a program of bilingual instruction to meet appellees' needs does not deny them equal protection of the law when such needs are not the result of discriminatory actions.[41]

On the issue of standing (a person's legal right to bring forth a lawsuit) and personal stake, the Tenth Circuit disagreed on both counts. Regarding standing, the court ruled that "National origin discrimination in equal educational opportunities is the alleged basis of this lawsuit. As the complaint and supporting evidence point out, 26 percent of the Portales school population is Spanish surnamed."[42] Regarding the appellants' claim that appellees have failed to show a personal stake in the outcome of the lawsuit, the court found,

> The complaint was filed by parents of school-age children and the Chicano Youth Association. Each minor child is allegedly a student in the Portales schools or was excluded therefrom. The complaint alleges that those and all Spanish surnamed school children have been subject to discrimination by the school district. We believe appellees have satisfactorily

alleged that appellants' discriminatory actions caused them injury in fact and hence they have standing to sue.[43]

With respect to the appellants' second challenge—the failure to provide a bilingual education to meet appellees' needs is not a denial of equal protection of the law when such needs do not arise from discriminatory actions—the Tenth Circuit felt no need to rule on this. The court noted in its opinion, "In light of the recent Supreme Court decision in Lau v. Nichols [1974] . . . however, we need not decide the equal protection issue. *Lau* is a case which appellants admit is almost identical to the present one."[44] The Tenth Circuit ruled that the district court did reach the correct decision on equal protection grounds, but the judges in the former court chose to follow the Supreme Court ruling in *Lau*—that is, "appellees were deprived of their statutory rights under Title VI of the 1964 Civil Rights Act."[45] Finally, the Tenth Circuit concluded,

> Under Title VI of the Civil Rights Act of 1964 *appellees have a right to bilingual education* [italics added]. And in following the spirit of *Swann, supra*, we believe the trial court, under its inherent equitable power, can properly fashion a bilingual-bicultural program which will assure that Spanish surnamed children receive a meaningful education. . . . We believe the trial court has formulated a just, equitable and feasible plan; accordingly we will not alter it on appeal.[46]

Serna is a highly significant case in the Mexican American community's struggle for bilingual education. This case, the first Mexican American–initiated lawsuit in bilingual education, and the first court-ordered mandate for such education, laid a strong legal foundation (Title VI, §601 of the 1964 Civil Rights Act) to compel school districts that were not adequately taking steps to meet the language needs of Mexican American students to provide bilingual education. We shall see, however, that in some post-*Serna* cases, legal indeterminacy shaped decisions, and the courts greatly weakened the *Serna* ruling.

Morales v. Shannon (1973)

Mexican American plaintiffs initiated this case in Uvalde, Texas, located in South Texas seventy-nine miles west of San Antonio and about sixty-eight miles from the Mexican border. Uvalde, based on South Texas standards, is a fairly old community, and the Uvalde Independent School District has deep roots, having been established in 1907.[47] Shortly before the filing of *Morales*, Mexican American–Anglo relations in Uvalde were extremely tense, culminating in a school blowout on April 14, 1970 (Sánchez, 1992). The school board's refusal to rehire Josué García, an elementary school teacher whom officials fired apparently for his political activity to improve the educational system in Uvalde, helped to trigger the blowout. Students also brought forth other issues, including assignments to undemanding, low-level classes and counselors who subtly discouraged them to apply to college. Throughout the final two months of the 1969–1970 school year, between 30% to 40% of the Mexican American student population had participated in the boycott (Sánchez, 1992). Aside from the educational issues that arose, individuals raised claims of Anglo discrimination toward the larger Mexican American community (e.g., sexual harassment of females; refusal to be served at the local restaurants; an at-large voting system that virtually locked out Mexican Americans from political office) (Sánchez, 1992).

At the time of filing *Morales*, the school district enrolled 3,853 students; 61% were Mexican American, and Anglos and African Americans made up 38.6% and 0.4%, respectively, of the total enrollment. The school district had the following schools (with respective enrollments of Mexican American students): four elementary schools (total Mexican American enrollment, 68%)—Dalton (35%), Benson (55%), Robb (97%), and Anthon (98%)[48]—one junior high school (60%), one senior high school (51%), and the West Garden kindergarten school (88%).[49] Based on the 1970 U.S. Census, Mexican Americans constituted approximately 60% of the adult population of Uvalde.[50]

Genoveva Morales, guardian ad litem for her son Daniel, and other unnamed individuals (i.e., not listed in the district court's decision) served as the plaintiffs in *Morales*. The defendants included E.P. Shannon, principal of Robb Elementary School, and other unnamed parties. Judge John H. Wood, Jr., heard *Morales* in the U.S. District Court for the Western District of Texas (Del Rio Division).

Plaintiffs based their claims on violations of the Equal Protection and Due Process Clauses of the Fourteenth Amendment and the Civil Rights Act of 1964. The complaint rested on four charges: (a) discriminatory segregation in the elementary schools; (b) discriminatory ability groupings in the elementary, junior high, and senior high schools; (c) failure of the school district to adequately address the "English language deficiencies"[51] of the Mexican American children; (d) discriminatory practices in the hiring of faculty and administrators. Given that the school segregation charge is covered in chapter 2 of this book, and because the discriminatory ability groupings and hiring claims are not particularly germane to the discussion here, the bilingual education aspect of the complaint is the sole focus.

In his decision, Judge Wood was fully aware of the U.S. District Court ruling for plaintiffs in *Serna* (the Tenth Circuit had not yet affirmed the district court's ruling in *Serna*). Yet he did not feel obliged to follow Judge Mechem's holding. Judge Wood noted,

> There [in *Serna*] the Court held that Mexican-American students were entitled, as a matter of substantive constitutional right, to be educated in public schools utilizing a bi-lingual–bi-cultural program. The *Serna* decision is the first opinion of any Federal Court to so hold. The Court cited not one judicial authority to support such a conclusion that the Fourteenth Amendment compels such result. I do not feel constrained to follow that decision of another District Court and specifically decline to do so.[52]

Judge Wood also found that plaintiffs' witnesses did not represent the district's Mexican American students as a whole, "but rather were an organized body of dissatisfied parents and teachers who had formed as a group for the purposes of this lawsuit and other Mexican-American political and civil-rights oriented causes."[53] Although Judge Wood wrote in his memorandum order that he possessed no "benefit of educational expertise"[54] regarding bilingual education, he went on to remark that this form of instruction is highly controversial with respect to its efficacy, and as such, bilingual education deals more with "educational and/or sociological issues but not constitutional issues."[55] Finally, Judge Wood commented that plaintiffs' witnesses who testified in favor of bilingual education were not experts, and their opinions were "subjective [and] unsubstantiated."[56] In light of these statements, it is not surprising that Judge Wood denied plaintiffs relief on the issue of bilingual education. He wrote,

> Accordingly, it is the conclusion of this Court that the plaintiff's complaints with respect to the existence of English language deficiencies on the part of many of the Mexican-American students and the claimed

failure of the School District to deal with them, even if it had so failed, would not and does not amount to a denial of equal educational opportunity protected by either the Fourteenth Amendment or the Civil Rights Act of 1964.[57]

Plaintiffs appealed to the Fifth Circuit Court of Appeals (*Morales v. Shannon*, 1975). Judge Griffin Bell, who wrote the opinion for the Fifth Circuit, noted that appellees reported bilingual education development in the school district. First, school officials instituted a bilingual program in the 1973–1974 school year. Second, in January 1974 the Texas Legislature enacted a statute that required bilingual education in Texas's elementary schools. Appellees informed the Fifth Circuit that the school district implemented such a program, commencing in the first grade in the 1974–1975 school year. One grade was to be added each consecutive year through the sixth grade.[58] Appellees also noted,

- Oral language development is taught in Spanish. It is also taught in English at another time period.
- Culture is taught in Spanish with an emphasis on an English vocabulary.
- Math is taught primarily in English with reinforcement in Spanish.
- Science is taught primarily in English with reinforcement in Spanish.
- Our classes are kept small, not over 20–22 students in each class. We have an aide in each classroom, either the teacher or aide, in most cases both, is bilingual.
- Our bilingual-bicultural teachers all attended a bilingual-bicultural workshop provided by the Texas Education Agency this past summer. The workshop was conducted by the Bilingual Institute of El Paso, Texas.[59]

In light of the "favorable" bilingual education program developments in the Uvalde Independent School District, the Fifth Circuit felt that the entire bilingual education issue was now a matter reserved for educators. The court did note, however, that given the off chance that the appellees "are engaging in discriminatory practices in the program as it currently exists, we pretermit decision here and remand to the district court for further consideration there on a fresh record in the event appellants determine to pursue the question."[60] The Fifth Circuit further ruled for the appellants by citing the authority of *Lau* (414 U.S. 563) and the Equal Educational Opportunity Act of 1974 (20 U.S.C. §1703(f)), in which the failure of districts "to take *appropriate action* [italics added] to overcome language barriers" is an unlawful educational practice.[61] Specifically, this landmark section of the Equal Educational Opportunity Act states,

> No state shall deny equal educational opportunity to an individual on account of his or her race, color, sex, or national origin, by—...
> (f) the failure by an educational agency to take appropriate action to overcome language barriers that impede equal participation by its students in its instructional programs.

Morales, in the end, proved to be an important case in the larger Mexican American community's legal resolve for bilingual education. At the district court level, the cards appeared to be stacked against the plaintiffs. Having a judge (Wood) who showed little knowledge about the efficacy of bilingual education and little sympathy toward its need for Mexican American students, coupled with the lack of expert testimony by the plaintiffs, worked against the Mexican American community in Uvalde. Upon appeal to the Fifth Circuit, however, the 1974 triangulation of the Supreme Court decision in *Lau*, the passage of the Equal Educational Opportunity Act, and the enactment of the bilingual education law in Texas helped appellants to prevail.

Keyes v. School District No. 1 of Denver (1974)

This lawsuit is one of the most complex and long-standing cases in bilingual education litigation, finally being resolved after a decade. *Keyes*'s complexity stems from the intertwining of segregation and bilingual education claims. In chapter 2 of this book, the segregation aspect of the case is discussed.

At the commencement of the 1973 school year, the large School District No. 1 of Denver, Colorado—coterminous with the city and covering one hundred square miles—enrolled 46,060 students at the elementary level (54.1% Anglo, 27% Spanish surnamed, and 17.6% Black). The total enrollments at the junior high and senior high school levels were 21,018 and 20,542, respectively. Spanish-surnamed and Black student enrollments, combined, at the latter two levels were 42.5% and 35.1%, respectively, while the Anglo enrollments were 56.6% and 63.8%, respectively.[62] Considerable school segregation existed at all three school levels (see chapter 2, this volume).

Plaintiff-intervenors in *Keyes*, represented by MALDEF attorneys, included thirteen unnamed Mexican American minors. The Congress of Hispanic Educators (CHE) also filed as intervenors. In *Keyes*, a class action lawsuit, class was defined as

(a) All Chicano school children [who] . . . are attending segregated schools and who are forced to receive unequal educational opportunity including *inter alia*, the absence of Chicano teachers and bilingual-bicultural programs;

(b) All those Chicano school children [who] . . . are attending segregated schools, and who will be and have been receiving an unequal educational opportunity.

(c) All those Chicano teachers, staff, and administrators who have been the victims of defendant's discriminatory hiring, promotion, recruitment, assignment, and selection practices and whose victimization has additionally caused educational injury to Chicano students in that Chicano teachers, staff, and administrators are either nonexistent or underemployed. Additionally, the class is composed of present and future teachers, staff, and administrators who may be affected by this court's impending relief in such a manner as to detrimentally affect Chicano children within said district.[63]

Defendants included the School District No. 1 of Denver and other parties (unnamed in the various opinions). Judge William E. Doyle presided over *Keyes* in the U.S. District Court for the District of Colorado.

Plaintiff-intervenors based their claims on violations of the Fourteenth Amendment and the Civil Rights Act of 1964. The heart of plaintiffs' desired remedy for bilingual education was a plan prepared by their language-rights expert, Dr. José A. Cárdenas, a prominent educator from Texas. The plan, referred to as the "Cárdenas Plan" in the *Keyes* proceedings, stemmed from the "theory of incompatibilities" posited by Cárdenas and his wife, Dr. Blandina Cárdenas (Cárdenas & Cárdenas, 1973). Broadly stated, the Cárdenas Plan—a reform strategy to improve the typically poor academic performance of minority students—hinges on the assertion that incompatibilities or incongruities exist between the needs and characteristics of children of color and the American school's orientation toward the education of English-speaking middle-class White children. The Cárdenas Plan groups

> the incompatibilities experienced by minority children into the broad categories of poverty, language, culture, mobility, and perceptions. The thrust of the plan is that the educational system should be altered where necessary to eliminate these incompatibilities, rather than requiring the minority child to reject his own cultural, linguistic, economic and other characteristics in order to adapt to an educational program imposed upon him.[64]

The Cárdenas Plan, comprehensive and systemic in scope, calls for bilingual and multicultural education (particularly at the elementary level) and extends to "matters of educational philosophy, governance, instructional scope and sequence, curriculum, student evaluation, staffing, noninstructional services and community involvement."[65]

In his memorandum opinion and order in *Keyes* (1974), Judge Doyle noted that the Cárdenas Plan, though not perfect, was "well balanced, most equitable and most feasible."[66] Thus, he ordered that the plan, or one similar to it, be adopted and that the parties submit a formal decree, and his formal entry of judgment would await presentation of the decree.[67]

Defendants appealed to the Tenth Circuit (*Keyes*, 1975), resting their claims on two basic issues. First, the district court's order left five predominantly Mexican American elementary schools highly segregated, with enrollments of students of color ranging from 77% to 88%. The district court justified such continued segregation because of the implementation or continuation of bilingual education programs.[68] The Tenth Circuit disagreed, citing the U.S. Supreme Court decision in *Lau v. Nichols* (1974) and its own decision in *Serna v. Portales Municipal Schools* (1974). The Tenth Circuit opinion noted, "*Bilingual education is not a substitute for desegregation* [italics added]. Although bilingual instruction may be required to prevent the isolation of minority students in a predominantly Anglo school system, . . . such instruction must be subordinate to a plan of school segregation."[69]

Second, appellants claimed that certain aspects of Judge Doyle's district court ruling "transgressed the limits of the court's power to fashion a desegregated remedy for the Denver school system."[70] On this issue of breach, the Tenth Circuit fully agreed, ruling that the district court's adoption of the Cárdenas Plan "oversteps the limits of its remedial powers."[71] More specifically, the Tenth Circuit stated that the Cárdenas Plan went well beyond helping Mexican American students reach English proficiency in order to learn other subjects. Instead of just removing barriers to effectively desegregate the school district, "the court's order would impose upon school authorities a pervasive and detailed system for the education of minority children. We believe this goes too far."[72]

In sum, the Tenth Circuit found that neither *Lau* nor its own holdings in *Serna* contradicted its position to refuse to affirm the district court's ruling regarding the adoption of the Cárdenas Plan. The district court's clear implication of arguments that students of color are entitled under the Fourteenth Amendment "to an educational experience tailored to their unique cultural and developmental needs"[73] did not stand a constitutional test. The Tenth Circuit also noted that in the 1973–1974 school year, the school district was providing special help to a substantial percentage (73%) of those Mexican American LEP students who needed English-language development.[74] As such, the court did not find any violation of §601 of the 1964 Civil Rights Act. The court vacated that part of the district court's order to adopt the Cárdenas Plan. The court, however, did remand the case for hearings to see if school officials were providing Mexican American students a curriculum sufficient to ensure that they acquired proficiency in English.[75]

From 1975—when the Tenth Circuit remanded *Keyes* for a determination of language relief—to 1980, the school district did very little to negotiate and compromise with plaintiffs regarding the issues relating to the LEP students. Thus, in 1980 CHE filed a supplemental complaint in intervention. Plaintiffs based their language claims on the Fourteenth Amendment, Title VI (§601) of the Civil Rights Act of 1964, and an added claim under the newly passed Equal Educational Opportunity Act (EEOA) of 1974 (§1703(f)). Parties litigated *Keyes* in the U.S. District Court for the District of Colorado (*Keyes*, 1983); Judge Richard P. Matsch presided.

Plaintiff-intervenors had many claims, including, for example, (a) "bilingual teachers" are inadequately trained in bilingual education methods; (b) many of the teachers in bilingual education classrooms are monolingual English; (c) there was an emphasis on oral English skills for LEP students; (d) the identification and placement of LEP students does not occur through a formal testing process.[76] Defendant school district asserted that it was providing good-faith efforts to remove language barriers via remedial instruction.[77] In deriving his opinion, Judge Matsch applied the holdings of *Castaneda v. Pickard* (1981), recognized as the most authoritative case construing §1703(f) of the 1974 EEOA (discussed later). Judge Matsch ruled that the school district failed to take "appropriate action" to eliminate language barriers for the LEP students.[78] In his opinion of December 30, 1983, Judge Matsch applied the *Castaneda* standards and ordered sweeping changes, including, for example, (a) hiring of bilingual teachers; (b) implementation of teacher training for bilingual education instructional staff; (c) implementation of adequate standards and testing of qualifications of bilingual education instructional staff; (d) implementation of adequate testing of LEP students for purposes of identification and placement.[79] Defendants did not appeal.

Finally, Judge Matsch ordered that the plaintiff-intervenors and the defendants attend a hearing on January 20, 1984, to begin discussions on the development of remedies as ordered by the district court. Seven months later, on August 17, 1984, Judge Matsch approved the consent decree as prepared and submitted by both parties. The content of the decree consisted of five discrete areas to be addressed: (a) identification, assessment, and reclassification of LEP students; (b) standards for bilingual teachers and teachers in English as a Second Language (ESL) programs; (c) elementary school programming, with a particular focus on elementary bilingual education for LEP students; (d) secondary school programming, with bilingual education in the "core" curriculum; (e) instructional needs of the Indo-Chinese LEP students (Roos, 1986).

Otero v. Mesa County Valley School District No. 51 (1975)

Mexican American plaintiffs brought forth this case in Mesa County, a far-western region in Colorado. The Mesa County Valley School District No. 51 is, geographically, one of the largest school districts in the state, covering 65% of Mesa County and 2,150 square miles.[80] At the time of the trial, nineteen elementary, six junior high, and three senior high schools constituted the school district. Of the total district enrollment, 90% of the students were Anglo, 8% Mexican American, and 2% other. At the junior and senior high school levels, the enrollments of students of color fairly reflected their percentage in the district. At the elementary school level, students of color ranged from 1% to 30% in the various schools. Of the nineteen elementary schools, only two had a concentration of students of color of more than 16%,[81] meaning that segregation was not a major problem in the school district.

Plaintiffs in *Otero* (class action), represented by MALDEF and Colorado Rural Legal Services attorneys, included ten named Mexican American minors. Several of the plaintiffs had dropped out of senior high school. Defendants comprised the Mesa County Valley School District No. 51, members of the Board of Education, Superintendent, Director of Federal Programs, Director of Personnel, and all twenty-eight school principals. Judge Fred M. Winner presided over the trial in the U.S. District Court for the District of Colorado.

Plaintiffs' claims rested on violations of the Fourteenth Amendment, the Civil Rights Act of 1964, and the EEOA of 1974. Two central issues formed plaintiffs' complaint. First, they asserted that the "District's curriculum, personnel, and other programs provide an inadequate or unequal educational service which does not take into account their [Mexican American students'] linguistic or cultural differences."[82] Plaintiffs sought remedy via a bilingual education program under the systemic reform features of the Cárdenas Plan (see previous discussion of *Keyes*). Second, plaintiffs claimed that the school district practiced racial discrimination in its hiring of personnel. In light of the disproportionately low percentages of Mexican American teachers and other supporting personnel, plaintiffs sought injunctive relief requiring the district to change its hiring practices to be more racially/ethnically inclusive.

Otero proved to be a "battle of the experts." Among others, four experts for plaintiffs and three for defendants testified; Dr. José A. Cárdenas, who testified as an expert witness in *Keyes*, served as one of the plaintiffs' experts. The case, which lasted two weeks, produced a voluminous record of more than ten thousand pages of depositions, briefs, reporter's transcripts, and so on. Judge Winner noted that defendants' experts gave the "more logical, believable testimony."[83]

Plaintiffs claimed that the school district inadequately met the language needs of the LEP students, and thus a bilingual education program was necessary. Defendants, however, argued that because the number of LEP students in the school district was so small, bilingual education was unwarranted. Based on two language assessment measures—the Screening Test for Auditory Comprehension of Language (STACL; Carrow, 1973) and the Dos Amigos Verbal Language Scales (Critchlow, 1974)—an examiner tested 628 Mexican American students for language dominance. Of these students, the assessor considered only seventeen (2.7%) to be Spanish dominant, Spanish proficient, or bilingual.[84] Given this finding that less than 3% of the students had any proficiency in speaking or understanding

Spanish, Judge Winner in his memorandum opinion relied on a quotation from defendant expert witness Dr. Edgar Ray Garrett, who did the language testing: "My opinion is that the presence of Spanish is not interfering with the English scores. *The list of 54* [students] *that we identified as being quite low in all cases had English scores that were higher than their Spanish scores.*"[85] Garrett's conclusion weighed heavily on Judge Winner when forming his opinion. He wrote, "Thus, accepting the validity of the tests, as I do, there is no deficiency on the part of a significant number of Mexican-American students in English language proficiency, and the students who are deficient in English are also deficient in Spanish."[86]

Also working against the plaintiffs in *Otero* were two other problems that arose regarding the language issue. First, plaintiffs—who objected to the language assessment procedures used by the school board—did their own language assessment. José Cruz, an employee of the Colorado Civil Rights Commission, acting under the direction of plaintiffs' counsel, conducted a survey "to ascertain if there was Spanish spoken in the homes of Spanish-surnamed students."[87] Judge Winner had harsh words for the survey, noting, "The survey was strictly a do-it-yourself poll, and it was supported by neither scientific design, training nor planning, nor was it taken by trained pollsters."[88] A second problem that did not bode well for the plaintiffs with respect to the language issue had to do with testimony by one of their own expert witnesses. Dr. Rolf Kjolseth, an expert in sociolinguistics, linguistics, and language development and assessment, had two children who attended schools in the district and were taught in English. Kjolseth's trial testimony, in part, consisted of the following:

> Q. Doctor, how many languages do you speak?
> A. Four. English, which is my mother tongue, Spanish, French and German.
>   I might add, if I may, that I never learned one in school. . . .
> Q. What language do you speak at home?
> A. Spanish exclusively. . . .
> Q. Are your children monolingual in Spanish?
> A. No, no, both children are completely bilingual. It's exclusively Spanish which is spoken at home, but in almost all of the other areas of social life it's English that is spoken so they are completely bilingual.[89]

Suffice it to say, Kjolseth proved to be a poor expert witness for the plaintiffs. Note the effect of his testimony on Judge Winner's opinion:

Dr. Kjolseth's children are doing quite well in school, but if the arguments [theory of incompatibilities] of Dr. Cardenas be accepted, they [the children] shouldn't be. Dr. Kjolseth is voluntarily putting his children in the environment about which plaintiffs complain, but the Kjolseth children do well.[90]

In conclusion, Judge Winner ruled against the plaintiffs regarding bilingual education as a remedy. He argued several major points. First, in light of the Ninth Circuit and the Supreme Court decisions in *Lau* not to rule on constitutional grounds, *Otero* plaintiffs had no Fourteenth Amendment basis on which to make a claim. Thus, plaintiffs have no constitutional right to bilingual education. Second, *Lau* and *Serna* dealt with large numbers of LEP students; in *Otero*, there were few such students. Therefore, defendants did not violate the 1964 Civil Rights Act. Third, in *Lau* and *Serna*, school boards made no real progress in meeting the language needs of LEP students. In *Otero*, however, the school board was "making a real, conscientious effort to recognize, face and solve any problem which may exist as to any student."[91] Judge Winner continued, "I confess that I wonder if school personnel should not be awarded combat pay for their efforts in trying to educate in today's climate."[92]

Judge Winner, in his memorandum opinion, spent considerably less time on plaintiffs' claim of discriminatory hiring practices of teachers and other supporting personnel. After citing numerous decisions on the standing question, including a handful of Supreme Court decisions, Judge Winner ruled that plaintiffs, as children, have no standing to challenge the school district's hiring practices because they have no constitutional right to bilingual education and "they failed miserably in their efforts to bring themselves within the *Lau-Serna* decisions."[93] Furthermore, Judge Winner wrote, "The Otero plaintiffs do not say that there has been any segregation, and they are not the victims of violation of any of their constitutional rights."[94] Finally, he noted, "Plaintiffs here have failed to show any actionable wrong against them."[95]

Plaintiffs appealed to the Tenth Circuit (*Otero v. Mesa County Valley School District No. 51*, 1977). Apparently seeing the futility of appealing the district court's ruling on the language complaint, appellants decided not to appeal the trial court's judgment that refused to require the defendants to implement a bilingual education program. On the discriminatory hiring claim, however, the Tenth Circuit vacated the district court's decision, ruling that given the disproportionately low number of Mexican American teachers and other supporting personnel, "this has an adverse effect upon the educational opportunity afforded the Mexican-American pupil."[96] Thus, the children had standing. The Tenth Circuit also noted that plaintiffs, at trial, showed "injury in fact."[97] Citing its own decision in *Serna*, the Tenth Circuit therefore ruled plaintiffs had standing. Finally, the appellate court ruled that the district court's findings of fact on the discriminatory hiring claim was insufficient according to Federal Rules of Civil Procedures (Rule 52(a)):

> In our view the trial court's findings of fact relative to the discrimination issue do not fully comply with Rule 52(a). They do not cover all of the material issues raised by the discrimination charge. Nor do they reveal in sufficient detail the factual basis for the trial court's ultimate finding of no discrimination. The trial court did not specify the statistics on which it relied in concluding that the district "doesn't look good." The court made no findings as to the racial impact of the various hiring practices of the district.[98]

The Tenth Circuit remanded the judgment to the district court with directions to make new findings of fact and conclusions of law regarding the discriminatory hiring claim, and then to enter judgment based on new findings and conclusions.

In sum, *Otero* represents a good example in bilingual education litigation as to how plaintiffs could have argued their case better. First, the way the district assessed the LEP students raised concerns. In light of (a) Dr. Garrett's likely conflict of interests as the assessor of the students' language status, coupled with the psychometric concerns of the instruments he used (see note 85, this chapter), and (b) the questionable nature of the language assessment survey conducted by plaintiffs, considerably more thought should have gone into how to conduct a valid language assessment. Perhaps plaintiffs could have negotiated with defendants to hire an independent party to conduct the language assessments, using psychometrically sound individually administered instruments *plus* a professionally developed, methodologically sound home survey. Second, the small-number argument was specious. As discussed earlier, Judge Winner made a big issue in *Otero* that because the district had so few LEP students, a bilingual education program was unwarranted. He cited the *Lau-Serna* holdings that only large numbers of LEP children, with unserved language needs, provided a basis for a Title VI violation. Counsel for plaintiffs should have sought case law to challenge the small-number argument. For example, legal scholar George A. Martínez (1994) notes that two other courts (in New York) found the failure to provide bilingual education in districts with small percentages of LEP students violated Title VI. In *Rios v. Read* (1978) only 7% of the district students were Latino, and in *Cintron v. Brentwood Union Free School District* (1978) about 20% were Latino.

Guadalupe Organization, Inc. v. Tempe Elementary School District No. 3 (1978)

This case had the same plaintiff organization and defendant school district described in the special education lawsuit (*Guadalupe*, 1972) in chapter 3 of this book. The reader is referred to chapter 3 for background on the plaintiff organization and community in which the instant case was initiated.

Guadalupe originated in the barrio of Guadalupe, located about five miles from Tempe, Arizona. Plaintiffs included Guadalupe Organization, Inc., and Mexican American and Yaqui Indian elementary school children.[99] Of the 12,280 students enrolled in the school district, about 18% were Mexican American or Yaqui. In the Guadalupe Elementary School, Mexican American and Yaqui students constituted 554 (92%) of the 605 students.[100] Plaintiffs initially filed *Guadalupe* (in 1973, it appears) in the U.S. District Court for the District of Arizona. Judge Walter E. Craig, the same judge who presided over the *Guadalupe* (1972) special education lawsuit (see chapter 4, this volume), also presided over the instant case.

Plaintiffs brought suit against the school district to compel it to provide bilingual education for the LEP students. The complaint—based on violations of the Fourteenth Amendment, the Civil Rights Act of 1964, and the EEOA of 1974—alleged four discriminatory acts. They were failure to

1. provide bilingual instruction which takes into account the special educational needs of Mexican-American and Yaqui Indian students;
2. hire enough teachers of Mexican-American or Yaqui Indian descent who can adequately teach bilingual courses and effectively relate to the educational and cultural needs of the appellants;
3. structure a curriculum that even minimally takes into account appellants' particular educational needs;

4. structure a curriculum that even minimally reflects the historical contributions of people of appellants' descent to the State of Arizona and
the United States.[101]

Judge Craig dismissed plaintiffs' complaint on May 21, 1973, on the basis
of the Ninth Circuit's January 8, 1973, holding in *Lau* (in which all relief
was denied; see note 44, this chapter).[102] Plaintiffs appealed to the Ninth
Circuit, which, in turn, remanded the case back to the district court on
April 5, 1975, "for further consideration in accordance" with the Supreme
Court's reversal of the Ninth Circuit's ruling in *Lau*.[103]

Upon remand, appellees made a motion to the court for appellants to
clarify the distinction between what was sought in the instant case and
what was ordered by the Supreme Court in *Lau*. In response to interrogatories (a means of pretrial discovery in which written questions are
provided by one litigant to another) of the appellees and in argument
before the district court, appellants "admitted that they did not complain of the school district's efforts to cure existing language deficiencies
of non-English-speaking children."[104] Instead, appellants asserted that
the district denied them an education from kindergarten to grade 12 in
which English and Spanish were vehicles of instruction. Appellants also
contended that the school district failed to provide a bicultural education.
Judge Craig granted the appellees' motion for summary judgment.

Once again, appellants appealed to the Ninth Circuit Court of Appeals
(*Guadalupe*, 1978). In this deliberation, the appellate court reviewed all
three sources of appellants' complaint.

• *Fourteenth Amendment*. In part, the Ninth Circuit cited the Supreme
Court decision in *San Antonio Independent School District v. Rodriguez*
(1973), which found that education was not guaranteed by the U.S. Constitution. Therefore, the appellate court ruled that if education is not a
fundamental right, then "Differences in treatment of students in the educational process, which in themselves do not violate specific constitutional
guarantees, do not violate the Fourteenth Amendment's Equal Protection
Clause if such differences are rationally related to legitimate state interests."[105] The appellate court cited *Keyes*, *Morales*, and *Otero*, noting that
these courts ruled that the respective school districts had taken affirmative steps to rectify language problems of LEP students. Thus, the district
did not intentionally discriminate against the plaintiffs.[106]

• *Civil Rights Act of 1964*. The Ninth Circuit found that appellants fared
no better under §601 of the Civil Rights Act. Appellants' claim that the

failure to provide the LEP students with a bilingual education program "forecloses them from meaningful education and that they receive fewer benefits from the district's educational program than do English-speaking students."[107] In contrast, the appellate court ruled that the district's provision of remedial instruction in English complied with *Lau*'s requirement of providing meaningful education. Therefore, the district did not violate §601.

• *EEOA of 1974.* Here, appellants argued that the "appropriate action" requirement of §1703(f) of the EEOA must include bilingual education (see *Morales* case, this chapter, for more on the "appropriate action" aspect of the EEOA). The Ninth Circuit, however, made the point that §1703(f) was a proposed amendment from the House, with little legislative history to guide the court as to Congress's intent. Furthermore, no previous legal decisions had interpreted the scope of the "appropriate action" mandate. Finally, the Ninth Circuit held that the "appropriate action" requirement need not mandate bilingual education. The court ruled, "The interpretation of floor amendments unaccompanied by illuminating debate should adhere closely to the ordinary meaning of the amendment's language."[108]

Although plaintiffs did not prevail in *Guadalupe*, the case proved important in at least one legal aspect: How does a court interpret the "appropriate action" requirement of §1703(f) of the EEOA? This issue is addressed next in the highly significant case of *Castaneda v. Pickard,* in which a standard is developed for bilingual education, thus forcing judges to be less discretionary in their decisions.

Castaneda v. Pickard (1981)

Mexican Americans initiated *Castaneda* in 1978 in Raymondville, Texas, situated in Willacy County in the lower Rio Grande Valley, about fifty miles from the Mexican border. In 1978, Willacy County—which contained a population of 77% Mexican American and nearly 23% Anglo—ranked 248th out of 254 Texas counties in average family income. In this agriculturally abundant region, migrant farm workers constituted about one-third of the Raymondville population.[109] At the time of *Castaneda*, the Raymondville Independent School District operated five schools—three elementary, one junior high, and one high school. Two of the elementary schools contained Mexican American enrollments of 100% and 83%; the Mexican American student bodies at the junior high and high school were 87% and 80%, respectively.[110]

Two Mexican American minors served as plaintiffs in *Castaneda*, a class action lawsuit. Texas Rural Legal Aid served as plaintiffs' counsel. Defendants included Mrs. A.M. "Billy" Pickard, President of the school district, the Board of Trustees, and unnamed others. Parties litigated *Castaneda* in June 1978 in the U.S. District Court for the Southern District of Texas (Brownsville Division). The record relied on here comes from the Fifth Circuit ruling, as the district court judge did not publish an opinion.

Plaintiffs' complaint at the district court level—which rested on violations of the Fourteenth Amendment, the Civil Rights Act of 1964, and the EEOA of 1974—alleged four claims of racial discrimination: (a) impermissible classroom segregation via ability grouping; (b) unfair hiring and promotion practices against Mexican American faculty and administrators; (c) inadequate bilingual education instruction; (d) unfair administration of the extracurricular programs with the purpose of denying Mexican American students an equal opportunity to partake in such activities.[111] In light of the focus of this chapter, the discussion here is confined to the claim that defendants failed to implement an adequate bilingual education program.

On August 17, 1978, the district court entered judgment in favor of the defendants on all points.[112] Regarding the bilingual education issue, the court found that the school district was operating a formal bilingual program for all K–3 students. In grades 4–5, the district provided only English instruction, and Spanish-speaking teacher aides available to assist LEP students. Finally, for older LEP students, the district provided assistance in the form of a learning center present at each school.[113] Plaintiffs argued that the school district's bilingual education efforts failed to comport with the requirements of the 1975 "Lau Guidelines," and thus the school district had fallen out of compliance with both Title VI of the Civil Rights Act of 1964 and §1703(f) of the EEOA of 1974. The district court disagreed and ruled against plaintiffs, finding that the Lau Guidelines lacked legal sufficiency and thus the school district did not violate Title VI. Also, the district court did not find a violation of the EEOA. This was not surprising. As discussed previously in *Guadalupe*, the Ninth Circuit held that the "appropriate action" mandate of §1703(f) had little legal authority given the virtual absence of legislative history and legal interpretation of the section's meaning.

Plaintiffs appealed to the Fifth Circuit (*Castaneda v. Pickard*, 1981), which affirmed the district court's ruling that the school district's bilingual education program did not violate Title VI. In its affirmance, the

Fifth Circuit noted that "serious doubt exists about the continuing vitality of Lau v. Nichols as a judicial interpretation of the requirements of Title VI or the Fourteenth Amendment."[114] The Fifth Circuit was referring to the *Bakke* case (*Regents of the University of California v. Bakke*, 1978), in which the Supreme Court held that a discriminatory purpose, not merely a disparate impact, must be found in order to establish a violation of the Equal Protection Clause of the Fourteenth Amendment.

Although the appellants did not prevail under Title VI, they hoped their claim that appellees had violated §1703(f) would prevail. The Fifth Circuit, however, showed some reluctance to deliberate on this claim in light of the unclear "appropriate action" aspect of §1703(f). Although the appellate court noted that "we have very little legislative history from which to glean the Congressional intent behind the EEOA's provisions,"[115] it moved to examine what "appropriate action" meant. The Fifth Circuit commented,

> Confronted, reluctantly, with this type of task in this case, we have attempted to devise a mode of analysis which will permit ourselves and the lower courts to fulfill the responsibility Congress has assigned to us without unduly substituting our educational values and theories for the educational and political decisions reserved to state or local school authorities or the expert knowledge of educators.[116]

The Fifth Circuit then proceeded to devise a set of criteria that a federal court should consider if a school district's language-remediation program is challenged under §1703(f) of the EEOA. The threefold set of responsibilities—commonly referred to as the *"Castaneda* standard"—is as follows:

- First, the court must examine carefully the evidence the record contains concerning the soundness of the educational theory or principles upon which the challenged program is based. . . . The court's responsibility, insofar as educational theory is concerned, is only to ascertain that a school system is pursuing a program informed by an educational theory recognized as sound by some experts in the field or, at least, deemed a legitimate experimental strategy.
- The court's second inquiry would be whether the programs and practices actually used by a school system are reasonably calculated to implement effectively the educational theory adopted by the school.
- Finally, a determination that a school system has adopted a sound program for alleviating the language barriers impeding the educational

progress of some of its students and made bona fide efforts to make the program work does not necessarily end the court's inquiry into the appropriateness of the system's actions. If a school's program, although premised on a legitimate educational theory and implemented through the use of adequate techniques, fails, after being employed for a period of time sufficient to give the plan a legitimate trial, to produce results indicating that the language barriers confronting students are actually being overcome, that program may, at that point, no longer constitute appropriate action as far as that school is concerned.[117]

The *Castaneda* standard can be compressed as such: (a) the school district's language-remediation program must be based on sound educational theory, recognized by experts in the field; (b) the program must be effectively implemented with the necessary practices, resources, and personnel; (c) the program must demonstrate, after a sufficient time for implementation, an effective reduction of language barriers.

The original plaintiffs in *Castaneda v. Pickard* (1981) filed suit again at the district court level, claiming that the Raymondville Independent School District continued discriminatory ability grouping, continued discriminatory hiring and promotion of Mexican American teachers and administrators, and failed to implement an adequate bilingual education program. As before, the discussion here will be limited to the language issue. And again, the appellate court's record is used, as the district court did not publish its opinion.

The district court in the second lawsuit ruled for the defendants. Subsequently, plaintiffs appealed to the Fifth Circuit (*Castaneda v. Pickard*, 1986—hereafter referred to as *Castaneda II*). Appellants argued that the school district had still failed to implement an adequate bilingual education program under §1703(f) of the EEOA. An interesting development here is that in 1981 the Texas Legislature passed the Texas Bilingual Education Act (popularly known as Senate Bill 477). Appellants in *Castaneda II* submitted that the new state law "is the appropriate standard against which to judge the RISD [bilingual] program in terms of its appropriateness for purposes of the EEOA, 20 U.S.C. §1703(f)."[118] The appellants particularly focused on their assertion that a number of the "bilingual teachers" had a very limited command of Spanish.[119] The district court found that the school district had corrected these deficiencies through in-service training and by hiring bilingual education teachers who were native speakers of Spanish. As such, the district court ruled that the school district's bilingual program "was in compliance with state law [and] and it passed muster under §1703(f)."[120] The Fifth Circuit in *Castaneda II* affirmed the judgment of the district court.

Castaneda v. Pickard (1981) is one of the most important Mexican American–initiated bilingual education lawsuits. The Fifth Circuit's interpretation of what Congress meant by the "appropriate action" notion of §1703(f) of the EEOA emerged as the *Castaneda* standard. This was certainly an advance in the litigation of bilingual education cases, as prior to the *Castaneda* standard, courts interpreted §1703(f) on a case-by-case approach, thus allowing considerable legal indeterminacy. The real test of the *Castaneda* standard's utility, however, would be to see how the courts actually used it in making their judgments. To explore this, we move to the next case.

Gomez v. Illinois State Board of Education (1985)

Mexican Americans in Onarga, Illinois (Iroquois West School District No. 10), and in Peoria, Illinois (Peoria School District No. 150), brought forth *Gomez*. Onarga lies about eighty-three miles due east from Peoria, in the north-central region of the state.

Six named Mexican American minors served as plaintiffs in *Gomez*.[121] MALDEF attorneys, who served as counsel for plaintiffs, filed the case as a class action lawsuit on behalf of Spanish-speaking children of limited English proficiency enrolled in various school districts in the state. Defendants included the Illinois State Board of Education, State Superintendent of Education Ted Sanders, and unnamed others. Judge Nicholas J. Bua presided over *Gomez* in the U.S. District Court for the Northern District of Illinois (Eastern Division).

Plaintiffs asserted that defendants violated chapter 122, §14C-3 of the Illinois Revised Statutes by not performing their duties to provide bilingual education to plaintiff children.[122] Plaintiffs also argued that the alleged breaches of state law constituted violations of their federal rights under §1703(f) of the EEOA of 1974, Title VI (§601) of the Civil Rights Act of 1964, and the Fourteenth Amendment. Regarding the state statute governing transitional bilingual education, the law requires

> school districts to identify students of limited English-speaking ability and classify them according to language, grade, age or achievement level. Any school district with 20 or more students of limited English speaking

proficiency must establish a transitional bilingual education program. The Illinois State Board of Education's responsibility under this statute is to develop certain regulations which must be adhered to by the school districts.[123]

Hence, plaintiffs asserted that the state officials neglected their duties regarding the statute requiring transitional bilingual education. Due to this neglect, plaintiffs' counsel claimed that school districts failed to assess plaintiffs' English-language proficiency and failed to provide bilingual education instruction or compensatory instruction.[124]

In *Gomez*, defendants filed a motion to dismiss on several grounds: (a) under the Eleventh Amendment to the U.S. Constitution, federal courts cannot order state officials to conform to state law; (b) states have considerable latitude to interpret §1703(f) of the EEOA given that the act does not specify the type of bilingual education program that schools should develop and implement; (c) because plaintiffs did not allege that defendants intentionally engaged in present or past de jure discrimination, plaintiffs had no legal bases under the Fourteenth Amendment or Title VI (§601) of the 1964 Civil Rights Act.[125] Judge Bua ruled for defendants on all counts and granted the motion to dismiss. He directed plaintiffs to file a new complaint, naming local school officials as defendants.

Subsequently, the *Gomez* plaintiffs appealed the district court's dismissal to the Seventh Circuit Court of Appeals (*Gomez v. Illinois State Board of Education*, 1987). They also reasserted their claims of violations of the Fourteenth Amendment, Title VI of the 1964 Civil Rights Act, and §1703(f) of the 1974 EEOA. The Seventh Circuit affirmed that the district court ruled correctly in finding that defendants did not act with discriminatory intent. Thus, the appellants' Fourteenth Amendment and Title VI claims failed.[126] Regarding the EEOA claim, however, the appellants prevailed. First, the Seventh Circuit disagreed with the appellees' assertion that the *Castaneda* standard only applied to local school districts. Citing the Fifth Circuit's ruling in *U.S. v. Texas* (1982), the Seventh Circuit noted that "the Castaneda guidelines [apply] to an entire state school system."[127] Second, the Seventh Circuit found that although the appellants had no quarrel with the school district's educational theory criterion of the *Castaneda* standard,[128] the appellees failed to meet the implementation criterion.[129] As such, the Seventh Circuit reversed the district court's dismissal of plaintiffs' EEOA claim. Yet, as we shall see in the next case, the use of the *Castaneda* standard did not always result in positive outcomes in Mexican American bilingual education lawsuits.

Teresa P. v. Berkeley Unified School District (1989)

A multiethnic group of plaintiffs initiated *Teresa P.* in Berkeley, California, located in the Bay Area, fifteen miles from San Francisco. The Berkeley Unified School District (BUSD) in 1988 enrolled about eight thousand students. The LEP population, which numbered 571 children and youths, consisted of thirty-eight language groups other than English. The largest LEP groups and their respective numbers were as follows: Spanish (268), Vietnamese (60), Cantonese (40), Laotian (32), Mandarin (32), and Tagalog (20).[130]

Six named individuals and all LEP students similarly situated in the school district served as plaintiffs in *Teresa P.* Attorneys from the Multicultural Education Training and Advocacy Project and the Legal Aid Society of Alameda County represented plaintiffs. Defendants included members of the Board of Education of the school district and the district Superintendent, Louis R. Zlokovich. Judge D. Lowell Jensen, a former official in President Reagan's administration, heard the case in the U.S. District Court for the Northern District of California.[131]

Plaintiffs, citing the *Gomez* court's ruling, alleged that defendants violated the three-prong approach of the *Castaneda* standard as well as Title VI of the 1964 Civil Rights Act. Regarding the *Castaneda* standard,

> Plaintiffs maintain that the BUSD remedial language program violates section 1703(f) of the EEOA. They claim that even if the program rests on a pedagogically sound basis its implementation violates the appropriate action standard of the EEOA. Plaintiffs argue that by failing to provide qualified teachers, sufficient supporting resources, and necessary monitoring systems, the BUSD has violated the EEOA. Plaintiffs also argue that the procedures utilized by the BUSD to identify, place, and exit students from the special language services program, violate the EEOA.[132]

After a lengthy trial (eighteen days of testimony and forty-six witnesses), Judge Jensen ruled for the defendants. Based on the defendants' expert witnesses' testimony, he found that the plaintiffs failed to meet their burden to show §1703(f) violations of the EEOA. In short, the school district met the *Castaneda* standard. Also, Judge Jensen found no violation of Title VI. It is noteworthy to add that the case appeared to be highly politicized and racialized. Crawford (1995) comments,

> *Teresa P.* was not decided in a political vacuum. Berkeley dipped into emergency reserves for $1.5 million to defend the lawsuit—more than three times what the district spent each year on LEP students—at a time of increasing hostility toward bilingualism. Resisting the demands of Hispanic parents proved popular, even in a community renowned for its liberalism. More important, the district received practical support and encouragement from an organized lobby. Throughout the litigation "expert" witnesses were recruited, "friend of the court" briefs were filed, and press coverage was orchestrated by a group known as U.S. English. (p. 59)

Conclusion

What can be concluded about the Mexican American community's legal struggle for bilingual education? To be sure, this quest has yielded both victories and losses, reflecting the indeterminacy of the courts. One of the greatest accomplishments emanating from this endeavor is the *Castaneda* standard. As García and Wiese (2002) note, the *Castaneda* standard "with deference to 'Lau' has become the most visible legal articulation of educational rights for Chicano, language minority students in public schools" (p. 163). The legal struggle discussed in this chapter, coupled with legislative advancements, has made it possible for hundreds of thousands of Mexican American English learners (ELs) and other language minority students to gain access to bilingual education. For example, as of the 2002–2003 school year, Texas public schools enrolled 490,380 English learners (overwhelmingly Mexican American) in bilingual/ESL education (early childhood, pre-K, and K–6) (Texas Education Agency, 2003b).

Notwithstanding the progress that Mexican Americans have made in the bilingual education arena, some states have suffered grave setbacks.[133] For example, in California on June 2, 1998, voters passed Proposition 227 ("English for the Children" initiative) with a margin of 61% "yes" to 39% "no," and thirty years of bilingual education came to an end (Cline, Necochea, & Rios, 2004; Johnson & Martínez, 2000).[134] Proposition 227, a direct attempt to dismantle bilingual education in California, has presented major obstacles to educational equality for Mexican American ELs, as well as other non-English-speaking students. In the 2005–2006 school year, there were 1,061,451 K–6 ELs in California, representing 32% of all K–6 students. Of these ELs, 907,979 (86%) were Spanish speakers (California Department of Education, 2006b). Proposition 227 eliminates instruction in the native language of these students and replaces it with "structured immersion" in English for one year (euphemism for the "sink-or-swim" practice of decades past). Baker and Hakuta (1997) describe the workings of Proposition 227 this way:

> As opposed to other measures that have been widely interpreted as "immigrant bashing," however, the Unz proposal (Proposition 227) recognizes the rights of immigrant students as a group. However, it focuses almost solely on their right to learn English, as opposed to content matter. In addition, it severely limits the availability of bilingual instruction: under the terms of the initiative, parents will have to go personally to their child's school site to enroll them in bilingual education, and children would have to meet eligibility criteria, such as minimum age and fluency in English. Also, parents will be able to sue school districts and teachers if they provide native language instruction in a manner that does not comply with the proposed law. That is, they will be able to file against districts if their students receive anything other than English-only instruction. (p. 6)

One day after Californians passed Proposition 227, six named plaintiffs (who appear to have been Latino) and a number of civil rights advocacy groups filed a lawsuit in the U.S. District Court for the Northern District of California, San Francisco Division (*Valeria G. v. Wilson,* 1998). Plaintiffs sought a preliminary injunction against the implementation of Proposition 227. Plaintiffs' legal bases rested, in part, on Title VI of the 1964 Civil Rights Act and the Fourteenth Amendment. The main thrust, however, was plaintiffs' claim that Proposition 227 failed to meet the three-prong test of the *Castaneda* standard. Presiding Judge Charles A. Legge ruled for the defendants. Plaintiffs appealed to the Ninth Circuit, and a three-member panel affirmed the district court's ruling (*Valeria v. Davis,* 2002). Appellants petitioned for a rehearing en banc, but the court denied it (*Valeria v. Davis,* 2003). In sum, the passage of Proposition 227 represents one of the greatest ironies in Mexican American educational history: the passage of this anti-bilingual-education law occurred in 1998, the sesquicentennial of the Treaty of Guadalupe Hidalgo, a treaty that agreed to protect the civil rights—including the language rights—of Mexicans living in the newly conquered area.[135] The centrality and intersectionality of race and racism in U.S. society, a major tenet of CRT, has proven useful in analyzing the Mexican American legal struggle for educational equality regarding language rights. This important premise can help us understand more fully the passage and implications of Proposition 227. For example, legal scholars Kevin R. Johnson and George A. Martínez (2000), in their article "Discrimination by Proxy: the Case of Proposition 227 and the Ban on Bilingual Education", assert that there is "core racial motivation behind the law's enactment" (p. 1230). Furthermore, the authors argue that Proposition 227 violates the Equal Protection Clause of the Fourteenth Amendment because, by utilizing language as a substitute for national origin, it is discriminatory against people of Mexican, other Latino, and Asian ancestry. In a similar vein, scholars Zulmara Cline, Juan Necochea, and Francisco Rios (2004), in their article "The Tyranny of Democracy: Deconstructing the Passage of Racist Propositions," have referred to the proposition as racist:

> In the case of Proposition 227, as with other race-based political propositions passed in California and other states, a largely uninformed electorate fed by the winds of racism, misinformation, hysteria, and half-truths exercised the majority rule to assert their will on educational and public policy issues. (p. 68)

In addition to the anti-bilingual-education referenda passed in some states, the second major problem that does not bode well for bilingual education is the recent demise of the Bilingual Education Act. James Crawford (2002) wrote an obituary that appeared on his website. He introduced matters this way:

> Title VII of the Elementary and Secondary Education Act, which transformed the way language-minority children are taught in the United States—promoting equal access to the curriculum, training a generation of educators, and fostering achievement among students—expired quietly on January 8 [2002]. The law was 34 years old. Its death was not unexpected, following years of attacks by enemies and recent desertions by allies in Congress. Title VII, also known as the Bilingual Education Act, was eliminated as part of a larger "school reform" measure known as No Child Left Behind, proposed by the Bush administration and passed with broad bipartisan support.

President George W. Bush's signing of the No Child Left Behind (NCLB) Act of 2002 (P.L. 107-110) was indeed the death knell of bilingual education. The new law reauthorized the BEA of 1994 as well as the ESEA (which was also amended). The BEA, which was known as Title VII of the ESEA, is now Title III of the NCLB Act. The official title is "Language Instruction for Limited English and Immigrant Children." The most significant aspect of Title III is that bilingual education is repealed and replaced with an English-only legislation (San Miguel, 2004). Furthermore, under the new law the word "bilingual" has been expunged (see Crawford, 2002).

From *Serna* to *Valeria*, the Mexican American community has vigorously fought for their right to have bilingual education. Yet this right is under siege. In light of the recent oppressive and repressive propositions passed by several states, Mexican Americans and other ELs are now faced with English-only schooling. This, coupled with the demise of federal-level support for bilingual education, means that the resolve of Mexican Americans' struggle for bilingual education needs to be stronger than ever.

5

School Closures

Four decades ago, many individuals hailed education in the United States as the new growth industry.[1] In the late 1960s and early 1970s, however, declining enrollments caught the K–12 educational system by surprise (Boyd, 1982; also, see Abramowitz & Rosenfeld, 1978). A decline in the birthrate (overwhelmingly among the White population) and an aging population meant fewer students enrolled in public schools. Adverse economic conditions (e.g., rising inflation) and a mounting societal dissatisfaction with levels of student achievement in the schools resulted in an erosion of public support and a diminished willingness to invest in education, particularly in a period of decline (see Boyd, 1982).[2] At the same time, competition between educational interest groups (e.g., bilingual education and special education) garnered the support of some politicians in passing legislation, resulting in "mandates without money" (Levine, 1979; cited in Boyd, 1982, p. 232). The resulting factionalism created enormous pressures for school districts throughout the country to deal head-on with the problems and conflicts of managing school systems with declining enrollments (Boyd & Wheaton, 1983). School administrators and school boards implemented numerous types of fiscal belt-tightening strategies (e.g., hiring freezes) to accommodate the decline in resources brought about by shrinking enrollments and exacerbated by growing inflation. One particular cost-saving measure that school districts used with some frequency—because school boards believed it made common and fiscal sense—was the closure of underutilized schools. In the 1970s, school boards closed over seven thousand public schools, affecting about 80% of the nation's school districts (Scott, 1983; also see Stinchcombe, 1984).

By the early 1980s, a voluminous and expanding literature on school closures had developed.[3] The bulk of these studies, however, was largely prescriptive.[4] These investigations dealt mainly with the advice and technical aspects of retrenchment (e.g., how to consolidate programs; how to decide the criteria for closures). Yet very few studies of the time examined the *policy implications* of closures on students and the community (Valencia, 1984a). These questions arose: (a) School closures increase enrollments in the remaining schools. Is bigger necessarily better? (b) School closures are purported to be cost-beneficial. Do closures actually result in substantial cost savings? (c) School closures are contentious technical and political processes. Do closures tend to erode public support for education? (d) School closures—by their very nature—are burdensome and raise issues of equity. Are such closures in multiracial communities "color blind"? Are closures in socioeconomically diverse communities equitable?[5] This chapter focuses on the latter concern, the equity issue, which arose from school closures in years past, particularly three school closure lawsuits filed by Mexican Americans.

A cold fact of life regarding retrenchment policymaking is that conflict-management decisions tend to result in clear winners and losers. On this point, Boyd and Wheaton (1983) note,

> The politics of school closings is more a "divide and conquer" than a "plan and agree" process. The secret of school closings, sensed by some school officials, is *concentrated cuts judiciously targeted* to minimize the likelihood of the formation of resistant coalitions. There always will be opposition to school closings, but if it is isolated it will have little effect. Because citizens in other neighborhoods do not mind seeing someone else's ox get gored, they will be unlikely to join forces with the losers unless they believe their neighborhood schools will be in jeopardy. (p. 31)

In urban, multiracial, socioeconomically diverse, segregated school districts (which characterize most of the nation's large urban centers then and now), school closures generated critical issues of educational equity. Based on a small number of case studies during the era of school closures, economically advantaged White students and their parents were the clear winners, while students of color and working-class students and their parents were the clear losers as a result of closure decisions. Investigations of school closures in Nashville, Tennessee (Berger, 1983; Scott, 1983), New York City, New York (Dean, 1983), Phoenix, Arizona (Valencia, 1984b), Santa Barbara, California (Valencia, 1980, 1984c), and St. Louis, Missouri (Colton & Frelich, 1979) reported that schools with primarily low-socioeconomic-status (SES) students of color suffered the brunt, if not the exclusive burden, of closings. In these cities, school boards closed schools attended by low-SES students of color, while economically advantaged White schools were disproportionately left open, though the White student population was overwhelmingly, if not exclusively, responsible for the decline in enrollment. In short, viewed within the context of CRT, school closures of the past were racialized and politically driven by White-dominated school boards' interests in protecting the privilege of their constituency, the White community.

This chapter discusses three school closure lawsuits brought forth by Mexican American plaintiffs: *Angeles v. Santa Barbara School District* (1979), *Castro v. Phoenix Union High School District # 210* (1982), and *Diaz v. San Jose Unified School District* (1985). In each of these cases, I served as an expert witness for plaintiffs and thus have an insider perspective to this litigation.

Angeles, Castro, *and* Diaz: *The Mexican American Community's Legal Struggle against Racialized School Closures*

Angeles v. Santa Barbara School District (1979)

As did many states in the 1960s and 1970s, California experienced a decline in the overall kindergarten through grade 12 (K–12) public school enrollment.[6] Foote, Espinosa, and García (1978) analyzed public school enrollment trends in California from 1967 to 1977 and found that the K–12 student body declined from 4,431,995 students in 1967 to 4,285,305 students in 1977, for a 3.3% net loss. The data are misleading, however, if one does not take racial differences into consideration. Foote et al. disaggregated the enrollment declines by race and uncovered an interesting pattern that is crucial to understanding the equity issue during the era of school closures. As shown in Figure 5.1, only White students showed an enrollment decline from 1967 to 1977 in California, sharply declining by 585,833 students, for an 18% decrease. On the other hand, all student groups of color showed enrollment increases, though varying in magnitude (in absolute numbers and percentages). For example, the Latino K–12 student enrollment (predominantly Mexican American) had the largest increase in absolute numbers ($n = 275,887$; a 46% increase). The demographic reality that White students in California and across the United States were responsible for all or most of enrollment declines, coupled with the consequences that school boards forced students of color to carry the exclusive

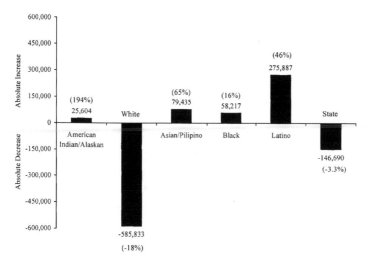

Figure 5.1. Absolute and Percentage Changes in California K–12 Enrollments by Race/Ethnicity: 1967–1977. *Note*: Percentages in parentheses refer to increases and decreases in enrollments. *Source*: Adapted from Foote, Espinosa, & García (1978, p. 3). With permission from Dr. Ruben W. Espinosa.

burden of school closures, formed the core of the equity issue in racially diverse communities.

In the late 1970s, Santa Barbara, California, a moderately sized coastal community (74,414 residents; U.S. Department of Commerce, Bureau of the Census, 1980) located one hundred miles north of Los Angeles, experienced a decline in elementary school enrollments. Because of the short-term and long-term financial losses facing the Santa Barbara School District (SBSD) due to heavy enrollment declines, members of the school board, the district Superintendent, and members of his staff began research on the possibility of closing elementary schools in the SBSD. In January 1979, the school board published a proposal (Thomas, 1979). The following three criteria were used by the SBSD to determine which schools would be closed: close those (a) with the least adequate facilities and sites; (b) that are the most utilitarian for other public or educational purposes; (c) that will lead to the least long-term socioeconomic and racial segregation. From late January through early February of 1979, a series of meetings were held throughout the SBSD for public review of the proposal. On March 1, 1979, the all-White school board voted on and approved the Superintendent's proposal. This decision soon set in motion a school boycott, charges of racial discrimination, and a lawsuit filed by Mexican American parents, because the three schools chosen for closure served the predominantly Mexican American low-income population of Santa Barbara's central area (Hurst, 1979).

In mid-April 1979, Channel Counties Legal Services Association, a federally funded legal aid firm based in Santa Barbara, and the Los Angeles–based Western Center on Law and Poverty, Inc., filed *Angeles v. Santa Barbara School District* in the Superior Court of Santa Barbara County. Judge Arden T. Jensen presided. Seven minor Mexican American elementary students, represented by their parents, served as plaintiffs. The Parents' Committee, a racially mixed group established to oppose the closure plans, also served as a plaintiff. The defendants in *Angeles* included the Santa Barbara School District, Santa Barbara High School District, the five members of the Santa Barbara School and High School District Board of Education, and the Superintendent and Assistant Superintendent of Schools.[7]

Litigation of *Angeles* began in mid-August 1979 and lasted for two weeks. The plaintiffs' attorneys based the lawsuit on numerous causes of action, including equal protection and due process violations of federal and state constitutions and statutes.[8] Plaintiffs complained that the closing of three predominantly Mexican American schools (a 50% or greater Mexican American enrollment), but no closing of any predominantly White schools (a 50% or greater White enrollment), and the "one-way busing" from the predominantly Mexican American schools to the predominantly White schools constituted racial discrimination.

Of the SBSD's twelve elementary schools, five were majority Mexican American, six primarily White, and one predominantly neither Mexican American nor White. Table 5.1 lists the schools with racial/ethnic percentages and predominant racial/ethnic classifications for the 1978–1979 school year. Under the SBSD's plan, three of the five predominantly Mexican American schools (60%) in the district would be eliminated. The percentage of Mexican American children enrolled in these schools was 30% ($n = 556$) of the total Mexican American children enrollment of 1,876 in the district. Although the Mexican American and White enrollments were nearly equal for the SBSD (46% White; 47% Mexican American), the district's plan forced 60% of the Mexican American schools and 30% of the Mexican American students and their parents to carry the exclusive burdens of school closures and one-way busing. Furthermore, the three schools proposed for closure—Lincoln, McKinley, and Wilson—were

TABLE 5.1
Racial/Ethnic Percentage by School: 1978–1979

School	Mexican American (%)	White (%)	Other (%)	Predominant Group
Franklin	68	19	13	Mexican American
McKinley[a]	65	30	5	Mexican American
Wilson[a]	62	32	6	Mexican American
Lincoln[a]	58	36	6	Mexican American
Harding	53	41	6	Mexican American
Cleveland	41	48	11	Neither
Roosevelt	38	57	5	White
Washington	31	64	5	White
Monroe	27	69	4	White
Adams	27	70	3	White
Peabody	16	79	5	White
Alternative[b]	10	85	5	White

Source: Thomas (1979, p. 31).

[a] Schools proposed for closure. [b] Not considered for closure due to its very small enrollment and programmatic necessity.

located in areas relatively adjacent to one another. The closure of the three schools would leave a substantial number of Mexican American families without a single neighborhood school in the central city, where a large percentage of the Mexican American community resided.

The litigation strategies of counsel for the plaintiffs chiefly consisted of a three-prong attack: (a) cross-examination of the SBSD Superintendent in an attempt to expose double standards and arbitrariness, hence racial discrimination; (b) testimony by plaintiffs' parents to show the parents' concerns about the school closures; (c) testimony by experts to show how the Mexican American children would be damaged.

Double standards and arbitrariness. Plaintiffs sought to show that the defendants acted arbitrarily and in a discriminatory manner in at least four areas related to (1) the nature of the enrollment decline, (2) the operational costs of small schools, (3) the adequacy of school sites and facilities, and (4) the nature of racial and socioeconomic segregation.

1. *Enrollment decline.* The SBSD declined 34% in enrollment from 1968 to 1978, primarily a White student decline (Thomas, 1979, p. 46). Plaintiffs asked, Why did the SBSD not emphasize intradistrict enrollment declines by examining the racial makeup of schools in its decision to implement closures?

2. *Operational costs.* In its proposal, the SBSD argued that small schools (enrollment of less than three hundred students) proved more inefficient to operate both economically and programmatically, compared to large

schools (enrollment of more than three hundred students). Of the three Mexican American schools proposed for closure, one was small (Lincoln) and two were large (McKinley and Wilson) (Thomas, 1979, p. 9). Of the five White schools (none proposed for closure), two were small (Cleveland and Monroe) and three were large (Adams, Peabody, and Washington).

Compared to the district average cost per student of $1,363, only one of the three Mexican American schools subject to closure (Lincoln, a small school) had a higher than district average cost per student (Thomas, 1979, p. 9). The other two Mexican American schools scheduled for closure (McKinley and Wilson, both large schools) had a cost per student less than the district average. On the other hand, of the five predominantly White schools, none proposed for closure, one (Adams, a large school) had a cost per student less than the district average, and the remaining four White schools (Cleveland and Monroe, small schools, and Roosevelt and Washington, large schools) all had costs per student greater than the district average (Thomas, 1979, p. 9). Therefore, using the SBSD's criterion dealing with operational costs, officials proposed for closure two "efficient" large schools (Mexican American) but not two "inefficient" small schools (White) and two "inefficient" large schools (White). Plaintiffs argued that this glaring inequity raised the question of the fairness in applying the district's criterion of cost efficiency in a color-blind fashion.

3. *School sites and facilities.* The closure of schools with the "least adequate facilities and sites" was another criterion. Lincoln and Wilson, two of the three predominantly Mexican American schools proposed for closure, had, according to the district school closure proposal, "clearly the least adequate facilities" (Thomas, 1979, p. 40). Both schools had the smallest acreage, mostly "sub-standard" temporary buildings, and noise and potential dangers from vehicular travel. In terms of buildings, Lincoln had 67% temporary classrooms; Wilson, 64%; and McKinley, 14%. Of the predominantly White schools, Adams had 57% temporary classrooms, and Roosevelt, a small-acreage school, had 100% temporary classrooms (Thomas, 1979, p. 6). Also, Adams, a large-acreage school located on one of the major arteries feeding into the freeway (U.S. Highway 101), experienced considerable noise and vehicular congestion. Again, plaintiffs asked, Did the district apply the closure proposal standards equitably?

4. *Racial and socioeconomic segregation.* The district also used the criterion of closing "those [schools] which lead to the least long-term racial/ethnic and socioeconomic segregation" (Thomas, 1979, p. 18). This criterion sparked considerable controversy during the trial. Plaintiffs' counsel

needed to argue that the district contained predominantly Mexican American as well as predominantly White schools. Yet the district proved successful in its argument that only the Mexican American schools were considered segregated, despite the reality that racial and socioeconomic segregation also existed in the five predominantly White schools.

The SBSD's decision to close only Mexican American schools and assign only Mexican American students for one-way busing becomes clearer in the context of economic power, as well in the context of CRT, in which school boards strive to protect White privilege. A *Los Angeles Times* article noted that the SBSD administration "admittedly gave heavy weight to a desire to spread the children of minority, low-income families into predominantly Anglo, middle class schools, without risking White flight through a reciprocal busing plan" (Hurst, 1979, p. 1). In addition, when speaking of Roosevelt School, one of the White schools, the district's proposal stated,

> The school's residential area is the highest socioeconomic area in the city. Maintaining this area as a predominantly public school attendance area is important to the District. Unless the District can attract and hold these upper middle class areas the entire Elementary School District is in danger of becoming progressively more ethnically and socioeconomically segregated. (Thomas, 1979, p. 46)

In simpler terms, if Roosevelt had been targeted for closure, the parents in this area would most likely have opted to enroll their children in private schools or leave the district. This was surely not an economic option that the low-income Mexican American parents in the central city schools had.

Parental testimony. As a second strategy, plaintiffs' counsel asked the parents of plaintiff children from the three Mexican American schools proposed for closure to give testimony. The parents went into depth about how the school closures would harm the Mexican American community. Their testimony centered around two major factors: (a) the need and desirability for neighborhood schools; (b) the consequences of school closure on parental participation. Regarding the former concern, the necessity and desirability for neighborhood schools in the central city of Santa Barbara was a focal point of the parental testimony. Here, drawing from CRT, we can see the experiential knowledge of parents as a major strength in contesting the closures. One parent from Lincoln School described the school as being "sacred, like a church." She spoke proudly of the school being free of graffiti and broken windows, as being the nexus of cultural activities, and as having an outstanding parental participation component and a strong bilingual/multicultural education program. Parents from the two other schools scheduled for closure spoke of their anxieties about the burdens of busing and the fact that their children would be away from the immediate neighborhood.

Parents also spoke of the anticipated problem of drastically decreased parental participation in the receiving schools. Because a substantial number of Mexican American parents from the three schools in question were of low-income status, many would not be able to afford the bus fare to the new schools; also, walking to the receiving schools would be physically prohibitive because of the distance, according to the parents. This factor of decreased parental participation (e.g., Parent Teacher Association [PTA] meetings; classroom volunteers) is a crucial variable in the schooling of young children. Research literature, then and now, demonstrates that parental participation in one way or another positively correlates with academic achievement of Mexican American and other students (see, e.g., Moreno & Valencia, 2002).

Expert testimony. The third and final strategy of plaintiffs' counsel included expert testimony as to how the Mexican American students and their parents would be harmed due to the school closures. Four experts testified in the areas of (a) demography, (b) testing, (c) educational and psychological development of racial minority children, and (d) bilingual-multicultural education.[9]

I served as an expert on the educational/psychological development of children of color, testifying that the closure of the Mexican American schools and the subsequent dispersion of the children to the predominantly middle- and upper-middle-class White schools would increase the probability of psychological disturbances and academic failure in the Mexican American students. Psychological theory related to cognitive dissonance, school stress, and responses to stress formed the basis of the expert testimony (Valencia, 1980). The main points advanced were the following:

1. Generally speaking, the public schools are failing Mexican American students, and there is a long history to this failure.

2. Because of the inequalities, negative experiences, and inferior schooling conditions that Mexican American students face in the schools, these students have a higher probability of failure in the school system.

3. All children face stress in the schools due to the demands placed on them to master the academic curriculum and the curriculum dealing with socialization.

4. School stress is particularly acute for Mexican American children, because the home culture is often not considered by the school culture.

5. The school creates stress for some Mexican American children because the environmental demands of the school (e.g., demands to speak and learn English) are dissonant with the characteristics of the child (e.g., Spanish speaking).

6. The Mexican American student's psychological responses to dissonance are often negative (e.g., denial of racial/ethnic membership; rebellion; withdrawal; passivity).

7. The preceding psychological responses are connected to low academic achievement, which in turn combines with the entire school culture to intensify the inequalities, negative experiences, and inferior schooling conditions that Mexican American students face as a group.

8. The district's proposal failed to address several key questions. Specifically, what had been the experiences of the White teachers, administrators, staff, parents, and students with the culturally, linguistically, and socioeconomically different Mexican American children and their parents? What would be the attitudes of the teachers, administrators, staff, parents, and students toward the Mexican American children and their parents in the majority White schools? The three Mexican American schools were far from perfect, but they were attempting to develop a good match, or "goodness of fit," between home and school. What did the receiving schools plan in order to reduce the school dissonance and stress that the Mexican American children and their parents would experience by the school closures? In short, what plans did the district have for *integration*?

The defendant school board members' testimony, for the most part, iterated the rationale presented in the SBSD closure proposal. The members testified that the decisions to close the schools in question were hard decisions, but the school board had no other choice based on the facts. The members stated that they had acted in good faith and that they did not discriminate against the Mexican American students. Such testimony was not at all surprising given that at the time of *Angeles*, the Santa Barbara Elementary School District School Board consisted of five White members of middle- and upper-socioeconomic-class background. The Mexican American community of Santa Barbara had always constituted a substantial percentage of the city and district population, but a Mexican

American had never been elected as a school board member since the SBSD's establishment in 1854.

Although the plaintiffs exposed the ubiquity of double standards in the district's decision-making process to close schools, legal indeterminacy arose. Judge Jensen ruled against the children and their parents, finding that the SBSD's school closure proposal was legitimate and did not constitute racial discrimination. In September 1979, the school board closed three inner-city predominantly Mexican American schools and dispersed 556 Mexican American children to majority-White schools. The plaintiffs appealed Judge Jensen's decision to the Court of Appeal, Second Appellate District, but the appellate court affirmed the lower court's decision. Kirk Ah Tye, counsel for the *Angeles* appellants, wrote that the "Court of Appeal in *Angeles* ruled that the district's desire to minimize segregation was a compelling interest and that the district had thus satisfied the strict scrutiny standard of review" (1982, p. 1013).

Before leaving the *Angeles* case, it is important to note that I conducted a follow-up study of the case about eighteen months after the school board closed the Mexican American schools (Valencia, 1984c). Bilingual Mexican American females interviewed mothers of fifty Mexican American families affected by the closures in order to confirm or disconfirm the prediction of adverse effects that I had proffered in the *Angeles* trial:[10]

1. The Mexican American children would generally experience serious psychological adjustment problems, which in turn would affect their school work.

2. The children would experience declines in academic achievement.

3. The children's parents would experience declines in parental participation in the receiving schools.

4. The children's parents would perceive the closures as having adverse consequences on the Mexican American community.

In brief, the results of my study confirmed the hypotheses. Many children, as reported by the parents, experienced serious adjustment problems and academic achievement declines. Regarding parental participation, 73% of the mothers reported that their participation levels were higher at the closed schools compared to the receiving schools, 13% reported higher participation levels at the receiving schools, 13% had similar levels at both schools, and 2% gave other responses. Calculations of the respondents' participation levels at the closed and receiving schools across ten different activity areas (e.g., PTA; parent-teacher conference; classroom volunteer) showed a consistent pattern: steep decreases across all participation activities in the receiving schools (see Valencia, 1984c, p. 157, Table 5).

Regarding hypothesis 4, overall consequences, 68% of the mothers reported that the increased distance between the home and the receiving school created problems, 30% said no problems arose, and 2% did not respond. In the study, I used a content analysis and classified 62% of the affirmative responses as community related (e.g., "child missed bus after school," "mother has no transportation, thus difficult to get to receiving school," and "mother misses having children close by"). The interviewers asked the mothers a global question containing three elements (children's school work, children's feelings, and parents' participation) that sought respondents' perception as to which school provided the best education. The majority of the mothers (52%) chose the closed schools, 10% chose the receiving schools, 32% selected both schools, and 6% gave other responses. The responses ranged broadly across all three dimensions and in varying combinations. The interviewers also asked the mothers a second global question: Had the closures affected—for the better or for the worse—their lives, their families, and the Mexican American community? Overwhelmingly (82%), the mothers reported that the closures had been for the worse. I classified the responses as predominantly community and psychological/community related. Typical answers included, "closures not to their advantage; no benefits for families," "closures resulted in feelings of aimlessness and helplessness, lost sense of security," "mother misses closeness of school to home," "children were negatively affected" (e.g., adjustment), "children were better students at closed schools," "buses are late and break down," and "children get home later and have to get up earlier."

Based on the empirical data collected in the *Angeles* follow-up study, it appears that the negative settling effects brought on by the closures began to take hold in a relatively short time. For a substantial percentage of the affected Mexican American student population, an already high probability of school problems and failure had been increased. This was a reasonable conclusion, given that students of color, in general, have been found to be more vulnerable, compared to their White peers, to academic achievement declines in normative school transitions such as those seen in transition to high school and school changes brought on by residential mobility (Felner, Primavera, & Cauce, 1981; Felner, Gintner, & Primavera, 1982).

In summary, the findings of the *Angeles* follow-up study raise serious questions regarding the complex set of policy considerations that the SBSD used in the closures of three inner-city elementary schools primarily serving Mexican American students. It appears that the short-term adverse effects experienced by the children and their families translated to long-term negative consequences as these young children progressed through the educational system.

Castro v. Phoenix Union High School District #210 (1982)

The second school closure case in which I served as an expert witness was *Castro v. Phoenix Union High School District #210*. Subsequent to this expert work in *Castro*, the Stanford Center for Chicano Research published a monograph that covered the background, trial, and outcome of the case (Valencia, 1984b). The following is a synopsis of the coverage in that monograph.

Phoenix Union High School District (PUHSD) #210 in the late 1970s was one of six high school districts in metropolitan Phoenix, Arizona. In the 1970–1971 school year, PUHSD #210 had an enrollment of 28,481 students. A decade later, in 1980–1981, the enrollment plummeted to 21,376 —a sharp decline of 25%.[11] Demographers projected that by the 1983–1984 school year, the district would lose another 2,000 students, thus bringing the total enrollment under 20,000 for the first time in twenty years. As was the situation in other multiracial communities across the country, White students overwhelmingly accounted for the enrollment declines in the district. In light of these enrollment declines, the highly segregated district faced a $6.5 million deficit for the 1982–1983 school year. Confronted with this severe financial crisis, the district administration and school board struck out in early 1979 to solve the budget crunch. Particular emphasis was placed on the study of school closures.

On October 4, 1979, the school board approved six general criteria to be used in the event of school closures.[12] The six criteria, with their respective weight values and number of "factors," were as follows:
1. Provision of Equal Educational Opportunity (30%; 8)
2. Membership Decline (15%; 2)
3. Population Balances (15%; 2)
4. Operational Cost Analysis (25%; 3)
5. Facility Flexibility (10%; 5)
6. Geographical Constraints (5%; 1).

TABLE 5.2

Rank Order Comparison between Total Criteria Score and Percentage of Minority Student Body Enrollment

School	Total Criteria Score		Minority Student Enrollment	
	Pts.[a]	Rank	%	Rank
Union	38	1	94.2	1
South	52	3	87.7	2
Hayden	58	4	75.0	3
North	49	2	64.4	4
East	67	6.5	56.7	5
West	65	5	25.7	6
Maryvale	74	9	19.5	7
Alhambra	67	6.5	13.2	8
Central	69	8	9.4	9
Camelback	75	10	7.8	10
Browne[b]	—	—	18.0	—

Source: Adapted from *An Analysis of Criteria for School Closure: A Report to the Board of Education*, pp. 48-53. Phoenix Union High School District, November 1, 1979.

[a] Total maximum was 105 points (21 factors × 5 points). The schools are ranked from least points obtained (Union) to most points obtained (Camelback). The lower the total criteria score, the more conducive for closure.
[b] Browne, built in 1972, was not given a score in the *Criteria Report* for the criterion of "membershp decline"; therefore, this school was not included in the analysis in this table.

Subsequently, on November 1, 1979, district staff presented to the school board a one-hundred-page report, entitled *An Analysis of Criteria for School Closure* (hereafter referred to as *Criteria Report*).[13] Staff members collected data for each of the six criteria, and used a scale of 1 to 5 to assign values to twenty-one factors, with a 1 deemed "most conducive to closure" and 5 "least conducive." Based on the school-by-school ratings in the *Criteria Report*, district staff rated the eleven high schools in the district for closure according to the total number of criteria points. The final rankings for closure are presented in Table 5.2, revealing that "minority" schools surfaced as most conducive for closure. In contrast, district staff ranked the "White" schools consistently toward the bottom, meaning evaluators judged them to be least conducive for closure.[14] I subjected this eyeball observation to a statistical analysis (Spearman rank order correlation) and found a highly significant relation between rankings of total criteria scores and racial enrollment percentages ($r_S = .90$, significant < .01). The higher the enrollment of students of color at a school, the higher the probability that district staff judged that school to be most conducive to closure.

On March 10, 1981, the school board decided by a 3–2 vote to close North High School, an inner-city school with a substantial enrollment of students of color (64% in 1979).[15] Furthermore, the district selected West High School, rapidly becoming a school predominantly of students of color, for closure and conversion to a vocational facility.[16] On November 19, 1981, by a 3–2 vote, the district also marked for closure Phoenix Union High School, the school with the greatest enrollment of students of color (94%). Finally, on January 7, 1982, a divided school board selected for closure East High School, an inner-city school with an enrollment that was two-thirds students of color.[17] As a result of these four closures, the plan had the potential to disembowel the inner city, leaving a thirty-square-mile area with no high school for the population of predominantly students of color.[18]

Mexican American and African American parents and students from Phoenix Union (94% combined minority) filed a federal lawsuit in March 1982, claiming racial discrimination. The lawsuit, litigated in the U.S. District Court for the District of Arizona, asked for injunctive relief. Judge Valdemar A. Cordova presided over the hearing. The plaintiffs asserted that the district had violated their rights under the Equal Protection and Due Process Clauses to the U.S. and Arizona Constitutions, and under Title VI of the Civil Rights Act of 1964 (42 U.S.C. §2000 et seq.).

Plaintiffs complained that school closures are indeed burdensome and that the school board's closure of Phoenix Union, plus the closures of the other schools, meant that the district placed the exclusive burden of the closures on students of color and exempted White students from such burdens. Albert M. Flores, counsel for the plaintiffs, noted that case law such as *Cisneros v. Corpus Christi Independent School District* (1972) and *U.S. v. Texas Education Agency* (1972) established that the imposition of burdens on students of color constitutes invidious discrimination and must be avoided. As such, plaintiffs employed a two-pronged legal strategy in *Castro*: to produce evidence of racially motivated intent and evidence of adverse impact.

The issue of intent: Discrimination in the decision-making process. As noted earlier, the school board approved, and eventually used, six criteria for school closure conduciveness. For trial testimony, I focused on the first criterion, "Provision of Equal Educational Opportunity." This standard proved critical for plaintiffs' legal strategy, as the criterion carried most of the weight (30%) compared to the other five closure criteria. Table 5.3 lists the eight factors subsumed under the Provision of Equal

TABLE 5.3
Provision of Equal Educational Opportunity

Factor No.	Factor Description
1	Comparison of Current Course Offerings
2	Assessment of Student Achievement Levels
3	Assessment of Special Education Needs
4	Assessment of Need for Gifted Programs
5	Length of Service or Experience of Teachers
6	Measure of Number of Teachers by Subject Areas
7	Campus Adequacy to Serve Handicapped Students
8	Adequacy of the School to Serve Educational Needs

Source: Adapted from *An Analysis of Criteria for School Closure: A Report to the Board of Education*, p. 4. Phoenix Union High School District, November 1, 1979.

Educational Opportunity criterion. By including this criterion for closure conduciveness, the district assumed that the eleven high schools in the district varied in their delivery of equal educational opportunities to the students. The district's logic was that schools that provide the least equal educational opportunities should be judged most conducive for closure. This appears to be a sound assumption. One must address two key questions, however, before deeming the components of the Provision of Equal Educational Opportunity criterion appropriate. First, do the factors of this criterion have sound "construct validity"? That is, do the factors measure what they are supposed to measure (equal educational opportunity)? Second, do the factors and the criterion, as a whole, have sound "predictive validity"? That is, can it be stated that the factors and criterion are systematically error (or bias) free in predicting which schools will be judged most conducive for closure? These two conditions, loosely drawn from test and measurement theory, served as guidelines in my analysis of the criterion under scrutiny and my subsequent court testimony regarding its inherent bias.

Substantial evidence demonstrated that this criterion for school closure conduciveness was inherently biased against the district's schools with predominantly students of color and toward the White schools.[19] The manner in which the district used the "factors" for this criterion led to the inevitable conclusion that schools with predominantly students of color would surface as most conducive for closure. Furthermore, I testified at the *Castro* hearing that most of the factors included within the Provision of Equal Educational Opportunity criterion were unsound because of faulty or unsupportable assumptions and/or lack of an empirical basis in the context of social science research. Finally, from a measurement standpoint, evidence showed that the scoring procedure for the factors contained arbitrary and capricious (a) scaling techniques, (b) assignment of values, and (c) interval cut-off points. It is beyond the scope of this section to comment on the unreliability of all eight factors that compose the Provision of Equal Educational Opportunity (see Valencia, 1984b, for a thorough discussion). A critique of one factor (Factor 2, "Assessment of Student Achievement Levels"), however, will serve as an example.

Although the *Criteria Report* did not explicitly state the rationale for Factor 2, defendants testified at the *Castro* hearing that schools with lower levels of academic achievement were not providing equal educational opportunity to the same degree as schools with higher levels of achievement. The inclusion of Factor 2 best illustrates that the decision-making index of the Provision of Equal Educational Opportunity criterion was biased against schools with predominantly students of color and biased in favor of White schools. Three interrelated observations from the educational literature regarding academic achievement of students of color support this assertion. Proportionately speaking, students of color, compared to White students, tend to (a) be from lower-SES background, (b) enroll in schools with predominantly students of color, and (c) perform lower on standardized achievement measures. Therefore, by including Factor 2, one could unequivocally predict, a priori, that schools with predominantly students of color would be identified as most conducive for closure. Furthermore, given the pervasive finding in the literature that SES positively correlates with academic achievement, and that collinearity exists between SES and race, it could be stated in advance of any analysis that the higher the enrollment of students of color at a high school in the district, the lower the achievement levels would be.

During cross-examination at the *Castro* hearing, a witness for defendants denied that school racial enrollment levels were excellent predictors of school achievement levels. However, upon inspecting the data in an exhibit that I prepared (showing a very strong statistical relation between enrollment of students of color and academic achievement in the district's eleven high schools), the witness changed her position. The analysis in the exhibit demonstrated a perfect rank order relation for the first five schools (the district's schools with predominantly students of color) (Valencia, 1984b, p. 25, Table 6; also, see Valencia, Menchaca, & Donato, 2002, p. 80, Table 3.5). It was not surprising, then, that the "Assessment of Student Achievement Levels" (Factor 2) identified the schools with predominantly students of color as being the most conducive for closure. The school with the highest enrollment of students of color and lowest achievement level, Phoenix Union, ranked number one for closure.

In conclusion, my analysis of the Equal Educational Opportunity criterion revealed that the inclusion of the eight factors (particularly Factors 1 through 6), in a singular and composite sense, served as inappropriate indices of equal educational opportunity and, hence, of closure conduciveness. The factors proved faulty on several accounts. First, several of the factors lacked clear assumptions and rationale. Second, some of the stated assumptions could not be supported in light of empirical evidence and/ or statistical analyses. Third, and most important, the factors appeared to be inherently biased against schools with predominantly students of color and in favor of White schools. In an a priori fashion, six of the eight factors served as excellent predictors of the racial composition of the district's schools. That is, the criterion factors were better predictors of racial enrollment percentage than of the intended criterion variable, namely, the delivery of equal educational opportunity. Table 5.4 contains data for the entire analysis and highlights this final point. The rank order calculation shows a strong and significant correlation between the total equal educational opportunity scores and the percentages of students of color enrolled in the eleven schools.

TABLE 5.4
Rank Order Comparison between the Total
Equal Educational Opportunity (EEO) Score and
Percentage of Minority Student Body Enrollment

| School | Total EEO Score | | Minority Student Enrollment | |
	Pts. (least)	*Rank*	%	*Rank*
Union	9	1	94.2	1
South	17	2	87.7	2
Hayden	21	4	75.0	3
North	18	3	64.4	4
East	27	6	56.7	5
West	30	8	25.7	6
Maryvale	31	9	19.5	7
Browne	26	5	18.0	8
Alhambra	29	7	13.2	9
Central	33	10	9.4	10
Camelback	35	11	7.8	11

Source: *Adapted from An Analysis of Criteria for School Closure: A Report to the Board of Education,* p. 48. Phoenix Union High School District, November 1, 1979.

$r_s = .89$ (significant < .01).

The issue of impact: Racial discrimination in the student-displacement process. The plaintiffs in the *Castro* case faced a second major challenge: produce evidence that the closure of Phoenix Union and the subsequent dispersion and displacement of the students was racially discriminatory in effect, in that the students' rights to an equal educational opportunity would be negatively affected. The major limitation, however, in providing evidence of adverse effects was that very little knowledge existed about the potential problems resulting from the closure of schools with predominantly students of color. Except for the theoretical (Valencia, 1980) and empirical bases (Valencia, 1984c) established in the *Angeles* school closure case in California, there was no other school closure literature and litigation from which to draw. Therefore, I had to draw from my work in *Angeles* and to seek elsewhere in the social science literature to study the issue of school closures and potential racialized effects on students of color.

As an anchor, the construct of "transition" (which was valuable as a way to frame the *Angeles* follow-up study; Valencia, 1984c) proved to be very useful in further understanding the potential adverse effects on students of color in the Phoenix closures. This impact testimony in *Castro* centered around three types of school transition research: (a) normative, (b) desegregation, and (c) school closure, as well as a fourth area—the school climate at the receiving school. In very brief form, the research findings on school transition, as well as the school climate of the receiving schools, suggested the following conclusions:

1. *Normative school transition research.* In general, cumulative school transfers and transitions into high school present students with heightened risks for academic problems, particularly for students of color (Felner et al., 1981; Levine, Wesolowski, & Corbett, 1966). Felner et al. (1981) note,

> It may be that factors such as socioeconomic status, the precipitants for the move, and the geographic distance it covers, which have also been suggested as potentially associated with vulnerability to school mobility . . . may be systematically different among the ethnic subgroups. . . . Of particular interest is that those students who seem most vulnerable during the transition to high school are those who may already be considered at risk either due to their prior history of school mobility or racial background. . . . sharp drops in academic performance, for whatever reason, are frequently associated with the development of enduring school difficulties and dropping out. (p. 456)

2. *Desegregation school transition research.* Researchers during the school desegregation era found that if the receiving schools (typically White) were not prepared for the bused-in students (typically of color), then the latter group tended to have academic and socioemotional problems. That is, if the receiving schools failed to implement a comprehensive integration plan, students of color were prone to receiving lower grades via "the normalization of instruction and grades" phenomenon,[20] dropping out,[21] and experiencing school stress and anxiety.[22]

3. *School closure transition research.* Based on the findings pursuant to the dispersion of Mexican American students in the *Angeles* school closure case and the subsequent adverse consequences that the students experienced (Valencia, 1980, 1984c), this line of school transition research proved useful to advance during the *Castro* hearing.

In summary, the three previous sections on research related to normative, desegregation, and school closure transition laid the theoretical and empirical foundations for my hypotheses of potential negative effects on students of color in the *Castro* case.

4. *The school climate at Central.* In the *Castro* case, as in the *Angeles* case, I testified that an important variable of concern was related to the nature of the receiving school, particularly its preparation, attitudes, receptivity, and goals for the incoming students of color displaced by the closures. The district designated Central High School, one of the highest-achieving high schools in the district, as the receiving school. Prior to the planned dispersion of students from the targeted school closures, Central had an enrollment of 2,044 students (90% White). Over 1,000 dispersed students (predominantly Mexican American and African American) would enroll in Central, resulting in a new total student body of 3,200 students (a 57% increase). Notwithstanding this massive influx of students, the defendants testified that no major problems in school management were likely to occur. On the basis of district reports, depositions, and defendants' trial testimony, my interpretation of Central's school climate differed sharply from the defendants' positive portrait. In my testimonial counterstory regarding school climate, I discussed five issues: (a) teacher attitudes; (b) academic excellence of Central's students of color; (c) tracking (academic resegregation); (d) systemic flux; (e) distance from home to school. In the interest of space, one issue, teacher attitudes, is discussed here.

Three concerns arose with regard to teacher attitudes at Central. First, Central teachers attended a half-day workshop, in which participants voiced some collective concerns, expectations, and dispositions that did not bode well for incoming students of color. Examples of summary quotes were, "Fear was expressed related to physical violence expected as directed toward staff and students"; "Graffiti will be more evident"; "Ethnic miscommunications will create potentially disruptive situations."

Second, the district held a five-day in-service for Central teachers in the summer of 1982 (before the influx of students of color in the fall semester). Phoenix Gang Squad officers facilitated one workshop devoted to "Phoenix Gangs." I testified that this workshop likely implanted or reinforced among the teachers a stereotype that students of color were gang members. This seemed probable because an entire workshop day had been devoted to a problem that involved only a small number of students of color.[23] Furthermore, because 90% of all Phoenix gang members were Mexican American, it is conceivable that a large number of Mexican American students would be entering Central stereotyped as gang members or potential gang members.

Third, facilitators held a workshop for Central teachers entitled "Multiethnic Considerations in the Curriculum." The group leaders asserted that African American and Mexican American students, in general, have different learning styles than do White students, and thus teachers should consider using different cognitive teaching styles. I testified that such pedagogical recommendations for different teaching styles for African American and Mexican American students actually stereotypes and unfairly pigeonholes them. Furthermore, empirical research fails to support the hypotheses that field dependence or field independence learning styles are good predictors of academic achievement and that they distinguish students of color from White students (e.g., Figueroa, 1980; Figueroa & Gallegos, 1978; Kagan & Buriel, 1977; Nelson, Knight, Kagan, & Gumbiner, 1980).

In sum, the attitudes held by Central teachers and the workshop information that was imparted to them carried generally unfavorable and negatively stereotypic perceptions, with potentially stigmatizing consequences for students of color. Given that the climate of a school in a desegregated setting is a critical factor for successful integration (Hughes, Gordon, & Hillman, 1980), particularly in the area of teacher expectations (e.g., Felice & Richardson, 1977a), some students of color might experience serious psychological and educational problems at Central.

After nine days of listening to testimony at the *Castro* injunctive relief hearing, Judge Cordova filed his memorandum of findings and order on August 30, 1982. The next day, the *Phoenix Gazette* blurted the front-page headline "Judge Rules PUHS Must Be Reopened" (McGowan, 1982, p. A1). Judge Cordova ruled that the closing of Phoenix Union was discriminatory in intent and had a negative effect on the plaintiffs' rights to an equal educational opportunity. His order included a number of points, including this granting of relief:

> That plaintiffs' motion or petition for preliminary injunction is granted, and the defendants are hereby enjoined from leasing, selling or otherwise disposing of the property of Phoenix Union High School, consisting of the realty and improvements thereon. . . . The defendants, effective the first day of the second semester of the 1982–83 school year, are enjoined from closing Phoenix Union High School. . . . This order will continue in full force and effect, pendente lite, or until the district has sooner considered and is prepared to put into effect an alternate plan which would fairly implement the constitutional and legal principles involved herein.[24]

Regarding discriminatory intent and impact, my testimony clearly influenced Judge Cordova's findings. On the issue of intent, he wrote,

> On October 4, 1979, the Board accepted criteria for the closure of one or more schools. The criteria and subsequent condensations thereof were prepared in such a manner that the conclusion was inevitable that a minority school would be subject to closure.[25]

He also found, "There is evidence that there would be substantial negative impact on the minority students and their parents."[26] Largely, his findings centered on negative consequences in the areas of distance, achievement, and dropping out. Regarding distance, Judge Cordova found,

> The students in many instances will be compelled to take a bus for much greater distances than before. . . . some are being compelled to expend money for bus fare; almost all students are far from walking distance to and from school; all must be up earlier than before; many because of the bus schedules are precluded from some extracurricular activities and athletics. The minority student is therefore being subjected to burdens which are not being imposed upon the non-minority student.[27]

On the issue of achievement, he noted,

> Because of the large sudden influx of minority students into Central High School and the fact that in general they scored lower in achievement tests they will be subjected to the "normalization of the instruction phenomenon" wherein it is expected that minorities will generally be receiving lower grades than the majority students at the receiving schools.[28]

Concerning the dropout issue, Judge Cordova found,

> There is a probability of an increase in the dropout rate. At the present time more than 50 students from Phoenix Union High School have not enrolled with a further expectation that of those that did enroll, an additional number will drop out.[29]

Before we leave the *Castro* case, there is an epilogue. During the months following the *Castro* decision, while the preliminary injunctive relief was in full force and effect, the district exercised its legal right to develop an alternate plan on the issue of school closures and budgetary problems that would meet the constitutional and legal principles ruled in the case. On November 23, 1982, the court accepted a plan, by which the district called for the original action to close Phoenix Union High School.[30] However, in order to solve the problem of not having a high school in the inner city to accommodate the population of predominantly students of color, the district proposed to reopen North High, a previously closed school with predominantly students of color, relatively nearby Phoenix Union. Furthermore, in order to tackle the issue of burden, the district ended the open enrollment policy for the Central, North, and Phoenix Union attendance areas and made some boundary changes. The district expected that these changes would result in a sharing, by Whites and students of color, of the burden of displacement to North and Central. For the 1982–1983 school year, North began operation with a freshman class of about six hundred students. In each of the three following years, a sophomore, junior, and senior class were respectively added, resulting in a four-year comprehensive high school by the 1985–1986 school year.

To some people, this major post-hearing development meant that the win by plaintiffs in the *Castro* injunctive relief hearing constituted a pyrrhic victory. This may be true. In the most optimistic sense, however, two points are noteworthy. First, the Mexican American and African American community, which predominated in population in the inner city of Phoenix, still had a school nearby that could serve it. Second, the ending of the open enrollment policy in the affected areas became a first step in desegregating the district's heavily segregated schools. Under the open enrollment policy, Whites residing in school attendance areas in which students of color predominated tended to flee to White schools. At the time, plaintiffs' counsel believed these two positive aspects worth considering in light of all that had transpired.

Diaz v. San Jose Unified School District (1985)

This lawsuit is more appropriately known as a desegregation case, and a long-standing one at that (see chapter 2, this volume, for a discussion of the desegregative aspects of *Diaz v. San Jose*). The action in *Diaz* initially began in 1971, followed by a series of decisions in the U.S. District Court for the Northern District of California and the Ninth Circuit Court of Appeals. In 1985, the San Jose Unified School District (SJUSD) sought to have the U.S. District Court approve a proposed desegregation plan (largely based on a voluntary magnet program). The plaintiffs, predominantly Mexican Americans, offered an alternative plan.

Although *Diaz* was a desegregation case, the SJUSD—in its plan—sought to close three predominantly Mexican American schools. They were, with their respective percentage of students of color, San Jose High School (83.8%), Peter Burnett Middle School (81.2%), and Gardner Elementary School (91.8%). The SJUSD did not propose any White schools for closure.[31] Given my reputation as the top expert on school closures involving students of color, counsel for plaintiffs asked me to testify in *Diaz*.[32]

Regarding the closure of San Jose High School, the SJUSD modified its plan to keep the school open but opted to convert it to a school for grades 6 to 12. Two other experts and I testified that this was a very unwise proposal. In his opinion, presiding Judge Robert F. Peckham found,

> The court finds persuasive testimony by plaintiffs' experts, Mr. Alves, Dr. Willie, and Dr. Valencia, indicating that such an idea is educationally unsound. They assert that this proposal runs counter to conventional wisdom about appropriate grade levels. Moving the middle school to the high school runs the unnecessary risk of exposing youths at too early an age to more pseudo-sophisticated ideas about social relationships, drugs,

and dropping out. The District did not counter this testimony with evidence that its plan was the product of a carefully considered change in educational policy.[33]

With respect to the closures of Peter Burnett Middle School and Gardner Elementary School, my testimony focused on the growing "goodness of fit" at these two schools.[34] Judge Peckham noted,

> Plaintiffs' expert, Dr. Richard Valencia, testified about the developing "goodness of fit" at Burnett School. He cited factors such as improving test scores, students' use of the media center before and after school, use of computer-assisted instruction lab by disadvantaged students, participation in extracurricular activities, the university outreach program, parental involvement, and the nature and conditions of the school facilities.[35]

Judge Peckham further commented, "The court, therefore, declines to place its imprimatur on the District's proposal as part of this desegregation plan. San Jose High, Peter Burnett, and Gardner [will remain open and] will become district-wide magnets at their current grade levels."[36] Although the SJUSD proved victorious in getting its very limited desegregation plan approved, and the plaintiffs lost their attempt to have their comprehensive plan (involving busing) approved by the court (see chapter 1, this volume), plaintiffs did win in preventing the closure of three predominantly Mexican American schools.

Conclusion

Although the *Angeles, Castro,* and *Diaz* cases may not be as well known as other Mexican American–initiated lawsuits (e.g., *Rodriguez* and *Cisneros*), these school closure cases deserve more than a mere footnote in the history of Mexican American educational litigation. They are important for the Mexican American community because they represented a *new form of denial* that did not previously exist (Valencia, 1980). In the past, whatever difficulties Mexican Americans experienced in education, they at least had neighborhood schools. In the 1980s, however, it appeared that even such schools for Mexican Americans were in jeopardy. The implication of this new form of denial held disastrous potential. By denying neighborhood schools to the Mexican American community in Santa Barbara,

Phoenix, and San Jose, district officials created conditions that hampered and even prevented Mexican American parents from participating in their children's education. Rather than school districts building on goodness-of-fit strengths existing within the Mexican American schools and the community in terms of academic achievement gains, school-community cohesiveness, bilingual education, and so forth, this new form of denial set in motion an erosion and disintegration of the very recent and small educational gains that Mexican Americans had made in Santa Barbara, Phoenix, San Jose, and elsewhere in the 1960s and 1970s.

Analyzing and understanding these racialized school closures through the lens of CRT, we can see how race and racism are so central in the political economy of the educational system. This analysis also helps to explain the actions of White-dominated school boards in these cases. School board members (overwhelmingly White) are elected by their constituents and are expected to serve them. In these cases, they protected White privilege. CRT also recognizes that the voices of the parents and their children in *Angeles, Castro,* and *Diaz* were central in providing their attorneys and experts, and the courts, with their experiential knowledge of the importance and value of having schools near their homes.

In conclusion, declining school enrollments and the school closure issue remain concerns of the past for our nation.[37] Given that our country's population is projected to increase from 281,422,000 people in the year 2000 to 570,954,000 in the year 2100 (a 103% increase),[38] the construction of new schools will be a priority for decades to come. Yet it is important to be cognizant that at one time in our nation's history school boards closed many schools, and in several communities, Mexican American schools were targeted for closure, resulting in a new form of educational denial. This chronicle shows how the Mexican American people—in *Angeles, Castro,* and *Diaz*—demonstrated unrelenting resolve in their legal struggle for social justice and educational equality.

6

Undocumented Students

On April 10, 2006, nearly two million people (mostly Latino) marched in seventy cities across the United States, protesting the restrictive immigration bills before Congress (Mangaliman, Rodriguez, & Gonzales, 2006). The current "immigration crisis" (López, 2005) reflects the historical vicissitudes of America's hostile attitudes and policies toward immigrants, especially the undocumented (Brinkley, 1993; Green, 2003; López, 2005).

Anti-immigration sentiment also characterized the 1970s, with calls to reestablish immigration exclusion (Green, 2003). The severe inflation that gripped the decade likely triggered these emotions (DeLong, 1995).[1] As the scapegoating theory of prejudice would predict (Schaefer, 2002), immigration exclusionists blamed undocumented people for the ailing economy. As a case in point, in 1975 the Texas Legislature amended the Texas Education Code to expel undocumented children (overwhelmingly Mexican origin) from the public schools. Proponents asserted that these children were an economic burden and should be removed from school *or* made to pay tuition. This legislative action sparked a major lawsuit by Mexican-origin people that the U.S. Supreme Court finally decided in their favor and "paved the way for the establishment of new rights for undocumented children" (Wilcoxen, 1985, p. 1101). From a CRT perspective, the chronicle discussed here represents a monumental challenge to dominant ideology (exclusion of the unwanted) and an unwavering commitment to social justice.

The rest of this chapter covers (a) the catalyst for undocumented student litigation: the amendment of Texas Education Code §21.031; (b) the Tyler Independent School District's compliance with §21.031: setting the stage for little Ana Flores and her peers to fight back; (c) *Hernandez v. Houston* (1977) and *Doe v. Plyler* (1978): the initial lawsuits; (d) *In re Alien Children Education Litigation*: lawsuits flood the federal district courts of

Texas; (e) *Plyler v. Doe* (1982): undocumented children prevail in the U.S. Supreme Court.

The Catalyst for Undocumented Student Litigation: The Amendment of Texas Education Code §21.031

Prior to the amendment of Texas Education Code (TEC) §21.031 by the Legislature in May 1975, the Education Code provided,

> (a) *All children* [italics added] without regard to color over the age of six years and under the age of 18 years . . . shall be entitled to the benefits of the Available School Fund for that year.
>
> (b) *Every child in this state* [italics added] over the age of six years and not over the age of 21 years . . . shall be permitted to attend the public free schools of the district in which he resides or in which his parent, guardian, or the person having lawful control of him resides.
>
> (c) The board of trustees of any public free school district of this state shall admit into the public free schools of the district *free of tuition all persons* [italics added] over six and not over 21 years of age . . . if such person or his parent, guardian or person having lawful control resides within the school district. (Vernon Supp. 1970, pp. 1480–1481)

The uncontrolled flow of the undocumented (mostly Mexicans in search of work) across the porous Texas-Mexico border and the subsequent enrollment of children from undocumented families in Texas's public schools prompted action by the Texas Legislature. State Representative Ruben Torres, sponsor of the amendment of TEC §21.031 (hereafter referred to as §21.031 or TEC §21.031), entered a resolution to the Texas House of Representatives warning that "As the number of illegal aliens in Texas continues to increase, many financially troubled districts find it difficult to provide educational services for alien children without adversely affecting the overall quality of such services" (Heberton, 1982, p. 122, n. 13). Not a scintilla of legislative history accompanied the amendment, nor did floor debate occur before the Legislature passed the new law by a voice vote.[2] At the time, no other state excluded undocumented children from enrolling in public schools.

Aside from some minor changes in the upper and lower age boundaries of students allowed to enroll in Texas schools, the changes in §21.031

had dire implications for undocumented children. Part "a" of §21.031 (Admission) was changed from "All children . . ." to "All children who are citizens of the United States or legally admitted aliens . . ." Part "b" was rewritten from "Every child in this state . . ." to "Every child in this State who is a citizen of the United States or legally admitted alien . . ." Finally, part "c" was changed from "shall admit into the public free schools of the district free of tuition all persons . . ." to "shall admit into the public free schools of the district free of tuition all persons who are citizens of the United States or legally admitted aliens . . ." (Vernon Supp. 1976, p. 23).[3] Notwithstanding the major change from universal access to education to access for students who were U.S. citizens, school districts had some latitude in interpreting the amendment of §21.031 of the Texas Education Code. First, districts could flatly exclude undocumented students from enrolling. Second, districts could charge a tuition fee as a condition of enrollment. Third, they could continue to enroll undocumented students on a tuition-free arrangement.[4] The Tyler Independent School District, for example, continued to allow undocumented students to enroll in its schools for the next two academic years before requiring tuition in the following year.[5]

The Tyler Independent School District's Compliance with §21.031: Setting the Stage for Little Ana Flores and Her Peers to Fight Back

The same year (1975) that the Legislature amended §21.031, the Flores family immigrated illegally from Mexico, finally settling in Tyler, Texas (Gamboa, 1994).[6] Similar to numerous undocumented families who immigrated to Texas in search of work, the Flores family—consisting of father, mother, Ana, and her seven siblings—followed this path. Tyler, located in East Texas about ninety miles from Dallas on Interstate 20, is known as the "Rose Capital of the World." In addition to employment in the growing, harvesting, and packaging of rose bushes, the local foundries (factories for the casting of iron pipes) provided employment. Jim Plyler, who became superintendent of the Tyler Independent School District (TISD) in 1969 and lead defendant in *Doe v. Plyler* (1978), recalled, "Local people wouldn't work for minimum wage, but the Hispanics would" (Gamboa, 1994, p. A7).

Regarding the new law, Superintendent Plyler noted, "The first year of the law we didn't implement it. We just let these youngsters come. We didn't have many." He continued, "But then they started coming in busloads and truckloads as soon as they [the parents] heard there were jobs here." Regarding the budgetary implications for the TISD, Plyler said, "I was the bad guy then. But the whole thing was we were trying to get some state money. We couldn't afford to educate all these kids locally" (Gamboa, 1994, p. A7).

The TISD Board of Trustees shared Plyler's trepidations about a financial shortfall. In July 1977, worried that the district "would become a 'haven' for illegal aliens,"[7] the Board of Trustees adopted the following policy:

The Tyler Independent School District shall enroll all qualified students who are citizens of the United States or legally admitted aliens, and who are residents of this school district, free of tuition charge. *Illegal alien children may enroll and attend schools in the Tyler Independent School District by payment of the full tuition fee* [italics added].[8]

The Board set the tuition fee at $1,000 per undocumented student per school year.[9] The amount of the tuition was arrived at by dividing TISD's yearly operational budget of $18.5 million by the estimated district enrollment of sixteen thousand students.[10] Given that the total number of undocumented students in the district ranged from between forty-six and fifty-six,[11] these students imposed a very small overall financial drain on the district.[12]

TISD officials notified the parents of the undocumented students that their children would not be able to attend school "without either producing the required documents or paying the $1,000 tuition fee."[13] The parents could not expect to be eligible for citizenship, as they would have difficulty providing the necessary family relationship with either a citizen of the United States or a permanent resident alien, *or* specific skills.[14] And the parents certainly could not pay the $1,000 tuition fee.[15] At the time, an undocumented family in Texas earned an average yearly salary of less than $4,000 (Osifchok, 1982). Because they could not satisfy either statutory option, TISD schools forcibly expelled the undocumented students. Ana Flores, the oldest of eight children, was eleven years old when she learned she could no longer attend school in the TISD. Flores, interviewed in 1994 at the age of twenty-eight, recalled, "I remember thinking, what's

going to happen to me?" (Gamboa, 1994, p. A1). Little did Ana know at
the time that her and her peers' dismissal from school in 1977 and their
subsequent lawsuit would lead to a landmark U.S. Supreme Court decision in 1982 that granted *all* children in the United States, irrespective of
their citizenship status, the right to a free public education. On September 6, 1977, four sets of undocumented parents who served as guardians
ad litem for their sixteen collective children (including the Flores family)
filed *Doe v. Plyler* in federal district court.[16]

Hernandez v. Houston (1977) *and* Doe v. Plyler (1978): *The Initial Lawsuits*

Hernandez v. Houston and *Doe v. Plyler* were filed months apart in 1977,
the former case in February and the latter in September. This chapter's
coverage of *Doe v. Plyler*, compared to *Hernandez*, is more comprehensive
because the legal chronicle is much more expansive and the opinion lays
out a bedrock of conclusions that survive, with some exceptions, all the
way to the U.S. Supreme Court.

Hernandez arose when a group of undocumented children and parents
brought suit against the Houston Independent School District (HISD).
Approximately five thousand of such children resided in the district[17] and
could enroll in school if they paid a monthly tuition fee.[18] Plaintiffs first
sought an administrative remedy but exhausted all these avenues, with
both the Commissioner of Education and the State Board of Education
denying their petitions.[19] The plaintiffs then filed suit in the 126th District
Court of Travis County, seeking an injunction to require the defendants
to admit the undocumented children.[20] They claimed that the HISD, by
denying admission to undocumented children under the full force of
§21.031, violated the Equal Protection Clause of both the U.S. and Texas
Constitutions.[21] The district court, however, affirmed the State Board of
Education's order and declared §21.031 constitutional.

Plaintiffs then appealed to the Texas Court of Civil Appeals, Third District, in Austin.[22] Although Judge Bob Shannon, who wrote the opinion
(November 16, 1977), did not mention it by name, he applied the "two-
tiered" test for determining if a heightened level of judicial scrutiny should
apply in an equal protection violation claim (see Cooper, 1995). Does the
new law violate a "fundamental right" or create a "suspect class"?[23] If so,
strict scrutiny must apply. In his opinion, Judge Shannon explained,

In an equal protection of the law analysis, the reviewing court, of necessity, must recognize the applicable standard of judicial scrutiny. If the questioned statute infringes upon a "fundamental right" or creates an inherently "suspect classification," the statute will be subjected to strict judicial scrutiny. Such scrutiny requires the state to establish a compelling interest in its enactment. To discharge such a burden the state must demonstrate that its purpose or interest is both constitutionally permissible and substantial, and that its use of the classification is necessary to the accomplishment of its purpose.[24]

Citing *San Antonio Independent School District v. Rodriguez* (1973), Judge Shannon found that a tuition-free education is not a fundamental right warranting "strict judicial scrutiny."[25] On the question of suspect classification, Judge Shannon ruled that classifications based on alienage in themselves are suspect and thus are bound to strict scrutiny.[26] Yet, he noted, the existing cases covered only classifications of *legal* aliens, not illegal ones. Judge Shannon concluded, "Those cases, then, are not authority for the premise that illegal aliens comprise a suspect classification subject to strict scrutiny."[27] In sum, the appellate court affirmed the district court's decision.[28] Judge Shannon also knew that the U.S. District Court in *Doe v. Plyler* (1978) had already entered a temporary injunctive order against the TISD. He wrote, however, that even if the appellate court were to consider the findings and conclusions of the *Doe v. Plyler* temporary injunction as an opinion of the court, "an unreported and unpublished opinion of a United States district court is of questionable precedential value in determining how the Supreme Court of the United States would decide the constitutional issues presented by §21.031."[29] A question arises: How might the *Hernandez* court have ruled had the published opinion from *Doe v. Plyler* been available, a landmark decision in which undocumented children plaintiffs prevailed?

Following on the heels of *Hernandez*, undocumented children in Tyler challenged the legality of §21.031, filing *Doe v. Plyler* on September 6, 1977 —about ten weeks before the Texas Court of Civil Appeals released the *Hernandez* ruling on November 16. Sixteen undocumented Mexican children, whose parents served as guardians ad litem, were plaintiffs.[30] Given their undocumented status, the four sets of parents feared disclosure of their identities and therefore filed their complaint using pseudonyms ("Doe," "Boe," "Roe," and "Loe").[31] The defendants included James Plyler, the TISD Superintendent, and the seven-member Board of Trustees of the

TISD. At a hearing on September 9, the court approved the State's motion to intervene as a defendant.[32] The trial, which lasted two days, was held in the U.S. District Court for the Eastern District of Texas (Tyler Division). The Honorable William Wayne Justice presided.[33]

Plaintiffs sought injunctive and declaratory relief against the TISD for excluding their children from attending school, pursuant to TEC §21.031, basing their claims on a violation of the Equal Protection Clause of the Fourteenth Amendment and 42 U.S.C. §1981.[34] Plaintiffs also asserted that the federal Immigration and Nationality Act, 8 U.S.C. §§1101 et seq., pre-empted §21.031.[35]

As seen in some other lawsuits covered in this book, the plaintiffs availed themselves of expert witnesses, who provided testimony on the following topics: "(1) the historical framework of illegal emigration from Mexico into the U.S.; (2) the general characteristics of illegal immigrants; (3) school financing in Texas; (4) the educational needs of Mexican children."[36] The defendants also had expert witnesses who provided testimony on the educational needs of Mexican children and immigration.[37]

The State asserted that the "wave of [illegal] migration has presented grave problems for the public schools of Texas,"[38] particularly overcrowding, resulting in a need to augment schools or build new ones. Yet, due to limited funds, some schools districts were unable to undertake the needed construction.[39] The State also argued that many of the illegal students spoke little or no English and thus needed bilingual education programs, but it was difficult to locate qualified personnel for these programs.[40] Defendants also claimed that undocumented children are generally from poor families. As such, the breadwinners of these families add little to the district tax base that goes to help support local school funding.[41] In sum, the State argued that the flow of undocumented Mexican children into Texas schools created severe financial hardships for many school districts.

Judge Justice found the defendant witnesses' testimony unconvincing. First, on the issue of alleged serious financial costs due to the education of the undocumented students in the TISD, the court found this consequence to be negligible.[42] Related to this claim of severe financial impact, the court noted that the federal government funds a wide variety of local school expenditures. For example, federal funds pay for "the free breakfast, lunch, and clothing programs for which many children of Mexican origin are eligible, whether or not they are legal residents."[43] Furthermore, the federal government serves as the largest single funding source for bilingual education programs, which funds about 45% of the total cost. Of the remaining 55% of funding, 80% comes from local funds, and the state pays for 20%.[44] Second, Judge Justice found the link between the "economy measure" of denying undocumented students access to the advantages of the Available School Fund[45] and providing increased quality for other students (i.e., legal residents) to be inaccurate and frequently "perverse in operation."[46] He noted,

> Prior to the enactment of section 21.031 in 1975, a district could include undocumented children in its ADA and receive state funds accordingly. Under section 21.031, however, a district is required to exclude undocumented children from its ADA, decreasing the amount of state funds it receives. Meanwhile, the diminished enrollment, by reason of the factors described above, is unlikely to have resulted in any savings to the local district. The school district is then forced to choose between increasing its own contribution, so as to maintain the current level of expenditures, or cutting back on its programs. Although the state will have saved money, it will not necessarily have improved the quality of education.[47]

Regarding judicial scrutiny, Judge Justice recognized, like Judge Shannon in the *Hernandez* case, the importance of the strict scrutiny standard.[48] Noting plaintiffs' assertion that the strict scrutiny standard should attach in the instant case, Judge Justice wrote,

> Plaintiffs[49] . . . argue that the challenged statute and policy should be subjected to close judicial scrutiny because: (1) plaintiffs are being absolutely deprived of any education; and (2) they are a politically powerless minority, forced to suffer because of the misdeeds of parents over whom they have no control.[50] The fiscal justifications advanced by the Tyler I.S.D. in support of their policy, plaintiffs contend, are insufficiently compelling to justify the discrimination imposed.[51]

With respect to plaintiffs' assertion that the undocumented children suffered absolute deprivation of education, Judge Justice noted that based on the holding of *Rodriguez* (see chapter 2, this volume), education is *not* a fundamental right guaranteed by the Constitution. The U.S. Supreme Court in *Rodriguez* limited its decision to the notion of *relative*, not absolute, deprivation. Judge Justice then noted that the Supreme Court opinion "is conspicuous in its efforts not to foreclose strict scrutiny in response to constitutional challenges to absolute deprivation of educational opportunity."[52] On the issue of a suspect class, Judge Justice found that undocumented people do not constitute a suspect class when they violate a state law or regulation whose central purpose is conformity with a federal objective. He commented, however, that a suspect class arises by reason of the undisputed history of exploitation and abuse of the undocumented in specific conditions that are not related to the federal bases that can be used for their exclusion.[53] In search of some middle ground, Judge Justice wrote,

> A reconciliation of this conflict might be accomplished by recognizing illegal aliens as a suspect class and requiring strict scrutiny in situations where the state acts independently of the federal exclusionary purposes,[54] accepts the presence of illegal aliens, and then subjects them to discriminatory laws.[55]

Judge Justice thus addressed the standard two-tiered test but found it unnecessary to establish a basis for strict scrutiny because the policies of §21.031 failed the much more lenient rational basis test.[56] One basis for his finding of irrationality is that undocumented children, as a class, are essentially indistinguishable from legally resident Mexican American children regarding their problems (e.g., poverty) and educational needs (e.g., bilingual education; free breakfast/lunch programs). "Viewed in light of the state's own statement of the issue with which section 21.031 attempts to deal, the irrationality of its choice of means is clearly revealed."[57]

Another significant issue arose in *Doe v. Plyler:* Were the undocumented children protected under the Fourteenth Amendment? Judge Justice reasoned that although the federal courts had not specifically extended equal protection to illegal aliens, neither the language nor logic of the Fourteenth Amendment precludes such an interpretation. He cited a number of cases where *due process* extends to illegal aliens, suggesting that equal protection applies as well.[58] The key to understanding the rationale for this extension lay in the structure of section 1 of the Fourteenth Amendment:

> No State shall make or enforce any laws which shall abridge the privileges or immunities of citizens of the United States; nor shall any State deprive *any person of life, liberty, or property, without due process of law; nor deny to any person within its jurisdiction the equal protection of the laws* [italics added].

Whereas due process is available to "any person," the Equal Protection Clause is afforded to "any person within its (the state's) jurisdiction." Judge Justice wrote that although the Fourteenth Amendment applies to illegal aliens, it does not guarantee exactly the same treatment as citizens or legal resident aliens. He quoted Justice Jackson, who denoted, in *Railway Express Agency v. New York* (1949), the "salutary doctrine" of the Equal Protection Clause: "cities, states and Federal Government must exercise their powers so as not to discriminate between their inhabitants except upon some reasonable differentiation fairly related to the object of regulation."[59] In a historic ruling on September 14, 1978, Judge Justice found,

> By virtue of its lack of rationality, section 21.031 of the Texas Education Code violates the equal protection clause of the Fourteenth amendment and hence is unconstitutional. Therefore, the defendants will be permanently enjoined from applying section 21.031 of the Texas Education Code and the policy adopted by the Board of Trustees of the Tyler I.S.D. on July 21, 1977, so as to deny free public education to any children in the Tyler I.S.D. solely on the basis of their status as undocumented Mexican aliens.[60]

The outcome of *Doe v. Plyler*, one of the most comprehensively examined Mexican American–initiated lawsuits,[61] stands as a monumental legal victory for the Mexican-origin community. But would Judge Justice's decision survive on appeal? Given the defendants' victory in *Hernandez*, an appeal of the *Doe v. Plyler* ruling to the Fifth Circuit was inevitable. Furthermore, given the legal indeterminacy that rose from opposite rulings in *Hernandez* and *Doe v. Plyler*, at least two school districts (HISD and TISD) in Texas operated under conflicting court orders.[62] School officials of the other 1,097 school districts must have asked at the time, How are we supposed to interpret these discordant orders?

In re Alien Children Education Litigation: *Lawsuits Flood the Federal District Courts of Texas*

On September 18, 1978—mere days after the Tyler District Court released the *Doe v. Plyler* ruling—a group of undocumented Mexican children filed *Martinez v. Reagen* in the U.S. District Court for the Southern District of Texas (Houston Division). Listed in Table 6.1, *Martinez* was one

TABLE 6.1

Consolidation of Seventeen Federal District Court Lawsuits Challenging the
Constitutionality of Texas Education Code §21.031

U.S. District Court	Parties	Case No.	Division	Filing Date
Southern	*Martinez v. Reagen*[a]	H-78-1797	Houston	9/18/78
	Mendoza v. Clark[a]	H-78-1831	Houston	9/22/78
	Cardenas v. Meyer[a]	H-78-1862	Houston	9/27/78
	Garza v. Reagen[a]	H-78-2132	Houston	11/6/78
	Cortes v. Wheeler[b]	H-79-1926	Houston	9/20/79
	Rodrigues v. Meyer[b]	H-79-1927	Houston	9/20/79
	Adamo v. Reagen[b]	H-79-1928	Houston	9/20/79
	Arguelles v. Meyer[b]	H-79-2071	Houston	10/4/79
Northern	*Boe v. Wright*[a]	3-79-0440-D	Dallas	4/79
Western	*Roe v. Holm*[a]	MO-79-CA-49	Midland/Odessa	6/79
	Coe v. Holm[a]	MO-79-CA-54	Midland/Odessa	7/79
Eastern	*Doe v. Lodestro*[b]	B-79-618-CA	Beaumont	9/18/79
	Roe v. Horn[b]	TY-79-338-CA	Tyler	9/24/79
	Doe v. Ford[b]	TY-79-351-CA	Tyler	9/28/79
	Roe v. Como-Pickton[b]	P-79-234-CA	Paris	10/19/79
	Doe v. Sulphur Springs[b]	P-79-31-CA	Paris	10/29/79
	Poe v. Chappel Hill[b]	TY-79-449-CA	Tyler	12/10/79

[a] Case was part of the original set of lawsuits ($n = 7$) that were consolidated. [b] Case was part of the second set of lawsuits ($n = 10$). Referred to as "tag-along actions," this second set was merged with the first set of cases to constitute an overall consolidation, known as *In re Alien Children Education Litigation* (1980).

of seventeen lawsuits challenging §21.031 of the Texas Education Code. Meanwhile, after *Martinez*, three other similar lawsuits (*Mendoza v. Clark, Cardenas v. Meyer*, and *Garza v. Reagen*) were filed in the Southern District. Next, *Boe v. Wright* was filed in the Northern District, followed by the filing of *Roe v. Holm* and *Coe v. Holm* in the Western District. Given the commonality of the various complaints, the State filed a petition with the Judicial Panel on Multidistrict Litigation (JPMDL) requesting the consolidation and centralization of the seven lawsuits (indicated by a superscript "a" in Table 6.1).[63] Pursuant to 28 U.S.C. §1407,[64] the JPMDL transferred the consolidated cases on November 16, 1979, to the U.S. District Court for the Southern District of Texas, with that court's consent, for consolidated pretrial proceedings. Beginning on September 18, 1979, and ending on December 10, 1979, a second deluge of lawsuits (referred to in legal terminology as "tag-along actions") were filed. These ten cases (indicated by a superscript "b" in Table 6.1) were filed in the Southern and Eastern Districts and then merged with the other seven cases to form an overall consolidation, known as *In re Alien Children Education Litigation* (*Alien Children*).[65]

Judge Woodrow B. Seals heard *Alien Children* in the U.S. District Court for the Southern District of Texas (Houston Division). Prior to hearing the case, on December 20, 1979, Judge Seals held a conference for the purpose of discussing the schedule for carrying out the consolidated pretrial proceedings. Both parties agreed to have the court rule on plaintiffs' claim that §21.031 was unconstitutional (Cantú & Garza, 1981). The plaintiffs in *Alien Children* consisted of the combined children noted in the seventeen actions listed in Table 6.1.[66] Defendants included the State of Texas and the Texas Education Agency (TEA), and later the Commissioner of Education and the Governor of Texas entered the case as defendants. Collectively, these defendants were referred to as the "State."[67]

On the strength of *Doe v. Plyler*, plaintiffs moved for summary judgment, using the doctrine of collateral estoppel[68] and arguing that *Doe v. Plyler* settled (a) whether §21.031 violates the Equal Protection Clause of the Fourteenth Amendment (it does) and (b) whether the Immigration and Naturalization Act preempts §21.031.[69] Judge Seals denied the summary judgment, noting that *Doe v. Plyler* and the instant case are not identical. The former case applied only to the TISD, whereas the latter multidistrict litigation case had a broader scope.[70]

The *Alien Children* hearing was protracted, covering twenty-four days of testimony and arguments[71] of several key points including (a) exclusionary consequence of §21.031 on plaintiffs' enrollment; (b) psychological effects on the excluded students; (c) the State's rationale for §21.031; (d) application of judicial scrutiny.

1. *Exclusionary consequence of §21.031 on plaintiffs' enrollment.* The exclusionary consequence of §21.031 on undocumented students in the TISD (*Doe v. Plyler* case) was quite small (see note 12, this chapter). In *Alien Children*, however, the exclusionary consequence was much larger. Plaintiffs conducted a survey of sixty Texas school districts (stratified random sample) and introduced the data as evidence obtained from twenty-nine districts with a student enrollment of ten thousand or greater, and thirty-one with an enrollment of ten thousand students or less. The results of the survey showed that of the participating school districts, 73% responded that they would (a) not allow undocumented students to enroll or (b) admit them only on the condition that they pay tuition.[72] In sum, although some school districts continued to enroll undocumented children, the vast majority excluded or charged them tuition.

2. *Psychological effects on the excluded children.* Testimony brought to bear in *Alien Children* dealt with the affective and cognitive harm on the undocumented children due to their exclusion from school. The plaintiffs'

experts unanimously concurred that the children experienced severe psychological damage.[73] Dr. Kenneth Williams, a specialist in child psychiatry, after observing some of the excluded children, commented that irreparable behavioral and emotional problems had set in. He stated,

> Children who are deprived of an education frequently suffer behavioral difficulties which can vary in extent from mild adjustment difficulties, through serious behavior difficulties, like hyperactivity, withdrawing behavior into fairly severe types of difficulties such as depression and breaks with reality. . . . When a child is not allowed to be educated, . . . there is a decrease in the cognitive function of the child and in the ultimate ability of that child to develop adult type thinking patterns. . . . The longer the exclusion goes, the more severe the effect would be.[74]

Dr. Thomas Carter, a frequent expert witness in Mexican American–initiated educational lawsuits,[75] testified that the State, by not allowing the undocumented children to attend school, denied them the most vital means for advancement in society—education. Moreover, Carter underscored the enduring nature of this disability by noting that these children, once adults, seldom gain literacy:

> We can very well say with perhaps a few individual exceptions that (an excluded) child would be illiterate, would be unable to read and unable to write. The child would also miss much of the . . . social training relative to the laws, the customs, the procedures, the organization of the society; that aspect of the formal (socialization) of the child would be missing. (These children) would probably be unable, with the lack of these skills, to integrate themselves into the society as productive members of society. The possibility of an illiterate person (growing) up and functioning at anything but marginal social levels in this industrial, technically advanced society is very hard to picture. He or she would be unable to complete the most rudimentary forms of application for work, which would restrict the individual to those kinds of jobs that would require no training, etc. As you know, these kinds of jobs are disappearing in our society. Cognitively, the child would be unequipped to cope with modern industrial society.[76]

3. *The State's rationale for §21.031.* Notwithstanding the expert testimony on harm and exclusion, the State pressed ahead in its defense of

the statute. In *Alien Children*, the State presented testimony regarding (a) the number of undocumented children residing in Texas; (b) the financial costs on state and local resources for educating these children; (c) the strain of educating these children on the overall quality of education and on compliance with bilingual education and court-ordered desegregation:

- An expert for the defendants estimated that 120,000 undocumented Mexican children resided in Texas.[77] Judge Seals heavily criticized the study as being methodologically unsound and thus unreliable.[78] The court found the estimate by plaintiffs' expert, Dr. Jorge Bustamante, of twenty thousand undocumented Mexican school-age children to be much more in line with estimates from other studies.[79] Even lower estimates were reported. A 1980 study by the Intercultural Development Research Association estimated that thirteen thousand undocumented Mexican children (in this case, students) resided in the state (Cárdenas & Cortez, 1986).

- Regarding fiscal costs, the State argued that §21.031 saved money and conserved the State's resources and that educating undocumented children would disperse the State's educational funding too thinly, resulting in a decline in overall quality of education and the necessity to reduce funding for other social services.[80]

Judge Seals found that without a reliable estimate of the count of undocumented children in Texas, the State could not measure the savings resulting from the exclusion of undocumented children pursuant to §21.031.[81] Nevertheless, based on the evidence, Judge Seals found that both the local school districts and the State could appropriate funds from the state budget surplus of $2.5 billion to provide a free public education to all undocumented children.[82]

- The State argued that the influx of undocumented Mexican children into the schools would strain the State's resources in providing bilingual education programs. As did Judge Justice in *Doe v. Plyler*, Judge Seals in *Alien Children* noted that the federal government provides the bulk of funding for bilingual education, not the State or local school districts. The court "was not convinced that it was necessary to exclude an identifiable portion of the children of limited English speaking ability in order to protect the Mexican-American and documented alien children in the State."[83]

With respect to school desegregation, the State contended that the inundation of undocumented children in schools may affect the number of minority students in some schools and thus make it quite difficult to comply with desegregation decrees. Judge Seals chastised the State: "The State did not even attempt to show that compliance with desegregation orders would be made more difficult. The State's bald assertion is insufficient to provide even a conceivable basis for the statute."[84]

4. *Application of judicial scrutiny.* Judge Seals concluded that the undocumented children suffered the absolute deprivation of education, particularly when such deprivation stems from one's complete inability to pay for the cost of an imposed tuition.[85] He remarked that when strict scrutiny applies, significant and lawful governmental interests are not enough to defend legislative classifications; the State must demonstrate a compelling interest.[86] Judge Seals ruled that financial stability does not constitute a compelling state interest. Moreover, the State failed to show that improving the overall quality of education in Texas requires the exclusion of undocumented children from school. Third, the State did not demonstrate that §21.031 actually advances the interest of the state. The State failed to distinguish between the educational needs of legal residents in Texas (particularly Mexican Americans) and those of the undocumented children. Likewise, the parents of the undocumented children, as do other parents, help finance public education through the taxes they pay. In sum, §21.031 is unnecessary to the attainment of the State's objective.[87] Judge Seals concluded, "The State never attempted to examine the impact of undocumented children on the schools before deciding to exclude them. It is thus not surprising that the classification used is in no way carefully tailored or drawn to advance the state interest."[88]

On July 21, 1980, Judge Seals released his opinion, noting that the denial of education to plaintiff children would ensure that many of them would become wards of society and create enormous social and financial costs to be borne in the future. Judge Seals highlighted this point by quoting from Bishop John Edward McCarthy, who testified in *Alien Children*:

> We are keeping certain people poor, and what we are manufacturing now is a monumental social cost to our society ten and fifteen and twenty years from now. . . . We are manufacturing ignorance; to be ignorant in society is to be nonproductive; to be nonproductive means for many instances to be forced into a state of crime. . . . (W)hether it be right now in the form of modest increases in tuition, in public school operating cost, or . . . in terms of social cost . . . fifteen years from now, we will pay this bill.[89]

Judge Seals also noted that having access to education results in the interchange of ideas and information. Education is central to those conditions that "make life in a free society so precious."[90] The court permanently enjoined the Texas Commissioner of Education from implementing §21.031 (parts a–c) of the Texas Education Code because the statute violated the plaintiffs' equal protection rights under the Fourteenth Amendment.

Soon after, the State appealed the *Alien Children* court's ruling, requesting a stay of the injunction. The Fifth Circuit granted the stay, pending appeal.[91] Thereafter, the plaintiffs applied to the U.S. Supreme Court, requesting that the stay be vacated. Supreme Court Justice Lewis F. Powell served as Circuit Justice for the Fifth Circuit. He rendered his ruling on September 4, 1980,[92] observing that a Circuit Justice has the power to dissolve a stay but must consider specific principles when reviewing the application:

> There must be a reasonable probability that four members of the Court would consider the underlying issue sufficiently meritorious for the grant of certiorari or the notation of probable jurisdiction; there must be a significant possibility of reversal of the lower court's decision; and there must be a likelihood that irreparable harm will result if that decision is not stayed.[93]

On Justice Powell's second point, he reasoned that the formulation must be modified, meaning that there must be a significant probability that a majority of the Court will *affirm* the district court's decision.[94] Justice Powell vacated the stay granted by the Fifth Circuit, finding it reasonable to think that five members of the Court may agree with the finding of the Seals court. He also concluded that the undocumented children would suffer irreparable harm if he did not cancel the stay.[95] On this issue of harm, Justice Powell wrote, "I conclude that the balance of harms weighs heavily on the side of the children, certainly in those school districts where the ability of the local schools to provide education will not be threatened."[96]

Seven weeks after Justice Powell vacated the stay, a three-judge panel of the Fifth Circuit finally ruled (October 20, 1980) on the *Doe v. Plyler* appeal.[97] In its review, the Fifth Circuit zeroed in on the issues of preemption and equal protection. As discussed earlier, Judge Justice in *Doe v. Plyler* found that the TISD's implementation of §21.031 violated the Supremacy Clause of the Constitution because federal immigration laws preempted the Texas statute. The Fifth Circuit agreed with the district court's application of the *DeCanas v. Bica* (1976)[98] standard in analyzing preemption but ruled that the district court applied it incorrectly. That is, the Fifth Circuit concluded, after reviewing the germane federal policy, that the perceived conflicts between state and federal levels were at most "illusory" and that §21.031 did not clash with federal policy.[99]

On the subject of equal protection, the Fifth Circuit examined three issues:

1. *The scope of the Equal Protection Clause.* As did the district court in *Doe v. Plyler*, the Fifth Circuit centered on the "within its jurisdiction" phrase of the Fourteenth Amendment. The appellants argued the illogicality of providing free public education to undocumented children in light of their illegal status. The Fifth Circuit countered, "This contention, however, fails to acknowledge the jurisdictional predicate of the equal protection clause."[100] Hence, the appellate court ruled that the Equal Protection Clause *does* apply to the undocumented.

2. *The applicable standard of review.* The plaintiffs in *Doe v. Plyler* argued that strict scrutiny should apply because §21.031 *absolutely* deprived them of a free public education, which denied them a fundamental interest, and a heightened standard of review is appropriate because the State was punishing the undocumented children for the sins of their parents. For their part, defendants in *Doe v. Plyler* asserted that in *Rodriguez* the Supreme Court held that education was not a fundamental right, and therefore strict scrutiny did not apply. The Fifth Circuit noted, however, that the Supreme Court left unresolved the question of whether an absolute deprivation of education would be constitutional. Although the appellate court acknowledged the importance of education for a child's development, it did not find any constitutional basis for applying strict scrutiny based on the fundamental right test.[101] Nevertheless, in light of the Supreme Court's opinion in *Rodriguez*, the Fifth Circuit refused to find that the Constitution permitted a complete denial of education.

Regarding the undocumented children's violation of immigration laws, the Fifth Circuit found that "they have committed no moral wrong."[102] As such, the Fifth Circuit concurred with the district court that plaintiffs belong to a suspect class, namely aliens, and thus §21.031 called for strict scrutiny. In making this ruling, the appellate court quoted the same passage from *Rodriguez* (see note 49, this chapter), sidestepping a final conclusion on the application of strict scrutiny, since "we need not dwell on that difficult decision, for we find that Section 21.031 is constitutionally infirm regardless of whether it is tested using the mere rational basis standard or some more stringent test."[103]

3. *The statute reviewed.* In summary, the Fifth Circuit boiled appellants' position down to this: "Texas concluded that, in order to protect the education of documented children, it must decrease or avoid increasing the total cost of education; to accomplish this result Texas excluded undocumented children from its free public schools."[104] Texas justified its policy on three grounds: (a) including undocumented students cost the state too much to bear economically; (b) the state feared that the undocumented who had communicable diseases would contaminate citizens and legal aliens; (c) denial of a free education will serve as a disincentive for others to immigrate illegally.[105] The court responded to these three assertions by the appellants as follows:

The court deferred to Texas's right to decide its own economic policy but asserted that Texas cannot devise a policy that violates the Constitution: excluding undocumented students simply to save money does not constitute a permissible reason, particularly when the Equal Protection Clause applies to them as well as to legal aliens. Regarding public health concerns, the Fifth Circuit ruled that excluding undocumented students would in no way control the spread of communicable diseases. Furthermore, the State presented no evidence that undocumented people are more prone to have such diseases compared to the general population. The Fifth Circuit concluded that Texas sought to control the health of the school children in an irrational manner.[106] Finally, as to the discouragement of illegal immigration, the court noted that undocumented families constitute a very small percentage of the total number of illegal immigrants; thus, §21.031 would result in little deterrence. The Fifth Circuit also remarked that Texas refused to pass a statute that restricts employers from hiring undocumented workers, thus casting doubt, in the court's eyes, that the statute rationally relates to its asserted objective.[107]

Accordingly, the Fifth Circuit affirmed the district court's order in *Doe v. Plyler* enjoining the defendants from applying TEC §21.031, as well as the tuition fee policy adopted by the TISD.[108] *Doe v. Plyler*, however, still lacked closure.

Plyler v. Doe (1982): *Undocumented Children Prevail in the U.S. Supreme Court*

Approximately six and a half months after the Fifth Circuit handed down its opinion, the U.S. Supreme Court, on May 4, 1981, noted probable jurisdiction over the *Doe v. Plyler* case,[109] invoking its original jurisdiction in cases involving aliens under 28 U.S.C. §1251(b).[110] Nearly six weeks later, on June 15, 1981, the Supreme Court again noted probable jurisdiction regarding *Certain Named and Unnamed Undocumented Alien Children* and consolidated the two cases under *Plyler v. Doe*.[111] Finally, on June 15, 1982, exactly one year after consolidation, the Supreme Court rendered its decision.[112] In this watershed ruling, widely acknowledged as one of the most significant civil rights cases of the 1980s, the Supreme Court, in a 5–4 decision, affirmed the Fifth Circuit's ruling: the new Texas law violates the Equal Protection Clause of the Fourteenth Amendment.[113]

The Supreme Court first addressed appellants' "outlaw" theory—the argument that undocumented children in Texas violated federal immigration law.[114] Appellants argued that given the undocumented status of the children, Texas was under no legal obligation to provide a free public education to this population, and therefore, §21.031 was justifiable and rational. In countering the outlaw theory, the Supreme Court asserted what the district courts and the Fifth Circuit had focused on: the "within its jurisdiction" phrase of the Fourteenth Amendment. Justice Brennan in his opinion wrote that the use of the phrase

> does not detract from, but rather confirms, the understanding that the protection of the Fourteenth Amendment extends to anyone, citizen or stranger, who is subject to the laws of a State, and reaches into every corner of a State's territory. That a person's initial entry into a State, or into the United States, was unlawful, and that he may for that reason be expelled, cannot negate the simple fact of his presence within the State's territorial perimeter. Given such presence, he is subject to the full range of obligations imposed by the State's civil and criminal laws. And until he leaves the jurisdiction—either voluntarily, or involuntarily in accordance with the Constitution and laws of the United States—he is entitled to the equal protection of the laws that a State may choose to establish.[115]

In summary, the Court concluded that the undocumented children plaintiffs may claim the benefit of the equal protection guarantee of the Fourteenth Amendment.

The second major issue before the *Plyler v. Doe* court had to do with the level of scrutiny. Because the Supreme Court (a) refused to define "illegal aliens" as a suspect class[116] and (b) hesitated to classify education as a fundamental right,[117] this reluctance precluded the application of the strict scrutiny standard as the required level of review. Also, the Court declined to apply the rational basis standard of review.[118] The court reasoned that §21.031 imposed a discriminatory burden on the grounds of a legal characteristic (the children's undocumented status) that the plaintiffs had no power to control. Justice Brennan observed that it was hard to think "of a rational justification for penalizing these children for their presence in the United States. Yet, that appears to be precisely the effect of §21.031."[119] The majority opinion continued by noting that Texas's new education code would create a permanent underclass of people by denying an education to blameless immigrant children. Justice Brennan wrote that the new Texas law will create

> a permanent caste of undocumented resident aliens, encouraged by some to remain here as a source of cheap labor, but nevertheless denied the benefits that our society makes available to citizens and lawful residents. The existence of such an underclass presents most difficult problems for a Nation that prides itself on adherence to principles of equality under law. . . . Section 21.031 imposes a lifetime hardship on a discrete class of children not accountable for their disabling status. The stigma of illiteracy will mark them for the rest of their lives. By denying these children a basic education, we deny them the ability to live within the structure of our civic institutions, and foreclose any realistic possibility that they will contribute in even the smallest way to the progress of our Nation. In determining the rationality of § 21.031, we may appropriately take into account its costs to the Nation and to the innocent children who are its victims. In light of these countervailing costs, the discrimination contained in § 21.031 can hardly be considered rational unless it furthers some substantial goal of the State.[120]

The Court, accordingly, selected an intermediate standard of review to utilize in its analysis of the new Texas education code.[121]

In its application of the intermediate scrutiny standard, the Supreme Court found that the undocumented are "special members" of the "underclass" referred to as illegal aliens.[122] In the legal literature, scholars describe this special classification as "sensitive" instead of "suspect."[123] The Court also applied the intermediate standard of review to §21.031 in regards to the fundamental importance of education. Here, the Court spoke in some detail about the supreme significance of an individual having an education and the subsequent positive consequences for society as a whole. Justice Brennan's opinion even quoted from the historic *Brown v. Board of Education of Topeka* (1954):

> Today, education is perhaps the most important function of state and local governments. Compulsory school attendance laws and the great expenditures for education both demonstrate our recognition of the importance of education to our democratic society. It is required in the performance of our most basic public responsibilities, even service in the armed forces. It is the very foundation of good citizenship. Today it is a principal instrument in awakening the child to cultural values, in preparing him for later professional training, and in helping him to adjust normally to his environment. In these days, it is doubtful that any child may reasonably be expected to succeed in life if he is denied the opportunity of an education. Such an opportunity, where the state has undertaken to provide it, is a right which must be made available to all on equal terms.[124]

In this context, the status of education carries a very important interest, a "special interest" (but not a "fundamental right").[125] To sum up, the Court justified its selection of the intermediate standard for §21.031 using the combination of undocumented children classified as a "sensitive class" and education considered a "special interest."

A third issue that the Supreme Court addressed was appellants' argument that §21.031 helps to preserve "the state's limited resources for the education of its lawful residents."[126] The Court commented on three points. First, the State presented no evidence to substantiate that the undocumented impose any burden of consequence on Texas's economy. To the contrary, the Court stated, plaintiffs provided ample evidence that the undocumented underutilize the various public services, while partaking in the labor market and paying taxes.[127] Second, the State provided no evidence whatsoever to support their claim that the exclusion of undocumented children from school will result in enough financial gain to improve the quality of education in Texas.[128] Third, the appellants suggested that they appropriately singled out the undocumented children because their illegal presence in the United States makes them less likely, compared to other children, to stay in Texas and put their schooling to productive political or social use. The Court noted that the State could neither quantify nor guarantee that any child, undocumented or citizen, will remain in Texas and put his or her education to good use.[129]

As *Plyler v. Doe* worked its way through the federal court structure during its four-year trek, few lawsuits since *Regents of the University of California v. Bakke* (1978) generated more controversy, as noted by media coverage and scholarly analysis, mostly in law reviews (Hull, 1983). The debate on the constitutionality of §21.031 led to considerable division, as expected, in the legal community. In addition to the U.S. Department of Justice, sixty other groups submitted briefs to the Supreme Court, urging it to sustain or oppose §21.031 (Hull, 1983). The Supreme Court in its deliberations was not immune to this split of authority (Hull, 1983). On June 15, 1982, when the Court announced its opinion, only five Justices—the slimmest majority—had voted to invalidate TEC §21.031. The dissenting opinion, written by Chief Justice Burger, contained language that attacked the majority view with atypical vehemence:[130] "The Constitution does not constitute us as 'Platonic Guardians' nor does it vest in this Court the authority to strike down laws because they do not meet our standards of desirable social policy, 'wisdom,' or 'common sense.'"[131] Chief Justice Burger also remarked, "The Court employs, and in my view abuses, the Fourteenth Amendment in an effort to become an omnipotent and omniscient problem solver."[132] Furthermore, he wrote, "In the end, we are told little more than that the level of scrutiny employed to strike down the Texas law applies only when illegal alien children are deprived of a public education." On this point, Chief Justice Burger continued, "If ever a court was guilty of an unabashedly result-oriented approach, this case is a prime example."[133]

Conclusion

Of the numerous Mexican American–initiated lawsuits discussed in this book, *Plyler* ranks at the top regarding the reach of civil rights on the Mexican-origin community. As a result of it, hundreds of thousands of undocumented Mexican schoolchildren (and undocumented children of other ethnic backgrounds) in the United States are able today to receive a free public education.[134] And this right to education, considered a "special interest" by the Court in *Plyler*, is protected under the Equal Protection Clause of the Fourteenth Amendment. Indubitably, in the field of Mexican American education and civil rights advancement, the *Plyler* decision— the nation's leading case in regard to undocumented students—continues to have far-reaching positive implications for the undocumented Mexican schoolchild and his or her family. One legal scholar comments, "It [*Plyler*] stands among a pantheon of landmark educational cases, such as *Brown v. Board of Education* and *Regents of the University of California v. Bakke*" (López, 2005, p. 1385). Another legal scholar heralds *Plyler* as "the high-water mark for the Latino community in the Supreme Court" (Johnson, 1995, p. 44). The same scholar compares *Plyler* with *Brown v. Board of Education of Topeka*. He asserts, however, that Latinos were part of a much smaller social movement than African Americans and that *Plyler* did not initiate a period of transformation in race relations or result in the principle of equality being deeply implanted in American jurisprudence.

The commitment to social justice, a major tenet of CRT, is clearly evident in the long road to *Plyler*. The year 2007 marked the thirtieth anniversary of when, in 1977, the TISD expelled little Ana Flores and her peers from school because they were undocumented. Because of their dire economic situation, the children could not afford the $1,000 tuition fee that would allow them to enroll in school. In protest, Ana and the excluded children formed a cadre of sixteen plaintiffs that brought forth a lawsuit that sparked a five-year struggle for social justice. This commitment eventually bore fruit in *Plyler* in 1982. In 1994, journalist Paul Feldman tracked down three of the four families, which included thirteen of the original sixteen youngsters (Feldman, 1994). He reported that ten of the thirteen finished high school in Tyler, and many of them went on to take college courses. Yet none had graduated from a four-year college or university. Most of the ten adults had full-time jobs—including employment as an auto mechanic, a stock clerk, and an assembly-line worker at a box factory; two worked as teacher's aides in the TISD. At the time of another interview in 1994, Ana Flores—married with four children—was working as a teacher's aide in the TISD, the same district that kicked her out in 1977 (Gamboa, 1994). All of the thirteen individuals, including Ana, gained legal residency, mainly through the federal amnesty program (see note 16, this chapter). Feldman writes, "In short, the 'Does' of Plyler v. Doe turned out a little like many other blue-collar schoolchildren across small-town America" (1994, p. A22).

What does *Plyler*, this vital ruling, represent? María Pabón López, Assistant Professor at the Indiana University School of Law, states, "Plyler stands for abolition of castes and an affirmation of equality—two precepts which should still be bedrock principles of the critical democratic movement in which we live" (López, 2005, p. 1377). *Plyler* also reminds us that Mexican-origin people in the United States are, in some respects, a conquered people, and "one of the defining features of any conquest is the subordination of the conquered" (Perea, 2003, p. 283). Conquest is, of course, a prime tenet of postcolonial discourse, as well. Texas's attempt to purge the public schools of undocumented children and youths appeared to be motivated by the perception that these students were draining the educational budget and that they therefore should be expelled. The U.S. Supreme Court ruled, however, that Texas's new education law lacked wisdom and, if enacted, would create a lasting caste of undocumented residents. As such, the politics of Texas's new law needs to be viewed in the racialized historical context of the conquest of Mexico by the United States between 1846 and 1848. Legal scholar Juan F. Perea comments,

> Events as large as the conquest of a neighboring country, and the seismic adjustments necessary to accommodate a conquest, have profound implications for both the conquerors and the conquered. The residue of conquest becomes like social DNA, producing and reproducing patterns and trajectories that resemble the originals. We can still sense the residue, the patterns and trajectories, in contemporary re-enactments of one of the themes of the conquest—the denial or limitation of political power to Mexicans, and later, Latino citizens and residents of the United States. (2003, p. 312)

Notwithstanding the civil rights advances realized by *Plyler*, we must ponder the contemporary movement to rid the public schools of undocumented children. As a case in point, voters in California passed Proposition 187 by a 59–41% margin on November 8, 1994. The initiative sought, in part, "to bar state and local governments . . . from providing nonemergency health care and social services and *public education to undocumented immigrants* [italics added]" (Johnson, 1996, p. 2). Section 7 of the initiative—entitled *Exclusion of Illegal Aliens from Public Elementary and Secondary Schools*—directly contravened *Plyler*. Not surprisingly, the vote on the highly controversial and debated Proposition 187 was racialized. Exit polls reported that Whites voted 63% "for" and 37% "against," while Latinos voted 23% "for" and 77% "against" (Johnson, 1996).[135]

A number of factors led to the passage of California's Proposition 187. These include, for example, the state's failing economy coupled with a severe budget crunch, Governor Pete Wilson's reelection campaign in which he sought a hot-button issue (e.g., "illegal aliens") to attract voters, and the cultural wars fueled by some racism and nativism (Johnson, 1996). The concerted political effort to overrule *Plyler* also served as a key factor in passing the referendum. For the architects of Proposition 187 the time to overturn *Plyler* appeared opportune. Writing in 1995, attorney Wayne C. Tobin noted that the U.S. Supreme Court's makeup had changed markedly since the *Plyler* Court of 1982. In 1994, Justice John P. Stevens was the sole remaining member from the majority. Two of the dissenters in *Plyler*, Justices Sandra Day O'Connor and William H. Rehnquist, remained on the Court. Three conservative Justices—Anthony M. Kennedy, Antonin G. Scalia, and Clarence Thomas—had been appointed since 1982. In sum, Tobin (1995) commented, "If the Supreme Court grants certiorari, Proposition 187 and the reasoning of *Plyler* will be analyzed by a Supreme Court less prone to benign judicial activism" (p. 210).

It is exceedingly clear that the designers of Proposition 187 placed Section 7 (exclusion of undocumented students from public schools) in the initiative with the intent for the U.S. Supreme Court to revisit and overrule *Plyler*. In 1995, Alan C. Nelson, coauthor of Proposition 187 and former Commissioner of the Immigration and Naturalization Service (1982–1989) wrote in a "Point/Counterpoint" feature in *Human Rights Brief*,

> The K–12 education provisions of Proposition 187 are the vehicle for the courts to re-visit the concept of free public education for illegal aliens. Current federal law, as established by the U.S. Supreme Court in its 5–4 *Plyler v. Doe* decision of 1982, holds that illegal aliens are entitled to free public education. Proposition 187, with its status checks for all enrollees and a provision on the transition of illegal aliens to their home countries, provides the Court with an opportunity to either hold that the California initiative meets the standards of *Plyler*, or to modify or overturn *Plyler* and allow the plan to stand. With the importance of the issue, it is essential that the Court revisit the issue of free public education of all present and future illegal aliens. By passing Proposition 187, California voters sent a strong message to political leaders that they want to stop illegal immigration and provided a strong catalyst for reasonable and responsible change, not only in California, but throughout the United States. (1995, p. 10)

Frank del Olmo, Deputy Editor of the editorial pages of the *Los Angeles Times*, countered Nelson this way:

> Perhaps no single argument against Proposition 187 makes its proponents so uneasy as what their initiative could wind up costing California

taxpayers. According to the California legislature's chief analyst, lost federal aid to schools, public hospitals, and clinics could add up to $15 billion. That made it hard for Proposition 187's proponents to sell it as a tax-saving initiative in the spirit of Proposition 13. So they changed strategy, and conceded that they did not expect 187 to go into effect right away. They then acknowledged their real goal: pushing the state into what is sure to be a long, costly lawsuit challenging the Supreme Court's *Plyler v. Doe* decision of 1982, which held that immigrant children are entitled to public education. In effect, Proposition 187's authors are gambling with California's tax money in the hope of winning a dubious legal battle. (1995, p. 12)

In sum, the architects of Proposition 187 explicitly included Section 7 in the referendum as part of their strenuous political efforts to achieve a political end: the overturning of *Plyler*. Although the designers succeeded in getting Proposition 187 passed, CRT would predict that a challenge to the orthodoxy would be imminent.

Many immigrants' rights advocates promptly confronted Proposition 187 after its passage. One lawsuit, *League of United Latin American Citizens v. Wilson* (1995, 1997), sought to invalidate Section 7 of the initiative (López, 2005). In the 1995 case, the court ruled that federal law preempted Section 7, as per the Supreme Court's equal protection analysis in *Plyler*.[136] Furthermore, in 1997, the same court cited *Plyler* as controlling case law by finding that §1643 of the California law directly expressed deference to *Plyler*.[137] Although a number of forces propelled the initiative (see Johnson, 1996), "there is no question that Proposition 187, at its core, was a direct challenge to *Plyler v. Doe*" (Cooper, 1995, p. 64).[138]

In light of the current and growing nativist campaign in the United States, the attack on *Plyler* will very likely escalate.[139] For example, on November 2, 2004, Arizona voters approved Proposition 200 (the Arizona Taxpayer and Citizen Protection Act) with a 56% "yes" vote.[140] The initiative would mandate that all Arizonans demonstrate proof of citizenship in order to vote and receive non-federally-mandated public benefits. Attorney General Terry Goddard stated that the children of undocumented workers would be exempt.[141] Four months after Arizona voters approved Proposition 200, the Arizona Legislature proposed a statute—in direct contravention of *Plyler*—that would require the state to verify the immigration status of students' parents before their children could enroll in primary and secondary school.[142] Furthermore, the Texas Legislature is attempting to revoke birthright citizenship (i.e., *jus soli* citizenship; see conclusion, this volume). Given that these anti-undocumented actions will very likely intensify across the nation, concomitantly there will need to be a renewed commitment to social justice for the educational rights of undocumented Mexican and other Latino students. As a number of post-colonial theorists, including Rodolfo Acuña and Frantz Fanon, point out, colonialism, once established, is very difficult to remove entirely. Education is a prime means by which a conquered people pass stories of their origins and treatment on from generation to generation. One lesson of this chapter, then, is that a dominant culture that demands assimilation as a condition of entry and places little premium on diversity will constantly seek means to deprive their colonized children of the training and tools they need to carry out the tasks of asserting their rights.

7

Higher Education Financing

The legal category of higher education financing significantly departs from the other groupings, with *higher education* as the target educational level. In 1990, Mexican Americans living in the "Border Region" of South Texas filed *LULAC v. Clements*, complaining that although 20% of all Texans reside there, the region only receives 10% of the state's higher education funds.[1] Although plaintiffs did not prevail, the attention generated by the case prompted the Texas Legislature to provide a considerable amount of funding to a number of targeted universities in the Border Region.

This chapter is structured as follows: (a) Mexican Americans' limited enrollment in higher education: Type I access problem; (b) limited funding for development of higher education institutions in high-density Mexican American geographic regions: Type II access problem; (c) *LULAC v. Clements* (1990) through *Richards v. LULAC* (1993); (d) a legal loss, but a legislative victory: the South Texas Border Initiative.

Mexican Americans' Limited Enrollment in Higher Education: Type I Access Problem

In light of the low academic achievement of many Mexican American students, their high dropout rate from secondary schools, their unmet language needs, and their limited access in secondary schools to high-status knowledge via curriculum differentiation (see Valencia, 2002b), it is not at all surprising that these students enroll in higher education in disproportionately low numbers. This limited access is referred to as a "Type I" access problem,[2] which has been a long-standing concern for Mexican Americans. From the 1920s through the mid-1940s, very few Mexican Americans attended institutions of higher education (San Miguel & Valencia, 1998). For example, nearly eighty years ago, Manuel (1930) surveyed institutions of higher education in Texas and reported that of the

38,538 students enrolled in colleges and universities in Texas, college officials classified only 188 (0.49%) as "Mexican." Of these 188 students, 34
(18.1%) claimed residence in Mexico.

At the end of World War II, however, Mexican American enrollment in
college increased as some Mexican American veterans took advantage of
the GI Bill of Rights of 1944 (officially known as the Servicemen's Read-
justment Act), which paid for a GI's complete college education (Morín,
1963). Notwithstanding this postwar increase of Mexican American students in higher education, they remained severely underenrolled in college
relative to their presence in the college-age population, and in comparison to their White peers. Based on 1950 U.S. Census data, Barrett (1966)
noted that only 2.2% of the "Spanish-speaking" people (overwhelmingly
Mexican American) in Texas had completed "college or more" (p. 181,
Table 9B), although they constituted 13.4% of the Texas population. This
disparity (underrepresentation), by my calculation, is 83.6%. Similar rates
of underrepresentation in college completion also existed for the Spanish-
speaking populations in the other Southwestern states of Arizona, California, Colorado, and New Mexico (compare Tables 1C and 9B in Barrett,
1966, pp. 161 and 181, respectively).

Even twenty years later, following the reporting of the 1950 Census
data, the Type I access problem regarding higher education persisted for
Mexican Americans. The Mexican American Education Study (MAES)
in its report no. 2—*The Unfinished Education: Outcomes for Minorities
in the Five Southwestern States* (U.S. Commission on Civil Rights, 1971b)
—found that for the combined five Southwestern states, 49% of White
students entered college, and 24% completed. By sharp contrast, 23% of
Mexican American students entered college, with only 5% finishing and
earning bachelor's degrees.

Many other studies over the years, including U.S. Census data, confirm that the low rates of college enrollment and completion for Mexican Americans reported by the MAES study more than three decades ago
stubbornly linger (e.g., Carter & Wilson, 1997; Cook & Cordova, 2006;
Harvey & Anderson, 2005; Keller, Deneen, & Magallán, 1991; Olivas, 1986;
Pérez & De La Rosa Salazar, 1993).[3] For example, Carter and Wilson conducted a national trend analysis (1975 to 1995) of college completion rates
by race/ethnicity of persons twenty-five to twenty-nine years of age. The
Latino completion rate of 6% in 1975 rose to 9% in 1995. By contrast, the
White completion rate of 15% in 1975 grew to 24% in 1995—thus pointing
to a sharp increase in the White/Latino gap (from 9 percentage points in

1975 to 15 percentage points in 1995). If these data had been disaggregated by Latino subgroup, the White/Mexican American completion gap would have been the largest—given that Mexican Americans have the lowest college completion rate of the various Latino subgroups (Chapa & Valencia, 1993, p. 173, Table 6; also see U.S. Department of Commerce, Bureau of the Census, 2000b).

Limited Funding for Development of Higher Education Institutions in High-Density Mexican American Geographic Regions: Type II Access Problem

Mexican Americans also experience another type of limited access to higher education: the lack of such institutions in geographic regions of high-density Mexican American populations. I refer to this limited entry as a "Type II" access problem. Legal scholar Michael Olivas notes that higher education connotes scores of things to numerous people, "but few persons consider the 'place-ness' of college, certainly not in the way people think of elementary and secondary schools as defining place" (2005, p. 169). Olivas also points out that the issue of place in higher education has been legally contested, for example,

> Whether colleges can locate in certain "service" areas, whether certain policies can be localized or tied to locales, whether regions and regional populations have legal claims to proportional college resources, or whether the setting of higher education can trigger racial claims. . . . Placing college near populations is a central feature of universal access. (p. 170)

Based on 2000 U.S. Census data, 20.9 million people resided in Texas, the second most populous state.[4] Regarding land area, Texas also ranks second, at 267,256 square miles.[5] Texas's southern proximity to the Mexican border and legacies of conquest and exploitation of the Mexican-origin people in the state (see Perea, 2003) has led to the formation of a region consisting of forty-one contiguous counties along the southernmost and westernmost part of the state (see Figure 7.1). Of these forty-one counties, fourteen traverse 1,254 miles along the Texas-Mexico border from the city of Brownsville in the south to El Paso in the west.[6] Scholars refer to this forty-one-county area by a number of names, including the "Border Region," "Border Area," "Borderlands," "Border" (or "*la frontera*"). Here,

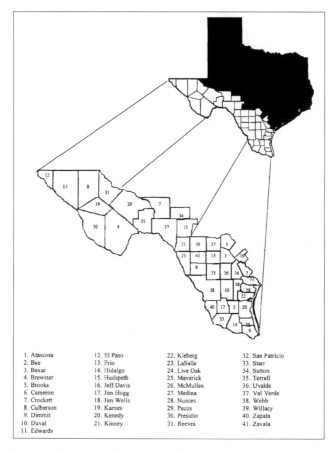

Figure 7.1. Names and Locations of the Forty-One Counties in the
Border Region of Texas. *Note:* The forty-one counties are listed in
Richards v. LULAC, 868 S.W.2d at 308 (note 2) (Tex. 1993).

"Border Region" is the most appropriate term.[7] The Border Region is so
large that if it were the fifty-first state in the union, it would be the six-
teenth largest in land area, with 79,423 square miles. Furthermore, if the
Border Region were a state, it would be the twenty-fifth largest in population count, with 4.1 million people (U.S. Department of Commerce, Bureau of the Census, 2000c).

In 1990, at the beginning of the *LULAC v. Clements* litigation, nearly
17 million people resided in Texas, with Mexican Americans and other
Latinos making up 25.5% (*n* = 4.3 million) of the total. Of the Mexican

American/Latino subtotal, 50.2% (*n* = 2.2 million) resided in the Border Region. This count of Mexican American/Latino people constituted 64.5% of the total Border Region population of 3.4 million residents (U.S. Department of Commerce, Bureau of the Census, 1990).[8] Regarding between-county variability in the forty-one-county Border Region, the Mexican American/Latino presence ranged from a low of 34.8% (Live Oak County) to a high of 97.2% (Starr County) (U.S. Department of Commerce, Bureau of the Census, 1990). The Border Region, primarily rural and sparsely populated,[9] has a higher unemployment rate (8%) compared to the remainder of the state (5%). Furthermore, because the region has predominantly agricultural and energy-based economies, it relies on sources of relatively inexpensive labor (Office of the Comptroller of Public Accounts, 1998).[10] The Border Region also possesses two conspicuous features, its high rate of poverty and low rate of educational attainment. In 1993, the poverty rate was nearly 30%. If the Border Region were a state, it would rank as the poorest in the country. Regarding educational attainment, in 1990 approximately 37% of all Border Region adults did not possess a high school diploma, a higher percentage than any state in the Union. In addition, if the Border Region were an entity unto itself, it would rank among the lowest ten states in the proportion of adults who hold bachelor's degrees (10%) and postgraduate degrees (5%) (Office of the Comptroller of Public Accounts, 1998). It is this latter concern, access to higher education in a place called the Border Region, that gave rise to a major lawsuit.

LULAC v. Clements (*1990*) *through* Richards v. LULAC (*1993*)

In December 1987, MALDEF, on behalf of LULAC, nine other organizations, and twenty-one Mexican American individuals, filed *LULAC v. Clements* (Mangan, 1991; Ramseyer, 2000).[11] Defendants included Texas Governor William P. Clements, the Texas Commissioner of Higher Education, the Chair and members of the Texas Higher Education Coordinating Board, and all individual members of the Board of Regents for fifteen universities and university systems in Texas.[12] Plaintiffs filed the lawsuit in the 107th District Court of Cameron County, located in Brownsville — Texas's southernmost city, situated on the Texas-Mexico border. Judge Benjamin Euresti, Jr., presided over a jury trial.[13]

The plaintiffs in *LULAC v. Clements*, a class action lawsuit,[14] challenged the constitutionality of Texas's system of higher education.[15] Plaintiffs based their complaint on two causes of action: defendants denied Mexican American residents of the Border Region (a) "participation in quality higher education programs" and (b) "access to equal education resources."[16] As such, plaintiffs claimed that both the choice and allocation of higher education sites plus the allocation of higher education resources created inequities between the Border and non-Border regions (Olivas, 2005).

The plaintiffs argued that the regional inequities caused by the defendants violated several requirements of the Texas Constitution and Texas statutes, namely,

- Article I, §3, the equal rights clause of the Texas Constitution, provides: All free men, when they form a social compact, have equal rights, and no man, or set of men, is entitled to exclusive separate public emoluments, or privileges, but in consideration of public services.
- Article I, §3a provides: Equality under the law shall not be denied or abridged because of sex, race, color, creed, or national origin. This amendment is self-operative.
- TEX. CIV. PRAC. & REM. CODE §106.001 provides in pertinent part: An officer or employee of the state or a political subdivision of the state who is acting or purporting to act in an official capacity may not, because of a person's race, religion, color, sex, or national origin: . . . (5) refuse to grant a benefit to the person; [or] (6) impose an unreasonable burden on the person.[17]

At the *LULAC v. Clements* jury trial, plaintiffs entered a number of incontrovertible findings of fact on specific statistical matters into the trial record:[18]

- About 20% of all Texans reside in the Border Region; however, the State allocates only about 10% of total expenditures for higher education to the region.
- Mexican Americans/Latinos make up the majority (54%) of the public university students in the Border Region; for the rest of Texas, Mexican Americans/Latinos constitute 7% of the public university student enrollment.[19]
- Of the approximately 590 doctoral programs in Texas universities, the Border Region universities house only three such programs.[20]
- About 15% of the Mexican American/Latino university students in the Border Region attend schools with an extensive range of master's and doctoral programs; for the rest of Texas, 61% of public university students attend schools with a wide range of such graduate programs.[21]

- Border Region universities account for about one-half of the physical plant value per capita and the number of library volumes per capita, compared to similar figures for the non–Border Region universities.[22]
- The average Border Region college or university student, compared to his or her peer in the rest of Texas, must travel a considerably farther distance to attend a comprehensive university.

This latter point about distance served as a focal point for plaintiffs during trial deliberations. Richard C. Jones and Albert Kauffman (1994) published an informative article on the distance issue, "Accessibility to Comprehensive Higher Education in Texas." Jones served as a research consultant for the plaintiffs in *LULAC v. Clements*, and Kauffman was senior litigating attorney for MALDEF in the case. First, Jones and Kauffman define a "comprehensive university." As accepted by both plaintiffs and defendants in *LULAC v. Clements*, the authors define a comprehensive university as "a public institution offering 20 or more Ph.D. degrees annually in at least one discipline; or ten or more Ph.D.s in three or more disciplines."[23] Second, in their analysis of relative access to comprehensive universities, Jones and Kauffman provide a map of Texas, divided into six regions, which the authors refer to as "cultural regions" (see Figure 7.2).

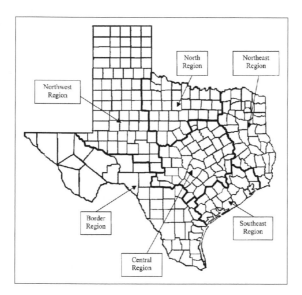

Figure 7.2. Six Cultural Regions of the State of Texas. *Source:* From Jones & Kauffman (1994, p. 270). Copyright © 1994 by JAI Press Inc. Adapted with permission from Elsevier.

TABLE 7.1
Road Distance to Closest Comprehensive Public University

Texas Region	Number of Counties	Average Distance (miles)	Total Students
7.1a. Six Regions			
Border	41	225	73,208
Northwest	69	100	28,145
North	36	31	90,851
Northeast	42	86	39,319
Southeast	19	29	92,037
Central	47	36	41,427
7.1b. Border Region vs. Rest of Texas			
Border	41	225	73,208
Rest of Texas	213	45	291,779
State Total	254	81	364,987

Source: Jones & Kauffman (1994, p. 271). Copyright © 1994 by JAI Press Inc. Adapted with permission from Elsevier.

Beginning in the northwestern part of the state and moving in a clockwise direction, the regions are Northwest, North, Northeast, Central, Southeast, and the Border.[24] Third, Jones and Kauffman provide a detailed data analysis of average road distances to the nearest comprehensive university, by each of the six cultural regions in Texas.[25] These data are presented in Table 7.1. Two salient points emerge from the data in sections 1a and 1b of Table 7.1:

1. The average student residing in the Border Region must travel an average distance of 225 miles to attend the closest comprehensive public university (Table 7.1a). The average student in the other five regions travels a considerably shorter distance to the nearest comprehensive public university (Table 7.1a). These average distances in ascending order are Southeast Region (29 miles), North Region (31 miles), Central Region (36 miles), Northeast Region (86 miles), and the Northwest Region (100 miles).

2. Compared to the rest of Texas regarding average distance to the closest comprehensive university (Table 7.1b), Border Region students must travel an average distance of 225 miles; students residing in the rest of Texas need to travel an average distance of only 45 miles. Stated in a similarly comparative way, Border Region students—compared to students in the rest of Texas—are required to travel *five times* as far in order to attend a comprehensive public university in Texas.

In November 1991 and after eight weeks of testimony, the *LULAC v.*

Clements jury reached a verdict.[26] The jury first considered the question of racial discrimination: Did the defendants treat "Plaintiffs differently, to their detriment, at least in part because Plaintiffs are Mexican Americans, in the process that leads to program approval or allocation of funds for Texas public institutions of higher education"?[27] The jury answered no for each defendant, concluding that the defendants had not discriminated against the residents of the Border Region, based on race/ethnicity.[28] In response to the other questions, however, the jury found the following:

1. The Legislature "failed to establish, organize or provide for the maintenance, support or direction of a system of education in which the Plaintiffs have substantially equal access to a 'University of the First Class.'"

2. The Legislature "failed to make suitable provisions for the support or maintenance of an Efficient System of public universities."

3. The State could have "reasonably located and developed university programs that provided more equal access to higher educational opportunities to Mexican Americans in the Border Region."[29]

In summary, the jury in *LULAC v. Clements* found that the Legislature failed to provide Border Region students equal access to a first-class university and an efficient system of public institutions of higher education and that the State could have located and developed university programs, with equal access, for Border Region students. Yet the jury ruled that these acts of omission did not constitute intentional discrimination.

On January 20, 1992, following the jury's verdict in *LULAC v. Clements*, a major development "stunned political leaders [and] appeared to contradict the findings of [the jury]," but the plaintiffs found it uplifting (Mangan, 1992, p. A25). Judge Euresti, the trial court judge, dismissed the jury's ruling and held that the Texas higher education system

1. Does not provide to the class that Plaintiffs represent equal rights under the law because of Plaintiffs' Mexican American national origin and discriminates against Plaintiffs and the class they represent because of their Mexican American national origin, in violation of Art. I §3 of the Texas Constitution, and denies Plaintiffs equal educational opportunity.

2. Has resulted in the expending of less state resources on higher education in geographic areas of significant Mexican American population than in other geographic areas of the state, and thereby denied to Mexican Americans equal rights and equality under the law, in violation of Texas Constitution Arts. I §3 and I §3a.

3. Expends less state resources on higher education in the border area of Texas . . . than its population would warrant thereby denying Plaintiffs and the class they represent equal rights and equality under the law guaranteed by the Texas Constitution in violation of Texas Constitution Art. I §3 and Texas Constitution Art. I §3a.[30]

In his ruling, Judge Euresti enjoined the defendants "from giving any force and effect to the sections of the Texas Education Code and the present or future appropriation acts relating to the financing of public universities and professional schools."[31] More specifically, Judge Euresti enjoined the defendants "from distributing, using, or dedicating funds from various specified sources, and from financing any permanent improvements under the Education Code, except as specifically excepted."[32] In sum, the trial court instructed the State to stop business as usual and "enact a constitutionally sufficient plan for funding the public universities."[33] To allow the State ample time to legislate such plan, Judge Euresti stayed the injunction until May 1, 1993.[34] The defendants appealed to the Texas Supreme Court requesting relief to ensure that the bonding efforts of the universities could continue unhindered. The Texas Supreme Court stayed (and extended) all injunctive relief granted by the trial court to preserve the former court's jurisdiction upon appeal.[35]

In all, the defendants and their counsel swiftly denounced Judge Euresti's ruling. State Higher Education Commissioner Kenneth H. Ashworth, one of the defendants, commented, "In effect, the judgment says the jury was wrong. After eight weeks of testimony, we thought that when they [the jury] rendered their decision it was pretty well informed." Ashworth continued, "I've been in this job almost 16 years, and I can certainly say there's been no discrimination during that time—not by me, not by my staff, or the Higher Education Coordinating Board" (Mangan, 1992, p. A30). Assistant Attorney General Jay Aguilar, who handled the lawsuit for the State, referred to Judge Euresti's decision as "legally incorrect." Aguilar commented that he was "confident the state would win on appeal" (Mangan, 1992, p. A30). Sharply differing from the defendants, Al Kauffman, MALDEF attorney, asserted that "the judge's decision did not contradict the jury's findings." Kauffman commented that "Even though the jury decided the individual defendants were not guilty of discrimination, the judge [Euresti] could still find the system itself discriminatory" (Mangan, 1992, p. A30).

Given what the State had at stake, an appeal to the Texas Supreme

Court was imminent. It appears that the State's possible loss of power highly motivated the defendants to appeal to the Texas Supreme Court (*Richards v. LULAC*, 1993).[36] Although the Texas Legislature was not a named defendant in this higher education lawsuit, "state leaders began to fear that a court-mandated 'equalization' of Texas' universities might result in the Legislature losing control of them" (Guerra, 2005, p. 1B).

On October 6, 1993, the Texas Supreme Court delivered its opinion. In a crushing blow to the appellees, the Court reversed the ruling of the trial court and rendered judgment in favor of the appellants. In brief, the Court based its ruling on the following reasons:

1. *Weak classification.* The Texas Supreme Court noted that the trial court's judgment rested on what appeared to be a primarily geographical "classification"—that is, the forty-one-county Border Region. The Court continued by finding that the plaintiffs created a class, *not of all* potential or actual Mexican American higher education students in Texas but only of those residing in a "carefully drawn region"—the Border Region.[37] In its opinion, the Court commented that the use of the Border Region as a classification was incomplete because the plaintiff class omitted nearly one-half of all Mexican Americans in Texas, given that they reside outside the Border Region.[38] As a case in point, the opinion noted that the plaintiff class excluded Mexican Americans in the Houston metropolitan area (which contains the largest number of Mexican Americans of any metropolitan area in Texas and has superior higher education resources).[39] In the conclusion of this chapter, I draw from CRT to explain how the Court's "weak classification" reason is baseless.

Another finding by the Texas Supreme Court regarding plaintiffs' questionable classification concerned case law. Quoting the U.S. Supreme Court in *McGowan v. Maryland* (1961), the Court noted that both state and federal guarantees of equality relate "equality between persons as such, rather than between areas, and . . . territorial uniformity is not a constitutional prerequisite."[40] In short, the Texas Supreme Court found that the plaintiffs failed to demonstrate "both disproportionate impact and discriminatory intent."[41] More specifically, the opinion stated,

> There is no direct evidence in this case of an intent to discriminate against Mexican-Americans in the border area on the part of the defendants. Thus, if intent is required to establish a violation of the Texas equal rights clause, plaintiffs must show a sufficiently high level of disparate impact, either alone or in conjunction with other factors, to raise an inference of

intent. They have not done so here. Even if intent is not required under the Texas equal rights clause, the evidence of impact in this case simply does not rise to an adequate level to show discrimination. The inherent flaws that call into question the plaintiffs' alleged classification also fatally weaken the evidence of impact. Whatever the effects of the Texas university system policies and practices, they fall upon the entire region and everyone in it, not just upon Mexican-Americans within the region. Conversely, they do not fall upon Mexican-Americans outside the region. The same decisions that plaintiffs allege show discrimination against Mexican Americans in the border area serve, at the same time, to afford greater benefits to the large number of Mexican Americans who live in metropolitan areas outside the border region.[42]

2. *Higher education is not a right.* In *LULAC v. Clements*, plaintiffs argued that higher education should be acknowledged as a "fundamental right" under the Texas Constitution.[43] Article VII ("Education"), §1 ("Support and Maintenance of System of Public Free Schools"), reads,

> A general diffusion of knowledge being essential to the preservation of the liberties and rights of the people, it shall be the duty of the Legislature of the State to establish and make suitable provision for the support and maintenance of an efficient system of public free schools.

Although the trial court found that the Legislature (acting through the defendants) violated this constitutional provision by failing "to make suitable provision for the support or maintenance of an efficient system of public universities,"[44] the Texas Supreme Court held that Article VII, §1, is not applicable to higher education.[45] The Court reasoned, (a) Article VII does not stipulate the number of years of public schooling to be provided;[46] (b) although the trial court found constitutional violations of other sections (i.e., §§10–18) of Article VII, the Texas Supreme Court contrarily ruled,

> Defendants correctly contend that the trial court erroneously found a duty to create a system of higher education in article I, §10, when in fact the section refers only to the creation of a particular university. The clear language of the section shows that the framers contemplated the founding of a single institution, to be located by the choice of the electorate. The election mandated by section 10 occurred in 1881, and the voters

chose Austin as the site of the main campus of that university. Therefore, this portion of the trial court's judgment must also be reversed.[47]

3. *Reliance on Fordice is misplaced.* In *LULAC v. Clements*, plaintiffs relied on *U.S. v. Fordice* (1992) for the argument that the use of race-neutral policies does not in itself cancel the State's constitutional duty to eradicate segregated higher education.[48] But the Texas Supreme Court in *Richards v. LULAC* held that the *Fordice* decision applied to the vestiges of de jure segregation. As such, the Texas Supreme Court ruled,

> Although Texas formerly operated a higher education system in which black students were segregated by law, plaintiffs have not shown that the policies and practices attacked in this suit—i.e., the placement of institutions in regions other than the border area and the allocation of resources to nonborder area schools—are in any way traceable to that *de jure* system of segregation.[49]

The Texas Supreme Court continued in its opinion by noting that plaintiffs attempted to invoke *Fordice* by relying on many forms of historical discrimination against Mexican Americans in Texas, rather than on a veritable system of de jure segregated colleges. *Fordice* relaxes the prerequisite of discriminatory action of the State because it applies when the State has *already* violated the Constitution by legally maintaining separate systems of higher education. As such, plaintiffs did not meet this initial burden of proof by demonstrating that the higher education system in Texas presently or previously denied them equal protection.[50]

Not surprisingly, the appellees and their supporters expressed considerable disappointment with the Texas Supreme Court's decision in *Richards v. LULAC* to reverse the 107th District Court's ruling. For example, Manuel L. Ibáñez, president of Texas A&M University–Kingsville, stated, "The Supreme Court's decision bodes ill for future funding of higher education in South Texas if the Legislature felt the MALDEF lawsuit was the only reason they should fund the South Texas institutions." Ibáñez continued, "I hope they remember how unbalanced the ratio is for funding of higher education north and south of [interstate highway] I-10" (Mangan, 1993, p. A25).

In conclusion, the Texas Supreme Court's decision created a major setback for Mexican Americans' legal struggle for increasing higher education funding for the Border Region. Yet all was not lost. Al Kauffman,

MALDEF attorney in the lawsuit, commented, "The lawsuit had brought the issue to the public's attention and galvanized support statewide for more equitable budgets" (Mangan, 1993, p. A28).

A Legal Loss but a Legislative Victory: The South Texas Border Initiative

The filing of the *LULAC v. Clements* lawsuit in 1987 gained considerable attention from the public as well as from Texas lawmakers (see, e.g., Fields, 1988a, 1988b). As noted previously, although the plaintiffs did not name the Texas Legislature as a defendant in this historic higher education financing lawsuit, it appears that the Legislature feared losing control of the universities via a court-ordered equalization of funding. In 1989, prior to Judge Euresti's decision in the 107th District Court (*LULAC v. Clements*) and the Texas Supreme Court's reversal of his ruling (*Richards v. LULAC*), the 71st Texas Legislature implemented the South Texas Border Initiative (STBI).[51] The Legislature targeted a $460 million funding package for the nine four-year colleges/universities in the Border Region.[52] The nine institutions were the University of Texas at Brownsville, the University of Texas at El Paso, the University of Texas–Pan American (Edinburg), the University of Texas at San Antonio, Texas A&M International University (Laredo), Texas A&M University–Corpus Christi, Texas A&M University–Kingsville, Sul Ross State University (including Sul Ross State University Rio Grande College), and the University of Texas Health Science Center at San Antonio.[53] The Legislature designed STBI funding in two forms. The first form of funding, "special item funding," is a direct sum of money from the Legislature that is above the regular, formula-based funding. From fiscal year 1990 to 2003, lawmakers provided the STBI institutions more than $800 million in special item funding. The second form of funding, "tuition revenue bonds," allows the institutions to issue bonds backed by institutional revenues, with the assumption that the Legislature will dispense general revenue money to service the debt.[54]

On December 6, 2002, the House Committee on Higher Education presented its report to the House of Representatives (78th Texas Legislature). The Committee noted, "The cumulative result of the South Texas Border Initiative has been an overwhelming success for the institutions toward which the Initiative was geared."[55] For example, as of August 2001, the nine targeted institutions in the Border Region offered many new degree programs (i.e., 675 bachelor's, master's, and doctoral programs). In addition, student enrollment increased, as did semester credit hours taken and student retention.[56]

Although the STBI has contributed to a number of impressive increases and improvements in the Border Region institutions of higher education, critics of the STBI have raised concerns. First, Ramseyer (2000) has found mixed results in his comprehensive analyses of the policy formulation and outcomes of the STBI. Overall, the STBI showed the most favorable consequences (e.g., increased student enrollment) on Texas A&M University–Corpus Christi, Texas A&M International University, and the University of Texas at San Antonio. Institutions that did not respond well, and that in some cases responded negatively, to the increased funding include the University of Texas–Pan American, Texas A&M University–Kingsville, and the University of Texas at El Paso.[57] A second issue concerns the continuation of STBI funding. In April 2005, Representative Vilma Luna (D-Corpus Christi), vice chair of the budget-writing Appropriations Committee, noted that the state budget shortfall of $10 billion in the previous session culminated in severe cuts of the STBI fundings. Luna commented, "I don't think the Legislature has lived up to the commitment" (Eaton, 2005, p. A1). President Flavius Killebrew of Texas A&M University–Corpus Christi agreed: "There's been a decline in the investment that the state has made in higher education, lacking further in South Texas than other parts of the state," he said. "The money just has not been there to keep up with the rapid growth rate down here" (Eaton, 2005, p. A1). President Rumaldo Juárez of Texas A&M University–Kingsville expressed similar worries. He warned that if further state cuts in funding occur, he may have to reduce or eliminate programs, including the honors program and the Ph.D. in Engineering: "It's becoming more difficult to maintain the quality and integrity of those programs" (Eaton, 2005, p. A5).

Conclusion

As discussed earlier, the Texas Supreme Court based its reversal in *Richards v. LULAC* on three reasons: (a) weak classification; (b) higher education is not a right; (c) reliance on *Fordice* is misplaced. In the context of CRT, it is necessary to comment on why the Texas Supreme Court's first reason, "weak classification," is specious. Citing case law, the Court ruled that state and federal equal protection guarantees apply to equality between persons, not geographic areas. This distinction is baseless. CRT begins from the premise that race and racism are endemic and enduring. This was the argumentative path that plaintiffs in *LULAC v. Clements* took when they contended that "their classification is primarily one of race or national origin rather than geography."[58] Yet the Texas Supreme Court held steadfastly that plaintiffs "carefully drew" the forty-one-county Border Region and left out nearly one-half of the Mexican American population in the state. Although 49.8% (2.1 million) of the total Mexican American population in the state indeed did not reside in the Border Region in 1990, it needs to be emphasized that a sizeable proportion, 50.2% (2.2 million) of the total Mexican American population did reside in the Border Region. As previously discussed, Mexican Americans constituted nearly two of three Border Region residents. Based on the 1990 Census data (U.S. Department of Commerce, Bureau of the Census, 1990), I conducted further analyses of the makeup of the forty-one counties by examining majority and plurality status by race/ethnicity. The results show,

MAJORITY GROUP	PLURALITY GROUP
Mexican American	Mexican American
($n = 34$ counties)	($n = 0$ counties)
White ($n = 6$ counties)	White ($n = 1$ county)

These data show that in 1990, around the time the trial court ruled in *LULAC v. Clements*, the Mexican American population made up the majority in thirty-four (83%) of the forty-one counties. This statistic demonstrates the centrality of race in this lawsuit, underscoring plaintiffs' assertion that their classification was chiefly one of race/national origin, not geography. Although the issue of travel distance to a comprehensive university proved paramount for many Border Region students (review Table 7.1), it is not the mere geographic expanse of the area that constituted the underlying concern of plaintiffs. The historical background of this "cultural region" needs to be placed in context. It is worth repeating plaintiffs' argument that their six incontrovertible findings of fact (see earlier discussion) need to be examined through a historical lens. The disparities and inequalities between the non–Border Region residents and the Border Region residents exist against a history of discrimination and civil rights violations of Mexican Americans in a number of ways, including, for example, lynchings (De Leon, 1983), forced segregation in hospitals (*Cisneros v. Corpus Christi Independent School District*, 324 F. Supp. at

613 [S.D. Tex. 1970]), forced stratification in the labor market (*Cisneros v. Corpus Christi Independent School District*, 324 F. Supp. at 614 [S.D. Tex. 1970]), "No Spanish" rules (see chapter 4, this volume), forced school segregation (see chapter 1, this volume), racially restrictive housing covenants (Ramos, 2001), inequities in financing of K–12 schools (see chapter 2, this volume), jury exclusion (Sheridan, 2003), and violations of voting rights (*Sierra v. El Paso Independent School District*, 591 F. Supp. 802 [W.D. Tex. 1984]). Examined in this historical context, the Texas Supreme Court's reversal in *Richards v. LULAC* was unsound by ignoring the centrality of race and racism and the intersectionality of racism with other forms of oppression.

For the sake of closure, several concluding observations are in order. First, this chapter on the Mexican American community's legal struggle for equity in higher education financing reminds us that the Mexican American campaign for educational equality does not end with the K–12 segments of the educational pipeline. Legal actions brought forth by Mexican Americans for the equitable access to comprehensive institutions of higher education remain equally important.

Second, the judicial outcome of *LULAC v. Clements*, compared to the ruling in *Richards v. LULAC*, informs us of the common theme that runs throughout the various chapters of this book: the existence of legal indeterminacy. By carefully analyzing the full legal record here, civil rights lawyers can get a better handle on sorting out the intricacies of these rulings as to how they have helped or hindered Mexican Americans' struggle in the area of equitable financing in higher education.

Third, as mentioned a number of times throughout this book, in CRT lies a fundamental proposition that the intersection of race and racism is central in helping scholars to identify and explain individual experiences of the law. In the *Richards v. LULAC* reversal, the Texas Supreme Court dismissed the centrality of race and racism, when clearly they were vital to plaintiffs' arguments.

Finally, the analysis presented needs to be contextualized within the demographic reality of the phenomenal growth of the Mexican American population (see Valencia, 2002a). Given the current funding shortfalls of the STBI, coupled with the projected large increase in the college student enrollment in the Border Region,[59] parents, students, administrators, and allies in the Texas Legislature must work together as advocates for a fully funded STBI.

8

High-Stakes Testing

Currently, an educational reform movement is sweeping across K–12 public education in the United States, affecting millions of school-children and youths.[1] This collective, pervasive, and top-down course of action—which I refer to as the "standards-based school reform movement" —holds students, educators, and administrators accountable for reaching specific benchmarks (e.g., minimum test performance by students on state-mandated tests). This movement has its roots in the 1983 volume *A Nation at Risk* (National Commission on Excellence in Education, 1983), produced by a commission appointed by Terrell H. Bell, Secretary of Education in the Reagan Administration. In its highly critical observations of the crisis in American education, *A Nation at Risk* commented, "If an unfriendly foreign power had attempted to impose on America the mediocre educational performance that exists today, we might have viewed it as an act of war" (p. 1).[2] This indictment of the "rising tide of mediocrity" (p. 1) laid the foundation of the standards-based school reform movement, including goals such as (a) combining the old basics with the new basics (e.g., computer literacy), (b) more time devoted to learning; (c) more testing, (d) measurable standards, and (e) higher-quality teaching (see Pearl, 2002).

"Accountability"—the standards-based school reform movement's mantra—is being driven by high-stakes testing, a form of assessment in which test results hold important consequences for students, their parents and teachers, schools, districts, and administrators. As of 2005, nineteen states had exit-level tests that all students must pass to graduate from high school, and seven other states will phase in exit exams by 2012 (Center on Education Policy, 2005).[3] About 72% of all U.S. students enrolled in high school in 2012 will be required to pass exit-level exams in order to graduate, a sharp increase from the 50% of students affected by such exams in 2005. High school exit-level exams will have an even greater effect on students of color. An estimated 82% of minority-group students and 87% of

English learners will be required to pass exit exams by 2012 (Center on Education Policy, 2005). In addition to the growing use of mandated exit-level high school tests, calls by politicians, policymakers, and others have influenced the implementation of test-based requirements in controlling grade promotion. The American Federation of Teachers (AFT) has provided comprehensive national information on states that have adopted these practices for ending social promotion. When the AFT first began to monitor such policies in 1996, only three states used test data, in part, to decide a student's promotion or retention. In its most recent report (2001), the AFT noted that sixteen states and the District of Columbia have institutionalized promotion policies at the elementary level.[4]

To be sure, critics have not let the standards-based school reform movement go uncontested. The issue is *not* over whether schools should be accountable for students' learning. The need for school accountability is indisputable (see, e.g., Valencia, Valenzuela, Sloan, & Foley, 2001; Valenzuela, 2005a). "It is the *type* of [accountability] system that becomes the point of contention" (Valencia et al., 2001, p. 321). Critics assert that the current standards-based school reform movement (a) narrows the curriculum via measurement-driven instruction (McNeil, 2005; Padilla, 2005; Valencia & Guadarrama, 1996; Valencia & Villarreal, 2003; Valenzuela, 2005a), (b) relies on the near exclusive use of single test scores, rather than multiple sources of assessment, to measure student performance (Valencia, Villarreal, & Salinas, 2002; Valenzuela, 2005a), and (c) is structurally misdirected because it treats the symptoms (poor academic performance), rather than the root cause (inferior schooling; see Valencia et al., 2001).[5]

In addition to these three critical observations of standards-based school reform, there is a fourth—the adverse impact that high-stakes testing has had, and continues to have, on certain populations of students of color, particularly Mexican Americans and African Americans. Adverse impact (also referred to as "disparate impact") on students of color and how such impact forms a basis for civil rights litigation is the focus of this chapter. What is adverse impact? Phillips's (2000a) conceptualization is informative:

> Differential performance occurs when passing rates for African-American and Hispanic students (minority groups) are lower than the passing rates for White students (majority group). When the differential performance between minority and majority groups becomes too great, it is labeled

adverse impact. An important issue in this context is determining when differential performance becomes large enough to qualify as adverse impact. (p. 363)

Racialized performance data on high-stakes testing abound. For example, in May 2005, officials of the Austin Independent School District (AISD) reported that 7% ($n=108$) of the White seniors failed the Texas Assessment of Knowledge and Skills (TAKS) test, the required state graduation exam that seniors need to pass in order to receive the high school diploma. By sharp contrast, 27% ($n=142$) of the African American seniors and 20% ($n=288$) of the Mexican American/other Latino seniors failed the TAKS test. Schools with predominantly students of color in the AISD demonstrated particularly elevated failure rates on the TAKS exit-level exam.[6] For example, at Johnston High School, with a "Hispanic" enrollment of 81.6%, 36% ($n=41$) of the Mexican American/other Latino seniors failed the TAKS test.[7]

Another example of how high-stakes testing has adversely affected students of color is seen in Louisiana. In 2000–2001, the state implemented high-stakes testing in which test scores would be used to make retention/promotion decisions. Students (in grades 4 and 8) in Louisiana are required to take the Louisiana Educational Assessment Program for the 21st Century, or LEAP 21. Based on data from the Louisiana Department of Education, Valencia and Villarreal (2003) calculated that during the years *before* officials implemented LEAP 21, placement committees retained about one in thirteen (8%) African American eighth-grade students (compared to one in twenty-one [5%] White eighth-graders). Yet, *after* LEAP 21 became official, placement committees retained about one in three (33%) African American eighth-graders (compared to one in ten [10%] Whites).[8]

In this final legal category covered in this book, high-stakes testing, three cases are discussed. CRT is helpful in understanding these lawsuits because they underscore the prominence of racialized test score patterns. CRT is also useful because these cases challenge the alleged objectivity and fairness of high-stakes tests. Two of the three lawsuits include Mexican American and African American plaintiffs; Mexican American, African American, and Asian American plaintiffs brought forth the third case. The first two cases cover adverse impacts resulting from high-stakes testing on students of color who aspire to become school teachers.[9] The first case is concerned with the requirement that students who desire to enroll in teacher education courses at colleges and universities in Texas must pass a preprofessional skills battery (*U.S. v. Texas*, 1985). The second lawsuit pertains to the requirement that individuals in California must pass a basic skills test to receive teacher certification (*Association of Mexican-American Educators v. California*, 1993). The third and final case discussed concerns a lawsuit brought forth by Mexican American and African American plaintiffs who failed the Texas high school exit-level test, and whom school officials subsequently denied a high school diploma (*GI Forum v. Texas Education Agency*, 2000).

U.S. v. Texas (1985)

The U.S. government's initial participation in this case was *U.S. v. Texas* (1970), one of a number of actions concerned with the desegregation of elementary and high schools in Texas. In 1970, the U.S. Department of Justice filed lawsuits against school districts all across Texas to secure compliance with desegregation orders under the omnibus title of "*U.S. v. Texas*." The vast majority of these cases involved only African American plaintiffs, but in some cases, Mexican Americans also entered into litigation. The first *U.S. v. Texas* case (321 F. Supp. 1043 [E.D. Tex. 1970]) involved the desegregation of four Independent School Districts and nine all-Black Common School Districts in East Texas. Because this case served as a bellwether for other desegregation cases, Mexican Americans have filed lawsuits that involve segregation or discriminatory school practices resulting from segregation (e.g., lack of bilingual education) under the aegis of *U.S. v. Texas* (1970). In the *U.S. v. Texas* (1985) case, the plaintiffs claimed that the court in *U.S. v. Texas* (1970) retained jurisdiction because they were still suffering from the vestiges of segregation. Given that the court in *U.S. v. Texas* (1970)—the U.S. District Court for the Eastern District of Texas (Tyler Division)—retained jurisdiction in the later case (*U.S. v. Texas*, 1985), the federal government entered as plaintiff in that case.[10] LULAC, GI Forum, and the NAACP (plaintiff-intervenors) and seven Latino (assumed to be Mexican American) and seven African American college and university students (applicants for intervention) joined the federal government in the 1985 case. The students sought to represent themselves and others similarly situated. Many of the applicants had finished high school, started families, and recently returned to higher education in an attempt to become teachers.[11]

Plaintiff-intervenors and applicants (shortened here to plaintiffs) in *U.S. v. Texas* (1985) challenged the legitimacy of the Pre-Professional Skills Test (PPST), a battery that tests skills in reading, writing, and mathematics. The PPST, developed by the Educational Testing Service (ETS), targeted the academic ability level of high school seniors or first-year college students.[12] As part of the nascent standards-based school reform movement in Texas, the Legislature enacted a requirement in 1981 that required "satisfactory performance on a competency examination on basic skills prescribed by [the Texas State Board of Education] as a condition to admission into an approved teacher education program."[13] The requirement further specified that if a student falls below the "preclusionary" (i.e., cut) scores set by the State Board of Education on any of the three sections of the PPST, he or she may not enroll in more than six hours of education courses until the student passes all components of the test.[14]

In March 1984, officials held the first administration of the PPST. Given the long-standing dual and inferior education experienced by Mexican American and African American students in Texas (see Valencia, 2000), it was not surprising that students of color, compared to their White peers, experienced the highest PPST failure rates.[15] Based on data compiled by the defendants in *U.S. v. Texas*, more than eighteen thousand students as of July 1985 had taken the PPST. When the data are disaggregated by race/ethnicity, evidence indisputably shows that students of color fared considerably poorer than White students (see Table 8.1). For all the PPST administrations from the initial testing in March 1984 to July 1985 (about sixteen months), White students clearly showed higher pass rates than did their peers of color. Whites had a pass rate (73%) about 2.2 times higher than that of Mexican Americans (34%) and approximately 3.2 times higher than

TABLE 8.1
Racial/Ethnic Pass and Fail Rates on the PPST: 1984–1985

Racial/Ethnic Group	Number of Examinees	Pass		Fail	
		n	%	*n*	%
White	14,969[a]	10,927	73	4,042	27
Hispanic	2,136	732	34	1,410	66
Black	895	203	23	689	77
TOTAL	18,000[a]	11,862	66	6,141	34

Source: My calculations are from data provided in *U.S. v. Texas*, 628 F. Supp. at 306 and 311 (E.D. Tex. 1985).

Note: PPST refers to the Pre-Professional Skills Test. All percentages are rounded to the nearest whole number.

[a] All data for White and Total rows are approximations.

that of African Americans (23%). Furthermore, Table 8.1 shows us that of the 3,031 Mexican American and African American students who took the PPST since its initial administration, only 935, or about 31%, were able to continue their preparation in teacher education. By contrast, nearly 75% of the White students were able to do so.

The plaintiffs in *U.S. v. Texas* (1985) sought a preliminary injunction to restrain the State of Texas (acting by and through the Texas Education Agency [TEA]) from preventing students who failed the PPST from enrolling in teacher education courses throughout colleges and universities in Texas. Plaintiffs' legal claims focused on the manner in which state authorities adopted the PPST—that is, it was hastily developed, very short notice was given to prospective examinees, and a questionable validity study was used to establish the psychometric integrity of the test.[16] Plaintiffs also raised the severity of the consequences of not passing the PPST, arguing that the teacher certification of students of color would be postponed by at least six months to a year.[17] Plaintiffs claimed that these problems with the PPST violated their rights (a) under the Equal Protection and Due Process Clauses of the Fourteenth Amendment, (b) under Title VI of the Civil Rights Act (42 U.S.C. §2000d), and (c) as third-party beneficiaries to contractual agreements between the United States and the State of Texas in which the parties guaranteed equal educational opportunity in Texas institutions of higher education.[18]

Judge William Wayne Justice, who presided over the case in the U.S. District Court for the Eastern District of Texas (Tyler Division), needed to consider four factors in determining whether to grant the plaintiffs a preliminary injunction:

1. irreparable harm to the plaintiff from failure to issue injunction;
2. the relative lack of harm to the defendant from issuance of the injunction;
3. the public interest; and
4. the probability that plaintiff will ultimately succeed on the merits.[19]

In brief, Judge Justice ruled on the four points as follows:

Irreparable harm. Due to the adverse impact of the PPST's preclusionary scores, the students would have their teacher certificates postponed at least six months to a year while parties litigated the instant case. Furthermore, the schoolchildren of Texas would be deprived of these teachers at a time of critical teacher shortage (particularly in general and bilingual education). Judge Justice, citing a Fifth Circuit ruling, found that a university's action of preventing a student from completing his or her degree that was a requisite for employment constituted "clear irreparable harm."[20]

Lack of harm to defendants. At the *U.S. v. Texas* (1985) hearing, Dr. William Kirby (TEA Commissioner of Education) noted three harms if the court allowed students to pursue their teacher education studies without having passed the PPST: (a) students would be permitted to take courses in which they lacked the basic skills; (b) negative public perception would arise; (c) allowing such students to pursue their course of study would be unfair to themselves if the PPST requirement was permitted to stand.[21]

Judge Justice found none of the alleged harms persuasive. For example, plaintiffs countered that the students, notwithstanding having difficulties passing the PPST, had been earning A's and B's in their classes and thus were quite academically capable. Also, many of the students missed the PPST preclusionary score by one or two points. Representatives of ETS testified that the standard error of measurement (SEM) on the PPST was about eight points.[22]

Public interest. Judge Justice ruled that the public interest was *not* disserved by permitting students to enroll in college courses and to serve as student teachers. On the contrary, the public interest was well served in a threefold fashion: (a) having sufficient numbers of teachers, particularly in areas that have historically suffered from the oppressive nature of the dual school system; (b) having competent teachers, capable of conveying knowledge and serving as role models; (c) having an integrated, unitary school system free of racial discrimination. In sum, the court noted, "The preliminary injunction herein sought would merely allow students to take courses and to perform student teaching; it would *not* permit teachers to be certified and teach in the schools of Texas without passing the PPST."[23]

Likelihood of success on the merits. Judge Justice found that plaintiffs demonstrated a likelihood of success on their four claims. In brief, the court ruled as follows:

1. *Equal protection.* In addition to the demonstration of clear disparate impact, Judge Justice found that the TEA's actions strongly suggested discriminatory intent.[24] The court commented that "the historical background of this decision is one of repeated and recent instances of intentional segregation, particularly in areas of South Texas where there is a substantial Mexican-American population."[25] Another indicator of racially

discriminatory intent noted by Judge Justice had to do with "alternative certification." In light of the severe teacher shortage in Texas, the alternative certification program allowed students to pass the PPST, graduate from college, and have an apprenticeship without taking any courses in teacher education.[26] The court commented,

> The choice to sacrifice the requirement of two years of training specifically directed at being a teacher, including student teaching, rather than change the PPST preclusionary scores or petition the Legislature to allow waiver of the PPST requirement . . . was one of the strongest indications of racial intent presented at the hearing. In effect, by the program of alternative certification, the defendant put itself on the record as considering the PPST more important than teacher education courses and student teaching. To use an analogy the defendant referred to repeatedly at the hearing, this is akin to allowing a person to get a driver's license simply by passing the eye examination, without taking either the written test or an actual driving test.[27]

2. *Due process.* As noted in Judge Justice's opinion, plaintiffs must show in claims of due process violations that the state has denied them of their *property* or *liberty* interests.[28] In the instant case, Judge Justice noted that the plaintiffs appeared to base their due process claims on the denial of property interests as seen in *Debra P. v. Turlington* (1981).[29] Yet he asserted that because the admission of a student into a teacher education program is in the hands of the universities and colleges, and not the State, the Fourteenth Amendment's Due Process Clause does not apply (it only applies to state actions).[30] However, given that the State failed to give the applicants ample notification of the nature and imminence of the PPST requirement (i.e., preclusionary scores) and made no effort to provide universities and colleges with PPST preparatory material or remediation funds, the State deprived the students of their liberty interests. That is, the TEA deprived them of their right to teach in Texas, and thus they were likely to be successful in their due process claim.[31]

3. *Title VI.* The defendants argued that because the PPST did not specifically receive federal funds, Title VI did not apply to address discrimination pertaining to the test. But Judge Justice ruled that because "The PPST is clearly part of the program of teacher education in Texas, and the teacher education program receives federal funds," the defendants' argument has no merit.[32] Furthermore, given that plaintiffs had a substantial

probability of success on constitutional causes of action (equal protection and due process), the court concluded that this likelihood extends to their Title VI cause of action (under 42 U.S.C. §2000d).[33]

4. *Equal Educational Opportunity Act (EEOA)*. The EEOA (20 U.S.C. §1703), passed in 1974, provides that

> No State shall deny equal educational opportunity to an individual on account of his or her race, color, sex, or national origin, by—
> (a) the deliberate segregation by an educational agency of students on the basis of race, color, or national origin, among or within schools;
> (b) the failure of an educational agency which has formerly practiced such deliberate segregation to take affirmative steps, consistent with part 4 of this subchapter, to remove the vestiges of a dual school system.[34]

In *Debra P. v. Turlington* (1981), the Fifth Circuit ruled that the use of a test to deny a diploma to students who had suffered under a dual school system perpetuated segregation and thus violated §1703(b) of the EEOA. The Eleventh Circuit later decided that sufficient time had passed to address the past discrimination and therefore reinstituted the diploma sanction. Given that many of the student applicants in the instant case had attended school under the dual system in Texas, left to raise a family, then returned to enter teacher education programs, Judge Justice found that they were still suffering from a dual system and were likely to succeed with their EEOA §1703(b) claim.

In his opinion, signed and entered on August 27, 1985, Judge Justice ruled, "By reason of the foregoing considerations, the defendants' motion to dismiss for lack of jurisdiction will be denied; and plaintiff-intervenors' motion for a preliminary injunction will be granted."[35] In light of what was at stake for the TEA and the incipient standards-based school reform movement in Texas, it was not at all surprising that the defendants appealed the decision in *U.S. v. Texas* (1985). It was also not unexpected that legal indeterminacy, a dominant theme of this book, arose at the appellate level.

The defendants in *U.S. v. Texas* (1985) appealed their case to the Fifth Circuit (*U.S. v. LULAC*, 1986).[36] Interestingly, and ironically, the United States, the original plaintiff in *U.S. v. Texas* (1985), joined the State in its defense of the PPST requirement. In its decision, the Fifth Circuit eviscerated the district court's opinion and reversed Judge Justice's order in which he issued a preliminary injunction. The foundation of the Fifth Circuit's ruling rested on the argument that the district court failed to determine whether or not the PPST is a "valid measure of the basic skills essential to perform satisfactorily in teacher-education courses."[37] Although the district court found that the PPST validity study undertaken by IOX Associates (contracted by the TEA) proved to be inadequately conducted (and thus the evidence insufficient),[38] the Fifth Circuit found the IOX report to be valid: "In the opinion of IOX" the PPST met the validity requirements for relevance to teacher education programs and to teacher performance in the classroom.[39] Based on my reading of the legal track regarding the validity of the PPST, the most scientifically sound decision comes from the district court, not the Fifth Circuit. This assertion is based on the likelihood of conflict of interests of IOX Associates. Note the following comments from the district court's opinion:

> [Dr. W. James] Popham and IOX Associates endeavored to discover whether the PPST tested subjects taught in Texas by conducting surveys of educators, students, and textbooks. The latter analysis looked at seventh through twelfth grade textbooks used in Texas public schools in 1981–82, and made no effort to determine how long those particular textbooks had been in use. The possibility exists, therefore, that virtually none of the students taking the PPST had used those textbooks. In addition, because the Educational Testing Service had not described the skills that the PPST was supposed to test with sufficient specificity, Dr. Popham and IOX prepared their own specifications, which were based on the single PPST test form available to them. In itself, this casts some doubt on the procedure; but, even worse, when the *independent textbook analyzers* [italics added] hired by IOX identified fewer textbook pages as relevant than did the verification-analysts, the textbook analyzers were told to go back and redo their analysis. Interestingly, the individuals referred to as "verification-analysts" in Dr. Popham's report were Dr. Popham himself and his associates. In light of these circumstances, the textbook analysis is entitled to little weight.[40]

The Fifth Circuit's ruling that the PPST is a fair and valid measure of the basic skills one needs to have in order to perform satisfactorily in teacher education courses indeed loomed large in the overall disposition of *U.S. v. LULAC*. Given the Fifth Circuit's finding that the district court did not determine whether or not the PPST is valid, and that the four factors to consider in determining whether to grant an injunction (e.g., irreparable harm to plaintiffs from failure to issue an injunction) all turned on whether the PPST is a fair measure, the district court erred in granting an injunction.[41]

In addition to vacating the preliminary injunction, the Fifth Circuit in *U.S. v. LULAC* ordered that the case proceed to trial on the merits. In personal communication with me, Albert Kauffman (counsel for LULAC, GI Forum, et al. in *U.S. v. LULAC*) explained that plaintiffs did not pursue the case because after the Fifth Circuit's decision in 1986, the TEA stopped using the PPST.[42] Mandated by the Legislature in 1987 and implemented in 1989, Texas replaced the PPST with the Texas Academic Skills Program (TASP) test, which also measures skills in reading, writing, and mathematics.[43] The state developed and owned the TASP, and thus it applied to all students in Texas public colleges and universities. However, the high rate of test failure by students of color continued unabated. In all, 2,841 teacher education candidates took the TASP exam in 1989, and the failure rates for Whites, Latinos, and African Americans were 14%, 39%, and 52%, respectively (G.X. García, 1989), meaning that Latino students had a failure rate 2.8 times greater than Whites, and African Americans had a failure rate 3.7 times greater than Whites. Kauffman and colleagues considered filing a separate lawsuit against the TASP, but at the time they focused most of their resources on the *Edgewood Independent School District v. Kirby* (1984) school financing litigation in Texas.[44]

Association of Mexican-American Educators v. California (1993)

The history of this teacher competency test lawsuit is similar to what transpired in *U.S. v. Texas* (1985) and *U.S. v. LULAC* (1986), including the clear presence of legal indeterminacy. The *AMAE v. California* case has a long and complex history, with legal action commencing in 1983 and a legal decision culminating in 2000. In July 1983, the Association of Mexican-American Educators (AMAE) filed discrimination charges against the State of California and several other defendants regarding teacher competency testing with the Equal Employment Opportunities Commission (EEOC) in Los Angeles, California. In May 1990, the EEOC issued a letter of determination and in December 1990 referred the AMAE case to the Justice Department. In May 1992, AMAE's counsel requested a right-to-sue letter from the EEOC, and the EEOC issued such a letter on June 17, 1992. AMAE filed a second discrimination charge on September 8, 1992, and subsequently the EEOC issued a second right-to-sue letter in October 1992. Plaintiffs filed *AMAE v. California* (*AMAE I*; 1993) in the U.S. District Court for the Northern District of California on September 23, 1992.[45]

Plaintiffs in *AMAE I*, a class action lawsuit, consisted of a racially/ethnically diverse group of organizations, demonstrating how within the framework of CRT diverse groups that join together to fight oppression frequently see that struggling to protect one group's fundamental rights is tightly linked to other groups' rights. These plaintiff organizations included the Association of Mexican-American Educators, the California Association for Asian-Pacific Bilingual Education, and the Oakland Alliance of Black Educators. Fifteen individual plaintiffs (eight Latino/Latina; four African American; three Asian/Pacific Islander) also joined.[46] The plaintiffs had failed the California Basic Educational Skills Test (CBEST), a battery assessing skills in reading, writing, and mathematics. Individuals are required to pass it for certification to teach in K–12 public schools in California.[47] An example of one of these plaintiffs is Rosa García (pseudonym), a Latina who

> took and failed the CBEST four times. [García] received an associate's degree from City College of San Francisco in 1972. She earned her bachelor's degree at San Francisco State University in developmental psychology in 1976. She completed a teacher credentialing program in multiple subjects/elementary education at San Francisco State University in 1978, but could not obtain a multiple-subject credential because she has not passed the CBEST. [García] does possess a general school services credential, which allows her to teach in child centers.[48]

Defendants in *AMAE I* included the State of California and the California Commission on Teacher Credentialing (CTC). Judge William H. Orrick presided over the case.

AMAE I asked a very basic legal question: Do Titles VI and VII apply to the State of California, the CTC, and/or the CBEST? Both parties moved for summary judgment regarding the applicability of Titles VI and VII. Plaintiffs asserted that the State and the CTC violated Title VI, given that they received federal funds to administer the CBEST, which resulted in disparate impact on racial minorities. In sum, Title VI contains a sweeping prohibition on the use of federal funds to subsidize racial discrimination.[49] Defendants, in turn, argued that Title VI did not apply, as they do not receive federal funds. Plaintiffs asserted that defendants were still covered because "the CTC is part of the California public school system which 'is extended' a large sum of 'federal financial assistance' on an annual basis."[50] Defendants also argued that disparate impact alone does not suffice to show a Title VI violation. Plaintiffs, however, argued that the Supreme Court ruling in *Lau v. Nichols* (1974) prohibits the use of federal funds with a discriminatory effect, regardless of the program's purpose.[51] In short, Title VI prohibits the utilization of federal money for programs that are discriminatory in effect, although not in purpose (i.e., intentional).

In *AMAE I*, the groups represented by the plaintiff class incontrovertibly experienced adverse impact as a result of taking the CBEST. In the beginning of this chapter, I introduced the concept of "adverse impact," which has to do with differential test performance between the majority group (White) and the minority group (e.g., Mexican American). When the differential performance (expressed as comparing pass rates on a high-stakes test) becomes too great, the result is labeled adverse impact. How is adverse impact measured? In *AMAE I*, both parties used the so-called 80-percent rule, prescribed by the Uniform Guidelines on Employee Selection Procedures.[52] Under the 80-percent rule, groups represented by the plaintiff class must demonstrate a pass rate that is less than 80% of the pass rate for the White group to show adverse impact. For example, in a case in which the pass rate on a high-stakes test is 90% for the White group and the pass rate for the plaintiff group (e.g., African American) is less than the 80% threshold (less than 72%), adverse impact can be legally noted.

In *AMAE I*, Dr. John Poggio (an expert for plaintiffs) noted that CBEST first-time pass rates were as follows:[53]

Whites	73.4%
Asians	53.0%
Latinos	49.4%
African Americans	37.7%

Applying the 80-percent rule here, the threshold was 58.7% (80% × 73.4% [White pass rate]). As such, all three groups of color demonstrated adverse impact.

AMAE I also differs from the previous case discussed (*U.S. v. Texas*; *U.S. v. LULAC*) in that it adds possible violations of Title VII of the Civil

Rights Act of 1964. Plaintiffs zeroed in on the section of Title VII that deals with hiring practices.

> It shall be an unlawful employment practice for an employer—
> (1) *to fail or refuse to hire* [italics added] or to discharge any individual, or otherwise to discriminate against any individual with respect to his compensation, terms, conditions, or privileges of employment, because of such individual's race, color, religion, sex, or national origin.[54]

With respect to Title VII, plaintiffs placed two highly significant and related questions before the court. First, is CBEST a licensing or employment exam? If it is the former, then Title VII does not apply. If it is the latter, then Title VII does apply. Second, is the State or the CTC liable, given that neither entity employs any of the plaintiffs or the class they represent? In regards to the first question—is the CBEST a licensing or employment exam—the defendants vigorously argued that the CBEST is simply a licensing exam, similar to the many other professional exams (e.g., accounting, legal, medical). However, in his summary judgment (a determination without a full trial) Judge Orrick found defendants' argument to be flawed, for one fundamental reason: "Passage of the CBEST is required only for those individuals who seek employment with public schools in California."[55] In short, the CBEST is functionally an employment exam. The individual who does not pass the CBEST is free to pursue a teaching position with any private school in California, but the unsuccessful CBEST examinee cannot be hired by the public school system in the state. Therefore, regarding the second question, Judge Orrick ruled that the State and the CTC, being entities of the public school system, were liable under Title VII, as the defendants placed obstacles in plaintiffs' path to employment as teachers.

AMAE II (1996) followed the summary judgment ruling in *AMAE I*. The purpose of *AMAE II* was to litigate whether the defendants actually violated Titles VI and VII of the Civil Rights Act of 1964. The same judge in the same court as *AMAE I* heard the case (Judge Orrick in the U.S. District Court for the Northern District of California).

As seen in *AMAE I*, defendants did not quarrel with the statistics that under the 80-percent rule, plaintiffs who were first-time CBEST examinees experienced adverse impact.[56] Defendants' major objective was to support their argument that (a) the CBEST is psychometrically valid and (b) the test has a business necessity. As such, the burden of proof was on defendants to demonstrate the validity of CBEST and, as required by the Ninth Circuit in *Contreras v. City of Los Angeles* (1981), to show that the test is "job-related" in that the skills, knowledge, and abilities measured are necessary for successful job performance.[57] In the area of test development this is known as "content validity," or "how well the sample of test tasks *represents* the domain of tasks to be measured" (Gronlund & Linn, 1990, p. 51). To develop a valid test (i.e., one that measures what it is supposed to measure), a "content validity study" needs to be undertaken. In the case of teacher tests (e.g., CBEST), a content validity study is necessary to ensure that the test measures skills and knowledge deemed essential to job performance, that is, teaching (see Hood & Parker, 1991).

The defendants presented three investigations pertaining to the CBEST's validity.[58] It appears that Judge Orrick found the job-analysis and content validity studies conducted in 1994 and 1995 by Dr. Kathleen Lundquist to be the most comprehensive and to contain the most compelling evidence. In the interest of space, this discussion is confined to Lundquist's investigation. In brief, Lundquist and her staff observed and interviewed a small sample of teachers and undertook a literature review regarding basic skill requirements for K–12 teachers. Next, panels of content experts reviewed the ascertained list of skills and abilities and linked the skill requirements to teacher activities on the job. Finally, the researcher created a job-analysis survey, which the CTC reviewed, pilot tested, and administered to samples of approximately 1,100 teachers and 230 administrators.[59]

Plaintiffs took issue with several parts of Lundquist's study. For example, plaintiffs asserted that the content validity study (the panels) inappropriately negated the results of the job analysis by restoring a large proportion of the mathematics skills, which should have been eliminated pursuant to the job analysis. In plaintiffs' view, "judgments of a small group of teachers were allowed to override the judgments of more than 1,100 teachers."[60] Plaintiffs also argued that Lundquist conducted her investigation *after* plaintiffs initiated the *AMAE v. California* lawsuit. That is, plaintiffs asserted that a test cannot be properly validated in the content domain without *first* undertaking a job analysis to demonstrate that the tasks or skills have importance to the job of teaching.[61] Notwithstanding plaintiffs' criticisms of the Lundquist study, the court found "that the skills tested on the CBEST are job related, and that the CBEST has been shown to be a valid measure of those skills."[62] Furthermore, the court found that because the defendants succeeded in showing the validity of the CBEST, and because the plaintiffs failed to demonstrate that alternatives to the CBEST (e.g., coursework alternative; required GPA) were workable, the CBEST was cost-effective, objective, and valid.[63]

In the end, *AMAE II* largely boiled down to the "battle of the experts," not uncommon in lawsuits in which tests are the focus. The reader should be aware, however, that the psychometric evidence pertaining to high-stakes testing is quite controversial. Issues (e.g., accuracy of evidence; relevance) abound regarding reliability, criterion-based validity, content-based validity, cultural bias and sensitivity studies, and cut-score determination (see, e.g., Valencia & Aburto, 1991b). Nonetheless, though defendants in *AMAE I* appeared to be not as well prepared as plaintiffs regarding their motion for summary judgment of the applicability of Titles VI and VII, defendants in *AMAE II*, via their experts, were highly influential in helping to shape Judge Orrick's opinion. On September 17, 1996, he ordered, "Defendants' requirement that plaintiffs pass the CBEST in order to obtain employment in the California public schools does not violate plaintiffs' rights under Title VI or Title VII of the Civil Rights Act of 1964.[64]

Plaintiffs, AMAE et al., appealed to the Ninth Circuit.[65] A three-member panel presided (Judges Robert Boochever, Andrew Kleinfield, and Stephen Wilson). The appellants contended that the district court erred in *AMAE II* in its finding that the CBEST was correctly validated and thus did not violate Titles VI and VII. Second, appellants argued that the district court violated Federal Rule of Evidence 706 by relying on an expert witness who did not prepare and submit a report and was not subject to cross-examination.[66] The appellees contended that the district court in *AMAE I* erred in holding that Title VI and VII apply regarding the administration of the CBEST. Second, appellees asserted that the district court in *AMAE II* abused its discretion by denying them $216,444 in legal costs.[67]

Regarding the applicability of Title VI, the Ninth Circuit held that although federal funds may have been provided to the Board of Education on the State's behalf, it is that agency—not the State as a whole—that is covered by Title VI. Given that neither the Department of Education, the Board of Education, nor the local school districts created the CTC (the California Legislature created it), such agencies are covered by Title VI, but the CTC is not covered by §2000d-4a(4) of Title VI. Therefore, the Ninth Circuit ordered the *AMAE I* court to dismiss plaintiffs' Title VI claim against the CTC.[68] With respect to the applicability of Title VII, the Ninth Circuit found that because the CBEST is a licensing exam, not an employment exam, Title VII does not apply. That is, the State is not the potential employer of teachers (school districts are). As such, the Ninth Circuit concluded that the CBEST is a valid licensing exam and is therefore exempt from liability under Title VII.[69]

The Ninth Circuit's ruling in *AMAE II* is yet another example of legal indeterminacy. Judge Boochever, a member of the three-judge panel, wrote a critical dissent. First, he noted that because the CTC had been receiving federal money since March 1996, there was no question that Title VI applies to the agency.[70] Second, Judge Boochever noted that because "local school districts are bound by a multitude of State constitutional and statutory mandates,"[71] school districts are agents of the State regarding the local operations of the school system. He cited an earlier Ninth Circuit ruling (*Gomez v. Alexian Bros. Hospital of San Jose*, 1983) in which the court held that for Title VII protections to apply there must be some employee-employer connection, but the relationship need not be direct. Therefore, Judge Boochever concluded that under Title VII the State is an employer of teachers.[72] In a blistering response to his fellow judges of the Ninth Circuit, Judge Boochever wrote,

> Under the majority opinion, the State is not subject to Title VII because it is not a direct employer. On the other hand, local school districts, which are the direct employers, are not subject to Title VII because it is the State and CTC that require and administer the CBEST. Given these circumstances, as a practical matter, the majority's reading of Title VII leaves minority public school teachers without any of the protections afforded by Title VII to challenge a state-imposed employment practice such as the CBEST. As a result of today's decision, California is no longer bound to follow Title VII's mandate when imposing its statewide hiring requirements for public school teachers, however invidious, discriminatory, or harmful those requirements may be. In reaching its decision, the majority ignores the political realities of public education in California and instead relies on the non-dispositive observation that the relationship between the State and public school teachers is not a traditional one. Because I believe that the majority has diminished the protections of Title VII for public school teachers beyond what Congress intended, I respectfully dissent.[73]

Perhaps motivated by Judge Boochever's dissent, AMAE et al. petitioned the Ninth Circuit for rehearing en banc.[74] After granting the request, the Ninth Circuit concluded that Title VII does apply to CBEST, but the test did not violate plaintiffs' rights because it was properly validated and job related. Furthermore, the court noted that Title VI does not need to be ruled on because plaintiffs' argument flows from their disparate impact theory under both Titles VI and VII. Thus, in light of the court's discussion of the merits under Title VII and the validation of the CBEST, the plaintiffs' claims on the merits of Title VI were resolved as well.[75] Accordingly, the Ninth Circuit en banc affirmed the *AMAE II* court's judgment in favor of the defendants.

In sum, the Texas and California teacher competency testing lawsuits initiated by Mexican American and other plaintiffs of color capture the legal and technical intricacies of this complex area of litigation. It appears that the linchpins of these cases lay in the issues of validity and job relatedness. Adverse impact, which is indisputable and so fundamental to plaintiffs' quest for justice, is, unfortunately, peripheral in the eyes of the court. The picture here, however, is not entirely bleak. As presented in note 9 of this chapter, African American plaintiffs have brought forth a number of teacher competency testing cases, and in the majority of these lawsuits, plaintiffs prevailed (e.g., *Groves v. Alabama Board of Education*, 1991), primarily winning on validity issues.

GI Forum v. Texas Education Agency (2000)

GI Forum v. Texas Education Agency (2000) concerned the use of high-stakes tests for awarding or denying students a high school diploma. I have an insider's perspective of this case. First, I served as an expert witness for the plaintiffs, and second, subsequent to the trial I served as Co-Guest Editor of a Special Issue of the case ("The Texas Assessment of Academic Skills [TAAS] Case: Perspectives of Plaintiffs' Experts"), published in the *Hispanic Journal of Behavioral Sciences* (Valencia & Bernal, 2000a). The experts for the defendants also produced a Special Issue germane to the lawsuit ("Defending a High School Graduation Test: *GI Forum v. Texas Education Agency*"), published in *Applied Measurement in Education* (Phillips, 2000b).

The plaintiffs included the GI Forum and *Image de Tejas* (two civil rights groups dedicated to the educational advancement of Mexican Americans in Texas), nine Mexican American and African American students whom the authorities denied a high school diploma,[76] and other students similarly situated in Texas. Defendants consisted of the Texas

Education Agency (TEA), members of the Texas State Board of Education, and Dr. Mike Moses (Texas Commissioner of Education). MALDEF attorneys filed the plaintiffs' complaint on October 14, 1997, in the U.S. District Court for the Western District of Texas (San Antonio Division); Judge Edward C. Prado presided.

The Texas Assessment of Academic Skills (TAAS) test—which measures reading, writing, and mathematics—lay at the center of controversy in the *GI Forum v. TEA* case.[77] The TEA required that students in grades 3, 5, 7, and 10 take the test; the grade 10 version of the TAAS served as the exit-level exam, and students needed to pass it to receive a high school diploma. Although school authorities first implemented the TAAS test in the 1990–1991 school year, the TEA did not provide exit-level pass and fail rates disaggregated by race/ethnicity until the 1993–1994 academic year. These data on the TAAS exit-level pass/fail rates showed a widespread and unwavering pattern: Mexican American and African American students, in comparison to their White peers, failed the TAAS exit-level test in significantly higher numbers. This occurred for all test administrations (initial, cumulative, and final) of the TAAS exam (see Fassold, 2000). Conversely, in terms of pass rates (for first-time test takers), White students passed the TAAS exit-level exam at nearly twice the rate of Mexican Americans and African Americans. While Whites passed the test at a rate of about 70%, Mexican Americans and African Americans passed the test at a rate of only around 40%.[78] According to the complaint submitted by MALDEF in late 1997, at the end of each academic year about forty-five hundred Mexican American and two thousand African American students had failed the TAAS test, and subsequently school officials denied them a high school diploma. While Mexican American and African American students constituted approximately 40% of all high school seniors, they constituted 85% of those who did not pass the final administration of the TAAS exam.[79] The exit-level TAAS testing had especially adverse impact on English learners. In 1995, teachers administered the exam (the English version) to eleven thousand English learner sophomores (identified as "Limited English Proficient," the vast majority being Mexican American). For these first-time test takers, only 14% passed the TAAS test.[80] In all, the overall negative consequences of the TAAS exit-level test on students of color proved grave. Dr. Walter Haney, an expert for plaintiffs in the case, estimated that the TEA prevented over one hundred thousand Mexican American and African American students, who were otherwise qualified, from receiving their high school diploma.[81]

The student plaintiffs in *GI Forum v. TEA* were, in all, quite similar.[82] They earned satisfactory or better grades in their course work. Some students made the honor roll. They had taken all the required courses to graduate. Some students participated in school activities, including positions of leadership. And they all had failed to pass the TAAS exam. In a number of cases, failure to pass the mathematics section of the test (usually by just one or two points) surfaced as the major obstacle. An example of such a student plaintiff is a Mexican American female (twenty-one years old at the time of the lawsuit). Her testimony, viewed from a CRT perspective, demonstrates the value of experiential knowledge. In her declaration, she wrote,

> I made good grades all through high school, generally I made A's and B's. I passed all of my courses. In my sophomore year I took my first TAAS test and passed the reading and writing sections, but not the math. I took the test again that summer of my sophomore year . . . and the next summer for a total of 4 times while I was still in school. . . . Since I left high school in 1997, I have taken the math part of the TAAS an additional 3 times, but have not been able to pass. I have missed the "70" passing grade mark by 1 point every time. *The last time I took the test was July 14, 1999.* . . . I applied at San Antonio College of Medical and Dental Assistants, to see if I could get in, but they need for me to pass my TAAS or get a GED. Project SER and Project Quest will pay for my education, but again, they want a GED or that I pass the TAAS. I refuse to get a GED. I do not want to get a GED, because I feel that since I went to school for 12 years I should be entitled to my diploma. This is the second reason I continue to take the TAAS test. I am a mother of two children. I applied at AVANCE for a position as a bus driver or cook in order that I could keep my children in their day care facilities, but because I do not have a high school diploma, I was denied the positions. I was NOT A HIGH SCHOOL DROPOUT. I finished all my courses and twelve years of school and expected to obtain a high school diploma. Only one part of the TAAS test is keeping me from obtaining a high school diploma and pursuing much better educational and employment opportunities.[83]

MALDEF attorneys presented seven claims in the *GI Forum v. TEA* lawsuit.[84] These claims can be further compressed to five assertions based on constitutional, statutory, and regulatory grounds (Saucedo, 2000).[85] In brief, plaintiffs grounded their claims in violations of (a) the State's duties to ensure that school districts provide equal educational opportunity pursuant to the desegregation order filed in *U.S. v. Texas* (1970); (b) the Equal Protection and Due Process Clauses of the Fourteenth Amendment; (c) Title VI of the Civil Rights Act of 1964, which prohibits discrimination by states that receive federal funds (42 U.S.C. §2000 *et seq.*); (d) the implementing regulations of Title VI by developing and mandating the use of an exam (the TAAS exit-level test) that discriminates against Mexican Americans and African Americans via its effects; (e) the EEOA (20 U.S.C. §1703) by failing to take appropriate measures to overcome language barriers that hinder equal participation by students (English learners) in instructional programs.[86]

MALDEF rested its Fourteenth Amendment claims on the assertion that the TEA, in its implementation of the TAAS exit-level exam, *knew in advance* that the test results would demonstrate unequivocal pass-rate differences between students of color and White examinees (Saucedo, 2000). Furthermore, MALDEF argued that the observable racial/ethnic test differences resulted, in part, from (a) an exam that was inherently flawed in its design and (b) the lack of opportunity of many students of color, attending historically segregated and inferior schools in Texas, to learn the content on the TAAS exit-level exam. Leticia M. Saucedo (co-counsel in the *GI Forum v. TEA* case) makes it clear that these equal protection and due process claims are not novel legal concepts (Saucedo, 2000). MALDEF based its legal theory in *GI Forum v. TEA* on the Fifth Circuit's landmark ruling that the use of exit-level exams to deny students' diplomas in Florida's public high schools was unconstitutional (*Debra P. v. Turlington*, 1981).[87] The appellate court ruled that students who had experienced past discrimination in Florida's public schools could not be forced to pass an exit-level exam to be awarded a high school diploma—unless the State could show that the exam overcame educational inequalities.[88] In sum, MALDEF in *GI Forum v. TEA* constructed its case on *Debra P.* and its progeny of lawsuits that sought to strike down standardized tests on grounds of validity (Saucedo, 2000).[89]

Approximately two months before commencement of trial, the State filed a motion for summary judgment requesting a dismissal of the plaintiffs' case (Saucedo, 2000). In all, only two of the plaintiffs' claims survived the court's review. Judge Prado dismissed plaintiffs' equal protection and Title VI claims. He reasoned that, notwithstanding the State's historical discrimination against Mexican American and African American students, the plaintiffs failed to demonstrate *present* intent to discriminate or that the TAAS exit-level exam requirement was connected to the State's past history of racial discrimination. In short, Judge Prado in his summary judgment ruled that the plaintiffs had neither direct nor circumstantial evidence of discrimination ample enough to support a claim of intentional discrimination.[90] Subsequently, the State requested that the court clarify the summary judgment's condition that limited the plaintiffs' ability to enter testimony regarding historical discrimination. Judge Prado ordered,

> The admissibility of [historical discrimination] evidence does not mean that the entire lengthy history of Texas's failures and success at educating minority students is admissible. Rather, Plaintiffs will be allowed to attempt to show that educational inequalities existed at the time the TAAS test was implemented and that those inequalities render the test unfair. Such a showing would be more a "snapshot" than of a historical narrative, however. In other words, the state of affairs at the time of the test's implementation need not be explained at length; it is enough to show that it existed and, perhaps, that the State was aware of it.[91]

As discussed later, the order of clarification severely diminished plaintiffs' experts' ability to introduce evidence of historical discrimination in Texas schools.

Judge Prado allowed the plaintiffs to proceed with their Title VI *regulation* discrimination claim. Three allegations make up a traditional Title VI regulation claim of discrimination (Saucedo, 2000). First, plaintiffs must prove that the implementation of the exam (in this case, the TAAS exit-level test) results in disparate impact on student plaintiffs. Second, the burden of proof then shifts to the defendants, who are required to show that the practice of requiring a pass on the exit-level exam is "educationally necessary." Or as Saucedo notes, "Is the practice manifestly related to a legitimate educational goal of the State?" (2000, p. 414). Third, the burden then shifts back to plaintiffs, who must demonstrate that there are alternatives (to the challenged practice) that are less discriminatory and equally efficacious.[92]

In an attempt to isolate the conflicting opinions, even antitheses, that abounded among the plaintiffs and defendants in the *GI Forum v. TEA* case, fellow expert witness, Dr. Ernesto M. Bernal, and I wrote an article entitled "An Overview of Conflicting Opinions in the TAAS Case" (Valencia & Bernal, 2000b).[93] We identified eight different issues and the

TABLE 8.2
Conflicting Opinions in the GI Forum v. TEA *Case*

Issue	Plaintiffs	Defendants
• Explanation of why some minority students fail the TAAS exam	Systemic in nature	Deficit thinking
• History of racial/ethnic minority discrimination in Texas schools	Important to include in testimony	Not relevant
• Opportunity to learn the TAAS exam content	Quite limited	Ample
• Alignment between teaching and the TAAS exam	Instructional validity	Curricular validity
• Adverse impact of the TAAS exam on minority students	Initial, cumulative, and final test administrations	Cumulative test administrations
• Psychometric integrity of the TAAS exam	Questionable; poor	Sound
• Decision model for awarding a high school diploma	Compensatory	Conjunctive
• Accountability model	Input, process, and output	Output only

Source: Adapted, with slight revisions, from Valencia & Bernal (2000b, p. 424). With permission of authors.

opinions that accompanied them.[94] These conflicting opinions are listed in Table 8.2. Due to space limitations, a discussion of only five of the eight opinions is presented here.

Explanation of why some minority students fail the TAAS exam. Defendants' position lay in deficit thinking. This discourse argues that many Mexican American and African American students of low-SES background fail in school (e.g., read below grade level; drop out of school) because of diminished intellectual capacity, poor motivation to achieve, and poor familial socialization for academic competence. Deficit thinkers assert that defects (or deficits) in children, their families, and their cultures thwart the learning process and lead to school failure. Schools are held exculpatory regarding school failure among students of color. This theoretical framework for explaining school failure among students of color has a long-standing position in American educational thought and practice (see Valencia, 1997c).

By sharp contrast, plaintiffs' experts asserted that school failure among many Mexican American and African American students is systemic and structural in nature. The focus of this model of school failure is on how schools have been organized to exclude students of color from learning by not providing equal educational opportunities.[95] The denial of equal educational opportunities—the driving force of school failure and diminished academic performance among students of color—manifests in school segregation, inequalities in school financing, curriculum differentiation (e.g., tracking in high school), substandard teachers, and a number of other schooling conditions that lead to racial/ethnic differentials in outcomes (see Valencia, 2002b). Parts of the depositional testimony provided by Dr. Mike Moses, Texas Commissioner of Education, were particularly disconcerting. Dr. Moses said nothing about structural or systemic problems in Texas schools (e.g., massive school segregation and its strong link to school failure) that can be posited to explain, in part, differences in the TAAS failure rates of White students and students of color. When asked by plaintiffs' co-counsel, Al Kauffman, about any possible systemic differences, the exchange went as follows:

> Q: Do you feel, at this time, there is a gap between the offerings available to minority students on the one hand and Anglo students on the other—
> A: No, sir.
> Q: —in the schools of Texas? None?
> A: No, sir. (Moses, 1998, p. 66)

History of racial/ethnic minority discrimination in Texas schools. Another issue in the *GI Forum v. TEA* case in which plaintiffs and defendants expressed sharp differences in opinion was the role of historical discrimination against students of color (see Table 8.2). Plaintiffs held the view that the history of educational discrimination against students of color in Texas links tightly to their current educational plight (see Valencia, 2000). The long history of racial discrimination and resultant school inequalities extends to the present day. As such, plaintiffs contended, this historical-contemporary connection is a key factor in understanding the discriminatory claims in the *GI Forum v. TEA* case. For example, current school segregation and its association with the inferior schooling of students of color are not merely the vestiges of historically forced separation of White students and students of color. Segregation and its invidious consequences continue from the past into the present—a lingering tradition that subtly allows the inferior educational preparation of students of color to take place (see, e.g., San Miguel & Valencia, 1998; Valencia, 2000; Valencia, Menchaca, & Donato, 2002; also, see chapter 2, this volume).

One of the charges for me as an expert for the plaintiffs in the *GI Forum v. TEA* case was to provide evidence of historical and contemporary discrimination against Mexican American and African American students in Texas's public schools (e.g., see Valencia, 1998). This line of reasoning, presented in trial testimony, was fairly straightforward. Linearly, the argument is as follows:[96]

1. Many Mexican American and African American students (particularly from a low-SES background) currently face various forms of schooling inequalities (e.g., segregation) in Texas public K–12 schooling.
2. These contemporary inequalities are not vestiges of past discrimination. Rather, they are part of a historical pattern that is continually being reproduced.
3. Existing schooling inequalities lead to diminished opportunities to learn the content on the TAAS exam.
4. The lower TAAS exam performance of Mexican American and African American students is primarily due to differences in opportunity to learn.
5. The TAAS exit-level test is being used unfairly because it places Mexican American and African American students in a double bind. Testing these students on what they have not been taught and then making crucial decisions (i.e., denial of a diploma) on the basis of their TAAS exam performance (failure in the case of the student plaintiffs) is a blatant form of discrimination.[97]

As previously discussed, the State proved successful in persuading the court to issue a motion in which it clarified the court's summary judgment order regarding past discrimination.[98] The court ruled that plaintiffs would be allowed to produce evidence of discrimination that existed at the time of TAAS implementation (which my trial testimony did), but even that, Judge Prado ordered, could only take the form of a "snapshot" rather than of a historical narrative. With all due respect to Judge Prado, historical discrimination in Texas schools (even in 1990, when TAAS was implemented) cannot be viewed as a snapshot. The true picture of such discrimination would constitute numerous reels of film. The court's inclination not to relate historical discrimination in Texas to contemporary racial/ethnic differences in TAAS exit-level performance strengthened the State's position that past discrimination did not link to the current and ubiquitous reality that Mexican American and African American students perform considerably lower than do their White peers on the TAAS exit-level exam (Saucedo, 2000).

It is my position that this ahistorical contention brought forth by the defendants and supported by Judge Prado is faulty and indefensible. At trial, I discussed two major points of schooling inequalities (Valencia, 2000). First, I raised the issue of long-standing school segregation and its strong association with diminished academic achievement of Mexican American and African American students. Second, I demonstrated the connection between the pervasiveness of substandard (noncertified) teachers in Texas public schools and lower TAAS exam performance of students of color.

Opportunity to learn the TAAS exam content. Table 8.2 lists a third issue, opportunity to learn (OTL), in which opinions of plaintiffs and defendants greatly differed. The notion of OTL is central to any discussion of the schooling of students of color, who as a group have experienced school failure. What is OTL? Valencia and Aburto (1991c) write that

> The notion of opportunity to learn deals with the fit—or lack of fit—between the content of a test (i.e., those samples of behavior that are measured), and the formal curriculum (i.e., that which is taught and learned in school). (p. 240)[99]

The implication for the testing of low-SES students of color attending segregated schools is clear. If they are not given the opportunity to learn the test material on which they later will be tested, then it is not surprising that their test scores will be lower, on the average, than their more economically advantaged White peers attending segregated White schools. Plaintiffs' in *GI Forum v. TEA* contended that students of color, on the whole, experience unfavorable schooling conditions (e.g., attend inferior, segregated schools; are taught, disproportionately, by less qualified teachers) and thus have reduced or quite limited opportunities to learn the content of the TAAS exam (see Valencia, 2000). Diminished OTL, plaintiffs argued, constitutes a major form of schooling inequality in the Texas public schools. In the broader sense, there are increasing instances in which claims such as the following are being registered: "Testing children on what they have not been taught and then stigmatizing their 'failure to achieve' is a fundamental form of discrimination" (Hanson, Schutz, & Bailey, 1980, p. 21; cited in Tittle, 1982, p. 46).

Defendants' experts' opinions on the OTL issue were, predictably, very different from the way plaintiffs' experts conceptualized this central concern in the *GI Forum v. TEA* case (see defendants' expert reports: Mehrens, 1999; Phillips, 1999). Defendants' expert witness Mehrens asserted,

"Students have had ample opportunity to learn the material tested on the TAAS" (1999, p. 8). He came to this conclusion based on the following logic:

> The schools in Texas are required by law to teach the essential elements outlined in the State Board of Education Rules of Curriculum. . . . To the extent that the TAAS content is taken from the essential elements, that State law requires schools to teach these elements, that schools must provide remediation to students who fail, that there are eight opportunities to take the test, and that there is at least some opinion by experts for the plaintiffs that schools emphasize the content tested by the TAAS, it seems obvious that students do have ample opportunity to learn the material. (pp. 8–9)

Phillips (1999), another expert for the defendants, shared Mehrens's views on the OTL issue:

> Opportunity to learn (OTL) means that students must be taught the skills tested on a graduation test. In practice, evidence of OTL is gathered by examining the official curricular materials used in instruction and by surveying teachers to determine whether they are teaching the tested content. For the TAAS exit-level tests, OTL has been established through the state-mandated essential elements and adequacy of preparation review by Texas educator committees and separate bias review panels. (pp. 10–11)

Valencia (1998) and Cárdenas (1998), experts for the plaintiffs, contended that the long history and effects of segregation, inequitable levels of school finance, and test abuse extends to the present day and thereby answer the question of equal OTL in the negative (see also Valencia, 2000). Fassold (1998), an expert for the plaintiffs, used data supplied by the TEA and calculated that many students of color attend "low quality" schools where, for example, teachers have lower levels of formal education and fewer teaching credentials, and many are assigned to teach courses for which they are not formally qualified (also, see Valencia, 2000). Furthermore, McNeil (1998), another expert for the plaintiffs, contended that the TAAS testing program has negatively affected instruction in schools with predominantly students of color, including the reallocation of relatively scarce resources (because of inequities in school finance) to direct instruction on the TAAS exam, or what Smith (1993) calls the narrowing of the curriculum.

The manner in which defendants' experts Mehrens and Phillips conceptualized OTL in the *GI Forum v. TEA* case is indefensible. Their expert opinion, it appears, is that OTL can come about by governmental fiat. Such a conception of OTL is specious and naïve. No governmental or legislative entity can mandate that all students be provided equal opportunity to learn material on which they will later be tested. The TEA might just as well decree that all students be taught by fully credentialed teachers in the areas taught, but that is clearly not the case in economically poor or historically segregated schools, mostly schools attended by students of color (Valencia, 2000). OTL and resultant school success can only be realized through assiduous efforts that lead to the provision of equal resources for all students—for example, via adequate school financing, qualified teachers, high-quality curricular offerings, high expectations of students' educability, and equal encouragement of students.

Alignment between teaching and the TAAS exam. As seen in Table 8.2, another issue in which conflicting opinions arose in the *GI Forum v. TEA* case was how to conceptualize the alignment between teaching in the classroom and TAAS test content. The issue here is closely related to the previous discussion regarding OTL. Heubert and Hauser (1999) have provided this useful distinction between curricular and instructional validity:

> There have been disagreements over how educational entities can demonstrate that a test measures what students have been taught. Some argue that it is sufficient for a state or school district to show that the formal written curriculum mentions the knowledge and skills that the test is designed to measure [i.e., curricular validity]. Others assert that what matters most is not the formal written curriculum but the actual curriculum and instruction in each classroom (Madaus, 1983)—that instructional rather than curricular validity is required. (p. 64)

Plaintiffs asserted that the alignment between classroom teaching and the TAAS test should be assessed through *instructional validity*, that is, through the link between actual teaching in the classroom and what is measured on the TAAS test. In the field of tests and measurements, this type of validity is known as "content validity."

Defendants asserted that *curricular validity*, not instructional validity, is more important in assessing whether there is a good alignment between classroom teaching and what TAAS measures. Once again, the defendants' experts relied on arguments that *imply* that the state-mandated curriculum drives test validity. Phillips (1999) asserted,

> The most important evidence of validity in this situation is a measure of the degree to which the items on each subject matter test measure the knowledge and skills prescribed by the state-mandated curriculum (essential elements). This type of validity evidence is often referred to as *content validity evidence*. (p. 3)

The issue of alignment between teaching and the TAAS test is central to understanding existing schooling inequalities in Texas. Phillips's view essentially allows the state to sidestep the requirement that it ensure that its curriculum is actually implemented by qualified teachers. One of the plaintiffs' experts, Haney (1999), in his supplementary expert report, generated his own analyses of TEA data (from spring of 1995) on the relation between TAAS exit-level scores and course grades. He computed correlations between TAAS scores (reading, mathematics, and writing) and English II grades for more than three thousand students (grade 10) in three school districts. Observed correlations between TAAS scores and grades were weak in magnitude, ranging from .32 to .37. Such analyses indicated that there were a large number of false positives—that is, students who failed TAAS but had passing grades. When the analyses were disaggregated by race/ethnicity, Haney found that the issue of misalignment was worse for students of color than for White students. He reported, "Of Grade 10 students . . . who are passing their English II courses, the rate of failure on the TAAS Reading test for Black and Hispanic students is more than double that of White [students]. A similar, but slightly smaller, disparity is apparent on the TAAS Writing sub-test" (1999, p. 33). As to explaining the disparity between TAAS scores and grades for minority and White students, Haney concluded,

> Such a disparity can result from one of two causes. First, if the TAAS Reading test is in fact a valid and unbiased test of reading skills, the fact that close to 30% of Black and Hispanic students who are *passing* their sophomore English courses as compared with only 10% of White students must indicate that minority students in these three districts are simply not receiving the same quality of education as their white counterparts

—especially when it is recalled that by 1995 Black and Hispanic students were being retained in grade 9 at much higher rates than white students. The only other explanation for the sharp disparity is that the TAAS-X [exit-level] tests and the manner in which they are being used (with a passing score of 70% correct) are simply not valid and fair measures of what students have had an opportunity to learn. (pp. 33–34)[100]

On a final point about the alignment issue, Haney (2002) surveyed 148 Texas teachers (secondary mathematics and English) regarding their opinions of the relation between mandated testing/teaching and the effects of mandated testing. Haney reported that in response to a question about the "similarity of content of mandated testing and their own instruction," only 52% of the respondents answered "quite" or "very similar." Thus, about one-half of the surveyed teachers believed that there was not a good match between what was mandated to teach and was required to be tested on the TAAS instrument (also, see Valenzuela, 2000).

Decision model for awarding a high school diploma. In our article regarding the *GI Forum v. TEA* lawsuit (Valencia & Bernal, 2000b), Ernesto Bernal and I discuss three issues germane to the decision model for awarding a high school diploma (standard, or pass score, setting; the use of the TAAS exit-level exam as a sole criterion; compensatory and conjunctive models). Because of space limitations, only the compensatory and conjunctive models are discussed here (see Table 8.2).

The issue here concerns the use of multiple critical scores for the areas of reading, writing, and mathematics. Crucial to understanding the clash of opinions between plaintiffs and defendants here is the difference between two decision-making models in awarding high school diplomas. Heubert and Hauser (1999) have described the distinction as follows:

> Two models are commonly used to combine data from multiple requirements and assessments: *conjunctive* and *compensatory*. A conjunctive model requires adequate performance on each measure, whereas a compensatory model allows performance on one measure to offset, or compensate for, substandard performance on another. (p. 165)

Defendants used a minimal Texas Learning Index score of 70 for each of the three subject areas, and failing any one area is sufficient to withhold the high school diploma, although the student may meet all other graduation requirements (e.g., adequate grades and attendance). This conjunctive use of criteria, defendants argued, is necessary to ensure the competencies desired for a high school diploma. Hills (1971), however, states that conjunctive criteria are most often adopted because they are "so simple" (p. 694) to use, not because they have been carefully evaluated.

Plaintiffs' expert Ernesto Bernal (1998) stated that evaluators ordinarily use multiple critical scores when external criteria have previously validated each cutting point (which would rarely be set empirically at the same score for all tests). Evaluators might also use multiple cut scores when internal criteria are clearly and separately so essential to a particular job or application that nothing can take their place or otherwise compensate for their absence (an example is the requirement to make both good takeoffs and safe landings to receive a pilot's license). Given that the State had not externally validated the TAAS exit-level exam, and it was not a basic skills test (unlike its predecessor, the Texas Educational Assessment of Minimum Skills), defendants failed to justify that TAAS scores cannot, within reason, be used together in a compensatory way to clear a student to receive a high school diploma. "Experience suggests . . . that in education at least . . . lack of one kind of talent can often be compensated for by possession of another relevant talent" (Hills, 1971, p. 694). Without this provision, a student who scores 70-70-70 on the three parts of the TAAS exit-level exam would pass, but one who scores a 75-75-69 would not, even though the latter student is probably better qualified. Intuitively, psychometrically, and statistically, this practice makes no sense and remains unjustified. Plaintiffs, then, argued for a comprehensive compensatory model. That is, a student who has a passing grade point average, has acceptable attendance, and has taken all required courses yet has difficulty in passing one or more parts of TAAS should be awarded a high school diploma (all plaintiff students were of such circumstances regarding academic requirements and TAAS status).[101]

After five weeks of trial (two hundred hours of testimony by many witnesses and showing of numerous exhibits), Judge Prado released his decision on January 7, 2000. He said that it was "probably the most challenging decision [he] had to make in 15 years on the bench" (Elliott, 1999, p. 1). Given that in 2000, eighteen states had high school graduation exams in place (Amrein & Berliner, 2002), the outcome of the *GI Forum v. TEA* lawsuit had national implications. States with existing exit-level exams, and those states that were planning to implement such tests, were attentively waiting for the decision in this landmark case. In a nutshell, Judge Prado ruled that the TAAS exit-level test did indeed result in adverse impact against the plaintiffs, but he also found that the use of the TAAS exam to deny student diplomas was not illegal because it served an educational necessity for Texas's accountability system. In sum, Judge Prado ruled in favor of the defendants—the State.[102] Next is a brief discussion of how the court came to its ruling.

Regarding the plaintiffs' due process claim, the court noted that it must first find that a protected interest of plaintiffs (either property or liberty) exists and that the State seeks to limit or deny it.[103] Based on the Texas Education Code[104] and *Debra P. v. Turlington* (1981), Judge Prado found that the State of Texas has created a protected interest in a student's receipt of a high school diploma. Citing the Fifth Circuit's ruling in *Debra P. v. Turlington* (1981), Judge Prado noted that the appellate court held that a state cannot prescribe a standardized test as a requirement for graduation without providing students *procedural* protection (i.e., adequate notice). Furthermore, the Fifth Circuit brought to bear the *substantive* component of students' rights. That is, it is illegal for a state to impose a graduation exam when the "imposition is arbitrary and capricious or frustrates a legitimate state interest or is fundamentally unfair, in that it encroaches upon concepts of justice lying at the basis of our civil and political institutions."[105] Judge Prado found that the use of the TAAS exit-level exam does not violate the due process rights of the students (minority or White).[106] Judge Prado found that the exam was sufficiently reliable, that it meets acceptable standards for curricular validity, that all students have reasonable opportunity to learn the material on which they will be tested, and that the state offers remediation for those students who fail the test. In sum, the court ruled that the TAAS exit-level exam is fair.[107]

With respect to the plaintiffs' claim that the defendants violated the implementing regulations of Title VI, the court ruled on the three allegations: disparate impact, educational necessity of the TAAS exit-level exam, and whether less discriminatory and equally efficient alternatives can be shown.

Disparate impact. Fassold (1998, 2000), plaintiffs' statistical expert, conducted a comprehensive analysis on the TAAS exit-level exam of adverse impact using the 80-percent rule[108] and three other statistical measures.[109] Judge Prado determined that plaintiffs had established a prima facie case of disparate impact. He credited Fassold's testimony and found that

> There is sufficient evidence that, on first-time administration of the exit-level test, a legally significant adverse impact exists. While an examination

of cumulative pass scores in more recent years does not evince adverse impact under the Four-Fifths Rule, the disparity there, too, is sufficient to give rise to legitimate concern.[110]

It was a major outcome for the plaintiffs to prevail on the disparate-impact claim. As a result, the burden of proof shifted to the State regarding the linchpin of the implementing regulations of a Title VI claim: Did the State sufficiently argue that the requirement of passing the TAAS exit-level exam is educationally necessary?

Educational necessity. At this point in Judge Prado's ruling, he began with a caveat, noting,

> The word "necessity," as an initial matter, is somewhat misleading; the law does not place so stringent a burden on the defendant as that word's common usage might suggest. Instead, an educational necessity exists where the challenged practice serves the *legitimate* educational goals of the institution.[111]

Or, as Saucedo (2000) notes, all the State needs to do is demonstrate that the practice is manifestly related to a legitimate educational goal of the State. Judge Prado found that the TEA had met its burden. He asserted that the TEA's articulated goals of the TAAS exit-level exam requirement —to hold students, teachers, and schools accountable for education and to ensure that all students receive equal educational opportunity—are "within the legitimate exercise of the State's power over public education."[112] Also, he ruled that the plaintiffs failed to demonstrate a causal relation between the TAAS exit-level test and increased minority dropout and retention rates[113] and that the exit-level-test graduation requirement "guarantees that students will be motivated to learn."[114]

Less discriminatory and equally efficient alternatives. Judge Prado ruled that the plaintiffs' suggestions for implementing less discriminatory and equally efficacious alternatives to the TAAS exit-level exam were not objective. First, plaintiffs sought the use of a sliding-scale compensatory model as an alternative to the TEA's conjunctive model (see earlier discussion). The court found that the sliding-scale system suggested by the plaintiffs would not "sufficiently motivate students to perform to their highest ability."[115] Second, the plaintiffs offered a compensatory model in which course grades, along with TAAS exit-level scores, could be used to award diplomas. Here, Judge Prado found that (a) grades are often inflated and thus "mask gaps in learning"[116] and (b) students' grades cannot be equated to TAAS exit-level test performance, "as grades can measure a variety of factors, ranging from effort and improvement to objective mastery."[117] In an apparent attempt to reify the TAAS exit-level exam as infallible, Judge Prado declared, *"The TAAS test is a solely objective measurement of mastery* [italics added]."[118]

At the end of his opinion, Judge Prado noted that he would have ruled for a due process violation if the TAAS exit-level exam "were used as a vehicle for holding students accountable for an educational system that failed them. The Court concludes, however, that the TAAS test is not used in such a manner."[119] He also commented that although Texas's problems in providing educational equality to all of its pupils have been well documented, some progress has been made. He stated, "It is only in the recent past that efforts have been made to provide equal funding to Texas public schools."[120] Although this is true, chapter 3 of this book underscores that serious near-future problems abound for Texas's public school finance system. Also regarding progress, Judge Prado noted, "Several schools in the state remain under desegregation orders."[121] He failed to mention, however, that Texas's public schools are extremely segregated and that such racial/ethnic isolation is on the rise (see chapter 1, this volume). Judge Prado also failed to note that such school segregation is intrinsically linked to school failure of many students of color, including diminished performance on Texas's state-mandated achievement tests (see Valencia, 2000; Valencia, Menchaca, & Donato, 2002; chapter 1, this volume). In the conclusion of his opinion, Judge Prado provided a compact summary of his ruling:

ACCORDINGLY, the Court finds that the TAAS exit-level examination does not violate regulations enacted pursuant to Title VI of the Civil Rights Act of 1964. While the TAAS test does adversely affect minority students in significant numbers, the TEA has demonstrated an educational necessity for the test, and the Plaintiffs have failed to identify equally effective alternatives. In addition, the Court concludes that the TAAS test violates neither the procedural nor the substantive due process rights of the Plaintiffs. The TEA has provided adequate notice of the consequences of the exam and has ensured that the exam is strongly correlated to material actually taught in the classroom. In addition, the test is valid and in keeping with current educational norms. Finally, the test does not perpetuate prior educational discrimination or unfairly hold Texas minority students accountable for the failures of the State's educational system. Instead, the test seeks to identify inequities and to address them. It is not for this Court to determine whether Texas has chosen the best of all possible means for achieving these goals. The system is not perfect, but the Court cannot say that it is unconstitutional. Judgment is GRANTED in favor of the Defendants, and this case is DISMISSED.[122]

Legal indeterminacy permeates Judge Prado's opinion. In light of the impressive evidence and arguments brought forth by plaintiffs, he easily could have ruled in their favor. Notwithstanding some praise (e.g., Phillips, 2000b) for the court's ruling in the *GI Forum v. TEA* lawsuit, many scholars have criticized the decision (see, e.g., Bernal & Valencia, 2000; Fassold, 2000; Fernández, 2001; Johnson, 2004; McNeil, 2000b; Moran, 2000; Valencia, 2000; Valenzuela, 2000). Some critics, for example, have commented on the irony in Judge Prado's ruling that he found that significant adverse impact resulted for Mexican American and African American students, yet he upheld the use of the TAAS exit-level exam because it achieves the legitimate educational objectives of Texas. Fassold, plaintiffs' statistical expert whose testimony was paramount in Judge Prado's finding of adverse impact, notes that the ruling was equivocal. "To plaintiffs this is a mixed ruling. It acknowledges their plight, but, at the same time, allows the State's inequitable accountability system to prevail" (Fassold, 2000, p. 478).

Other critics have noted that the ruling in *GI Forum v. TEA* reflects the modern era of conservative ascendancy in the federal courts in which the judiciary consistently shows almost total deference to state educational agencies (see, e.g., Fernández, 2001; Moran, 2000).[123] These critics (who are typically legal scholars) trace this deference to the early 1970s, when the U.S. Supreme Court held steadfastly to the position that education is not a fundamental right guaranteed by the Constitution (see *San Antonio Independent School District v. Rodriguez* [1973], chapter 2, this volume) but is, rather, a state concern.[124] The issue of judicial deference presents the major obstacle preventing plaintiffs from prevailing in high-stakes testing litigation. Plaintiffs could come to trial well prepared with credible, convincing evidence of a claim involving the implementing regulations of Title VI, yet plaintiffs would still face a formidable challenge. As this book has underscored, Mexican Americans and other students of color have continually turned to the courts for relief from educational injustices. In commenting on the plight of the disenfranchised, Fernandez notes, "By granting states unmitigated latitude in education policies, however, the judiciary has effectively denied those members of our community with the least status and least political access any remedy against policies that unfairly affect them or their children" (2001, p. 145).

Notwithstanding their grave reservations about both the contemporary and future use of the TAAS exit-level exam, MALDEF attorneys decided not to appeal the district court's ruling to the Fifth Circuit, as several legal concerns were at stake. Al Kauffman, plaintiffs' co-counsel, states, "Although we identified several reversible errors in the opinion, we faced a risk of reversal of the District Court's correct holdings on adverse impact, the state's duty to prove both instructional and curricular validity and a student's property interest in a high school diploma" (Kauffman, 2000, p. 243).

Conclusion

In light of the daunting challenge that plaintiffs faced in the cases discussed in this chapter (*U.S. v. Texas*, *AMAE v. California*, and *GI Forum v. TEA*), it appears that high-stakes testing litigation is likely to go on hiatus. Opponents of high-stakes testing vis-à-vis students of color have become exceedingly cognizant of the difficulty in prevailing in the courts. Thus, critics have centered on an assessment strategy that emerged in the *GI Forum v. TEA* case—the use of multiple criteria (including test data). Advocating for multiple criteria assessment has taken on a two-pronged focus: (a) legislative bills[125] and (b) scholarly writing.[126] Interest and efforts in multiple criteria assessment are rapidly gaining momentum and are so widespread that one scholar has referred to them as "the movement for multiple criteria."[127]

The advocacy for using multiple criteria in assessment (e.g., test scores, student grades, portfolios, classroom observations, teacher recommendations, medical records) is not a new idea. For example, in the 1970 *Diana v. State Board of Education* case of nearly four decades ago (discussed in chapter 3, this volume), plaintiffs and defendants agreed (in the stipulation and order) on ten major points, one being that "multiple information" shall be collected before a child is enrolled in a class for the mentally retarded. As far as my own writings on multiple criteria assessment, I have advocated such use for over twenty-five years (Valencia, 1982).[128] In any event, the movement for multiple criteria assessment is certainly receiving attention. The major impediment for successful implementation, however, is the disconnect between academe and state legislatures. In order to bridge the gap, it behooves policymakers to understand and embrace the following dictum from the measurement community: "In all . . . educational decisions, test scores provide just one type of information and should be supplemented by past records of achievement and other types of assessment data. *No major educational decision should ever be based on test scores alone*" (Gronlund, 1985, p. 480).[129]

In conclusion, high-stakes testing has now become entrenched as a popular mechanism of the standards-based school reform movement in the United States. As discussed in the introduction to this chapter, within a few years the majority of states will require exit-level exams to award, or to deny, students their high school diploma. This is an explosive growth of 2,500%, from one state in 1979 to twenty-six states projected to have exit-level exams in 2012.[130] What is particularly inauspicious is that by 2012, high school exit-level exams will likely have the greatest consequences for students of color (especially Latino and African American students), as their proportion of the school-age population swells. Concomitantly, high-stakes testing will assuredly expand. If the quality of schooling does not commensurately increase for Mexican American/other Latino and African American students—along with the certain growth of high-stakes testing—considerable school failure among these students is imminent. We must, however, continue to struggle for relief from the oppressive nature of high-stakes testing. Although high-stakes testing litigation appears to be in a respite, we must not abandon the legal struggle for educational equality in this area.

In these final thoughts, let us draw from the wisdom of Leticia M. Saucedo, plaintiffs' co-counsel in the *GI Forum v. TEA* case. Saucedo (2000) offers some valuable suggestions for future litigation in the high-stakes testing arena. First, it is incumbent on both civil rights attorneys and experts, working together, to further isolate and underscore the linkages between race and test performance. Second, experts trained in historical analysis must continue to research and document patterns of discrimination. Particular emphasis needs to be placed on examining how current practices and past discrimination are "causally" linked. Third, experts should actively participate in understanding how their testimony will support the legal claims of plaintiffs. "Such an understanding will undoubtedly enhance the plaintiffs' development of an overall story for judge and jury" (Saucedo, 2000, p. 420). In sum, Saucedo's advice for future litigation in the high-stakes testing realm is well taken. As she notes, the *GI Forum v. TEA* case, and lawsuits like it, are becoming increasingly arduous to litigate due to the growing disinclination of the courts to establish "race as a factor in a cause-and-effect factor analysis of discrimination" (p. 420). Saucedo further comments that current courts, compared to past ones, are much more disposed to accept the reasoning that factors other than race (e.g., SES; poor student motivation) are the explanation for differential effects of state policy on Whites and students of color. As seen in the *GI Forum v. TEA* lawsuit, as a case in point, the State was quite successful in deflecting arguments that the TAAS exit-level exam discriminated based on race. Herein lies the value of CRT in understanding these sharp differences in views. In CRT, there is a proposition that race and racism in society are deep-seated and unwavering in identifying and explaining individual experiences of the law. On the other hand, the deficit thinking discourse—so pronounced in the *GI Forum v. TEA* case—racializes school failure among students of color and blames them for their "inability" to pass the TAAS exam. In future high-stakes testing litigation brought forth by students of color, for justice to prevail the courts must understand these antithetical explanations of why some students succeed and some fail. In particular, this case reveals that if students of color do not receive equal opportunity to learn, then their poor performance on high-stakes tests reflects inferior schooling, not the inability to learn.

Conclusion

The Contemporary and Future Status of Mexican American–Initiated School Litigation; What We Have Learned from This Legal History

In this final chapter, I offer some thoughts on the contemporary and future status of school litigation brought forth by the Mexican American community. First, I discuss two lawsuits that have been recently litigated. My coverage is brief because the cases may be appealed. Second, I speculate on the types of educational lawsuits Mexican Americans may file in the very near future. I close the chapter by reflecting on what we have learned from this legal history, particularly regarding race and education in the United States.

Recently Litigated Educational Lawsuits Brought Forth by Mexican Americans

The Mexican American–initiated school litigation covered in this book ranges over more than eight decades, from the 1925 *Romo v. Laird* desegregation case in Arizona to the 2006 ruling in the 250th District Court of Travis County (Texas) that brought closure to the *Edgewood* school financing case (*West Orange-Cove v. Neeley*, 2006). To be sure, the chronicle of Mexican American school litigation does not end there. Two recent cases deserve our attention. The first lawsuit deals with school desegregation; the second one concerns bilingual education.

Santamaria v. Dallas Independent School District (2006)

This desegregation lawsuit differs radically from the type of school segregation cases discussed in chapter 1, which concerned "between-school segregation," or the isolation of Mexican American students in very high-enrollment Mexican American schools.[1] Historically, scholars and educators alike have described schools in which the students enrolled were exclusively Mexican-origin as "Mexican" schools. Contemporarily, the courts adjudge schools with predominantly Mexican American enrollments as "de facto" segregated (i.e., due to residential housing patterns).

The type of segregation seen in the *Santamaria* case, however, concerns racial isolation in a racially diverse elementary school. This isolation, or "within-school segregation," refers to the segregation of students of color (in this case, Mexican Americans and other Latinos) from their White peers in self-contained, separate classrooms. Within-school segregation is quite uncommon in elementary schools, but it occurs frequently at the high school level in the form of "tracking" (see, e.g., Oakes, 1985, 2005; Oakes & Guiton, 1995; Page, 1991). The focal point in the *Santamaria* lawsuit was Preston Hollow Elementary School, located in an affluent, predominantly White neighborhood in North Dallas.[2] In the 2005–2006 school year, Preston Hollow's enrollment contained 66% Latino students, 18% White, 14% African American, and 2% Asian American.[3]

On April 18, 2006, MALDEF filed a complaint for plaintiff Lucresia Mayorga Santamaria on behalf of her three children (Does 1, 2, and 3) and for plaintiff *Organización Para El Futuro de Los Estudiantes* (Organization for the Children's Future) on behalf of their Latino children who attend Preston Hollow. Plaintiffs claimed that their children, who were overwhelmingly classified as not limited-English-proficient (non-LEP), were, nevertheless, enrolled in ESL (English as a Second Language) classes.[4] School officials had deemed these students English proficient based on a language assessment instrument. These "non-LEP" Latino children were segregated for instruction from their White peers, who were disproportionately enrolled in "General Education" sections.[5] Plaintiffs asserted that school officials denied their children "the opportunity to learn in integrated classrooms, which contributes to a sense of inferiority."[6] The complaint alleged that school authorities intentionally segregated the Latino children on the basis of race, color, or national origin, in violation of the Equal Protection Clause of the Fourteenth Amendment to the U.S. Constitution, as well as Title VI of the Civil Rights Act of 1964.[7] Defendants in *Santamaria* were the Dallas Independent School District (DISD), DISD Board of Trustees, Michael Hinojosa (DISD Superintendent), and Teresa Parker (Principal of Preston Hollow). Parties litigated *Santamaria* in the U.S. District Court for the Northern District of Texas (Dallas Division), with Judge Sam A. Lindsay presiding. MALDEF counsel asked me to serve as an expert witness for the plaintiffs.

The bench trial of *Santamaria* lasted from August 9 to August 21, 2006. I testified, based on extensive data analyses, that the within-school segregation of Latino and White children at Preston Hollow had no justifiable pedagogical rationale.[8] First, I testified that because the strong majority of the Latino students labeled "ESL" *did not*, in fact, qualify as LEP based on a valid and reliable language assessment instrument, language status did not justify their within-school segregation. Second, I ruled out between-class ability grouping as a justifiable rationale for the within-school segregation. I based my assertion on a comprehensive analysis of Iowa Test of Basic Skills scores that found considerable overlap in measured achievement scores of the Latino and White children. Thus, the assumption of homogeneity of ability—the major premise for the use of between-class ability grouping—was unwarranted.[9]

On November 16, 2006, after numerous witnesses for both the plaintiffs and defendants provided testimony, Judge Lindsay ruled that Principal Parker intentionally discriminated against the Latino children by segregating them from the White children.[10] For conspicuous violation of the constitutional rights of Doe children 1 and 3, Judge Lindsay assessed punitive damages of $20,000 against Principal Parker; the damages were to be paid to the two children.[11] Finally, Judge Lindsay ordered that by January 17, 2007, Principal Parker eliminate the racial segregation at Preston Hollow.[12]

References to the protection of White privilege, a dominant theme of this book, resounded in Judge Lindsay's decision:

> In reserving certain classrooms for Anglo students, Principal Parker was, in effect, operating, at taxpayer's expense, a private school for Anglo children within a public school that was predominantly minority. [Moreover, the purpose of such isolation was] to prevent white flight from Preston Hollow.[13]

Reminiscent of claims that segregation stigmatized students of color (cf. *Mendez* and *Brown*), Judge Lindsay noted,

> It does not require a mathematician or educational psychologist to conclude that being segregated and placed in ESL classrooms in different hallways from one's Anglo counterparts would adversely affect a minority

student's self esteem, leading to feelings of being stigmatized based on race and national origin, as well as adversely affect a minority student's ability to obtain the same benefit from schooling as his or her Anglo counterpart.[14]

Furthermore, the centrality of race and racism—another dominant theme of this book—arose in the court's ruling. In a follow-up Memorandum and Opinion issued on April 10, 2007 ("Memorandum Opinion II"), Judge Lindsay concluded that Principal Parker's actions were "a clear and unequivocal violation of a long-established constitutional right [and declared] . . . The court can think of no constitutional violations more damaging and indelible than those based on immutable characteristics such as race and ethnicity at issue in this case."[15]

The *Santamaria* ruling represents a major victory for the Mexican American/Latino community. It is unknown if other racially diverse elementary schools practice within-school segregation. If they do, *Santamaria* stands as a precedent from which plaintiffs' lawyers can draw. The case reminds us of the centrality of race and racism in education, as well as the extent to which an individual school administrator will go in protecting White privilege.

U.S. v. Texas (2006)

This bilingual education lawsuit has a long and complicated history. In the late 1960s, the U.S. Department of Justice began a campaign to force state educational agencies into compliance with new federal desegregation rulings. *U.S. v. Texas* (1970) began as just such a case, targeting nine all–African American school districts in East Texas.[16] As discussed earlier in this book, at about this same time Mexican Americans were gaining recognition as an identifiable ethnic group in school cases (e.g., *Cisneros v. Corpus Christi Independent School District*, 1970; *Keyes v. School District No. 1 of Denver*, 1973; see chapter 1, this volume), and thus the courts entitled them to the same protections afforded African Americans under *Brown v. Board of Education*. Furthermore, this recognition helped to open the door for Mexican Americans to demand bilingual-bicultural education under the Equal Protection Clause of the Fourteenth Amendment (e.g., *Serna v. Portales Municipal Schools*, 1972).

The first such bilingual education case was an extension of the original *U.S. v. Texas* desegregation case, filed on behalf of Mexican American students in the San Felipe–Del Rio Consolidated Independent School District. San Felipe and Del Rio School Districts, located in Del Rio, Texas, along the U.S.-Mexico border, originally were two separate districts, the former exclusively Mexican American and the latter exclusively White.[17] In the original *U.S. v. Texas* suit, the U.S. Department of Justice alleged that the State of Texas unconstitutionally segregated Mexican Americans in its public schools. On August 13, 1971, Judge William W. Justice of the U.S. District Court for the Eastern District of Texas (Tyler Division) ordered the consolidation and desegregation of both districts.[18] In a subsequent order clarifying his original opinion, Judge Justice noted that an essential feature of equal opportunity for plaintiffs was schooling designed for Mexican American students who did not speak English. Although *Serna* (1972) was the first Mexican American lawsuit in the nation that mandated bilingual education, *U.S. v. Texas* is important because now the court ordered Texas, at the time the third most populous state in the country, to provide bilingual-bicultural education.[19]

Despite Judge Justice's ruling, Texas was very slow to comply, prompting LULAC and the American GI Forum (who were represented by MALDEF) to intervene in 1972 on behalf of all Mexican American students. On June 3, 1975, the plaintiff-intervenors filed a motion to enforce decree and for supplemental relief to compel the State of Texas to establish the bilingual-bicultural education programs that Judge Justice's order required. This motion was predicated, in part, on alleged violations of Title VI of the 1964 Civil Rights Act, the Equal Protection Clause of the Fourteenth Amendment, and the Equal Education Opportunities Act of 1974, 20 U.S.C. §1703(f).[20] After nearly six years of litigation, Judge Justice again ruled for plaintiff-intervenors, finding Texas culpable for the alleged violations, and ordered defendants to develop a comprehensive bilingual education plan.[21] Texas appealed to the Fifth Circuit, which in 1982 reversed the district court ruling, citing that the recent passage of Texas's new bilingual education law (SB 477) was to provide funding for bilingual education programs from kindergarten to grade 6 and ESL programs for higher grades.[22] The issue remained dormant for *nearly twenty-five years*, until February 9, 2006, when MALDEF, once again representing movants LULAC and the American GI Forum, filed a motion for further relief.[23] Defendants were the State of Texas, the Texas Commissioner of Education (as of December 2006, Dr. Shirley J. Neeley), and the Texas Education Agency (TEA). Parties argued the motion in the U.S. District Court for the Eastern District of Texas (Tyler Division). As before, Judge William W. Justice presided.

The plaintiff-intervenors maintained that Texas had been guilty of an "Evisceration of Monitoring and Enforcement of the Bilingual Education/ESL Program in Violation of 20 U.S.C. §1703(f) and the Order of this Court."[24] This, in turn, led to a number of academic problems for LEP children in Texas schools, whose population increased by 244% from 1979 to the 2004–2005 school year.[25] Plaintiff-intervenors claimed that the failures of the defendants' bilingual education program in the areas of monitoring and enforcement were of particular concern in light of the grave academic difficulties faced by LEP students. Based on TEA data, LEP students—compared to both White students and all students statewide—had higher rates of (a) failure in meeting the state's standards on the Texas Assessment of Knowledge and Skills (TAKS),[26] (b) dropping out, and (c) grade retention.[27] In *U.S. v. Texas* (2006), plaintiff-intervenors requested that the court "issue an order for injunctive relief requiring TEA to design, sufficiently staff, and promptly implement a program for monitoring of programs for LEP students, including the bilingual education/ESL program."[28] Judge Justice commenced a five-day bench trial on October 24, 2006, and released his decision on July 27, 2007, ruling for the State (see *U.S. v. Texas*, 2007). He found that the plaintiffs failed to provide evidence that Texas's bilingual education/ESL program was not taking "appropriate action to overcome language barriers" (20 U.S.C. §1703[f]). In sum, the State was not in violation of the *Castaneda* standard (see chapter 4, this volume).

Likely Future Mexican American–Initiated School Litigation

Based on my sense of the past and current state of public education for school-age Mexican American students (Valencia, 2002b), along with the extraordinary growth of the Mexican American population (Valencia, 2002a) and the escalating anti-immigrant sentiment across the United States (López, 2005; Mangaliman, Rodríguez, & Gonzales, 2006), matters do not bode well for the educational futures of Mexican-origin people. Given the overall current status of race relations in the United States, Mexican Americans may face regressive and oppressive legislative acts and local laws that will force them to seek justice in the courts. Here, I offer conjectures as to what might be some types of lawsuits that Mexican Americans will bring forth in the near future. These cases are likely to revolve around (a) continuing inequities in interdistrict funding and (b) attempts by state legislatures to deny birthright citizenship to children born in the United States to undocumented immigrants.

Continuing inequities in interdistrict funding. A new wave of litigation on this issue seems likely. Consider Texas, for example. As noted earlier in this book, some critics have asserted that the Legislature's recent plan (HB 3) is seriously flawed because the new taxes collected would result in a major shortfall (Robin Hood plan, 2006; also, see Embry, 2006).[29]

Indeed, Dr. Albert Cortez, Director of the Institute for Policy and Leadership of the Intercultural Development Research Association (IDRA),[30] has asserted that the Texas Legislature's latest school funding plan is a dramatic regression in school finance equity. Cortez (2006) reports that the fifty wealthiest school districts in Texas—which have student enrollments of approaching three-quarters White, 25% Latino, and 3% African American—will receive $671 more in per-pupil expenditures under the new plan. By contrast, the fifty poorest school districts—which have enrollments of about 5% White, 94% Latino, and 1% African American students—will receive only $294 more in per-pupil expenditures (a 56% less increase in per-pupil funding, compared to the fifty richest districts).[31] Cortez comments that the bottom line is that billions of dollars will be spent under the new school funding scheme, but equity will suffer. In language very similar to that of decades past (e.g., *Serrano*; see chapter 3, this volume), Cortez notes that educational quality in Texas is closely tied to local district wealth. He writes,

> Ultimately the students in the great majority of Texas schools will suffer as a result of a system that is grossly under-funded and produces schools where the quality of education that a child receives—even more than it has been over the last few years—is based on the wealth of the neighborhood in which he or she happens to live. (2006, p. 4)

Another type of school finance lawsuit that may arise will challenge funding inequities for the construction of new schools and the renovation of older school buildings (Scharrer, 2006). The recent Texas school finance reform plan, HB 3, did not address funding for new schools or the renovation of old ones.[32] Senator Leticia Van de Putte (D-San Antonio), a member of the Texas Senate Education Committee, commented that if the Legislature does not attend to the issue of funding inequities regarding school facilities, then a lawsuit is to be expected (Scharrer, 2006).

Attempts by state legislatures to deny birthright citizenship to children born in the United States to undocumented immigrants. As part of the anti-immigration sentiment raging across the country, at least twenty cities and towns in the nation have approved or discussed English-only laws (Moscoso, 2006a). Some communities have resorted to even more draconian measures by passing anti-immigration ordinances that are comprehensive in nature.[33] For example, in Farmers Branch, Texas (a suburb of Dallas), the City Council in a 6-0 vote passed ordinances on November 13, 2006, that, in addition to designating English as the official language, authorized fines of landlords who rent to "illegal aliens." Also, an ordinance authorized the city police to enter into an agreement with officials of the Immigration and Naturalization Service to single out criminal aliens. LULAC and MALDEF have vowed to file a lawsuit (Aynesworth, 2006).[34]

Anti-immigration forces have recently targeted another population —schoolchildren—by attempting to deny services (particularly access to public education) to children born in the United States to undocumented immigrants (Castillo, 2006). What is at stake here is of great importance in the area of civil rights and political justice. One of the pillars of U.S. democracy is birthright citizenship, or *jus soli* citizenship (a literal translation is "right of the soil"). *Jus soli* is defined as "A rule of law that a child's citizenship is determined by his or her place of birth."[35] The origins of the United States' conception of birthright citizenship lie deep in the foundations of English common law in the medieval past (Price, 1997).[36] One of the most important discussions of birthright citizenship in the United States occurred in *Dred Scott v. Sandford* (1857), in which the plaintiff, Dred Scott, a native-born slave, sought citizenship, but the U.S. Supreme Court denied it. In response to *Dred Scott*, Congress passed the Civil Rights Act of 1866, in which "citizens" under the U.S. Constitution and laws referred to free individuals that were born in the United States or naturalized. Soon after, on July 9, 1868, birthright citizenship became lawful with the ratification of the Fourteenth Amendment to the U.S. Constitution (Dellinger, 1995), whose Citizenship Clause provided that "All persons born or naturalized in the United States, and subject to its jurisdiction thereof, are citizens of the United States wherein they reside" (U.S. Constitution, Amendment XIV, §1).

The principle of birthright citizenship found its most comprehensive articulation in *U.S. v. Wong Kim Ark* (1898) (Meyler, 2001). Wong Kim

Ark was born in 1873 in San Francisco, California. In 1895 he left for a trip to China. Upon his return to the United States, customs officials denied him entry on the grounds that he was not a citizen. Thomas Riordan, an attorney for the Chinese Consulate in San Francisco and the Chinese Six Companies, filed a federal writ of habeas corpus on behalf of Wong Kim Ark, based on Ark having been born in the United States. Riordan also relied on the authority of *In re Look Tin Sing* (1884), a case very similar to *U.S. v. Wong Kim Ark*. The court ordered that Wong Kim Ark be released from custody. Immediately, the case was appealed to the U.S. Supreme Court, where Wong Kim Ark prevailed. In its decision, the U.S. Supreme Court relied on the Citizenship Clause of the Fourteenth Amendment.[37]

Although the principle of birthright citizenship has its roots in the United States about 140 years ago, it is of particular interest that contemporary attention to and awareness of birthright citizenship appeared recently, about a decade ago. Writing in 1997, law professor Christopher L. Eisgruber commented,

> Until recently it [birthright citizenship] has also been remarkably little known. Many lawyers (and some law professors) are surprised to learn that the Constitution confers citizenship upon the American-born children of illegal aliens. With few exceptions, the vast literature on constitutional theory has largely ignored the principle. Recently, however, politicians have discovered the Fourteenth Amendment's Citizenship Clause and have attacked it. (p. 55)

Not surprisingly, the practice of birthright citizenship is contentious, drawing both proponents and opponents. Peter H. Schuck and Rogers M. Smith (1985) have proffered one of the better-known positions against birthright citizenship (*Citizenship without Consent: Illegal Aliens in the American Polity*).[38] The authors challenge the practice of birthright citizenship at three levels (normative theory, law, and policy). In the same vein, Wood (1999) argues that birthright citizenship for "illegal aliens" is harmful for a number of reasons, including that it leads to an increased number of citizens without traditional American values, creates an incentive for illegal immigration, and leads to higher welfare costs. To be sure, some writers defend the practice of birthright citizenship (e.g., Dellinger, 1995; Drimmer, 1995; Eisgruber, 1997; *Harvard Law Review*, 1994; Houston, 2000) and maintain that any denial of birthright citizenship is a threat to equality and is unconstitutional.

The political realm is likely to see attempts to eliminate birthright citizenship. In 1995, the "Citizenship Reform Act of 1995" (H.R. 1363, 104th Congress), would have

limited the number of children who automatically become U.S. citizens simply because they are born on U.S. soil. It would have granted automatic birthright citizenship only to:

1. Children born in the United States to married parents either of whom was a U.S. citizen or legal permanent resident; or

2. Children born in the United States to an unmarried mother who was a U.S. citizen or legal permanent resident.[39]

Congress failed to pass the Citizenship Reform Act.

At the state level, on November 13, 2006, Texas Representative Leo Berman (R-Tyler) filed HB 28, which is a direct challenge to birthright citizenship. The bill would have excluded U.S.-born children of "illegal aliens" from receiving

- Public assistance benefits, including welfare payments, food stamps, or food assistance from this state or a political subdivision of this state.
- Health care or public assistance health benefits.
- Disability benefits or assistance.
- Public housing or public housing assistance.
- *Instruction in primary or secondary education* [italics added].
- *Instruction from a public institution of higher education* [italics added].
- An unemployment benefit.[40]

Subsequently, Representative Berman decided to remove the denial of health care benefits and education from HB 28, commenting that the U.S. Supreme Court affirmed them as constitutional rights. He also noted that these provisions could hurt his bill's chance of passing (Castillo, 2006). According to the Texas Legislature Online, HB 28 was read for the first (and only) time on the House floor on January 29, 2007, and was referred to the House State Affairs Committee, where it appears to have died in committee.[41]

Given the escalating anti-immigration sentiment in the United States, it is likely that these forces will make more attempts to eliminate *jus soli* citizenship. As scholar Michael R.W. Houston puts it, "These [federal] bills are essentially constitutional amendments under the guise of legislation"

(Houston, 2000, p. 727). He further notes that if such a bill passed (requiring a simple majority of both houses of Congress coupled with the President's signature), this in effect would amount to an amendment of the Citizenship Clause via the legislative process, which is a violation of the separation of powers. At the state level, any successful attempts by legislatures to eliminate birthright citizenship will spark challenges on constitutional grounds. Organizations like MALDEF are sure to pounce on such laws, arguing that they contradict the Citizenship Clause of the Fourteenth Amendment of the U.S. Constitution and thus are unconstitutional (see, e.g., Dellinger, 1995; Eisgruber, 1997; Houston, 2000). If the Citizenship Clause were to be modified to do away with birthright citizenship, this could only come through a constitutional amendment. This route would be quite difficult, requiring a super majority vote (i.e., two-thirds) of both houses and ratification by the legislatures of three-quarters of the states.[42]

In any event, the Mexican-origin community and other affected groups must be vigilant and prepared to file lawsuits countering either federal or state legislative attempts to eliminate *jus soli* citizenship. As attorney James C. Ho has noted, "Stay tuned: *Dred Scott II* could be coming soon to a federal court near you" (2006, p. 378).

What We Have Learned from This Legal History

This book has demonstrated that the Mexican American people have been tenacious in their struggle for educational equality. Despite the odds against prevailing in a judicial system filled with legal indeterminacy, the Mexican American community has accomplished much. We have learned, for example, the following:

• *School financing litigation*: *Serrano* and *Rodriguez* (and the numerous variants of *Edgewood*) led to the reallocation of billions of dollars to property-poor school districts throughout the nation, benefiting students of all racial backgrounds.

• *Special education litigation*: The trinity of cases—*Diana*, *Covarrubias*, and *Guadalupe*—initiated a sea change in special education in shaping nondiscriminatory assessment practices via federal legislation and professional standards. These practices and standards have benefited not only Mexican American children but other groups of color—other Latinos,

African Americans, American Indians, and Asian Americans have also seen assessment improvements.

- *Bilingual education litigation*: The *Castaneda* standard, emanating from *Castaneda v. Pickard*, has become the most prominent legal articulation for the language rights of Mexican American English learners and other language-minority children.

- *Undocumented students litigation*: *Plyler v. Doe* is the capstone of constitutionally guaranteed rights for one of the nation's most vulnerable populations, undocumented school-age students.

- *High-stakes testing litigation*: Although plaintiffs did not prevail in *GI Forum v. Texas Education Agency*, the case helped indirectly to generate, at least in Texas, a political agenda to replace state-mandated testing with end-of-course examinations.[43]

Notwithstanding the educational gains that the Mexican American community has made by means of litigation, the struggle for educational equality continues. Numerous inequalities characterize the current schooling experience of many Mexican American school-age students: increasing segregation, low academic achievement, loss of bilingual education (e.g., in California and Arizona), disproportionately high rates of grade retention, soaring dropout rates, inequities in school financing, unfavorable teacher-student interactions, disproportionately high rates of being taught by noncertified teachers, unfavorable curriculum differentiation, underrepresentation in gifted/talented education, adverse impact of high-stakes testing, and disproportionately low rates of college matriculation (Valencia, 2002b). Many of these inequalities also apply to other Latino groups (e.g., Puerto Ricans), as well as to other students of color, particularly African Americans.

In light of the educational plight faced by Mexican American students, as well as by other students of color, an important question is, What is needed to improve Mexican American education? To address this, I draw on several recommendations from my 2002 edited volume, *Chicano School Failure and Success: Past, Present, and Future* (Valencia, 2002c). One of the major problems experienced by numerous Mexican American secondary students is their very high dropout rate—one of the highest in the nation. If one views the dropout issue as an entrenched social problem affecting most urban, low-SES, high-enrollment Mexican American schools, then the solution needs to be based on systemic and policy approaches. Such strategies would have schools work "in concert with other social service agencies, to support the students, their families, and community members who together forge a vision for community success" (Rumberger & Rodríguez, 2002, p. 137; also see Secada et al., 1998; Verstegen, 1994).

Another salient issue has to do with Mexican American parental participation in the education of their children.[44] Numerous empirical research studies have demonstrated that parental involvement (e.g., supervising of, and assisting with, their children's homework) can improve the educational achievement of both White students and students of color, particularly at the elementary school level (see Moreno & Valencia, 2002; Valencia & Black, 2002). Notwithstanding the importance of Mexican American parental participation in their children's education, we need to be aware of the personal/psychological, contextual, and sociocultural variables related to parental involvement (Moreno & Valencia, 2002). Especially important in discussions of promoting Mexican American school success is the contextual level. As the literature informs us, some Mexican American parents view schools as being cold and indifferent toward them. Such feelings of Mexican American parents underscore the reality that parental participation is a two-way process. Schools and teachers need to be encouraging, hospitable, and respectful toward Mexican American parents, especially non-English-speaking parents who may be unfamiliar with the policies and procedures of schools.

A third and final example as to how to improve education for Mexican American students deals with the notion of "democratic education." Since the beginning of public education in the United States, there has never been agreement that schools promote school success for *all* students. Hence, there has been an ongoing debate about what constitutes workable school reform. Art Pearl's (2002) analysis points rather clearly to those strategies that have *not* shown to be successful (e.g., compensatory education). On the other hand, his ideas about democratic education offer us a promising vision of what it will take, in part, to achieve Mexican American school success. I believe that his notions of students' rights, equal encouragement, useful knowledge, and so forth can serve as beacons for structuring and implementing school success for Mexican Americans. As Pearl notes, the bottom line of workable school reform is to connect education with political action. In the years ahead, failure to pay attention to the linkages of schooling with a number of social issues, macrolevel policies, and the features of democratic education will very likely result in the continuation of Mexican American schooling problems.

As I discussed in the book's preface (note 7), the Mexican American community's historical and contemporary struggle for educational equality has taken five forms: advocacy organizations, individual activists, political demonstrations, legislation, and the subject of this book—litigation. In order for the Mexican American people to optimize their campaign for equality in education, they must draw from all five forms of struggle. Each one in itself is important, but all five streams flowing simultaneously and eventually becoming one fast-moving river have the potential to create a powerful confluence for systemic change in education.

We have learned that the lens of CRT can serve as a valuable source of navigation in this collective struggle. First, CRT informs us that race and racism are entrenched in U.S. society. Thus, we need to proceed with awareness of their centrality in the educational system. In each chapter of this book, insights from CRT and postcolonial theory help us understand the course of Mexican American school litigation, particularly how each case shows the link between race and education. We have learned that racialized opportunity structures lead to racialized academic performance patterns.

Second, CRT calls for heterodoxy. Challenges to the dominant ideology (e.g., the prevailing view of meritocracy) are necessary. We have learned from this legal history that in many instances (e.g., school segregation lawsuits) that the protection of White privilege abounded. The earlier cases (e.g., *Salvatierra, Mendez*) demonstrated that school boards' educational justification for segregation (language grounds) was merely a smokescreen for school officials' race-based opposition to mixing young Mexican American and White students in the same classrooms.

Third, CRT includes, as a major pillar, a firm duty to social justice. Schools are seen as political institutions. Therefore, the elimination of subordination and oppression in the educational system requires political responses. Public education is the repository and transmitter of cultural knowledge and, for that reason, is the site of contestation over divergent or minority views and hopes (Bowles & Gintis, 1976). With this in mind, change is very slow in coming, but it is worth the effort nonetheless. As the United States moves toward an increasingly multiracial future, the contestation over diverse perspectives of public education will concomitantly increase. Furthermore, we have learned from this legal history that the judicial system has thrown up obstacles for Mexican American children and youths because it still has not figured out how to surmount the Black/White binary paradigm of race in order to cope with this country's increasingly multiracial society.

Fourth, CRT recognizes the importance of experiential knowledge of people of color. The voices of parents and their children are seen as valuable strengths that need to be incorporated in the ongoing discourse regarding social change. This is especially important in the area of the right to have bilingual education, which is currently under siege. Our discussion of language rights (stemming from the Treaty of Guadalupe Hidalgo) and bilingual education has shown how a colonized people must constantly struggle to maintain a thread of cultural memory.

Fifth, CRT asserts that the struggle to eliminate race and racism in education must incorporate interdisciplinary perspectives and multiracial categories. Many of the legal issues discussed in this book have implications for other groups of color, as well as for poor Whites. Asian Americans, for example, have many of the same language issues as Mexican Americans do. Many Asian-origin people are immigrants too. African Americans have many of the same problems as Mexican American students (e.g., school segregation; underfunded schools; adverse impact via high-stakes testing; special education concerns). Latino-African coalitions, like the ones developed around *Mendez v. Westminster* (Valencia, 2005), seem distinctly possible. The litigation discussed in this book cuts quite broadly into the "big picture"—issues that affect a number of groups who experience inferior education. In sum, much work lies ahead if Mexican Americans, Puerto Ricans, other Latinos, African Americans, Asian Americans, American Indians, and poor Whites are to win recognition as groups who require attention to their schooling. Renewed litigation on behalf of these groups can reinforce the call for systemic reform so all groups who receive substandard education may benefit.

Notes

1. Portions of this preface build on Valencia & Black (2002, pp. 82, 90–94). For a critique of Sowell's reasoning, see *Id.* (p. 88).

2. See, for example, Booth & Dunn (1996); Chavkin (1993); Chavkin & Williams (1989); Comer (1986); Dornbusch & Ritter (1988); Englund, Luckner, Whaley, & Egeland (2004); Marburger (1990); Sheldon & Epstein (2005). Also, see Cotton & Wikelund (1989) for a synthesis of forty-one documents covering the positive effects of parental involvement on children's academic achievement and affective development.

3. For research on Latino parental participation, see, for example, Achor & Morales (1990); Anguiano (2004); Delgado-Gaitán (1992); Eamon (2005); Gándara (1982); Immerwahr & Foleno (2000); Keith & Lichtman (1994); Martínez, DeGarmo, & Eddy (2004); Moll, Amanti, Neff, & González (1992); Moreno & López (1999); Okagaki & Frensch (1998); Treviño (2004).

4. This quote by Graglia is from a newsclip (September 10, 1997, news conference at UT) shown on NBC's *Today*, September 12, 1997.

5. It appears that Graglia's views on affirmative action have hurt him. According to D.H. Martin, reporter for the UT *Daily Texan*, "Former President Ronald Reagan [in 1986] pulled away from appointing Graglia to the 5th U.S. Circuit Court of Appeals after complaints about his remarks regarding affirmative action" (1997, p. 2).

6. The phrase "Mexican American community," which I frequently use in this book, is extensively seen in the extant literature. On November 27, 2006, I conducted a Google search using "Mexican American community" as a descriptor, and I retrieved 304,000 hits. Conceptualizing the notion of Mexican American community is no easy task. This fast-growing group of people, who have roots in Mexico, numbered 20.6 million based on the 2000 Census and constitute approximately 59% of the total 35.3 million Latinos residing in the United States (Valencia, 2002a, p. 55, Table 2.2). Mexican Americans reside in every state in the United States but are largely concentrated in the Southwest region (Arizona, California, Colorado, New Mexico, and Texas), where 75% of the total are located (Valencia, 2002a, p. 55, Table 2.3).

The Mexican American community is not a monolithic social group. Considerable variability exists along lines of language status, acculturation, immigrant status, schooling attainment, socioeconomic status, religion, political party affiliation, and much more. In this book, I use "Mexican American community" in a collective sense in which there is a sense of peoplehood, of shared elements of culture, and of being victims of oppression, largely racial in nature. In the context of Mexican American–initiated school litigation, the "community" can range from thousands and thousands of parent and child plaintiffs in a class action lawsuit in a particular state (e.g., *Diana v. State Board of Education*, 1970; see chapter 3) to a handful of parent and child plaintiffs in a particular school (e.g., *Santamaria v. Dallas Independent School District*, 2006; see conclusion).

7. The course is an analysis of how Mexican Americans have struggled for better education via five historical and contemporary processes. In brief, they are the following:

a. *Advocacy organizations.* In their pursuit of improved education for their community, Mexican American parents, scholars, lawyers, and youths have founded a number of advocacy organizations. Beginning with the establishment of the League of United Latin American Citizens (LULAC) in 1929 (Márquez, 1993), many advocacy groups—in which better education is a rallying point for action—have been founded over the years. Examples of these highly visible organizations are American GI Forum (Ramos, 1998), Mexican American Legal Defense and Educational Fund (MALDEF; O'Connor & Epstein, 1984), and Movimiento Estudiantil Chicano de Aztlán (MEChA; Muñoz, 1989). These advocacy organizations, and many others, have played critical roles in the identification of schooling issues and in the advancement of improved educational conditions and outcomes for Mexican American students. For example, San Miguel and Valencia (1998) note, "Over the last three decades, MALDEF has evolved into a chief source of successful education litigation for the Mexican American community, winning many lawsuits and setting highly influential case law" (p. 388).

b. *Individual activists.* Another indication that Mexican Americans value education stems from the work of scores of individuals who have championed the cause—that is, the Mexican American community's historical and contemporary resolve for the pursuit and attainment of educational equality. Historically, there have been, for example, the likes of grassroots organizer Eleuterio Escobar in San Antonio, Texas, in the 1930s through the 1950s (García, 1979); Dr. Héctor García, founder of the American GI Forum in Texas in 1948 (Ramos, 1998); Professor George I. Sánchez, scholar/civil rights activist from the 1930s to 1970s (Romo, 1986); attorney Pete Tijerina, founder of MALDEF in San Antonio, Texas, in 1968 (O'Connor & Epstein, 1984); and Professor Mari-Luci Jaramillo, pioneer of bilingual/bicultural education in New Mexico (Vásquez, 1994). To this illustrious list, we can add numerous other individual activists: university professors, lawyers, students, parents, community organizers, schoolteachers, politicians, and so forth.

c. *Political demonstrations.* For decades, Mexican Americans have expressed their collective interest and action in promoting better education for children and youths by engaging in public confrontations in a display of dissatisfaction with oppression, with the goal of gaining resources. One of the more common forms of political demonstrations has been the strategy of a "blowout" (school walkout). It appears that the first such blowout occurred in 1910 in San Angelo, Texas—lasting through 1915 (De León, 1974). At the heart of the blowout was the Tejano community's demand that its children be allowed to attend the superior White schools. Other well-known blowouts transpired in East Los Angeles in 1968 (Rosen, 1974) and in Crystal City, Texas, in 1969 (Navarro, 1995).

d. *Legislation.* Another form of struggle in which Mexican Americans have expressed their resolve in improving the educational lot for their children and youths is seen in legislative efforts. One example is the long struggle for bilingual education in Texas in which state senator Joe Bernal and state representative Carlos Truan persevered from 1969 to 1981 to institutionalize bilingual education (San Miguel, 1987; Vega, 1983). Another example is the "Top Ten Percent Plan," a law that went into effect in Texas in fall 1998. The bill, written by the late state representative Irma Rangel and now retired state senator Gonzalo Barrientos, allows high school students who graduate in the top 10% of their graduating classes to be automatically admitted to any public four-year institution of higher education in Texas, including its premier institutions (see Chapa, 1997, 2005; Dickson, 2006; Horn & Flores, 2003).

e. *Litigation.* From 1925 to the present, Mexican Americans have brought forth scores of lawsuits of various types in efforts to improve the education of their children and youths. This legal struggle is the subject of the present book. Notwithstanding the range of outcomes of this litigation as a whole (bittersweet ones, some losses, and some victories), taking their cases to court for over the past eight-plus decades speaks to the reality that Mexican Americans highly value education.

NOTES TO THE INTRODUCTION

1. A portion of this first paragraph draws from, with minor revisions, Valencia (2005, p. 390).

2. Also, see Ruiz Cameron (1998) for a discussion of the Black/White binary paradigm of race as it relates to Latinos.

3. Portions of this discussion of CRT build on, with minor revisions, Valencia (2005, pp. 392–393).

4. For overviews of CRT, see Araujo (1997); Crenshaw, Gotanda, Peller, &

Thomas (1995); Delgado (1995); Delgado & Stefancic (1993, 2001); Litowitz (1997); Taylor (1998); Valdés, Culp, & Harris (2002).

5. The following are examples of publications exploring educational issues in the context of CRT: Ladson-Billings & Tate (1995); López (2003); López & Parker (2003); Parker, Deyhle, & Villenas (1999); Solórzano (1998); Solórzano & Yosso (2000, 2002); Villenas & Deyhle (1999).

6. For examples of LatCrit publications, see García (1995); Martínez (1994); Revilla (2001); Solórzano & Delgado Bernal (2001); Solórzano & Yosso (2001); Stefancic (1998); Valdés (1996).

7. For examples of writings on the idea of legal indeterminacy, see Coleman & Leiter (1993); Dorf (2003); Herget (1995); Kress (1989); Lawson (1996); Madry (1999); Martínez (1994); Meyer (1996); Ruiz Cameron (1998); Yablon (1992).

8. For an essay on the origins and evolution of legal indeterminacy, see Herget (1995), who introduces his treatise this way:

There is a puzzle here for intellectual history. Legal Indeterminacy, so widely (but certainly not universally) accepted in one form or another today, itself now competes to become part of the accepted wisdom. Yet, strangely, it was grasped only a little over a century ago after some two millennia of specu-lation about law in the western tradition. (p. 59)

9. Lawson (1996) pointed out that an economist might write the formula as $I = f (U, S)$, where I is indeterminacy, and U and S are uncertainty and standard of proof, respectively. That is, "The *cause* of indeterminacy is therefore always a combination of uncertainty and the standard of proof" (p. 421).

10. These three standards, in order from lowest to highest standard of proof are (a) the rational basis test, (b) the intermediate scrutiny standard, and (c) the strict scrutiny test or standard (see Wilcoxen, 1985; also, see chapter 2, this vol-ume, for a discussion of these standards).

11. In addition to educational litigation (i.e., school segregation and bilingual education), Martínez (1994) also discusses noneducational litigation (i.e., restric-tive covenants, public accommodations, land grants, and racial slurs).

12. Martínez (1994, p. 559) expands on this point:

Providing judges with counterstories or alternative perspectives on civil rights issues is one way to help them overcome the "unthinking conviction that [their] way of seeing the world is the only one—that the way things are is inevitable, natural, just, and best" [quoted from Delgado, 1989, p. 2439]. By acknowledging their limited perspective, judges can avoid serious moral error and promote justice in civil rights cases.

13. See, for example, Acuña (2007); Ashcroft, Griffiths, & Tiffin (2006); Fanon (1963); Memmi (1991); Said (1979); Thomas (2000).

NOTES TO CHAPTER 1

1. Portions of this introductory text ("Historical Prevalence of School Segregation" and "School Segregation: Inferior Schooling and Adverse Effects") build on Valencia, Menchaca, & Donato (2002, pp. 70–72, 75, 77–79, 81) and San Miguel & Valencia (1998, p. 366).

2. See, for example, Álvarez (1988), Donato (1997), González (1990), Menchaca & Valencia (1990), San Miguel (1987), San Miguel & Valencia (1998), Valencia (2005), and Valencia, Menchaca, & Donato (2002).

3. Cisneros v. Corpus Christi Independent School District, 324 F. Supp. at 613 (S.D. Tex. 1970).

4. Orfield (1988a) reported data for Latinos as a whole, not disaggregated by Latino subgroups (e.g., Mexican American, Puerto Rican). Given that Mexican American students constitute the strong majority of Latino students (see Valencia, 2002a), any findings about Latinos (as a whole) in this chapter can safely be generalized to Mexican Americans.

5. See Valencia, Menchaca, & Donato (2002, pp. 75–77) for a discussion of school segregation in AISD.

6. The TAKS tests were taken in Reading and Mathematics in grade 3; Reading, Mathematics, and Writing in grade 4; and Reading, Mathematics, and Science in grade 5. All tests were administered in English or Spanish.

7. The seventy-four elementary schools had a total enrollment (Early Childhood Education to grade 5) of 41,937 students. Racial/ethnic enrollments, in descending order, were the following: Mexican American and other Latino (55.8%); White (27.0%); African American (14.2%); Asian/Pacific Islander (2.8%); American Indian (0.3%).

8. Findings of Fact and Order, Romo v. Laird, Civil Action No. 21617 (Superior Court, Maricopa County, Arizona October 5, 1925). (Appended in Muñoz, 2001, pp. 31–32). Findings of Fact and Order, the court's Judgment, and minutes of the school district's Board of Trustees can also be obtained online; see *Romo v. Laird* reference, this volume.

9. *Id.*

10. *Id.*

11. *Id.*

12. Paragraph 2750, Revised Statute Arizona 1913 (Civil Code). See Findings of Fact and Order, Romo v. Laird, Civil Action No. 21617 (Superior Court, Maricopa County, Arizona October 5, 1925). Also see Segregation of School Children. Mexican Children Not Embraced in Segregation Law. Biennial Report of the Attorney General of Arizona, 1915–1916. (Appended in Muñoz, 2001, p. 34).

13. Dameron v. Bayless, 14 Ariz. at 182 (1912). For background on this case, see Luckingham (1994, pp. 136–137).

14. Judgment, Romo v. Laird, Civil Action No. 21617 (Superior Court, Maricopa County, Arizona October 5, 1925). (Appended in Muñoz, 2001, p. 32).

15. Meeting Minutes of the Board of Trustees, Tempe School District No. 3, October 9 and 21, 1925, Tempe, Arizona. (Appended in Muñoz, 2001, pp. 33–34).

16. A point of clarification is needed here. The first challenge to the segregation of Mexican American children in Texas preceded *Salvatierra* by two years in *Vela v. Board of Trustees of Charlotte Independent School District* (Charlotte, Texas, is located forty-three miles south of San Antonio). In 1928, Felipe Vela filed a complaint on behalf of his adopted daughter, Amada (unknown racial/ethnic background), who was forced to attend the segregated Mexican school. The young girl sought admission to the White school. It appears that the case did not enter litigation, as Mr. Vela appealed directly to the State Superintendent of Public Instruction, S.M.N. Marrs—who ruled in favor of the Vela child. For further discussion of the case, see San Miguel (1987, pp. 76–78). Also, see Manuel (1930, pp. 82–85), who provides a reprint of the facts of and decision in the case (written by Superintendent Marrs).

17. Independent School District v. Salvatierra, 33 S.W.2d at 791 (Tex. Civ. App., San Antonio 1930). It appears that the judge of the District Court of Val Verde County did not publish his opinion. Thus, for discussion of *Salvatierra*, I rely on the opinion rendered by the Court of Civil Appeals, San Antonio.

18. *Id.*

19. *Id.* at 793–794.

20. See Article VII, Section 7 of the Texas Constitution. The Texas Legislature reenacted codifications of the original statute several times from 1893 to 1925. See Gammel (1898, 1905); *Complete Texas Statutes* (1920); Jenkins (1925).

21. Rangel and Alcala (1972) have commented that the "other White" strategy argued in *Salvatierra* rested on the prevailing doctrine of the *Plessy v. Ferguson* (1896) case. Likewise, as Weinberg (1977) has noted, "In the absence of a state law requiring segregation of Mexican-Americans, they claimed equal treatment with all other 'whites.' The crucial point was to leave little leeway to be treated as blacks under both state law and U.S. Supreme Court ruling" (p. 166). The Mexican American community employed the other-White strategy in desegregation cases for four decades, but finally abandoned it in *Cisneros v. Corpus Christi Independent School District* (1970).

22. Independent School District v. Salvatierra, 33 S.W.2d at 792 (Tex. Civ. App., San Antonio 1930).

23. *Id.* The Superintendent did, however, state this: "Yes, it's true, generally the best way to learn a [second] language is to be associated with the people who speak the language" (*Id.* at 793). I will underscore later, in our discussion of the *Mendez v. Westminster* (1946) case, that the language-learning proposition loomed large.

24. *Id.* at 792.

25. *Id.* at 795.

26. *Id.* at 794.

27. Certiorari: "a writ (order) of a higher court to a lower court to send all the documents in a case to it so the higher court can review the lower court's decision" (Hill & Hill, 1995, s.v. "certiorari").

28. Independent School District v. Salvatierra, 33 S.W.2d at 793.

29. *Id.*

30. Balderrama (1982) notes that the overcrowding situation provided an opportunity for the local chamber of commerce and the Parent Teacher Association to pressure the school board into voting for the construction of a school exclusively for the Mexican American children.

31. Some scholars, for example, Bowman (2001) and Montoya (2001), have cited this case as *Alvarez v. Owen.* Technically, it should be *Alvarez v. Owen et al.* Defendants were E.L. Owen, Anna E. Wight, and Henry A. Anderson (school board members) and Jerome J. Green (principal). Yet most scholars—including the foremost expert on the case, Robert R. Álvarez, Jr.—cite this case as *Alvarez v. Lemon Grove School District.* Legal documents pertaining to *Alvarez* are difficult to obtain. Robert R. Álvarez, Jr., related that he discovered the case while undertaking field research on the migration and adaptation of Mexican families from Baja California to the United States, including his own family. His father (Roberto Álvarez) was lead plaintiff in *Alvarez,* and this appears to have motivated him to learn more about the lawsuit (see Álvarez, 1988, p. 48, n. 3). In constructing what is known about the case, Alvarez studied the aging, but still readable, microfilm that contains the court records. He also undertook extensive interviews. For the most detailed accounts of *Alvarez,* see Álvarez (1986, 1988); Balderrama (1982). Also, see the award-winning docudrama "The Lemon Grove Incident," produced by KPBS (San Diego) in 1985.

32. See Petition for Writ of Mandate, Alvarez v. Lemon Grove School District (Superior Court, San Diego County, California *filed,* February 13, 1931) (No. 66625). See Álvarez (1988) for other citations germane to the case (i.e., Order for Alternate Writ of Mandate, Alternative Writ of Mandate, Findings of Fact and Conclusions of Law). A writ of mandate (a more modern term for "writ of mandamus") is "a court order to a government agency, including another court, to follow the law by correcting prior actions or ceasing illegal acts" (Hill & Hill, 1995, s.v. "writ of mandate").

33. This section on the *Mendez v. Westminster* (1946) case, which follows, is drawn, with minor revisions, from the *Mendez* discussion in Valencia (2005, pp. 399–401, 403–411, and 413–418).

34. A number of scholars have mentioned or briefly discussed the *Mendez* case. Several publications, however, stand out as the most detailed and informative: Arriola (1995); González (1990, pp. 147–156); Valencia (2005); Wollenberg (1974).

35. The four districts are described this way in Phillips (1949).

36. Mendez v. Westminster, 64 F. Supp. at 545 (S.D. Cal. 1946).

37. Section 8003 reads,

The governing board of any school district may establish separate schools for Indian children, excepting children of Indians who are the wards of the United States Government and children of all other Indians who are descendants of the original American Indians of the United States, and for children of Chinese, Japanese, or Mongolian parentage. (Mendez v. Westminster, 64 F. Supp. at 548 [S.D. Cal. 1946])

Also pertinent is Section 8004, which reads, "When separate schools are established for Indian children or children of Chinese, Japanese or Mongolian parentage, the Indian children or children of Chinese, Japanese or Mongolian parentage shall not be admitted to any other school" (quoted in Peters, 1948, p. 78).

38. Mendez v. Westminster, 64 F. Supp. at 546 (S.D. Cal. 1946).

39. *Id.* at 545. Congress passed Amendment XIV to the U.S. Constitution on June 13, 1866, and ratified it on July 9, 1868. The Equal Protection Clause is mentioned in Section 1 of the Fourteenth Amendment:

All persons born or naturalized in the United States, and subject to the jurisdiction thereof, are citizens of the United States and of the State wherein they reside. No State shall make or enforce any law which shall abridge the privileges or immunities of citizens of the United States; nor shall any State deprive any person of life, liberty, or property, without due process of law; nor deny to any person within its jurisdiction the equal protection of the laws.

40. Reporter's Transcript Proceeding, Mendez v. Westminster, 64 F. Supp. 544 (S.D. Cal. 1946). Available at Mendez v. Westminster: Research Materials, 1879–1955 (Collection number: M0938), Department of Special Collections and University Archives, Stanford University Libraries, Stanford, California. I wish to thank Christopher Arriola (who donated these *Mendez* papers to Stanford) for informing me about the collection. I also wish to thank Polly Armstrong, Public Service Specialist, Department of Special Collections, who provided me with the *Mendez* trial transcripts, amicus briefs filed at the Ninth Circuit Court of Appeals, and other germane materials. Guide to the *Mendez* papers can be viewed at: *http://www-sul.stanford.edu/depts/spc.*

41. Reporter's Transcript Proceeding (p. 670), Mendez v. Westminster, 64 F. Supp. 544 (S.D. Cal. 1946).

42. *Id.* at 676.

43. *Id.*

44. *Id.* at 668.

45. *Id.* at 675.

46. *Id.* at 676–677.

47. *Id.* at 691.

48. *Id.* at 695–696.

49. Mendez v. Westminster, 64 F. Supp. at 546 (S.D. Cal. 1946).

50. *Id.* at 547–548.

51. The late Judge Motley was Senior District Judge, U.S. District Court for the Southern District of New York. She joined the legal staff of the NAACP in October 1945.

52. Motley (1991, note no. 10, p. 26).

53. Mendez v. Westminster, 64 F. Supp. at 549 (S.D. Cal. 1946).

54. *Id.*

55. *Id.* at 546.

56. *Id.*

57. *Id.* at 550.

58. *Id.* at 549–550.

59. *Id.* at 549.

60. *Id.* at 551.

61. *La Opinión* (March 22, 1946). The English translation of Marcus's statement was first cited in Wollenberg (1974). The accuracy of the translation was confirmed, by Dr. Bruno J. Villarreal, for this book.

62. No authors are listed for the reviews published in these law journals. Thus, I have cited these in the References this way: *Columbia Law Review* (1947); *Harvard Law Review* (1946–1947); *Illinois Law Review* (1947); *Minnesota Law Review* (1946); *Yale Law Journal* (1947).

63. Also, see coverage by Davies (1946b).

64. Appellant's Opening Brief, p. 7, Westminster v. Mendez, 161 F.2d 774 (9th Cir. 1947).

65. Westminster v. Mendez, 161 F.2d at 775 (9th Cir. 1947). Amicus curiae, in Latin, literally means "friend of the court." In legal terms, an amicus curiae is "a party or an organization interested in an issue which files a brief or participates in the argument in a case in which that party or organization is not one of the litigants" (Hill & Hill, 1995, s.v. "amicus curiae"). In the *Mendez* case, the Ninth Circuit granted permission each to the NAACP, the American Jewish Congress, the Attorney General of the State of California, and the American Civil Liberties Union (together with the National Lawyers Guild) to file an amicus curiae brief (or amicus brief, for short), the legal document that an amicus curiae writes for the court to consider.

66. Motion and Brief for the National Association for the Advancement of Colored People as *Amicus Curiae*, Westminster v. Mendez, 161 F.2d 774 (9th Cir. 1947) (No. 11310).

67. *Id.* at 30.

68. *Id.*

69. *Id.* at 13.

70. Brief for the American Jewish Congress as *Amicus Curiae*, Westminster v. Mendez, 161 F.2d 774 (9th Cir. 1947) (No. 11310).

71. *Id.* at 3–4.

72. *Id.* at 4.

73. *Id.*

74. *Id.* at 35.

75. Brief for the American Civil Liberties Union, and the National Lawyers Guild, Los Angeles chapter, as *Amici Curiae*, Westminster v. Mendez, 161 F.2d 774 (9th Cir. 1947) (No. 11310).

76. Appellants' Reply Brief to American Civil Liberties Union, and the National Lawyers Guild, Los Angeles chapter, and The Attorney General of the State of California, as *Amici Curiae*, Westminster v. Mendez, 161 F.2d 774 (9th Cir. 1947) (No. 11310).

77. Motion and Brief for The Attorney General of the State of California as *Amicus Curiae*, Westminster v. Mendez, 161 F.2d 774 (9th Cir. 1947) (No. 11310).

78. Westminster v. Mendez, 161 F.2d at 778 (9th Cir. 1947).

79. *Id.* at 779.

80. *Id.*

81. *Id.* at 781.

82. This aspect of the Ninth Circuit's ruling has captured considerable attention in scholarly writings on the *Mendez* case (see, e.g., Arriola, 1995; González, 1990; Perea, 1997; Wollenberg, 1974).

83. Westminster v. Mendez, 161 F.2d at 779 (9th Cir. 1947).

84. *Id.* at 780. Also, see concurring opinion of Judge William Denman (*Id.* at 781–785), in which he uses strong language in denouncing the defendant districts' segregative policy. His key points are that (a) the Ninth Circuit should have considered in its opinion the importance of *Lopez v. Seccombe* (see earlier discussion of *Lopez* in this chapter); (b) had the segregative actions of Orange County officials been allowed to continue, perhaps other national-origin groups in California would have been segregated; (c) the actions of defendant districts were so discriminatory that they should be criminally liable.

85. The *Yale Law Journal* noted, "There is little doubt that the Supreme Court will be presented with a case involving segregation in schools within the next year or two" (1947, p. 1067). This was communicated to the journal by Robert L. Carter, Assistant Special Counsel, NAACP.

86. Mendez v. Westminster, 64 F. Supp. at 549 (S.D. Cal. 1946).

87. *Id.*

88. *Id.*

89. The research works referred to by the journal are cited in notes 16 to 26 (pp. 1060–1062).

90. Brown v. Board of Education of Topeka, 347 U.S. at 495 (1954).

91. *Id.*

92. Calderón refers to the Mexican American children as "Spanish-speaking" and the White children as "Anglo-American," fairly typical nomenclature for the time.

93. Based on the raw data presented in Calderón's master's thesis, there appears to be some slight errors in his analysis of ranges and means. As such, I have recalculated the analyses.

94. Analyses were not reported for Elsa Elementary School due to incomplete raw data.

95. During this period, the term "retardation" was used in several different ways (see Taylor, 1927). *Psychological* retardation conveyed mental retardation; *physiological* retardation had to do with physical growth of children; and *pedagogical* retardation referred to students who were overage for their grade level. It was this latter type of retardation to which Calderón was most likely referring.

96. Complaint to Enjoin Violation of Federal Civil Rights and for Damages (November 17, 1947; pp. 2–5), Delgado v. Bastrop Independent School District of Bastrop County et al., Civil Action No. 388 (W.D. Tex. June 15, 1948).

97. *Id.* at 6–9.

98. Deposition of P.J. Dodson (April 30, 1948, p. 49), Delgado v. Bastrop Independent School District of Bastrop County et al., Civil Action No. 388 (W.D. Tex. June 15, 1948).

Attorney General Price Daniel's opinion, dated April 8, 1947 (less than a week before Judge McCormick handed down his decision in *Mendez*) was another development that appeared to prompt *Delgado*'s filing. The Attorney General, drawing from the authority of *Salvatierra* (1930), stated that based only on deficiencies in language or other individual aptitudes or needs, "separate classes or schools may be maintained for pupils who, after examinations equally applied, come within such classifications. No part of such classification or segregation may be based solely upon Latin-American or Mexican descent" (*Digest of Opinions of the Attorney General of Texas*, V-128, at 39 [1947]). In turn, on August 18, 1947 (three months before filing the complaint in *Delgado*), Gus García sent Attorney General Daniel a letter requesting clarity in the opinion. García inquired whether the opinion disallowed segregation except that which was based on scientific tests applied "equally to all students regardless of racial ancestry," and whether inferior facilities were forbidden (letter from García to Daniel; see Sánchez & Strickland [1948] for full text of letter). In unambiguous terms, Attorney General Daniel responded,

> I am certainly pleased to know that your interpretation of this opinion certainly agrees with ours. We meant that the law prohibits discrimination against or segregation of Latin-Americans on account of race or descent, and that *the law permits no subterfuge to accomplish such discrimination* [italics added]. (letter from Daniel to García, August 21, 1947; see Sánchez & Strickland [1948] for full text of letter)

99. García passed the bar exams in 1938. After serving in World War II, he joined LULAC and became quite active in educational problems faced by Mexican American students. García is also well known for successfully arguing (with co-counsel Carlos Cadena) the landmark jury exclusion case, *Hernandez v. State of Texas* (1954), in front of the U.S. Supreme Court (see Allsup, 1982, for more on García).

100. One can surmise that Wirin (of the Los Angeles Civil Rights Union) brought to *Delgado* a wealth of experience and knowledge based on his work as an attorney for plaintiffs in *Mendez*.

101. For discussion of Dr. García's endeavors on the part of Mexican American students, see Allsup (1982).

102. According to Romo (1986), Sánchez obtained a copy of the *Mendez* decision and assisted Gus García in preparing the factual part of the brief for *Delgado*. See Romo for discussion of Sánchez's work in the legal and civil rights realm.

103. Complaint to Enjoin Violation of Federal Civil Rights and for Damages (November 17, 1947), Delgado v. Bastrop Independent School District of Bastrop County et al., Civil Action No. 388 (W.D. Tex. June 15, 1948).

104. Memorandum of Points and Authorities in Support of Plaintiffs Application for Injunction Pendente Lite (November 17, 1947), Delgado v. Bastrop Independent School District of Bastrop County et al., Civil Action No. 388 (W.D. Tex. June 15, 1948).

105. *Id.* at 1. The complaint argued that defendant districts segregated the Mexican American children pursuant to "custom, usage, and/or common plan" (p. 9).

106. Memorandum of Points and Authorities in Support of Plaintiffs Application for Injunction Pendente Lite (November 17, 1947; p. 2), Delgado v. Bastrop Independent School District of Bastrop County et al., Civil Action No. 388 (W.D. Tex. June 15, 1948).

107. Complaint to Enjoin Violation of Federal Civil Rights and for Damages (November 17, 1947; pp. 14–15), Delgado v. Bastrop Independent School District of Bastrop County et al., Civil Action No. 388 (W.D. Tex. June 15, 1948). Subsequently, the plaintiffs dismissed the monetary cause of action. Final Judgment (p. 2), Delgado v. Bastrop Independent School District of Bastrop County et al., Civil Action No. 388 (W.D. Tex. June 15, 1948).

108. Final Judgment, Delgado v. Bastrop Independent School District of Bastrop County et al., Civil Action No. 388 (W.D. Tex. June 15, 1948).

109. *Id.* at 2.

110. *Id.* at 3. In light of the class action nature of *Delgado*, Judge Rice also permanently restrained and enjoined State Superintendent L.A. Woods from allowing the segregation of Mexican American children (*Id.* at 4).

111. *Id.* at 3.

112. *Id.*

113. Texas State Department of Education (1948–1949), *Standards and Activities of the Division and Accreditation of School Systems*, Bulletin No. 507, pp. 45–46 (Austin: Author). For full text of Superintendent Woods's order, see Sánchez (1951, pp. 74–75).

114. Sánchez (1951, p. 75).

115. See, for example, Allsup (1982, pp. 85–90); Rangel & Alcala (1972, pp. 338–342); San Miguel (1987, pp. 125–134).

116. *Id.*

117. *Id.*

118. Gonzales v. Sheely, 96 F. Supp. 1004 (D. Ariz. 1951).

119. *Id.* at 1006–1007.

120. *Id.* at 1005.

121. As discussed by Greenfield and Kates (1975, pp. 681–682, n. 92), Arizona initially required segregation of "pupils of the African race from pupils of the White races" (Act of May 20, 1912, ch. 77, §41 [1912] Laws of Ariz. 364, 382), and then made segregation of "pupils of the African race from pupils of the Caucasian race" mandatory in the lower grades of public schools, but dependent in the high schools on a majority vote of the electorate.

122. Gonzales v. Sheely, 96 F. Supp. at 1008 (D. Ariz. 1951).

123. *Id.* at 1007.

124. *Id.*

125. *Id.*

126. *Id.* at 1008.

127. *Id.*

128. See San Miguel (1987, p. 132). Also, for citations for these cases, see References, this volume.

129. See Allsup (1982, p. 92).

130. Rangel & Alcala (1972, p. 341).

131. *Id.*

132. *Id.* at 340.

133. *Id.*

134. *Id.* As noted by San Miguel (1983, p. 358, n. 59), nine local districts were brought to the Commissioner of Education for special hearings. The districts were as follows: Carrizo Springs, Driscoll, Hondo, Kingsville, Kyle, Mathis, Nixon, Pecos, and Sanderson.

135. Romero v. Weakley, 131 F. Supp. 818 (S.D. Cal. 1955). Initially, *Romero* consisted of two separate complaints, one brought forth on behalf of Mexican American minors (No. 1712-SD) and one brought forth by African American minors (No. 1713-SD). By stipulation of the parties, the two cases were consolidated.

136. *Id.*

137. Recall our earlier discussion regarding the 1947 repeal of sections of the Education Code that allowed separate schools for certain ethnic minority groups.

138. Romero v. Weakley, 131 F. Supp. at 837 (S.D. Cal. 1955).

139. Romero v. Weakley, 226 F.2d 399 (9th Cir. 1955).

140. *Id.* at 401.

141. Hernandez v. Driscoll, 2 Race Rel. L. Rep. 329 (1957).

142. *Id.* at 330.

143. See notes 113 and 114, this chapter.

144. Hernandez v. Driscoll, 2 Race Rel. L. Rep. at 329 (1957).

145. Hernandez v. Driscoll, 2 Race Rel. L. Rep. at 40 (1956).

146. Hernandez v. Driscoll, 2 Race Rel. L. Rep. at 330 (1957).

147. *Id.* Under this policy, the first grade typically required three years to complete, divided into classes as follows: (a) beginners, (b) low first, and (c) high first, each taking one year for completion. After one year in a segregated class in the second grade, the Mexican American pupil was then allowed to enroll into the mixed third grade.

148. Hernandez v. Driscoll, 2 Race Rel. L. Rep. at 42 (1956).

149. Hernandez v. Driscoll, 2 Race Rel. L. Rep. at 333 (1957).

150. *Id.* at 331. The identification of existing individual differences in English proficiency, as well as in academic achievement, within and between groups is a powerful legal strategy. By not looking at individual differences, blanket classifications are frequently made, and underinclusiveness and overinclusiveness can result. As noted by Rangel and Alcala (1972), if the goal of educational separation is to disallow Mexican American students from retarding the progress of their Anglo peers, which may be deemed legitimate, the classification is similarly arbitrary, because of underinclusiveness and overinclusiveness. Rangel and Alcala note, "The classification is underinclusive because some Anglo underachievers also hold back a class's progress. It is overinclusive because it includes Chicano high achievers who do not retard class progress" (p. 364). Legally, underinclusiveness and overinclusiveness do not meet permissive standards and thus result in classifications that are unconstitutionally discriminatory.

151. Hernandez v. Driscoll, 2 Race Rel. L. Rep. at 331 (1957).

152. *Id.*

153. See the earlier discussion of noncompliance and subterfuges following the *Delgado* decree.

154. Chapa v. Odem Independent School District, Civil Action No. 66-C-72 (S.D. Tex. July 28, 1967). The legal record on *Chapa* was unpublished. Due to time constraints, I was unable to request the record from the National Archives and Records Administration, Southwest Region. As such, I have relied on secondary sources (Rangel & Alcala, 1972, pp. 347–348; Salinas, 1971, p. 941).

155. José Cisneros, interview by *Weekly Current Magazine*, September 16, 1970, p. 9 (cited in U.S. Commission on Civil Rights [1977], p. 8).

156. *Id.*

157. *Cisneros* is extraordinary as it is the first education lawsuit wholly funded by a labor union.

158. Cisneros v. Corpus Christi Independent School District, 324 F. Supp. 599 (S.D. Tex. 1970).

159. *Id.* at 611.

160. *Id.* at 609.

161. *Id.* at 609–610.

162. The concept of ethnic imbalance/balance stems from the 1960s, when state education agencies (see, e.g., Cal. Admin. Code, Title V, §10421) and other governmental entities (e.g., U.S. Commission on Civil Rights, 1971a) sought to ascertain the degree of segregation of Whites and students of color within the schools of a district. The arithmetical formula commonly used to calculate the ethnic imbalance/balance in a district was the "±15%" rule of thumb. As I and my associates have noted elsewhere,

> One takes the percentage of the *combined* total enrollment of minority students in a school district, and then adds 15 percentage points to obtain the *upper limit* of the band and also subtracts 15 percentage points to obtain the *lower limit* of the band. Individual schools that fall *within* the band's upper and lower limits in combined minority percentage are deemed racially/ethnically "balanced." Schools that fall *outside* the lower or upper limits are considered "imbalanced." (Valencia, Menchaca, & Donato, 2002, p. 75)

163. For more on Title VI, see note 17 and accompanying chapter text, chapter 4 of this book.

164. Cisneros v. Corpus Christi Independent School District, 324 F. Supp. at 604 (S.D. Tex. 1970).

165. Cisneros v. Corpus Christi Independent School District, 330 F. Supp. 1377 (S.D. Tex. 1971).

166. Cisneros v. Corpus Christi Independent School District, 324 F. Supp. at 606 (S.D. Tex. 1970).

167. *Id.* at 608. The cases to which Judge Seals referred were the following: *Hernandez v. Texas* (1954); *Hernandez v. Driscoll* (1957); *Mendez v. Westminster* (1946); *Perez v. Sonora Independent School District* (1970). In this latter case, Judge Seals noted that it was particularly important because it was the first desegregation case in which the federal government (Justice Department) had intervened on behalf of Mexican American plaintiffs (also, see Salinas [1971, p. 943]).

168. Cisneros v. Corpus Christi Independent School District, 324 F. Supp. at 607 (S.D. Tex. 1970). In all, Carter—then a Professor of Education and Sociology at the University of Texas at El Paso and the author of the classic volume *Mexican Americans in Schools: A History of Educational Neglect* (1970)—was a highly influential expert witness in the *Cisneros* case. For more on Carter's influence on the course of Mexican American education, see Valencia (2006a).

169. *Id.* at 614.

170. *Id.* at 600.

171. *Id.* at 616.

172. *Id.* at 617. The "corridor" referred to the residential location (running from the northeast corner of the district to the southwesterly direction) where most Mexican American and African Americans were concentrated. White neighborhoods were concentrated in the south and southeast of the corridor.

173. *Id.*

174. *Id.* at 617–619.

175. *Id.* at 627. For details of the committee's composition, work, and controversies, see *Cisneros II* (Cisneros v. Corpus Christi, 350 F. Supp. 1377 [S.D. Tex. 1971]) and U.S. Commission on Civil Rights (1977).

176. See Cisneros v. Corpus Christi Independent School District, 404 U.S. 1211 (1971); Cisneros v. Corpus Christi Independent School District, 448 F.2d 1392 (5th Cir. 1971); Cisneros v. Corpus Christi Independent School District, 459 F.2d 13 (5th Cir. 1972); Cisneros v. Corpus Christi Independent School District, 413 U.S. 920 (1973); Corpus Christi Independent School District v. Cisneros, 413 U.S. 922 (1973); Cisneros v. Corpus Christi Independent School District, 414 U.S. 881 (1973); Cisneros v. Corpus Christi Independent School District, 560 F.2d 190 (5th Cir. 1977).

177. Cisneros v. Corpus Christi Independent School District, 467 F.2d 142 (5th Cir. 1972). Typically, an appeal is heard by a panel of three judges in U.S. courts of appeals. One or both parties, however, can petition the court to rehear the case en banc. When a case is heard en banc, all the judges of the appeals court hear the case, not just a three-judge panel; "the larger number sit in judgment when the court feels there is a particularly significant issue at stake" (Hill & Hill, 1995, s.v. "en banc").

178. Ross v. Eckels, 317 F. Supp. 512 (S.D. Tex. 1970).

179. Ross v. Rogers, 2 Race Rel. L. Rep. 114 (S.D. Tex. 1957).

180. Ross v. Houston Independent School District, 699 F.2d 218 (5th Cir. 1983). The term "unitary" is used by the courts "to describe a school system that has made the transition from a segregated or 'racially dual' system to a desegregated or 'unitary' system" (Sneed & Martin, 1997). Prior to the early 1990s, many courts used the term "unitary" in their decisions. The problem, however, was that the courts failed to interpret the term in a uniform manner (Sneed & Martin, 1997). As such, the U.S. Supreme Court in *Board of Education of Oklahoma City Public Schools v. Dowell* (1991) and *Freeman v. Pitts* (1992) developed standards for deciding whether a school district had attained unitary status. In these two cases, the U.S. Supreme Court drew from the *Green v. County School Board of New Kent County* case (391 U.S. 430 [1968]) to craft remedies for desegregation. Six factors, known as the *Green* factors, emerged from *Green*: racial composition of the student body; faculty; staff; transportation; extracurricular activities; facilities.

In desegregation proposals, the courts scrutinize the district's efforts in actively working toward meeting a sense of racial equity across the *Green* factors.

181. Ross v. Eckels, 317 F. Supp. at 513–514 (S.D. Tex. 1970).

182. *Id.* at 514.

183. Ross v. Eckels, 434 F.2d 1140 (5th Cir. 1970).

184. Ross v. Eckels, 317 F. Supp. at 515–516 (S.D. Tex. 1970).

185. *Id.* at 519.

186. *Id.* at 523.

187. Ross v. Eckels, 434 F.2d 1140 (5th Cir. 1970).

188. *Id.* at 1150.

189. *Id.*

190. *Id.* Judge Clark noted that the Fifth Circuit judges knew that African Americans and Mexican Americans resided, for the most part, in the same areas (also, see Salinas, 1971; San Miguel, 2001). Because many African Americans and Mexican Americans lived in adjacent neighborhoods, and because Mexican Americans were considered White (in the HISD) for purposes of desegregation, it was a given that many children of these two minority groups would be attending the same schools under the pairing order.

191. Ross v. Eckels, 434 F.2d at 1150 (5th Cir. 1970).

192. *Id.*

193. For a listing of the paired schools, see *Id.* at 1148.

194. Ross v. Eckels, 468 F.2d 649 (5th Cir. 1972). If an outside group (or individual) believes that the proceedings or outcomes of a court case directly affects them, they can petition the court for permission to participate, or *intervene,* in the proceedings. In this case, Mexican Americans petitioned the District Court to intervene in the *Ross* case (originally begun by African American plaintiffs) to assert their newly won protections under *Brown* that were first established in *Cisneros* in the HISD's desegregation plans. To *intervene* means "to obtain the court's permission to enter into a lawsuit which has already started between other parties and to file a complaint stating the basis for a claim in the existing lawsuit" (Hill & Hill, 1995, s.v. "intervene").

195. U.S. v. Texas Education Agency, 467 F.2d 848 (5th Cir. 1972).

196. Ross v. Eckels, 468 F.2d at 650 (5th Cir. 1972).

197. *Id.*

198. Keyes v. School District No. 1 of Denver, Colorado, 313 F. Supp. 61 (D. Colo. 1970).

199. Keyes v. Congress of Hispanic Educators v. School District No. 1 of Denver, Colorado, 902 F. Supp. 1274 (D. Colo. 1995).

200. Keyes v. School District No. 1 of Denver, Colorado, 445 F.2d at 996 (10th Cir. 1971).

201. Keyes v. School District No. 1 of Denver, Colorado, 413 U.S. at 189 (1973). The State of Colorado had no statutory provision for the segregation of

any students by race. To the contrary, the Colorado Constitution clearly prohibits "any classification of pupils . . . on account of race or color" (Article IX, Section 8). Yet, in *Keyes* it was found that the school board segregated schools throughout the district via neighborhood school policy, school site selection, and gerrymandering of attendance zones (*Id.* at 191).

202. Keyes v. School District No. 1 of Denver, Colorado, 313 F. Supp. at 69 (D. Colo. 1970).

203. *Id.*

204. Keyes v. School District No. 1 of Denver, Colorado, 445 F.2d 990 (10th Cir. 1971).

205. Keyes v. School District No. 1 of Denver, Colorado, 404 U.S. 1036 (1972).

206. Keyes v. School District No. 1 of Denver, Colorado, 406 U.S. 941 (1972).

207. Keyes v. School District No. 1 of Denver, Colorado, 413 U.S. at 216 (1973).

208. *Id.* at 201. Also see note 201, this chapter. Yet a problem existed. As discussed by Martínez (1994), although the opinion in *Keyes* refers to de jure segregation, the Supreme Court failed to address whether de facto segregation created a constitutional violation. Martínez comments, "By declining to resolve the question, the Supreme Court sustained the legal indeterminacy on the issue" (p. 596). Hence, in post-*Keyes* cases, lower courts were split on the de facto issue and frequently exploited the equivocation in *Keyes* in coming to their decisions. Martínez goes on (pp. 596–602) and illustrates this legal indeterminacy by discussing five cases.

209. Keyes v. School District No. 1 of Denver, Colorado, 413 U.S. at 197 (1973). Judge Brennan's lead cite for authority here was the landmark Mexican American jury-exclusion case, *Hernandez v. Texas* (1954), decided by the Supreme Court. Judge Brennan also cited a number of Mexican American desegregation cases, for example, *Soria v. Oxnard School District* (1971); *Alvarado v. El Paso Independent School District* (1971); *Cisneros v. Corpus Christi Independent School District* (1972).

210. Soria v. Oxnard School District Board of Trustees, 328 F. Supp. 155 (C.D. Cal. 1971).

211. Soria v. Oxnard School District Board of Trustees, 488 F.2d at 581 (9th Cir. 1973). The junior high schools were not part of the lawsuit, as it was conceded that they were ethnically balanced (*Id.*).

212. *Id.*

213. *Id.*

214. Soria v. Oxnard School District Board of Trustees, 328 F. Supp. at 157 (C.D. Cal. 1971).

215. Soria v. Oxnard School District Board of Trustees, 467 F.2d at 60 (9th Cir. 1972).

216. Soria v. Oxnard School District Board of Trustees, 488 F.2d at 586 (9th Cir. 1973).

217. *Id.*

218. *Id.*

219. *Id.* at 580.

220. *Id.* at 585.

221. *Id.* at 588.

222. Soria v. Oxnard School District Board of Trustees, 386 F. Supp. 539 (C.D. Cal. 1974).

223. McCurdy (1975, p. 3).

224. Soria v. Oxnard School District Board of Trustees, 386 F. Supp. at 541 (C.D. Cal. 1974).

225. *Id.*

226. *Id.*

227. *Id.*

228. *Id.* at 542.

229. McCurdy (1975, p. 3).

230. Soria v. Oxnard School District Board of Trustees, 386 F. Supp. at 542 (C.D. Cal. 1974).

231. *Id.* at 543.

232. *Id.* at 545.

233. Diaz v. San Jose Unified School District, 412 F. Supp. 310 (N.D. Cal. 1976).

234. Diaz v. San Jose Unified School District, 861 F.2d 591 (9th Cir. 1988).

235. Diaz v. San Jose Unified School District, 633 F. Supp. at 809 (N.D. Cal. 1985).

236. *Id.*

237. Diaz v. San Jose Unified School District, 412 F. Supp. at 311 (N.D. Cal. 1976).

238. *Id.* at 311, 317.

239. *Id.* at 312.

240. Diaz v. San Jose Unified School District, 612 F.2d at 415 (9th Cir. 1979).

241. *Id.*

242. *Id.* The Ninth Circuit based its ruling in light of U.S. Supreme Court decisions in *Columbus Board of Education v. Penick,* 443 U.S. 449 (1979), and *Dayton Board of Education v. Brinkman,* 443 U.S. 526 (1979).

243. Diaz v. San Jose Unified School District, 518 F. Supp. 622 (N.D. Cal. 1981).

244. Diaz v. San Jose Unified School District, 705 F.2d 1129 (9th Cir. 1983).

245. *Id.* at 1136.

246. Diaz v. San Jose Unified School District, 733 F.2d 660 (9th Cir. 1984).

247. *Id.* at 667, 670, and 674.

248. Diaz v. San Jose Unified School District, 633 F. Supp. at 809 (N.D. Cal. 1985). For an interesting case note on *Diaz,* see Galván (1991), who discusses how

contemporary courts face the challenge of desegregating diverse groups and how the courts use a growing corpus of social science findings in the process of formulating a desegregation remedy.

249. Defendants' Brief in Support of Its Proposed Desegregation Plan and in Opposition to Plaintiffs' Proposed Plan, Diaz v. San Jose Unified School District, 633 F. Supp. 808 (N.D. Cal. 1985) (No. 71-2130-RFP).

250. Diaz v. San Jose Unified School District, 633 F. Supp. at 809, 810 (N.D. Cal. 1985).

251. *Id.* at 810.

252. *Id.* at 810–811.

253. *Id.* at 814.

254. *Id.* at 815.

255. Diaz v. San Jose Unified School District, 861 F.2d 591 (9th Cir. 1988).

256. For a brief history of this antidesegregation era, see, for example, Frankenberg, Lee, & Orfield (2003), Orfield (2001), and Orfield & Yun (1999).

257. For the other two 1990 court decisions that have created obstacles to desegregation efforts, see *Freeman v. Pitts* (1992) and *Missouri v. Jenkins* (1995).

258. Board of Education of Oklahoma City Public Schools v. Dowell, 498 U.S. at 238 (1991).

259. See for example, Frankenberg, Lee, & Orfield (2003), Orfield (2001), and Orfield & Yun (1999).

260. See Valencia, Menchaca, & Donato (2002) for a discussion of Mexican American/other Latino hypersegregation trends at the national, regional, Southwestern, and local levels.

261. See Valencia, Menchaca, & Donato (2002, pp. 99–104) and Orfield (2001, pp. 105–106).

262. The U.S. Supreme Court jointly heard two cases: *Parents Involved in Community Schools v. Seattle School District No. 1*, No. 05-908, slip op. (U.S. June 28, 2007) and *Crystal D. Meredith v. Jefferson County Board of Education*, No. 05-915, slip op. (U.S. June 28, 2007). The joint cases are cited as *Parents Involved in Community Schools v. Seattle School District No. 1*, 551 U.S. __ (2007). The slip opinions (opinions not yet published in *U.S. Reports*) are available online at: *http://www. supremecourtus.gov/opinions/06slipopinion.html.*

263. Parents Involved in Community Schools v. Seattle School District No. 1, slip op. at 6 (U.S. June 28, 2007) (Roberts, C.J., majority).

264. *Id.* at 27. Chief Justice Roberts was joined by conservative Justices Samuel A. Alito, Anthony M. Kennedy, Antonin G. Scalia, and Clarence Thomas.

265. *Id.* at 36. See chapter 2, this volume, for a discussion of strict scrutiny.

266. Concurring opinions "agree with the result [majority opinion] but apply different emphasis, precedents, or logic to reach the determination" (Hill & Hill, 1995, s.v. "concurring opinion").

267. Parents Involved in Community Schools v. Seattle School District No. 1, slip op. at 2–3 (U.S. June 28, 2007) (Kennedy, J., concurring).

268. *Id.* at 7.

269. *Id.*

270. He was joined by Justices Ruth Bader Ginsburg, David H. Souter, and John Paul Stevens.

271. Parents Involved in Community Schools v. Seattle School District No. 1, slip op. at 2 (U.S. June 28, 2007) (Breyer, J., dissenting).

272. *Id.* at 65.

273. *Id.* at 68.

NOTES TO CHAPTER 2

1. The issue of financing education equitably is not confined to public elementary and secondary schools. This concern is also applicable to public higher education (see chapter 7, this volume).

2. This paragraph builds on, with minor modifications, Valencia (2002b, p. 19).

3. The teacher-student ratios are my calculations based on the data presented in García (1979, p. 66).

4. For a list of the disposition and parties of these lawsuits, see Brimley & Garfield (2005, pp. 242–245; also, see Minorini & Sugarman, 1999, pp. 41–47). The earlier lawsuits sought parity between property-rich and property-poor school districts. The more recent lawsuits (known as "educational adequacy" complaints), however, are intended to seek sufficient funds for property-poor districts to meet the targeted goals of the 2002 No Child Left Behind Act (NCLBA; Dobbs, 2004). According to the Center for American Progress (2004), President Bush's budget has allocated $9.4 billion less than the financial levels originally authorized by the NCLBA.

5. Also, see Henke (1986) for a discussion of *McInnis*. On the matter of educational needs and standards, respectively, the court held,

> There is no Constitutional requirement that public school expenditures be made only on the basis of pupils' educational needs without regard to the financial strength of local school districts. Nor does the Constitution establish the rigid guideline of equal dollar expenditures for each student. . . . Even if the Fourteenth Amendment required that expenditures be made only on the basis of pupils' educational needs, this controversy would be non-justiciable. While the complaint does not present a "political question" in the traditional sense of the term, there are no "discoverable and manageable standards" by which a court can determine when the Constitution is satisfied and when it is violated. . . . Even if there were some guidelines

available to the judiciary, the courts simply cannot provide the empirical research and consultation necessary for intelligent educational planning. (*McInnis v. Shapiro*, 293 F. Supp. at 335–336 [N.D. Ill. 1968])

6. The principle of fiscal neutrality as proffered by Coons et al. (1970) has been frequently discussed in the literature on school finance litigation. See for example, Areen (1973), Berke & Callahan (1972), Dayton & Dupre (2004), Gitlin (1980), Goldstein (1972), Henke (1986), and Kramer (2002).

7. For the basis of this argument, see Coons et al. (1970, pp. 355–358).

8. For the basis of this argument, see *Id.* at 151–160.

9. The importance of *Serrano v. Priest* is clearly seen in the sheer number of times the case is cited. In December 2006, I conducted a Google search (using "Serrano v. Priest" as a descriptor) and obtained 23,600 hits. For a partial list of scholarly journal articles that cover *Serrano v. Priest*, in part or whole, see Areen (1973); Berke & Callahan (1972); Crowley (1982); Dayton (2003); Dayton & Dupre (2004); Fischel (1989, 1996, 2004); Gitlin (1980); Goldstein (1972); Grubb & Michelson (1973); Guthrie (1983); Henke (1986); Hirji (1999); Joondeph (1995); Karst (1972, 1974); Kramer (2002); Schoettle (1971); Shanks (1972); Stark & Zasloff (2003); Thro (1990).

10. Serrano v. Priest, 5 Cal.3d at 591 (Cal. 1971).

11. A real property tax, or an ad valorem tax (according to the value), is imposed at a rate percentage of value. *Real* property, as opposed to *personal* property, is not considered readily movable (e.g., buildings, improvements, land). Typically, real property is classified as commercial, residential, agricultural, industrial, and unused (vacant) (Brimley & Garfield, 2005).

12. Serrano v. Priest, 5 Cal.3d at 592 (Cal. 1971).

13. *Id.*

14. *Id.*

15. *Id.* at 594.

16. This brief account of John Serrano, Jr., is based on Fischel (2004). According to Fischel, descriptions of Serrano's life before the lawsuit was filed have been quite inaccurate (e.g., some authors noted that he was a poor Mexican American who lived in Baldwin Park in Los Angeles County).

17. Serrano v. Priest, 5 Cal.3d at 589 (Cal. 1971).

18. *Id.*

19. *Id.* at 584, 590–591.

20. A "general demurrer" is defined as "a demurrer that challenges the sufficiency of the substance of allegation" (*Merriam-Webster's Dictionary of Law*, 1996, s.v. "general demurrer"; available online at: *http://dictionary.lp.findlaw.com/*). By and large, with a general demurrer a defendant neither admits nor denies the allegations of the plaintiff but says, in effect, "so what?" In short, this is a mechanism by which defendants can make a clear statement that the allegations have

no teeth and that the plaintiffs' case is wholly without merit and lacking in legal substance.

21. Serrano v. Priest, 5 Cal.3d at 584 (Cal. 1971). As noted by Odden and Picus (2000), the defendants cited *McInnis v. Shapiro* (1968) in Illinois and *Burruss v. Wilkerson* (1969) in Virginia as precedents that school finance cases are nonjusticiable. See Odden & Picus (2000, pp. 27–28) for further discussion of *McInnis* and *Burruss*.

22. The Court of Appeal of California (Second District, Division 4) rendered its decision on September 1, 1970 (89 Cal. Rptr. 345, 10 Cal. App.3d 1110 [Ct. App. 1970]). In its opinion, the appellate court considered two questions: (a) Was there a violation of the Equal Protection Clause of the Fourteenth Amendment? and (b) Was there a violation of Article IX, §5 (establishment of common schools) of the California Constitution? Answers to these questions led the appellate court to rule that the complaint did not state any actionable claims under these two provisions and to affirm the trial court's decision to grant the demurrers.

23. Serrano v. Priest, 5 Cal.3d at 598 (Cal. 1971). "Suspect class" is defined as "A class of individuals marked by immutable characteristics (as of race or national origin) and entitled to equal protection of the law by means of judicial scrutiny of a classification that discriminates against or otherwise burdens or affects them" (*Merriam-Webster's Dictionary of Law*, 1996, s.v. "suspect class"; available online at: *http://dictionary.lp.findlaw.com/*).

24. Serrano v. Priest, 5 Cal.3d at 598 (Cal. 1971).

25. *Id.* at 599.

26. *Id.*

27. *Id.* at 600.

28. *Id.* at 589.

29. *Id.* at 604.

30. *Id.* According to *Black's Law Dictionary* (Garner, 2004, p. 697), a "fundamental interest" is synonymous with a "fundamental right," which is defined as "A right that is considered by a court (as the U.S. Supreme Court) to be explicitly or implicitly expressed in a constitution (as the U.S. Constitution)" (*Merriam-Webster's Dictionary of Law*, 1996, s.v. "fundamental right"; available online at: *http://dictionary.lp.findlaw.com/*).

31. Serrano v. Priest, 5 Cal.3d at 605 (Cal. 1971).

32. See chapter 6, this volume, for a quotation by Justice Brennan from the *Brown* decision regarding the fundamental importance of education.

33. Serrano v. Priest, 5 Cal.3d at 605 (Cal. 1971).

34. *Id.*

35. The application of the strict scrutiny standard is also critical in the *Rodriguez v. San Antonio Independent School District* (1971; see later discussion, this chapter). Also see discussion of *Plyler v. Doe* in chapter 6, this volume.

36. A "compelling state interest" is defined as "a governmental interest (as in educating children or protecting the public) which is so important that it outweighs individual rights" (*Merriam-Webster's Dictionary of Law*, 1996, s.v. "compelling state interest"; available online at: *http://dictionary.lp.findlaw.com/*).

37. Serrano v. Priest, 5 Cal.3d at 610 (Cal. 1971).

38. *Id.* at 611.

39. *Id.* at 619.

40. Serrano v. Priest, 18 Cal.3d at 736 (Cal. 1976). As noted by Slayton (1997), the primary purpose of SB 90 and AB 1267 was to prevent property tax rates from increasing out of control. The new law also contained features designed to alter specific parts of the state's school finance system.

> The law placed a ceiling on how quickly districts were allowed to increase their revenues. High spending districts were limited to smaller increases than low spending districts. The theory was that over time, low spending districts could catch up with high spending districts. This was based on the assumption that high spending districts would not exercise their prerogative under SB 90 and AB 1267 to vote for a tax override that would lift the ceiling on expenditure increases. Yet between 1972, when SB 90 and AB 1267 became law, and 1974, voters approved approximately 40 percent of 580 referenda brought before them to override the ceiling on expenditure increases. In other words, SB 90 failed to reduce expenditure disparities in any meaningful way. (Slayton, 1997, p. 2)

41. Serrano v. Priest, 18 Cal.3d at 736, 767 (Cal. 1976).

42. *Id.* at 736–737.

43. *Id.* at 736.

44. Judge Jefferson did not rule, however, that the state's school financing system was in violation of the Equal Protection Clause of the Fourteenth Amendment. His conclusion was based on the U.S. Supreme Court decision in *San Antonio Independent District v. Rodriguez* (1973), which was made subsequent to *Serrano I*. The basis for this significant decision by the U.S. Supreme Court will be discussed later in this chapter.

45. Serrano v. Priest, 18 Cal.3d at 747 (Cal. 1976).

46. The basic concept underlying the public school financing system of California at the time of the rehearing of *Serrano v. Priest* was referred to as the "foundation approach" or the "foundation program." In general, the program was designed

> to insure a certain guaranteed dollar amount for the education of each child in each school district, and to defer to the individual school district for the provision of whatever additional funds it deems necessary to the furtherance of its particular educational goals. . . . The mechanisms by which this concept was implemented prior to the adoption of S.B. 90 and A.B. 1267 were basically four: (1) basic aid, (2) equalization aid, (3) supplemental aid,

and (4) tax rate limitations and overrides. The new law retained three of these, the element of supplemental aid . . . being discontinued. The basic aid component remained the same, i.e., $125 per ADA. Thus it was fundamentally through adjustments and alterations in the remaining two areas —equalization aid and tax rate limitations and overrides—that the Legislature sought to bring the system into constitutional conformity. (Serrano v. Priest, 18 Cal.3d at 741–742 [Cal. 1976])

47. As described in note 40, the SB 90 and AB 1267 law was designed to be a revenue limit for high-wealth districts. At the time, there was also a statutory provision that allowed high-wealth districts, who felt they were being squeezed by the new law, to increase their revenue via a voted override (see Goldfinger, 1999). That is, some high-wealth districts could get revenue limits increased by having a majority vote of the electorate to pass an override of the tax rate.

48. These four points are from Serrano v. Priest, 18 Cal.3d at 747 (Cal. 1976).

49. *Id.* at 750.

50. *Id.*

51. *Id.* at 776.

52. In the 2003–2004 school year, California ranked thirty-third in per-pupil expenditures. The figure was $7,860, considerably below the national average of $8,807 (California Department of Education, 2006a).

53. Serrano v. Priest, 226 Cal. Rptr. 584, 200 Cal. App.3d 897 (Ct. App. 1986).

54. In December 2006, I conducted a Google search (using "San Antonio Independent School District v. Rodriguez" as a descriptor) and obtained 16,100 hits. This is 7,500 fewer hits than I obtained for "Serrano v. Priest" (see note 9, this chapter), yet it appears that *Rodriguez* is more well known that *Serrano*. This is likely true for three reasons. First, *Rodriguez* was heard in the federal courts; thus, the case had national implications. Second, the U.S. Supreme Court's decision in *Rodriguez* soundly excluded plaintiffs who sought to utilize the U.S. Constitution and the federal court system as an instrument to achieve school funding equity. Finally, *Serrano*, as the nation's first *successful* school financing case, was already part of case law at the time of *Rodriguez* (and was even cited in the Supreme Court's opinion), and thus was likely to be included in the hits for *Rodriguez*.

55. In 1949, the Texas Legislature created the Gilmer-Aiken Committee to design a new public school finance system for the remaining half of the twentieth century (see Yudof & Morgan, 1974). A major aspect of the new finance scheme was the Minimum Foundation Program, which was based on

a set of formulas for allocating state funds for personnel and operations. In most instances, the state would pay the bulk of the costs of the program, later established at eighty per cent, while the local districts would contribute the remainder. By the use of an "economic index," additional funds were to be allocated to poorer districts, in effect forgiving all or part of their required twenty per cent share, to enable them to provide an education at the state established minimum. Local districts were, of course, free to enrich their educational programs beyond the state minimum in accordance with their fiscal capacity and willingness to tax. (Yudof & Morgan, 1974, p. 386)

56. San Antonio Independent School District v. Rodriguez, 411 U.S. at 11 (1973). Based on information provided in *San Antonio Independent School District v. Rodriguez* (at 37), I deduced that the other six schools districts were Alamo Heights Independent School District, Harlandale Independent School District, North East Independent School District, Northside Independent School District, South San Antonio Independent School District, and Southwest Independent School District.

57. *Id.* at 12.

58. In the available literature, *Rodriguez v. San Antonio Independent School District* (1971) and *San Antonio Independent School District v. Rodriguez* (1973) are not referred to as *Rodriguez I* and *Rodriguez II*, respectively. In the present discussion, however, I refer to the two decisions in this way for the ease of communication.

59. San Antonio Independent School District v. Rodriguez, 411 U.S. at 5 (1973). Subsequent to a pretrial conference, the District Court issued an order that dismissed six of the seven school districts from the lawsuit (*Id.*). Also, see Yudof & Morgan (1974).

60. San Antonio Independent School District v. Rodriguez, 411 U.S. at 4 (1973).

61. It is of interest to note that when Gochman first began to advise the parents that they may have a claim under the Fourteenth Amendment, he approached MALDEF for its assistance. Gochman knew that the parents would not be able to bear the costs of litigation. Unfortunately, MALDEF refused to participate, and Gochman pressed ahead at his personal expense (Yudof & Morgan, 1974). One possible reason why MALDEF opted not to participate in the case was that the organization had just been incorporated—in 1968, the same year the *Rodriguez I* complaint had been filed. MALDEF, a very young organization, lacked experienced civil rights attorneys, and was finding its way vis-à-vis the Mexican American community (O'Connor & Epstein, 1984). It is important to note, however, that MALDEF eventually did participate in the case. Mario Obledo, general counsel of MALDEF, was with Gochman on the brief when Gochman argued the *Rodriguez* case for appellees before the U.S. Supreme Court (San Antonio Independent School District v. Rodriguez, 411 U.S. 1 [1973]); also, see O'Connor & Epstein (1984) for a brief discussion of MALDEF's participation in *Rodriguez*.

62. Rodriguez v. San Antonio Independent School District, 337 F. Supp. at 281, 284 (W.D. Tex. 1971).

63. *Id.* at 282.

64. *Id.*

65. The city of Alamo Heights was incorporated in 1922 and has always been considered as one of the wealthiest areas in the San Antonio area. In the year 2000, Alamo Heights (population of 7,319; 84% White and 14% Latino residents) had a median household income of $64,688. By sharp contrast, the city of San Antonio in 2000 (population 1.1 million; 32% White and 59% Latino residents) had a median income of $36,214. Information available at: *http://www.city-data.com/city/Alamo-Heights-Texas.html* and *http://factfinder.census.gov/servlet/QTTable?_bm = y&-qr_name = DEC_2000_SF1_U_DP1&-ds_name = DEC_2000_SF1_U&-_lang = en&-geo_id = 16000US4865000.*

66. San Antonio Independent School District v. Rodriguez, 411 U.S. at 11 (1973).

67. Rodriguez v. San Antonio Independent School District, 337 F. Supp. at 282 (W.D. Tex. 1971).

68. *Id.* at 283.

69. *Id.*

70. *Id.* at 284.

71. *Id.*

72. *Id.* at 286.

73. *Id.* It is important to note that the trial court had previously allowed (in 1969) the Legislature an opportunity to correct the school finance system (see earlier discussion of *Rodriguez I*).

74. Following their defeat in *Rodriguez I*, defendants, rather than appeal to the Fifth Circuit, petitioned the U.S. Supreme Court to review the case directly, via appellate jurisdiction. With this type of appeal, a litigant must file a "jurisdictional statement" that sets forth the grounds for appellate jurisdiction, and then demonstrate that a substantial question is at issue in the case necessitating review by the U.S. Supreme Court (U.S. Department of Justice, Office of the Solicitor General, 2006). In the instant case, the U.S. Supreme Court agreed to review the case, noting "probable jurisdiction" in *San Antonio Independent School District v. Rodriguez*, 406 U.S. 966 (1972).

75. San Antonio Independent School District v. Rodriguez, 411 U.S. at 3 (1973).

76. *Id.* In a bizarre twist of events, the SAISD—one of the original defendants —"realizing that it stood to gain from school finance reform and despite its nominal designation as a defendant, also urged affirmance" (Yudof & Morgan, 1974, p. 399).

77. As was done in *Rodriguez I*, Gochman provided evidence in his *Rodriguez II* brief of the funding disparities between EISD and AHISD. See San Antonio Independent School District v. Rodriguez, 411 U.S. at 12–15 (1973).

78. *Id.* at 43.

79. Chief Justice Warren Burger and Justices Harry Blackmun, William H. Rehnquist, and Potter Stewart joined Justice Powell. Justice Byron White, joined

by Justices William J. Brennan and William O. Douglas, wrote a dissenting opinion. Justice Thurgood Marshall also wrote a dissenting opinion, with whom Justice Douglas concurred.

80. San Antonio Independent School District v. Rodriguez, 411 U.S. at 22–23 (1973).

81. *Id.* at 23.

82. *Id.* at 35.

83. *Id.* at 37.

84. *Id.* at 55.

85. *Id.*

86. *Id.* at 89.

87. *Id.* at 90.

88. *Id.* at 92.

89. *Id.* at 111. To underscore the ubiquitous importance of education in the nation, Justice Marshall remarked that in its last term, the U.S. Supreme Court noted, "Providing public schools ranks at the very apex of the function of a State" (*Wisconsin v. Yoder*, 406 U.S. at 213 [1972]). He also stated that the importance of education is clearly borne out by the fact that in forty-eight of the fifty states providing public education is constitutionally mandated.

90. San Antonio Independent School District v. Rodriguez, 411 U.S. at 98 (1973).

91. *Id.* at 99.

92. *Id.* at 100.

93. *Id.* at 103.

94. *Id.*

95. *Id.* at 102–103. The notion of a "sliding scale," though not mentioned by name or formally defined, is more fully explicated by Gunther (1972).

96. For further discussion of this impact, see, for example, Guthrie (1983) and Roos (1974).

97. Citations for this development, and other chronological events discussed in this section are, in part, from the sources provided at the bottom of Table 2.3 and Table 2.7, this chapter.

98. The case was originally filed as *Edgewood Independent School District v. Bynum*, as the Commissioner of Education at the time of filing was Dr. Raymon L. Bynum. By the time of trial, however, Kirby had replaced Bynum as Commissioner, thus the case is known as *Edgewood v. Kirby* (Cárdenas, 1997).

99. Kirby v. Edgewood Independent School District, 761 S.W.2d at 860 (Tex. App.–Austin 1988). Judge Clark did not prepare a published opinion in *Edgewood I*. Thus, all prior history from the district court deliberations discussed here is derived from the first appellate opinion (*Kirby v. Edgewood Independent School District*, 761 S.W.2d 859 [Tex. App.–Austin 1988]).

100. *Id.* at 867.

101. *Id.*

102. *Id.* at 868.

103. *Id.*

104. *Id.*

105. *Id.*

106. *Id.*

107. *Id.* at 860.

108. *Id.* at 860–861.

109. *Id.* at 861.

110. *Id.* at 862.

111. *Id.* at 863.

112. *Id.* at 864. Judge Shannon also wrote the opinion for the Third Court of Appeals in *Hernandez v. Houston Independent School District* (1977); see chapter 6, this volume.

113. Kirby v. Edgewood Independent School District, 761 S.W.2d at 870 (Tex. App.–Austin 1988).

114. Edgewood Independent School District v. Kirby, 777 S.W.2d at 393 (Tex. 1989).

115. *Id.*

116. The SEISD is located in San Elizario, Texas, a small community on the Texas-Mexico border that is about eighteen miles southeast of El Paso. In the year 2000, San Elizario had a population of 11,046 people; 98% were Mexican-origin (information available online at: *http://www.city-data.com/city/San-Elizario-Texas.html*).

117. Edgewood Independent School District v. Kirby, 777 S.W.2d at 393 (Tex. 1989).

118. *Id.*

119. *Id.* at 394.

120. *Id.*

121. *Id.*

122. *Id.* at 395.

123. *Id.* at 396.

124. *Id.* at 397.

125. *Id.*

126. *Id.* at 399.

127. Former Texas Supreme Court Justice William W. Kilgarlin, as Master in Chancery, and Drs. Billy D. Walker and José A. Cárdenas, as Associate Masters, composed the master group.

128. Edgewood Independent School District v. Kirby, Civil Action No. 362,516 (250th District Court, Travis County, Texas, September 20, 1990).

129. Kirby v. Edgewood Independent School District, 804 S.W.2d 491 (Tex. 1991).

130. The CEDs were not so much traditional school districts, but served more as taxing districts (see Sracic [2006] for a discussion of the two-tiered nature of the CEDs).

131. These asserted constitutional violations were in regards to (a) Article VIII, §1-e (state ad valorem tax), (b) Article VII, §3 (ad valorem tax without voter approval), and (c) Article VII, §3, and Article III, §§56 and 64(a) (creation of county education districts ["CEDs"]).

132. Dr. Lionel R. Meno replaced William Kirby as Texas Commissioner of Education on July 1, 1991; hence the referent *Edgewood v. Meno*.

133. Three of the five consolidated cases—*Carrollton-Farmers Branch Independent School District v. Edgewood Independent School District*, Cause No. D-1469; *Andrews Independent School District v. Edgewood Independent School District*, Cause No. D-1477; and *Highland Park Independent School District v. Edgewood Independent School District*, Cause No. D-1560—were originally filed in intervention, but were severed from *Edgewood III*, as these cases challenged the constitutionality of SB 351 on different grounds. The two other cases that were consolidated on similar grounds were *McCarty v. County Education District No. 21*, Cause No. D-1493, on appeal from a judgment on September 4, 1991, from the 18th District Court of Somervell County, Texas; and *Reyes v. Mitchell County Education District*, Cause No. D-1544, on appeal from a judgment on September 5, 1991, from the 32nd District Court of Mitchell County, Texas.

134. Carrollton-Farmers Branch v. Edgewood, 826 S.W.2d 489 (Tex. 1992).

135. See Sracic (2006) for a brief discussion of the nature of SB 7.

136. Edgewood Independent School District v. Meno, Civil Action No. 362,516 (250th District Court, Travis County, Texas, April 26, 1994).

137. Edgewood Independent School District v. Meno, 917 S.W.2d 717 (Tex. 1995).

138. The case was originally filed as *West Orange-Cove Consolidated Independent School District v. Nelson*, Civil Action No. GV100528 (250th District Court, Travis County, Texas *filed*, April 9, 2001). The named defendant in this case was James Nelson, then Texas Commissioner of Education. Given that the district court did not publish an opinion, by the time the case reached the Third Court of Appeals, the case became known as *West Orange-Cove Consolidated Independent School District v. Alanis*, as Dr. Felipe Alanis succeeded Nelson as Commissioner of Education on April 1, 2002.

139. West Orange-Cove v. Alanis, 78 S.W.3d at 541 (Tex. App.–Austin 2002).

140. West Orange-Cove v. Alanis, 78 S.W.3d 529 (Tex. App.–Austin 2002, rev'd and rem'd).

141. West Orange-Cove v. Alanis, 107 S.W.3d 558 (Tex. 2003).

142. *Id.* at 579–583.

143. West Orange-Cove Consolidated Independent School District v. Neeley,

Civil Action No. GV100528 (250th District Court, Travis County, Texas, September 15, 2003).

144. Neeley v. West Orange-Cove Consolidated Independent School District, 176 S.W.3d 746 (Tex. 2005).

NOTES TO CHAPTER 3

1. These data are from Tables AA2, AA4, AA5, and AF9 in U.S. Department of Education, Office of Special Education Programs (2002). For a disaggregation by race/ethnicity of students classified in the various special education categories, see U.S. Department of Education, Office for Civil Rights (2001). Also, for a discussion of such disaggregated data, by race/ethnicity from the penultimate U.S. Department of Education, Office for Civil Rights (1997) survey, see Valencia & Suzuki (2001, pp. 201–205).

2. This section on intelligence testing in 1920s Los Angeles builds on, with revisions, Valencia, Villarreal, & Salinas (2002, pp. 257–258).

3. González (1974a) drew this median IQ data from McAnulty (1929), whose study in turn drew on a compilation of IQ test data surveyed in Los Angeles from 1926 through 1928. The observed median IQ of 91.2 of Mexican American children in 1920s Los Angeles was about two-thirds of a standard deviation below the typical White median (and mean) of 100. This difference of two-thirds of a standard deviation was frequently found in other race psychology studies of the time. Furthermore, Valencia (1985), in a comprehensive review of research on intelligence testing and Chicano school-age children, estimated an aggregated mean IQ of 87.3 for these children and youths. His analysis is based on 10,739 Chicano children in seventy-eight studies spanning six decades. Valencia noted, however, that this aggregated mean IQ of 87.3 is entirely misleading and greatly confounded by the failure of researchers to control for critical variables (e.g., English proficiency of participants).

4. This section is drawn, with revisions, from Valencia & Suzuki (2001, pp. 21–22).

5. This section is drawn, with revisions, from Valencia & Suzuki (2001, pp. 22–23).

6. In 1963, about 90% of children with EMR were taught in full-time, special classes; about 10% of these children were taught, part-time, in regular classes (Goldberg, 1971).

7. Theimer and Rupiper (1975) have devised a typology to understand the nature of special education litigation. First, the authors discuss "right-to-education" lawsuits in which plaintiffs (White in some cases, minority in some cases) filed suit for *inclusion* in educational services denied to them in the past. See, for example, *Pennsylvania Association for Retarded Children v. Commonwealth of*

Pennsylvania (1971) and *Mills v. Board of Education of the District of Columbia* (1972). Second, Theimer and Rupiper explain "right-to-placement" cases in which plaintiffs (only minority students) brought suit for *exclusion* from inappropriate special education placement (e.g., *Diana; Covarrubias; Guadalupe*).

8. Although *Diana, Covarrubias,* and *Guadalupe* are considered the most important special education lawsuits involving Mexican American students deemed EMR, there are lesser known and less influential cases. See, for example, *Arreola v. Santa Ana Board of Education* (1968) and *Ruiz v. State Board of Education* (1971). For brief reviews of *Arreola* and *Ruiz,* see Ross et al. (1971) and Abeson & Bolick (1974), respectively.

9. Complaint for Injunction and Declaratory Relief (Civil Rights) (p. 5), Diana v. State Board of Education, Civil Action No. C-70-37 (N.D. Cal. 1970). Children diagnosed with educable (or mild) mental retardation typically score between 52 and 68 IQ on the Stanford-Binet and between 55 and 69 IQ on the Wechsler Intelligence Scale for Children. These "children can master basic academic skills while adults at their level may maintain themselves independently or semi-independently in the community" (Grossman, 1973, p. 149).

10. A second group of plaintiffs ($n = 4$) from the same families of the main plaintiff group also served. Some of the children in the second group were preschoolers about to enter school or were in grades 1 and 2 who were about to be administered IQ tests. The parents of these four children feared that the special education system in Soledad would inevitably lead to the children's EMR placement (Complaint for Injunction and Declaratory Relief [Civil Rights] [p. 3], Diana v. State Board of Education, Civil Action No. C-70-37 [N.D. Cal. 1970]).

11. *Id.*

12. *Id.*

13. *Id.*

14. *Id.*

15. *Id.* at 4.

16. It is not stated in the complaint that plaintiffs hired Ramírez to conduct the evaluations, but I assume that was the arrangement.

17. Psychological Evaluation of Nine Plaintiffs Conducted by School Psychologist, Victor Ramírez (Exhibit A), Diana v. State Board of Education, Civil Action No. C-70-37 (N.D. Cal. 1970). (Note: Exhibit A was an untitled memo from Ramírez to plaintiffs' counsel. I have provided a title for ease of communication.)

18. In plaintiffs' complaint (pp. 9–10), reference is made to a study by John Plakos of the California Department of Education. Plakos's study (undertaken in June 1969, five months before Ramírez did his retesting of the *Diana* plaintiffs) provided corroborative data for the value of Spanish-language testing. Plakos randomly selected forty-seven Mexican American children enrolled in EMR classes in two districts (a rural and an urban area). All children were individually administered the *Escala de Inteligencia Wechsler Para Niños,* the Spanish version of

the WISC. The results showed that forty-two (89%) of the forty-seven children scored above the IQ cut score for EMR classification. Further analyses found that thirty-seven (79%) of the children scored IQs of 75 or higher, over one-half scored higher than 80, and about 17% scored IQs in the 90s and 100s. Plakos observed the mean gain score over earlier testing to be 13.2 IQ points, nearly one standard deviation (the mean score for the initial testing was 68.6, and the mean score for the second testing was 81.8). Plakos's study was later published as Chandler & Plakos (1969).

19. This average of 9.6 points is my calculation of the FSIQ scores provided in Table 3.3. I base this average in the context of a WISC cut score of 70 IQ. In the plaintiffs' complaint (p. 4), however, an average of "8½ points" is noted. This calculation appears to be in error. In any event, my calculation of the average and the average presented in the complaint are quite similar.

20. Complaint for Injunction and Declaratory Relief (Civil Rights) (p. 4), Diana v. State Board of Education, Civil Action No. C-70-37 (N.D. Cal. 1970).

21. Valencia (1985) analyzed twenty-two research studies (spanning decades) in which Mexican American children were administered intelligence tests. The children's mean IQs on verbal and performance tests were 85.6 and 94.7, respectively, a difference of 9.1 points. Valencia's finding was very similar to an earlier report by Klineberg (1935), who found, in a much smaller corpus of investigations with Mexican American children, a 10-point P>V difference.

22. In the 1969 Plakos study (see note 18, this chapter), the average P>V difference was 8 IQ points; nine (19%) of the forty-seven children scored at least 20 points higher on the performance test.

23. Psychological Evaluation of Nine Plaintiffs Conducted by School Psychologist, Victor Ramírez (Exhibit A), Diana v. State Board of Education, Civil Action No. C-70-37 (N.D. Cal. 1970).

24. Complaint for Injunction and Declaratory Relief (Civil Rights) (p. 3), Diana v. State Board of Education, Civil Action No. C-70-37 (N.D. Cal. 1970).

25. *Id.* at 5.

26. Psychological Evaluation of Nine Plaintiffs Conducted by School Psychologist, Victor Ramírez (Exhibit A, p. 4), Diana v. State Board of Education, Civil Action No. C-70-37 (N.D. Cal. 1970).

27. For the other two children, Ramírez recommended that they "should also be reassigned with a great deal of caution exercised to determine whether these 2 students can make the adjustment through intensive training to a regular program" (*Id.* at 1).

28. *Id.* at 2.

29. Complaint for Injunction and Declaratory Relief (Civil Rights) (p. 10), Diana v. State Board of Education, Civil Action No. C-70-37 (N.D. Cal. 1970).

30. *Id.*

31. *Id.*

32. *Id.* at 11.

33. *Id.*

34. *Id.* at 12.

35. Plaintiffs also wrote in the complaint,

It [this action] also arises under the Constitution and Laws of the State of California, including Art. 9 §5 of the Constitution, Education Code §§ 1051, 1054, 5051, and 5054 [right to education], and Education Code §§ 6902 et seq. [education of mentally retarded minors]. A declaration of rights is sought under the Declaratory Judgment Act, 28 U.S.C. §§ 2201. Jurisdiction of this court is invoked under Title 28 U.S.C. §§ 1331, 1337, 1343 and Title 42 U.S.C. §§ 1983 and 1985. (*Id.* at 2).

36. *Id.* at 15–16.

37. *Id.* at 16.

38. *Id.*

39. Stipulation and Order, Diana v. State Board of Education, Civil Action No. C-70-37 (N.D. Cal. 1970).

40. *Id.* at 4, 9.

41. *Id.* at 4. The stipulation and order also states that in the event a school psychologist or other qualified person is unavailable, an interpreter may be used (see *Id.* at 10 for types of interpreters and charge of the interpreter).

42. *Id.* at 4.

43. *Id.*

44. *Id.* at 2–3. The racial/ethnic exclusivity of the standardization groups for the WISC and Stanford-Binet served as the impetus for the development of an intelligence test normed on Mexican Americans. White, native-born American children exclusively served in the norming of both tests (see plaintiffs' complaint, pp. 8–9; also, see discussion earlier in this chapter). Regarding the development of an intelligence test designed for Mexican Americans, it appears that the project was never begun (Reschly, 1979).

45. Stipulation and Order (p. 5), Diana v. State Board of Education, Civil Action No. C-70-37 (N.D. Cal. 1970). I am assuming here that "special" refers to mental retardation, particularly EMR.

46. *Id.*

47. *Id.* at 4.

48. *Id.* at 9–11.

49. *Id.*

50. *Id.* at 2. The issue of significant variance proved to be highly contentious in *Diana*. Although the stipulation required defendants to provide EMR enrollment data, they claimed that no agreement on the statistical formula to determine significant variance had been reached, and thus they refused to provide plaintiffs with any survey data (Memorandum of Points and Authorities, Diana v. State Board of Education, Civil Action No. C-70-37, N.D. Cal. 1970). This recalcitrance

resulted in Judge Peckham finding the defendants in contempt of court and ordering them to provide the plaintiffs with survey data (Memorandum and Order, Diana v. State Board of Education, Civil Action No. C-70-37, N.D. Cal. 1970). Despite Judge Peckham's order, defendants steadfastly continued to refuse to provide plaintiffs with survey data, resulting in plaintiffs submitting Motions to Compel three times between 1974 and 1981, and submitting Interrogatories in 1980 and 1983. In November 1983, *ten years* after being found in contempt, defendants finally provided EMR enrollment data and listings of districts with significant variance (Defendants' Response to Plaintiffs' First Request for Admissions, First Request for Productions, Second Set of Interrogatories, Diana v. State Board of Education, Civil Action No. C-70-37, N.D. Cal. 1970).

51. The inability to get a more precise count of the number of decertified students was due to not knowing

> (a) how many reassigned students were cases of pending placement but not placed in view of new guidelines; (b) how many were removed without formal decertification; and (c) how large was the usual proportion of students leaving school by dropout or graduation. (Yoshida et al., 1976, p. 216)

52. One important case was *Covarrubias v. San Diego Unified School District* (1971), which I discuss in the next section. The other highly influential case was *Larry P. v. Riles* (1972), a class action lawsuit filed on behalf of African American students in EMR classes in San Francisco. *Larry P.*, fundamentally different from *Diana*, went much further in asking for relief. Whereas *Diana* plaintiffs requested "*revision* and *reform* of current assessment practices," the plaintiffs in *Larry P.* "originally requested *elimination* of all standardized tests including, of course, individual intelligence tests" (Reschly, 1979, p. 221). *Larry P.* also differed from *Diana* in that the former case was litigated and resolved in a federal district court (U.S. District Court for the Northern District of California; Judge Peckham, who presided over *Diana*, also presided over *Larry P.*). Thus, *Larry P.* was decided by highly influential judicial opinion, not by the more interpretive and controversial nature of a consent decree, as seen in the resolution of *Diana*. The litigation in *Larry P.* lasted a number of years (see *Larry P.* [1972] reference) and produced a voluminous record. The results were far-reaching:

> In 1974 the plaintiffs requested and obtained an expansion of the original injunction to include all school districts in the state of California. This resulted in California State Board of Education action forbidding the use of individual intelligence tests for *all* students in California schools *if* the outcome of such tests was a classification decision of mental retardation (California State Board of Education, 1975). Intelligence tests were not banned generally by the courts in California as is commonly believed, and use of intelligence tests in California was permissible as long as a decision of mental retardation was not under consideration. (Reschly, 1979, p. 221)

It appears that other special education categories are also off-limits to the use of intelligence tests to assess students in California. In 2004, Pamela Lewis, a mother of an African American child, wanted her six-year-old son, Nicholas, to be given a standardized intelligence test to determine if he could qualify for special education speech therapy. The district denied her request, due to the statewide policy that has its origin in 1979 (Associated Press, 2004).

53. The twelve districts selected represented a wide variation regarding size of total enrollment, size of racial/ethnic enrollment, and community SES.

54. It appears that OCR Director Pottinger mailed the well-known OCR memorandum on May 25, 1970. Yet the *Federal Register* did not codify the actual memo until July 18, 1970 (35 F.R. 11595). Following the 1970 OCR memorandum, a November 28, 1972, OCR memorandum contained a comprehensive set of federal guidelines and procedures for evaluating and placing minority students in EMR classes. See Oakland (1977, pp. 148–155, Appendix D) for the full text of the draft of the "Memorandum from OCR to State and Local Education Agencies on Elimination of Discrimination in the Assignment of Children to Special Education Classes for the Mentally Retarded." See Gerry (1973) for a discussion of the 1972 OCR memorandum.

55. Complaint for Damages, for Injunction and for Declaratory Relief (Civil Rights) (p. 3), Covarrubias v. San Diego Unified School District, Civil Action No. 70-394-T (S.D. Cal. 1971).

56. *Id.*

57. Affidavit of Scott C. Gray in Support of Motion to Dismiss Second Cause of Action (Rule 12 (b)(6)) (Exhibit A), Covarrubias v. San Diego Unified School District, Civil Action No. 70-394-T (S.D. Cal. 1971).

58. Complaint for Damages, for Injunction and for Declaratory Relief (Civil Rights) (p. 8), Covarrubias v. San Diego Unified School District, Civil Action No. 70-394-T (S.D. Cal. 1971). The complaint did not state what the examiner used as compensatory techniques. Given that a P>V pattern was reported, I assume that the Mexican American plaintiffs were likely administered the Spanish version of the WISC. It is not clear what the African American plaintiffs were administered. I assume, however, that they were given the WISC and that subsequent scrutiny was given to the Performance Scale versus Verbal Scale comparisons, as these children also demonstrated a P>V pattern.

59. Id.

60. *Id.* at 9.

61. *Id.* at 11.

62. *Id.* at 4. 42 U.S.C. §1983.

63. *Id.* at 4. 42 U.S.C. §1985(3).

64. *Id.* at 4.

65. See *Id.* at 17–19 for complete list of points for injunctive and declaratory relief.

66. *Id.* at 13–14.

67. This claim for monetary damages in *Covarrubias* is similar to what transpired in the *Stewart v. Phillips* (1970) case. African American plaintiffs placed in EMR classes in the Boston Public School System sought $20,000 each for compensatory and punitive damages.

68. Complaint for Damages, for Injunction and for Declaratory Relief (Civil Rights) (pp. 12, 14), Covarrubias v. San Diego Unified School District, Civil Action No. 70-394-T (S.D. Cal. 1971).

69. *Id.* at 10.

70. *Id.* at 18.

71. It is noteworthy that the two powerful legal arms of the Mexican American and African American communities—MALDEF and the NAACP LDF, respectively—represented the plaintiffs.

72. See Settlement Agreement (Exhibit A), Covarrubias v. San Diego Unified School District, Civil Action No. 70-394-T (S.D. Cal. 1971).

73. Complaint for Injunction and Declaratory Relief (Civil Rights) (p. 3), Guadalupe Organization, Inc. v. Tempe Elementary School District No. 3, Civil Action No. 71-435 (D. Ariz. 1972). In the *Guadalupe* case, the term "handicapped" was used, not "retarded" as seen in *Diana* and *Covarrubias*. Trainable mental retardation, which refers to a moderate degree of mental retardation (as opposed to a mild or educable mental retardation), describes individuals who have a measured IQ between 40 and 54 on the WISC, or 36 and 51 on the Stanford-Binet (Grossman, 1973; Ysseldyke & Algozzine, 1984). Individuals with moderate retardation "usually can learn self-help, communication, and simple occupational skills but only limited academic or vocational skills" (Grossman, 1973, p. 149).

74. Complaint for Injunction and Declaratory Relief (Civil Rights) (p. 9), Guadalupe Organization, Inc. v. Tempe Elementary School District No. 3, Civil Action No. 71-435 (D. Ariz. 1972). In the complaint, no corresponding data were provided for the Yaqui Indian students.

75. *Id.* at 4.

76. The Yaquis in Arizona, whose ancestors come from Sonora, Mexico, crossed over the border at the turn of the century. The Mexican Yaquis "are widely known for their long, armed struggle with the Mexican government to keep their tribal lands in Sonora and to maintain their self-determination" (Brewster, 1976, p. 1). Arizona served as a refuge for the Sonoran Yaquis, who eventually gathered in villages around Tucson and Phoenix. At the time of *Guadalupe* five centers of Yaqui life existed in Arizona: "Barrio Libre, Old Pascua, New Pascua, and Marana in the Tucson area; and Guadalupe in the Phoenix area" (Brewster, 1976, p. 70). Brewster describes the Guadalupe Organization, Inc., lead plaintiff in *Guadalupe*, as follows:

> Since this barrio [Guadalupe] is shared with Mexican Americans, the Mexican Americans form a sizeable proportion of the clientele of Guadalupe

Organization. This Organization performs many services which are of the "expediter" sort. They cut red tape to make the services offered by various agencies more readily available to their clients, the Yaquis and Chicanos of Guadalupe. There is also a medical clinic in Guadalupe, serving all segments of the community. In Guadalupe, as in Old Pascua, the nature of the barrio is that of an urban ghetto—but on the edge of the city rather than at its center. (p. 72)

77. Compared to the *Diana* and *Covarrubias* complaints, the *Guadalupe* complaint was quite brief and limited in its description of the plaintiff children. It did not provide separate counts for the number of Mexican American and Yaqui children. It is not possible to distinguish the Mexican American from the Yaqui children by inspection of surname. Brewster (1976) notes, "Almost all Arizona Yaquis use Spanish surnames" (p. 134). Finally, the complaint did not provide information for the age or grade of the plaintiffs, SES background, or data on IQs.

78. First Amended Complaint for Injunction and Declaratory Relief (Civil Rights) (p. 4), Guadalupe Organization, Inc. v. Tempe Elementary School District No. 3, Civil Action No. 71-435 (D. Ariz. 1972).

79. Complaint for Injunction and Declaratory Relief (Civil Rights) (p. 3), Guadalupe Organization, Inc. v. Tempe Elementary School District No. 3, Civil Action No. 71-435 (D. Ariz. 1972).

80. By inspection of the names of the plaintiffs' representatives (e.g., mother) in groups 1 and 2, it appears that considerable overlap existed, meaning that plaintiff children in both groups were, with some exceptions, siblings.

81. Complaint for Injunction and Declaratory Relief (Civil Rights) (p. 5), Guadalupe Organization, Inc. v. Tempe Elementary School District No. 3, Civil Action No. 71-435 (D. Ariz. 1972).

82. *Id.* at 8.

83. The duties of Dr. Margaret Fauci, school psychologist, included the "administration of intelligence tests to children of Mexican-American and Yaqui Indian family background" (*Id.* at 6). In my view, the naming of a school psychologist as a defendant (which did not occur in *Diana* and *Covarrubias*) served as a potent tactic. Given that the school psychologist does the clinical assessment and recommends placement in a class for the mentally retarded, it appears that plaintiffs strengthened their case by placing some of the culpability for inappropriate diagnosis at the level of the individual school psychologist.

84. *Id.* at 3.

85. For the complete list of points for injunctive and declaratory relief, see *Id.* at 11–12.

86. *Id.* at 11.

87. Order, Guadalupe Organization, Inc. v. Tempe Elementary School District No. 3, Civil Action No. 71-435 (D. Ariz. 1972).

88. Stipulation and Order (p. 3), Guadalupe Organization, Inc. v. Tempe Elementary School District No. 3, Civil Action No. 71-435 (D. Ariz. 1972).

89. *Id.* at 3–7.

90. *Id.* at 3–4.

91. *Id.* at 4.

92. In 1990, Congress passed P.L. 101-476 (*Federal Register*, October 30, 1990), amending P.L. 94-142 and changing the name of the law to the Individuals with Disabilities Education Act (IDEA). Among the amendments in IDEA: (a) an expansion of special education categories to include physical, cognitive, communication, social or emotional, and adaptive development, and (b) an extension of the age range (ages three to twenty-one) in which students would be eligible for services.

93. Donovan and Cross (2002) note that the P.L. 94-142 PEP regulations of 1977 did not undergo revision until 1999 (*Federal Register*, March 12, 1999), when the government published 1997 regulations for the IDEA as the Procedures for Evaluation and Determination of Eligibility (PEDE) (34 C.F.R. 300.530–543). See Donovan & Cross (2002, pp. 234–239, Appendix 6-A) for the PEDE regulations.

94. These three organizations first published the collaborative version of the *Standards* in 1966. Revisions were published in 1974, 1985, and 1999 (American Educational Research Association, American Psychological Association, & National Council on Measurement in Education, 1999, p. v).

95. Note the implicit tone in the *Standards* regarding the legal and regulatory requirements of testing:

The standards do not attempt to repeat or to incorporate the many legal or regulatory requirements that might be relevant to the issues they address. In some areas, such as the collection, analysis, and use of test data and results for different subgroups, the law may both require participants in the testing process to take certain actions and prohibit those participants from taking other actions. Where it is apparent that one or more standards or comments address an issue on which established legal requirements may be particularly relevant, the standard, comment, or introductory material may make note of that fact. Lack of specific reference to legal requirements, however, does not imply that no relevant requirement exists. In all situations, participants in the testing process should separately consider and, where appropriate, obtain legal advice on legal and regulatory requirements. (American Educational Research Association, American Psychological Association, & National Council on Measurement in Education, 1999, p. 4)

NOTES TO CHAPTER 4

1. The Cherokee achieved this very high 90% literacy rate by using Sequoyah's syllabary, or phonetic writing system (Crawford, 1995).

2. This first paragraph draws from, with minor modifications, San Miguel & Valencia (1998, p. 354).

3. This 1858 bill stipulated that no school would receive state funding unless English was "principally taught" (*School Law of 1858*, in Eby, 1919). In the 1850s, California suspended the 1849 constitutional provision allowing the state government to publish its laws in Spanish. In 1855, the State Bureau of Public Instruction formalized the campaign against Spanish and all other non-English languages when it issued an administrative ruling requiring all schools to teach strictly in English (Beck, 1975; Kloss, 1977, Pitt, 1968).

4. Governor William Lane, for instance, proposed in the early 1850s that, for efficiency's sake, the legislature should replace Spanish with English as the official state language. Due to fierce resistance by the large Spanish-speaking community, the territorial legislature soundly defeated his proposal. White legislators in 1856 proposed the establishment of an English-only public school system. Mexican American voters rejected the monolingual public school system by a wide margin (Eiband, 1978).

5. On the Texas law, see *School Law of 1870* (in Eby, 1919). For the law in California, see California Statutes (1870). Legislators strengthened and broadened the California provision to include all public institutions with the passage in 1879 of a new constitution that made English the only "official language of the state" (California Constitution, 1879). For a comprehensive historical and legal analysis of language-rights issues in Texas, see Juárez (1995).

6. See *School Law of 1891* (cited in Meyer, 1977). For a Mexican American response to this law and its aftermath, see Espinosa (1917).

7. The second, third, and fourth sentences of the first paragraph of this section, the penultimate paragraph, a portion of the final paragraph, and note 9 build on, with revisions, Valencia (2002b, pp. 7–9, 41).

8. The other states of the Southwest (i.e., Arizona, California, Colorado, and New Mexico) were less restrictive on the "No Spanish" rule (see U.S. Commission on Civil Rights, 1972b, Figure 7, p. 16).

9. In addition to language exclusion, officials also subjected Mexican American students to cultural exclusion in the school curricula. The MAES reported, in detail, the extent of such cultural exclusion (U.S. Commission on Civil Rights, 1972b). The report found that only 4.3% of the elementary schools surveyed in the five Southwestern states in 1969 offered Mexican American "units" in their social studies curriculum; only 4.7% of these schools offered Mexican history units. At the secondary level, only 7.3% of the schools provided Mexican American history in their curriculum, and merely 5.8% provided Mexican history. The report noted, "In spite of the rich bicultural history of the Southwest, the schools offer little opportunity for Mexican Americans to learn something about their roots —who they are and where they came from and what their people have achieved" (p. 30).

10. San Miguel's *Contested Policy* is a comprehensive treatise of the politically charged history of federal bilingual education in the United States. He covers the 1960s origins of the 1968 Bilingual Education Act and its turbulent six re-authorizations from 1974 to 2001. San Miguel examines the major actors, events, and developments that led to the rise and fall of federally sponsored bilingual education.

11. The United States experienced its greatest period of immigration from 1830 to 1930. Historians typically divide this century-long era into two periods: the "old" immigration (1830–1882) and the "new" immigration (1882–1930). See Chorover (1979).

12. See Peal & Lambert (1962) for a review of early international research on the relation of bilingualism to intelligence. The authors' reviews are divided among studies supporting the detrimental effects of bilingualism to intelligence (the modal group), studies supporting favorable effects, and studies finding no effects.

13. See Hakuta (1986) for a discussion of research findings on the relation between bilingualism and intelligence.

14. For a discussion of the struggle for Black equality (1950s and 1960s), see Sitkoff (1993). Also see, for example, Brooks (1974), Civil Rights Education Project (1989), and Davis (1998).

15. For a discussion of how the resurgence of bilingual education was tied to the Civil Rights Movement, also see Castellanos (1985) and Malakoff & Hakuta (1990).

16. Malakoff and Hakuta (1990) discuss the Bilingual Education Act (BEA) of 1968 as part of this first avenue. For the sake of chronological flow, however, I discuss the BEA later.

17. Title VI requires the following:
No person in the United States shall, on the ground of race, color, or national origin, be excluded from participation in, be denied the benefits of, or be subjected to discrimination under any program or activity receiving Federal financial assistance. (42 U.S.C. §2000d)

18. For other coverages of the Chicano(a) Movement, see, for example, Barrera (1988); Gómez-Quiñones (1978, 1990); Muñoz (1989).

19. For discussions of the Coral Way experience, see, for example, Castellanos (1985); Crawford (1995); Hakuta (1986). For an exceptionally comprehensive coverage of the Coral Way program, see Mackey & Beebe (1977).

20. Note the subtitle of the NEA report: *The NEA-Tucson Survey on the Teaching of Spanish to the Spanish-Speaking.*

21. See the Appendix (pp. 37–39) of the NEA (1966) report for a listing of the forty-five schools.

22. *Congressional Record* (January 17, 1967), "Two proposals for a better way of life for Mexican-Americans of the Southwest," p. 599.

23. *Id.* at 600.

24. *Congressional Record* (January 17, 1967), §704(b), p. 601.

25. 20 U.S.C. §880(b).

26. Castellanos (1985) comments on the relation between the ambiguous purpose of the BEA and the accompanying fiscal problems this way:

> Guidelines were unclear. While the Act was passed "in recognition of the special educational needs . . . of children of limited English-speaking ability," these special needs, as well as the parameters from bilingual programs, were left up to the imagination of local educational agencies (LEAs). While the Office of Education defended the generous latitude with the rationale that these were "seed" monies intended to fund innovative projects, the absence of a clear-cut bilingual policy led to the misuse, misapplication, and general waste of funds which were already critically limited. (p. 86)

27. An additional problem along with the voluntary basis of the 1968 BEA was the large number of states—including some Southwestern states—that had English-only instruction laws at the time. Castellanos (1985) notes,

> Another problem at the time of the enactment of Title VII [BEA] was the fact that 21 states—including California, Louisiana, New Mexico, New York, Pennsylvania, and Texas—had English-only laws. Dr. Max Rafferty, who was the California chief school officer from 1963 to 1971, was vehemently against bilingual instruction. Ronald Reagan, who served as governor of California from 1966 to 1974, did not favor the bilingual approach either, but his public pronouncements were carefully guarded—tempered by the inevitable needs of his State. In seven states, including Texas, teachers risked criminal penalties or revocation of their licenses if caught teaching in other languages. Obviously, these districts were ineligible to receive funding that required instruction in languages other than English. Interestingly, when monies became available, many (not all) of these states scurried to change their laws to permit them to teach bilingually. Others simply ignored their own laws, procured the funds, and implemented the programs —albeit "illegally." (p. 86)

28. For other discussions on the complexities of legal claims for the right to bilingual education, see Carter, Brown, & Harris (1978); Johnson (1974); McFadden (1983).

29. Mexican Americans have not been the only minority group that has brought suit for bilingual education. In addition to the landmark Chinese American–initiated *Lau v. Nichols* (1974) case (which is discussed in note 44, this chapter), Puerto Ricans have also been actively involved. In *Aspira of New York v. Board of Education of the City of New York* (1974), Aspira (a Puerto Rican advocacy group) and students and their parents brought suit in 1972 on behalf of 150,000 Spanish-speaking students in New York City public schools. As discussed by Castellanos (1985),

The suit alleged that the school system had failed either to teach Spanish-speaking children in a language that they understood or to provide them with the English language skills needed to progress effectively in school. Plaintiffs charged they were faced with unequal treatment based on language and, thus, were denied equal educational opportunity as compared with English-speaking students. This was the first major [bilingual education] case involving Puerto Rican children's rights. (p. 119)

In January 1974, the Supreme Court decided *Lau v. Nichols* (1974), prompting plaintiffs to move for a summary judgment. After nearly two years of bitter resistance, the defendants relented in August 1974, and both parties worked out a consent decree. The school board acknowledged plaintiffs' rights to bilingual education under Title VI (§601) of the 1964 Civil Rights Act. The parties agreed to an extensive bilingual education plan, and the board was ordered to pay plaintiffs' attorney fees (Carter et al., 1978). By 1976, however, the school board still had not fully implemented the consent decree, and the court subsequently held it in contempt for failing to comply (*Aspira of New York v. Board of Education of the City of New York*, 1976).

In *Rios v. Read* (1978), another lawsuit initiated by Puerto Ricans (and other Latinos), plaintiffs sued the Patchogue-Medford School District (Long Island, NY) that the bilingual education program being employed was ineffective. The U.S. District Court for the Eastern District of New York ruled in favor of the plaintiffs, ruling,

A denial of educational opportunities to a child in the first years of schooling is not justified by demonstrating that the educational program employed will teach the child English sooner than programs comprised of more extensive Spanish instruction. While the District's goal of teaching Hispanic children the English language is certainly proper, it cannot be allowed to compromise a student's right to meaningful education before proficiency in English is obtained. (Rios v. Read, 480 F. Supp. at 22 [E.D.N.Y. 1978])

30. The U.S. Commission on Civil Rights (1972b, p. 14) noted that 47% of all Mexican American first graders did not speak English as well as the average Anglo first grader. Thus, through implication, about one in two Mexican American first graders could have benefited from bilingual education. The U.S. Commission on Civil Rights also reported, based on its 1969 survey, that "With the exception of a few districts in Texas, almost all bilingual education today is offered in small, scattered pilot programs" (p. 22). Furthermore, the report estimated that of over one million Mexican American students in districts with 10% or greater Mexican American enrollment, only twenty-nine thousand (3%) were enrolled in bilingual education classes.

31. Serna v. Portales Municipal Schools, 351 F. Supp. at 1281 (D.N.M. 1972).

32. *Id.* at 1280.

33. In his memorandum opinion, Judge Mechem wrote,

In the current school year, six Spanish-American teachers are employed at Lindsey. The school is continuing a bilingual-bicultural program for first graders which was instituted in the 1971–1972 school year and also provides a limited program in English as a second language which reaches approximately 40 students in the second through sixth grades. Neither of these programs or any other bilingual-bicultural program is offered in the other Portales elementary schools nor are any Spanish-surnamed teachers employed in those three schools. (*Id.* at 1281)

34. *Id.*

35. *Id.* The hiring of Spanish-surnamed teachers was recent. Judge Mechem noted,

Until 1970 none of the teachers in Portales schools was Spanish surnamed, including those teaching the Spanish language in junior and senior high school; there had never been a Spanish surnamed principal or vice-principal and there were no secretaries who spoke Spanish in the elementary grades (Serna v. Portales Municipal Schools, 499 F.2d at 1149 [10th Cir. 1974]).

36. Examiners administered intelligence and achievement tests *solely in English*. Regarding reading performance, the students at Lindsey—compared to the pupils at the three predominantly Anglo elementary schools—were nearly a full grade equivalent behind in language mechanics and language expression. With respect to intelligence test performance, the Lindsey students' IQ scores declined as they moved from first to fifth grade. Finally, the court record noted that as the disparity in achievement levels increased between the Mexican American and Anglo students, so did the disparities in school attendance and dropout rates (Serna v. Portales Municipal Schools, 499 F.2d at 1149–1150 [10th Cir. 1974]). These findings showing the relation between language status and school failure are not unexpected. As LEP students were promoted to the next grade, and in the absence of bilingual education, the students were faced with the sink-or-swim challenge. As learning demands (in English) increased in successive grades, school failure was imminent for many of these students.

Expert witnesses for plaintiffs also provided testimony regarding the deleterious affective effects of the children not having bilingual education. The Spanish-speaking Mexican American children, the experts testified, experienced feelings of inadequacy, lowered self-esteem, withdrawal, emotional disorders, and discipline problems (*Id.* at 1150).

37. Serna v. Portales Municipal Schools, 351 F. Supp. at 1282 (D.N.M. 1972).

38. *Id.*

39. Serna v. Portales Municipal Schools, 499 F.2d at 1151 (10th Cir. 1974).

40. *Id.* at 1151–1152.

41. *Id.* at 1152.

42. *Id.*

43. *Id.*

44. *Id.* at 1152–1153. *Lau v. Nichols* (1974), originally heard in the U.S. District Court for the Northern District of California, began as a class action lawsuit against the San Francisco Unified School District on behalf of 2,856 Chinese-speaking students. The plaintiffs alleged violations of the Fourteenth Amendment and the 1964 Civil Rights Act for the school district's failure to provide a remedy for Chinese-speaking students' lack of English proficiency. The district court denied all relief, and plaintiffs appealed to the Ninth Circuit. The appellate court affirmed the district court's decision, holding that appellees had provided the same facilities, materials, teachers, and curriculum to the Chinese-speaking students as to other students. Appellants petitioned for a rehearing en banc but were denied. In a strongly worded dissent on the denial of rehearing en banc, Judge Shirley Hufstedler wrote,

> The majority opinion concedes that the children who speak no English receive no education. . . . In short, discrimination is admitted. Discriminatory treatment is not constitutionally impermissible, they say, because all children are offered the same educational fare, *i.e.,* equal treatment of unequals satisfies the demands of equal protection. The Equal Protection Clause is not so feeble. Invidious discrimination is not washed away because the able bodied and the paraplegic are given the same state command to walk. (Lau v. Nichols, 483 F.2d at 806 [9th Cir. 1973])

Appellants petitioned for certiorari, which the U.S. Supreme Court granted in June 1973 (Lau v. Nichols, 412 U.S. 938 [1973]), and parties argued the case in December 1973. The Supreme Court, in its unanimous, landmark decision, embraced Judge Hufstedler's logic and reversed the Ninth Circuit's ruling: "there is no equality of treatment merely by providing students with the same facilities, textbooks, teachers, and curriculum; for students who do not understand English are effectively foreclosed from any meaningful education" (Lau v. Nichols, 414 U.S. at 566 [1974]). The justices did not, however, reach the Fourteenth Amendment to base their ruling but relied solely on §601 of the Civil Rights Act of 1964. Thus, the Supreme Court's ruling can be interpreted to mean that bilingual education is not a right guaranteed by the Constitution.

Although the Supreme Court in its *Lau* decision did find a violation of appellants' rights under Title VI (§601) of the Civil Rights Act of 1964, it needs to be underscored that the Court did *not* specify a remedy (nor did the appellants). Justice William O. Douglas wrote in his opinion,

> No specific remedy is urged upon us. Teaching English to students of Chinese ancestry who do not speak the language is one choice. Giving instructions to this group in Chinese is another. There may be others. Petitioners ask only that the Board of Education be directed to apply its expertise to the problem and rectify the situation. (*Lau v. Nichols*, 414 U.S. at 564–565 [1974])

As one can see, the *Lau* decision fell short of requiring bilingual education. The Supreme Court's ruling, however, left the subject of remedy open to interpretation. As such, bilingual education proponents were quick to act. The Department of Health, Education, and Welfare appointed a task force to establish guidelines to implement the *Lau* ruling (Castellanos, 1985; Crawford, 1995). The guidelines, which came to be known as the "Lau Remedies," were available in 1975. The Lau Remedies—though they lacked the legal status of federal legislation—informed districts

> how to identify and evaluate children with limited English skills, what instructional treatments would be appropriate, when children were ready for mainstream classrooms, and what professional standards teachers should meet. They also set timetables for meeting these goals. Most significant, the remedies went beyond the *Lau* decision, requiring that where children's rights had been violated, districts must provide bilingual education for elementary school students who spoke little or no English. "English as a second language is a necessary component" of bilingual instruction, the guidelines said, but "since an ESL program does not consider the affective or cognitive development of the students . . . an ESL program [by itself] is *not* appropriate." For secondary students, English-only compensatory instruction would usually be permissible. (Crawford, 1995, p. 46)

45. Serna v. Portales Municipal Schools, 499 F.2d at 1153 (10th Cir. 1974).

46. *Id.* at 1154.

47. Morales v. Shannon, 366 F. Supp. at 816 (W.D. Tex. 1973).

48. *Id.*

49. Morales v. Shannon, 512 F.2d at 412 (5th Cir. 1975).

50. Morales v. Shannon, 366 F. Supp. at 816 (W.D. Tex. 1973).

51. *Id.*

52. *Id.* at 823. Judge Wood, in his memorandum order, was aware of the Ninth Circuit Court of Appeals' ruling in the *Lau* case and the Supreme Court's as yet unreported ruling on *Lau* (see note 44, this chapter, for a brief discussion of *Lau*).

53. Morales v. Shannon, 366 F. Supp. at 824 (W.D. Tex. 1973). Prior to the filing of *Morales*, HEW officials came to Uvalde to hear complaints against the school district regarding bilingual education and other issues. Judge Wood did not give much credence to the findings of the HEW hearing, noting that the investigation was cursory and misinterpreted data (*Id.*)

54. *Id.* at 822.

55. *Id.*

56. *Id.*

57. *Id.* at 824.

58. Morales v. Shannon, 516 F.2d at 415 (5th Cir. 1975).

59. *Id.*

60. *Id.*

61. *Id.* As noted by Malakoff and Hakuta (1990), several months after the Supreme Court decided *Lau* in 1974, Congress codified the ruling into the Equal Educational Opportunity Act. This new legislation extended the *Lau* ruling to *all* public school districts, not only those receiving federal funds. The problem with the "appropriate action" requirement of §1703(f) of the Equal Educational Opportunity Act was what constituted the mandate of the term. As such, "courts varied in their interpretation, in line with the case-by-case remedy approach" (Malakoff & Hakuta, 1990, p. 35).

62. Keyes v. School District No. 1 of Denver, 380 F. Supp. at 674 (D. Colo. 1974).

63. Keyes v. School District No. 1 of Denver, 576 F. Supp. at 1505 (D. Colo. 1983).

64. Keyes v. School District No. 1 of Denver, 380 F. Supp. at 681 (D. Colo. 1974).

65. Keyes v. School District No. 1 of Denver, 521 F.2d at 481 (10th Cir. 1975).

66. Keyes v. School District No. 1 of Denver, 380 F. Supp. at 694 (D. Colo. 1974).

67. *Id.* at 694, 696.

68. Keyes v. School District No. 1 of Denver, 521 F.2d at 479–480 (10th Cir. 1975).

69. *Id.* at 480.

70. *Id.*

71. *Id.* at 481.

72. *Id.* at 482.

73. *Id.*

74. *Id.* at 483.

75. *Id.*

76. Keyes v. School District No. 1 of Denver, 576 F. Supp. at 1512–1513, 1518 (D. Colo. 1983).

77. *Id.* at 1519. For an interesting perspective from the school district on language-rights issues, see the analysis by Michael Jackson (1986), who served as chief litigator for the school district in *Keyes*.

78. Keyes v. School District No. 1 of Denver, 576 F. Supp. at 1520 (D. Colo. 1983).

79. *Id.*

80. Otero v. Mesa County Valley School District No. 51, 408 F. Supp. at 165 (D. Colo. 1975).

81. *Id.*

82. *Id.* at 163.

83. *Id.* at 164.

84. *Id.* at 165.

85. *Id.* at 165–166. Garrett's opinion is troublesome for two reasons. First, given that he served as an expert witness for the defendants and as the examiner of the language assessments, might there have been a conflict of interests? May Garrett have had some examiner bias? That is, having a low incidence rate of LEP students best served the interest of defendants. Second, a concern arises about the psychometric properties of the language-assessment instruments used. For example, the Dos Amigos Verbal Language Scales—a picture-elicitation measure that assesses expressive and receptive single-word vocabulary in both Spanish and English to derive a dominance score (Damico, 1991)—is noted to have psychometric issues. Hamayan and Damico (1991) comment,

> The standardization of this norm-referenced tool is good. However, *no reliability or validity information is presented in the manual* [italics added]. Some authorities suspect that the test may *underestimate Spanish dominance* [italics added] and that the task may be too difficult if the child does not understand the concept of opposite. (pp. 328–329)

The other language assessment instrument used, the STACL, is a short form of the parent test, the Tests for Auditory Comprehension of Language. The weaknesses are that neither the parent nor the short form have norms in Spanish. Also, the Spanish items are direct translations of the English items. This is a major shortcoming, as "A translation procedure implies that complexities of one language can be equated to complexities of another on a one-to-one basis" (Molina, 1978, p. 613).

It should be noted, however, that Dr. Gene Glass, defendants' expert in statistics and measurement, "established their [the two language-assessment instruments'] psychometric properties as being sufficient to assess English-Spanish proficiency" (Otero v. Mesa County Valley School District No. 51, 408 F. Supp. at 168 (D. Colo. 1975). Based on the limited legal record available on *Otero*, it is difficult to evaluate the accuracy of this assertion.

86. Otero v. Mesa County Valley School District No. 51, 408 F. Supp. at 166 (D. Colo. 1975).

87. *Id.* at 167.

88. *Id.*

89. *Id.* at 166.

90. *Id.*

91. *Id.* at 171.

92. *Id.* at 170.

93. *Id.* at 175–176.

94. *Id.* at 176.

95. *Id.*

96. Otero v. Mesa County Valley School District No. 51, 568 F.2d at 1314 (10th Cir. 1977).

97. *Id.*

98. *Id.* at 1316.

99. See note 76, chapter 3, this volume, for a description of the Yaqui Indians in Arizona.

100. Guadalupe Organization, Inc. v. Tempe Elementary School District, 587 F.2d at 1024 (9th Cir. 1978).

101. *Id.*

102. Given Judge Craig's dismissal of plaintiffs' complaint, he published no opinion. As such, all discussion provided here stems from the Ninth Circuit's ruling in *Guadalupe* (1978).

103. Guadalupe Organization, Inc. v. Tempe Elementary School District, 587 F.2d at 1024 (9th Cir. 1978).

104. *Id.* Interrogatories allow parties to a legal proceeding the opportunity to obtain necessary information from the other side long before trial, and this obtained information can help shape the litigation and strategy.

105. *Id.* at 1026.

106. *Id.* at 1028–1029.

107. *Id.* at 1029.

108. *Id.* at 1030.

109. Castaneda v. Pickard, 648 F.2d at 993 (5th Cir. 1981).

110. *Id.*

111. *Id.* at 992.

112. *Id.*

113. *Id.* at 1005.

114. *Id.* at 1008.

115. *Id.* at 1007.

116. *Id.* at 1009.

117. *Id.* at 1009–1010.

118. Castaneda v. Pickard, 781 F.2d at 470 (5th Cir. 1986).

119. *Id.* at 471.

120. *Id.* at 470.

121. None of the opinions I have read that are germane to the *Gomez* case mentioned the ethnicity of the plaintiffs. In personal communication (January 23, 2004), however, with law professor Fernando Colón-Navarro, he informed me that Mexican Americans served as the named plaintiffs and as the overwhelming majority of the other plaintiffs in this class action lawsuit. Professor Colón-Navarro, a MALDEF attorney, represented plaintiffs in *Gomez*.

122. Gomez v. Illinois State Board of Education, 614 F. Supp. at 344 (N.D. Ill. 1985).

123. *Id.*

124. *Id.*

125. *Id.* at 345–357.

126. Gomez v. Illinois State Board of Education, 811 F.2d at 1044 (7th Cir. 1987).

127. *Id.* at 1042.

128. *Id.* That is, the appellants approved the transitional bilingual education model chosen by the State of Illinois.

129. *Id.* Furthermore, given that the program did not meet the implementation criterion, the third criterion—proper evaluation—was a moot point for the Seventh Circuit.

130. Teresa P. v. Berkeley Unified School District, 724 F. Supp. at 700 (N.D. Cal. 1989).

131. Crawford (1995, p. 59).

132. Teresa P. v. Berkeley Unified School District, 724 F. Supp. at 713 (N.D. Cal. 1989).

133. This first paragraph on Proposition 227 draws from, with minor revisions, San Miguel & Valencia (1998, pp. 391–392).

134. Voters passed mandates for English-only schooling in Arizona in 2000 (see Crawford, 2000–2001) and Massachusetts in 2002 (Vaishnav, 2002). Colorado attempted to pass an English-only schooling plebiscite in 2002, but voters defeated it (Mitchell, 2002).

135. This sentence draws from, with minor revisions, San Miguel & Valencia (1998, p. 392).

NOTES TO CHAPTER 5

1. The introduction to this chapter draws, with revisions, from Valencia (1984a, pp. 1–2, 7–8, and 17) and Valencia (1980, p. 16).

2. The tax limitation movement that swept the nation in the late 1970s and early 1980s best exemplifies the widespread public resistance to invest further money in education. For example, in June 1978, California homeowners were so upset with exceedingly higher and ever-increasing property taxes that they overwhelmingly passed Proposition 13, a law that sliced property taxes an average of 56% (statewide). This heavy loss of revenue resulted in a deficit of $7 billion in the coffers of California public schools and local governments in fiscal year 1978–1979 (for a brief discussion of these developments, also see the *Serrano* case, chapter 3, this volume). In 1979, the financial crisis in California worsened as taxpayers passed Proposition 4, which put a lid on state spending (Valencia, 1980).

3. Zerchykov (1982) undertook the most comprehensive review of the literature on declining enrollments. Of the 250 studies reviewed, 57 (23%) dealt with school closures.

4. Although the literature was mainly prescriptive in nature, some scholarship sought to be more theoretical and empirical. See, for example, the entire

volumes of *Education and Urban Society* (1983, 15) and *Peabody Journal of Education* (1983, 60).

5. See Valencia (1984a) for a discussion of these four policy implications of school closures.

6. This section on the *Angeles* case draws, with revisions, from Valencia (1980, pp. 5–13).

7. Angeles v. Santa Barbara School District, Civil Action No. 127040, Superior Court, Santa Barbara County, California, August 1979.

8. See Ah Tye (1982) for a discussion of germane case law involving equal protection considerations. Ah Tye served as counsel for the plaintiffs in *Angeles*.

9. Experts and their respective fields and universities were Dr. Ruben W. Espinosa (demography, San Diego State University); Dr. Steven Moreno (testing, San Diego State University); Dr. Richard R. Valencia (educational/psychological development of racial minority children, University of California at Santa Cruz); Dr. M. Beatriz Arias (bilingual-multicultural education, University of California at Los Angeles). For a discussion of the experts' testimony, see Valencia (1980).

10. For further details on the sampling procedure, participants, interview instrument, and procedure, see Valencia (1984c).

11. Interested readers who wish to see my cites for these facts or sources in this coverage of *Castro* are directed to the endnotes in Valencia (1984b).

12. L.M. Stewart and Associates, *Investigation reports on the school closure decision by the Phoenix Union High School District*, at 3. U.S. Department of Education, Office for Civil Rights, June 17, 1981.

13. *An analysis of criteria for school closure: A report to the Board of Education.* Phoenix Union High School District, November 1, 1979.

14. Within the district and during litigation, observers had a common perception and consensus that a "minority" school was a school that had a combined enrollment of students of color of greater than 50%, and a "White" school had a White enrollment of greater than 50%.

15. A.M. Flores, Pre-Hearing Memorandum, August 3, 1982, at 1, Castro v. Phoenix Union High School District #210, Civil Action No. 82-302 (D. Ariz. August 30, 1982). Albert M. Flores, of the Phoenix law firm of Cordova, Flores, Morales, and Iníguez, was lead counsel for plaintiffs in *Castro*.

16. *Id.*

17. *Id.* at 2.

18. Memorandum of Findings and Order, August 30, 1982, at 5, Castro v. Phoenix Union High School District #210, Civil Action No. 82-302 (D. Ariz. August 30, 1982).

19. Here, I used the term "biased" to denote the notion of "unfairness." In this context, one can speak of how scores on some measure can be used in a decision-making or selection process. When viewed in this way, issues of social justice (i.e., fairness/unfairness) sometimes arise, and members of one group benefit more

than members of another group (for further discussion, see Valencia & Suzuki, 2001, p. 116).

20. See Gerard & Miller (1975); also, see Valencia (1984b) for discussion of this notion.

21. See Bryant (1968); Clement, Eisenhart, & Wood (1976); Felice & Richardson (1977a, 1977b).

22. See Edwards (1979); Gerard & Miller (1975); Mercer, Coleman, & Harloe (1974; cited in Epps, 1975); Schilhab (1976; cited in Phillips, 1978).

23. Based on personal communication I had with a detective from the Phoenix Gang Squad in August 1982, the police department's concerns were with a very small number of rival gang members who were expected to enroll at Central.

24. Memorandum of Findings and Order, August 30, 1982, at 9–10, Castro v. Phoenix Union High School District #210, Civil Action No. 82-302 (D. Ariz. August 30, 1982).

25. *Id.* at 3–4.

26. *Id.* at 6.

27. *Id.* at 6–7.

28. *Id.*

29. *Id.* at 6.

30. J.W. Brammer, Defendants' Petition for Approval of Alternate to Opening Phoenix Union High School, November 5, 1982, Castro v. Phoenix Union High School District #210, Civil Action No. 82-302 (D. Ariz. August 30, 1982). Brammer, of the Phoenix firm of DeConcini, McDonald, and Brammer, served as the counsel for the defendants.

31. Plaintiffs' Brief in Opposition to Entry of SJUSD's Proposed Desegregation Plan and in Support of Plaintiffs' Proposed Plan, Diaz v. San Jose Unified School District, 633 F. Supp. 808 (N.D. Cal. 1985).

32. Cynthia L. Rice, Stephen Kociol, and Gilbert P. Carrasco of the Legal Aid Society of Santa Clara County and Norma V. Cantú and Antonio Hernández of the Mexican American Legal Defense and Educational Fund served as counsel for plaintiffs.

33. Memorandum and Order Re: Desegregation Remedy, Diaz v. San Jose Unified School District, 633 F. Supp. at 821–822 (N.D. Cal. 1985).

34. See Reporter's Transcript Proceeding (at 9-19 to 9-107) for my court testimony regarding the closure of Gardner Elementary School and Peter Burnett Middle School and the conversion of San Jose High School to a school for grades 6 to 12, Diaz v. San Jose Unified School District, 633 F. Supp. 808 (N.D. Cal. 1985).

35. Diaz v. San Jose Unified School District, 633 F. Supp. at 820 (N.D. Cal. 1985).

36. *Id.* at 822.

37. There are some exceptions to this assertion. Bhatt (2005) reports that more

than a dozen cities across the country are experiencing declining enrollments. As such, school boards are considering school closures in order to save money. An example is the Detroit Public Schools (DPS), a district that has been experiencing severe enrollment declines over the past decade. The DPS School Board has closed some schools and plans to close dozens more. The closings have prompted a lawsuit by parents and advocacy groups who seek injunctive relief from further closings (*Orozco v. Detroit Board of Education*, 2007).

38. See Valencia (2002a, p. 56, Table 2.4).

NOTES TO CHAPTER 6

1. As discussed in chapter 5 of this book, declining student enrollments in the 1970s, coupled with inflation, forced school boards across the country to survive on austere budgets. One common belt-tightening strategy was to close schools and consolidate student bodies.

2. In re Alien Children Education Litigation, 501 F. Supp. at 555 (S.D. Tex. 1980).

3. The complete amendment of Texas Education Code §21.031 reads as follows:

(a) All children who are citizens of the United States or legally admitted aliens and who are over the age of five years and under the age of 21 years on the first day of September of any scholastic year shall be entitled to the benefits of the Available School Fund for that year.

(b) Every child in this state who is a citizen of the United States or a legally admitted alien and who is over the age of five years and not over the age of 21 years on the first day of September of the year in which admission is sought shall be permitted to attend the public free schools of the district in which he resides or in which his parent, guardian, or the person having lawful control of him resides at the time he applies for admission.

(c) The board of trustees of any public free school district of this state shall admit into the public free schools of the district free of tuition all persons who are either citizens of the United States or legally admitted aliens and who are over five and not over 21 years of age at the beginning of the scholastic year if such a person or his parent, guardian or person having lawful control resides within the school district. (Vernon Supp. 1976, p. 23)

4. In re Alien Children Education Litigation, 501 F. Supp. at 555 (S.D. Tex. 1980).

5. Doe v. Plyler, 458 F. Supp. at 571–572 (E.D. Tex. 1978).

6. This account of the Flores family and the events leading up to the *Doe v. Plyler* lawsuit is taken, in part, from a newspaper article written by Suzanne Gamboa (1994).

7. Doe v. Plyler, 458 F. Supp. at 572 (E.D. Tex. 1978).

8. *Id.*

9. *Id.* at 574.

10. *Id.* The actual quotient, which I calculated, is $1,156.

11. *Id.*

12. Based on my calculations, I estimate that the financial cost of the un-documented students (approximately $N = 52$) on the TISD was about 0.56%. This was calculated by multiplying 52 by $2,000 (the average per pupil expenditure in Texas at the time; see Cárdenas & Cortez, 1986) and dividing this product by the TISD budget of $18.5 million. Also, see *Doe v. Plyler*, 458 F. Supp. at 577 (E.D. Tex. 1978).

13. Doe v. Plyler, 458 F. Supp. at 574 (E.D. Tex. 1978).

14. *Id.* at 575.

15. The *Doe v. Plyler* opinion noted, "Because of their poverty, none of the parents of the named plaintiffs can afford to pay the tuition fee of $1,000 or any other significant sum" (458 F. Supp. at 575 [E.D. Tex. 1978]).

16. A few days after her dismissal, Ana Flores was allowed to return to school while the lawsuit worked its way through the courts. In the seventh grade, Ana withdrew from school due to her parents' divorce. Yet she persisted and later earned her high school equivalency (GED) degree. Under the auspices of the 1986 amnesty program (Immigration Reform and Control Act), Ana became a legal resident (Gamboa, 1994).

17. Hernandez v. Houston Independent School District, 558 S.W.2d at 125 (Tex. Civ. App.–Austin 1977, writ ref'd n.r.e.).

18. *Id.* at 123.

19. Doe v. Plyler, 458 F. Supp. at 573 (E.D. Tex. 1978).

20. *Id.*

21. Hernandez v. Houston Independent School District, 558 S.W.2d at 123 (Tex. Civ. App.–Austin 1977, writ ref'd n.r.e.).

22. Hernandez v. Houston Independent School District, 558 S.W.2d 121 (Tex. Civ. App.–Austin 1977, writ ref'd n.r.e.).

23. See chapter 3 of this book (notes 23 and 30, respectively) for definitions of "suspect class" and "fundamental right."

24. As Judge Shannon noted, the pertinent cases are listed in *Norwick v. Nyquist*, 417 F. Supp. at 917 (S.D. N.Y. 1976).

25. Hernandez v. Houston Independent School District, 558 S.W.2d at 124 (Tex. Civ. App.–Austin 1977, writ ref'd n.r.e.).

26. See *Graham v. Richardson*, 403 U.S. 365 (1971).

27. Hernandez v. Houston Independent School District, 558 S.W.2d at 124 (Tex. Civ. App.–Austin 1977, writ ref'd n.r.e.).

28. *Id.* at 125. This is referred to as a "point of error," which is defined as "a challenge by a party to a finding, ruling, or judgment of a trial court on the basis

that it is contrary to the evidence or to the law" (*Merriam-Webster's Dictionary of Law*, 1996, s.v. "point of error"; available online at: *http://dictionary.lp.findlaw. com/*). The appellants had other points of error designed to attack §21.031 on additional constitutional grounds. The Court of Civil Appeals ruled that those points of error would not be considered because the grounds for those points were not pleaded and were therefore waived.

29. Hernandez v. Houston Independent School District, 558 S.W.2d at 124 (Tex. Civ. App.–Austin 1977, writ ref'd n.r.e.).

30. All plaintiff children, except two, attended TISD schools in the 1976–1977 academic year. The exceptions were enrolled in the TISD Head Start program in summer 1977. Before the issuance of Judge Justice's preliminary injunction, none of the plaintiffs were attending TISD schools (they had been expelled).

31. Doe v. Plyler, 458 F. Supp. at 569, 572 (E.D. Tex. 1978).

32. *Id.* at 572.

33. Plaintiffs were fortunate to have Judge Justice hear their case. Appointed to the federal bench by President Lyndon B. Johnson in 1968, fellow jurists considered Judge Justice a liberal judge. Many of his rulings have protected the rights of racial/ethnic minorities, the politically powerless, and the poor. An extended version of this biographical note is available online at: *http://www.utexas.edu/ law/academics/centers/publicinterest/about/judgejustice.html*. Also, see Vara-Orta (2006) for a brief sketch of Judge Justice's career.

34. The Civil Rights Act of 1866, 42 U.S.C. §1981 (Equal rights under the law) reads as follows:

(a) Statement of equal rights

All persons within the jurisdiction of the United States shall have the same right in every State and Territory to make and enforce contracts, to sue, be parties, give evidence, and to the full and equal benefit of all laws and proceedings for the security of persons and property as is enjoyed by white citizens, and shall be subject to like punishment, pains, penalties, taxes, licenses, and exactions of every kind, and to no other.

35. Doe v. Plyler, 458 F. Supp. at 572 (E.D. Tex. 1978).

36. *Id.* at 573.

37. *Id.*

38. *Id.* at 576.

39. *Id.*

40. *Id.*

41. *Id.*

42. See discussion in preceding section and note 12 of this chapter.

43. Doe v. Plyler, 458 F. Supp. at 577 (E.D. Tex. 1978).

44. *Id.*

45. This fund "is currently made up of money set aside by the state from

current or annual revenues for the support of the public school system." See the Handbook of Texas Online at: *http://www.tsha.utexas.edu/handbook/online/ articles/AA/khakg.html.*

46. Doe v. Plyler, 458 F. Supp. at 577 (E.D. Tex. 1978).

47. *Id.* ADA is average daily attendance. This head count of students is used in formulating the amount of funding that schools receive.

48. Doe v. Plyler, 458 F. Supp at 580 (E.D. Tex. 1978).

49. In *Doe v. Plyler*, the U.S. Department of Justice was granted leave to submit an amicus curiae brief.

50. Plaintiffs, along with the U.S. Department of Justice via its amicus curiae brief, urged that strict scrutiny should be utilized because illegal aliens are, fundamentally, a suspect class. They meet all the traditional indices of suspectness: "(t)he class is . . . saddled with such disabilities, or subjected to such a history of purposeful unequal treatment, or relegated to such a position of political powerlessness as to command extraordinary protection from the majoritarian political process" (San Antonio Independent School District v. Rodriguez, 411 U.S. at 28 [1973]; quoted in *Doe v. Plyler*, 458 F. Supp. at 582 [E.D. Tex. 1978]).

51. Doe v. Plyler, 458 F. Supp. at 579 (E.D. Tex. 1978).

52. *Id.* at 580.

53. *Id.* at 583. It should be mentioned that the *Doe v. Plyler* court identified an additional indicator demonstrating that heightened scrutiny might be appropriate: suspect classification of wealth. That is, two relatively wealthy undocumented children were able to attend TISD schools by paying the $1,000 tuition fee, while poor undocumented children were excluded (see *Id.* at 581).

54. Judge Justice found that §21.031, as implemented in the TISD, violated the Supremacy Clause of the Constitution and was preempted by federal laws of immigration (e.g., Immigration and Nationality Act).

55. Doe v. Plyler, 458 F. Supp. at 584 (E.D. Tex. 1978).

56. *Id.* at 585.

57. *Id.* at 589. The court also reasoned that some of the undocumented children's parents, although in the United States illegally, owned property, paid taxes, and had minor children who were born in the United States and thus were citizens. As such, "The court can . . . invalidate state efforts that fail to demonstrate a rational basis that make scapegoats of a defenseless group, in an arbitrary, or even invidious manner" (*Id.* at 590).

58. *Id.* at 579. See, for example, *Mathews v. Diaz*, 426 U.S. 67 (1976) (dictum); *Wong Wing v. U.S.*, 163 U.S. 228 (1896).

59. Doe v. Plyler, 458 F. Supp. at 580 (E.D. Tex. 1978). See *Railway Express Agency v. New York*, 336 U.S. 106 (1949) (Jackson, J., concurring).

60. Doe v. Plyler, 458 F. Supp. at 593 (E.D. Tex. 1978).

61. Examples of analyses (mostly by legal scholars) of *Doe v. Plyler* and aspects

of the subsequent legal record are Bernal (1979); Cantú & Garza (1981); Cárdenas & Cortez (1986); Cooper (1995); Flores (1984); García y Griego (1986); Heberton (1982); Hull (1981, 1983); Langford (1979); Leboo (1984); Osifchok (1982); Porter (1983); Sax (1979); Towler (1981); Wilcoxen (1985).

62. The rulings in *Hernandez* and *Doe v. Plyler* epitomize a classic instance of legal indeterminacy, a major theme of this book. Both Judge Shannon in *Hernandez* and Judge Justice in *Doe v. Plyler* heard—within a year of each other—identical complaints (the unconstitutionality of excluding Mexican-origin undocumented children from school) and reviewed the identical section of the TEC (§21.031), yet the two judges' rulings were starkly contrasting.

63. In re Alien Children Education Litigation, 482 F. Supp. 326 (JPMDL 1979).

64. 28 U.S.C. §1407 (Multidistrict Litigation): "When civil actions involving one or more common questions of fact are pending in different districts, such actions may be transferred to any district for coordinated or consolidated pretrial proceedings."

65. In re Alien Children Education Litigation, 501 F. Supp. 544 (S.D. Tex. 1980).

66. *Id.* at 550. The class was defined
as all children who are over five and not over twenty-one years of age at the beginning of the scholastic year and have been or will be denied admission to the public schools in the State of Texas on a tuition-free basis because of the alienage provisions of section 21.031 of the Texas Education Code. (*Id.* at 553)

67. *Id.* at 550.

68. "Collateral estoppel" is defined as "barring the relitigation of issues litigated by the same parties on a different cause of action" (*Merriam-Webster's Dictionary of Law*, 1996, s.v. "collateral estoppel"; available online at: *http://dictionary. lp.findlaw.com/*).

69. In re Alien Children Education Litigation, 501 F. Supp. at 552 (S.D. Tex. 1980).

70. *Id.*

71. *Id.*

72. *Id.* at 555.

73. *Id.* at 561. Particularly ironic about this aspect of psychological harm is that the seventeen cases of *Alien Children* were consolidated in 1979, the "International Year of the Child" (see *Id.* at 549).

74. *Id.* at 561.

75. See, for example, his role in the *Cisneros* case (chapter 1, this volume; see Valencia [2006a] for a tribute to Carter's contributions to the field of Mexican American education).

76. In re Alien Children Education Litigation, 501 F. Supp. at 562 (S.D. Tex. 1980).

77. *Id.* at 576.

78. *Id.*

79. *Id.* at 577. In 1979, the TEA reported that 2,872,719 students were enrolled in K–12 public schools (see Motion for Further Relief, p. 7, U.S. v. Texas, Civil Action No. 6:71-CV-5281 [E.D. Tex. February 9, 2006]). If Dr. Bustamante's estimate of twenty thousand undocumented school-age children living in Texas is correct, then they constituted an infinitesimal proportion, 0.70%, of the total school enrollment.

80. In re Alien Children Education Litigation, 501 F. Supp. at 579 (S.D. Tex. 1980).

81. *Id.* at 579. It is interesting that nowhere in the *Alien Children* opinion is it mentioned that the State provided an estimate of the monetary cost due to the enrollment of undocumented students. The cost can be easily estimated, however, using several bits of data in existence around the time of *Alien Children*: (a) the average per-pupil expenditure in Texas, which was $2,000, (b) the estimated number of undocumented children in school, which was about thirteen thousand, and (c) the annual state expenditure for K–12 education, which was $3,000,000,000 (all data are from Cárdenas & Cortez, 1986). Based on my calculation, the financial cost of the undocumented students on the State's education budget is a minuscule 0.87% (i.e., $26,000,000 ÷ $3,000,000,000). Even using the larger estimate of twenty thousand undocumented children (Texas residents) provided by Dr. Bustamante (see previous discussion), the estimated fiscal cost is still extremely small (1.33%). Finally, using the estimate of 120,000 undocumented children (Texas residents) that the State presented, I calculate the estimated financial cost to be a mere 8.0%.

82. *Id.* at 579–580. It appears that by 1979, Texas had worked its way through the hardship of the 1970s widespread inflation across the country.

83. *Id.* at 581.

84. *Id.* at 581–582.

85. *Id.* at 582.

86. *Id.*

87. *Id.* at 583.

88. *Id.*

89. *Id.* at 597.

90. *Id.*

91. The Fifth Circuit's opinion was not published. The case pending appeal was the *Doe v. Plyler* case, also under review by the Fifth Circuit.

92. Certain Named and Unnamed Non-Citizen Children and Their Parents v. Texas, 448 U.S. 1327 (1980). For reasons unknown, somewhere between the U.S. District Court for the Southern District of Texas and the U.S. Supreme Court, the

name of the case "*In re Alien Children Education Litigation*," was changed to "*Certain Named and Unnamed Non-Citizen Children and Their Parents v. Texas*."

93. *Id.* at 1330.

94. *Id.*

95. *Id.* at 1332.

96. *Id.* at 1334.

97. Doe v. Plyler, 628 F.2d 448 (5th Cir. 1980).

98. DeCanas v. Bica, 424 U.S. 351 (1976).

99. Doe v. Plyler, 628 F.2d at 452–453 (5th Cir. 1980).

100. *Id.* at 455.

101. *Id.* at 457.

102. *Id.* This legal theory has been referred to as the "corruption of blood principle" (Shulman, 1995). Children born in the United States of undocumented immigrants are morally faultless for the illegal acts of their parents and thus should not be penalized for their parents' actions (also, see Houston, 2000).

103. Doe v. Plyler, 628 F.2d at 458 (5th Cir. 1980).

104. *Id.* at 459.

105. *Id.* at 459–461.

106. *Id.* at 460.

107. *Id.* at 461.

108. *Id.*

109. Plyler v. Doe, 451 U.S. 968 (1981).

110. 28 U.S.C. §1251(b) reads,

The Supreme Court shall have original but not exclusive jurisdiction of:

(1) All actions or proceedings to which ambassadors, other public ministers, consuls, or vice consuls of foreign states are parties;

(2) All controversies between the United States and a State;

(3) All actions or proceedings by a State against the citizens of another State or against aliens.

111. Texas v. Certain Named and Unnamed Undocumented Alien Children, 452 U.S. 937 (1981).

112. Plyler v. Doe, 457 U.S. 202 (1982).

113. Justice William J. Brennan wrote the opinion, and he was joined by Justices Harry Blackmun, Thurgood Marshall, Lewis F. Powell, and John P. Stevens. Chief Justice Warren Burger wrote the dissenting opinion, and he was joined by Justices Sandra Day O'Connor, William H. Rehnquist, and Byron White.

114. For a comprehensive discussion of the "outlaw" theory, see Oren (1979).

115. Plyler v. Doe, 457 U.S. at 215 (1982).

116. *Id.* at 219.

117. *Id.* at 221.

118. *Id.* at 220.

119. *Id.*

120. *Id.* at 218–219, 223–224.

121. *Id.* at 218. See Osifchok (1982) for an excellent discussion on the Supreme Court's utilization of intermediate scrutiny in *Plyler v. Doe* (1982).

122. Plyler v. Doe, 457 U.S. at 219 (1982).

123. See Tribe (1978; cited in Osifchok, 1982).

124. Brown v. Board of Education of Topeka, 347 U.S. at 493 (1954); quoted in *Plyler v. Doe*, 457 U.S. at 222–223 (1982).

125. Also, see Osifchok (1982).

126. Plyler v. Doe, 457 U.S. at 227 (1982).

127. *Id.* at 228.

128. *Id.* at 229. Also, see notes 12 and 81, this chapter.

129. *Id.* at 229–230.

130. It should also be noted, however, that in the very first line of Chief Justice Burger's dissenting opinion it appeared that the minority agreed with Justice Brennan's opinion regarding the irrationality of §21.031. Chief Justice Burger wrote, "Were it our business to set the Nation's social policy, I would agree without hesitation that it is senseless for an enlightened society to deprive any children—including illegal aliens—of an elementary education" (*Id.* at 242).

131. *Id.* For more discussion on Chief Justice Burger's dissenting opinion, see Hull (1983).

132. Plyler v. Doe, 457 U.S. at 243 (1982).

133. *Id.* at 244.

134. It is difficult to derive an accurate count of the number of undocumented Mexican schoolchildren in the United States. Thus, one needs to extrapolate. According to a recent report by the Urban Institute (Passel, Capps, & Fix, 2004), there are an estimated 9.3 million undocumented immigrants in the United States, of whom over half (57%) are Mexican origin. Of the 9.3 million undocumented, about 1.6 million (17.2%) are children under eighteen years of age.

135. The voting patterns for other groups of color were intermediate between Whites and Latinos. Both African Americans and Asian Americans voted 47% "for" and 53% "against" (Johnson, 1996).

136. League of United Latin American Citizens v. Wilson, 908 F. Supp. 755 (C.D. Cal. 1995). Also, see López (2005). See Favish (n.d.) for an opinion that the judge who ruled in this case made four errors.

137. League of United Latin American Citizens v. Wilson, 997 F. Supp. 1244 (C.D. Cal. 1997). Also, see López (2005).

138. López (2005) also raises two other concerns in addition to the attack on *Plyler* via state plebiscites. First, she asserts that "the continued vitality of *Plyler* lies in the renewed call for immigration reform, so that once the undocumented student is educated in our country, he or she will have the opportunity to work legally in the United States" (p. 1404). Second, she discusses the serious problems

that undocumented Latino students have in gaining access to higher education and obtaining loans and in being charged for nonresident tuitions. López also discusses the federal efforts that are in progress to remedy these latter obstacles.

139. See Carter (1997) for a comprehensive analysis of what it would take for *Plyler* to survive an attack at the U.S. Supreme Court in the event a Proposition 187–like initiative is passed by a state, a lawsuit emerges, and the case is eventually granted certiorari by the Supreme Court.

140. See Vote Yes on Arizona Proposition 200 website: *http://yesonprop200. com/.*

141. "What You Should Know about the Latest on Proposition 200," *Arizona Republic,* November 14, 2004; available online at: *http://www.azcentral.com/specials/ special03/articles/1114Prop200QA14.html.*

142. "Arizona to Clamp Down Even Harder on Illegals," NewsMax.com, March 4, 2005; available online at: *http://www.newsmax.com/archives/articles/2005/ 3/4/112027.shtml.*

NOTES TO CHAPTER 7

1. Richards v. LULAC, 868 S.W.2d at 309 (Tex. 1993).

2. This section on the Type I access problem draws, with some revisions, from Valencia (2002b, pp. 28–29).

3. For a discussion of factors that lead to the Type I access problem for Mexican Americans, see Valencia (2002b, pp. 29–32).

4. California, with 33.9 million residents, had the largest population. U.S. Census website, "State and County QuickFacts," *http://quickfacts.census.gov.*

5. Alaska is largest in area, at 616,240 square miles. nationalatlas.gov website, *http://nationalatlas.gov/articles/mapping/a_general.html.*

6. The United States has 2,000 miles coterminous with Mexico, of which 1,254 (63%) are along the border of Texas (*Special Report: State Functions at the Texas-Mexico Border and Cross-Border Transportation,* January 2001, Office of the Comptroller of Public Accounts; available online at: *http://www.window.state. tx.us/specialrpt/border/*).

7. Although the term "Border Area" is used in the legal record (e.g., *Clements v. LULAC,* 800 S.W.2d 948 [Tex. App.–Corpus Christi 1990]), the referent "Border Region" is more appropriate. The term "region" is used by a number of scholars to capture the historical and cultural roots, as well as the physical geography, of different locales—particularly within states (see Jones & Kauffman, 1994). It should also be noted that the large concentration of low-SES students of color located far distances from comprehensive universities within a state are not confined to the Border Region of Texas. Other examples include the southern regions of Georgia and Arkansas (see Jones & Kauffman, 1994).

8. The percentages of the other racial/ethnic groups, in descending order, were White (30.8%), Black (3.6%), Asian/Pacific Islander (0.7%), American Indian (0.2%), and Other (0.2%) (U.S. Department of Commerce, Bureau of the Census, 1990).

9. Although the huge Border Region is predominantly rural, data from the 1990 U.S. Census showed that 2.9 million (85.9%) of the 3.4 million residents lived in six Metropolitan Statistical Areas (MSAs) within the Border Region. These MSAs, in alphabetical order, are Brownsville-Harlingen, Corpus Christi, El Paso, Laredo, McAllen-Edinburg-Pharr, San Antonio (U.S. Department of Commerce, Bureau of the Census, 1990). The San Antonio and Corpus Christi MSAs, however, also include some counties that are not considered to be part of the Border Region. The populations from those non–Border Region counties were therefore excluded from my calculations for these two MSAs.

10. In this 1998 report of the Office of the Comptroller of Public Accounts, it is noted that for "analytical reasons" the study defined the Border Region as covering the forty-three (not forty-one) counties west of Interstate 37 and south of Interstate 10.

11. It is noted, however, in the opinion issued by the Texas Supreme Court in this case that *fifteen* individual Mexican Americans served as plaintiffs (*Richards v. LULAC*, 868 S.W.2d at 308 [Tex. 1993]).

12. The fifteen universities and university systems are the University of Texas system, the Texas A&M University system, the Texas State University system, East Texas State University, Stephen F. Austin State University, West Texas State University, Midwestern State University, the University System of South Texas, North Texas State University, Texas Southern University, Texas Women's University, Lamar State University, Texas Tech University, the University of Houston system, and Pan American University.

13. Unfortunately, Judge Euresti did not provide a published opinion. As such, for analyses of the trial's deliberation and his decision, I relied on the published rulings from the Texas Court of Appeals and the Texas Supreme Court. I also relied on some secondary sources (e.g., Fields, 1988a, 1988b; Jones & Kauffman, 1994; Mangan, 1991; Ramseyer, 2000).

14. Class was defined as

All persons of Mexican-(Hispanic) ancestry who reside in the Border Area consisting of these forty-one contiguous counties along the border in Texas . . . and who are now or will be students at Texas public senior colleges and universities or health related institutions (or who would be or would have been students at Texas public senior colleges and universities or health related institutions were it not for the resource allocation policies and practices complained of in Plaintiffs' petition). This class does not include persons with claims for specific monetary or compensatory relief. (Richards v. LULAC, 868 S.W.2d at 308 [Tex. 1993])

15. In its opinion, the Texas Supreme Court limited the term "higher education" to institutions of "state universities, senior colleges, and professional schools" (*Id.*).

16. *Id.*

17. *Id.* at 310.

18. *Id.* at 309. Plaintiffs argued that the six findings of fact needed to be contextualized against a historical backdrop. The legal record noted, "These disparities exist against a history of discriminatory treatment of Mexican Americans in the border area (with regard to education and otherwise), and against a present climate of economic disadvantage for border area residents" (*Id.*).

19. In 1988, twelve public colleges and universities were located near the Texas-Mexico border. Corpus Christi State University, Laredo State University, and Texas A&I University constituted the "University System of South Texas" (Ramseyer, 2000). In alphabetical order, the other nine institutions are Bee County College, Del Mar College, El Paso Community College, Laredo Junior College, Pan American University, Pan American University at Brownsville, Texas Southmost College, Texas State Technical Institute–Rio Grande Campus, and the University of Texas at El Paso (see Fields [1988a] for a figure showing the location of the twelve institutions). For reasons unclear, Fields (1988a) fails to mention two other Border Region institutions of higher education that existed in 1988: Sul Ross State University and the University of Texas at San Antonio.

20. According to Guerra (2005), these three doctoral programs were in bilingual education ($n=2$) and mining engineering ($n=1$).

21. Regarding the availability of master's degree programs around the time of the *LULAC v. Clements* lawsuit, the Border Region offered the fewest ($n=6$) for every one hundred thousand residents compared to other regions. For example, Central Texas had fourteen for every hundred thousand residents, and West Texas offered sixteen for every hundred thousand residents (Fields, 1988a). With respect to public medical schools, law schools, or other professional schools, none existed in the Border Region (Fields, 1988a).

22. Salaries of faculty teaching at colleges and universities along the Texas-Mexico border also lagged behind the state as a whole. In 1987–1988, at Texas colleges and universities the top-three faculty ranks had a mean salary of $38,179. In comparison, professors in the Border Region received lower salaries (e.g., the University of Texas at El Paso, $35,155; Corpus Christi State University, $32,399; Pan American University, $32,392; Laredo State University, $31,661) (Fields, 1988b).

23. Jones and Kauffman (1994) note that this definition is the Carnegie Foundation's definition for a "Doctoral I" institution (see Carnegie Foundation for the Advancement of Teaching, 1987).

24. Jones and Kauffman (1994) note, "Such regions are defined by the common heritage of their lands and peoples—i.e., differentiating settlement history, ethnicity, political and religious characteristics, underlain by their physical geography"

(p. 269). For example, the Border Region "reflects Spanish and Mexican settlement history, in addition to the physiographic, climatic, and vegetational regions of the South Texas Plain and the Trans-Pecos or Mountain and Basin" (p. 269).

It should be stated that the plaintiffs in *LULAC v. Clements* constructed the forty-one-county Border Region as a palpable locale, but defendants did not necessarily accept it. As noted in the legal record, the Border Region was a "carefully drawn region, labeled the 'Border Area.' This particular zone was defined solely by plaintiffs and does not constitute a regional designation recognized in the administration of the Texas higher education system" (Richards v. LULAC, 868 S.W.2d at 311 [Tex. 1993]).

25. Jones and Kauffman (1994) note that the mileages to the closest comprehensive university are averaged by region. That is, each average is weighted by the number of students in each county "actually attending a public, 4-year university somewhere in the state in 1989. This is done so that the average mileages will reflect where potential students for the comprehensive universities are located within the region" (p. 272).

26. Two years prior to the jury verdict in *LULAC v. Clements*, defendants appealed Judge Euresti's certification of the plaintiff class to the Texas Court of Appeals, Corpus Christi, arguing that the plaintiffs lacked standing to sue (Clements v. LULAC, 800 S.W.2d 948 [Tex. App.–Corpus Christi 1990]). For example, appellants complained that three plaintiffs, who based their lawsuit on the lack of a law school in the Rio Grande Valley, had already graduated from law school. The appellate court ruled, "A class so defined does not preclude one from its membership who has already graduated, if other criteria denoting that the representative has a claim typical of the class is present" (*Id.* at 953). In all, the appellate court affirmed the trial court's certification of the class.

27. Richards v. LULAC, 868 S.W.2d at 309 (Tex. 1993).

28. *Id.* at 310.

29. *Id.*

30. *Id.*

31. *Id.*

32. Richards v. LULAC, 863 S.W.2d at 449 (Tex. 1993).

33. Richards v. LULAC, 868 S.W.2d at 310 (Tex. 1993).

34. *Id.*

35. *Id.*

36. *Id.* at 306. In light of Ann Richards's election as Governor on November 6, 1990, she replaced Governor William C. Clements as lead defendant in this lawsuit.

37. *Id.* at 311.

38. *Id.*

39. *Id.*

40. McGowan v. Maryland, 366 U.S. at 427 (1961). Other examples of germane

case law cited by the Texas Supreme Court in *Richards v. LULAC* are *Mouton v. State*, 627 S.W.2d 765, 767 (Tex. App.–Houston [1st Dist.] 1981, no pet.); *Salsburg v. Maryland*, 346 U.S. 545 (1954).

41. Richards v. LULAC, 868 S.W.2d at 312 (Tex. 1993).

42. *Id.* at 314. Olivas (2005) succinctly captures this passage by noting, "The [Texas Supreme] Court determined that the [plaintiffs'] theory of the case was both under-inclusive and over-inclusive" (p. 184).

43. Richards v. LULAC, 868 S.W.2d at 314 (Tex. 1993).

44. *Id.* at 316.

45. *Id.*

46. *Id.*

47. *Id.* at 317.

48. *Id.* at 315. *U.S. v. Fordice* (505 U.S. 717 [1992]), which plaintiffs initially brought forth in 1975 and which was ruled on by the U.S. Supreme Court in 1992, was concerned with the de jure segregation of the public university system in Mississippi. Notwithstanding the Court's historic decision in *Brown v. Board of Education of Topeka* (i.e., *Brown I*, 347 U.S. 483 [1954]; *Brown II*, 349 U.S. 294 [1955]), by the early 1990s Mississippi still maintained its de jure system of segregation in higher education, as evidenced by the existence of five nearly all-White universities and three almost exclusively African American universities. The Fifth Circuit left overwhelmingly undisturbed the lower court's findings and conclusions that the State had brought itself into compliance with the Equal Protection Clause. The U.S. Supreme Court, however, ruled that the lower courts did not use the correct legal standard in their rulings. As such, the Court vacated *Fordice* and remanded it for further proceedings consistent with its opinion.

49. Richards v. LULAC, 868 S.W.2d at 316 (Tex. 1993).

50. *Id.*

51. Texas House of Representatives, House Committee on Higher Education (2002), *Interim Report 2002* (p. 55). Available online at: *http://www.house.state. tx.us/committees/reports/77interim/higher_education.pdf.*

52. *Id.* Although the Legislature passed funding in 1989, lawmakers did not approve the actual dispersal of money until 1993. See Bracco (1997), *Texas Case Study Summary* (p. 6). Available online at: *http://www.capolicycenter.org/texas/ texas.html.*

It appears that the passage of the STBI and the accompanying funding plans likely worked to the advantage of the appellants in the Texas Supreme Court's ruling in *Richards v. LULAC*. The opinion noted that the State, via the STBI, was attempting "to increase educational opportunities for minority students in Texas" (Richards v. LULAC, 868 S.W.2d at 314 [Tex. 1993]).

53. Texas House of Representatives, House Committee on Higher Education (2002), *Interim Report 2002* (p. 55). Available online at: *http://www.house.state. tx.us/committees/reports/77interim/higher_education.pdf.*

As part of the STBI, a major change occurred in institutional affiliations. Prior to the STBI implementation, the Legislature incorporated Corpus Christi State University, Laredo State University, and Texas A&I University into the Texas A&M system, and Pan American University at Brownsville and Pan American University (located in the city of Edinburg) into the UT system. Many individuals viewed the incorporation of these five universities into the two major higher education systems in Texas as an upgrade by giving them "more political clout." See *State Structures: Texas Case Study: Characteristics of the Texas Higher Education System* (p. 6). Available online at: *http://www.capolicycenter.org/texas/texas3. html*.

54. *House Committee on Higher Education Texas House of Representatives Interim Report 2002* (p. 56). Available online at: *http://www.house.state.tx.us/ committees/reports/77interim/higher_education.pdf.*

55. *Id.*

56. *Id.*

57. It is beyond the scope of this discussion to examine the underlying factors related to the mixed outcomes of the STBI, as presented by Ramseyer (2000). A brief example, however, concerns the detrimental consequences seen at the University of Texas–Pan American. Located in Edinburg, the University of Texas–Pan American competes with South Texas Community College, situated about ten miles away in McAllen (the largest city in the McAllen-Edinburg-Pharr MSA). At the time, South Texas Community College had been undergoing construction of newer facilities. This development of the community college, being situated in a larger urban population and having considerably lower costs in tuition and fees, appeared to have a negative effect on the enrollment at the University of Texas–Pan American. For further analyses of the mixed findings as related to the STBI funding of the targeted Border Region institutions, see Ramseyer (2000), particularly chapters 7 and 8.

58. Richards v. LULAC, 868 S.W.2d at 312 (Tex. 1993). The Texas Supreme Court aptly noted that the U.S. Supreme Court has ruled that the Equal Protection Clause protects groups that are easily identifiable and singled out for discrimination in the community. In particular, the Court has recognized that Mexican Americans, as a separate class, experience discrimination, and such unequal treatment amounts to racial discrimination. See *Hernandez v. Texas*, 347 U.S. 475 (1954), which dealt with discrimination in the process of petit jury selection; *Keyes v. School District No. 1 of Denver, Colorado*, 413 U.S. 189 (1973), discrimination in the school desegregation process; *White v. Regester*, 412 U.S. 755 (1973), discrimination in legislative reapportionment; *Castaneda v. Partida*, 430 U.S. 482 (1977), discrimination in the process of grand jury selection.

59. A report from the Texas Higher Education Coordinating Board (1997) notes that college student enrollment in South Texas (which is defined in this re-

port as including the lower half of the Border Region [*n* = 30 counties] and seventeen additional counties) is projected to increase by over forty thousand by 2010.

NOTES TO CHAPTER 8

1. Portions of the first, second, and third paragraphs draw, with revisions, from Valencia, Villarreal, & Salinas (2002, p. 287), and Valencia & Villarreal (2005, p. 116).

2. See Berliner and Biddle's (1995) book, *The Manufactured Crisis: Myths, Fraud, and the Attack on America's Public Schools,* for a powerful critique of *A Nation at Risk* and other sources that have proffered groundless criticisms of American public schools.

3. The twenty-six states are Alabama, Alaska, Arizona, California, Florida, Georgia, Idaho, Indiana, Louisiana, Maryland, Massachusetts, Minnesota, Mississippi, Nevada, New Jersey, New Mexico, New York, North Carolina, Ohio, Oklahoma, South Carolina, Tennessee, Texas, Utah, Virginia, and Washington.

4. The sixteen states are Arkansas, California, Connecticut, Delaware, Florida, Georgia, Hawaii, Louisiana, Mississippi, New Mexico, North Carolina, Oklahoma, South Carolina, Texas, Virginia, and Wisconsin (see American Federation of Teachers, 2001, p. 33, Table 12). Of these sixteen states, all but Arkansas, Georgia, and Hawaii have promotion policies at the middle school level (D.C. also does not have a promotion policy at this level).

5. For an in-depth critique of one state's accountability system (i.e., Texas), see Valenzuela (2005b). Regarding other scholars who have leveled criticisms at high-stakes testing and the standards-based school reform movement, see, for example, Amrein & Berliner (2002), Darling-Hammond (2004), Darling-Hammond & Wise (1985), Flores & Clark (1997), Gunzenhauser (2003), Haney (2002), Horn (2003), McNeil (2000a), Meier (2002), Nichols, Glass, & Berliner (2005), Orfield & Kornhaber (2001), Pearl (2002), Valencia & Guadarrama (1996), Valencia, Valenzuela, Sloan, & Foley (2001), and Valencia & Villarreal (2003). For a comprehensive volume that offers commentaries from both sides of the equity/accountability debate, see Skrla & Scheurich (2004).

In addition to criticisms of high-stakes testing expressed in scholarly publications, numerous professional organizations have opposed high-stakes testing. A computer search I conducted in January 2006 identified over seventy such organizations (available online at: *http://www.educationalequity.net/opposition.htm*). These professional organizations include, for example, the International Reading Association, the American Association of School Administrators, the American Psychological Association, and the American Educational Research Association. The position statements of these various organizations are thematically similar in their opposition to high-stakes testing (e.g., the narrowing of the curriculum;

excessive weight of high-stakes testing in decision making). The position statement of the American Psychological Association (APA) is particularly germane to
this chapter. The APA noted,

> Some public officials and educational administrators are increasingly call-
> ing for the use of tests to make high-stakes decisions, such as whether a
> student will move on to the next grade level or receive a diploma. School
> officials using such tests must ensure that students are tested on a curricu-
> lum they have had a fair opportunity to learn, so that certain subgroups
> of students, such as racial and ethnic minority students or students with
> a disability or limited English proficiency, are not systematically excluded
> or disadvantaged by the test or the test-taking conditions. Furthermore,
> high-stakes decisions should not be made on the basis of a single test score,
> because a single test can only provide a "snapshot" of student achievement
> and may not accurately reflect an entire year's worth of student progress
> and achievement. (Available online at: *http://www.apa.org/pubinfo/testing.
> html*)

6. "1 in 10 Seniors Is Left Behind," *Austin American-Statesman*, May 24, 2005,
p. A10.

7. *Id.*

8. For a fuller discussion of the Louisiana retention data, see Valencia & Villarreal (2003, 2005). Given the serious consequences of failure on the LEAP 21
for a substantial proportion of Louisiana's fourth- and eighth-grade students (particularly African Americans), parents initiated a class action lawsuit in *Parents for
Educational Justice v. Picard* (2000), challenging the high-stakes use of the LEAP
21 to make promotion/retention decisions as unfair. In her unpublished opinion,
Judge Edith Brown Clement of the U.S. District Court for the Eastern District of
Louisiana ruled that none of the individual plaintiffs had suffered "actual injury"
(i.e., grade retention) at the time of the filing of the case (the results of the LEAP
21 testing had not yet become available). As such, Judge Clement dismissed the
case for plaintiffs' lack of standing. Plaintiffs were undaunted, however, and re-
filed the case as *Parents Against Testing Before Teaching v. Orleans Parish School
Board* (2000), requesting a three- to five-year moratorium of the LEAP 21 for
grade-promotion purposes "until all responsible parties are held fully accountable
for their part in maintaining quality public schools" (quoted in Robelen, 2001, p.
9). The District Court, however, rejected plaintiffs' request. Plaintiffs appealed the
decision, first to the Fifth Circuit, which upheld the district court ruling (*Parents
Against Testing Before Teaching v. Orleans Parish School Board,* 2001), then petitioned the U.S. Supreme Court for certiorari to hear the case, which was denied
(*Parents Against Testing Before Teaching v. Orleans Parish School Board,* 2002).

9. There are other lawsuits regarding teacher-competency testing. These cases,
which were brought forth by African American prospective and incumbent

teachers, are (listed in chronological order) *Armistead v. Starkville Separate School District*, 325 F. Supp. 560 (N.D. Miss. 1971), *aff'd in part, rev'd in part*, 461 F.2d 276 (5th Cir. 1972); *U.S. v. North Carolina Association of Educators v. North Carolina*, 400 F. Supp. 343 (E.D. N.C. 1975); *York v. Alabama State Board of Education*, 581 F. Supp. 779 (M.D. Ala. 1983), 631 F. Supp. 78 (M.D. Ala. 1986); *Allen v. Alabama State Board of Education*, 612 F. Supp. 1046 (M.D. Ala. 1985), *rev'd*, 816 F.2d 575 (11th Cir. 1987); *Richardson v. Lamar County Board of Education*, 729 F. Supp. 806 (M.D. Ala. 1989), *aff'd*, 935 F.2d 1240 (11th Cir. 1991); *Groves v. Alabama State Board of Education*, 776 F. Supp. 1518 (M.D. Ala. 1991); *Fields v. Hallsville Independent School District*, 906 F.2d 1017 (5th Cir. 1990); *Frazier v. Garrison Independent School District*, 980 F.2d 1514 (5th Cir. 1993).

10. Although the federal government brought forth the initial action in *U.S. v. Texas* (1970), its own counsel described its appearance in the 1985 case as having the role of amicus curiae. See *U.S. v. Texas*, 628 F. Supp. at 306 (E.D. Tex. 1985).

11. *Id.* at 323.

12. *Id.* at 304–305.

13. *Id.* at 305. See Texas Education Code §13.032(e).

14. *U.S. v. Texas*, 628 F. Supp. at 305–306 (E.D. Tex. 1985).

15. Texas was not alone in exhibiting this pattern of considerably lower fail rates among students of color, compared to Whites, on teacher competency tests during the early to mid-1980s. Similar patterns were also seen in Arizona, California, Florida, New Mexico, and New York (see Valencia & Aburto, 1991a, pp. 193–194, Table 6).

16. *U.S. v. Texas*, 628 F. Supp. at 306–321 (E.D. Tex. 1985).

17. *Id.* at 313.

18. *Id.* at 306.

19. *Id.* at 312–313.

20. *Id.* at 313; the Fifth Circuit ruling is *Camenisch v. University of Texas*, 616 F.2d 127 (5th Cir. 1980).

21. *U.S. v. Texas*, 628 F. Supp. at 313 (E.D. Tex. 1985).

22. *Id.* at 313–314. The SEM is used to estimate the range, with varying degrees of statistical confidence, in which the "true" score of an individual falls on a particular test. The testimony by the ETS representatives actually boded well for the plaintiff students, given that their observed scores were very slightly below the PPST preclusionary scores and that the SEM of the PPST was approximately eight points.

23. *Id.* at 314.

24. *Id.* at 315–318. Judge Justice noted that "Discriminatory purpose is elusive and difficult to prove, especially when what must be proven is discriminatory intent on the part of a state agency or board" (*Id.* at 315). It appeared that the Supreme Court ruling in *Arlington Heights v. Metropolitan Housing Corp.* (429 U.S.

252 [1977]) assisted Judge Justice in his decision making. In *Arlington Heights* the High Court commented,

> Rarely can it be said that a legislature or administrative body operating under a broad mandate made a decision motivated solely by a single concern, or even that a particular purpose was the "dominant" or "primary" one. . . . Determining whether invidious discriminatory purpose was a motivating factor demands a sensitive inquiry into such circumstantial and direct evidence of intent as may be available. The impact of the official action— whether it "bears more heavily on one race than another," may provide an important starting point. (*Id.* at 265–266)

25. U.S. v. Texas, 628 F. Supp. at 315 (E.D. Tex. 1985). See, e.g., *U.S. v. Texas Education Agency*, 679 F.2d 1104 (5th Cir. 1982) (Port Arthur Independent School District); *U.S. v. Texas Education Agency*, 647 F.2d 504 (5th Cir. 1981) (South Park Independent School District).

26. U.S. v. Texas, 628 F. Supp. at 316 (E.D. Tex. 1985).

27. *Id.* Judge Justice wrote,

> At the hearing, defendant's witnesses compared the requirements of teacher's education courses, student teaching, and the PPST to the requirements of a written examination, a driving test, and an eye examination for a driver's license. To carry the analogy further, it is similar to allowing an applicant to receive a driver's license simply by passing the eye examination, when it is not at all certain that the eye examination actually measures the ability to see, when the eye examination has only been in effect for a year, and when it is well known that minorities fail the eye examination at much higher rates than Whites, although they do well on the driving test and have been driving on the roads of Texas for years. (*Id.*; written as note 22 in the opinion)

28. *Id.* at 318. See *Board of Regents v. Roth*, 408 U.S. 564 (1972).

29. U.S. v. Texas, 628 F. Supp. at 318 (E.D. Tex. 1985). In *Debra P. v. Turlington*, 644 F.2d 397 (5th Cir. 1981), it was argued that students have a property interest in a high school diploma.

30. U.S. v. Texas, 628 F. Supp. at 318 (E.D. Tex. 1985).

31. *Id.* at 319–320.

32. *Id.* at 322.

33. *Id.*

34. The EEOA was introduced in chapter 4 (*Morales v. Shannon*, 1973), this volume.

35. U.S. v. Texas, 628 F. Supp. at 323 (E.D. Tex. 1985).

36. U.S. v. LULAC, 793 F.2d 636 (5th Cir. 1986). The careful reader might wonder why the case changed names when it was appealed from the district court to the Fifth Circuit. This confusion is due to certain conventions that the courts use to name cases. At the district court level, although LULAC was an intervenor, as

noted earlier in this section, the case was filed under the aegis of the original *U.S. v. Texas* (1970) suit; thus, the case name was retained. At the appellate level, however, the United States switched sides, joining Texas as appellants, and LULAC was appellee. Given that the United States and LULAC are the first two parties listed on the opinion, the case was renamed *U.S. v. LULAC* (1986).

37. *Id.* at 639.

38. U.S. v. Texas, 628 F. Supp. at 320–321 (E.D. Tex. 1985).

39. U.S. v. LULAC, 793 F.2d at 640 (5th Cir. 1986).

40. U.S. v. Texas, 628 F. Supp. at 320 (E.D. Tex. 1985).

41. U.S. v. LULAC, 793 F.2d at 639 (5th Cir. 1986).

42. Albert Kauffman, e-mail message to author, January 23, 2006.

43. Texas Education Code, §51.306(b). By law, authorities required first-year students to pass the TASP to enroll in upper-division courses. Also, students needed to pass the TASP to receive an associate degree or to enter teacher education programs.

44. See chapter 3, this volume, for discussion of *Edgewood* and other school financing cases.

45. For this history, see *Association of Mexican-American Educators v. California*, 937 F. Supp. at 1400 (N.D. Cal. 1996).

46. The court records note the race/ethnicity of eight of the fifteen plaintiffs (*Id.* at 1401–1402). For the other seven plaintiffs, I have used their surnames to deduce race/ethnicity.

47. The CBEST, developed by ETS, is a virtual clone of the PPST (also developed by ETS). Drawing from Peterson (1984), Valencia and Aburto (1991b) have noted that the CBEST and PPST "share virtually identical test specifications and similar moderate reliabilities" (p. 197).

48. Association of Mexican-American Educators v. California, 937 F. Supp. at 1401 (N.D. Cal. 1996).

49. Association of Mexican-American Educators v. California, 836 F. Supp. at 1539–1540 (N.D. Cal. 1993).

50. *Id.* at 1544. See subsection (2)(B) of the Civil Rights Restoration Act of 1987 (Pub. L. No. [100–259], 102 Stat. 28 [1987]). The Restoration Act amended Title VI by affixing a broader definition of the terms "program or activity."

51. Lau v. Nichols, 414 U.S. 563 (1974).

52. 29 C.F.R. §1607 (1978). The Civil Service Commission, the EEOC, the Department of Justice, and the Department of Labor jointly promulgated the "Uniform Guidelines" (29 C.F.R. §1607.1[A]). The Uniform Guidelines do not obligate the courts to follow the 80-percent rule, but the principle can have persuasive force. For other ways of measuring adverse impact, see later discussion of the *GI Forum v. Texas Education Agency* (2000) case in this chapter.

53. Association of Mexican-American Educators v. California, 937 F. Supp. at 1409 (N.D. Cal. 1996).

54. 42 U.S.C. §2000e-2(a)(1).

55. Association of Mexican-American Educators v. California, 836 F. Supp. at 1549 (N.D. Cal. 1993).

56. Association of Mexican-American Educators v. California, 937 F. Supp. at 1407 (N.D. Cal. 1996).

57. Contreras v. City of Los Angeles, 656 F.2d 1267 (9th Cir. 1981).

58. In his opinion, Judge Orrick spoke at some length of the CBEST validity studies. See Association of Mexican-American Educators v. California, 937 F. Supp. at 1412–1420 (N.D. Cal. 1996).

59. *Id.*

60. *Id.* at 1417.

61. *Id.* at 1419.

62. *Id.*

63. *Id.* at 1427–1428.

64. *Id.* at 1428.

65. Original appeal was *Association of Mexican-American Educators v. California*, 183 F.3d 1055 (9th Cir. 1999). The opinion was initially issued on July 12, 1999, but amended on October 28, 1999. Also, the original opinion was not published. The amended opinion appears as *Association of Mexican-American Educators v. California*, 195 F.3d 465 (9th Cir. 1999).

66. Association of Mexican-American Educators v. California, 195 F.3d at 473–474 (9th Cir. 1999). Due to space limitations I do not discuss appellants' second claim regarding the expert witness. See *Id.* at 492–493.

67. *Id.* at 474. Also due to space limitations I do not discuss appellees' second claim about legal costs. See *Id.* at 493–495.

68. *Id.* at 481.

69. *Id.* at 482–484.

70. *Id.* at 495.

71. *Id.* at 498.

72. *Id.* at 497.

73. *Id.* at 499–500.

74. Association of Mexican-American Educators v. California, 208 F.3d 786 (9th Cir. 2000). See note 177 of chapter 1, this volume, for a full explication of "en banc."

75. Association of Mexican-American Educators v. California, 231 F.3d at 589–590 (9th Cir. 2000).

76. The court dismissed three students, who did not appear to testify, for failure to prosecute. GI Forum v. Texas Education Agency, 87 F. Supp.2d at 668 (W.D. Tex. 2000).

77. In the 2002–2003 school year, the TEA replaced the TAAS testing program with the Texas Assessment of Knowledge and Skills (TAKS) testing pro-

gram. Present students need to pass the TAKS exam to receive a high school diploma.

78. Complaint (p. 4), GI Forum v. Texas Education Agency, Civil Action No. SA-97-CA-1278 (W.D. Tex. 1997). Available online at: *http://www.bc.edu/research/csteep/CTESTWEB/TAAS/taasleg.html.*

79. *Id.* at 4–5.

80. *Id.* at 5.

81. Expert report of Dr. Walter Haney, Plaintiffs' Exhibit P36, GI Forum v. Texas Education Agency, Civil Action No. SA-97-CA-1278 (W.D. Tex. 1997).

82. Complaint (pp. 2–3), GI Forum v. Texas Education Agency, Civil Action No. SA-97-CA-1278 (W.D. Tex. 1997).

83. In order to protect the identity of this plaintiff, I have selected not to cite the legal document (i.e., declaration) from which this quote is excerpted.

84. Complaint (pp. 7–8), GI Forum v. Texas Education Agency, Civil Action No. SA-97-CA-1278 (W.D. Tex. 1997).

85. At my request, Leticia M. Saucedo (co-counsel in the *GI Forum v. TEA* case) graciously agreed to write an article ("The Legal Issues Surrounding the TAAS Case") for the Special Issue co-edited by Valencia and Bernal (2000a).

86. For a comprehensive analysis of the legal issues and theory of the *GI Forum v. TEA* case, see Fernández (2001); also, see Moran (2000). For the reader who is interested in reading excerpted portions of most of the experts' reports (plaintiffs' and defendants' experts) who participated in *GI Forum v. TEA*, see Gómez, Kastely, & Holleman (2000). For broader analyses of high-stakes testing mandates and litigation, see Elul (1999) and O'Neill (2003). Finally, for a historical perspective of high-stakes testing and high school graduation, see Dorn (2003).

87. Debra P. and similarly situated African American twelfth-grade students who had failed, or who thereafter failed, Florida's exit-level exam (the State Student Assessment Test) brought forth *Debra P. v. Turlington*. The litigation record of the *Debra P.* case is 474 F. Supp. 244 (M.D. Fla. 1979), *aff'd in part, vac'd and rem'd in part*, 644 F.2d 397 (5th Cir. 1981), *pet. for reh'g en banc denied*, 654 F.2d 1079 (5th Cir. 1981), 564 F. Supp. 177 (M.D. Fla. 1983), *aff'd*, 730 F.2d 1405 (11th Cir. 1984).

88. Regarding the *GI Forum v. TEA* defendants' position on the relationship between *GI Forum* and *Debra P.*, see the article by defendants' expert witness, Phillips (2000a, pp. 242–245).

89. See, for example, *Debra P. v. Turlington* (1981), *Larry P. v. Riles* (1984), *Cureton v. NCAA* (1999), *Groves v. Alabama Board of Education* (1991), *Sharif v. New York State Education Department* (1989), and *Richardson v. Lamar County Board of Education* (1989). See Saucedo (2000, pp. 420–421, n. 1) for a brief statement of judicial findings in these cases.

90. Saucedo (2000), however, points out that plaintiffs indeed did produce

evidence that the defendants knowingly discriminated. For example, the State Board of Education was shown empirically based investigations that documented the White/minority gap in TAAS exit-level exam pass rates *before* it arbitrarily set the cut (i.e., pass) score on the exit exam at 70. This assertion by plaintiffs, plus two other evidential points, are—as noted by Saucedo (p. 415)—"all elements of a claim of intentional discrimination based on circumstantial evidence" (see *Arlington Heights v. Metropolitan Housing Development Corporation*, 1977).

91. Quoted in Saucedo (2000, p. 416). Order granting in part and denying in part defendants' motion for clarification, GI Forum v. Texas Education Agency, Civil Action No. SA-97-CA-1278 (W.D. Tex. 1997). Order is on file with Leticia M. Saucedo. Also, see Prado (1999).

92. These three elements were also germane to the Title VI claim in *AMAE v. California* (1996), which was previously discussed in this chapter.

93. Portions of this overview (as well as accompanying notes) draw, with revisions, from Valencia and Bernal (2000b, pp. 425–433, 436–437, and 440).

94. Our summary of opinions (Valencia & Bernal, 2000b) is based not only on our understanding of views expressed through direct means (e.g., depositional and trial testimony by witnesses, both expert and nonexpert; reports and documents submitted as evidence) but also on our broader sense of the substantive issues that helped shape this significant educational case. We need to underscore, however, that the framework of issues presented in Table 8.2 is based on our perceptions. The framework does not necessarily reflect the views of all experts (and nonexperts) and counsel involved in the *GI Forum v. TEA* case.

95. There is considerable literature available to support this major position of structural inequality in schooling. Regarding African American students, see, for example, Feagin & Feagin (1999), Kozol (1991), and Lomotey (1990). With respect to Mexican American students, see, for example, Donato (1997), Moreno (1999), San Miguel (1987), San Miguel & Valencia (1998), and Valencia (1991, 2002c).

96. This section regarding my argument draws, with minor revisions, from Valencia (2000, pp. 446–447).

97. Plaintiffs advanced a very similar argument in *Debra P. v. Turlington* (1979).

98. It appears that the defendants' ahistorical position regarding discrimination hit its mark with the court. In his order regarding defendants' motion for summary judgment, Prado (1999) wrote,

> The United States Supreme Court, in *United States v. Fordice*, 505 U.S. 717 (1992), held that plaintiffs alleging that a state practice that was rooted in prior discriminatory policies could be prohibited without a finding that the State, in engaging in the practice, acted with a discriminatory purpose. *See Fordice*, 505 U.S. at 734 n.8. Because Plaintiffs have alleged that the TEA [Texas Education Agency] here acted against a backdrop of prior discrimination, the Defendants argue that they must, as in *Fordice*, demonstrate

that the discriminatory effects of the TAAS test are rooted in Texas' history of discriminatory educational practices. The Court disagrees.

First, it is unclear whether Plaintiffs are bringing a specific *"Fordice"* claim. To the extent that they are, the Court agrees with Defendants that such a claim must be rejected. While Plaintiffs have demonstrated that a history of discrimination exists in the State, they have not shown that the TAAS test itself is rooted in that history. *See Fordice*, 505 U.S. at 729–30 & n.4. . . . There is no evidence that the implementation of the TAAS test, which is a tool to identify problems in education and hold schools and students accountable for those problems, stems from this discrimination.

The Plaintiffs are not limited to *Fordice* in bringing their equal protection claim, however. A finding that the challenged practices are not rooted in prior segregation simply means that the Plaintiffs may proceed with their claim under traditional equal protection standards. *Id.* at 737 n.6. Thus, the Plaintiffs are required to demonstrate intentional discrimination and may attempt to do so by relying, in part, on circumstantial evidence, including a history of prior discrimination by the state actor. In that event, however, the history of prior discrimination is relevant only insofar as it supports an inference of *intent*, which remains the threshold showing. The Court finds that the evidence presented here does not support an inference of intent. (pp. 7–8)

99. For a similar understanding of the OTL construct, see Husen (1967). For a review of the notion of OTL, see Anderson (1985).

100. Regarding the weak association between TAAS performance and course grades, the defendants' position was that the poor connection was due to the high unreliability of grades as indicators of students' mastery of subjects (see Treisman, 1999). Such assertions influenced Judge Prado's decision (see *GI Forum v. Texas Education Agency*, 87 F. Supp.2d at 680 [W.D. Tex. 2000]). See Haney (2002) for his perspective on why Judge Prado's reasoning was flawed.

101. Furthermore, as discussed earlier, most of the student plaintiffs failed to pass a TAAS exam section (typically mathematics) by just one or two points. In light of the SEM of tests (see note 22, this chapter), it would have been psychometrically allowable, and morally correct, to conclude that the student plaintiffs' true score on the TAAS exit-level exam was likely *above* the cut score.

102. These two sentences draw, with slight revisions, from Valencia & Bernal (2000c, p. 407).

103. See *Michael H. v. Gerald D.*, 491 U.S. 110 (1989); *Regents of University of Michigan v. Ewing*, 474 U.S. 214 (1985).

104. §§28.085, 4.002, and 28.025.

105. GI Forum v. Texas Education Agency, 87 F. Supp.2d at 682 (W.D. Tex. 2000). For the Fifth Circuit's discussion of procedural and substantive aspects, see *Debra P. v. Turlington*, 644 F.2d at 404 (5th Cir. 1981).

106. GI Forum v. Texas Education Agency, 87 F. Supp.2d at 682 (W.D. Tex. 2000).

107. *Id.*

108. See earlier discussion of *AMAE v. California* (1996) for introduction of the 80-percent rule.

109. Fassold referred to the 80-percent rule as the "four-fifths rule." The other measures of disparate impact that he used were (a) the Hazelwood rule, (b) the Shoben rule, and (c) the rule of practical significance. Data analyses using these four rules can detect whether the differences between the pass rates of White and minority examinees are statistically significant. See Fassold (2000) for discussion of these various measures to examine adverse impact.

110. GI Forum v. Texas Education Agency, 87 F. Supp.2d at 676 (W.D. Tex. 2000).

111. *Id.* at 679. Here, Judge Prado cited *Wards Cove Packing Co. v. Atonio*, 490 U.S. 642 (1989), an employment-discrimination claim filed under Title VII of the 1964 Civil Rights Act. According to Rebell (1991), the Supreme Court in *Wards Cove* reversed the long-standing *Griggs v. Duke Power Co.* doctrine (401 U.S. 424 [1971]) by substantially lessening the burden of proof on employers in Title VII lawsuits.

112. GI Forum v. Texas Education Agency, 87 F. Supp.2d at 679 (W.D. Tex. 2000).

113. *Id.* at 676.

114. *Id.* at 681.

115. *Id.*

116. *Id.* at 673.

117. *Id.* at 680.

118. *Id.*

119. *Id.* at 683.

120. *Id.*

121. *Id.*

122. *Id.* at 683–684.

123. Regarding the issue of judicial deference to states, also see Elul (1999), written before the *GI Forum v. TEA* ruling.

124. See, for example, *San Antonio Independent School District v. Rodriguez*, 411 U.S. 1 (1973).

125. For legislative efforts in Texas, as a case in point, see Valenzuela (2005a). Also, see Hinton (2005) and Jackson & Prieto (2005). At the time of completing this book, proponents of multiple criteria assessment have proved unsuccessful in getting germane bills passed in Texas (see Valenzuela, 2005a).

126. See, for example, Valencia & Aburto (1991c); Valencia & Villarreal (2003); Valencia, Villarreal, & Salinas (2002); Valenzuela (2002).

127. See Johnson (2004, pp. 70–76).

128. In Valencia (1982), I refer to multiple criteria assessment as "multiple data sources in assessment" (pp. 79–81).

129. This principle discussed by Gronlund has also been advocated by the Board on Testing and Assessment of the National Research Council: "An educational decision that will have a major impact on a test taker should not be made solely or automatically on the basis of a single test score" (Heubert & Hauser, 1999, p. 3). Although information/data other than test scores are used in high-stakes testing decision making, high-stakes exam scores usually have *determinative weight* (see Valencia, Villarreal, & Salinas, 2002, p. 296).

130. The 2,500% increase is my calculation derived from data in Amrein & Berliner (2002) and the Center on Education Policy (2005).

NOTES TO THE CONCLUSION

1. Mexican American student isolation can also occur when these students attend schools with African American students, hence forming a very high-enrollment and racially identifiable "minority" school.

2. The Preston Hollow neighborhood is well known for a number of wealthy people who reside there (e.g., Dallas Mavericks owner Mark Cuban and billionaire H. Ross Perot) or are former residents (e.g., President George W. Bush). Presently, the value of homes in Preston Hollow range from $200,000 to $9 million, with a median value of $251,000. Information available online at *http://en.wikipedia.org/wiki/Preston_Hollow* and *http://dallas.housealmanac.com/subdivision-preston-hollow.htm*.

3. Memorandum Opinion and Order, p. 12, Santamaria v. Dallas Independent School District, Civil Action No. 3:06-CV-692-L (N.D. Tex. November 16, 2006).

4. *Id.* at 4–5. Also see Supplementary Expert Report (Valencia, 2006c).

5. See Preliminary Expert Report (Valencia, 2006b) and Supplementary Expert Report (Valencia, 2006c).

6. Memorandum Opinion and Order, p. 2, Santamaria v. Dallas Independent School District, Civil Action No. 3:06-CV-692-L (N.D. Tex. November 16, 2006). Also see Preliminary Expert Report (Valencia, 2006b).

7. Complaint (April 18, 2006), Santamaria v. Dallas Independent School District, Civil Action No. 3:06-CV-692-L (N.D. Tex. November 16, 2006).

8. For a comprehensive explication, see Supplementary Expert Report (Valencia, 2006c).

9. *Id.*

10. The other defendants (the DISD, the DISD Board of Trustees, and DISD Superintendent Hinojosa) were not found liable.

11. Memorandum Opinion and Order, p. 102, Santamaria v. Dallas Independent School District, Civil Action No. 3:06-CV-692-L (N.D. Tex. November 16, 2006).

12. *Id.* at 108.

13. *Id.* at 79.

14. *Id.* at 104.

15. Memorandum Opinion and Order, p. 18, Santamaria v. Dallas Independent School District, Civil Action No. 3:06-CV-692-L (N.D. Tex. April 10, 2007).

16. U.S. v. Texas, 321 F. Supp. 1043 (E.D. Tex. 1970).

17. U.S. v. Texas, 342 F. Supp. 24 (E.D. Tex. 1971).

18. *Id.* at 24.

19. *Id.* at 30.

20. Motion for Further Relief, U.S. v. Texas, Civil Action No. 6:71-CV-5281 (E.D. Tex. February 9, 2006). See note 194 of chapter 1 for a full explanation of "intervene."

21. U.S. v. Texas, 506 F. Supp. 405 (E.D. Tex. 1981).

22. U.S. v. Texas, 680 F.2d 356 (5th Cir. 1982).

23. Motion for Further Relief, U.S. v. Texas, Civil Action No. 6:71-CV-5281 (E.D. Tex. February 9, 2006).

24. *Id.* at 10.

25. *Id.* at 7. This is my calculation. In the Motion for Further Relief (p. 7), the record noted that in 1979 the TEA reported that K–12 public schools enrolled 2,872,719 students, of whom 198,618 (6.9%) were deemed LEP. For the 2004–2005 school year, the TEA reported that 4,440,644 total students were enrolled in Texas's public schools, and 684,007 (15.4%) were considered LEP.

26. TAKS is Texas's state-mandated achievement test for students in grades 3–11, covering, for example, reading, writing, and mathematics.

27. These three academic problems are described in Motion for Further Relief, pp. 8–9, U.S. v. Texas, Civil Action No. 6:71-CV-5281 (E.D. Tex. February 9, 2006). In a similar Mexican American–initiated bilingual education case, *Flores v. Arizona* (2005), involving the academic problems of LEP students, the record noted,

> The Court was also asked to preclude the State from requiring ELL students to pass the Arizona's Instrument to Measure Standards ("AIMS") test as a necessary criteria to receive a diploma and graduate from high school until the State has properly funded ELL programs for a sufficient period of time to provide ELL students with a meaningful opportunity to achieve the State's academic standards that are measured by the AIMS test. (p. 1113)

28. Motion for Further Relief, p. 17, U.S. v. Texas, Civil Action No. 6:71-CV-5281 (E.D. Tex. February 9, 2006).

29. HB 1, which the Legislature passed prior to HB 3, had the intent to correct the constitutional violation ruled on in *Neeley v. West Orange-Cove* (2005) (see chapter 2, this volume) by providing considerably more state revenue to fund public schools and to allow local school districts to exercise discretion in setting property tax rates. By contrast, the Legislature intended HB 3 to close the

loopholes in the franchise tax by requiring certain businesses to pay taxes. Also, HB 3 broadened the tax base and lowered the rate (Texas Legislature Online, 2006).

30. IDRA, located in San Antonio, Texas, is an independent, private organization whose goal is to strengthen public schools for all children, particularly students of color, the poor, and those who are non-English speaking.

31. The disparity is my calculation.

32. The way such funding in Texas occurs is through local bond elections. In their report, Dawn and McLaughlin (1996) estimated that construction and renovation costs for new and older school facilities was about $4.8 billion, covering about 38% of Texas schoolchildren and youths. Not surprisingly, a need for this funding is disproportionately seen in property-poor school districts in the Border Region (Valencia, 2002b). Rapidly growing suburban districts are also in need.

33. Examples of cities and towns that have passed ordinances intended to crack down on illegal immigration are Escondido, California; Farmers Branch, Texas; Hazelton, Pennsylvania; Pahrump, Nevada; and Valley Park, Missouri (Moscoso, 2006b). On July 26, 2007, U.S. District Court Judge James M. Munley (Middle District of Pennsylvania) struck down Hazelton's stern anti-immigration ordinance (Associated Press, 2007). He ruled that federal law preempted the ordinance and that it violated plaintiffs' due process rights. Hazelton's legislation was emulated by local communities across the country.

34. The ordinances are available online at: *http://www.ci.farmers-branch.tx.us/ Communication/Ordinance%20No%202892.html*.

35. *Merriam-Webster's Dictionary of Law* (1996, s.v. "jus soli"). Available online at: *http://dictionary.lp.findlaw.com/*. *Jus soli* is typically contrasted with *jus sanguinis*, which is defined as "A rule of law that a child's citizenship is determined by that of his or her parents" (*Merriam-Webster's Dictionary of Law,* 1996, s.v. "jus sanguinis").

36. See *Calvin v. Smith,* 77 Eng. Rep. 377 (K.B. 1608).

37. See "All Persons Born or Naturalized . . . The legacy of *U.S. v. Wong Kim Ark*" (UC Hastings College of the Law Library, Summer 2001). Available online at: *http://library.uchastings.edu/library/Library%20Collections/Displays/wkadisplay/ index.htm*.

38. For an extensive review of the Schuck and Smith (1985) book, see Carens (1987). For a critique, see Eisgruber (1997).

39. Available online at: *http://www.numbersusa.com/text?ID=218*. See David Dellinger's (1995) statement against H.R. 1363 before the Subcommittees on Immigration and Claims and on the Constitution of the House Committee on the Judiciary.

40. The wording of HB 28 is available online via the Texas Legislature's search engine at: *http://www.capitol.state.tx.us/Home.aspx*.

41. The legislative history of HB 28 is available online via the Texas Legisla-

ture's website: *http://www.capitol.state.tx.us/BillLookup/History.aspx?LegSess=80R &Bill=HB28.*

42. U.S. Constitution, Article V.

43. As we have seen in chapter 8, Mexican American and African American plaintiffs failed in their efforts in *GI Forum v. Texas Education Agency* (2000) to have the State modify the use of the Texas Assessment of Academic Skills test to make it nondiscriminatory. The trial helped to raise the serious issues surrounding high-stakes testing for students of color. As Angela Valenzuela (2005a) has noted,

> Following the trial, a small, multiethnic group of university faculty, gradu-
> ate students, and grassroots advocates for children (Parents United to Re-
> form TAAS Testing) united into a coalition working toward twin goals: to
> increase awareness of the harmful effects of high-stakes testing and to pro-
> mote the use of multiple compensatory criteria for academic assessment.
> . . . Through our published work, as well as through opinion-editorial
> pieces, scholarly conferences, community presentations, and the dissemina-
> tion of pertinent information through listservs and websites . . . we have
> been able to reach a variety of audiences. One especially successful effort
> to educate communities of color and other stakeholders throughout the
> state and nation took place during the opening days of the Texas legisla-
> tive session on January 26, 2001. The event brought . . . together legislators,
> legislative staff, and an 800-strong, statewide representation of Latino stu-
> dents, parents, educators, and community activists. During the open-mike
> session, researchers, community members, and Latino educational leaders
> repeatedly voiced concern over test abuse. This public exchange, along with
> the federal trial and a rally organized by League of United Latin American
> Citizens (LULAC) activists in Houston on January 27, 2001 to challenge the
> accountability system, were among the first broad-based expressions of dis-
> enchantment in the Latino community regarding high-stakes testing. (p. 5)

In sum, the early political agitation described by Valenzuela eventually generated agendas among Texas legislators to eliminate the oppressive nature of the
one-size-fits-all state-mandated testing program. These collective efforts demonstrate that in some instances political, rather than litigative, strategies are more
likely to bear fruit. As a case in point, Texas State Senator and Chair of the Senate Education Committee Florence Shapiro (R-Plano) proposed a bill in the 80th
Legislature to replace the Texas Assessment of Knowledge and Skills examination
with end-of-course examinations for grades 9–12. The Legislature passed SB 1031,
and Governor Rick Perry signed the resolution into law on June 15, 2007. It will
go into effect in the 2011–2012 school year. See a summary of SB 1031 online at:
http://www.capitol.state.tx.us/tlodocs/80R/billtext/html/SB01031F.htm.

44. The text in this paragraph and the next one draws, with revisions, from
Moreno & Valencia (2002, p. 227) and Valencia (2002d, pp. 367–368).

References

Abeson, A., & Bolick, N. (1974). *A continuing summary of pending and completed legislation regarding the education of handicapped children.* Reston, VA: Council for Exceptional Children.

Abramowitz, S., & Rosenfeld, S. (1978). Setting the stage. In S. Abramowitz & S. Rosenfeld (Eds.), *Declining enrollment: The challenge of the coming decade* (pp. 1–17). Washington, DC: National Institute of Education.

Achor, S., & Morales, A. (1990). Chicanas holding doctoral degrees: Social reproduction and cultural ecological approaches. *Anthropology & Education Quarterly, 21,* 269–287.

Acosta, T.P. (2001). Edgewood ISD v. Kirby. *Handbook of Texas.* Austin: Texas State Historical Association. Available online at: *http://www.tsha.utexas.edu/handbook/online/articles/EE/jre2.html.*

Acuña, R.F. (2007). *Occupied America: A history of Chicanos* (6th ed.). New York: Longman.

Ah Tye, K. (1982). Equal protection considerations in school closures. *Clearinghouse Review, 15,* 1010–1014.

Alemán, E., Jr. (2005). Is Robin Hood the "Prince of Thieves" or a pathway to equity? Applying Critical Race Theory to school finance political discourse. *Educational Policy, 20,* 113–142.

Allen v. Alabama State Board of Education, 612 F. Supp. 1046 (M.D. Ala. 1985), *rev'd,* 816 F.2d 575 (11th Cir. 1987).

Allsup, V.C. (1982). *The American G.I. Forum: Origins and evolution.* Austin: University of Texas Press.

Alvarado v. El Paso Independent School District, 326 F. Supp. 674 (W.D. Tex. 1971), *rev'd and rem'd,* 445 F.2d 1011 (5th Cir. 1971).

Alvarez v. Lemon Grove School District, Civil Action No. 66625 (Superior Court, San Diego County, California March 30, 1931). Alvarez case information available at San Diego State University, Department of Chicana and Chicano Studies website, "San Diego's Mexican and Chicano History": *http://www-rohan.sdsu.edu/dept/mas/chicanohistory/chapter07/c07s02.html.*

Álvarez, R., Jr. (1986). The Lemon Grove incident: The nation's first successful desegregation court case. *Journal of San Diego History, 32,* 116–135.

Álvarez, R., Jr. (1988). National politics and local responses: The nation's first successful desegregation court case. In H. Trueba & C. Delgado-Gaitán (Eds.), *School and society: Learning content through culture* (pp. 37–52). New York: Praeger.

American Educational Research Association, American Psychological Association, & National Council on Measurement in Education. (1999). *Standards for educational and psychological testing.* Washington, DC: Author.

American Federation of Teachers. (2001). *Making standards matter 2001: A fifty-state report on efforts to implement a standards-based system.* Washington, DC: Author.

Amrein, A.L., & Berliner, D.C. (2002). High-stakes testing, uncertainty, and student learning. *Education Policy Analysis Archives, 10*(18). Available online at: *http://epaa.asu.edu/epaa/v10n18/.*

Anastasi, A. (1988). *Psychological testing* (6th ed.). New York: Macmillan.

Anderson, L.W. (1985). Opportunity to learn. In T. Husen & T.N. Postlethwaite (Eds.), *The international encyclopedia of education* (Vol. 6, pp. 3682–3686). Oxford, UK: Pergamon.

Angeles v. Santa Barbara School District, Civil Action No. 127040 (Superior Court, Santa Barbara County, California, August 1979).

Anguiano, R.P.V. (2004). Families and schools: The effect of parental involvement on high school completion. *Journal of Family Issues, 25,* 61–85.

Araujo, R.J. (1997). Critical Race Theory: Contributions to and problems for race relations. *Gonzaga Law Review, 32,* 537–575.

Areen, J. (1973). The judiciary and education reform: A reassessment. *Georgetown Law Journal, 61,* 1009–1026.

Arlington Heights v. Metropolitan Housing Development Corp., 429 U.S. 252 (1977).

Arlington National Cemetery Website. (2006). Thurgood Marshall: Associate Justice, United States Supreme Court. Available online at: *http://www.arlington cemetery.net/tmarsh.htm.*

Armistead v. Starkville Separate School District, 325 F. Supp. 560 (N.D. Miss. 1971), *aff'd in part, rev'd in part,* 461 F.2d 276 (5th Cir. 1972).

Arreola v. Santa Ana Board of Education, Case No. 160577 (Superior Court, Orange County, California, November 1968).

Arriola, C. (1995). Knocking on the schoolhouse door: *Mendez v. Westminster,* equal protection, public education, and Mexican Americans in the 1940's. *La Raza Law Journal, 8,* 166–207.

Artiles, A.J., & Trent, S.C. (1994). Overrepresentation of minority students in special education: A continuing debate. *Journal of Special Education, 27,* 410–437.

Arvizu v. Waco Independent School District, 373 F. Supp. 1264 (W.D. Tex. 1973).

Ashcroft, B., Griffiths, G., & Tiffin, H. (Eds.). (2006). *The post-colonial studies reader* (2nd ed.). London: Routledge.

Aspira of New York v. Board of Education of the City of New York, Civil Action No. 72-4002 (S.D.N.Y. August 29, 1974), 423 F. Supp. 647 (S.D.N.Y. 1976).

Associated Press. (2004, July 2). Black children denied IQ tests in California. Available online at: *http://www.papillonsartpalace.com/blacck.htm*.

Associated Press. (2007, July 26). Widely imitated "relief act" rejected. *Austin American-Statesman*, p. A10.

Association of Mexican-American Educators v. California, 836 F. Supp. 1534 (N.D. Cal. 1993), 937 F. Supp. 1397 (N.D. Cal. 1996), 183 F.3d 1055 (9th Cir. 1999) (*orig. op. unpub'd*), *aff'd*, 195 F.3d 465 (9th Cir. 1999) (*amended op.*), *pet. for reh'g en banc granted*, 208 F.3d 786 (9th Cir. 2000), *aff'd en banc*, 231 F.3d 572 (9th Cir. 2000).

Atkins, J.C. (1978). *Who will educate? The schooling question in territorial New Mexico, 1846-1911*. Unpublished doctoral dissertation, University of New Mexico, Albuquerque.

August, D., & García, E.E. (1988). *Language minority education in the United States: Research, policy, and practice*. Springfield, IL: Charles C. Thomas.

Aynesworth, H. (2006, November 15). Texas town cracks down on illegal aliens, expects suit. *Washington Times*. Available online at: *http://washingtontimes.com/national/20061114-114126-4331r.htm*.

Baker, S., & Hakuta, K. (1997, December). *Bilingual education and civil rights*. Paper presented at the Harvard University Civil Rights Project Conference on the Latino Civil Rights Crisis, Los Angeles, CA, and Washington, DC.

Balderrama, F.E. (1982). *In defense of La Raza*. Tucson: University of Arizona Press.

Barraza v. Pecos Independent School District, decided by Commissioner of Education, J.W. Edgar, November 25, 1953. Decision on file at Texas State Archives. Also available at the George I. Sánchez Papers, Benson Latin American Collection, The University of Texas at Austin.

Barrera, M. (1988). *Beyond Aztlán: Ethnic awareness in comparative perspective*. New York: Praeger.

Barrett, D.N. (1966). Demographic characteristics. In J. Samora (Ed.), *La Raza: Forgotten Americans* (pp. 159–199). Notre Dame, IN: University of Notre Dame Press.

Beck, N.P. (1975). *The other children: Minority education in California public schools from statehood to 1890*. Unpublished doctoral dissertation, University of California, Los Angeles.

Bell, D. (1980). *Brown v. Board of Education* and the interest-convergence dilemma. *Harvard Educational Review, 93*, 518–534.

Bell, D. (1995). Serving two masters: Integration ideals and client interests in school desegregation litigation. In R. Delgado (Ed.), *Critical Race Theory: The cutting edge* (pp. 228–240). Philadelphia: Temple University Press.

Berger, M.A. (1983). Neighborhood schools: The new (?) legal response to enrollment decline and desegregation. *Urban Education, 18*, 7–28.

Berke, J., & Callahan, J. (1972). *Serrano v. Priest*: Milestone or millstone for school finance. *Journal of Public Law, 21*, 23–71.

Berliner, D.C., & Biddle, B.J. (1995). *The manufactured crisis: Myths, fraud, and the attack on America's public schools.* Reading, MA: Addison-Wesley.

Bernal, D.V. (1979). Constitutional law—A statute which denies an education to undocumented is unconstitutional—*Doe v. Plyler. Texas International Law Review, 14*, 289–316.

Bernal, E.M. (1998). Expert report. GI Forum v. Texas Education Agency, Civil Action No. SA-97-CA-1278 (W.D. Tex. 1997).

Bernal, E.M., & Valencia, R.R. (2000). The TAAS case: A recapitulation and beyond. *Hispanic Journal of Behavioral Sciences, 22*, 540–556.

Bersoff, D.N. (1982). The legal regulation of psychology. In C.R. Reynolds & T.B. Gutkin (Eds.), *The handbook of school psychology* (pp. 1043–1074). New York: Wiley.

Bhatt, S. (2005, February 21). School closures are a risk, experts say. *Seattle Times.* Available online at: *http://seattletimes.nwsource.com/html/localnews/2002185891_closures21m.html.*

Bialystok, E. (2001). *Bilingualism in development: Language, literacy, and cognition.* Cambridge: Cambridge University Press.

Bilingual Education Act, Pub. L. No. (90-247), 81 Stat. 816 (1968).

Blair, B. (2006, April 13). Meeting the June 1 school finance deadline. *House Research Organization, Texas House of Representatives, Interim News, 79*, 1, 6–12. Available online at: *http://www.hro.house.state.tx.us/interim/int79-4.pdf.*

Board of Education of Oklahoma City Public Schools v. Dowell, 498 U.S. 237 (1991).

Board of Regents v. Roth, 408 U.S. 564 (1972).

Booth, A., & Dunn, J.F. (1996). *Family-school links: How do they affect educational outcomes?* Mahwah, NJ: Lawrence Erlbaum.

Bowles, S., & Gintis, H. (1976). *Schooling in capitalist America: Education reform and the contradictions of economic life.* New York: Basic Books.

Bowman, K.L. (2001). The new face of school desegregation. *Duke Law Journal, 50*, 1751–1808.

Boyd, W.L. (1982). The politics of declining enrollments and school closings. In N.H. Cambron-McCabe & A. Odden (Eds.), *The changing politics of school finance* (pp. 231–267). Cambridge, MA: Ballinger.

Boyd, W.L., & Wheaton, D.R. (1983). Conflict management in declining school districts. *Peabody Journal of Education, 60*, 25–36.

Bracco, K.R. (1997). *Texas case study summary.* California Higher Education Policy Center. Available online at: *http://www.capolicycenter.org/texas/texas3.html.*

Brady, P.M., Manni, J.L., & Winikur, D.W. (1983). Implications of ethnic disproportion in programs for the educable mentally retarded. *Journal of Special Education, 17*, 295–302.

Brewster, S.A. (1976). *The Yaqui Indians of Arizona: Trilingualism and cultural change*. Unpublished doctoral dissertation, The University of Texas at Austin.

Brimley, V., Jr., & Garfield, R.R. (2005). *Financing education in a climate of change* (9th ed.). Boston: Allyn and Bacon.

Brinkley, A. (1993). *The unfinished nation*. New York: McGraw-Hill.

Brooks, T.R. (1974). *Walls come tumbling down: A history of the civil rights movement, 1940–1970*. Englewood Cliffs, NJ: Prentice-Hall.

Brown v. Board of Education of Topeka, 347 U.S. 483 (1954), *supp. op.*, 349 U.S. 294 (1955).

Bryant, J.C. (1968). *Some effects of racial integration of high school students on standardized achievement test scores, teacher grades, and drop-out rates in Angleton, Texas*. Unpublished doctoral dissertation, University of Houston, TX.

Burruss v. Wilkerson, 310 F. Supp. 572 (W.D. Va. 1969), *aff'd*, 397 U.S. 44 (1970).

Calderón, C.I. (1950). *The education of Spanish-speaking children in Edcouch-Elsa, Texas*. Unpublished master's thesis, The University of Texas at Austin.

California Constitution, Art. 4, §24 (1879).

California Department of Education. (2005). *2004–05 district and school enrollment report by ethnicity*. Sacramento, CA: Author. Report available online using DataQuest search engine at: *http://data1.cde.ca.gov/dataquest*.

California Department of Education. (2006a). *Comparing California*. Report available online using Ed-Data database at: *http://www.ed-data.k12.ca.us/Articles/article.asp?title=California%20comparison*.

California Department of Education. (2006b). *Statewide enrollment by gender, grade, and ethnic designation, 2005–06; Statewide number of English learners in California public schools, by language and grade, ranked by total, 2005–06*. Sacramento, CA: Author. Reports available online via DataQuest search engine at: *http://data1.cde.ca.gov/dataquest*.

California Legislature. (1947). *Senate final history*, 57th Session (p. 499). Sacramento: State Printing Office.

California State Board of Education (1975, January 15). *News release*. Sacramento, CA: Author.

California Statutes, Ch. 556, §55 (1870).

Calvert, R.A., & De León, A. (1990). *The history of Texas*. Arlington Heights, TX: Harlan Davidson.

Calvin v. Smith, 77 Eng. Rep. 377 (K.B. 1608).

Camenisch v. University of Texas, 616 F.2d 127 (5th Cir. 1980).

Cantú, M.G., & Garza, F. (1981). The Seals decision—Landmark in education for children of undocumented aliens. *Agenda, 11*, 23–26.

Cárdenas, B., & Cárdenas, J.A. (1973, February). Chicano—bright-eyed, bilingual, brown, and beautiful. *Today's Education, 62*, 49–51.

Cárdenas, J.A. (1997). *Texas school finance reform: An IDRA perspective*. San Antonio, TX: Intercultural Development Research Association.

Cárdenas, J.A. (1998). Expert report. GI Forum v. Texas Education Agency, Civil Action No. SA-97-CA-1278 (W.D. Tex. 1997).

Cárdenas, J.A., & Cortez, A. (1986). The impact of *Plyler v. Doe* upon Texas public schools. *Journal of Law & Education, 15,* 1–17.

Carens, J.H. (1987). Who belongs? Theoretical and legal questions about birthright citizenship in the United States. *University of Toronto Law Journal, 37,* 413–443.

Carnegie Foundation for the Advancement of Teaching. (1987). *A classification of institutions of higher education.* Princeton, NJ: Author.

Carroll, P. (2003). *Felix Longoria's wake: Bereavement, racism, and the rise of Mexican American activism.* Austin: University of Texas Press.

Carrow, E. (1973). *Screening Test for Auditory Comprehension of Language.* Austin, TX: Learning Concepts.

Carter, D.G., Brown, F., & Harris, J.J., III. (1978). Bilingual-bicultural education: A legal analysis. *Education and Urban Society, 10,* 295–304.

Carter, D.J., & Wilson, R. (1997). *Minorities in higher education, 1996–1997: 15th annual report.* Washington, DC: American Council on Education, Office of Minorities in Higher Education.

Carter, L.E. (1997). Intermediate scrutiny under fire: Will *Plyler* survive state legislation to exclude undocumented children from schools? *University of San Francisco Law Review, 31,* 345–398.

Carter, T.P. (1970). *Mexican Americans in school: A history of educational neglect.* New York: College Entrance Examination Board.

Castaneda v. Partida, 430 U.S. 482 (1977).

Castaneda v. Pickard, 648 F.2d 989 (5th Cir. 1981), *aff'd,* 781 F.2d 456 (5th Cir. 1986).

Castellanos, D. (1985). *The best of two worlds: Bilingual-bicultural education in the U.S.* (Rev. ed.). Trenton: New Jersey State Department of Education.

Castillo, J. (2006, November 18). Debate on birthright citizenship is revived. *Austin American-Statesman,* pp. A1, A19.

Castro v. Phoenix Union High School District #210, Civil Action No. 82-302 (D. Ariz. August 30, 1982).

Center for American Progress. (2004, April 6). The failed promise to leave no child behind. Available online at: *http://www.americanprogress.org/site/pp.asp?c =biJRJ8OVF&b=44515.*

Center on Education Policy. (2005). *State high school exit exams: States try harder, but gaps exist.* Washington, DC: Author.

Chandler, J.T., & Plakos, J. (1969). Spanish-speaking pupils classified as educable mentally retarded. *Integrated Education, 7,* 28–33.

Chang, R.S. (1993). Toward an Asian American legal scholarship: Critical race theory, post-structuralism, and narrative space. *California Law Review, 81,* 1241–1323.

Chapa v. Odem Independent School District, Civil Action No. 66-C-72 (S.D. Tex. July 28, 1967).

Chapa, J. (1997, December). *The Hopwood decision in Texas as an attack on Latino access to selective higher education programs.* Paper presented at the Harvard University Civil Rights Project, Research Conference on the Latino Civil Rights Crisis, Los Angeles, CA, and Washington, DC.

Chapa, J. (2005). Affirmative action and percent plans as alternatives for increasing successful participation of minorities in higher education. *Journal of Hispanic Higher Education, 4,* 181–196.

Chapa, J., & Valencia, R.R. (1993). Latino population growth, demographic characteristics, and educational stagnation: An example of recent trends. *Hispanic Journal of Behavioral Sciences, 15,* 165–187.

Chapman, P.D. (1988). *Schools as sorters: Lewis M. Terman, applied psychology, and the intelligence testing movement, 1890–1930.* New York: New York University Press.

Chavkin, N.F. (1993). *Families and schools in a pluralistic society.* Albany: State University of New York Press.

Chavkin, N.F., & Williams, D.L. (1989). Low-income parents' attitudes toward parent involvement in education. *Journal of Sociology and Social Welfare, 16,* 17–28.

Chorover, S.L. (1979). *From genius to genocide: The meaning of human nature and the power of behavior control.* Cambridge, MA: MIT Press.

Cintron v. Brentwood Union Free School District, 455 F. Supp. 57 (E.D.N.Y. 1978).

Cisneros v. Corpus Christi Independent School District, 324 F. Supp. 599 (S.D. Tex. 1970), 330 F. Supp. 1377 (S.D. Tex. 1971), *stay reinstated,* 404 U.S. 1211 (1971), *pet. for reh'g en banc denied,* 448 F.2d 1392 (5th Cir. 1971), *enjoined pending appeal,* 459 F.2d 13 (5th Cir. 1972), *aff'd in part, modified in part, and rem'd,* 467 F.2d 142 (5th Cir. 1972), *cert. denied,* 413 U.S. 920 (1973), *cert. denied,* 413 U.S. 922 (1973), *cert. denied,* 414 U.S. 881 (1973), *aff'd,* 560 F.2d 190 (5th Cir. 1977).

Civil Rights Act, Pub. L. No. (88-352), 78 Stat. 255 (1964).

Civil Rights Education Project. (1989). *Free at last: A history of the civil rights movement and those who died in the struggle.* Montgomery, AL: Southern Poverty Law Center.

Clement, D.C., Eisenhart, M., & Wood, J.W. (1976). School desegregation and educational inequality: Trends in the literature, 1960–1975. In R. Rist (Ed.), *The desegregation literature: A critical appraisal* (pp. 1–77). Washington, DC: National Institute of Education.

Clements v. LULAC, 800 S.W.2d 948 (Tex. App.–Corpus Christi 1990, *aff'd*).

Cline, Z., Necochea, J., & Rios, F. (2004). The tyranny of democracy: Deconstructing the passage of racist propositions. *Journal of Latinos and Education, 3,* 67–85.

Coleman, J.L., & Leiter, B. (1993). Determinacy, objectivity, and authority. *University of Pennsylvania Law Review, 142,* 549–637.

Collings, G.D. (1973). Case review: Rights of the retarded. *Journal of Special Education, 7,* 27–37.

Colton, D., & Frelich, A. (1979). Enrollment decline and school closings in a large city. *Education and Urban Society, 11,* 396–417.

Columbia Law Review. (1947). Segregation in schools as a violation of the XIVth Amendment. *47,* 325–327.

Columbus Board of Education v. Penick, 443 U.S. 449 (1979).

Comer, J.P. (1986). Parent participation in the schools. *Phi Delta Kappan, 67,* 442–446.

Complete Texas statutes. (1920). Kansas City, MO: Vernon Law Book Co.

Contreras v. City of Los Angeles, 656 F.2d 1267 (9th Cir. 1981).

Cook, B.J., & Cordova, D.L. (2006). *Minorities in higher education: 22nd annual report.* Washington, DC: American Council on Higher Education, Center for Policy Analysis, and Center for Advancement of Racial and Ethnic Equity.

Coon, A.F., & Sommer, S.A. (1999, December 2). Separate and unequal: *Serrano* played an important role in development of school-district policy. *Los Angeles Daily Journal, 112,* 7. Available online at: *http://library.findlaw.com/1999/Dec/1/129939.html.*

Coons, J.E., Clune, W.H., III, & Sugarman, S.D. (1970). *Private wealth and public education.* Cambridge, MA: Belknap Press of Harvard University Press.

Cooper, P.J. (1995). *Plyler* at the core: Understanding the Proposition 187 challenge. *Chicano-Latino Law Review, 17,* 64–87.

Copelin, L. (2003, December 1). Rich, poor schools join forces on finance; Lawsuit to be filed today allies districts in quest for more money. *Austin American-Statesman,* pp. A1, A6.

Cortez v. Carrizo Springs Independent School District, Civil Action No. 832 (W.D. Tex. *dism'd w.o.j., filed,* April 20, 1955). Case file documents available at the George I. Sánchez Papers, Benson Latin American Collection, The University of Texas at Austin.

Cortez, A. (2006, August). Perspectives on the Texas Legislature's latest school funding plan. *IDRA Newsletter.* Available online at: *http://www.idra.org/IDRA_Newsletters/August_2006_Community_Engagement/Latest_School_Funding_Plan/.*

Cotton, K., & Wikelund, K.R. (1989). *Parent involvement in education* (Closeup #6). School Improvement Research Series, Northwest Regional Education Laboratory. Available online at: *http://www.nwrel.org/scpd/sirs/3/cu6.html.*

Covarrubias v. San Diego Unified School District, Civil Action No. 70-394-T (S.D. Cal. *filed,* December 1, 1971).

Crawford v. Board of Education of Los Angeles, 17 Cal.3d 280 (Cal. 1976).

Crawford, J. (1995). *Bilingual education: History, politics, theory, and practice* (3rd ed.). Los Angeles: Bilingual Education Services.

Crawford, J. (2000–2001). Bilingual education: Strike two. *Rethinking schools, 15.*

Available online at: *http://ourworld.compuserve.com/homepages/JWCRAWFORD/RS-az.htm.*

Crawford, J. (2002). Obituary: The Bilingual Education Act: 1968–2002. Available online at: *http://ourworld.compuserve.com/homepages/JWCRAWFORD/T70bit.htm.*

Crenshaw, K., Gotanda, N., Peller, G., & Thomas, K. (Eds.). (1995). *Critical Race Theory: The key writings that formed the movement.* New York: New Press.

Critchlow, D.E. (1974). *Dos Amigos Verbal Language Scales.* San Rafael, CA: Academic Therapy Publications.

Crowley, D.W. (1982). Implementing *Serrano*: A study in judicial impact. *Law and Policy Quarterly, 4,* 299–326.

Cureton v. NCAA, 37 F. Supp.2d 687 (E.D. Pa. 1999), *rev'd on other grounds,* 198 F.3d 107 (3rd Cir. 1999).

Dameron v. Bayless, 14 Ariz. 180 (1912).

Damico, J.S. (1991). Descriptive assessment of communicative ability in limited English proficient students. In E.V. Hamayan & J.S. Damico (Eds.), *Limiting bias in the assessment of bilingual students* (pp. 157–217). Austin, TX: PRO-ED.

Darling-Hammond, L. (2004). Standards, accountability, and school reform. *Teachers College Record, 106,* 1047–1085.

Darling-Hammond, L., & Wise, A.E. (1985). Beyond standardization: State standards and school improvement. *Elementary School Journal, 85,* 315–336.

Davies, L.E. (1946a, December 22). Segregation of Mexicans stirs school-court fight. *New York Times,* p. 6e.

Davies, L.E. (1946b, December 10). Pupil segregation on coast is fought. *New York Times,* p. 28.

Davis, T. (1998). *Weary feet, rested souls: A guided history of the Civil Rights Movement.* New York: Norton.

Dawn, L., & McLaughlin, M. (1996). *Financing public school facilities in Texas.* Austin: Texas Center for Educational Research.

Dayton Board of Education v. Brinkman, 443 U.S. 526 (1979).

Dayton, J. (2003). Rural children, rural schools, and public school funding litigation: A real problem in search of a real solution. *Nebraska Law Review, 82,* 99–132.

Dayton, J., & Dupre, A. (2004). School funding litigation: Who's winning the war? *Vanderbilt Law Review, 57,* 2351–2413.

De León, A. (1974). Blowout 1910 style: A Chicano school boycott in West Texas. *Texana, 12,* 125–140.

De León, A. (1983). *They called them greasers: Anglo attitudes towards Mexicans in Texas, 1821–1900.* Austin: University of Texas Press.

Dean, J. (1983). Neighborhood impacts of school closings: The case in New York City. *Education and Urban Society, 15,* 245–254.

Debra P. v. Turlington, 474 F. Supp. 244 (M.D. Fla. 1979), *aff'd in part, vac'd and rem'd in part*, 644 F.2d 397 (5th Cir. 1981), *pet. for reh'g en banc denied*, 654 F.2d 1079 (5th Cir. 1981), 564 F. Supp. 177 (M.D. Fla. 1983), *aff'd*, 730 F.2d 1405 (11th Cir. 1984).

DeCanas v. Bica, 424 U.S. 351 (1976).

Delgado v. Bastrop Independent School District of Bastrop County, Civil Action No. 388 (W.D. Tex. June 15, 1948).

Delgado, R. (1989). Storytelling for oppositionists and others: A plea for narrative. *Michigan Law Review, 87,* 2411–2441.

Delgado, R. (Ed.). (1995). *Critical Race Theory: The cutting edge.* Philadelphia: Temple University Press.

Delgado, R., & Stefancic, J. (1993). Critical Race Theory: An annotated bibliography. *Virginia Law Review, 79,* 461–516.

Delgado, R., & Stefancic, J. (2001). *Critical Race Theory: An introduction.* New York: New York University Press.

Delgado-Gaitán, C. (1992). School matters in the Mexican American home: Socializing children to education. *American Educational Research Journal, 29,* 495–513.

Dellinger, W. (1995, December 13). Statement before the Subcommittees on Immigration and Claims and on the Constitution of the House Committee on the Judiciary. Available online at: *http://www.usdoj.gov/olc/deny.tes.31.htm.*

DeLong, J.B. (1995). America's only peacetime inflation: The 1970s. Available online at: *http://www.j-bradford-delong.net/pdf_files/Peacetime_inflation.pdf.*

del Olmo, F. (1995). Point/Counterpoint—Proposition 187: Unfounded and ineffective. *Human Rights Brief, 2*(2), 10–12. Available online at: *http://www.wcl.american.edu/hrbrief/v2i2/point.htm.*

Deutsch, M., Fishman, J., Kogan, L., North, R., & Whiteman, N. (1964). Guidelines for testing minority group children. *Journal of Social Issues, 20,* 127–145.

Diana v. State Board of Education, Civil Action No. C-70-37 (N.D. Cal. *filed*, January 7, 1970).

Diaz v. San Jose Unified School District, 412 F. Supp. 310 (N.D. Cal. 1976), *vac'd and rem'd*, 612 F.2d 411 (9th Cir. 1979), 518 F. Supp. 622 (N.D. Cal. 1981), *aff'd*, 705 F.2d 1129 (9th Cir. 1983), *en banc, rev'd and rem'd*, 722 F.2d 660 (9th Cir. 1984), 633 F. Supp. 808 (N.D. Cal. 1985), *aff'd*, 861 F.2d 591 (9th Cir. 1988).

Dickson, L. (2006). Does ending affirmative action in college admissions lower the percent of minority students applying to college? *Economics of Education Review, 25,* 109–119.

Digest of opinions of the Attorney General of Texas, Vol. 128 at 39, 1947. Austin: Texas Legislature.

Dobbs, M. (2004, June 7). Poor schools sue for funding: Higher standards are basis for seeking 'educational adequacy.' *Washington Post,* p. A13. Available online at: *http://www.washingtonpost.com/wp-dyn/articles/A20727-2004Jun6.html.*

Doe v. Plyler, 458 F. Supp. 569 (E.D. Tex. 1978), *aff'd* 628 F.2d 448 (5th Cir. 1980), *prob. juris. noted*, 451 U.S. 968 (1981), *consol'd* with Texas v. Certain Named and Unnamed Alien Children, 452 U.S. 937 (1981), *aff'd* 457 U.S. 202 (1982).

Doll, E.E. (1941). The essentials of an inconclusive concept of mental deficiency. *American Journal of Mental Deficiency, 46*, 214–219.

Doll, E.E. (1962). Historical survey of research and management of mental retardation in the United States. In E.P. Trapp & P. Himelstein (Eds.), *Readings on the exceptional child* (pp. 21–68). New York: Appleton-Century-Crofts.

Domínguez, J.R. (1977). School finance: The issues of equity and efficiency. *Aztlán: International Journal of Chicano Studies Research, 8*, 175–199.

Donato, R. (1997). *The other struggle for equal schools: Mexican Americans during the civil rights era.* Albany: State University of New York Press.

Donovan, M.S., & Cross, C.T. (Eds.). (2002). *Minority students in special and gifted education.* Committee on Minority Representation in Special Education, Division of Behavioral and Social Sciences and Education, National Research Council. Washington, DC: National Academy Press.

Dorf, M.C. (2003). Legal indeterminacy and institutional design. *New York University Law Review, 78*, 875–981.

Dorn, S. (2003). High-stakes testing and the history of graduation. *Education Policy Analysis Archives, 11*(1). Available online at: *http://epaa.asu.edu/epaa/v11n1.*

Dornbusch, S.M., & Ritter, P.L. (1988). Parents of high school students: A neglected resource. *Educational Horizons, 6*, 75–77.

Dred Scott v. Sandford, 60 U.S. 393 (1857).

Drimmer, J.C. (1995). The nephews of Uncle Sam: The history, evolution, and application of birthright citizenship in the United States. *Georgetown Immigration Law Journal, 9*, 667–717.

Dudziak, M.L. (1995). Desegregation as a Cold War imperative. In R. Delgado (Ed.), *Critical Race Theory: The cutting edge* (pp. 110–121). Philadelphia: Temple University Press.

Dunn, L.M. (1968). Special education of the mildly retarded—is much of it justifiable? *Exceptional Children, 35*, 5–22.

Eamon, M.K. (2005). Social-demographic, school, neighborhood, and parenting influences on the academic achievement of Latino young adolescents. *Journal of Youth and Adolescence, 34*, 163–174.

Eaton, T. (2005, April 5). College funds fall short, South Texas officials say: Border Initiative monies reduced as budget tightened. *Corpus Christi Caller-Times*, pp. A1, A5.

Eby, F. (1919). *Education in Texas: Source materials.* Austin: University of Texas Press.

Eby, F. (1925). *The development of education in Texas.* New York: Macmillan.

Economic Opportunity Act, Pub. L. No. (88-452), 78 Stat. 508 (1964).

Edgewood Independent School District v. Bynum, Civil Action No. 362,516 (250th District Court, Travis County, Texas *filed*, May 23, 1984).

Edgewood Independent School District v. Kirby, Civil Action No. 362,516 (250th District Court, Travis County, Texas April 29, 1987), *rev'd sub nom* Kirby v. Edgewood Independent School District, 761 S.W.2d 859 (Tex. App.–Austin 1988), *rev'd and rem'd*, 777 S.W.2d 391 (Tex. 1989), *trial ct. aff'd*, 804 S.W.2d 491 (Tex. 1991), *reh'd sub nom* Edgewood Independent School District v. Meno, Civil Action No. 362,516 (250th District Court, Travis County, Texas August 27, 1991), *trial ct. rev'd sub nom* Carrollton-Farmers Branch Independent School District v. Edgewood Independent School District, 826 S.W.2d 489 (Tex. 1992), *trial ct. aff'd sub nom* Edgewood Independent School District v. Meno, 917 S.W.2d 717 (Tex. 1995).

Education for All Handicapped Children Act, Pub. L. No. (94-142), 89 Stat. 773 (1975).

Edwards, E. (1979). Effects of midterm integration on state and trait anxiety in Black and White elementary school children. *American Journal of Community Psychology, 7*, 57–70.

Eiband, D.M. (1978). *The dual language policy in New Mexico.* Unpublished master's thesis, The University of Texas at Austin.

Eisgruber, C.L. (1997). Birthright citizenship and the Constitution. *New York University Law Review, 72*, 54–96.

Elementary and Secondary Education Act, Pub. L. No. (89-10), 79 Stat. 27 (1965).

Elliott, J. (1999, November 1). Pass or fail? Does the TAAS test unfairly discriminate against minorities? *Texas Lawyer, 15*, 1, 17.

Elul, H. (1999). Making the grade, public education reform: The use of standardized testing to retain students and deny diplomas. *Columbia Human Rights Law Review, 30*, 495–536.

Embry, J. (2004, September 16). Judge rules state must fix school financing; Lawmakers have one year to find solution; state plans to appeal. *Austin American-Statesman*, pp. A1, A6.

Embry, J. (2005, August 20). Politicians may soon learn failure to act has consequences. *Austin American-Statesman*, pp. A1, A10.

Embry, J. (2006, May 26). Districts shelve challenges to school finance system. *Austin American-Statesman*, p. B1.

Englund, M.M., Luckner, A.E., Whaley, G.J.L., & Egeland, B. (2004). Children's achievement in early elementary school: Longitudinal effects of parental involvement, expectations, and quality of assistance. *Journal of Educational Psychology, 96*, 723–730.

Epps, E.G. (1975). The impact of school desegregation on aspirations, self-concepts, and other aspects of personality. *Law and Contemporary Problems, 39*, 300–313.

Equal Educational Opportunity Act, Pub. L. No. (93-380), 88 Stat. 515 (1974).

Escamilla, K. (1980). German-English bilingual schools, 1870–1917: Cultural and linguistic survival in St. Louis. *Bilingual Journal, 2,* 16–20.

Espinosa, A.M. (1917). Speech mixture in New Mexico: The influence of the English language on New Mexican Spanish. In H.M. Stephens & H.E. Bolton (Eds.), *The Pacific Ocean in history* (pp. 408–428). New York: Macmillan.

Espinosa, R.W., & Ochoa, A. (1986). Concentration of California Hispanic students in schools with low achievement: A research note. *American Journal of Education, 95,* 77–95.

F.S. Royster Guano Co. v. Virginia, 253 U.S. 412 (1920).

Fanon, F. (1963). *The wretched of the earth* (C. Harrington, Trans.). New York: Grove. (Original work published in 1961.)

Fassold, M. (1998). Expert report. GI Forum v. Texas Education Agency, Civil Action No. SA-97-CA-1278 (W.D. Tex. 1997).

Fassold, M. (2000). Disparate impact analyses of TAAS scores and school quality. *Hispanic Journal of Behavioral Sciences, 22,* 460–480.

Favish, A.J. (n.d.) A decision under fire. Available online at: *http://www.allanfavish. com/pfael1187.htm.*

Feagin, J.R., & Feagin, C.B. (1999). *Racial and ethnic relations* (6th ed.). Upper Saddle River, NJ: Prentice Hall.

Feldman, P. (1994, October 23). Texas case looms over Prop. 187's legal future. *Los Angeles Times,* pp.A1, A21–A22.

Felice, L.G., & Richardson, R.L. (1977a). The effects of busing and school desegregation on majority and minority student dropout rates. *Journal of Educational Research, 70,* 242–246.

Felice, L.G., & Richardson, R.L. (1977b). Effects of desegregation on minority student dropout rates. *Integrated Education, 15,* 47–50.

Felner, R.D., Gintner, M., & Primavera, J. (1982). Primary prevention during school transitions: Social support of environmental structure. *American Journal of Community Psychology, 10,* 277–290.

Felner, R.D., Primavera, J., & Cauce, A.M. (1981). The impact of school transitions: A focus for preventive efforts. *American Journal of Community Psychology, 9,* 449–459.

Ferg-Cadima, J.A. (2004). *Black, white, and brown: Latino school desegregation efforts in the pre- and post-Brown v. Board of Education era.* Los Angeles: Mexican American Legal Defense and Education Fund. Available online at: *http:// www.maldef.org/publications/pdf/LatinoDesegregationPaper2004.pdf.*

Fernández, B.L. (2001). Comment: TAAS and *GI Forum v. Texas Education Agency:* A critical analysis and proposal for redressing problems with the standardized testing in Texas. *St. Mary's Law Journal, 33,* 143–198.

Ferris, D.F. (1962). *Judge Marvin and the founder of the California public school system.* Berkeley: University of California Press.

Fields v. Hallsville Independent School District, 906 F.2d 1017 (5th Cir. 1990).

Fields, C.M. (1988a, March 2). Hard-time budgets for universities in southern Texas perpetuate historic discrimination, Hispanics charge. *Chronicle of Higher Education*, pp. A17–A18.

Fields, C.M. (1988b, March 16). Texas' border campuses hope to capitalize on political clout of their region's growing Mexican-American population. *Chronicle of Higher Education*, pp. A26–A27.

Figueroa, R.A. (1980). Field dependence, ethnicity, and cognitive styles. *Hispanic Journal of Behavioral Sciences, 2*, 35–42.

Figueroa, R.A., & Gallegos, E.A. (1978). Ethnic differences in school behavior. *Sociology of Education, 51*, 289–298.

Fine, B. (1949, September 18). More and more, the IQ idea is questioned. *New York Times Magazine*, pp. 7, 72–74.

Finn, J.D. (1982). Patterns in special education placement as revealed by the OCR surveys. In K.A. Keller, W.H. Holtzman, & S. Messick (Eds.), *Placing children in special education: A strategy for equity* (pp. 322–381). Washington, DC: National Academy Press.

Fischel, W.A. (1989). Did *Serrano* cause Proposition 13? *National Tax Journal, 42*, 465–473.

Fischel, W.A. (1996). How *Serrano* caused Proposition 13. *Journal of Law & Politics, 12*, 607–636.

Fischel, W.A. (2004). Did John Serrano vote for Proposition 13? A reply to Stark and Zasloff's "Tiebout and tax revolts: Did *Serrano* really cause Proposition 13?" *UCLA Law Review, 51*, 887–932.

Flores v. Arizona, 405 F. Supp.2d 1112 (D. Ariz. 2005).

Flores, B.B., & Clark, E.R. (1997). High-stakes testing: Barriers for prospective bilingual education teachers. *Bilingual Research Journal, 21*, 334–356.

Flores, E.T. (1984). Research on undocumented immigrants and public policy: A study of the Texas school case. *International Migration Review, 18*, 505–523.

Foote, T.H., Espinosa, R.W., & Garcia, J.O. (1978). *Ethnic groups and public education in California.* San Diego: California School Finance Project and the California Association for Bilingual Education.

Frankenberg, E., Lee, C., & Orfield, G. (2003). *A multiracial society with segregated schools: Are we losing the dream?* The Civil Rights Project, Harvard University. Cambridge, MA: Harvard University Press. Available online at: *http://www.civilrightsproject.harvard.edu/research/reseg03/AreWeLosingtheDream.pdf.*

Frazier v. Garrison Independent School District, 980 F.2d 1514 (5th Cir. 1993).

Freeman v. Pitts, 503 U.S. 467 (1992).

Friedman, M.S. (1978). *An appraisal of the role of the public school as an acculturating agency of Mexican Americans in Texas, 1850–1968.* Unpublished doctoral dissertation, New York University, New York.

Frost, J.F., & Hawkes, G.R. (Eds.). (1966). *The disadvantaged child: Issues and innovations.* Boston: Houghton Mifflin.

Galván, A. (1991). Case note: *Diaz v. San Jose Unified School District. La Raza Law Journal, 4,* 98–123.

Gamboa, S. (1994, November 28). Testing a landmark. *Austin American-Statesman,* pp. A1, A7.

Gammel, H.P.N. (1898). (Compiler). *The laws of Texas, 1822–1897.* Austin, TX: H.P.N. Gammel Book Co.

Gammel, H.P.N. (1905). (Compiler). *General laws of the state of Texas passed at the regular session of the 29th Legislature.* Austin, TX: State Printing Co.

Gándara, P. (1982). Passing through the eye of the needle: High-achieving Chicanas. *Hispanic Journal of Behavioral Sciences, 4,* 167–179.

García, E.E., & Wiese, A.-M. (2002). Language, public policy, and schooling: A focus on Chicano English learners. In R.R. Valencia (Ed.), *Chicano school failure and success: Past, present, and future* (2nd ed., pp. 149–169). London: RoutledgeFalmer.

García, G.X. (1989, November 25). 74% of graduates pass TASP tests: Failure rate among Black students 52%. *Austin American-Statesman,* pp. A1, A8.

García, I.M. (1989). *United we win: The rise and fall of La Raza Unida Party.* Tucson: Mexican American Studies and Research Center, University of Arizona.

García, I.M. (1997). *Chicanismo: The forging of a militant ethos among Mexican Americans.* Tucson: University of Arizona Press.

García, M.T. (1979). *Mexican Americans: Leadership, ideology, and identity, 1930–1960.* New Haven, CT: Yale University Press.

García, R. (1995). Critical race theory and Proposition 187: The racial politics of immigration law. *Chicano-Latino Law Review, 17,* 118–148.

García y Griego, M. (1986). The rights of undocumented Mexicans in the United States after *Plyler v. Doe*: A sketch of moral and legal issues. *Journal of Law & Education, 15,* 57–82.

Garner, B.A. (Ed.). (1999). *Black's law dictionary* (7th ed.). St. Paul, MN: West Group.

Garner, B.A. (Ed.). (2004). *Black's law dictionary* (8th ed.). St. Paul, MN: West Group.

Gerard, H.B., & Miller, N. (1975). *School desegregation: A long-term study.* New York: Plenum.

Gerry, M. (1973). Cultural myopia: The need for a corrective lens. *Journal of School Psychology, 11,* 307–315.

GI Forum v. Texas Education Agency, 87 F. Supp.2d 667 (W.D. Tex. 2000).

Gilbert, E.H. (1947). *Some legal aspects of the education of Spanish-speaking children in Texas.* Unpublished master's thesis, The University of Texas at Austin.

Gilbert, H.B. (1966). On the IQ ban. *Teachers College Record, 67,* 282–285.

Gitlin, B. (1980). The constitutionality of public school financing laws: Judicial and legislative interaction. *Fordham Urban Law Journal, 8,* 673–693.

Goldberg, I.I. (1971). Human rights for the mentally retarded in the school system. *Mental Retardation, 9*, 3–7.

Goldfinger, P.M. (1999). A history of revenue limits—Or, why is your base revenue limit bigger than mine? *Fiscal Report, 19*, 1–18. Available online at: *http://www.sscal.com/histrvlm.htm.*

Goldstein, H., Arkell, C., Ashcroft, S.C., Hurley, O.L., & Lilly, M.S. (1975). Schools. In N. Hobbs (Ed.), *Issues in the classification of children: Volume 2* (pp. 4–61). Washington, DC: Jossey-Bass.

Goldstein, S.R. (1972). Interdistrict inequalities in school financing: A critical analysis of *Serrano v. Priest* and its progeny. *University of Pennsylvania Law Review, 120*, 504–544.

Gomez v. Alexian Bros. Hospital of San Jose, 698 F.2d 1019 (9th Cir. 1983).

Gomez v. Illinois State Board of Education, 614 F. Supp. 342 (N.D. Ill. 1985), rev'd, 811 F.2d 1030 (7th Cir. 1987).

Gómez, P., Kastely, A., & Holleman, M. (2000). The Texas Assessment of Academic Skills exit test: "Driver of equity" or "ticket to nowhere"? *The Scholar: St. Mary's Law Review on Minority Issues, 2*, 187–247.

Gómez-Quiñones, J. (1978). *Mexican students por la raza: The Chicano student movement in Southern California.* Santa Barbara, CA: Editorial La Causa.

Gómez-Quiñones, J. (1990). *Chicano politics: Reality and promise, 1940–1990.* Albuquerque: University of New Mexico Press.

Gong Lum v. Rice, 275 U.S. 78 (1927).

Gonzales v. Sheely, 96 F. Supp. 1004 (D. Ariz. 1951).

González, G.G. (1974a). *The system of public education and its function within the Chicano communities, 1910–1930.* Unpublished doctoral dissertation, University of California, Los Angeles.

González, G.G. (1974b). Racism, education, and the Mexican community in Los Angeles, 1920–1930. *Societas, 4*, 287–301.

González, G.G. (1990). *Chicano education in the era of segregation.* Philadelphia: Balch Institute Press.

González, G.G. (1999). Segregation and the education of Mexican children, 1900–1940. In J.F. Moreno (Ed.), *The elusive quest for equality: 150 years of Chicano/Chicana education* (pp. 53–76). Cambridge, MA: Harvard Educational Review.

Gould, B. (1932). *Methods of teaching Mexicans.* Unpublished master's thesis, University of Southern California, Los Angeles.

Graham v. Richardson, 403 U.S. 365 (1971).

Gray v. Sanders, 372 U.S. 368 (1963).

Grebler, L., Moore, J.W., & Guzmán, R.C. (1970). *The Mexican-American people: The nation's second largest minority.* New York: Free Press.

Green v. County School Board of New Kent County, 391 U.S. 430 (1968).

Green, P.E. (2003). The undocumented: Educating the children of migrant workers in America. *Bilingual Research Journal, 27*, 51–71.

Greenfield, G.A., & Kates, D.B., Jr. (1975). Mexican Americans, racial discrimination, and the Civil Rights Act of 1866. *California Law Review, 63,* 662–731.

Griffin v. Illinois, 351 U.S. 12 (1956).

Griggs v. Duke Power Co., 401 U.S. 424 (1971).

Griswold del Castillo, R. (1990). *The Treaty of Guadalupe Hidalgo: A legacy of conflict.* Norman: University of Oklahoma Press.

Gronlund, N.E. (1985). *Measurement and evaluation in teaching* (5th ed.). New York: Macmillan.

Gronlund, N.E., & Linn, R.L. (1990). *Measurement and evaluation in teaching* (6th ed.). New York: Macmillan.

Grossman, H.H. (Ed.). (1973). *Manual on terminology and classification in mental retardation.* Washington, DC: American Association on Mental Deficiency.

Groves v. Alabama State Board of Education, 776 F. Supp. 1518 (M.D. Ala. 1991).

Grubb, E.B. (1974). Breaking the language barrier: The right to bilingual education. *Harvard Civil Rights–Civil Liberties Law Review, 9,* 52–94.

Grubb, W.N., & Michelson, S. (1973). Public school finance in a post-Serrano world. *Harvard Civil Rights–Civil Liberties Law Review, 8,* 550–570.

Guadalupe Organization, Inc. v. Tempe Elementary School District No. 3, Civil Action No. 71-435 (D. Ariz. *filed,* August 10, 1972).

Guadalupe Organization, Inc. v. Tempe Elementary School District No. 3, 587 F.2d 1022 (9th Cir. 1978).

Guerra, C. (2005, February 22). Time to review what has changed in border area's higher ed. *San Antonio Express News,* p. 1B.

Gunther, G. (1972). Forward: In search of evolving doctrine on a changing court: A model for a newer equal protection. *Harvard Law Review, 86,* 1–48.

Gunzenhauser, M.G. (2003). High-stakes testing and the default of education. *Theory into Practice, 42,* 51–58.

Guthrie, J. (1983). United States school finance policy, 1955–1980. *Educational Evaluation and Policy Analysis, 5,* 207–230.

Hakuta, K. (1986). *Mirror of language: The debate on bilingualism.* New York: Basic Books.

Hakuta, K. (1987). Degree of bilingualism and cognitive ability in mainland Puerto Rican children. *Child Development, 58,* 1372–1388.

Hakuta, K. (1990). Language and cognition in bilingual children. In A.M. Padilla, H.F. Fairchild, & C.M. Valadez (Eds.), *Bilingual education: Issues and strategies* (pp. 47–59). Newbury Park, CA: Sage.

Hamayan, E.V., & Damico, J.S. (Eds.). (1991). *Limiting bias in the assessment of bilingual students.* Austin, TX: PRO-ED.

Haney, W.M. (1999). Expert report (supplementary). GI Forum v. Texas Education Agency, Civil Action No. SA-97-CA-1278 (W.D. Tex. 1997).

Haney, W.M. (2002). The myth of the Texas miracle in education. *Education Policy Analysis Archives, 8*(41). Available online at: *http://epaa.asu.edu/epaa/v8n41/.*

Hanson, R.A., Schutz, R.E., & Bailey, J.D. (1980). *What makes achievement tick: Investigation of alternative instrumentation for instructional program evaluation.* Los Alamitos, CA: Southwest Regional Laboratory for Educational Research and Development.

Hargrave v. McKinney, 413 F.2d 320 (5th Cir. 1969).

Harris, K.G. (2002). *A legislator's guide to public education in Virginia: Public school finance.* Richmond: Virginia Division of Legislative Services. Available online at: *http://dls.state.va.us/pubs/lgpe/lgpe2b.pdf.*

Harvard Law Review. (1946–1947). Constitutional law—equal protection of the laws—segregation of children of Mexican descent by school officials without legislative authority held unconstitutional. *60,* 1156–1158.

Harvard Law Review. (1994). The birthright citizenship amendment: A threat to equality. *107,* 1026–1043.

Harvey, W.B., & Anderson, E.L. (2005). *Minorities in higher education, 2003–2004: 21st annual report.* Washington, DC: American Council on Education, Center for Advancement of Racial and Ethnic Equity, Center for Policy Analysis.

Hayashi, B.M. (2004). *Democratizing the enemy: The Japanese American internment.* Princeton, NJ: Princeton University Press.

Heber, R. (1961). Modifications in the Manual on Terminology and Classification in Mental Retardation. *American Journal of Mental Deficiency, 65,* 499–500.

Heberton, C., IV. (1982). To educate or not to educate: The plight of undocumented alien children in Texas. *Washington University Law Quarterly, 60,* 119–159.

Hellmuth, J. (Ed.). (1967). *Disadvantaged child* (Vol. 1). New York: Brunner/Mazel.

Hendrick, I.G. (1977). *The education of non-whites in California, 1848–1970.* San Francisco: R&E Associates.

Hendrick, I.G. (1980). *California education: A brief history.* San Francisco: Boyd Fraser.

Henke, J.T. (1986). Financing public schools in California: The aftermath of *Serrano v. Priest* and Proposition 13. *University of San Francisco Law Review, 21,* 1–39.

Herget, J.E. (1995). Unearthing the origins of a radical idea: The case of Legal Indeterminacy. *American Journal of Legal History, 39,* 59–70.

Hernandez v. Driscoll, 2 Race Rel. L. Rep. 34 (1956), 2 Race Rel. L. Rep. 329 (1957).

Hernandez v. Houston Independent School District, 558 S.W.2d 121 (Tex. Civ. App.-Austin 1977, *writ ref'd n.r.e.*).

Hernandez v. Texas, 347 U.S. 475 (1954).

Heubert, J.P., & Hauser, R.M. (Eds.). (1999). *High stakes: Testing for tracking, promotion, and graduation.* Committee on Appropriate Test Use, Board on Testing and Assessment, Commission on Behavioral and Social Sciences and Education, National Research Council. Washington, DC: National Academy Press.

Hill, G.N., & Hill, K.T. (1995). *Real life dictionary of the law: Taking the mystery out of legal language.* Los Angeles: General Publishing Group. Search engine available online at: *http://dictionary.law.com/.*

Hills, J.R. (1971). Use of measurement in selection and placement. In R.L. Thorndike (Ed.), *Educational measurement* (2nd ed., pp. 680–732). Washington, DC: American Council on Education.

Hinsley, J.C. (1968). *The handbook of Texas school law* (4th ed.). Austin, TX: Steck-Vaugh.

Hinton, K.A. (2005). Multiple criteria assessment: A proposed amendment to the Texas Education Code. Unpublished manuscript. Available online at: *http://lonestar.utsa.edu/khinton/taksboycott/mca_amendment.pdf.*

Hirji, H.S.P. (1999). Inequalities in California's public school system: The undermining of *Serrano v. Priest* and the need for a minimum standards system of education. *Loyola of Los Angeles Law Review, 32,* 583–609.

Ho, J.C. (2006). Defining "American": Birthright citizenship and the original understanding of the 14th Amendment. *Green Bag, 9,* 367–378.

Hobson v. Hansen, 269 F. Supp. 401 (D.D.C. 1967).

Hood, S., & Parker, L. (1991). Minorities, teacher testing, and recent U.S. Supreme Court holdings: A regressive step. *Teachers College Record, 92,* 603–618.

Horn, C. (2003). High-stakes testing and students: Stopping or perpetuating a cycle of failure. *Theory into Practice, 42,* 30–41.

Horn, C.L., & Flores, S.M. (2003). *Percent plans in college admissions: A comparative analysis of three states' experiences.* The Civil Rights Project, Harvard University. Cambridge, MA: Harvard University. Available online at: *http://www.civilrightsproject.harvard.edu/research/affirmativeaction/tristate.php.*

Houston, M.R.W. (2000). Birthright citizenship in the United Kingdom and the United States: A comparative analysis of the common law basis for granting citizenship to children born of illegal immigrants. *Vanderbilt Journal of Transnational Law, 33,* 693–738.

Hughes, L.W., Gordon, W.M., & Hillman, L.W. (1980). *Desegregating American schools.* New York: Longman.

Hull, E. (1981). Undocumented aliens and the equal protection clause: An analysis of *Plyler v. Doe. Brooklyn Law Review, 48,* 43–74.

Hull, E. (1983). Undocumented alien children and free public education: An analysis of *Plyler v. Doe. University of Pittsburgh Law Review, 44,* 409–432.

Hurst, J. (1979, April 12). Santa Barbara Latins suing school board: Chicanos also staging boycott to block 3 shutdowns. *Los Angeles Times,* part II, p. 1.

Husen, T. (1967). *International study of achievement in mathematics: A comparison of twelve countries.* New York: Wiley.

Illinois Law Review. (1947). Segregation of race in public schools and its relation to the Fourteenth Amendment. *42,* 545–549.

Immerwahr, J., & Foleno, T. (2000). *Great expectations: How the public and par-*

ents—*White, African American, and Hispanic—view higher education.* New York: Public Agenda.

In re Alien Children Education Litigation, 501 F. Supp. 326 (JPMDL 1979), 501 F. Supp. 544 (S.D. Tex. 1980), *stay vac'd sub nom* Certain Named and Unnamed Non-Citizen Children and Their Parents v. Texas, 448 U.S. 1327 (1980), *consol'd sub nom* Texas v. Certain Named and Unnamed Alien Children *with* Plyler v. Doe, 452 U.S. 937 (1981).

In re Look Tin Sing, 21 F. 905 (Cir. D. California 1884).

Independent School District v. Salvatierra, 33 S.W. 2d 790 (Tex. Civ. App., San Antonio 1930), *cert. denied sub nom* Salvatierra v. Independent School District, 284 U.S. 580 (1931).

Individuals with Disabilities Education Act, Pub. L. No. (101-476), 104 Stat. 1103 (1990).

Jackson, L.G., & Prieto, L. (2005). Policy brief: Integrating multiple criteria in the Texas accountability system. Unpublished manuscript. Available online at: *http://texasassessment.edb.utexas.edu/MCAPolicyBrief.pdf.*

Jackson, M. (1986). Bilingual education in Denver: The school district's perspective. *La Raza Law Journal, 1,* 250–256.

Jaeger, C. (1987). *Minority and low income high schools: Evidence of educational inequality in metro Los Angeles* (Working Paper No. 8). Chicago: Metropolitan Opportunity Project, University of Chicago.

Jastak, J.E., & Jastak, S.R. (1965). *Manual: The Wide Range Achievement Test.* Wilmington, DE: Guidance Associates.

Jenkins, C.H. (1925). *The revised civil statutes of Texas, 1925, annotated.* Austin, TX: H.P.N. Gammel Book Co.

Johnson, A.W. (2004). *Objectifying measures: Mapping the terrain of statistical discourse in the hegemony and racial politics of high-stakes testing.* Unpublished doctoral dissertation, The University of Texas at Austin.

Johnson, K.R. (1995). Civil rights and immigration: Challenges for the Latino community in the twenty-first century. *La Raza Law Journal, 8,* 42–89.

Johnson, K.R. (1996). *Proposition 187: The nativist campaign, the impact on the Latino community, and the future.* JSRI Research Report No. 15. East Lansing: Julian Samora Research Institute, Michigan State University. Available online at: *http://www.jsri.msu.edu/RandS/research/irr/rr15.html.*

Johnson, K.R., & Martínez, G.A. (2000). Discrimination by proxy: The case of Proposition 227 and the ban on bilingual education. *U.C. Davis Law Review, 33,* 1227–1276.

Johnson, W.E. (1974). The constitutional right of bilingual children to an equal educational opportunity. *Southern California Law Review, 47,* 943–997.

Jones, R.C., & Kauffman, A. (1994). Accessibility to comprehensive higher education in Texas. *Social Science Journal, 31,* 263–283.

Joondeph, B.W. (1995). The good, the bad, and the ugly: An empirical analysis of litigation-prompted school finance reform. *Santa Clara Law Review*, 35, 763–824.

Juárez, J.R., Jr. (1995). The American tradition of language rights: The forgotten right to government in a "known tongue." *Law and Inequality: A Journal of Theory and Practice*, 13, 443–642.

Kagan, S., & Buriel, R. (1977). Field dependence-independence and Mexican American culture and education. In J.L. Martínez (Ed.), *Chicano psychology* (pp. 279–328). New York: Academic Press.

Karst, K.L. (1972). *Serrano v. Priest*: A state court's responsibilities and opportunities in the development of federal constitutional law. *California Law Review*, 60, 720–756.

Karst, K.L. (1974). California: *Serrano v. Priest*'s inputs and outputs. *Law and Contemporary Problems*, 38, 333–349.

Kauffman, A. (2000). Epilogue. In P. Gómez, A. Kastely, & M. Holleman, The Texas Assessment of Academic Skills exit test: "Driver of equity" or "ticket to nowhere?" (pp. 242–243). *The Scholar: St. Mary's Law Review on Minority Issues*, 2, 187–247.

Keith, P.B., & Lichtman, M.V. (1994). Does parental involvement influence the academic achievement of Mexican-American eighth graders? Results from the National Education Longitudinal Study. *School Psychology Quarterly*, 9, 256–272.

Keller, G.D., Deneen, J.R., & Magallán, R.J. (1991). *Assessment and access: Hispanics in higher education*. Albany: State University of New York Press.

Keyes v. School District No. 1 of Denver, Colorado, *prelim. inj. entered*, 313 F. Supp. 61 (D. Colo. 1970), *aff'd in part, rev'd in part, and rem'd*, 445 F.2d 990 (10th Cir. 1971), *cert. granted*, 404 U.S. 1036 (1972), *leave granted*, 406 U.S. 966 (1972), *modified and rem'd*, 413 U.S. 189 (1973), *dism'd*, 902 F. Supp. 1274 (D. Colo. 1995).

Keyes v. School District No. 1 of Denver, 380 F. Supp. 673 (D. Colo. 1974), *aff'd in part, rev'd in part, rem'd*, 521 F.2d 465 (10th Cir. 1975), 576 F. Supp. 1503 (D. Colo. 1983).

Klarman, M.J. (2004). *From Jim Crow to civil rights: The Supreme Court and the struggle for racial equality*. New York: Oxford University Press.

Klineberg, O. (1935). *Race differences*. New York: Harper.

Kloss, H. (1977). *The American bilingual tradition*. Rowley, MA: Newberry House.

Kluger, R. (1976). *Simple justice: The history of Brown v. Board of Education and black America's struggle for equality*. New York: Knopf.

Kozol, J. (1991). *Savage inequalities: Children in America's schools*. New York: Crown.

Kramer, L. (2002). Achieving equitable education through the courts: A comparative analysis of three states. *Journal of Law & Education*, 31, 1–51.

Kress, K. (1989). Legal indeterminacy. *California Law Review*, 77, 283–337.

La Opinión. (1946, March 22). *Termina la segregación* [Segregation ends], pp. 1, 8.

Ladson-Billings, G., & Tate, W. (1995). Toward a critical race theory of education. *Teachers College Record, 97,* 47–68.

Langford, S.B. (1979). Constitutional law—Equal protection—Charge of tuition to illegal alien schoolchildren pursuant to Texas statute violates Fourteenth Amendment. *St. Mary's Law Journal, 11,* 549–569.

Larry P. v. Riles, *prelim. inj. granted,* 343 F. Supp. 1306 (N.D. Cal. 1972), *aff'd* 502 F.2d 63 (9th Cir. 1974), *dec. on merits,* 495 F. Supp. 926 (N.D. Cal. 1979), *aff'd* 793 F.2d 969 (9th Cir. 1984).

Lau v. Nichols, 483 F.2d 791 (9th Cir. 1973), *cert. granted,* 412 U.S. 938 (1973), *rev'd,* 414 U.S. 563 (1974).

Lauer, M. (1997, September 12). *Today.* New York: National Broadcasting Corporation.

Lawerence, G. (1978). Indian education: Why bilingual-bicultural? *Education and Urban Society, 10,* 305–320.

Lawson, G. (1996). Legal indeterminacy. *Harvard Journal of Law & Public Policy, 19,* 411–428.

League of United Latin American Citizens v. Wilson, 908 F. Supp. 755 (C.D. Cal. 1995), 997 F. Supp. 1244 (C.D. Cal. 1997).

Leboo, C.A. (1984). Undocumented alien children and free public education— *Plyler v. Doe. Howard Law Journal, 27,* 301–328.

Leibowitz, A.H. (1980). *The Bilingual Education Act: A legislative analysis.* Rosslyn, VA: InterAmerica Research Associates.

Levine, C.H. (1979). More on cutback management: Hard questions for hard times. *Public Administration, 39,* 179–183.

Levine, M., Wesolowski, J.C., & Corbett, F.J. (1966). Pupil turnover and academic performance in an inner city school. *Psychology in the Schools, 3,* 153–156.

Litowitz, D.E. (1997). Some critical thoughts on Critical Race Theory. *Notre Dame Law Review, 72,* 503–529.

Lomotey, K. (Ed.). (1990). *Going to school: The African-American experience.* Albany: State University of New York Press.

Lopez v. Seccombe, 71 F. Supp. 769 (S.D. Cal. 1944).

López, G.R. (2003). The (racially neutral) politics of education: A Critical Race Theory perspective. *Educational Administrative Quarterly, 39,* 68–94.

López, G.R., & Parker, L. (Eds.). (2003). *Interrogating racism in qualitative research methodology.* New York: Peter Lang.

López, M.P. (2005). Reflections on educating Latino and Latina undocumented children: Beyond *Plyler v. Doe. Seton Hall Law Review, 35,* 1373–1406.

Luckingham, B. (1994). *Minorities in Phoenix: A profile of Mexican American, Chinese American, and African American communities, 1860–1992.* Tucson: University of Arizona Press.

LULAC v. Clements, Civil Action No. 13-90-146-CV (107th District Court, Cameron County, Texas January 20, 1992), *stay granted sub nom* Richards v. LU-LAC, 863 S.W.2d 306 (Tex. 1993), *rev'd*, 868 S.W.2d 449 (Tex. 1993).

Lyon, L.L. (1933). *Investigation of the program for the adjustment of Mexican girls to the high schools of the San Fernando Valley.* Unpublished master's thesis, University of Southern California, Los Angeles.

Macías, R.F. (1984). *Cauldron-boil and bubble: United States language policy towards indigenous language groups during the nineteenth century.* Unpublished manuscript.

Mackey, W.F., & Beebe, V.N. (1977). *Bilingual schools for a bicultural community: Miami's adaptation to the Cuban refugees.* Rowley, MA: Newbury House.

Madaus, G. (Ed.). (1983). *The courts, validity, and minimum competency testing.* Boston: Kluwer-Nijhoff.

Maddux, H. (1932). *Some conditions which influence the Mexican children in Greeley, Colorado, and its vicinity.* Unpublished master's thesis, Colorado State Teachers College, Greeley, CO.

Madry, A.R. (1999). Legal indeterminacy and the bivalence of legal truth. *Marquette Law Review, 82,* 581–599.

Malakoff, M., & Hakuta, K. (1990). History of language minority education in the United States. In A.M. Padilla, H.F. Fairchild, & C.M. Valadez (Eds.), *Bilingual education: Issues and strategies* (pp. 27–43). Newbury Park, CA: Sage.

Mangaliman, J., Rodriguez, J., & Gonzales, S. (2006, April 11). Festive crowd joins nationwide rallies for illegal immigrants. *San Jose Mercury News,* pp. A1, A15.

Mangan, K.S. (1991, November 27). Texas jury faults states on equal access to top universities. *Chronicle of Higher Education,* pp. A25–A26.

Mangan, K.S. (1992, January 29). Judge finds discrimination against Hispanics in Texas; corrective plan ordered. *Chronicle of Higher Education,* pp. A25, A30.

Mangan, K.S. (1993, October 13). Top Texas court sees no evidence state was biased against Mexican Americans. *Chronicle of Higher Education,* pp. A25, A28.

Manuel, H.T. (1930). *The education of Mexican and Spanish-speaking children in Texas.* Austin: Fund for Research in the Social Sciences, The University of Texas.

Marans, A.E., & Lourie, R. (1967). Hypotheses regarding the effects of child-rearing patterns on the disadvantaged child. In J. Hellmuth (Ed.), *Disadvantaged child* (Vol. 1, pp. 17–41). New York: Brunner/Mazel.

Marburger, C.L. (1990). The school site level: Involving parents in reform. In S.B. Bacharach (Ed.), *Education reform: Making sense of it all* (pp. 82–91). Boston: Allyn & Bacon.

Márquez, B. (1993). *LULAC: The evolution of a Mexican American political organization.* Austin: University of Texas Press.

Martin, D.H. (1997, September 12). Remarks raise lawmakers' ire. *Daily Texan,* pp. 1–2.

Martínez, C.R., Jr., DeGarmo, D.S., & Eddy, J.M. (2004). Promoting academic success among Latino youths. *Hispanic Journal of Behavioral Sciences, 26*, 128–151.

Martínez, G.A. (1994). Legal indeterminacy, judicial discretion and the Mexican-American litigation experience: 1930–1980. *U.C. Davis Law Review, 27*, 555–618.

Martínez, P.E. (1979). *Serna v. Portales*: The plight of bilingual education four years later. *Journal of Ethnic Studies, 7*, 109–114.

Mathews v. Diaz, 426 U.S. 67 (1976).

McAnulty, E.A. (1929). Distribution of intelligence in the Los Angeles elementary schools. *Los Angeles Educational Research Bulletin, 8*, 6–8.

McCurdy, J. (1975, January 19). School board minutes play big role in Oxnard desegregation. *Los Angeles Times*, Part II, pp. 1, 3.

McFadden, B.J. (1983). Bilingual education and the law. *Journal of Law & Education, 12*, 1–27.

McGowan v. Maryland, 366 U.S. at 427 (1961).

McGowan, D. (1982, August 31). Judge rules PUHS must be reopened. *Phoenix Gazette*, pp. A1, A4.

McInnis v. Shapiro, 293 F. Supp. 327 (N.D. Ill. 1968).

McLaurin v. Oklahoma State Regents, 339 U.S. 637 (1950).

McNeil, L.M. (1998). Expert report. GI Forum v. Texas Education Agency, Civil Action No. SA-97-CA-1278 (W.D. Tex. 1997).

McNeil, L.M. (2000a). *Contradictions of reform: The educational costs of standardization*. New York: Routledge.

McNeil, L.M. (2000b). Sameness, bureaucracy, and the myth of educational equity: The TAAS system of testing in Texas public schools. *Hispanic Journal of Behavioral Sciences, 22*, 508–523.

McNeil, L.M. (2005). Faking equity: High-stakes testing and the education of Latino youth. In A. Valenzuela (Ed.), *Leaving children behind: How "Texas-style" accountability fails Latino youth* (pp. 57–111). Albany: State University of New York Press.

Mehrens, W.A. (1999). Expert report. GI Forum v. Texas Education Agency, Civil Action No. SA-97-CA-1278 (W.D. Tex. 1997).

Meier, D. (2002). *In schools we trust*. Boston: Beacon.

Meier, K.J., Stewart, J., & England, R.E. (1989). *Race, class, and education: The politics of second-generation discrimination*. Madison: University of Wisconsin Press.

Memmi, A. (1991). *The colonizer and the colonized*. Boston: Beacon.

Menchaca, M. (2001). *Recovering history, constructing race: The Indian, Black, and White roots of Mexican Americans*. Austin: University of Texas Press.

Menchaca, M., & Valencia, R.R. (1990). Anglo-Saxon ideologies and their impact on the segregation of Mexican students in California, the 1920s-1930s. *Anthropology & Education Quarterly, 21,* 222–249.

Mendez v. Westminster, 64 F. Supp. 544 (S.D. Cal. 1946), *aff'd sub nom* Westminster v. Mendez, 161 F.2d 774 (9th Cir. 1947).

Mendoza v. Tucson Unified School District, 623 F.2d 1338 (9th Cir. 1980).

Mercer, J.R. (1973). *Labeling the mentally retarded: Clinical and social system perspectives on mental retardation.* Berkeley: University of California Press.

Mercer, J.R., Coleman, M., & Harloe, J. (1974). Racial/ethnic segregation and desegregation in American public education. In C.W. Gordon (Ed.), *The uses of the sociology of education—The seventy-third yearbook of the National Society for the Study of Education, Part II* (pp. 279–329). Chicago: University of Chicago Press.

Merriam-Webster, Inc. (1996). *Merriam-Webster's dictionary of law.* Springfield, MA: Merriam-Webster. Available online at: *http://dictionary.lp.findlaw.com/.*

Meyer, D.L. (1977). The language issue in New Mexico, 1880–1900: Mexican American resistance against cultural erosion. *Bilingual Review, 4,* 99–106.

Meyer, L.R. (1996). When reasonable minds differ. *New York University Law Review, 71,* 1467–1528.

Meyler, B. (2001). The gestation of birthright citizenship, 1868–1898: states' rights, the law of nations, and mutual consent. *Georgetown Immigration Law Journal, 15,* 519–562.

Michael H. v. Gerald D., 491 U.S. 110 (1989).

Mills v. Board of Education of the District of Columbia, 348 F. Supp. 866 (D.D.C. 1972).

Minnesota Law Review. (1946). Constitutional law—equal protection of the laws—schools—requirement that children of Mexican or Latin descent attend separate schools held invalid. *30,* 646–647.

Minorini, P.A., & Sugarman, S.D. (1999). School finance litigation in the name of educational equity: Its evolution, impact, and future. In H.F. Ladd, R. Chalk, & J.S. Hansen (Eds.), *Equity and adequacy in education finance: Issues and perspectives* (pp. 34–71). Committee on Education Finance, Commission on Behavioral and Social Sciences and Education, National Research Council. Washington, DC: National Academy Press.

Missouri ex rel. Gaines v. Canada, 305 U.S. 337 (1938).

Missouri v. Jenkins, 515 U.S. 70 (1995).

Mitchell, N. (2002, November 6). Colorado hands English immersion backer his first loss. *Rocky Mountain News,* p. 29A.

Molina, H. (1978). Review of the *Tests for Auditory Comprehension of Language.* In O.K. Buros (Ed.), *Eighth Mental Measurements Yearbook* (pp. 612–614). Highland Park, NJ: Gryphon.

Moll, L.C., Amanti, C., Neff, D., & González, N. (1992). Funds of knowledge for teaching: Using a qualitative approach to connect homes and classrooms. *Theory into Practice, 31*, 132–141.

Montoya, M.E. (2001). A brief history of Chicana/o school segregation: One rationale for affirmative action. *Berkeley La Raza Law Journal, 12*, 159–172.

Morales v. Shannon, 366 F. Supp. 813 (W.D. Tex. 1973), *rev'd and rem'd*, 512 F.2d 411 (5th Cir. 1975).

Moran, R.F. (2000). Sorting and reforming: High-stakes testing in the public schools. *Akron Law Review, 34*, 107–135.

Moreno, J.F. (Ed). (1999). *The elusive quest for equality: 150 years of Chicano/Chicana education*. Cambridge, MA: Harvard Educational Review.

Moreno, R.P., & López, J.A. (1999). Latino parent involvement: The role of maternal acculturation and education. *School Community Quarterly, 9*, 83–101.

Moreno, R.P., & Valencia, R.R. (2002). Chicano families and schools: Myths, knowledge, and future directions for understanding. In R.R. Valencia (Ed.), *Chicano school failure and success: Past, present, and future* (2nd ed., pp. 227–249). London: RoutledgeFalmer.

Morín, R. (1963). *Among the valiant: Mexican Americans in WWII and Korea*. Los Angeles: Borden.

Morse, T.E. (2000). Ten events that shaped special education's century of dramatic change. *International Journal of Educational Reform, 9*, 32–38.

Mortiz, J. (2006a, May 19). Perry signs first bill in education package. *Fort Worth Star-Telegram*, p. B1.

Mortiz, J. (2006b, May 26). Judge rescinds ruling on school finance. *Fort Worth Star-Telegram*, p. B1.

Moscoso, E. (2006a, December 6). English-only laws are fighting words. *Austin American-Statesman*, p. A13.

Moscoso, E. (2006b, November 23). City immigration laws draw fire from ACLU. *Austin American-Statesman*, pp. A1, A5.

Moses, M. (1998, March). Deposition. GI Forum v. Texas Education Agency, Civil Action No. SA-97-CA-1278 (W.D. Tex. 1997).

Motley, C.B. (1991). Standing on his shoulders: Thurgood Marshall's early career. *Howard Law Journal, 35*, 23–36.

Mouton v. State, 627 S.W.2d 765 (Tex. App.–Houston [1st Dist.] 1981).

Muñoz, C., Jr. (1989). *Youth, identity, power: The Chicano movement*. London: Verso.

Muñoz, L.K. (2001). Separate but equal? A case study of *Romo v. Laird* and Mexican American education. *OAH Magazine of History, 15*, 28–34.

National Commission on Excellence in Education. (1983). *A nation at risk: The imperatives for educational reform*. Washington, DC: Government Printing Office.

National Education Association. (1966). *The invisible minority . . . pero no vencibles*. Washington, DC: Author.

Navarro, A. (1995). *Mexican American Youth Organization: Avant-garde of the Chicano movement in Texas*. Austin: University of Texas Press.

Nelson, A.C. (1995). Point/Counterpoint—Proposition 187: An important approach to prevent illegal immigration. *Human Rights Brief*, 2(2), 8–10. Available online at: *http://www.wcl.american.edu/hrbrief/v2i2/point.htm*.

Nelson, W., Knight, G.P., Kagan, S., & Gumbiner, J. (1980). Locus of control, self-esteem, and field independence as predictors of school achievement among Anglo American and Mexican American children. *Hispanic Journal of Behavioral Sciences*, 2, 323–335.

Nichols, S.L., Glass, G.V., & Berliner, D.C. (2005). *High-stakes testing and student achievement: Problems for the No Child Left Behind Act*. Education Policy Studies Laboratory, Education Policy Research Unit, Arizona State University, Tempe. Available online at: *http://www.asu.edu/educ/epsl/EPRU/epru_2005_Research_Writing.htm*.

No Child Left Behind Act, Pub. L. No. (107-110), 115 Stat. 1425 (2002).

Norwick v. Nyquist, 417 F. Supp. at 917 (S.D.N.Y. 1976).

O'Connor, K., & Epstein, L. (1984). A legal voice for the Chicano community: The activities of the Mexican American Legal Defense and Educational Fund, 1968–1982. *Social Science Quarterly*, 65, 245–256.

O'Neill, P.T. (2003). High stakes testing law and litigation. *Brigham Young University Education and Law Journal*, 32, 623–662.

Oakes, J. (1985). *Keeping track: How schools structure inequality*. New Haven, CT: Yale University Press.

Oakes, J. (2005). *Keeping track: How schools structure inequality* (2nd ed.). New Haven, CT: Yale University Press.

Oakes, J., & Guiton, G. (1995). Matchmaking: The dynamics of high school tracking decisions. *American Educational Research Journal*, 32, 3–33.

Oakland, T. (Ed.). (1977). *Psychological and educational assessment of minority children*. New York: Brunner/Mazel.

Oakland, T., & Goldwater, D.L. (1979). Assessment and interventions for mildly retarded and learning disabled children. In G.D. Phye & D.J. Reschly (Eds.), *School psychology: Perspectives and issues* (pp. 123–155). New York: Academic Press.

Oakland, T., & Laosa, L.M. (1977). Professional, legislative, and judicial influences on psychoeducational assessment practices in schools. In T. Oakland (Ed.), *Psychological assessment of minority children* (pp. 21–51). New York: Brunner/Mazel.

Odden, A.R., & Picus, L.O. (2000). *School finance: A policy perspective* (2nd ed.). Boston: McGraw-Hill.

Office of the Comptroller for Public Accounts. (1998). *Life on the line: Comptroller's study looks at conditions along the Texas-Mexico border*. Comptroller for Public Accounts Publication, June. Austin, TX: Author.

Okagaki, L. & Frensch, P.A. (1998). Parenting and children's school achievement: A multiethnic perspective. *American Educational Research Journal, 35*, 123–144.

Olivas, M.A. (Ed.). (1986). *Latino college students*. New York: Teachers College Press.

Olivas, M.A. (2005). Higher education as "place": Location, race, and college attendance policies. *Review of Higher Education, 28*, 169–189.

Oquendo, A.R. (1995). Re-imagining the Latino(a) race. *Harvard Blackletter Law Journal, 12*, 93–129.

Oren, L. (1979). Comment: The legal status of undocumented aliens: In search of a consistent theory. *Houston Law Review, 16*, 667–709.

Orfield, G. (1988a, July). *The growth and concentration of Hispanic enrollment and the future of American education*. Paper presented at the National Council of La Raza Conference, Albuquerque, NM.

Orfield, G. (1988b). School desegregation in the 1980s. *Equity and Choice, 4*, 25–28.

Orfield, G. (2001). *Schools more separate: Consequences of a decade of research*. The Civil Rights Project, Harvard University. Cambridge, MA: Harvard University. Available online at: *http://www.civilrightsproject.harvard.edu/research/ deseg/Schools_More_Separate.pdf*.

Orfield, G., & Kornhaber, M.L. (Eds.). (2001). *Raising standards or raising barriers? Inequality and high-stakes testing in public education*. New York: Century Foundation Press.

Orfield, G., & Yun, J.T. (1999). *Resegregation in American schools*. The Civil Rights Project, Harvard University. Cambridge, MA: Harvard University. Available online at: *http://www.civilrightsproject.harvard.edu/research/deseg/Resegregation _American_Schools99.pdf*.

Orozco v. Detroit Board of Education, Civil Action No. 07-715043 CZ (Circuit Court, Wayne County, Michigan *filed*, June 5, 2007).

Orozco, C.E. (2001). Rodriguez v. San Antonio ISD. *Handbook of Texas*. Austin: Texas State Historical Association. Available online at: *http://www.tsha.utexas. edu/handbook/online/articles/RR/jrrht.html*.

Orta v. Hondo Independent School District, decided by Commissioner of Education, J.W. Edgar, September, 1953. Decision on file at Texas State Archives. Also available at the Dr. Héctor P. García Papers, Mary and Jeff Bell Library, Texas A&M University-Corpus Christi.

Ortiz v. Jack, Civil Action No. 1723 (D. Ariz. *dism'd w.o.j., filed*, September 20, 1952).

Osifchok, D.I. (1982). The utilization of intermediate scrutiny in establishing the right to education for undocumented alien children: *Plyler v. Doe. Pepperdine Law Review, 10*, 139–165.

Otero v. Mesa County Valley School District No. 51, 408 F. Supp. 162 (D. Colo. 1975), rev'd, 568 F.2d 1312 (10th Cir. 1977).

Padilla, R.V. (2005). High-stakes testing and educational accountability as social constructions across cultures. In A. Valenzuela (Ed.), *Leaving children behind: How "Texas-style" accountability fails Latino youth* (pp. 249–262). Albany: State University of New York Press.

Page, R.N. (1991). *Lower track classrooms: A curricular and cultural perspective.* New York: Teachers College Press.

Parents Against Testing Before Teaching v. Orleans Parish School Board, Civil Action No. 00-CV-2525-N (E.D. La. 2000), aff'd, 273 F.3d 1107 (5th Cir. 2001), cert. denied, 534 U.S. 1162 (2002).

Parents for Educational Justice v. Picard, U.S. Dist. LEXIS 6382 (E.D. La. 2000).

Parents Involved in Community Schools v. Seattle School District No. 1, 551 U.S. __ (2007) (Kennedy, J., concurring; Breyer, J., dissenting).

Parker, L., Deyhle, D., & Villenas, S. (Eds.). (1999). *Race is . . . race isn't: Critical race theory and qualitative studies in education.* Boulder, CO: Westview.

Passel, J.S., Capps, R., & Fix, M.E. (2004). *Undocumented immigrants: Facts and figures.* Washington, DC: Urban Institute. Available online at: *http://www.urban. org/url.cfm?ID=1000587.*

Patrick, J., & Reschly, D.J. (1982). Relationship of state demographic variables to school-system prevalence of mental retardation. *American Journal of Mental Deficiency, 86,* 351–360.

Peal, E., & Lambert, W.E. (1962). The relation of bilingualism to intelligence. *Psychological Monographs, 76,* 1–23.

Pearl, A. (1997). Cultural and accumulated environmental deficit models. In R.R. Valencia (Ed.), *The evolution of deficit thinking: Educational thought and practice* (pp. 132–159). Stanford Series on Education and Public Policy. London: Falmer.

Pearl, A. (2002). The big picture: Systemic and institutional factors in Chicano school failure and success. In R.R. Valencia (Ed.), *Chicano school failure and success: Past, present, and future* (2nd ed., pp. 335–364). London: Routledge-Falmer.

Pearson v. Murray, 169 Md. 478 (1936).

Pennsylvania Association for Retarded Children v. Commonwealth of Pennsylvania, 334 F. Supp. 1257 (E.D. Pa. 1971).

People ex rel. Lynch v. San Diego Unified School District, 96 Cal. Rptr. 658, 19 Cal. App.3d 252 (Cal. App. 1971).

Perea, J.F. (1997). The Black/White binary paradigm of race: The "normal science" of American racial thought. *California Law Review, 85,* 1213–1258.

Perea, J.F. (2003). A brief history of race and the U.S.-Mexican border: Tracing the trajectories of conquest. *UCLA Law Review, 51,* 283–312.

Perez v. Sonora Independent School District, Civil Action No. 6-224 (N.D. Tex. November 5, 1970).

Pérez, S.M., & De La Rosa Salazar, D. (1993). Economic, labor force, and social implications of Latino educational and population trends. *Hispanic Journal of Behavioral Sciences, 15*, 188–229.

Peters, M.M. (1948). *The segregation of Mexican American children in the elementary schools of California: Its legal and administrative aspects.* Unpublished master's thesis, University of California, Los Angeles.

Peterson, R.E. (1984, April). *CBEST, NTE, and other mensurations: Notes on testing would-be teachers in California, and elsewhere.* Paper presented at the Conference of the California Council on the Education of Teachers, San Diego, CA.

Phillips, B.N. (1978). *School stress and anxiety: Theory, research, and intervention.* New York: Human Sciences Press.

Phillips, L.H. (1949). Segregation in education: A California case study. *Phylon, 10*, 407–413.

Phillips, S.E. (1999). Expert report. GI Forum v. Texas Education Agency, Civil Action No. SA-97-CA-1278 (W.D. Tex. 1997).

Phillips, S.E. (2000a). GI Forum v. Texas Education Agency: Psychometric evidence. *Applied Measurement in Education, 13*, 343–385.

Phillips, S.E. (Ed.). (2000b). Defending a high school graduation test: GI Forum v. Texas Education Agency [Special issue]. *Applied Measurement in Education, 13*(4).

Pitt, L. (1968). *The decline of the Californios: A social history of the Spanish-speaking Californians, 1846–1890.* Berkeley: University of California Press.

Plessy v. Ferguson, 163 U.S. 537 (1896).

Plyler v. Doe, 457 U.S. 202 (1982).

Porter, C.D. (1983). Constitutional law—Undocumented alien children, equal protection, and "special constitutional sensitivity"—*Plyler v. Doe*, 457 U.S. 202 (1982). *Mississippi College Law Review, 3*, 295–318.

Prado, E.C. (1999, July). Order granting, in part, and denying, in part, defendants' motion for summary judgment. GI Forum v. Texas Education Agency, Civil Action No. SA-97-CA-1278 (W.D. Tex. 1997).

Pratt, R.A. (2002). *Brown v. Board of Education* revisited. *Reviews in American History, 30*, 141–148.

President's Commission on Mental Retardation. (1970). *The six-hour retarded child.* Washington, DC: U.S. Government Printing Office.

Price, P.J. (1997). Natural law and birthright citizenship in Calvin's Case (1608). *Yale Journal of Law & the Humanities, 9*, 73–145.

Pulliam, J.D. (1987). *History of education in America* (4th ed.). Columbus, OH: Merrill.

Railway Express Agency v. New York, 336 U.S. 106 (1949).

Ramos, C. (2001). The educational legacy of racially restrictive housing covenants:

Their long term impact on Mexican Americans. *Scholar: St. Mary's Law Review on Minority Issues, 4,* 149–184.

Ramos, H.A.J. (1998). *The American GI Forum: In pursuit of the dream, 1948–1953.* Houston: Arte Público.

Ramseyer, M.J. (2000). *Financing higher education in the 1990s: The case of the South Texas Border Initiative.* Unpublished doctoral dissertation, University of Texas at Dallas.

Rangel, S.C., & Alcala, C.M. (1972). Project report: De jure segregation of Chicanos in Texas schools. *Harvard Civil Rights–Civil Liberties Law Review, 7,* 307–391.

Rebell, M.A. (1991). Ward's Cove one year later: An update on recent development on Title VII law. Unpublished manuscript. Available online at: *http://www.nesinc.com/PDFs/1991_05Rebell.pdf.*

Regents of the University of California v. Bakke, 438 U.S. 265 (1978).

Regents of the University of Michigan v. Ewing, 474 U.S. 214 (1985).

Rendón, A.B. (1971). *Chicano manifesto.* New York: Macmillan.

Rendón, R. (2001, April 10). Districts feel robbed by tax law; La Porte, others sue over "Robin Hood." *Houston Chronicle,* p. A15.

Reschly, D.J. (1979). Nonbiased assessment. In G.D. Phye & D.J. Reschly (Eds.), *School psychology: Perspectives and issues* (pp. 215–253). New York: Academic Press.

Revilla, A.T. (2001). LatCrit and CRT in the field of education: A theoretical dialogue between two colleagues. *Denver University Law Review, 78,* 622–632.

Reynolds, A. (1933). *The education of Spanish-speaking children in five southwestern states* (Bulletin 1933, No. 11). Washington, DC: Government Printing Office.

Richardson v. Lamar County Board of Education, 729 F. Supp. 806 (M.D. Ala. 1989), *aff'd,* 935 F.2d 1240 (11th Cir. 1991).

Rios v. Read, 480 F. Supp. 14 (E.D.N.Y. 1978).

Robelen, E.W. (2001, September 26). Appellate court rejects challenge to Louisiana high-stakes testing. *Education Week, 21,* p. 9.

Roberts v. City of Boston, 59 Mass. 198 (1849).

Robin Hood plan. (2006, September 10). Available online at: *http://en.wikipedia.org/wiki/Robin_Hood_plan.*

Robinson, H.B., & Robinson, N.M. (1965). *The mentally retarded child.* New York: McGraw-Hill.

Rodriguez v. San Antonio Independent School District, 337 F. Supp. 280 (W.D. Tex. 1971), *prob. juris. noted,* 406 U.S. 966 (1972), *rev'd sub nom* San Antonio Independent School District v. Rodriguez, 411 U.S. 1 (1973) (Marshall, J., dissenting).

Romero v. Weakley, 131 F. Supp. 818 (S.D. Cal. 1955).

Romo v. Laird, Civil Action No. 21617 (Superior Court, Maricopa County, Arizona

October 5, 1925). Unpublished *Romo* decision and case file documents available at the Organization of American Historians website: *http://www.oah.org/pubs/magazine/deseg/munoz.html.*

Romo, R. (1986). George I. Sánchez and the civil rights movement: 1940–1960. *La Raza Law Journal*, *1*, 342–362.

Roos, P.D. (1974). The potential impact of *Rodriguez* on other school reform litigation. *Law and Contemporary Problems*, *38*, 566–581.

Roos, P.D. (1986). Implementation of the federal bilingual education mandate: The *Keyes* case as a paradigm. *La Raza Law Journal*, *1*, 257–276.

Rosen, G. (1974). The development of the Chicano movement in Los Angeles from 1967 to 1969. *Aztlán—International Journal of Chicano Studies Research*, *4*, 155–183.

Roser, M.A. (1997, September 11). UT group praises Hopwood ruling. *Austin American-Statesman*, p. B1.

Roser, M.A., & Tanamachi, C. (1997, September 17). Jackson urges UT to fight racism. *Austin American-Statesman*, pp. A1, A10.

Ross v. Eckels, 317 F. Supp. 512 (S.D. Tex. 1970), *originally filed sub nom* Ross v. Rogers, 2 Race Rel. L. Rep. 1114 (S.D. Tex. 1957), *aff'd in part, rev'd in part, and rem'd*, 434 F.2d 1140 (5th Cir. 1970), *vac'd and rem'd*, 468 F.2d 649 (5th Cir. 1972), *unitary status aff'd*, 699 F.2d 218 (5th Cir. 1983).

Ross, S.L., Jr., DeYoung, H.G., & Cohen, J.S. (1971). Confrontation: Special education placement and the law. *Exceptional Children*, *38*, 5–12.

Rueda, R. (1991). An analysis of special education as a response to the diminished academic achievement of Latino students. In R.R. Valencia (Ed.), *Chicano school failure and success: Research and policy agendas for the 1990s* (pp. 252–270). Stanford Series on Education and Public Policy. London: Falmer.

Ruiz Cameron, C.D. (1998). How the García cousins lost their accents: Understanding the language of Title VII decisions approving English-only rules as the product of racial dualism, Latino invisibility, and legal indeterminacy. *California Law Review*, *85*, 1347–1393.

Ruiz v. State Board of Education, Case No. 218394, Superior Court, Sacramento County, California, December 1971.

Rumberger, R.W., & Rodríguez, G.M. (2002). Chicano dropouts: An update of research and policy issues. In R.R. Valencia (Ed.), *Chicano school failure and success: Past, present, and future* (2nd ed., pp. 114–146). London: Routledge-Falmer.

Russell, M. (1992). Entering great America: Reflections on race and the convergence of progressive legal theory and practice. *Hastings Law Journal*, *43*, 749–767.

Saghaye-Biria, H. (2001, April 22). Robin Hood is working. *World Internet News Cooperative*. Available online at: *http://soc.hfac.uh.edu/artman/publish/article_137.shtml.*

Said, E. (1979). *Orientalism*. New York: Vintage Books.

Salinas v. Kingsville Independent School District, Civil Action No. 1309 (S.D. Tex. *dism'd w.o.j., filed*, February 25, 1956). Case file documents available at the George I. Sánchez Papers, Benson Latin American Collection, The University of Texas at Austin.

Salinas, G. (1971). Mexican Americans and the segregation of schools in the Southwest. *Houston Law Review, 8*, 929–951.

Salsburg v. Maryland, 346 U.S. 545 (1954).

San Francisco Unified School District v. Johnson, 3 Cal.3d 937 (Cal. 1971).

San Miguel, G., Jr. (1983). The struggle against separate and unequal schools: Middle class Mexican Americans and the desegregation campaign in Texas, 1929–1957. *History of Education Quarterly, 23*, 343–359.

San Miguel, G., Jr. (1987). *"Let all of them take heed": Mexican Americans and the campaign for educational equality in Texas, 1910–1981*. Austin: University of Texas Press.

San Miguel, G., Jr. (2001). *Brown, not White: School integration and the Chicano movement in Houston*. College Station: Texas A&M University Press.

San Miguel, G., Jr. (2004). *Contested policy: The rise and fall of federal bilingual education in the United States, 1960–2001*. Denton: University of North Texas Press.

San Miguel, G., Jr., & Valencia, R.R. (1998). From the Treaty of Guadalupe Hidalgo to *Hopwood*: The educational plight and struggle of Mexican Americans in the Southwest. *Harvard Educational Review, 68*, 353–412.

Sánchez, G.I. (1951). *Concerning segregation of Spanish-speaking children in the public schools*. Inter-American Education Occasional Papers, no. IX. Austin: University of Texas Press.

Sánchez, G.I., & Strickland, V. (1948). *A study of the educational opportunities provided Spanish-name children in ten Texas school systems*. Reprinted from *The Nation's Schools, 41*(1) (January 1948) and available online at the George I. Sánchez Papers, Benson Latin American Collection, General Libraries, The University of Texas at Austin: *http://www.lib.utexas.edu/photodraw/sanchez/study.html*.

Sánchez, J.O. (1992). Walkout cabrones! The Uvalde school walkout of 1970. *West Texas Historical Yearbook, 68*, 122–133.

Sandoval, J., & Irvin, M.G. (1990). Legal and ethical issues in the assessment of children. In C.R. Reynolds & R.W. Kamphaus (Eds.), *Handbook of psychological and educational assessment: Intelligence and achievement* (pp. 86–104). New York: Guilford.

Santamaria v. Dallas Independent School District, Civil Action No. 3:06-CV-692-L, 2006 U.S. Dist. LEXIS 83417 (N.D. Tex. November 16, 2006), *motion granted in part, and denied in part*, 2007 U.S. Dist. LEXIS 26821 (N.D. Tex. April 10, 2007).

Sattler, J.M. (1992). *Assessment of children* (3rd ed., revised & updated). San Diego: Sattler.

Saucedo, L.M. (2000). The legal issues surrounding the TAAS case. *Hispanic Journal of Behavioral Sciences, 22,* 411–422.

Sax, S.M. (1979). Texas statute's denial of free education to illegal aliens violates equal protection clause and is preempted by the Immigration and Nationality Act. *Vanderbilt Journal of Transnational Law, 12,* 787–793.

Schaefer, R.T. (2002). *Racial and ethnic groups.* Upper Saddle River, NJ: Prentice Hall.

Scharrer, G. (2006, November 27). School issues still big issues at Capitol. *Houston Chronicle,* pp. B1, B5.

Schilhab, J.E. (1976). *Influences of psycho-social factors in a newly integrated school.* Unpublished doctoral dissertation, The University of Texas at Austin.

Schoettle, F.P. (1971). The equal protection clause in public education. *Columbia Law Review, 61,* 1355–1419.

Schuck, P.H., & Smith, R.M. (1985). *Citizenship without consent: Illegal aliens in the American polity.* New Haven, CT: Yale University Press.

Scott, H.J. (1983). Desegregation in Nashville: Conflicts and contradictions in preserving schools in black neighborhoods. *Education and Urban Society, 15,* 235–244.

Secada, W.G., Chávez-Chávez, R., García, E., Muñoz, C., Oakes, J., Santiago-Santiago, I., & Slavin, R. (1998). *No more excuses: The final report of the Hispanic dropout project.* Washington, DC: U.S. Department of Education.

Serna v. Portales Municipal Schools, 351 F. Supp. 1279 (D.N.M. 1972), *aff'd,* 499 F.2d 1147 (10th Cir. 1974).

Serrano v. Priest, Civil Action No. 938254, Superior Court, Los Angeles County, California, January 8, 1969, *aff'd,* 89 Cal. Rptr. 345, 10 Cal. App.3d 1110 (Ct. App. 1970), *rev'd and rem'd,* 5 Cal.3d 584, 96 Cal. Rptr. 601, 487 P.2d 1241 (Cal. 1971), *aff'd,* 18 Cal.3d 728, 135 Cal. Rptr. 345, 557 P.2d 929 (Cal. 1976), *aff'd,* 226 Cal. Rptr. 584, 200 Cal. App.3d 897 (Ct. App. 1986).

Shanks, H. (1972). Educational financing and equal protection: Will the California Supreme Court's breakthrough become the law of the land? *Journal of Law & Education, 1,* 73–95.

Sharif v. New York State Education Department, 709 F. Supp. 345 (S.D.N.Y. 1989).

Sheldon, S.B., & Epstein, J.L. (2005). Involvement counts: Family and community partnerships and mathematics achievement. *Journal of Educational Research, 98,* 196–206.

Sheridan, C. (2003). "Another white race": Mexican Americans and the paradox of whiteness in jury selection. *Law and History Review, 21,* 195–205.

Shulman, R.J. (1995). Children of a lesser god: Should the Fourteenth Amendment be altered or repealed to deny automatic citizenship rights and privileges to American born children of illegal aliens? *Pepperdine Law Review*, 22, 669–725.

Sierra v. El Paso Independent School District, 591 F. Supp. 802 (W.D. Tex. 1984).

Sitkoff, H. (1993). *The struggle for black equality, 1954–1992* (Rev. ed.). New York: Hill and Wang.

Skrla, L., & Scheurich, J.J. (Eds.). (2004). *Educational equity and accountability: Paradigms, policies, and politics*. New York: RoutledgeFalmer.

Slayton, J. (1997). School finance in California and the consequences and implications for LAUSD. Available online at: *http://www.gseis.ucla.edu/gseisdoc/study/finance1.html*.

Smith, M.L. (1993). *The role of high-stakes testing in school reform*. Washington, DC: National Education Association, Professional Standards and Practice.

Sneed, M., & Martin, C. (1997, March). Practical guide to issues related to unitary status. *Inquiry and Analysis*. Retrieved July 9, 2007, from: *http://www.nsba.org/site/doc_cosa.asp?TRACKID=vid=50&CID=1348&DID=3713*.

Solórzano, D.G. (1998). Critical race theory, race and gender microaggressions, and the experience of Chicana and Chicano scholars. *Qualitative Studies in Education*, 11, 121–136.

Solórzano, D.G., & Delgado Bernal, D. (2001). Examining transformational resistance through a critical race and LatCrit theory framework: Chicana and Chicano students in an urban context. *Urban Education*, 36, 308–342.

Solórzano, D.G., & Yosso, T. (2000). Toward a critical race theory of Chicana and Chicano education. In C. Tejada, C. Martínez, Z. Leonardo, & P. McLaren (Eds.), *Charting new terrains of Chicana(o)/Latina(o) education* (pp. 35–65). Cresskill, NJ: Hampton.

Solórzano, D.G., & Yosso, T. (2001). Critical race and LatCrit theory and method: Counterstorytelling Chicana and Chicano graduate school experiences. *International Journal of Qualitative Studies in Education*, 14, 471–495.

Solórzano, D.G., & Yosso, T. (2002). Critical race methodology: Counterstorytelling as an analytical framework for education research. *Qualitative Inquiry*, 8, 23–44.

Soria v. Oxnard School District Board of Trustees, 328 F. Supp. 155 (C.D. Cal. 1971), *denied*, 467 F.2d 59 (9th Cir. 1972), *vac'd*, 488 F.2d 579 (9th Cir. 1973), 386 F. Supp. 539 (C.D. Cal. 1974).

Sowell, T. (1981). *Ethnic America: A history*. New York: Basic Books.

Sracic, P.A. (2006). *San Antonio v. Rodriguez and the pursuit of equal education: The debate over discrimination and school funding*. Lawrence: University Press of Kansas.

Stanley, G. (1920). Special schools for Mexicans. *The Survey*, 44, 714–715.

Stark, K., & Zasloff, J. (2003). Tiebout and tax revolts: Did *Serrano* really cause Proposition 13? *UCLA Law Review*, 50, 801–858.

State-Federal Information Clearinghouse for Exceptional Children. (1973). *Second dimensions: Special educators view the field.* Imprint series. Arlington, VA: Council for Exceptional Children.

Stefancic, J. (1998). Latino and Latina critical theory: An annotated bibliography. *La Raza Law Journal, 10,* 423–498.

Stewart v. Phillips, Civil Action No. 70-1199-F (D. Mass. 1970).

Stinchcombe, J. (1984). *Response to declining enrollment: School-closing in suburbia.* Lanham, MD: University Press of America.

Stone, G.R., Seidman, L.M., Sunstein, C.R., & Tushnet, M.V. (1991). *Constitutional law* (2nd ed.). Boston: Little, Brown.

Swadener, B.B., & Lubeck, S. (Eds.). (1995). *Children and families 'at promise': Deconstructing the discourse of risk.* Albany: State University of New York Press.

Sweatt v. Painter, 339 U.S. 629 (1950).

Tasby v. Estes, 444 F.2d 124 (5th Cir. 1971).

Taylor, E. (1998). A primer on critical race theory: Who are the critical race theorists and what are they saying? *Journal of Blacks in Higher Education, 19,* 122–124.

Taylor, M.C. (1927). *Retardation of Mexican children in the Albuquerque schools.* Unpublished master's thesis, Stanford University, Stanford, CA.

Taylor, P.S. (1929). *Mexican labor in the United States: Racial school statistics.* Los Angeles: University of California Publications in Economics.

Teresa P. v. Berkeley Unified School District, 724 F. Supp. 698 (N.D. Cal. 1989).

Terman, L.M., & Merrill, M.A. (1960). *Stanford-Binet Intelligence Scale: 1960 norms edition.* Boston: Houghton Mifflin.

Texas Education Agency. (2003a). *Academic Excellence Indicator System.* Austin, TX: Author.

Texas Education Agency. (2003b). *2002–03 state performance report.* Academic Excellence Indicator System. Austin, TX: Author. Available online at: *http://www.tea.state.tx.us/perfreport/aeis/2003/state.html.*

Texas Education Agency. (2004). *Academic Excellence Indicator System.* Austin, TX: Author.

Texas Education Agency. (2005). *Academic Excellence Indicator System.* Austin, TX: Author.

Texas Higher Education Coordinating Board. (1997). *Responding to projected increases in student enrollment.* Austin, TX: Author. Available online at: *http://www.thecb.state.tx.us/Reports/.*

Texas House of Representatives, House Committee on Higher Education. (2002). *Interim report 2002.* Austin, TX: Author. Available online at: *http://www.house. state.tx.us/committees/reports/77interim/higher_education.pdf.*

Texas Legislature Online (2006). Bill Lookup search engine available online at: *http://www.capitol.state.tx.us/BillLookup/BillNumber.aspx.*

Texas State Department of Education. (1948–1949). *Standards and Activities of the*

Division and Accreditation of School Systems, Bulletin No. 507, pp. 45–46. Austin, TX: Author.

Theimer, R.M., & Rupiper, O.J. (1975). Special education litigation and school psychology. *Journal of School Psychology, 13*, 324–334.

Thomas v. Bryan Independent School District, Civil Action No. 13850 (S.D. Tex. *inj. granted*, July 23, 1971).

Thomas, C. (2000). Critical race theory and postcolonial development theory: Observations on methodology. *Villanova Law Review, 45*, 1195–1220.

Thomas, D.N. (1979). *A proposal to close schools in the Santa Barbara Elementary School District.* Santa Barbara, CA: Santa Barbara School District.

Thompson, D. (2006). *Texas public school finance: A look at where we have been— and where we are headed.* Houston, TX: Bracewell & Patterson. Available online at: *www.citizensoneducation.org/files/school_finance_hstory.pdf?PHPSESSID =9a3b59055f68b152e1aa3308a4e15279*.

Thro, W.E. (1990). Third wave: The impact of the Montana, Kentucky, and Texas decisions on the future of public school finance reform litigation. *Journal of Law & Education, 19*, 219–250.

Tittle, C.K. (1982). Use of judgmental methods in item bias studies. In R.A. Berk (Ed.), *Handbook of methods for detecting test bias* (pp. 31–63). Baltimore: Johns Hopkins University Press.

Tobin, W.C. (1995). *Plyler v. Doe*: Will it stop Proposition 187? *Journal of Juvenile Law, 16*, 210–224.

Torres, M.A. (2001). *Edgewood v. Kirby: Tax warfare in Texas.* Unpublished doctoral dissertation, University of Texas at El Paso.

Towler, K. (1981). Does the Constitution guarantee a free public education to undocumented children? *Baylor Law Review, 33*, 637–655.

Treisman, P.U. (1999). Expert report (preliminary). GI Forum v. Texas Education Agency, Civil Action No. SA-97-CA-1278 (W.D. Tex. 1997).

Treviño, R. (2004). Against all odds: Lessons from parents of migrant high-achievers. Chapter 11 in *Scholars in the field: the challenge of migrant education* (ERIC Document Reproduction Service No. 481 645).

Tribe, L.H. (1978). *American constitutional law.* Mineola, NY: Foundation Press.

Tussman, J., & tenBrock, J. (1949). The equal protection of the laws. *California Law Review, 37*, 341–381.

Tyack, D. (1974). *The one best system: A history of American urban education.* Cambridge, MA: Harvard University Press.

U.S. Commission on Civil Rights. (1971a). *Mexican American education study, report 1: Ethnic isolation of Mexican Americans in the public schools of the Southwest.* Washington, DC: Government Printing Office.

U.S. Commission on Civil Rights. (1971b). *Mexican American education study, report 2: The unfinished education. Outcomes for minorities in the five southwestern states.* Washington, DC: Government Printing Office.

U.S. Commission on Civil Rights. (1972a). *Mexican American education study, report 4: Mexican American education in Texas: A function of wealth.* Washington, DC: Government Printing Office.

U.S. Commission on Civil Rights. (1972b). *Mexican American education study, report 3: The excluded student. Educational practices affecting Mexican Americans in the Southwest.* Washington, DC: Government Printing Office.

U.S. Commission on Civil Rights. (1977). *School desegregation in Corpus Christi, Texas.* A report of the Texas Advisory Committee to the United States Commission on Civil Rights. Washington, DC: U.S. Government Printing Office.

U.S. Department of Commerce, Bureau of the Census. (1980). *Characteristics of the population, California* (PC80-1-A6). Washington, DC: Author.

U.S. Department of Commerce, Bureau of the Census. (1990). *1990 Census of Population and Housing in the United States, Summary Tape File 1—100 Percent Data, Table P010.* Washington, DC: Author. Available online at: *http://www.census.gov/main/www/cen1990.html.*

U.S. Department of Commerce, Bureau of the Census. (2000a). *Detailed list of languages spoken at home for the population 5 years and over by state: 2000.* Washington, DC: Author. Available online at: *http://www.census.gov/population/www/cen2000/phc-t20.html.*

U.S. Department of Commerce, Bureau of the Census. (2000b). *Current Population Survey, March, 2000.* Ethnic and Hispanic Statistics Branch, Population Division.

U.S. Department of Commerce, Bureau of the Census. (2000c). *2000 Census of Population and Housing in the United States, Summary File 1—100 Percent Data, Table P8.* Washington, DC: Author. Available online at: *http://www.census.gov/main/www/cen2000.html.*

U.S. Department of Commerce, Bureau of the Census. (2006). *Public education finance, 2004.* Washington, DC: Author. Available online at: *http://www.census.gov/govs/www/school.html.*

U.S. Department of Education, Office for Civil Rights. (1997). *Fall 1994 elementary and secondary school civil rights compliance report.* Washington, DC: Author.

U.S. Department of Education, Office for Civil Rights. (2001). *Fall 1998 elementary and secondary school civil rights compliance report.* Washington, DC: Author.

U.S. Department of Education, Office for Civil Rights. (2004). *Fall 2002 elementary and secondary school civil rights compliance report.* Washington, DC: Author.

U.S. Department of Education, Office of Special Education Programs. (2002). *Twenty-fourth annual report to Congress on the implementation of the Individuals with Disabilities Education Act.* Washington, DC: Author.

U.S. Department of the Interior, Bureau of Education. (1926). *Cities reporting the use of homogenous grouping and of the Winnetka technique and the Dalton plan* (City School Leaflet No. 22). Washington, DC: Government Printing Office.

U.S. Department of Justice, Office of the Solicitor General. (2006). Help/Glossary. Available online at: *http://www.usdoj.gov/osg/briefs/help.html.*

U.S. v. CRUCIAL, West Odessa Parents for Quality Neighborhood Schools v. Ector County Independent School District, 722 F.2d 1182 (5th Cir. 1983).

U.S. v. Fordice, 505 U.S. 717 (1992).

U.S. v. Lubbock Independent School District, 316 F. Supp. 1310 (N.D. Tex. 1970).

U.S. v. Midland Independent School District, 443 F.2d 1180 (5th Cir. 1971), *rev'd* 519 F.2d 1084 (5th Cir. 1975).

U.S. v. North Carolina Association of Educators v. North Carolina, 400 F. Supp. 343 (E.D. N.C. 1975).

U.S. v. Texas, Civil Action No. 6:71-CV-5281 (E.D. Tex. February 9, 2006).

U.S. v. Texas, 321 F. Supp. 1043 (E.D. Tex. 1970), *supp. op.*, 330 F. Supp. 235 (E.D. Tex. 1970), *aff'd with modifications*, 447 F.2d 441 (5th Cir. 1971), *stay denied sub nom* Edgar v. U.S., 404 U.S. 1206 (1971), *cert. denied*, 404 U.S. 1016 (1972).

U.S. v. Texas, 628 F. Supp. 304 (E.D. Tex. 1985), *rev'd sub nom* U.S. v. LULAC, 793 F.2d 636 (5th Cir. 1986).

U.S. v. Texas (Del Rio), 342 F. Supp. 24 (E.D. Tex. 1971); 506 F. Supp. 405 (E.D. Tex. 1981); *inj. vac'd*, 680 F.2d 356 (5th Cir. 1982), *motion for further relief denied*, Civil Action No. 6:71-CV-5281 (E.D. Tex. July 27, 2007).

U.S. v. Texas Education Agency (Austin), 467 F.2d 848 (5th Cir. 1972).

U.S. v. Texas Education Agency (Port Arthur Independent School District), 679 F.2d 1104 (5th Cir. 1982).

U.S. v. Texas Education Agency (South Park Independent School District), 647 F.2d 504 (5th Cir. 1981).

U.S. v. Wong Kim Ark, 169 U.S. 649 (1898).

Vaishnav, A. (2002, November 6). English immersion plan wins over bilingual ed. *Boston Globe*, p. A1.

Valdés, F. (1996). Forward: Latina/o ethnicities, critical race theory and post-identity politics in postmodern legal education: From practice to possibilities. *La Raza Law Journal, 9*, 1–31.

Valdés, F., Culp, J.M., & Harris, A.P. (Eds.). (2002). *Crossroads, directions, and a new Critical Race Theory*. Philadelphia: Temple University Press.

Valencia, R.R. (1980). The school closure issue and the Chicano community. *Urban Review, 12*, 5–21.

Valencia, R.R. (1982). Psychoeducational needs of minority children: The Mexican American child, a case in point. In S. Hill & B.J. Barnes (Eds.), *Young children and their families: Needs of the 90s* (pp. 73–87). Lexington, MA: Lexington Books, D.C. Heath.

Valencia, R.R. (1984a). *School closures and policy issues* (Policy Paper No. 84-C3). Stanford, CA: Stanford University, Institute for Research on Educational Finance and Governance.

Valencia, R.R. (1984b). *Understanding school closures: Discriminatory impact on*

Chicano and Black students (Policy Monograph Series, No. 1). Stanford, CA: Stanford University, Stanford Center for Chicano Research.

Valencia, R.R. (1984c). The school closure issue and the Chicano community: A follow-up study of the *Angeles* case. *Urban Review, 16*, 145–163.

Valencia, R.R. (1985). *Chicanos and intelligence testing: A descriptive state of the art.* Unpublished manuscript.

Valencia, R.R. (1988). The McCarthy scales and Hispanic children: A review of psychometric research. *Hispanic Journal of Behavioral Sciences, 10*, 81–104.

Valencia, R.R. (Ed.). (1991). *Chicano school failure and success: Research and policy agendas for the 1990s.* Stanford Series on Education and Public Policy. London: Falmer.

Valencia, R.R. (1997a). Genetic pathology model of deficit thinking. In R.R. Valencia (Ed.), *The evolution of deficit thinking: Educational thought and practice* (pp. 41–112). Stanford Series on Education and Public Policy. London: Falmer.

Valencia, R.R. (1997b). Conceptualizing the notion of deficit thinking. In R.R. Valencia (Ed.), *The evolution of deficit thinking: Educational thought and practice* (pp. 1–12). Stanford Series on Education and Public Policy. London: Falmer.

Valencia, R.R. (Ed.). (1997c). *The evolution of deficit thinking: Educational thought and practice.* Stanford Series on Education and Public Policy. London: Falmer.

Valencia, R.R. (1998). Expert report. GI Forum v. Texas Education Agency, Civil Action No. SA-97-CA-1278 (W.D. Tex. 1997).

Valencia, R.R. (2000). Inequalities and the schooling of minority students in Texas: Historical and contemporary conditions. *Hispanic Journal of Behavioral Sciences, 22*, 445–459.

Valencia, R.R. (2002a). The explosive growth of the Chicano/Latino population: Educational implications. In R.R. Valencia (Ed.), *Chicano school failure and success: Past, present, and future* (2nd ed., pp. 52–69). London: RoutledgeFalmer.

Valencia, R.R. (2002b). The plight of Chicano students: An overview of schooling conditions and outcomes. In R.R. Valencia (Ed.), *Chicano school failure and success: Past, present, and future* (2nd ed., pp. 3–51). London: RoutledgeFalmer.

Valencia, R.R. (Ed.). (2002c). *Chicano school failure and success: Past, present, and future* (2nd ed.). London: RoutledgeFalmer.

Valencia, R.R. (2002d). Conclusions: Towards Chicano school success. In R.R. Valencia (Ed.), *Chicano school failure and success: Past, present, and future* (2nd ed., pp. 365–369). London: RoutledgeFalmer.

Valencia, R.R. (2005). The Mexican American struggle for equal educational opportunity in *Mendez v. Westminster*: Helping to pave the way for *Brown v. Board of Education. Teachers College Record, 107*, 389–423.

Valencia, R.R. (2006a). A tribute to Thomas P. Carter (1927–2001): Activist scholar, and pioneer in Mexican American education. *Journal of Latinos and Education, 5*, 237–252.

Valencia, R.R. (2006b, April). Preliminary Expert Report. Submitted to plaintiffs' counsel, David G. Hinojosa. Santamaria v. Dallas Independent School District, Civil Action No. 3:06-CV-692-L (N.D. Tex. November 16, 2006).

Valencia, R.R. (2006c, July). Supplementary Expert Report. Submitted to plaintiffs' counsel, David G. Hinojosa. Santamaria v. Dallas Independent School District, Civil Action No. 3:06-CV-692-L (N.D. Tex. November 16, 2006).

Valencia, R.R., & Aburto, S. (1991a). Competency testing and Latino student access to the teaching profession: An overview of issues. In G.D. Keller, J. Deneen, & R. Magallán (Eds.), *Assessment and access: Hispanics in higher education* (pp. 167–194). Albany: State University of New York Press.

Valencia, R.R., & Aburto, S. (1991b). Research directions and practical strategies in teacher testing and assessment: Implications for improving Latino access to teaching. In G.D. Keller, J. Deneen, & R. Magallán (Eds.), *Assessment and access: Hispanics in higher education* (pp. 195–232). Albany: State University of New York Press.

Valencia, R.R., & Aburto, S. (1991c). The uses and abuses of educational testing: Chicanos as a case in point. In R.R. Valencia (Ed.), *Chicano school failure and success: Research and policy agendas for the 1990s* (pp. 203–251). Stanford Series on Education and Public Policy. London: Falmer.

Valencia, R.R., & Bernal, E.M. (Eds.). (2000a). The Texas Assessment of Academic Skills (TAAS) case: Perspectives of plaintiffs' experts [Special issue]. *Hispanic Journal of Behavioral Sciences, 22*(4).

Valencia, R.R., & Bernal, E.M. (2000b). An overview of conflicting opinions in the TAAS case. *Hispanic Journal of Behavioral Sciences, 22*, 423–444.

Valencia, R.R., & Bernal, E.M. (2000c). Guest editors' introduction. *Hispanic Journal of Behavioral Sciences, 22*, 405–410.

Valencia, R.R., & Black, M.S. (2002). "Mexican Americans don't value education!": On the basis of the myth, mythmaking, and debunking. *Journal of Latinos and Education, 2*, 81–103.

Valencia, R.R., & Guadarrama, I.N. (1996). High-stakes testing and its impact on racial and ethnic minority students. In L.A. Suzuki, P.J. Meller, & J.G. Ponterotto (Eds.), *Multicultural assessment: Clinical, psychological, and educational applications* (pp. 561–610). San Francisco: Jossey-Bass.

Valencia, R.R., Menchaca, M., & Donato, R. (2002). Segregation, desegregation, and integration of Chicano students: Old and new realities. In R.R. Valencia (Ed.), *Chicano school failure and success: Past, present, and future* (2nd ed., pp. 70–113). London: RoutledgeFalmer.

Valencia, R.R., & Suzuki, L.A. (2001). *Intelligence testing and minority students: Foundations, performance factors, and assessment issues.* Thousand Oaks, CA: Sage.

Valencia, R.R., Valenzuela, A., Sloan, K., & Foley, D.E. (2001). At odds—Let's treat the cause, not the symptoms: Equity and accountability in Texas revisited. *Phi Delta Kappan, 83*, 318–321, 326.

Valencia, R.R., & Villarreal, B.J. (2003). Improving students' reading performance via standards-based school reform: A critique. *Reading Teacher, 56*, 612–621.

Valencia, R.R., & Villarreal, B.J. (2005). Texas' second wave of high-stakes testing: Anti-social promotion legislation, grade retention, and adverse impact on minorities. In A. Valenzuela (Ed.), *Leaving children behind: How "Texas-style" accountability fails Latino youth* (pp. 113–152). Albany: State University of New York Press.

Valencia, R.R., Villarreal, B.J., & Salinas, M.F. (2002). Educational testing and Chicano students: Issues, consequences, and prospects for reform. In R.R. Valencia (Ed.), *Chicano school failure and success: Past, present, and future* (2nd ed., pp. 253–309). London: RoutledgeFalmer.

Valenzuela, A. (2000). The significance of the TAAS test for Mexican immigrant and Mexican American adolescents: A case study. *Hispanic Journal of Behavioral Sciences, 22*, 524–539.

Valenzuela, A. (2002). High-stakes testing and U.S.-Mexican youth in Texas: The case of multiple compensatory criteria in assessment. *Harvard Journal of Hispanic Policy, 14*, 97–116.

Valenzuela, A. (2005a). Introduction: The accountability debate in Texas: Continuing the conversation. In A. Valenzuela (Ed.), *Leaving children behind: How "Texas-style" accountability fails Latino youth* (pp. 1–32). Albany: State University of New York Press.

Valenzuela, A. (Ed.). (2005b). *Leaving children behind: How "Texas-style" accountability fails Latino youth.* Albany: State University of New York Press.

Valeria G. v. Wilson, 12 F. Supp.2d 1007 (N.D. Cal. 1998), *aff'd sub nom* Valeria v. Davis, 307 F.3d 1036 (9th Cir. 2002), *pet. for reh'g en banc denied*, 320 F.3d 1014 (9th Cir. 2003).

Vara-Orta, F. (2006, August 12). 'Activist' judge still battling injustice. *Austin American-Statesman*, pp. A1, A10–A11.

Vásquez, O. (1994). Mari-Luci Jaramillo. In M.S. Seller (Ed.), *Women educators in the United States, 1820–1993: A biographical sourcebook* (pp. 258–264). Westport, CT: Greenwood.

Vaughan, R.W. (1973). Community, courts, and conditions of special education today: Why? *Mental Retardation, 11*, 43–47.

Vega, J.E. (1983). *Education, politics, and bilingualism in Texas.* Washington, DC: University Press of America.

Vernon's Texas Codes Annotated. (1970). Supplement. Kansas City, MO: Vernon Law Book.

Vernon's Texas Codes Annotated. (1976). Cumulative Annual Pocket Part, 1976–1977. St. Paul, MN: West.

Verstegen, D.A. (1994). Reforming American education policy for the 21st century. *Educational Administration Quarterly, 30*, 365–390.

Villarreal v. Mathis Independent School District, Civil Action No. 1385 (S.D. Tex.

dism'd w.o.j., filed, May 2, 1957). Case file documents available at the George I. Sánchez Papers, Benson Latin American Collection, The University of Texas at Austin.

Villenas, S., & Deyhle, D. (1999). Critical Race Theory and ethnographies challenging the stereotypes: Latino families, schooling, resilience and resistance. *Curriculum Inquiry, 29*, 413–445.

Wards Cove Packing Co. v. Atonio, 490 U.S. 642 (1989).

Wechsler, D. (1949). *Manual for the Wechsler Intelligence Scale for Children.* New York: Psychological Corporation.

Weinberg, M. (1977). *A chance to learn: The history of race and education in the United States.* Cambridge: Cambridge University Press.

West Orange-Cove Consolidated Independent School District v. Nelson, Civil Action No. GV100528 (250th District Court, Travis County, Texas July 24, 2001), *aff'd sub nom* West Orange-Cove Consolidated Independent School District v. Alanis, 78 S.W.3d 529 (Tex. App.–Austin 2002), *rev'd and rem'd* 107 S.W.3d 558 (Tex. 2003), *reh'd sub nom* West Orange-Cove Consolidated Independent School District v. Neeley, Civil Action No. GV100528 (250th District Court, Travis County, Texas September 15, 2003), *aff'd sub nom* Neeley v. West Orange-Cove Consolidated Independent School District, 176 S.W.3d 746 (Tex. 2005), *reh'd sub nom* West Orange-Cove Consolidated Independent School District v. Neeley, Civil Action No. GV100528 (250th District Court, Travis County, Texas May 26, 2006).

White v. Regester, 412 U.S. 755 (1973).

Whitman, M. (Ed.). (1993). *Removing a badge of slavery: The record of Brown v. Board of Education.* Princeton, NJ: Markus Wiener.

Wilcoxen, J.M. (1985). Equal protection: Can California offer more for undocumented alien children? *Pacific Law Journal, 16*, 1101–1121.

Wisconsin v. Yoder, 406 U.S. 205 (1972).

Wise, A.E. (1965). Is denial of equal educational opportunity constitutional? *Administrator's Network, 13*, 1–4.

Wise, A.E. (1967). *The Constitution and equality: Wealth, geography, and educational opportunity.* Unpublished doctoral dissertation, University of Chicago.

Wise, A.E. (1968). *Rich schools, poor schools: The promise of equal educational opportunity.* Chicago: University of Chicago Press.

Wollenberg, C. (1974). *Mendez v. Westminster:* Race, nationality, and segregation in California schools. *California Historical Quarterly, 53*, 317–332.

Wong Wing v. United States, 163 U.S. 228 (1896).

Wood, C. (1999). Losing control of America's future—The census, birthright citizenship, and illegal aliens. *Harvard Journal of Law & Public Policy, 22*, 465–522.

Wright, P., & Santa Cruz, R. (1983). Ethnic composition of special education programs in California. *Learning Disability Quarterly, 6*, 387–394.

Yablon, C. (1992). Timeless rules: Can normative closure and legal indeterminacy be reconciled? *Cardozo Law Review, 13*, 1605–1618.

Yale Law Journal. (1947). Segregation in public schools—a violation of "equal protection of the law." *56*, 1059–1067.

York v. Alabama State Board of Education, 581 F. Supp. 779 (M.D. Ala. 1983), 631 F. Supp. 78 (M.D. Ala. 1986).

Yoshida, R.K., MacMillan, D.L., & Meyers, C.E. (1976). The decertification of minority group EMR students in California: Student achievement and adjustment. In R.L. Jones (Ed.), *Mainstreaming and the minority child* (pp. 215–233). Reston, VA: Council for Exceptional Children.

Yosso, T.J. (2006). *Critical race counterstories along the Chicana/Chicano educational pipeline.* New York: Routledge.

Ysseldyke, J.E., & Algozzine, B. (1984). *Introduction to special education.* Boston: Houghton Mifflin.

Yudof, M.G., & Morgan, D.C. (1974). Rodriguez v. San Antonio Independent School District: Gathering the ayes of Texas—The politics of school finance reform. *Law and Contemporary Problems, 38*, 383–414.

Zamora v. New Braunfels Independent School District, 362 F. Supp. 552 (W.D. Tex. 1973), rev'd 519 F.2d 1084 (5th Cir. 1975).

Zerchykov, R. (1982). *A review of the literature and an annotated bibliography on managing decline in school systems.* Boston: Institute for Responsive Education, Boston University.

Zettel, J.J., & Ballard, J. (1982). The Education for All Handicapped Children Act of 1975 (P.L. 94-142): Its history, origins, and concepts. In J.J. Ballard, B.A. Ramírez, & F.J. Weintraub (Eds.), *Special education in America: Its legal and governmental foundations* (pp. 11–22). Reston, VA: Council for Exceptional Children.

Index

Aboussie, Marilyn, 105
Aburto, S., 293
academic achievement: African American students, xiii–xiv, 84; Austin Independent School District (AISD) (Texas), 11–12; bilingual education, 156, 159, 364n36; Border Region of South Texas, 255; California Assessment Program (CAP), 11; *Castro v. Phoenix Union High School District #210* (1982), 214–215, 220; children with Spanish surnames, 163; graduation rates, 12–13; inability to learn, xviii; inferior schooling, xviii; Los Angeles Unified School District (LAUSD), 84; Mexican American students, xiii–xiv, 14, 84, 206–207, 208, 317, 318; minority students, xiii–xiv, 11, 12–13; normalization of instruction and grades, 217; parental participation, xiii, 318; racial stereotyping, xiii–xiv; racialized opportunity structures, 319; *Romo v. Laird* (1925), 14; school closures, 214–215, 220; school segregation, 7–9, 11–13, 14; school transition research, 216; schools with primarily low-socioeconomic status (SES) students of color, 214; students of color, 318; "theory of incompatibilities," 177–178, 183; White enrollment, 11; White students, 318.
See also intelligence testing
Acuña, Rodolfo, 250
affirmative action, 321n5
African American students: academic achievement, xiii–xiv, 84; California Basic Educational Skills Test (CBEST), 280; high-stakes testing, 269–270; learning style, 218; Los Angeles Unified School District (LAUSD), 84; Louisiana, 270; Mexican American student isolation, 397n1; Mexican American students, pairing with, 61, 65; overrepresentation among educable mentally retarded (EMR), 126, 136–137, 138–139, 152; Pre-Professional Skills Test (PPST), 272–273; segregation of, 74; Texas Academic Skills Program (TASP), 278; Texas Assessment of Academic Skills (TAAS), 286, 290, 296–297
African Americans: *Dameron v. Bayless* (1912), 14; desegregation legislation, 42; *Groves v. Alabama Board of Education* (1991), 285; high-

stakes testing, 285; *Hobson v. Hansen* (1967), 122; *Keyes v. School District No. 1 of Denver* (1973), 9; *Larry P. v. Riles* (1972), 355n52; Mexican Americans and, similarities between, 66; *Roberts v. City of Boston* (1849), 42; *Ross v. Eckels* (1970), 337n190, 337n194; teacher competency testing, 285
Aguilar, Jay, 260
Alabama, school financing, 81
Alamo Heights, Texas, 347n65
Alamo Heights Independent School District (AHISD) (Texas), 95–97, 345n56, 347n77
Alaska, school financing, 81
Alcala, C.M., 58, 326n21, 334n15
Allred, James, 56, 57–58
Álvarez, Robert R., Jr., 327n31
Álvarez, Roberto, 20, 21, 327n31
Alvarez v. Lemon Grove School District (1931), 19–22; Álvarez and, Robert R., Jr., 327n31; Álvarez and, Roberto, 20, 21, 327n31; Anderson, Henry A., 327n31; Bowman and, K.L., 327n31; Brinkley and, 20; Chambers and, 20, 21; citations of, 327n31; *Comité de Vecinos de Lemon Grove* (Lemon Grove Neighborhood Committee), 20; constitutionality of separating Mexican American students on racial grounds, 20, 21; Green and, Jerome J., 19–20; *La Caballeriza* (the stable), 19–20; Lemon Grove Grammar School, 19–21; Mexican Americans' English language development needs, 20–21; Mexican Americans' need for Americanization, 20–21; Montoya and, M.E., 327n31; Noon and, 20; overcrowding, 19; Owen and, E.L., 327n31; Petition for Write of Mandate, 327n31; *San Diego Evening Tribune*, 20; San Diego Superior Court, 20; Wright and, Anna E., 327n31
Amarillo, Texas, enrollment in, 75
American Association on Mental Deficiency (AAMD), 146–147
American Civil Liberties Union (ACLU): *Mendez v. Westminster* (1946), 4, 32, 34, 329n65; *San Antonio Independent School District v. Rodriguez* (1973) (*Rodriguez II*), 98
American Federation of Teachers (AFT), 269
American GI Forum. *See* GI Forum